The Hymn Fake Book

A Collection of Over 1000 Multi-Denominational Hymns

MELODY, LYRICS, CHORDS

ISBN 0-634-01043-3

HAL•LEONARD® CORPORATION

7777 W. BLUEMOUND RD. P.O. BOX 13819 MILWAUKEE, WI 53213

ABOUT THIS BOOK

This is one of the largest, if not *the* largest, comprehensive collections of hymns ever assembled. It contains a huge variety of cross-denominational hymns, spanning several centuries. In the research phase of this book, over 75 hymnals were consulted, some dating back to the mid-1800s.

It is a common practice in hymnals to alter the text in various ways for the sake of modern perceptions. In this book, however, we have made every effort to retain the original texts whenever possible. We have also attempted to include most, if not all, of the original verses, generally up to six. The chord symbols allow players to harmonize their own arrangements, while preserving the authentic chord progressions.

For those who are unfamiliar with this format, a "fake book" attempts to provide a shorthand version of all essential elements: melody, lyrics and chords. In other words, "faking it." Although the four-part harmonies typically found in hymnals are not included, these arrangements are intended for players, soloists, or group singing.

–The Editors

CONTENTS

ALPHABETICAL INDEX OF TUNE NAMES

ABIDE IN GRACE, LORD JESUS

CHRISTUS, DER IST MEIN LEBEN
music by
Melchior Vulpius (c.1560-1615)

words by
Josua Stegmann (1588-1632)
tr. by F.W. Detterer (1861-1893)

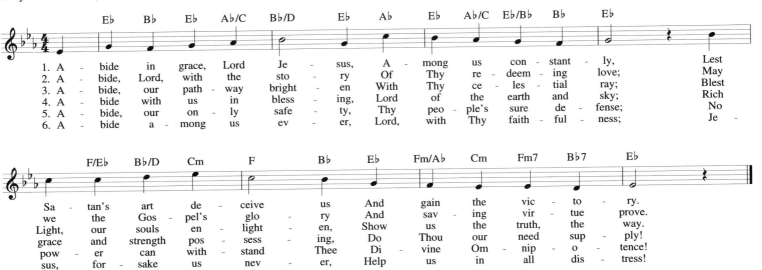

1. A - bide in grace, Lord Je - sus, A - mong us con - stant - ly, Lest
2. A - bide, Lord, with the sto - ry Of Thy re - deem - ing love; May
3. A - bide, our path - way bright - en With Thy ce - les - tial ray; Blest
4. A - bide with us in bless - ing, Lord of the earth and sky; Rich
5. A - bide, our on - ly safe - ty, Thy peo - ple's sure de - fense; No
6. A - bide a - mong us ev - er, Lord, with Thy faith - ful - ness; Je

Sa - tan's art de - ceive us And gain the vic - to - ry.
we the Gos - pel's glo - ry And sav - ing vir - tue prove.
Light, our souls en - light - en, Show us the truth, the way.
grace and strength pos - sess - ing, Do Thou our need sup - ply!
pow - er can with - stand Thee Di - vine Om - nip - o - tence!
sus, for - sake us nev - er, Help us in all dis - tress!

ABIDE WITH ME

EVENTIDE
music by
William H. Monk, 1861

words by
Henry F. Lyte, 1847

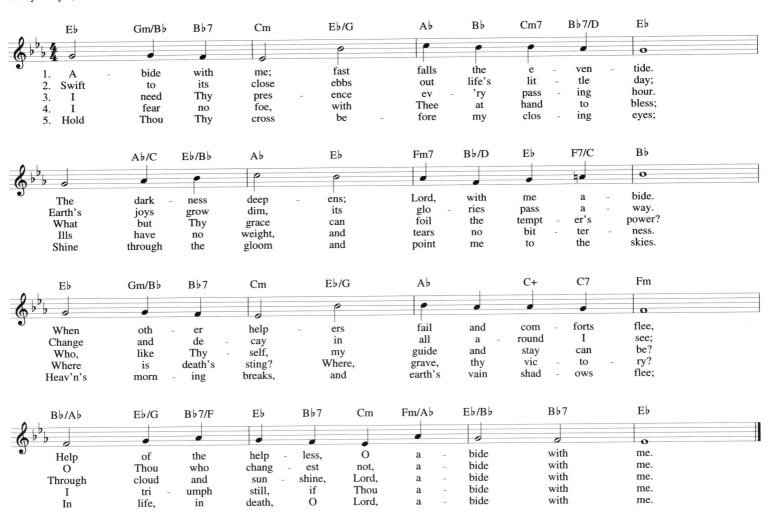

1. A - bide with me; fast falls the e - ven - tide.
2. Swift to its close ebbs out life's lit - tle day;
3. I need Thy pres - ence ev - 'ry pass - ing hour.
4. I fear no foe, with Thee at hand to bless;
5. Hold Thou Thy cross be - fore my clos - ing eyes;

The dark - ness deep - ens; Lord, with me a - bide.
Earth's joys grow dim, its glo - ries pass a - way.
What but Thy grace can foil the tempt - er's power?
Ills have no weight, and tears no bit - ter - ness.
Shine through the gloom and point me to the skies.

When oth - er help - ers fail and com - forts flee,
Change and de - cay in all a - round I see;
Who, like Thy - self, my guide and stay can be?
Where is death's sting? Where, grave, thy vic - to - ry?
Heav'n's morn - ing breaks, and earth's vain shad - ows flee;

Help of the help - less, O a - bide with me.
O Thou who chang - est not, a - bide with me.
Through cloud and sun - shine, Lord, a - bide with me.
I tri - umph still, if Thou a - bide with me.
In life, in death, O Lord, a - bide with me.

3

AH, HOLY JESUS

words by
Johann Heermann, 1630
tr. by Robert Bridges, 1899

HERZLIEBSTER JESU
music by
Johann Crüger, 1640

ALAS, AND DID MY SAVIOR BLEED

words by
Isaac Watts (1674-1748)

MARTYRDOM
music by
Hugh Wilson (1764-1824)

ALL CREATURES OF OUR GOD AND KING

words by
Francis of Assisi, 1225
tr. by William Henry Draper

LASST UNS ERFREUEN
music from
Geistliche Kirchengesäng, 1623

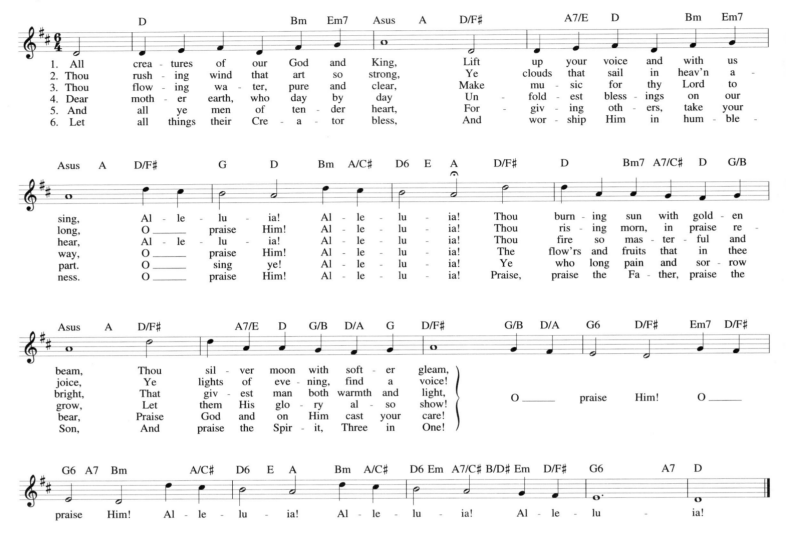

1. All crea - tures of our God and King, Lift up your voice and with us
2. Thou rush - ing wind that art so strong, Ye clouds that sail in heav'n a -
3. Thou flow - ing wa - ter, pure and clear, Make mu - sic for thy Lord to
4. Dear moth - er earth, who day by day Un - fold - est bless - ings on our
5. And all ye men of ten - der heart, For - giv - ing oth - ers, take your
6. Let all things their Cre - a - tor bless, And wor - ship Him in hum - ble -

sing, Al - le - lu - ia! Al - le - lu - ia! Thou burn - ing sun with gold - en
long, O _____ praise Him! Al - le - lu - ia! Thou ris - ing morn, in praise re -
hear, Al - le - lu - ia! Al - le - lu - ia! Thou fire so mas - ter - ful and
way, O _____ praise Him! Al - le - lu - ia! The flow'rs and fruits that in thee
part. O _____ sing ye! Al - le - lu - ia! Ye who long pain and sor - row
ness. O _____ praise Him! Al - le - lu - ia! Praise, praise the Fa - ther, praise the

beam, Thou sil - ver moon with soft - er gleam, O _____ praise Him! O _____
joice, Ye lights of eve - ning, find a voice!
bright, That giv - est man both warmth and light,
grow, Let them His glo - ry al - so show!
bear, Praise God and on Him cast your care!
Son, And praise the Spir - it, Three in One!

praise Him! Al - le - lu - ia! Al - le - lu - ia! Al - le - lu - ia!

ALL DAY LONG

Traditional Spiritual

Traditional Spiritual

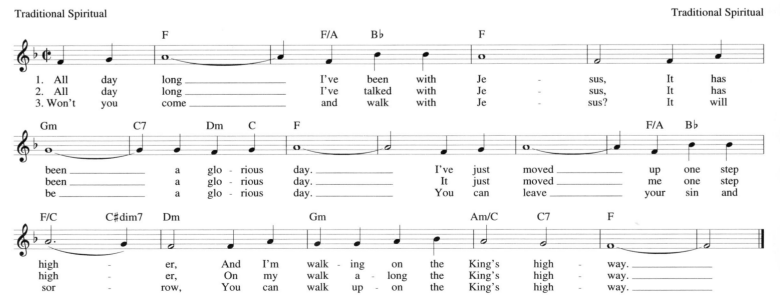

1. All day long _____ I've been with Je - sus, It has
2. All day long _____ I've talked with Je - sus, It has
3. Won't you come _____ and walk with Je - sus? It will

been _____ a glo - rious day. _____ I've just moved _____ up one step
been _____ a glo - rious day. _____ It just moved _____ me one step
be _____ a glo - rious day. _____ You can leave _____ your sin and

high - er, And I'm walk - ing on the King's high - way. _____
high - er, On my walk a - long the King's high - way. _____
sor - row, You can walk up - on the King's high - way. _____

ALL DEPENDS ON OUR POSSESSING

words from
Nürnberg Gesang-Buch, 1676
tr. by C. Winkworth (1827-1878)

ALLES IST AN GOTTES SEGEN
music by
J.B. König (1691-1758)

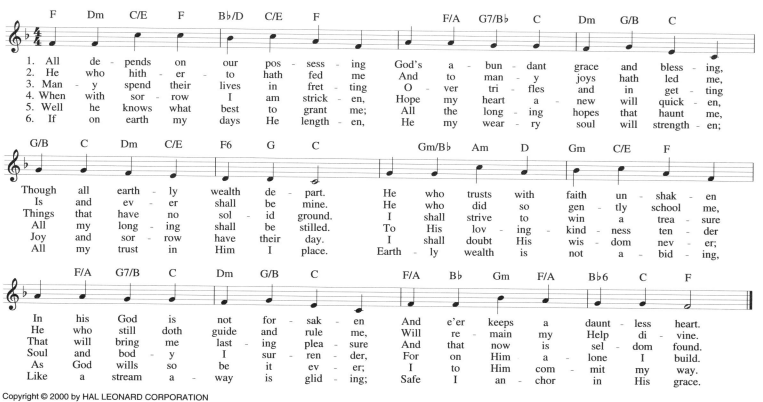

ALL FOR JESUS

words by
Mary D. James (1810-1883)

CONSTANCY
Composer unknown

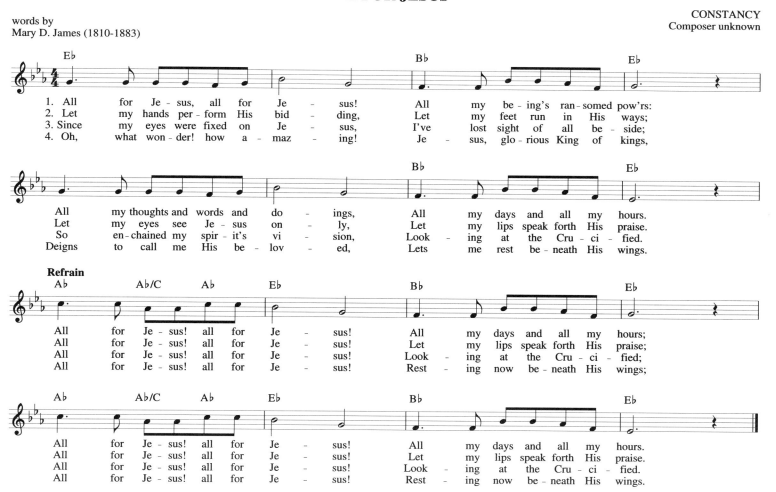

ALL GLORY, LAUD AND HONOR

words by
Theodulph of Orleans, c. 820
tr. by John Mason Neale (1818-1866)

ST. THEODULPH
music by
Melchior Teschner (1584-1635)
arr. by William Henry Monk, 1861

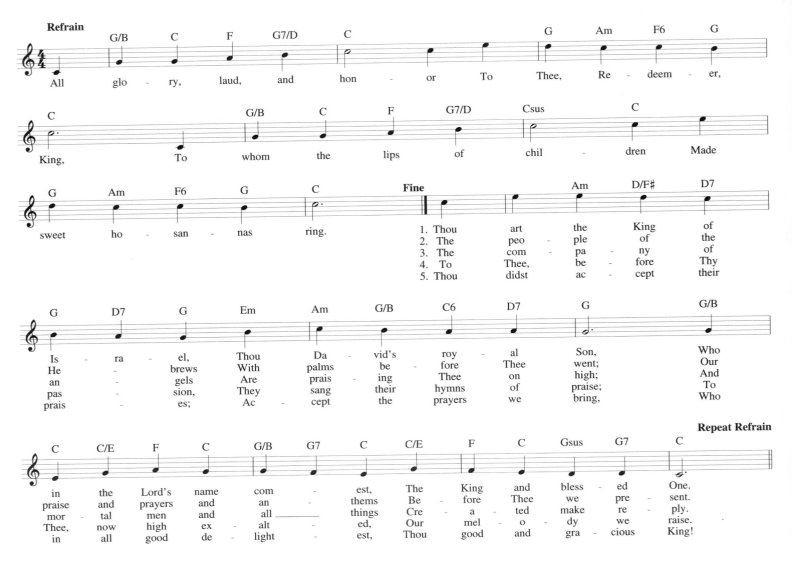

ALL HAIL THE POWER OF JESUS' NAME

words by
Edward Perronet, 1779
alt. by John Rippon, 1787

CORONATION
music by
Oliver Holden, 1792

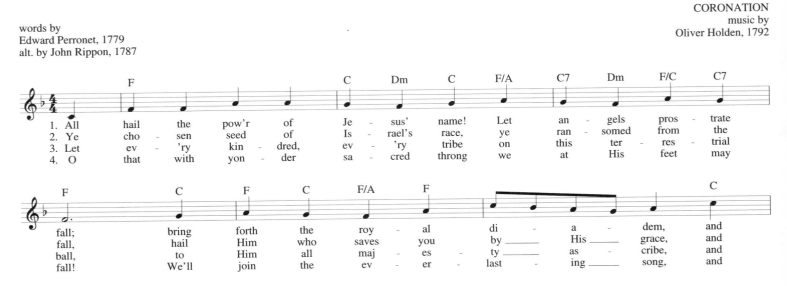

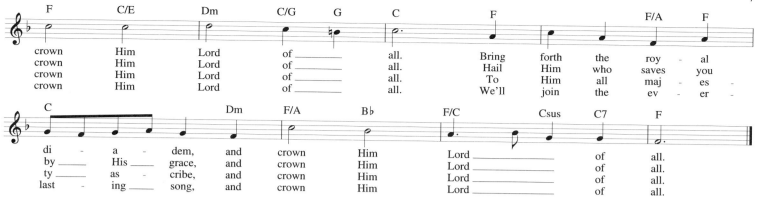

crown Him Lord of _____ all. Bring forth the roy- al
crown Him Lord of _____ all. Hail Him who saves you
crown Him Lord of _____ all. To Him all maj- es-
crown Him Lord of _____ all. We'll join the ev- er-

di- a- dem, and crown Him Lord _____ of all.
by _____ His grace, and crown Him Lord _____ of all.
ty as- cribe, and crown Him Lord _____ of all.
last- ing _____ song, and crown Him Lord _____ of all.

ALL HAIL THE POWER OF JESUS' NAME

words by
Edward Perronet, 1779
alt. by John Rippon, 1787

DIADEM
music by
James Ellor, 1838

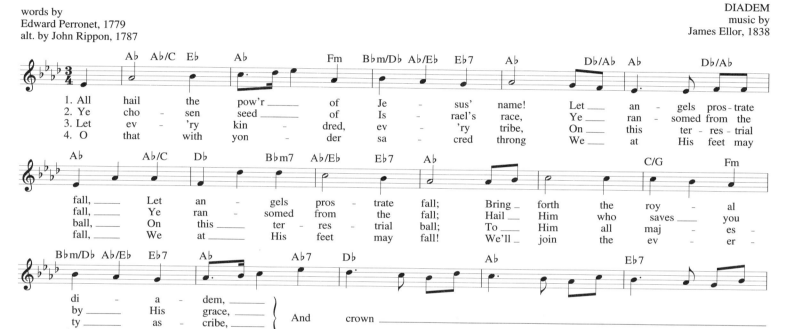

1. All hail the pow'r _____ of Je- sus' name! Let _____ an- gels pros- trate
2. Ye cho- sen seed _____ of Is- rael's race, Ye _____ ran- somed from the
3. Let ev- 'ry kin- dred, ev- 'ry tribe, On _____ this ter- res- trial
4. O that with yon- der sa- cred throng We _____ at His feet may

fall, _____ Let an- gels pros- trate fall; Bring _ forth the roy- al
fall, _____ Ye ran- somed from the fall; Hail _ Him who saves _____ you
ball, _____ On this _____ ter- res- trial ball; To _____ Him all maj- es-
fall, _____ We at _____ His feet may fall! We'll _ join the ev- er-

di- a- dem, _____ by _____ His grace, _____ And crown _____
ty as- cribe, _____
last- ing song, _____

_____ Him, crown Him, crown Him, crown Him, And crown _____ Him Lord of all.

ALL HAIL THE POWER OF JESUS' NAME

words by
Edward Perronet, 1779
alt. by John Rippon, 1787

MILES LANE
music by
William Shrubsale (1760-1806)

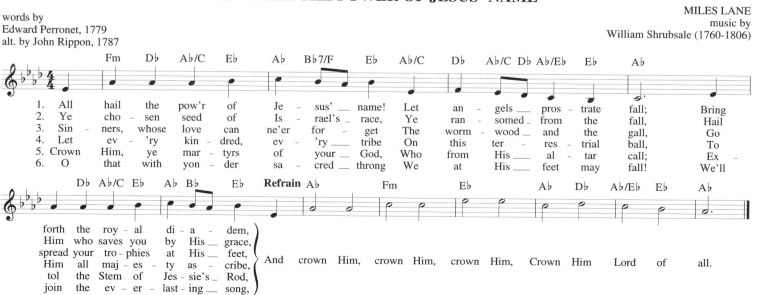

1. All hail the pow'r of Je- sus' name! Let an- gels _____ pros- trate fall; Bring
2. Ye cho- sen seed of Is- rael's race, Ye ran- somed _____ from the fall, Hail
3. Sin- ners, whose love can ne'er for- get The worm- wood and the gall, Go
4. Let ev- 'ry kin- dred, ev- 'ry _____ tribe On this ter- res- trial ball, To
5. Crown Him, ye mar- tyrs of your _____ God, Who from His _____ al- tar call; Ex-
6. O that with yon- der sa- cred _____ throng We at His _____ feet may fall! We'll

forth the roy- al di- a- dem,
Him who saves you by His _____ grace,
spread your tro- phies at His _____ feet, And crown Him, crown Him, crown Him, Crown Him Lord of all.
Him all maj- es- ty as- cribe,
tol the Stem of Jes- sie's _ Rod,
join the ev- er- last- ing _____ song,

ALL PEOPLE THAT ON EARTH DO DWELL

OLD HUNDREDTH
music from
Genevan Psalter, 1551
attr. to Louis Bourgeois (1510-1561)

words by
William Kethe, from *Scottish Psalter,* 1565;
based on Psalm 100

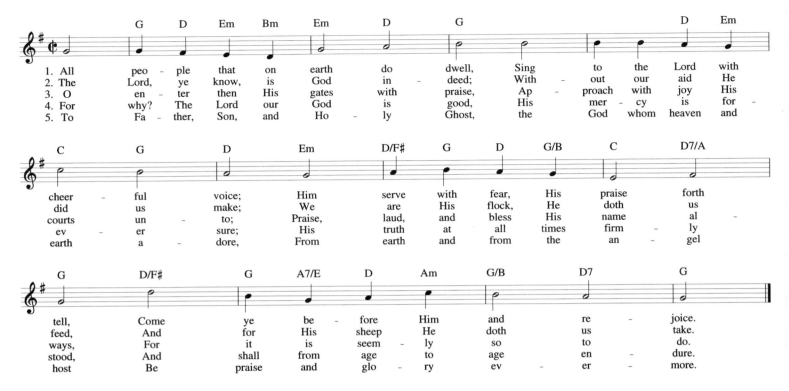

1. All peo - ple that on earth do dwell, Sing to the Lord with
2. The Lord, ye know, is God in - deed; With - out our aid He
3. O en - ter then His gates with praise, Ap - proach with joy His
4. For why? The Lord our God is good, His mer - cy is for -
5. To Fa - ther, Son, and Ho - ly Ghost, the God whom heaven and

cheer - ful voice; Him serve with fear, His praise forth
did us make; We are His flock, He doth us
courts un - to; Praise, laud, and bless His name al -
ev - er sure; His truth at all times firm - ly
earth a - dore, From truth earth and from the an - gel

tell, Come ye be - fore Him and re - joice.
feed, And for His sheep He doth us take.
ways, For it is seem - ly so to do.
stood, And shall from age to age en - dure.
host Be praise and glo - ry ev - er more.

ALL PRAISE TO OUR REDEEMING LORD

ARMENIA
music by
Sylvanus B. Pond, 1836

words by
Charles Wesley, 1747

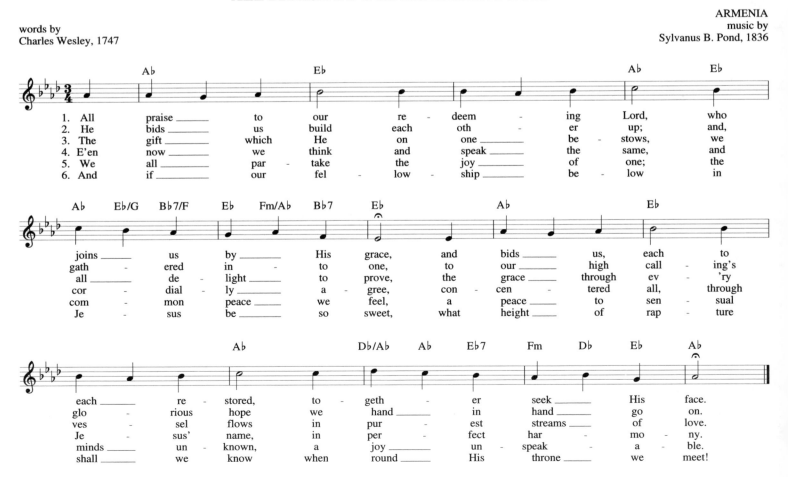

1. All praise to our re - deem - ing Lord, who
2. He bids us build each oth - er up; and,
3. The gift which He on one be - stows, we
4. E'en now we think and speak the same, and
5. We all par - take the joy of one; the
6. And if our fel - low - ship be - low in

joins us by His grace, and bids us, each to
gath - ered in - to our high call - ing's
all de - light to prove, the grace through ev - 'ry
cor - dial - ly a - gree, con - cen - tered all, through
com - mon peace we feel, a peace to sen - sual
Je - sus be so sweet, what height of rap - ture

each re - stored, to - geth - er seek His face.
glo - rious hope we hand in hand go on.
ves - sel flows in pur - est streams of love.
Je - sus' name, in per - fect har - mo - ny.
minds un - known, a joy un - speak - a - ble.
shall we know when round His throne we meet!

ALL PRAISE TO THEE, MY GOD, THIS NIGHT

words by
Thomas Ken, c. 1674

TALLIS' CANON
music by
Thomas Tallis, c. 1567

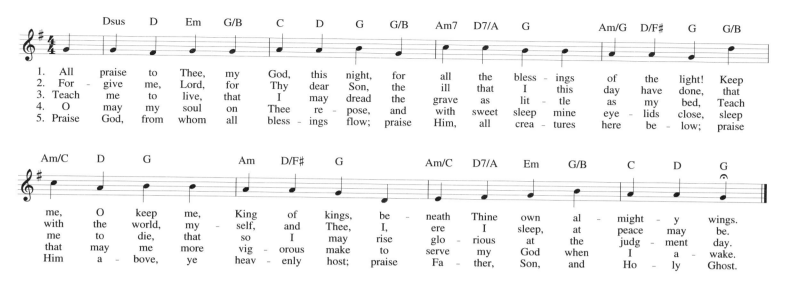

1. All praise to Thee, my God, this night, for all the bless - ings of the light! Keep
2. For - give me, Lord, for Thy dear Son, the ill that I this day have done, that
3. Teach me to live, that I may dread the grave as lit - tle as my bed, Teach
4. O may my soul on Thee re - pose, and with sweet sleep mine eye - lids close, sleep
5. Praise God, from whom all bless - ings flow; praise Him, all crea - tures here be - low; praise

me, O keep me, King of kings, be - neath Thine own al - might - y wings.
with me to die, that so I may rise glo - rious at the judg - ment day.
Him a - bove, ye heav - en - ly host; praise Fa - ther, Son, and Ho - ly Ghost.

the world, my - self, of and Thee, I, ere I sleep, at peace may be.
that may me more vig - orous make to serve my God when I a - wake.

Copyright © 2000 by HAL LEONARD CORPORATION

ALL THE WAY ALONG

words by
Ada Blenkhorn, 1904

music by
Lewis E. Jones, 1904

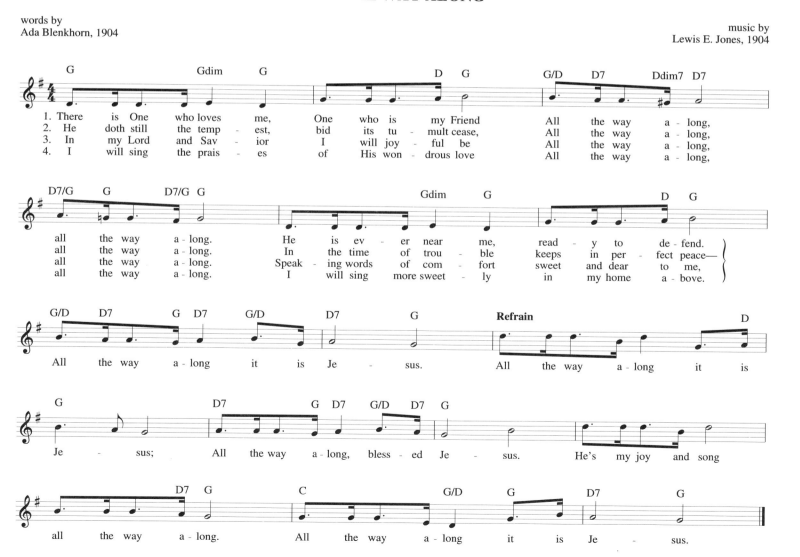

1. There is One who loves me, One who is my Friend All the way a - long,
2. He doth still the temp - est, bid its tu - mult cease, All the way a - long,
3. In my Lord and Sav - ior I will joy - ful be, All the way a - long,
4. I will sing the prais - es of His won - drous love All the way a - long,

all the way a - long. He is ev - er near me, read - y to de - fend.
all the way a - long. In the time of trou - ble keeps in per - fect peace—
all the way a - long. Speak - ing words of com - fort sweet and dear to me,
all the way a - long. I will sing more sweet - ly in my home a - bove.

Refrain
All the way a - long it is Je - sus. All the way a - long it is

Je - sus; All the way a - long, bless - ed Je - sus. He's my joy and song

all the way a - long. All the way a - long it is Je - sus.

Copyright © 2000 by HAL LEONARD CORPORATION

ALL THE WAY MY SAVIOR LEADS ME

ALL THE WAY
music by
Robert Lowry, 1875

words by
Fanny J. Crosby, 1875

ALL THINGS BRIGHT AND BEAUTIFUL

ALL THINGS BRIGHT
music by
William Henry Monk (1823-1889)

words by
Cecil Frances Alexander (1818-1895)

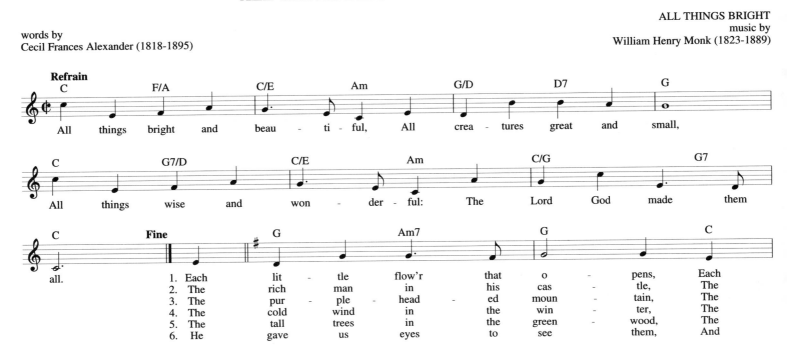

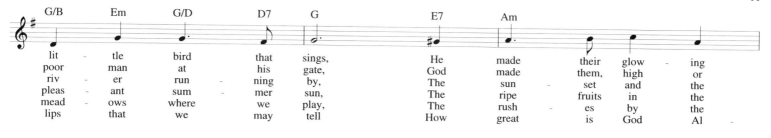

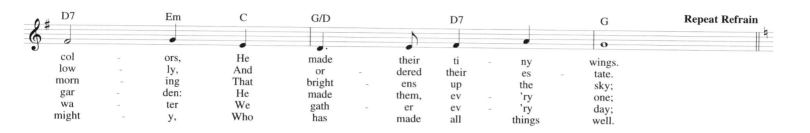

ALL THINGS BRIGHT AND BEAUTIFUL

words by
Cecil Frances Alexander, 1848

ROYAL OAK
17th century English melody

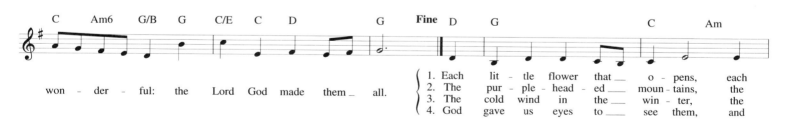

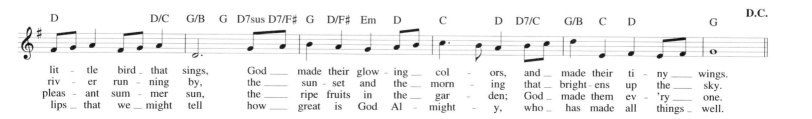

ALL WHO BELIEVE AND ARE BAPTIZED

ES IST DAS HEIL
music from
Etlich christlich Lieder, Wittenberg, 1524

words by
Thomas H. Kingo (1634-1703)
tr. by George T. Rygh (1860-1943)

1. All who believe and are baptized Shall see the Lord's salvation;
Baptized into the death of Christ, Each is a new creation;
Through Christ's redemption we shall stand Among the glorious heav'nly band Of ev'ry tribe and nation.
2. With one accord, O God, we pray, Grant us Your Holy Spirit;
Help us in our infirmity Through Jesus' blood and merit;
Grant us to grow in grace each day That, as is promised here, we may Eternal life inherit.

ALL YE WHO SEEK A COMFORT SURE

KINGSFOLD
Traditional English melody

Latin text, 18th century
tr. by Edward Caswall (1814-1878)

1. All ye who seek a comfort sure In trouble and distress,
What ever sorrow vex the mind, Or guilt the soul oppress,
Jesus who gave Himself for you Upon the Cross to die:
O pens to you His sacred Heart; O to that Heart draw nigh.
2. Ye hear how kindly He invites; Ye hear His words so blest—
"All ye that labour come to Me, And I will give you rest."
Jesus joy of Saints on high, Thou hope of sinners here,
At tracted by those loving words To Thee I lift my prayer.

ALL YOUR ANXIETY

words by
Edward Henry Joy, 1920

music by
Edward Henry Joy, 1920

ALLELUIA! ALLELUIA! LET THE HOLY ANTHEM RISE

Author unknown

LET THE HOLY ANTHEM RISE
music from
St. Basil's Hymnal, 1889

ALLELUIA! ALLELUIA!

HYMN TO JOY
music by
Ludwig van Beethoven (1770-1827)
adapted by Edward Hodges (1796-1867)

words by
Christopher Wordsworth (1807-1885)

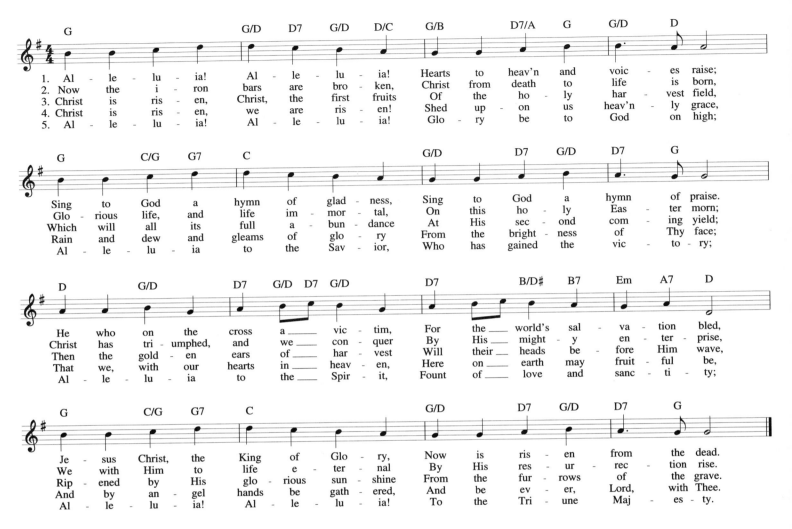

1. Al - le - lu - ia! Al - le - lu - ia! Hearts to heav'n and voic - es raise;
2. Now the i - ron bars are bro - ken, Christ from death to life is born,
3. Christ is ris - en, Christ, the first fruits Of the ho - ly har - vest field;
4. Christ is ris - en, we are ris - en! Shed up - on us heav'n - ly grace,
5. Al - le - lu - ia! Al - le - lu - ia! Glo - ry be to God on high;

Sing to God a hymn of glad - ness, Sing to God a hymn of praise.
Glo - rious life, and life im - mor - tal, On this ho - ly Eas - ter morn;
Which will all its full a - bun - dance At His sec - ond com - ing yield;
Rain and dew and gleams of glo - ry From the bright - ness of Thy face;
Al - le - lu - ia to the Sav - ior, Who has gained the vic - to - ry;

He who on the cross a vic - tim, For the world's sal - va - tion bled,
Christ has tri - umphed, and we con - quer By His might - y en - ter - prise,
Then the gold - en ears of har - vest Will their heads be - fore Him wave,
That we, with our hearts in heav - en, Here on earth may fruit - ful be,
Al - le - lu - ia to the Spir - it, Fount of love and sanc - ti - ty;

Je - sus Christ, the King of Glo - ry, Now is ris - en from the dead.
We with Him to life e - ter - nal By His res - ur - rec - tion rise.
Rip - ened by His glo - rious sun - shine From the fur - rows of the grave.
And by an - gel hands be gath - ered, And be ev - er, Lord, with Thee.
Al - le - lu - ia! Al - le - lu - ia! To the Tri - une Maj - es - ty.

ALLELUIA! ALLELUIA!

LUX EOI
music by
Arthur Seymour Sullivan (1842-1900)

words by
Christopher Wordsworth (1807-1885)

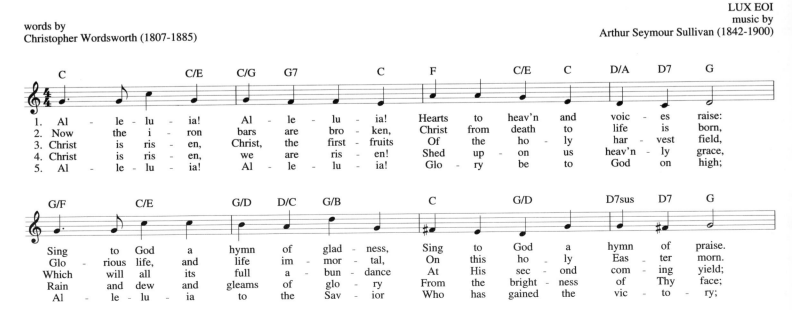

1. Al - le - lu - ia! Al - le - lu - ia! Hearts to heav'n and voic - es raise:
2. Now the i - ron bars are bro - ken, Christ from death to life is born,
3. Christ is ris - en, Christ, the first fruits Of the ho - ly har - vest field,
4. Christ is ris - en, we are ris - en! Shed up - on us heav'n - ly grace,
5. Al - le - lu - ia! Al - le - lu - ia! Glo - ry be to God on high;

Sing to God a hymn of glad - ness, Sing to God a hymn of praise.
Glo - rious life, and life im - mor - tal, On this ho - ly Eas - ter morn.
Which will all its full a - bun - dance At His sec - ond com - ing yield;
Rain and dew and gleams of glo - ry From the bright - ness of Thy face;
Al - le - lu - ia to the Sav - ior Who has gained the vic - to - ry;

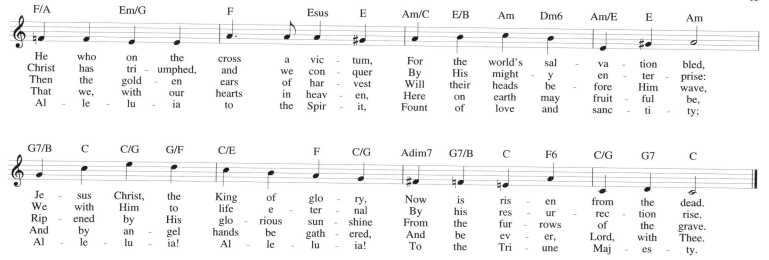

ALLELUIA! SING TO JESUS

words by
William Chatterton Dix (1837-1898)

ALLELUIA
music by
Samuel Sebastian Wesley (1810-1876)

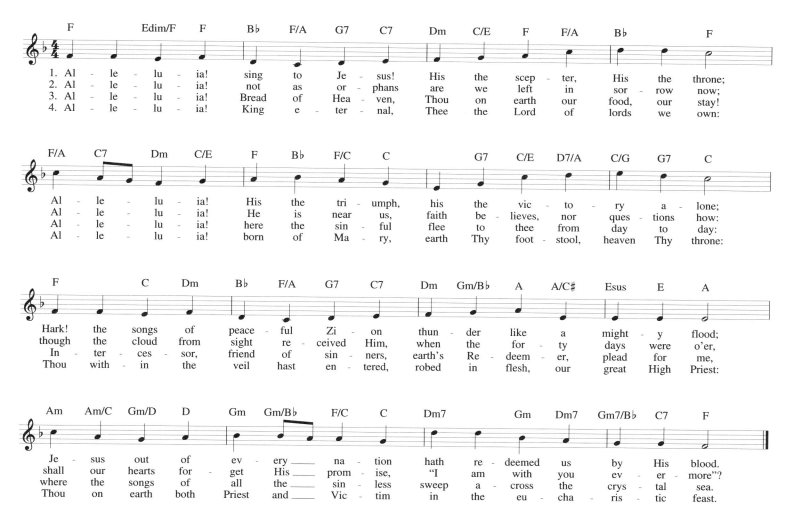

ALLELUIA! SING TO JESUS

HYFRYDOL
music by
Rowland Hugh Prichard, 1831

words by
William Chatterton Dix, 1866

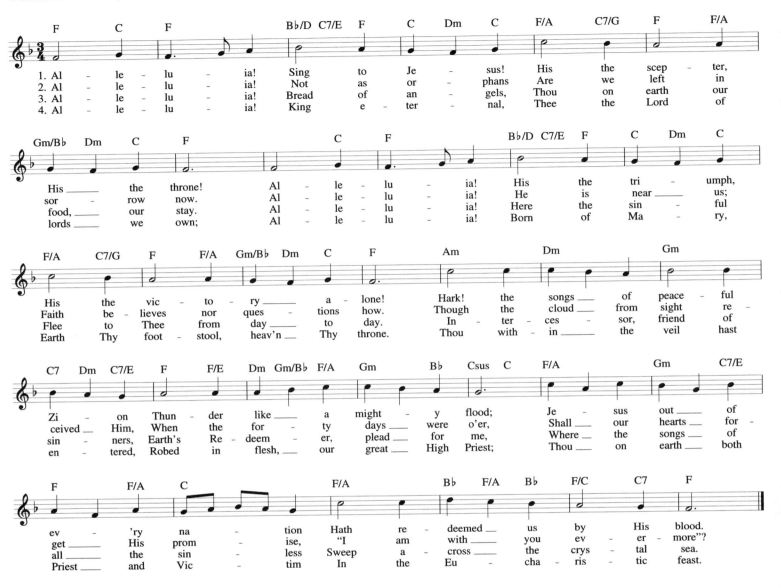

1. Al - le - lu - ia! Sing to Je - sus! His the scep - ter,
2. Al - le - lu - ia! Not as or - phans Are we left in
3. Al - le - lu - ia! Bread of an - gels, Thou on earth our
4. Al - le - lu - ia! King e - ter - nal, Thee the Lord of

His _____ the throne! Al - le - lu - ia! His the tri - umph,
sor - row now. Al - le - lu - ia! He is near us;
food, _____ our stay. Al - le - lu - ia! Here the sin - ful
lords _____ we own; Al - le - lu - ia! Born of Ma - ry,

His the vic - to - ry _____ a - lone! Hark! the songs _____ of peace - ful re -
Faith be - lieves nor ques - tions how. Though the cloud _____ from sight friend of
Flee to Thee from day _____ to day. In - ter - ces - sor, friend of
Earth Thy foot - stool, heav'n _____ Thy throne. Thou with - in _____ the veil hast

Zi - on Thun - der like _____ a might - y flood; Je - sus out _____ of
ceived _____ Him, When the for - ty days _____ were o'er, Shall _____ our hearts _____ for
sin - ners, Earth's Re - deem - er, plead _____ for me, Where the songs _____ of
en - tered, Robed in flesh, _____ our great _____ High Priest; Thou _____ on earth _____ both

ev - 'ry na - tion Hath re - deemed _____ us by His blood.
get _____ His prom - ise, "I am with _____ you ev - er - more"?
all _____ the sin - less Sweep a - cross _____ the crys - tal sea.
Priest _____ and Vic - tim In the Eu - cha - ris - tic feast.

ALMIGHTY GOD, THY WORD IS CAST

ST. FLAVIAN
music from
John Day's *Psalter*, 1562

words by
John Cawood (1775-1852)

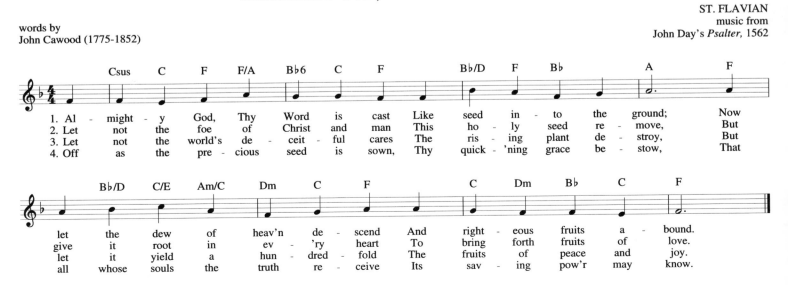

1. Al - might - y God, Thy Word is cast Like seed in - to the ground; Now
2. Let not the foe of Christ and man This ho - ly seed re - move, But
3. Let not the world's de - ceit - ful cares The ris - ing plant de - stroy, But
4. Off as the pre - cious seed is sown, Thy quick - 'ning grace be - stow, That

let the dew of heav'n de - scend And right - eous fruits a - bound.
give it root in ev - 'ry heart To bring forth fruits of love.
let it yield a hun - dred - fold The fruits of peace and joy.
all whose souls the truth re - ceive Its sav - ing pow'r may know.

ALLELUIA, SONG OF GLADNESS

Latin text, 11th century
tr. by John Mason Neale (1818-1866)

DULCE CARMEN
music from
Essay on the Church Plain Chant, 1782

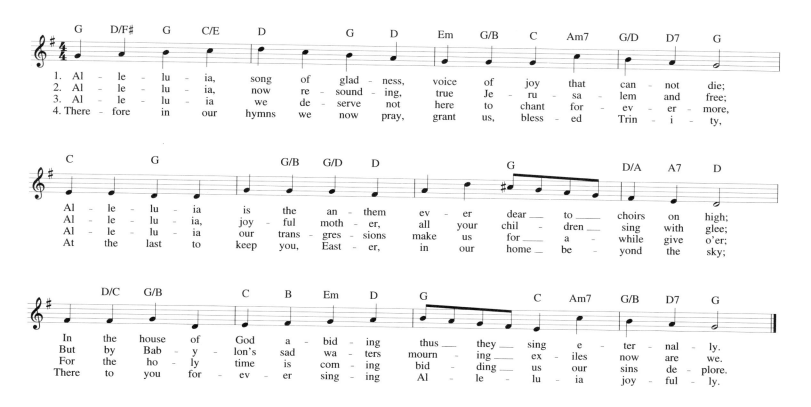

1. Al - le - lu - ia, song of glad - ness, voice of joy that can - not die;
2. Al - le - lu - ia, now re - sound - ing, true Je - ru - sa - lem and free;
3. Al - le - lu - ia we de - serve not here to chant for ev - er - more,
4. There - fore in our hymns we now pray, grant us, bless - ed Trin - i - ty,

Al - le - lu - ia is the an - them ev - er dear to choirs on high;
Al - le - lu - ia, joy - ful moth - er, all your chil - dren sing with glee;
Al - le - lu - ia our trans - gres - sions make us for a - while give o'er;
At the last to keep you, East - er, in our home be - yond the sky;

In the house of God a - bid - ing thus they sing e - ter - nal - ly.
But by Bab - y - lon's sad wa - ters mourn - ing ex - iles now are we.
For the ho - ly time is com - ing bid - ding us our sins de - plore.
There to you for - ev - er sing - ing Al - le - lu - ia joy - ful - ly.

Copyright © 2000 by HAL LEONARD CORPORATION

ALMOST PERSUADED

words by
Philip P. Bliss (1838-1876)

music by
Philip P. Bliss (1838-1876)

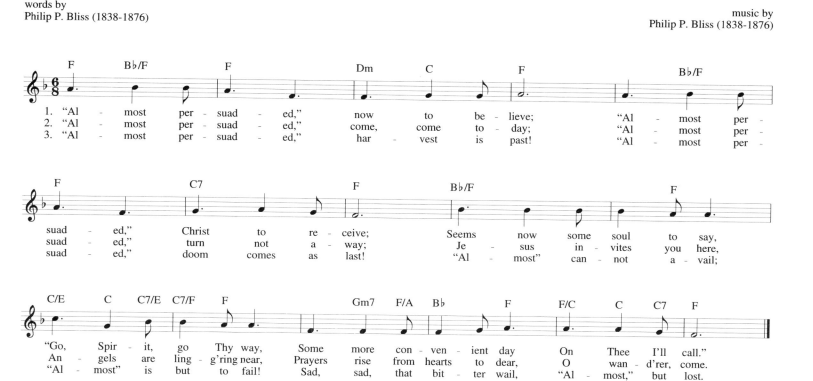

1. "Al - most per - suad - ed," now to be - lieve; "Al - most per -
2. "Al - most per - suad - ed," come, come to - day; "Al - most per -
3. "Al - most per - suad - ed," har - vest is past! "Al - most per -

suad - ed," Christ to re - ceive; Seems now some soul to say,
suad - ed," turn not a - way; Je - sus in - vites you here,
suad - ed," doom comes as last! "Al - most" can - not a - vail;

"Go, Spir - it, go Thy way, Some more con - ven - ient day On Thee I'll call."
An - gels are ling - g'ring near, Prayers rise from hearts to dear, O wan - d'rer, come.
"Al - most" is but to fail! Sad, sad, that bit - ter wail, "Al - most," but lost.

Copyright © 2000 by HAL LEONARD CORPORATION

AM I A SOLDIER OF THE CROSS

ARLINGTON

words by
Isaac Watts (1674-1748)

music by
Thomas A. Arne (1710-1778)

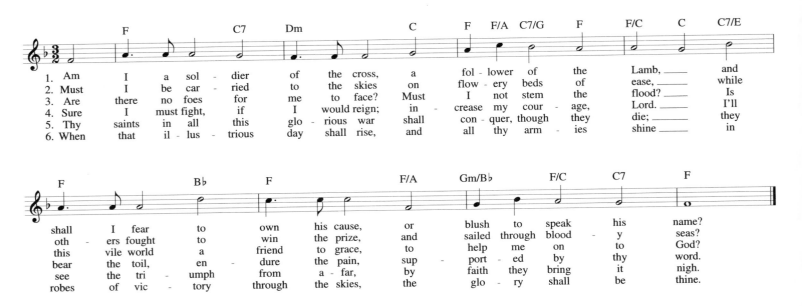

1. Am I a sol-dier of the cross, a fol-lower of the Lamb, and
2. Must I be car-ried to the skies on flow-ery beds of ease, while
3. Are there no foes for me to face? Must I not stem the flood? Is
4. Sure I must fight, if I would reign; in-crease my cour-age, Lord. I'll
5. Thy saints in all this glo-rious war shall con-quer, though they die; they
6. When that il-lus-trious day shall rise, and all thy arm-ies shine in

shall I fear to own his cause, or blush to speak his name?
oth-ers fought to win the prize, and sailed through blood-y seas?
this vile world a friend to grace, to help me on to God?
bear the toil, en-dure the pain, sup-port-ed by thy word.
see the tri-umph from a-far, by faith they bring it nigh.
robes of vic-tory through the skies, the glo-ry shall be thine.

AMAZING GRACE

words by John Newton (1725-1807), v. 1-4
v. 5 from *A Collection of Sacred Ballads*, 1790

Traditional American melody
from Carrell and Clayton's *Virginia Harmony*, 1831
arr. by Edwin O. Excell, 1900

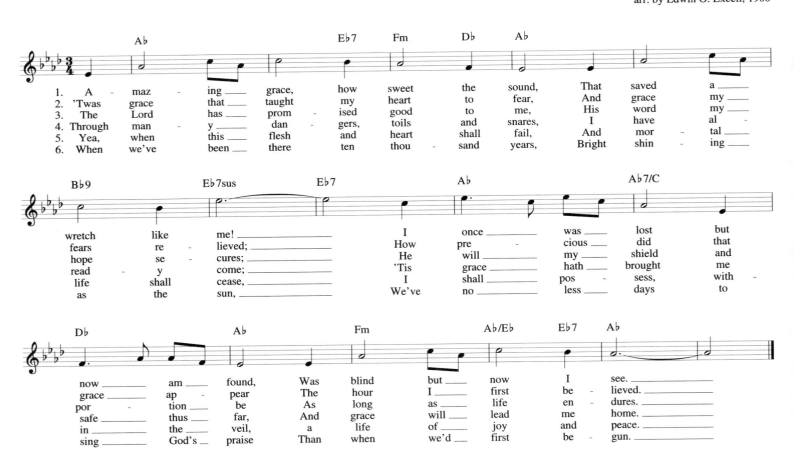

1. A-maz-ing grace, how sweet the sound, That saved a
2. 'Twas grace that taught my heart to fear, And grace my
3. The Lord has prom-ised good to me, His word my
4. Through man-y dan-gers, toils and snares, I have al-
5. Yea, when this flesh and heart shall fail, And mor-tal
6. When we've been there ten thou-sand years, Bright shin-ing

wretch like me! I once was lost but
fears re-lieved; How pre-cious did that
hope se-cures; He will my shield and
read-y come; 'Tis grace hath brought me
life shall cease, I shall pos-sess, with
as the sun, We've no less days to

now am found, Was blind but now I see.
grace ap-pear The hour I first be-lieved.
por-tion be As long as life en-dures.
safe thus far, And grace will lead me home.
in the veil, a life of joy and peace.
sing God's praise Than when we'd first be-gun.

AMERICA, THE BEAUTIFUL

words by
Katharine Lee Bates, 1904

MATERNA
music by
Samuel A. Ward, 1888

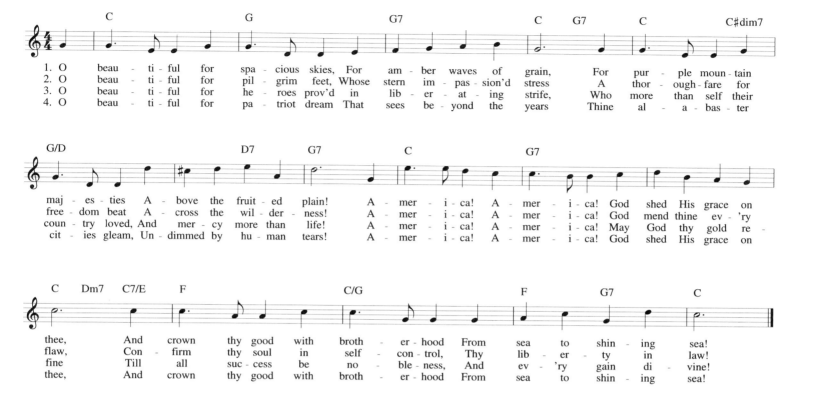

1. O beau - ti - ful for spa - cious skies, For am - ber waves of grain, For pur - ple moun - tain
2. O beau - ti - ful for pil - grim feet, Whose stern im - pas - sion'd stress A thor - ough - fare for
3. O beau - ti - ful for he - roes prov'd in lib - er - at - ing strife, Who more than self their
4. O beau - ti - ful for pa - triot dream That sees be - yond the years Thine al - a - bas - ter

maj - es - ties A - bove the fruit - ed plain! A - mer - i - ca! A - mer - i - ca! God shed His grace on
free - dom beat A - cross the wil - der - ness! A - mer - i - ca! A - mer - i - ca! God mend thine ev - 'ry
coun - try loved, And mer - cy more than life! A - mer - i - ca! A - mer - i - ca! May God thy gold re -
cit - ies gleam, Un - dimmed by hu - man tears! A - mer - i - ca! A - mer - i - ca! God shed His grace on

thee, And crown thy good with broth - er - hood From sea to shin - ing sea!
flaw, Con - firm thy soul in self - con - trol, Thy lib - er - ty in law!
fine Till all suc - cess be no - ble - ness, And ev - 'ry gain di - vine!
thee, And crown thy good with broth - er - hood From sea to shin - ing sea!

AND ARE WE YET ALIVE

words by
Charles Wesley, 1749

DENNIS
music by
Johann G. Nägeli
arr. by Lowell Mason, 1845

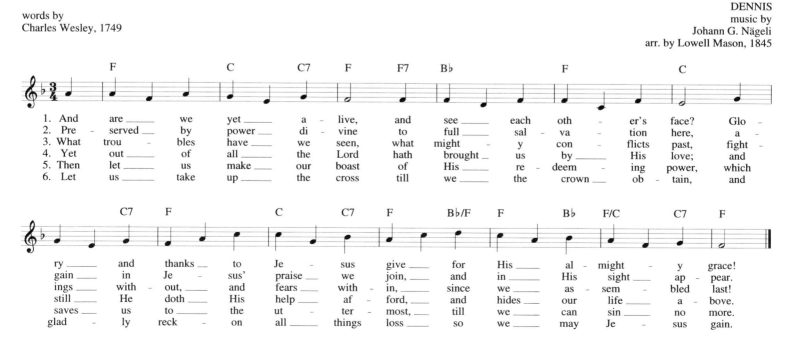

1. And are we yet a - live, and see each oth - er's face? Glo -
2. Pre - served by power di - vine to full sal - va - tion here, a -
3. What trou - bles have we seen, what might - y con - flicts past, fight -
4. Yet out of all the Lord hath brought us by His love; and
5. Then let us make our boast of His re - deem - ing power, which
6. Let us take up the cross till we the crown ob - tain, and

ry and thanks to Je - sus give for His al - might - y grace!
gain in Je - sus' praise we join, and in His sight ap - pear.
ings with - out, and fears with - in, since we as - sem - bled last!
still He doth His help af - ford, and hides our life a - bove.
saves us to the ut - ter - most, till we can sin no more.
glad - ly reck - on all things loss so we may Je - sus gain.

AND NOW, O FATHER, MINDFUL OF THE LOVE

UNDE ET MEMORES

words by
William Bright (1824-1901)

music by
William Henry Monk (1823-1889)

AND CAN IT BE THAT I SHOULD GAIN

SAGINA

words by
Charles Wesley (1707-1788)

music by
Thomas Campbell (1777-1844)

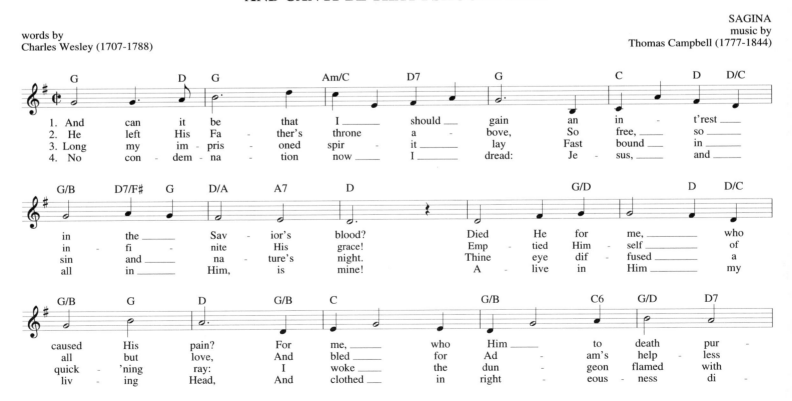

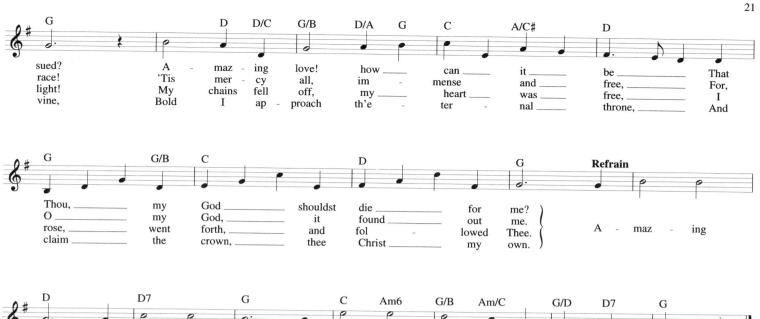

sued?   A - maz - ing love! how ___ can ___ it be ___ That
race!   'Tis mer - cy all, im - mense and ___ free, ___ For,
light!   My chains fell off, my ___ heart ___ was ___ free, ___ I
vine,   Bold I ap - proach th'e - ter - nal ___ throne, ___ And

Thou, ___ my God ___ shouldst die ___ for me?
O, ___ my God, ___ it found ___ out me.
rose, ___ went forth, ___ and fol - lowed Thee.
claim ___ the crown, ___ thee Christ ___ my own.

A - maz - ing

love! How can it be That Thou, my God, shouldst _ die for me!

ANGELS FROM THE REALMS OF GLORY

words by
James Montgomery (1771-1854)

REGENT SQUARE
music by
Henry T. Smart (1813-1879)

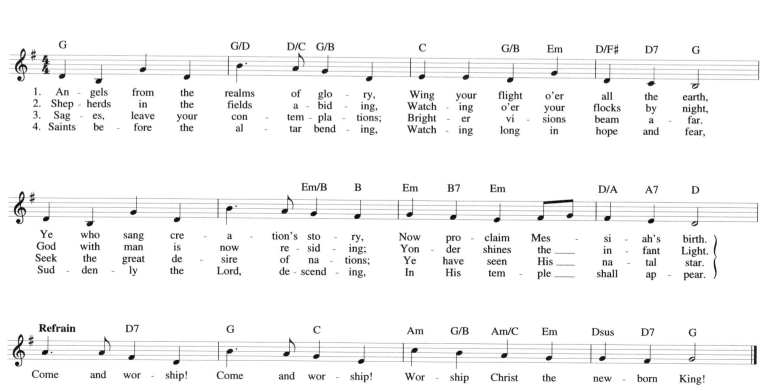

1. An - gels from the realms of glo - ry, Wing your flight o'er all the earth,
2. Shep - herds in the fields a - bid - ing, Watch - ing o'er your flocks by night,
3. Sag - es, leave your con - tem - pla - tions; Bright - er vi - sions beam a - far.
4. Saints be - fore the al - tar bend - ing, Watch - ing long in hope and fear,

Ye who sang cre - a - tion's sto - ry, Now pro - claim Mes - si - ah's birth.
God with man is now re - sid - ing; Yon - der shines the ___ in - fant Light.
Seek the great de - sire of na - tions; Ye have seen His ___ na - tal star.
Sud - den - ly the Lord, de - scend - ing, In His tem - ple ___ shall ap - pear.

Refrain
Come and wor - ship! Come and wor - ship! Wor - ship Christ the new - born King!

ANGELS WE HAVE HEARD ON HIGH

GLORIA
Traditional French melody

Traditional French carol
tr. by James Chadwick (1813-1882)

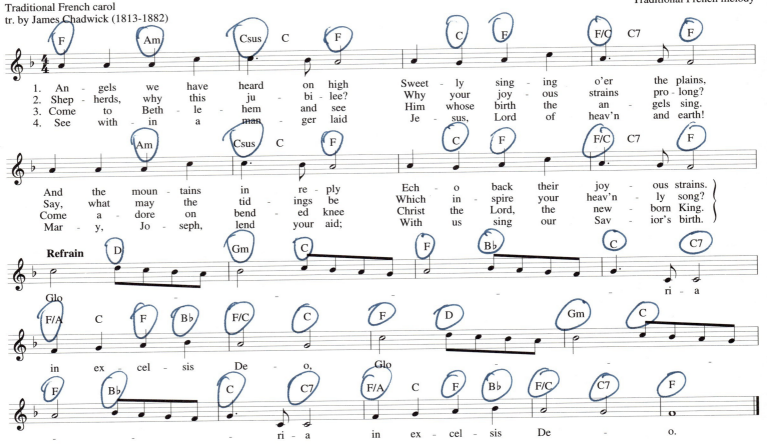

ANOTHER YEAR IS DAWNING

AURELIA
music by
Samuel S. Wesley (1810-1876)

words by
Frances Ridley Havergal (1836-1879)

ANYWHERE WITH JESUS

words by
Jessie B. Pounds (v. 1,2,4), 1887
and Helen C. Dixon (v. 3), 1915

SECURITY
music by
Daniel B. Towner, 1887

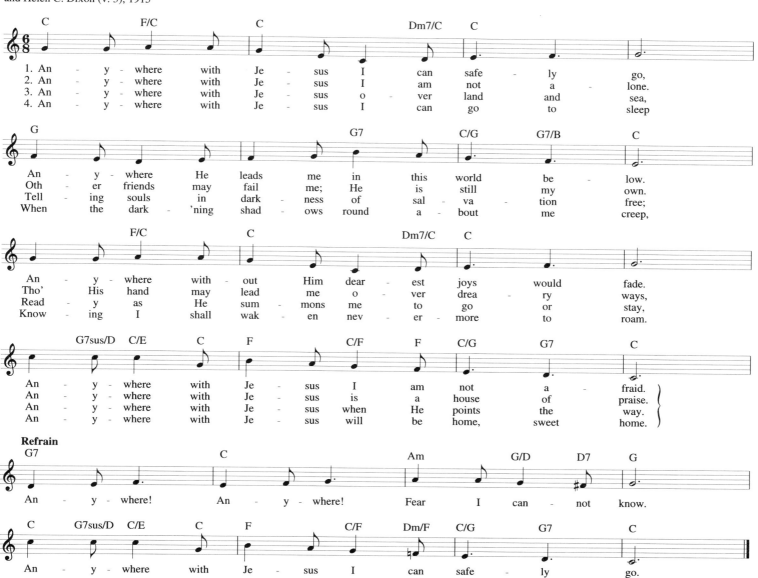

1. An - y - where with Je - sus I can safe - ly go,
2. An - y - where with Je - sus I am not a - lone.
3. An - y - where with Je - sus o - ver land and sea,
4. An - y - where with Je - sus I can go to sleep

An - y - where He leads me in this world be - low.
Oth - er friends may fail me; He is still my own.
Tell - ing souls in dark - ness of sal - va - tion free;
When the dark - 'ning shad - ows round a - bout me creep,

An - y - where with - out Him dear - est joys would fade.
Tho' His hand may lead me o - ver drea - ry ways,
Read - y as He sum - mons me to go or stay,
Know - ing I shall wak - en nev - er - more to roam.

An - y - where with Je - sus I am not a - fraid.
An - y - where with Je - sus is a house of praise.
An - y - where with Je - sus when He points the way.
An - y - where with Je - sus will be home, sweet home.

Refrain

An - y - where! An - y - where! Fear I can - not know.

An - y - where with Je - sus I can safe - ly go.

AS PANTS THE HART FOR COOLING STREAMS

words by Nahum Tate (1652-1715)
and Nicholas Brady (1659-1726)

MARTYRDOM
music by
Hugh Wilson (1764-1824)
adapted by Robert Smith (1780-1829)

1. As pants the hart for cool - ing streams When heat - ed in the
2. For Thee, my God, the liv - ing God, My thirst - y soul doth
3. Why rest - less, why cast down, my soul? Hope still, and thou shalt
4. To Fa - ther, Son and Ho - ly Ghost, The God whom we a -

chase, So longs my soul, O God, for Thee And Thy re - fresh - ing grace.
pine: O when shall I be - hold Thy face, Thou Maj - es - ty di - vine?
sing The praise of Him who is thy God, Thy health's e - ter - nal spring.
dore, Be glo - ry as it was, is now, And shall be ev - er - more.

ARE YOU WASHED IN THE BLOOD?

WASHED IN THE BLOOD
music by
Elisha A. Hoffman, 1878

words by
Elisha A. Hoffman, 1878

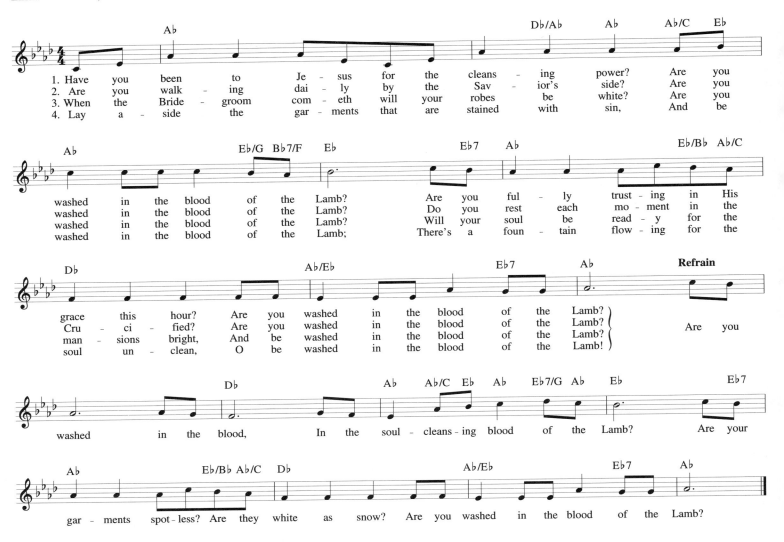

ARISE, MY SOUL, ARISE

LENOX
music by
Lewis Edson (1748-1820)

words by
Charles Wesley (1707-1788)

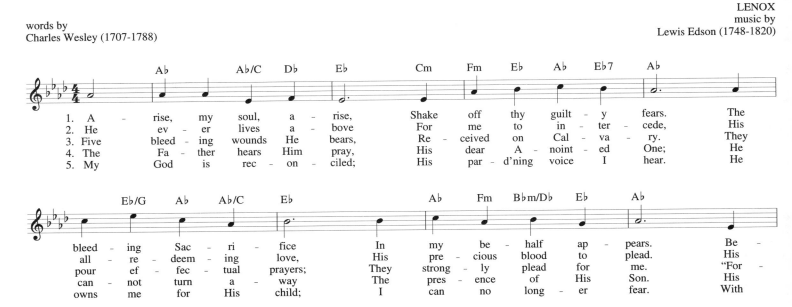

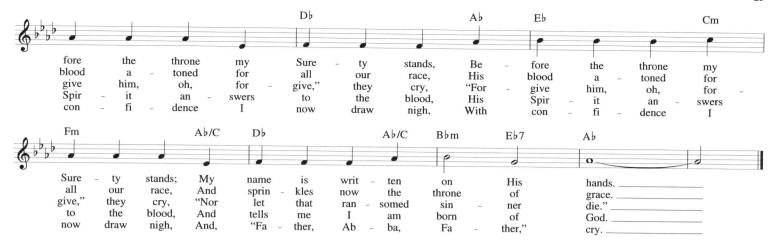

			Db			Ab	Eb		Cm

fore the throne my Sure - ty stands, Be - fore the throne my
blood a - toned my for - give," they race, cry, "For His blood a - toned my for
Spir - it an - swers give," to they the cry, His "For Spir - it an - swers
con - fi - dence I now draw blood, nigh, With con - fi - dence I

Sure - ty stands; My name is writ - ten on His hands. _____
all our race, And sprin - kles now the throne of grace. _____
give," they cry, "Nor let that ran - somed sin - ner die." _____
to the blood, And tells me I am born of God. _____
now draw nigh, And, "Fa - ther, Ab - ba, Fa - ther," cry. _____

AS THE SUN DOTH DAILY RISE

Latin Hymn Text
tr. by J. Masters
adapt. by Horatio Nelson, 1864

INNOCENTS
music from
The·Parish Choir, 1850

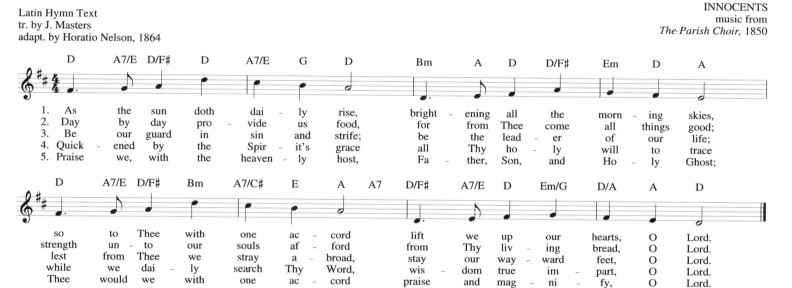

1. As the sun doth dai - ly rise, bright - ening all the morn - ing skies;
2. Day by day doth pro - vide us food, for from Thee come all things good;
3. Be our guard in sin and strife; be the lead - er of our life;
4. Quick - ened by the Spir - it's grace, all Thy ho - ly will to trace
5. Praise we, with the heaven - ly host, Fa - ther, Son, and Ho - ly Ghost;

so to Thee with one ac - cord lift we up our hearts, O Lord.
strength un - to our souls af - ford from Thy liv - ing bread, O Lord.
lest from Thee we stray a - broad, stay our way - ward feet, O Lord.
while we dai - ly search Thy Word, wis - dom true im - part, O Lord.
Thee would we with one ac - cord praise and mag - ni - fy, O Lord.

AS WITH GLADNESS MEN OF OLD

words by
William Chatterton Dix (1837-1898)

DIX
music by
Conrad Kocher (1786-1872)

1. As with glad - ness men of old Did the guid - ing star be - hold;
2. As with joy - ful steps they sped To that low - ly man - ger bed,
3. As they of - fered gifts most rare At that man - ger rude and bare,
4. Ho - ly Je - sus, ev - 'ry day Keep us in the nar - row way;

As with joy they hailed its light, Lead - ing on - ward, beam - ing bright;
There to bend the knee be - fore Him whom heav'n and earth a - dore;
So may we with ho - ly joy, Pure and free from sin's al - loy,
And when earth - ly things are past, Bring our ran - somed souls at last

So, most gra - cious Lord, may we Ev - er - more be led to Thee.
So may we with will - ing feet Ev - er seek Thy mer - cy seat.
All our cost - liest trea - sures bring, Christ, to Thee, our heav'n - ly King.
Where they need no star to guide, Where no clouds Thy glo - ry hide.

ASK YE WHAT GREAT THING I KNOW

words by
Johann C. Schwedler, 1741
tr. by Benjamin H. Kennedy, 1863

HENDON
music by
H.A. César Malan, 1827

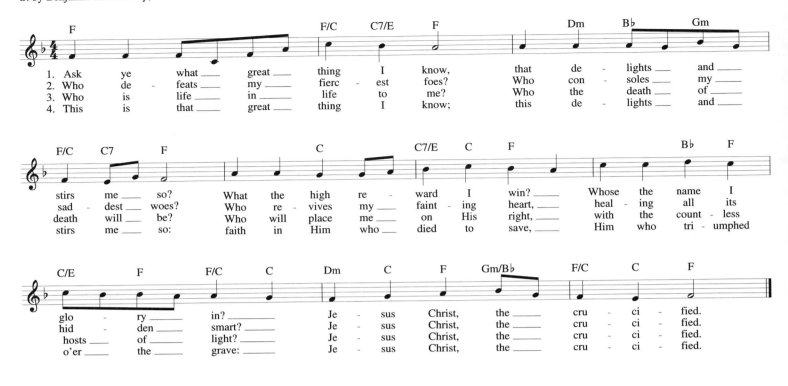

1. Ask ye what great thing I know, that de - lights and
2. Who de - feats my fierc - est foes? Who con - soles my
3. Who is life in life to me? Who the death of
4. This is that great thing I know; this de - lights and

stirs me so? What the high re - ward I win? Whose the name I
sad - dest woes? Who re - vives my faint - ing heart, heal - ing all its
death will be? Who will place me on His right, with the count - less
stirs me so: faith in Him who died to save, Him who tri - umphed

glo - ry in? Je - sus Christ, the cru - ci - fied.
hid - den smart? Je - sus Christ, the cru - ci - fied.
hosts of light? Je - sus Christ, the cru - ci - fied.
o'er the grave: Je - sus Christ, the cru - ci - fied.

AT CALVARY

words by
William R. Newell, 1895

CALVARY
music by
Daniel B. Towner, 1895

1. Years I spent in van - i - ty and pride, Car - ing not my Lord was cru - ci - fied,
2. By God's Word at last my sin I learned; Then I trem - bled at the law I'd spurned,
3. Now I've giv'n to Je - sus ev - 'ry - thing, Now I glad - ly own Him as my King,
4. O the love that drew sal - va - tion's plan! O the grace that brought it down to man!

Know - ing not it was for me He died on Cal - va - ry.
Till my guilt - y soul im - plor - ing turned to Cal - va - ry.
Now my rap - tured soul can on - ly sing of Cal - va - ry.
O the might - y gulf that God did span at Cal - va - ry!

Mer - cy there was great and grace was free, Par - don there was mul - ti - plied to me,

There my bur - dened soul found lib - er - ty, at Cal - va - ry.

AT THE CROSS

words by Isaac Watts, 1707 (verses)
and Ralph E. Hudson, 1885 (refrain)

HUDSON
music by
Ralph E. Hudson, 1885

AT THE CROSS, HER VIGIL KEEPING

words by
Jacopone da Todi, 13th century
tr. by Edward Caswall (1814-1878)

STABAT MATER
music from
Maintzisch Gesangbuch, 1661

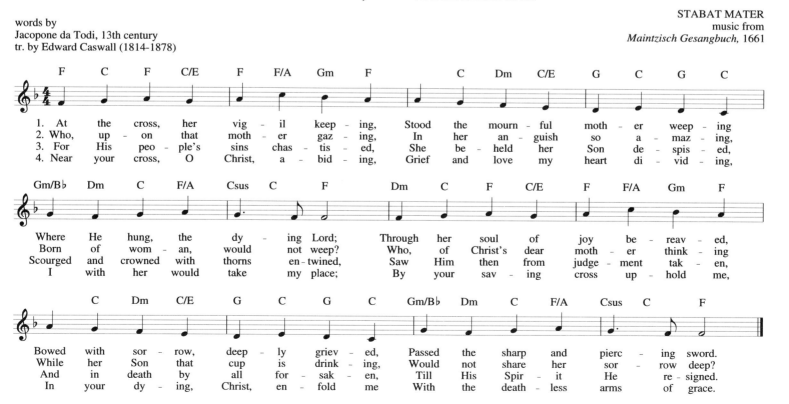

AT THE LAMB'S HIGH FEAST WE SING

SALZBURG
music by
Jakob Hintze (1622-1702)

4th century Latin text
tr. by Robert Campbell (1814-1868)

1. At the Lamb's high feast we sing Praise to our vic-to-rious King.
2. Where the Pas-chal blood is poured, Death's dark an-gel sheathes his sword;
3. Might-y Vic-tim from the sky, Hell's fierce pow'rs be-neath Thee lie;

Who hath washed us in the tide Flow-ing from His pierc-ed side;
Is-rael's hosts tri-um-phant go Through the wave that drowns the foe.
Thou hast con-quered in the flight, Thou hast brought us life and light;

Praise we Him whose love di-vine, Gives His sa-cred Blood for wine,
Praise we Christ, whose blood was shed, Gives Pas-chal Vic-tim, Pas-chal Bread;
Now no more can death ap-pall, Now no more the grave en-thrall;

Gives His Bod-y for the feast, Christ the Vic-tim, Christ the Priest.
With sin-cer-i-ty and love Eat we man-na from a-bove.
Thou hast o-pened par-a-dise, And in Thee Thy saints shall rise.

Copyright © 2000 by HAL LEONARD CORPORATION

AT THE NAME OF JESUS

WYE VALLEY
music by
James Mountain, 1876

words by
Caroline M. Noel, 1870

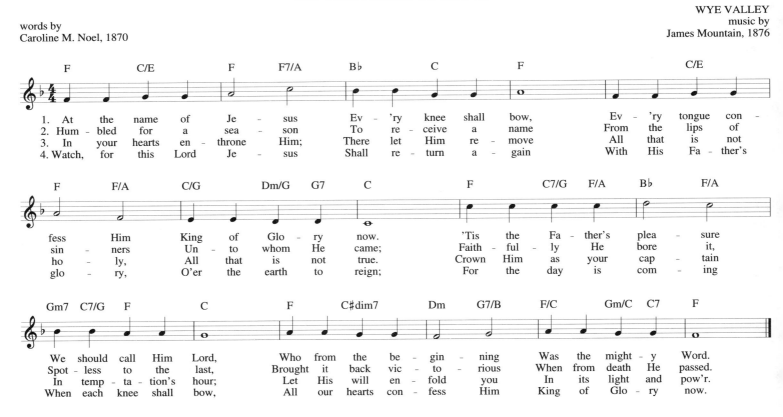

1. At the name of Je-sus Ev-'ry knee shall bow, Ev-'ry tongue con-
2. Hum-bled for a sea-son To re-ceive a name From the lips of
3. In your hearts en-throne Him; There let Him re-move All that is not
4. Watch, for this Lord Je-sus Shall re-turn a-gain With His Fa-ther's

fess Him King of Glo-ry now. 'Tis the Fa-ther's plea-sure
sin-ners Un-to whom He came; Faith-ful-ly He bore it,
ho-ly, All that is not true. Crown Him as your cap-tain
glo-ry, O'er the earth to reign; For the day is com-ing

We should call Him Lord, Who from the be-gin-ning Was the might-y Word.
Spot-less to the last, Brought it back vic-to-rious When from death He passed.
In temp-ta-tion's hour; Let His will en-fold you In its light and pow'r.
When each knee shall bow, All our hearts con-fess Him King of Glo-ry now.

Copyright © 2000 by HAL LEONARD CORPORATION

AWAKE AND SING THE SONG

words by
William Hammond (1719-1783)

ST. ETHELWALD
music by
William Henry Monk (1823-1889)

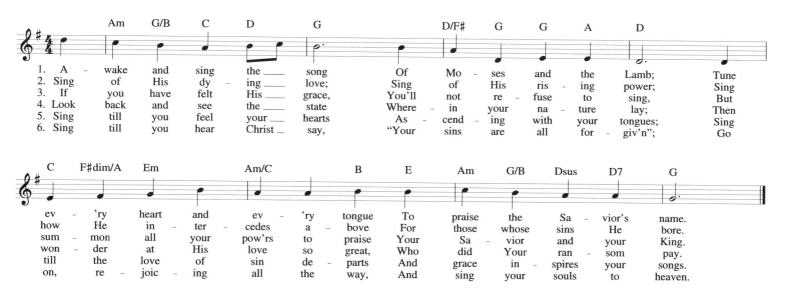

1. A - wake and sing the ____ song Of Mo - ses and the Lamb; Tune
2. Sing of His dy - ing ____ love; Sing of His ris - ing power; Sing
3. If you have felt His ____ grace, You'll not re - fuse to sing, But
4. Look back and see the ____ state Where in your na - ture lay; Then
5. Sing till you feel your ____ hearts As - cend - ing with your tongues; Sing
6. Sing till you hear Christ ____ say, "Your sins are all for - giv'n"; Go

ev - 'ry heart and ev - 'ry tongue To praise the Sa - vior's name.
how He in - ter - cedes a - bove For those whose sins He bore.
sum - mon all your pow'rs to praise Your Sa - vior and your King.
won - der at His love so great, Who did Your ran - som pay.
till the love of sin de - parts And grace in - spires your songs.
on, re - joic - ing all the way, And sing your souls to heaven.

AWAKE, AWAKE TO LOVE AND WORK

words by
Geoffrey Anketel Studdert-Kennedy (1883-1929)

MORNING SONG
music from
Wyeth's *Repository of Sacred Music, Part Second*, 1813

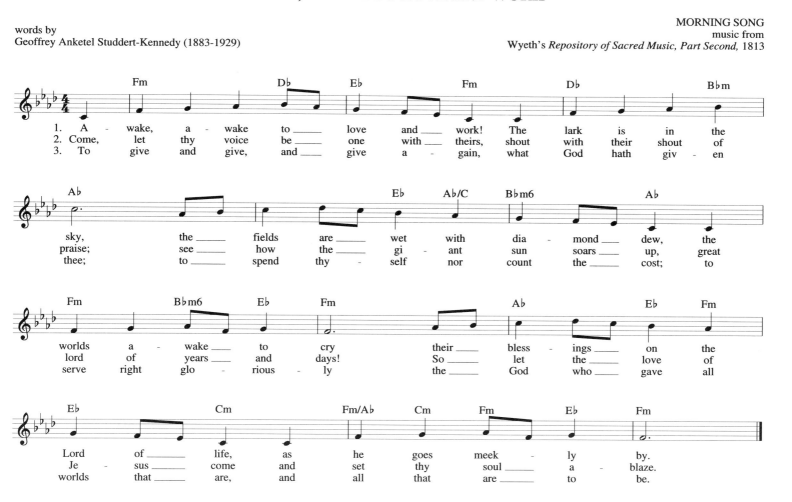

1. A - wake, a - wake to ____ love and ____ work! The lark is in the
2. Come, let thy voice be ____ one with ____ theirs, shout with their shout of
3. To give and give, and ____ give a - gain, what God hath giv - en

sky, the ____ fields are ____ wet with dia - mond ____ dew, the
praise; see ____ how the ____ gi - ant sun soars ____ up, the great
thee; to ____ spend thy - self nor count the ____ cost; to

worlds a - wake ____ to cry their ____ bless - ings ____ on the
lord of years ____ and days! So ____ let the ____ love of
serve right glo - rious - ly the ____ God who ____ gave all

Lord of ____ life, as he goes meek - ly by.
Je - sus ____ come and set thy soul ____ a - blaze.
worlds that ____ are, and all that are ____ to be.

AWAKE, MY HEART, WITH GLADNESS

AUF, AUF, MEIN HERZ

words by
Paul Gerhardt (1607-1676)
tr. by John Kelly (1833-1890)

music by
Johann Crüger (1598-1662)

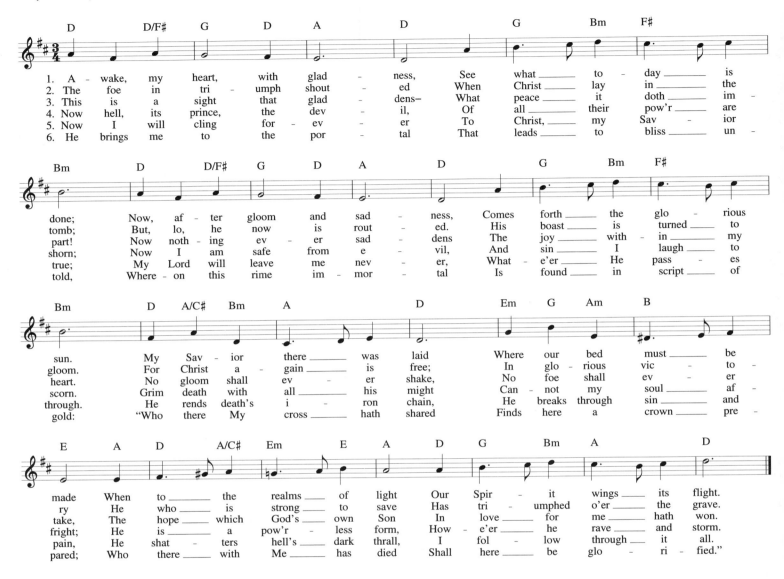

1. A - wake, my heart, with glad - ness, See what to - day is
2. The foe in tri - umph shout - ed When Christ lay in the
3. This is a sight that glad - dens— What peace it doth im -
4. Now hell, its prince, the dev - il, Of all their pow'r are
5. Now I will cling for - ev - er To Christ, my Sav - ior
6. He brings me to the por - tal That leads to bliss un -

done; Now, af - ter gloom and sad - ness, Comes forth the glo - rious
tomb; But, lo, he now is rout - ed, His boast is turned to
part! Now noth - ing ev - er sad - dens The joy with - in my
shorn; Now I am safe from e - vil, And sin I laugh to
true; My Lord will leave me nev - er, What - e'er He pass - es
told, Where - on this rime im - mor - tal Is found in script of

sun. My Sav - ior there was laid Where our bed must be
gloom. For Christ a - gain is free; In glo - rious vic - to -
heart. No gloom shall ev - er shake, No foe shall ev - er
scorn. Grim death with all his might Can - not my soul af -
through. He rends death's i - ron chain, He breaks through sin and
gold: "Who there My cross hath shared Finds here a crown pre -

made When to the realms of light Our Spir - it wings its flight.
ry He who is strong to save Has tri - umphed o'er the grave.
take, The hope which God's own Son In love for me hath won.
fright; He is a pow'r - less form, How - e'er he rave and storm.
pain, He shat - ters hell's dark thrall, I fol - low through it all.
pared; Who there with Me has died Shall here be glo - ri - fied."

Copyright © 2000 by HAL LEONARD CORPORATION

AWAKE, MY SOUL, STRETCH EVERY NERVE

SIROË

words by
Philip Doddridge (1702-1751)

music by
George Frideric Handel (1685-1759)
adapt. in *Melodia Sacra*, 1815

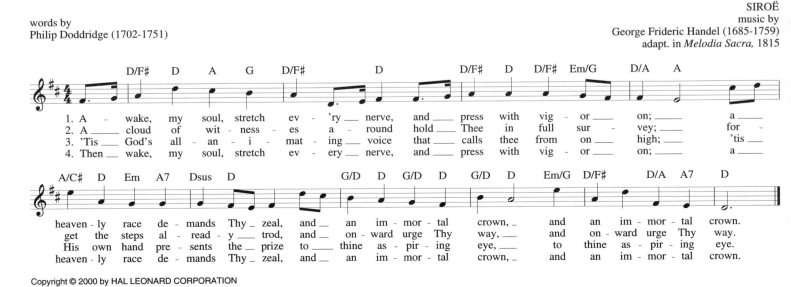

1. A - wake, my soul, stretch ev - 'ry nerve, and press with vig - or on; a -
2. A cloud of wit - ness - es a - round hold Thee in full sur - vey; for -
3. 'Tis God's all - an - i - mat - ing voice that calls thee from on high; 'tis
4. Then wake, my soul, stretch ev - ery nerve, and press with vig - or on; a -

heaven - ly race de - mands Thy zeal, and an im - mor - tal crown, and an im - mor - tal crown.
get the steps al - read - y trod, and on - ward urge Thy way, and on - ward urge Thy way.
His own hand pre - sents the prize to thine as - pir - ing eye, to thine as - pir - ing eye.
heaven - ly race de - mands Thy zeal, and an im - mor - tal crown, and an im - mor - tal crown.

Copyright © 2000 by HAL LEONARD CORPORATION

AWAKE, MY SOUL, AND WITH THE SUN

words by
Thomas Ken (1637-1711)

MORNING HYMN
music by
François H. Barthélémon (1741-1808)

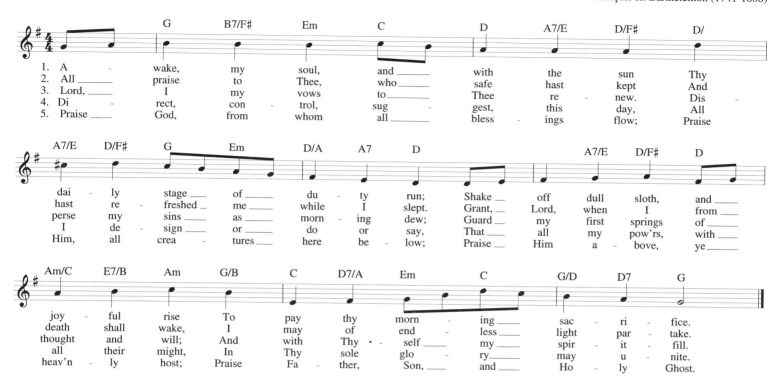

1. A - wake, my soul, and with the sun Thy
2. All praise to Thee, who safe hast kept And
3. Lord, I my vows to Thee re - new. Dis
4. Di - rect, con - trol, sug - gest, this day, All
5. Praise God, from whom all bless - ings flow; Praise

dai - ly stage of du - ty run; Shake off dull sloth, and
hast re - freshed me while I slept. Grant, Lord, when first springs of
perse my sins as morn - ing dew; Guard my first springs of
I de - sign or do or say, That all my pow'rs, with
Him, all crea - tures here be - low; Praise Him a - bove, ye

joy - ful rise To pay thy morn - ing sac - ri - fice.
death shall wake, To I may of end - less light par - take.
thought and will; And with Thy - self my spir - it - fill.
all their might, In Thy sole glo - ry may u - nite.
heav'n - ly host; Praise Fa - ther, Son, and Ho - ly Ghost.

AWAY IN A MANGER

Author unknown (v. 1,2)
v. 3 by John T. McFarland (1851-1913)

CRADLE SONG
music by
William J. Kirkpatrick (1838-1921)

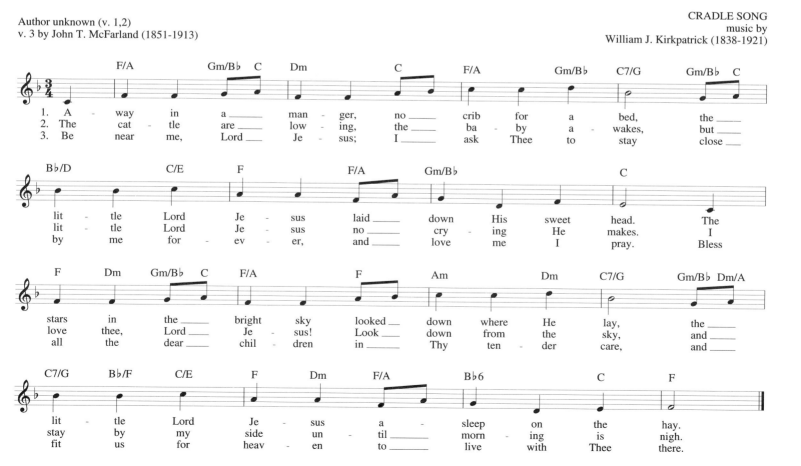

1. A - way in a man - ger, no crib for a bed, the
2. The cat - tle are low - ing, the ba - by a - wakes, but
3. Be near me, Lord Je - sus; I ask Thee to stay close

lit - tle Lord Je - sus laid down His sweet head. The
lit - tle Lord Je - sus no cry - ing He makes. I
by me for - ev - er, and love me I pray. Bless

stars in the bright sky looked down where He lay, the
love thee, Lord Je - sus! Look down from the sky, and
all the dear chil - dren in Thy ten - der care, and

lit - tle Lord Je - sus a - sleep on the hay.
stay by my side un - til morn - ing is nigh.
fit us for heav - en to live with Thee there.

AWAY IN A MANGER

MUELLER
music by
James R. Murray (1841-1905)

Author unknown (v. 1,2)
v. 3 by John T. McFarland (1851-1913)

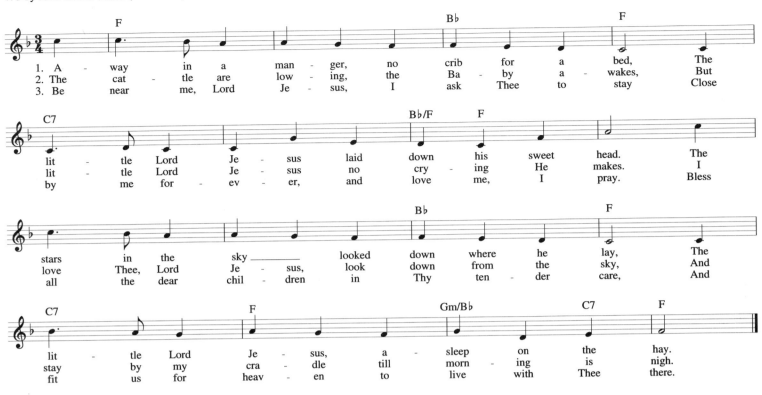

1. A - way in a man - ger, no crib for a bed, The
2. The cat - tle are low - ing, no the Ba - by a - wakes, But
3. Be near me, Lord Je - sus, I ask Thee to stay Close

lit - tle Lord Je - sus laid down his sweet head. The
lit - tle Lord Je - sus no cry - ing He makes. I
by me for - ev - er, and love me, I pray. Bless

stars in the sky _____ looked down where he lay, The
love Thee, Lord Je - sus, look down from the sky, And
all the dear chil - dren in Thy ten - der care, And

lit - tle Lord Je - sus, a - sleep on the hay.
stay by my cra - dle till morn - ing is nigh.
fit us for heav - en to live with Thee there.

Copyright © 1992 by HAL LEONARD CORPORATION

THE BANNER OF THE CROSS

ROYAL BANNER
music by
James McGranahan (1840-1907)

words by
Daniel W. Whittle (1840-1901)

1. There's a roy - al ban - ner giv - en for dis - play To the sol - diers of the
2. Though the foe may rage and gath - er as the flood, Let the stand - ard be dis -
3. O - ver land and sea, wher - ev - er man may dwell, Make the glo - rious tid - ings
4. When the glo - ry dawns— 'tis draw - ing ver - y near— It is has - t'ning day by

King; As an en - sign fair we lift it up to - day, While as ran - somed ones we
played; And be - neath its folds, as sol - diers of the Lord, For the truth be not dis -
known; Of the crim - son ban - ner now the sto - ry tell, While the Lord shall claim His
day; Then be - fore our King the foe shall dis - ap - pear, And the cross the world shall

sing.
mayed.
own!
sway!   March - ing on, march - ing on, For Christ count ev - 'ry-thing but loss! And to

crown Him King, toil and sing 'Neath the ban - ner of the cross!

Copyright © 2000 by HAL LEONARD CORPORATION

BAPTIZED INTO THY NAME MOST HOLY

words by
J.J. Rambach (1693-1735)
tr. by Catherine Winkworth (1827-1878)

O DASS ICH TAUSEND ZUNGEN HÄTTE
music by
K.H. Dretzel (1697-1775)

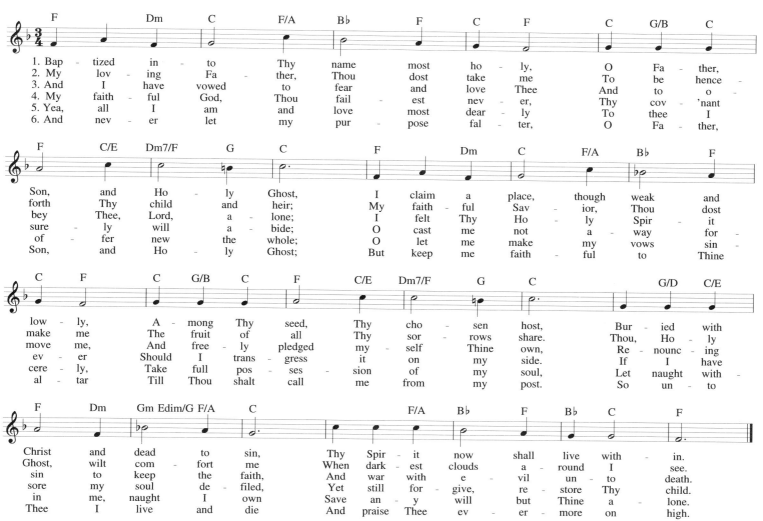

1. Bap - tized in - to Thy name most ho - ly, O Fa - ther,
2. My lov - ing Fa - ther, Thou dost take me To be hence -
3. And I have vowed to fear and love Thee And to o -
4. My faith - ful God, Thou fail - est nev - er, Thy cov - 'nant
5. Yea, all I am and love most dear - ly To thee I
6. And nev - er let my pur - pose fal - ter, O Fa - ther,

Son, and Ho - ly Ghost, I claim a place, though weak and
forth Thy child, Thy child, My faith - ful Sav - ior, Thou dost
bey Thee, Lord, a - lone; I felt Thy Ho - ly Spir - it
sure of - fer new the whole; O cast me not a - way for
Son, and Ho - ly Ghost; But keep me faith - ful to Thine

low - ly, A - mong Thy seed, Thy cho - sen host, Bur - ied with
make me, The fruit of all Thy sor - rows share. Thou, Ho - ly
move me, And free - ly pledged my - self Thine own, Re - nounc - ing
ev - er, Should I trans - gress it on my side. If I have
cere - ly, Take full pos - ses - sion of my soul, Let naught with -
al - tar Till Thou shalt call me from my post. So un - to

Christ and dead to sin, Thy Spir - it now shall live with - in.
Ghost, wilt com - fort me, When dark - est clouds a - round I see.
sin, to keep the faith, And war with e - vil un - to death.
sore my soul de - filed, Yet still for - give, re - store Thy child.
in me, naught I own, Save an - y will but Thine a - lone.
Thee I live and die And praise Thee ev - er - more on high.

Copyright © 2000 by HAL LEONARD CORPORATION

BE JOYFUL, MARY

Latin text, 17th century
tr. in *Psallite*, 1901

REGINA CAELI
music from
Leisentritt's *Catholicum Hymnologium Germanicum, 1584*

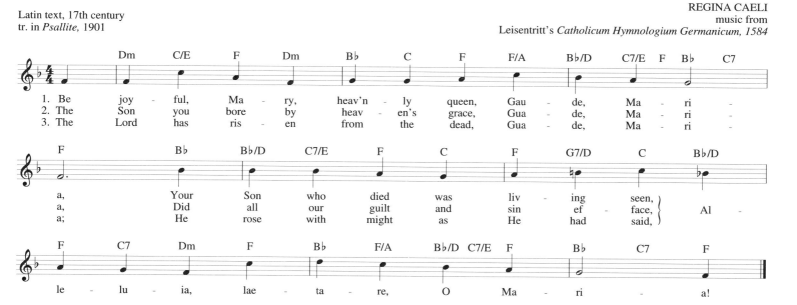

1. Be joy - ful, Ma - ry, heav'n - ly queen, Gau - de, Ma - ri -
2. The Son you bore by heav - en's grace, Gua - de, Ma - ri -
3. The Lord has ris - en from the dead, Gua - de, Ma - ri -

a, Your Son who died was liv - ing seen, Al -
a, Did all our guilt and sin ef - face, Al -
a; He all rose with might as He had said, Al -

le - lu - ia, lae - ta - re, O Ma - ri - a!

Copyright © 2000 by HAL LEONARD CORPORATION

BATTLE HYMN OF THE REPUBLIC

BATTLE HYMN
Traditional American melody, 19th century

words by
Julia Ward Howe (1819-1910)

1. Mine eyes have seen the glo-ry of the com-ing of the Lord, He is tram-pling out the vin-tage where the
2. seen Him in the watch-fires of a hun-dred cir-cling camps, They have build-ed Him an al-tar in the
3. sound-ed forth the trum-pet that shall nev-er sound re-treat, He is sift-ing out the hearts of men be-
4. beau-ty of the lil-ies Christ was born a-cross the sea, With a glo-ry in His bos-on that trans-

grapes of wrath are stored. He hath loos'd the fate-ful light-ning of His ter-ri-ble swift sword; His
eve-ning dews and damps. I can read His right-eous sen-tence by the dim and flar-ing lamps; His
fore His judg-ment seat. O be swift, my soul, to an-swer Him! Be ju-bi-lant, my feet! Our
fig-ures you and me. As He died to make men ho-ly, let us die to make men free, While

truth is march-ing on.
day is march-ing on.
God is march-ing on.
God is march-ing on.

Glo-ry, glo-ry, hal-le-lu-jah! Glo-ry, glo-ry, hal-le-

lu-jah! Glo-ry, glo-ry, hal-le-lu-jah! His truth is march-ing on.

(2.) I have on.
(3.) He has
(4.) In the

BE KNOWN TO US IN BREAKING BREAD

ST. FLAVIAN
music from
Day's *Psalter*, 1562

words by
James Montgomery, 1825

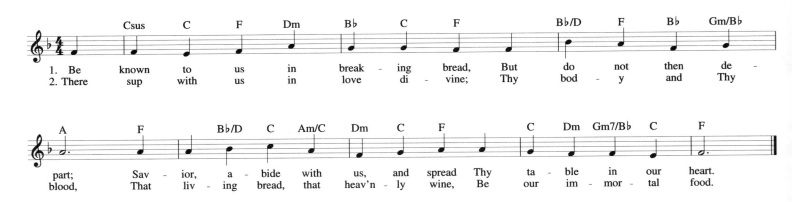

1. Be known to us in break-ing bread, But do not then de-
2. There sup with us in love di-vine; Thy bod-y and Thy

part; Sav-ior, a-bide with us, and spread Thy ta-ble in our heart.
blood, That liv-ing bread, that heav'n-ly wine, Be our im-mor-tal food.

BE PRESENT AT OUR TABLE, LORD

words by
John Cennick, 1741

OLD HUNDREDTH
music attr. to
Louis Bourgeois, 1551

1. Be pres - ent at our ta - ble, Lord; be here and ev - 'ry - where a - dored; Thy
2. We thank Thee, Lord, for this our food, but more be - cause of Je - sus' blood; let

crea - tures bless, and grant that we may feast in par - a - dise with Thee.
man - na to our souls be giv'n, the bread of life sent down from heav'n.

BE STILL AND KNOW

Author unknown
based on Psalm 46:10, Exodus 15:26

Composer unknown

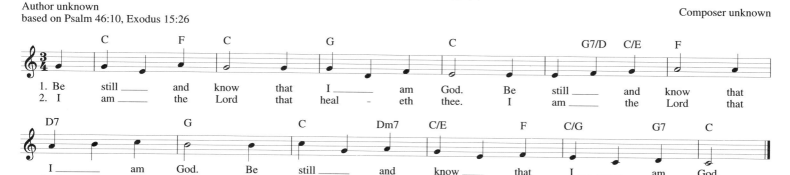

1. Be still and know that I am God. Be still and know that
2. I am the Lord that heal - eth thee. I am and the know Lord that

I am God. Be still and know that I am God.
heal - eth thee. I am the Lord that heal - eth thee.

BE STILL, MY SOUL

words by
Katharina von Schlegel, 1752
tr. by Jane L. Borthwick, 1855

FINLANDIA
music by
Jean Sibelius, 1899

1. Be still, my soul! The Lord is on thy side; Bear pa - tient - ly the
2. Be still, my soul! Thy God doth un - der - take To guide the fu - ture
3. Be still, my soul! The hour is has - t'ning on When we shall be for -

cross of grief or pain. Leave to thy God to or - der and pro - vide;
as He has the past. Thy hope, thy con - fi - dence let noth - ing shake;
ev - er with the Lord, When dis - ap - point - ment, grief, and fear are gone,

In ev - 'ry change He faith - ful will re - main. Be still, my soul! Thy
All now mys - te - rious shall be bright at last. Be still, my soul! The
Sor - row for - got, love's pur - est joys re - stored. Be still, my soul! The

best, thy heav'n - ly Friend Thro' thorn - y ways leads to a joy - ful end.
waves and winds still know His voice who ruled them while He dwelt be - low.
change and tears are past, All safe and bless - ed we shall meet at last.

BE THOU MY VISION

SLANE
Traditional Irish melody

Ancient Irish poem
tr. by Mary E. Byrne, 1905

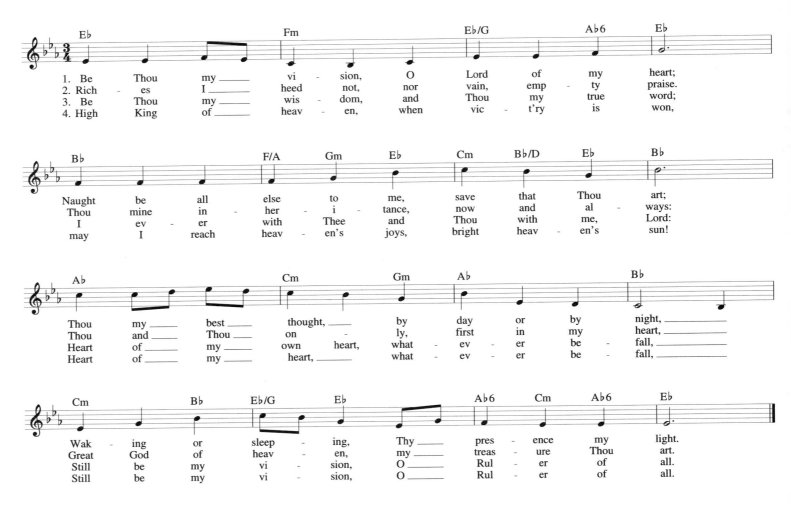

1. Be Thou my vi - sion, O Lord of my heart;
2. Rich - es I heed not, nor vain, emp - ty praise.
3. Be Thou my wis - dom, and Thou my true word;
4. High King of heav - en, when vic - t'ry is won,

Naught be all else to me, save that Thou art;
Thou mine in - her - i - tance, now and al - ways:
Thou and Thou on - ly, first in my heart,
may I reach heav - en's joys, bright heav - en's sun!

Thou my best thought, by day or by night,
Thou and Thou on - ly, first in my heart,
Heart of my own heart, what - ev - er be - fall,
Heart of my heart, what - ev - er be - fall,

Wak - ing or sleep - ing, Thy pres - ence my light.
Great God of heav - en, my treas - ure Thou art.
Still be my vi - sion, O Rul - er of all.
Still be my vi - sion, O Rul - er of all.

BEAMS OF HEAVEN AS I GO

SOMEDAY
music by
Charles Albert Tindley, c. 1906

words by
Charles Albert Tindley, c. 1906

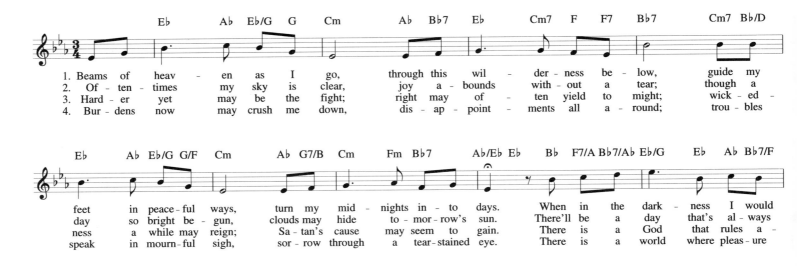

1. Beams of heav - en as I go, through this wil - der - ness be - low, guide my
2. Of - ten - times my sky is clear, joy a - bounds with - out a tear; though a
3. Hard - er yet may be the fight, right may of - ten yield to might; wick - ed
4. Bur - dens now may crush me down, dis - ap - point - ments all a - round; trou - bles

feet in peace - ful ways, turn my mid - nights in - to days. When in the dark - ness I would
day so bright be - gun, clouds may hide to - mor - row's sun. There'll be a day that's al - ways
ness a while may reign; Sa - tan's cause may seem to gain. There is a God that rules a -
speak in mourn - ful sigh, sor - row through a tear - stained eye. There is a world where pleas - ure

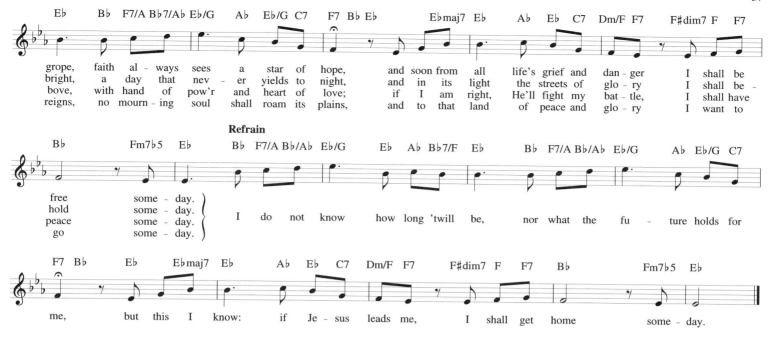

grope, faith al - ways sees a star of hope, and soon from all life's grief and dan - ger I shall be

bright, a day that nev - er yields to night, and in its light the streets of glo - ry I shall be -

bove, with hand of pow'r and heart of love; if I am right, He'll fight my bat - tle, I shall have

reigns, no mourn - ing soul shall roam its plains, and to that land of peace and glo - ry I want to

Refrain

free some - day.

hold some - day.

peace some - day.

go some - day.

I do not know how long 'twill be, nor what the fu - ture holds for

me, but this I know: if Je - sus leads me, I shall get home some - day.

THE BEAUTIFUL GARDEN OF PRAYER

words by
Eleanor Allen Schroll

BEAUTIFUL GARDEN
music by
James H. Fillmore (1849-1936)

1. There's a gar - den where Je - sus is wait - ing, ____ There's a place that is

2. There's a gar - den where Je - sus is wait - ing, ____ And I go, with my

3. There's a gar - den where Je - sus is wait - ing, ____ O can aught with His

4. There's a gar - den where Je - sus is wait - ing; ____ And He bids you to

won - drous - ly fair, ____ For it glows with the light of His pres - ence;

bur - den and care, ____ Just to learn from His lips words of com - fort ____

glo - ry com - pare? ____ Just to walk and to talk with my Sav - ior ____

come meet Him there, ____ Just to bow and re - ceive a new bless - ing ____

____ 'Tis the beau - ti - ful gar - den of prayer. ____

____ In the beau - ti - ful gar - den of prayer. ____

____ In the beau - ti - ful gar - den of prayer. ____

____ In the beau - ti - ful gar - den of prayer. ____

Refrain

O the

beau - ti - ful gar - den, the gar - den of prayer, O the beau - ti - ful

gar - den of prayer! ____ There my Sav - ior a - waits, and He

o - pens the gates To the beau - ti - ful gar - den of prayer. ____

BEAUTIFUL ISLE OF SOMEWHERE

BEAUTIFUL ISLE
music by
J.S. Fearis, 1897

words by
Jessie B. Pounds, 1897

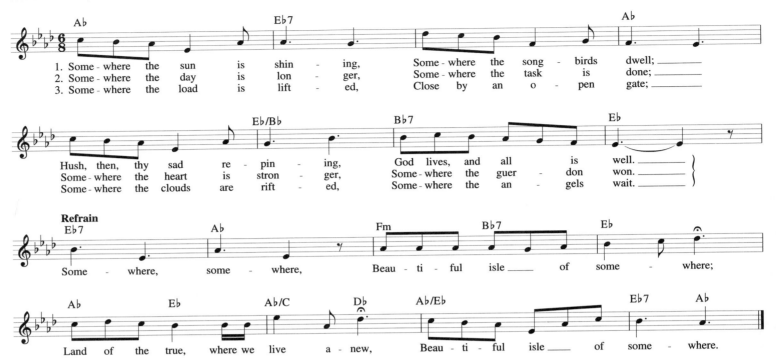

1. Some - where the sun is shin - ing, Some - where the song - birds dwell;_____
2. Some - where the day is lon - ger, Some - where the task is done;_____
3. Some - where the load is lift - ed, Close by an o - pen gate;_____

Hush, then, thy sad re - pin - ing, God lives, and all is well._____
Some - where the heart is stron - ger, Some - where the guer - don won._____
Some - where the clouds are rift - ed, Some - where the an - gels wait._____

Refrain

Some - where, some - where, Beau - ti - ful isle_____ of some - where;

Land of the true, where we live a - new, Beau - ti - ful isle_____ of some - where.

BEAUTIFUL SAVIOR

SCHÖNSTER HERR JESU (I)
Silesian folk tune, 19th century

words from
Münsterisch Gesangbuch, 1677
tr. by Joseph A. Seiss (1823-1904)

1. Beau - ti - ful Sav - ior, King of cre - a - tion,
2. Fair are the mead - ows, Fair are the wood - lands,
3. Fair is the sun - shine, Fair is the moon - light,
4. Beau - ti - ful Sav - ior, Lord of the na - tions,

Son of_____ God and_____ Son of_____ Man!
Robed in_____ flow'rs of_____ bloom - ing spring;
Bright the_____ spar - kling_____ stars on_____ high;
Son of_____ God and_____ Son of_____ Man!

Tru - ly I'd love_____ thee, Tru - ly I'd serve_____ thee,
Je - sus is fair - er, Je - sus is pur - er,
Je - sus shines bright - er, Je - sus shines pur - er,
Glo - ry and hon - or, Praise, ad - o - ra - tion,

Light of my soul, my joy, my crown.
He makes our sor - r'wing spir - it sing.
Than all the an - gels in the sky.
Now and for - ev - er - more be thine!

BECAUSE THOU HAST SAID

words by
Charles Wesley, 1748

PADERBORN
music from
Paderborn Gesangbuch, 1765

1. Be - cause Thou hast said: "Do ____ this for My sake," the mys - ti - cal
2. 'Tis here we look up and ____ grasp at Thy mind, 'tis here that we

bread we ____ glad - ly par - take; we ____ thirst for the Spir - it that
hope Thine ____ im - age to find; the ____ means of be - stow - ing that Thy

flows ____ from a - bove, and long to in - her - it Thy ____ full - ness of love.
gifts ____ we em - brace; and but all things are ____ ow - ing to ____ Je - sus' grace.

BEFORE JEHOVAH'S AWFUL THRONE

words by
Isaac Watts (1674-1748)
alt. by John Wesley, 1736

OLD HUNDREDTH
music by
Louis Bourgeois (c. 1510-1561)

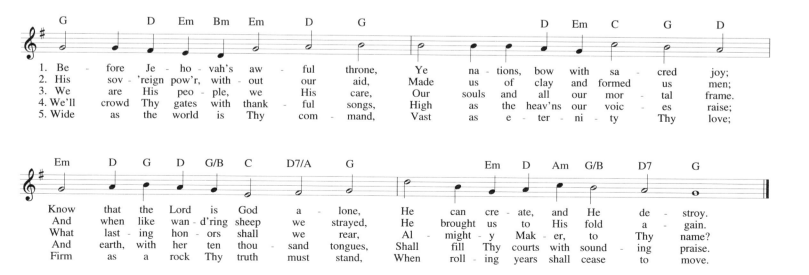

1. Be - fore Je - ho - vah's aw - ful throne, Ye na - tions, bow with sa - cred joy;
2. His sov - 'reign pow'r, with - out our aid, Made us of clay and formed us men;
3. We are His peo - ple, we His care, Our souls and all our mor - tal frame.
4. We'll crowd Thy gates with thank - ful songs, High as the heav'ns our voic - es raise;
5. Wide as the world is Thy com - mand, Vast as e - ter - ni - ty Thy love;

Know that the Lord is God a - lone, He can cre - ate, and He de - stroy.
And when like wan - d'ring sheep we strayed, He brought us to His fold a - gain.
What last - ing hon - ors shall we rear, Al - might - y Mak - er, to Thy name?
And earth, with her ten thou - sand tongues, Shall fill Thy courts with sound - ing praise.
Firm as a rock Thy truth must stand, When roll - ing years shall cease to move.

BEFORE JEHOVAH'S AWFUL THRONE

PARK STREET
music by
Frederick M.A. Venua (1788-1872)

words by
Isaac Watts (1674-1748)
alt. by John Wesley, 1736

BEFORE JEHOVAH'S AWFUL THRONE

WINCHESTER NEW
music from
Musicalisch Hand-Buch, 1690

words by
Isaac Watts (1674-1748)
alt. by John Wesley, 1736

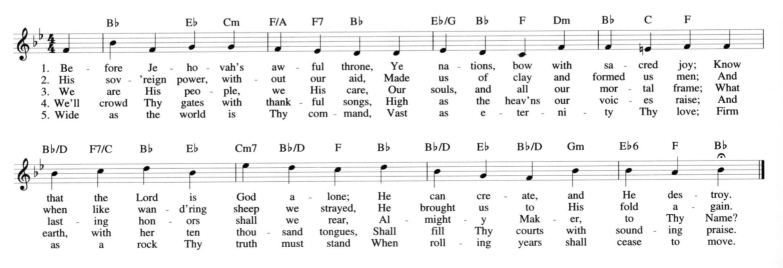

BEFORE THE LORD WE BOW

words by
Francis Scott Key (1779-1843)

DARWALL'S 148TH
music by
John Darwall (1731-1789)

BEFORE THY THRONE, O GOD, WE KNEEL

words by
William Boyd Carpenter (1841-1918)

ST. PETERSBURG
music by
Dimitri S. Bortniansky (1751-1825)

BEGIN, MY TONGUE, SOME HEAVENLY THEME

MANOAH
music from
Henry W. Greatorex's *Collection*, 1851

words by
Isaac Watts (1674-1748)

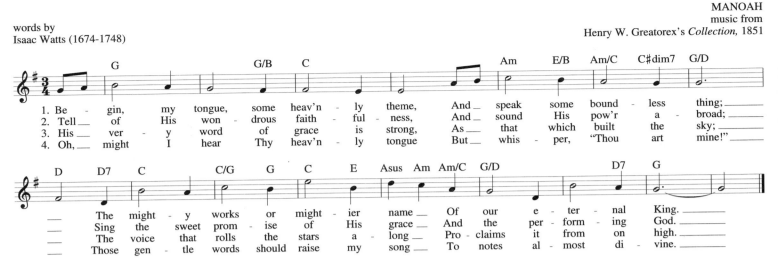

BEHOLD THE AMAZING GIFT OF LOVE

ST. STEPHEN
music by
William Jones, 1789

words by
Isaac Watts, 1709
para. by William Cameron, 1781

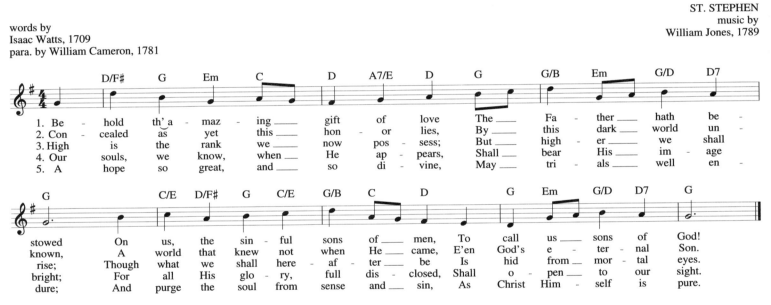

BEHOLD THE THRONE OF GRACE

ST. THOMAS
music by
Aaron Williams, 1763

words by
John Newton, 1779

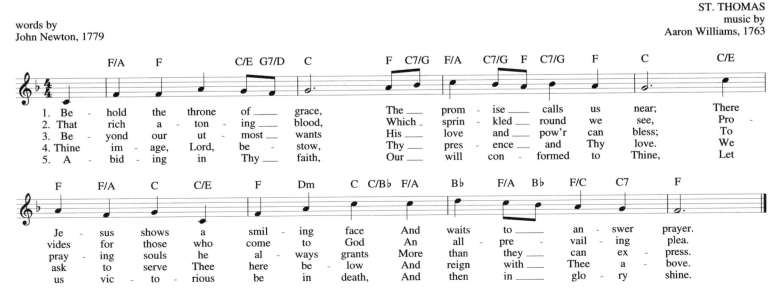

BELOVED, LET US LOVE

words by
Horatius Bonar (1808-1889)
based on I John 4:7

SONG 46
music by
Orlando Gibbons (1583-1625)

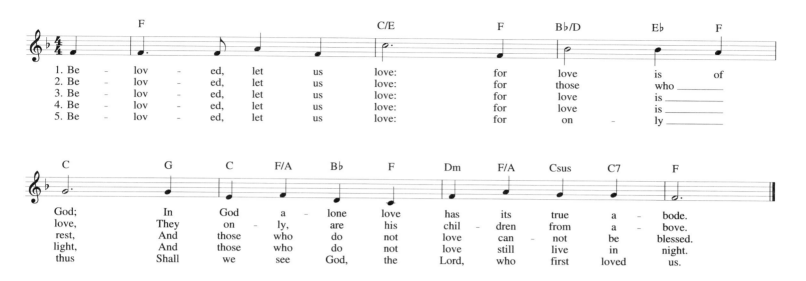

1. Be - lov - ed, let us love: for love is of God; In God a - lone love has its true a - bode.
2. Be - lov - ed, let us love: for those who _____ love, They on - ly, are his chil - dren from a - bove.
3. Be - lov - ed, let us love: for love is _____ rest, And those who do not love can - not be blessed.
4. Be - lov - ed, let us love: for love is _____ light, And those who do not love still live in night.
5. Be - lov - ed, let us love: for on - ly _____ thus Shall we see God, the Lord, who first loved us.

BENEATH THE CROSS OF JESUS

words by
Elizabeth Cecilia Douglas Clephane, 1872

ST. CHRISTOPHER
music by
Frederick Charles Maker, 1881

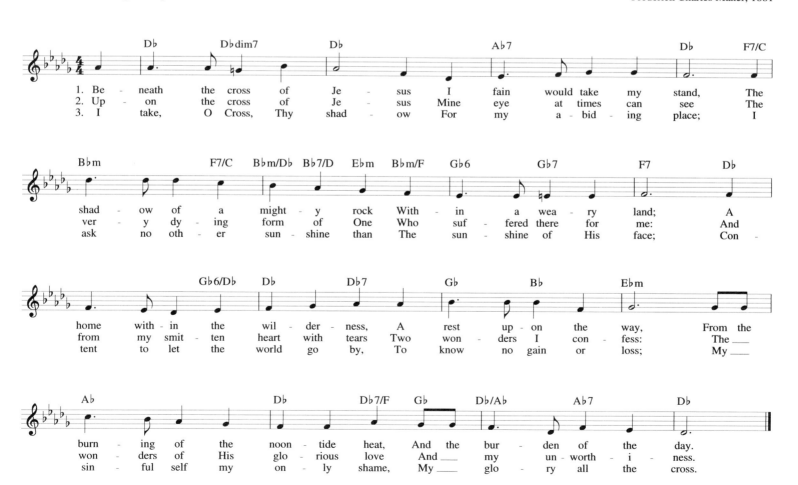

1. Be - neath the cross of Je - sus I fain would take my stand, The shad - ow of a might - y rock With - in a wea - ry land; A home with - in the wil - der - ness, A rest up - on the way, From the burn - ing of the noon - tide heat, And the bur - den of the day.
2. Up - on the cross of Je - sus Mine eye at times can see The ver - y dy - ing form of One Who suf - fered there for me: And _____ my smit - ten heart with tears Two won - ders I con - fess: The _____ won - ders of His glo - rious love And _____ my un - worth - i - ness.
3. I take, O Cross, Thy shad - ow For my a - bid - ing place; I ask no oth - er sun - shine than The sun - shine of His face; Con - tent to let the world go by, To know no gain or loss, My _____ sin - ful self my on - ly shame, My _____ glo - ry all the cross.

BEULAH LAND

words by
Edgar Page Stites (1836-1921)

music by
John R. Sweney (1837-1899)

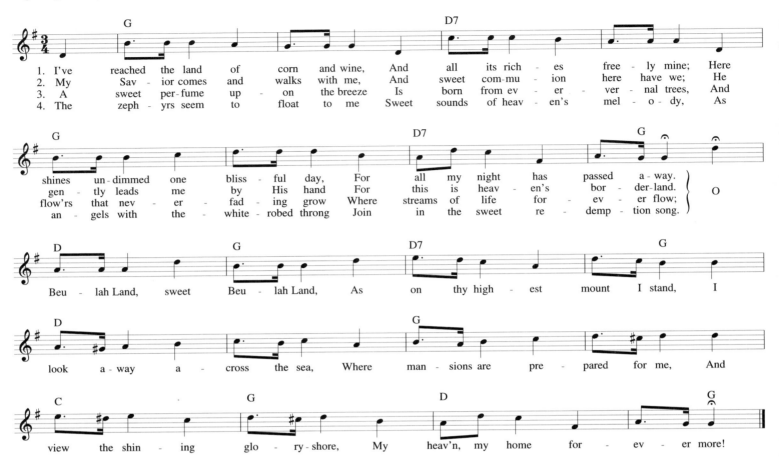

1. I've reached the land of corn and wine, And all its rich - es free - ly mine; Here
2. My Sav - ior comes and walks with me, And sweet com-mu - ion here have we; He
3. A sweet per-fume up - on the breeze Is born from ev - er - ver - nal trees, And
4. The zeph - yrs seem to float to me Sweet sounds of heav - en's mel - o - dy, As

shines un - dimmed one bliss - ful day, For all my night has passed a - way.
gen - tly leads me by His hand For this is heav - en's bor - der-land.
flow'rs that nev - er - fad - ing grow Where streams of life for - ev - er flow;
an - gels with the - white - robed throng Join in the sweet re - demp - tion song.

O

Beu - lah Land, sweet Beu - lah Land, As on thy high - est mount I stand, I

look a - way a - cross the sea, Where man - sions are pre - pared for me, And

view the shin - ing glo - ry-shore, My heav'n, my home for - ev - er more!

BLESS, O MY SOUL, THE LIVING GOD

PARK STREET
music by
Frederick M.A. Venua, c. 1810

words by
Isaac Watts, 1719
based on Psalm 103

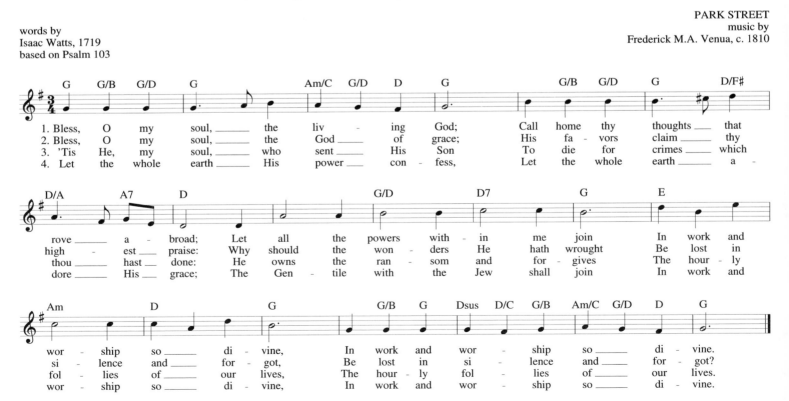

1. Bless, O my soul, the liv - ing God; Call home thy thoughts that
2. Bless, O my soul, the God of grace; His fa - vors claim thy
3. 'Tis He, my soul, who sent His Son To die for crimes which
4. Let the whole earth His power con - fess, Let the whole earth a -

rove a - broad; Let all the powers with - in me join In work and
high - est praise: Why should the won - ders He hath wrought Be lost in
thou hast done: He owns the ran - som and for - gives The hour - ly
dore His grace; The Gen - tile with the Jew shall join In work and

wor - ship so di - vine, In work and wor - ship so di - vine.
si - lence and for - got: Be lost in si - lence and for - got?
fol - lies of our lives, The hour - ly fol - lies of our lives.
wor - ship so di - vine, In work and wor - ship so di - vine.

BLESS THE LORD, O MY SOUL

Author unknown
based on Psalm 103:1

BLESS THE LORD
Composer unknown

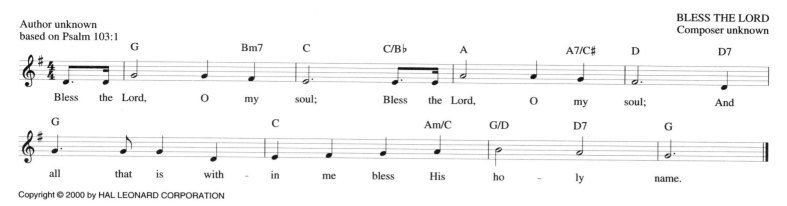

Bless the Lord, O my soul; Bless the Lord, O my soul; And all that is with-in me bless His ho-ly name.

BLESS THOU THE GIFTS

words by
Samuel Longfellow, c. 1886

DEUS TUORUM MILITUM
music from
Grenoble Antiphoner, 1753
adapt. by Ralph Vaughan Williams, 1906

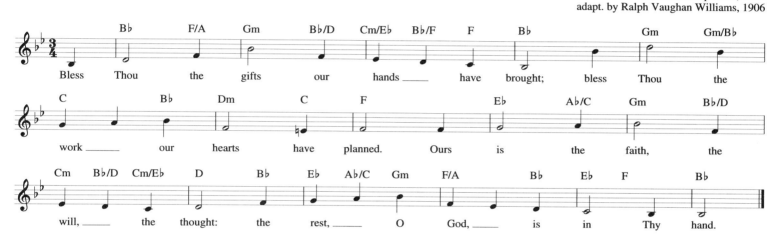

Bless Thou the gifts our hands have brought; bless Thou the work our hearts have planned. Ours is the faith, the will, the thought: the rest, O God, is in Thy hand.

BLESSED ASSURANCE

words by
Fanny J. Crosby (1820-1915)

ASSURANCE
music by
Phoebe Palmer Knapp (1839-1908)

1. Bless-ed as-sur-ance, Je-sus is mine! Oh, what a fore-taste of glo-ry di-vine! Heir of sal-va-tion, pur-chase of God, Born of His Spir-it, washed in His blood. This is my
2. Per-fect sub-mis-sion, per-fect de-light! Vi-sions of rap-ture now burst on my sight. An-gels de-scend-ing bring from a-bove Ech-oes of mer-cy, whis-pers of love.
3. Per-fect sub-mis-sion, all is at rest, I in my Sav-ior am hap-py and blest. Watch-ing and wait-ing, look-ing a-bove, Filled with His good-ness, lost in His love.

sto-ry, this is my song, Prais-ing my Sav-ior all the day long. This is my
sto-ry, this is my song, Prais-ing my Sav-ior all the day long.

BLESSED BE THE NAME

words by William H. Clark (verses)
and Ralph E. Hudson (refrain)

Composer unknown
arr. by Ralph E. Hudson and William J. Kirkpatrick

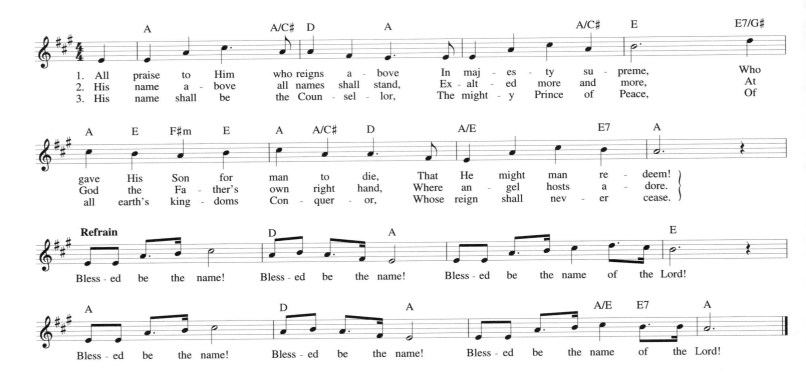

1. All praise to Him who reigns a - bove In maj - es - ty su - preme, Who
2. His name a - bove all names shall stand, Ex - alt - ed more and more, At
3. His name shall be the Coun - sel - lor, The might - y Prince of Peace, Of

gave His Son for man to die, That He might man re - deem!
God the Fa - ther's own right hand, Where an - gel hosts a - dore.
all earth's king - doms Con - quer - or, Whose reign shall nev - er cease.

Refrain

Bless - ed be the name! Bless - ed be the name! Bless - ed be the name of the Lord!

Bless - ed be the name! Bless - ed be the name! Bless - ed be the name of the Lord!

BLESSED BE THE NAME

words by Charles Wesley (verses)
and Ralph E. Hudson (refrain)

Composer unknown
arr. by Ralph E. Hudson and William J. Kirkpatrick

1. O for a thou - sand tongues to sing— Bless - ed be the name of the Lord! The
2. Je - sus, the name that charms our fears— Bless - ed be the name of the Lord! 'Tis
3. He breaks the pow'r of can - celled sin— Bless - ed be the name of the Lord! His
4. I nev - er shall for - get that day— Bless - ed be the name of the Lord! When

glo - ries of my God and King— Bless - ed be the name of the Lord!
mu - sic in the sin - ner's ears— Bless - ed be the name of the Lord!
blood can make the foul - est clean— Bless - ed be the name of the Lord!
Je - sus washed my sins a - way— Bless - ed be the name of the Lord!

Refrain

Bless - ed be the name, bless - ed be the name; Bless - ed be the name of the Lord!

Bless - ed be the name, bless - ed be the name; Bless - ed be the name of the Lord!

BLESSED JESUS, AT THY WORD

v. 1-3 by T. Clausnitzer (1619-1684)
tr. by C. Winkworth (1827-1878)
v. 4 from *Gesangbuch,* Berlin, 1707
translator unknown

LIEBSTER JESU, WIR SIND HIER
music by
J.R. Ahle (1625-1673)

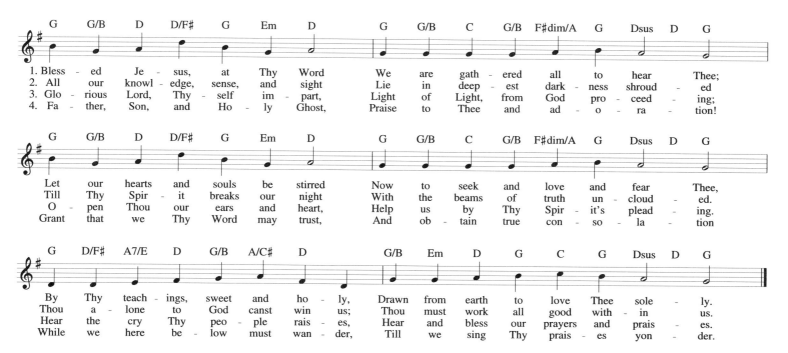

1. Bless - ed Je - sus, at Thy Word We are gath - ered all to hear Thee;
2. All our knowl - edge, sense, and sight Lie in deep - est dark - ness shroud - ed
3. Glo - rious Lord, Thy - self im - part, Light of Light, from God pro - ceed - ing;
4. Fa - ther, Son, and Ho - ly Ghost, Praise to Thee and ad - o - ra - tion!

Let our hearts and souls be stirred Now to seek and love and fear Thee,
Till Thy Spir - it breaks our night With the beams of truth un - cloud - ed.
O - pen Thou our ears and heart, Help us by Thy Spir - it's plead - ing.
Grant that we Thy Word may trust, And ob - tain true con - so - la - tion

By Thy teach - ings, sweet and ho - ly, Drawn from earth to love Thee sole - ly.
Thou a - lone to God canst win us; Thou must work all good with - in us.
Hear the cry Thy peo - ple rais - es, Hear and bless our prayers and prais - es.
While we here be - low must wan - der, Till we sing Thy prais - es yon - der.

BLESSED QUIETNESS

words by
Manie Payne Ferguson, c. 1897

music by
W.S. Marshall, c. 1897
arr. by James M. Kirk, 1900

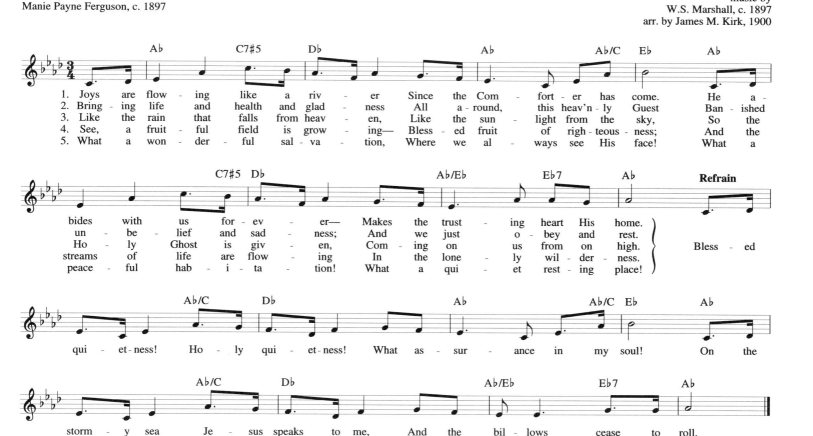

1. Joys are flow - ing like a riv - er Since the Com - fort - er has come. He a -
2. Bring - ing life and health and glad - ness All a - round, this heav'n - ly Guest Ban - ished
3. Like the rain that falls from heav - en, Like the sun - light from the sky, So the
4. See, a fruit - ful field is grow - ing— Bless - ed fruit of righ - teous - ness; And the
5. What a won - der - ful sal - va - tion, Where we al - ways see His face! What a

bides with us for - ev - er— Makes the trust - ing heart His home.
un - be - lief and sad - ness; And we just o - bey and rest.
Ho - ly Ghost is giv - en, Com - ing on us from on high.
streams of life are flow - ing In the lone - ly wil - der - ness.
peace - ful hab - i - ta - tion! What a qui - et rest - ing place! } Bless - ed

Refrain

qui - et - ness! Ho - ly qui - et - ness! What as - sur - ance in my soul! On the

storm - y sea Je - sus speaks to me, And the bil - lows cease to roll.

BLESSED REDEEMER

REDEEMER
words by
Avis B. Christiansen, 1921
music by
Harry Dixon Loes, 1921

BLESSING AND HONOR

AMERICAN HYMN
words by
Horatius Bonar (1808-1889)
music by
Matthias Keller (1813-1875)

BLESSING AND HONOR

words by
Horatius Bonar (1808-1889)

O QUANTA QUALIA
music from
Paris *Antiphoner,* 1681
as in La Feillée's *Méthode du plain-chant,* 1808

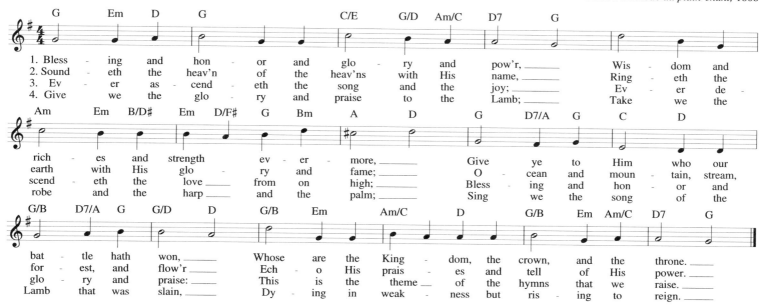

BLEST ARE THE PURE IN HEART

words by
John Keble (1792-1866)

FRANCONIA
music by
Johann Balthasar König (1691-1758)

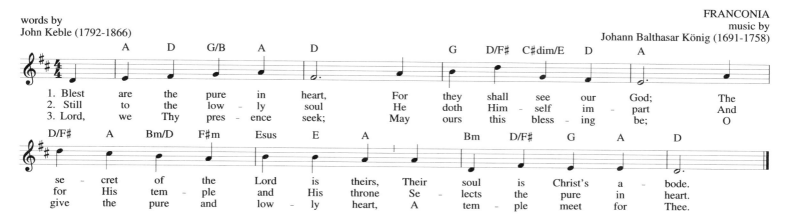

BLEST BE THE DEAR UNITING LOVE

words by
Charles Wesley, 1742

EVAN
music by
William Havergal, 1847
arr. by Lowell Mason, 1850

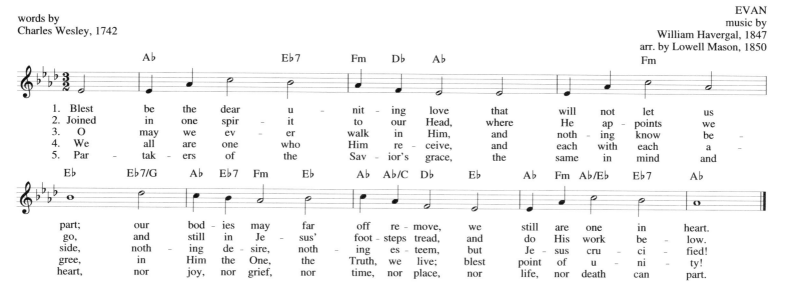

BLEST BE THE TIE THAT BINDS

DENNIS
music by
Johann G. Nägeli, 1828
arr. by Lowell Mason, 1845

words by
John Fawcett, 1782

1. Blest be the tie that binds our hearts in Christ - ian love; the
2. Be - fore our Fa - ther's throne we pour our ar - dent prayers; our
3. We share each oth - er's woes, our mu - tual bur - dens bear; and
4. When we a - sun - der part, it gives us in - ward pain; but

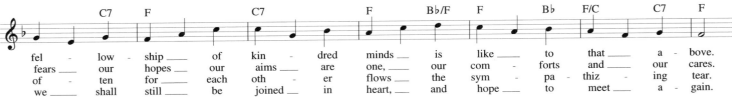

fel - low - ship of kin - dred minds is like to that a - bove.
fears our hopes our aims are one, our com - forts and our cares.
of - ten for each oth - er flows the sym - pa - thiz - ing tear.
we shall still be joined in heart, and hope to meet a - gain.

THE BLOOD WILL NEVER LOSE ITS POWER

MARTIN
music by
Stillman Martin, 1912

words by
Civilla D. Martin, 1912

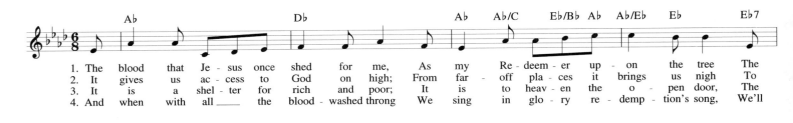

1. The blood that Je - sus once shed for me, As my Re - deem - er up - on the tree, The
2. It gives us ac - cess to God on high; From far - off pla - ces it brings us nigh To
3. It is a shel - ter for rich and poor; It is to heav - en the o - pen door, The
4. And when with all the blood - washed throng We sing in glo - ry re - demp - tion's song, We'll

blood that set - teth the pris - 'ner free Will nev - er lose its pow'r. ____
pre - cious bless - ings that nev - er die. It will nev - er lose its pow'r. ____
sin - ner's mer - it for ev - er - more. It will nev - er lose its pow'r. ____
pass the glo - ri - ous truth a - long: It has nev - er lost its pow'r. ____

It will

Refrain

nev - er lose its pow'r. ____ It will nev - er lose its pow'r. ____ The

blood that cleans - es from all sin Will nev - er lose its pow'r. ____

BLOW YE THE TRUMPET, BLOW

words by
Charles Wesley, 1750

LENOX
music by
Lewis Edson, c. 1782

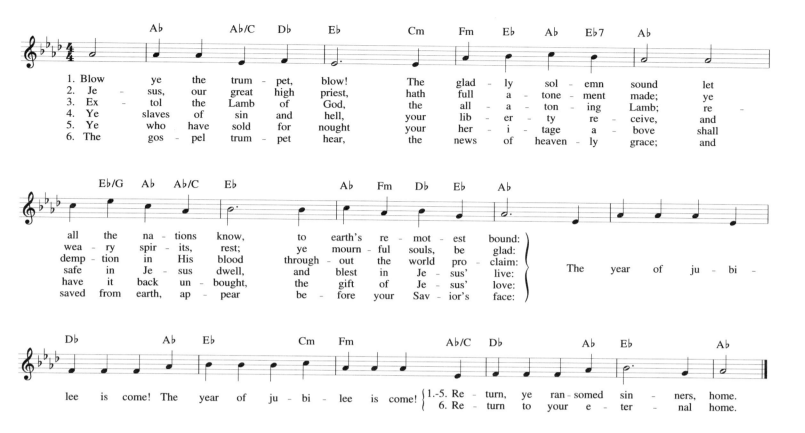

1. Blow ye the trum - pet, blow! The glad - ly sol - emn sound let
2. Je - sus, our great high priest, hath full a - tone - ment made; ye
3. Ex - tol the Lamb of God, the all - a - ton - ing Lamb; re -
4. Ye slaves of sin and hell, your lib - er - ty re - ceive, and
5. Ye who have sold for nought your her - i - tage a - bove shall
6. The gos - pel trum - pet hear, the news of heaven - ly grace; and

all the na - tions know, to earth's re - mot - est bound:
wea - ry spir - its, rest; ye mourn - ful souls, be glad:
demp - tion in His blood through - out the world pro - claim:
safe in Je - sus dwell, and blest in Je - sus' live:
have it back un - bought, the gift of Je - sus' love:
saved from earth, ap - pear be - fore your Sav - ior's face:

The year of ju - bi -

lee is come! The year of ju - bi - lee is come! { 1.-5. Re - turn, ye ran - somed sin - ners, home.
6. Re - turn to your e - ter - nal home.

BOW DOWN THINE EAR, ALMIGHTY LORD

words by
Thomas E. Powell (1823-1901)

HERR JESU CHRIST, MEINS
music from
As Hymnodus Sacer, Leipzig, 1625

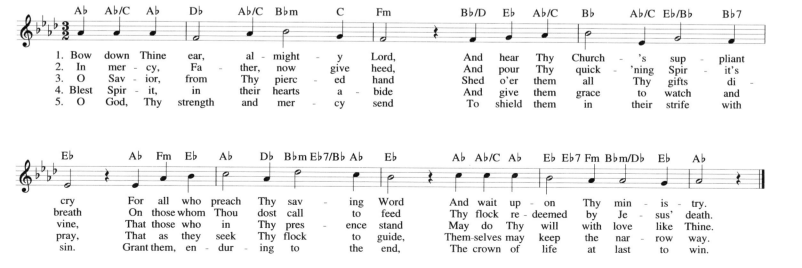

1. Bow down Thine ear, al - might - y Lord, And hear Thy Church - 's sup - pliant
2. In mer - cy, Fa - ther, now give heed, And pour Thy quick - 'ning Spir - it's
3. O Sav - ior, Fa - from Thy pierc - ed hand Shed o'er them all Thy gifts di -
4. Blest Spir - it, in their hearts a - bide And give them grace to watch and
5. O God, Thy strength and mer - cy send To shield them in their strife with

cry For all who preach Thy sav - ing Word And wait up - on Thy min - is - try.
breath On those whom Thou dost call to feed Thy flock re - deemed by Je - sus' death.
vine, That those who in Thy pres - ence stand May do Thy will with love like Thine.
pray, That as they seek Thy flock to guide, Them-selves may keep the nar - row way.
sin. Grant them, en - dur - ing to the end, The crown of life at last to win.

BREAD OF HEAVEN, ON THEE I FEED

ARFON
French and Welsh melody

words by
Josiah Conder, 1824

1. Bread of heav-en, on ____ thee I feed, For thy flesh is meat, ____ in-deed;
2. Vine of heav-en, thy ____ blood sup-plies This blest cup of sac-ri-fice;

Ev-er may my soul be fed With this ____ true and liv-ing Bread; ____
'Tis thy ____ wounds my heal-ing give; To thy ____ cross I look, and live; ____

Day by day ____ with ____ strength sup-plied Through the life of him ____ who ____ died.
Thou my Life, ____ oh, ____ let me be Root-ed, graft-ed, built ____ on ____ thee!

BREAD OF HEAVEN, ON THEE I FEED

JESU, JESU, DU MEIN HIRT
music by
Paul Heinlein (1626-1686)

words by
Josiah Conder (1789-1855)

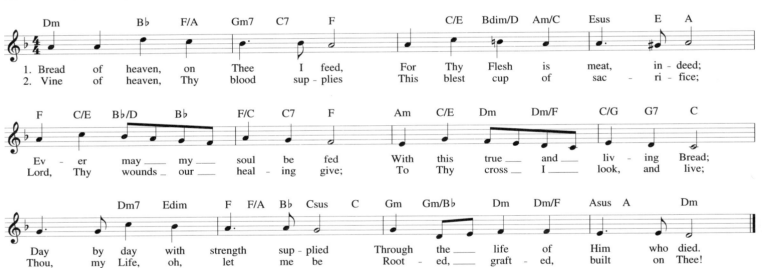

1. Bread of heaven, on Thee I feed, For Thy Flesh is meat, in-deed;
2. Vine of heaven, Thy blood sup-plies This blest cup of sac-ri-fice;

Ev-er may ____ my ____ soul be fed With this true ____ and liv-ing Bread;
Lord, Thy wounds _ our ____ heal-ing give; To Thy cross ____ I look, and live;

Day by day with strength sup-plied Through the ____ life of Him who died.
Thou, my Life, oh, let me be Root-ed, ____ graft-ed, built on Thee!

BREAD OF THE WORLD

RENDEZ À DIEU
music by
Louis Bourgeois (1510-1561)

words by
Reginald Heber (1783-1826)

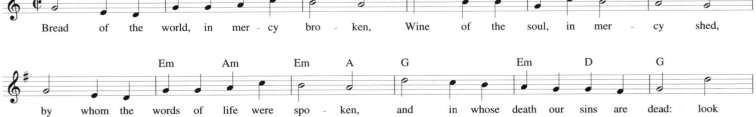

Bread of the world, in mer-cy bro-ken, Wine of the soul, in mer-cy shed,

by whom the words of life were spo-ken, and in whose death our sins are dead: look

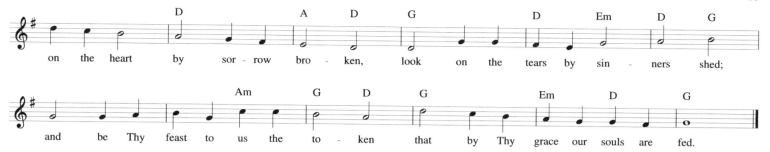

on the heart by sor - row bro - ken, look on the tears by sin - ners shed;

and be Thy feast to us the to - ken that by Thy grace our souls are fed.

BREAK THOU THE BREAD OF LIFE

words by
Mary Artemesia Lathbury, 1877

BREAD OF LIFE
music by
William Fiske Sherwin, 1877

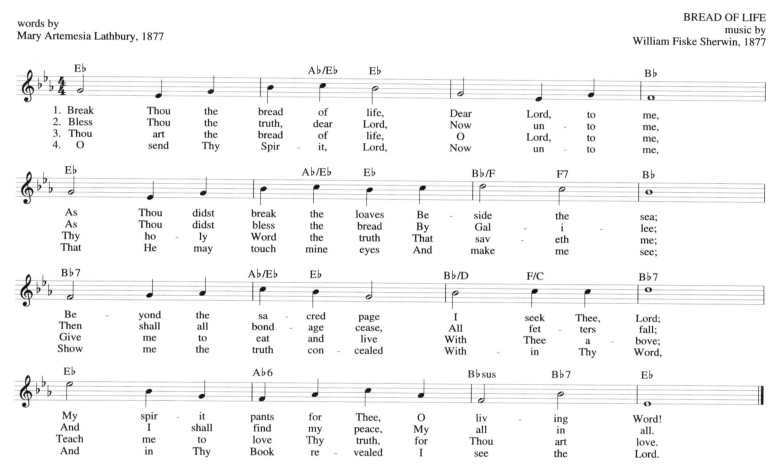

1. Break Thou the bread of life, Dear Lord, to me,
2. Bless Thou the truth, dear Lord, Now un - to me,
3. Thou art the bread of life, O Lord, to me,
4. O send Thy Spir - it, Lord, Now un - to me,

As Thou didst break the loaves Be - side the sea;
As Thou didst bless the bread By Gal - i - lee;
Thy ho - ly Word the truth That sav - eth me;
That He may touch mine eyes And make me see;

Be - yond the sa - cred page I seek Thee, Lord;
Then shall all bond - age cease, All fet - ters fall;
Give me to eat and live With Thee a - bove;
Show me the truth con - cealed With - in Thy Word,

My spir - it pants for Thee, O liv - ing Word!
And I shall find my peace, My all in all.
Teach me to love Thy truth, for Thou art love.
And in Thy Book re - vealed I see the Lord.

BREATHE ON ME, BREATH OF GOD

words by
Edwin Hatch, 1886

TRENTHAM
music by
Robert Jackson, 1894

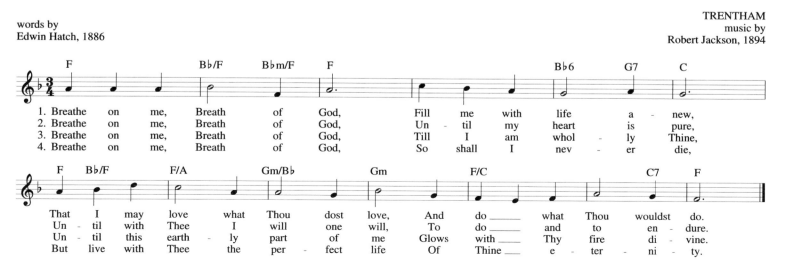

1. Breathe on me, Breath of God, Fill me with life a - new,
2. Breathe on me, Breath of God, Un - til my heart is pure,
3. Breathe on me, Breath of God, Till I am whol - ly Thine,
4. Breathe on me, Breath of God, So shall I nev - er die,

That I may love what Thou dost love, And do ____ what Thou wouldst do.
Un - til with Thee I will one will, To do ____ and to en - dure.
Un - til this earth - ly part of me Glows with ____ Thy fire di - vine.
But live with Thee the per - fect life Of Thine ____ e - ter - ni - ty.

BRETHREN, WE HAVE MET TO WORSHIP

HOLY MANNA
music by
William Moore, 1825

words by
George Atkins, 19th Century

1. Breth - ren, we have met to wor - ship And a - dore the Lord our God. Will you pray with all your pow - er While we try to preach the Word? All is vain un - less the Spir - it Of the Ho - ly One comes down. Breth - ren, pray, and ho - ly man - na Will be show - ered all a - round.

2. Breth - ren, see poor sin - ners round you? Slum - b'ring on the brink of woe. Death is com - ing; hell is mov - ing; Can you bear to let them go? See our fa - thers and our moth - ers And our chil - dren sink - ing down. Breth - ren, pray, and ho - ly man - na Will be show - ered all a - round.

3. Sis - ters, will you join and help us? Mo - ses' sis - ter aid - ed him. Will you help the trem - bling mourn - ers Who are strug - gling hard with sin? Tell them all a - bout the Sav - ior; Tell them that He will be found. Sis - ters, pray, and ho - ly man - na Will be show - ered all a - round.

4. Let us love our God su - preme - ly; Let us love each oth - er too. While we try to preach the Word? All is vain un - less the Spir - it Till our God makes all things new. Then He'll call us home to heav - en; At His ta - ble we'll sit down. Christ will gird Him - self and serve us With sweet man - na all a - round.

BRIGHTEN THE CORNER WHERE YOU ARE

music by
Charles H. Gabriel

words by
Ina Duley Ogdon

1. Do not wait un - til some deed of great - ness you may do, Do not wait to shed your light a - far. To the man - y du - ties ev - er near you now be true, Bright - en the cor - ner

2. Just a - bove are cloud - ed skies that you may help to clear, Let not nar - row self your way de - bar. Though in - to one heart a - lone may fall your song of cheer,

3. Here for all your tal - ent you may sure - ly find a need, Here re - flect the Bright and Morn - ing Star. E - ven from your hum - ble hand the bread of life may feed,

where you are. Bright-en the cor-ner where you are! Bright-en the cor-ner where you are!

Some-one far from har-bor you may guide a-cross the bar, Bright-en the cor-ner where you are.

BRING THEM IN

words by
Alexcenah Thomas, 19th century

music by
William A. Ogden (1841-1897)

1. Hark! 'tis the Shep - herd's voice I hear, Out in the des - ert dark and drear,
2. Who'll go and help this Shep - herd kind, Help Him the wan - d'ring ones to find?
3. Out in the des - ert hear their cry, Out on the moun - tains wild and high;

Call - ing the sheep who've gone a - stray Far from the Shep - herd's fold a - way.
Who'll bring the lost ones to the fold Where they'll be shel - tered from the cold?
Hark! 'tis the Sav - ior speaks to thee, "Go find my sheep wher - e'er they be."

Bring them in, bring them in, Bring them in ____ from the fields of sin;

Bring them in, bring them in, Bring the wan - d'ring ones to Je - sus.

BRINGING IN THE SHEAVES

words by
Knowles Shaw (1834-1878)

HARVEST
music by
George A. Minor

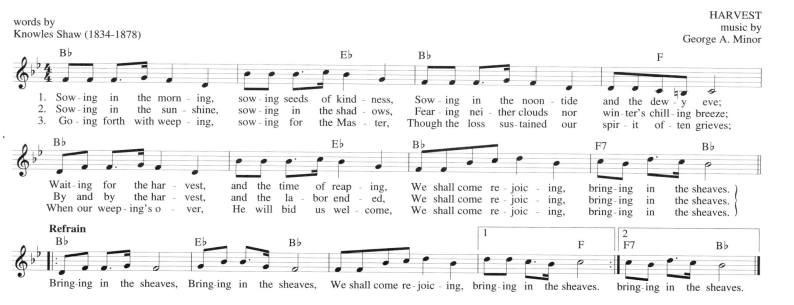

1. Sow - ing in the morn - ing, sow - ing seeds of kind - ness, Sow - ing in the noon - tide and the dew - y eve;
2. Sow - ing in the sun - shine, sow - ing in the shad - ows, Fear - ing nei - ther clouds nor win - ter's chill - ing breeze;
3. Go - ing forth with weep - ing, sow - ing for the Mas - ter, Though the loss sus - tained our spir - it of - ten grieves;

Wait - ing for the har - vest, and the time of reap - ing, We shall come re - joic - ing, bring - ing in the sheaves.
By and by the har - vest, and the la - bor end - ed, We shall come re - joic - ing, bring - ing in the sheaves.
When our weep - ing's o - ver, He will bid us wel - come, We shall come re - joic - ing, bring - ing in the sheaves.

Refrain

Bring-ing in the sheaves, Bring-ing in the sheaves, We shall come re-joic - ing, bring-ing in the sheaves. bring-ing in the sheaves.

BRING YOUR VESSELS, NOT A FEW

BRING YOUR VESSELS

words by
Lelia N. Morris, 1912

music by
Lelia N. Morris, 1912

1. Are you long - ing for the full - ness of the bless - ing of the Lord In your
2. Bring your emp - ty earth - en ves - sels, clean thro' Je - sus' pre - cious blood. Come, ye
3. Like the cruse of oil un - fail - ing is His grace for - ev - er - more, And His

heart and life to - day? Claim the prom - ise of your Fa - ther; come ac -
need - y, one and all; And in hu - man con - se - cra - tion wait be -
love un - chang - ing still; And ac - cord - ing to His prom - ise, with the

cord - ing to His Word, In the bless - ed, old - time way.)
fore the throne of God Till the Ho - ly Ghost shall fall. } He will fill your heart to-day to o - ver -
Ho - ly Ghost and pow'r He will ev - 'ry ves - sel fill.)

flow - ing. As the Lord com-mand - eth you, "Bring your ves - sels, not a few." He will

fill your heart to - day to o - ver - flow - ing With the Ho - ly Ghost and pow'r.

BUILT ON THE ROCK THE CHURCH DOTH STAND

KIRKEN

words by
Nicolai F.S. Grundtvig, 1837
tr. by Carl Döving, 1909

music by
Ludvig M. Lindeman, 1871

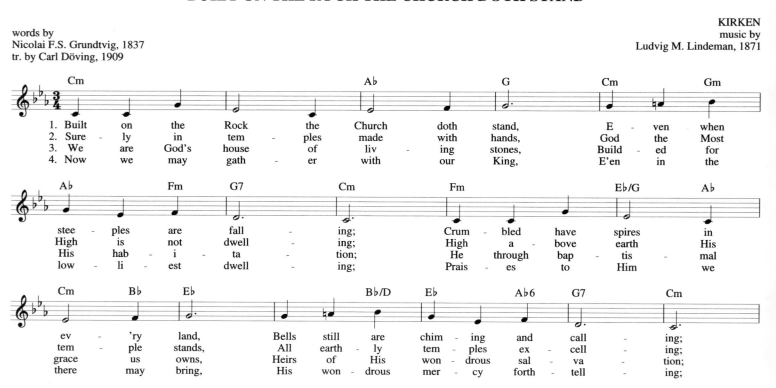

1. Built on the Rock the Church doth stand, E - ven when
2. Sure - ly in tem - ples made with hands, God the Most
3. We are God's house of liv - ing stones, Build - ed for
4. Now we may gath - er with our King, E'en in the

stee - ples are fall - ing; Crum - bled have spires in
High is not dwell - ing; High a - bove earth His
His hab - i - ta - tion; He through bap - tis - mal
low - li - est dwell - ing; Prais - es to Him we

ev - 'ry land, Bells still are chim - ing and call - ing;
tem - ple stands, All earth - ly tem - ples ex - cell - ing;
grace us owns, Heirs of His won - drous sal - va - tion;
there may bring, His won - drous mer - cy forth - tell - ing;

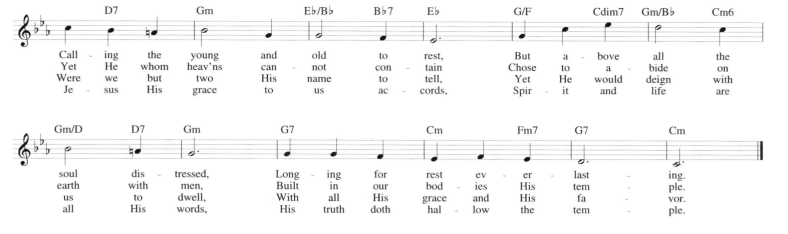

Call - ing the young and old to rest, But a - bove all the
Yet He whom heav'ns can - not con - tain Chose to a - bide on
Je - sus His grace to us ac - cords, Spir - it and life are

soul dis - tressed, Long - ing for rest ev - er - last - ing.
earth with men, Built in our bod - ies His last tem - ple.
all His words, His truth doth hal - low the tem - ple.

CALVARY

African-American Spiritual

African-American Spiritual

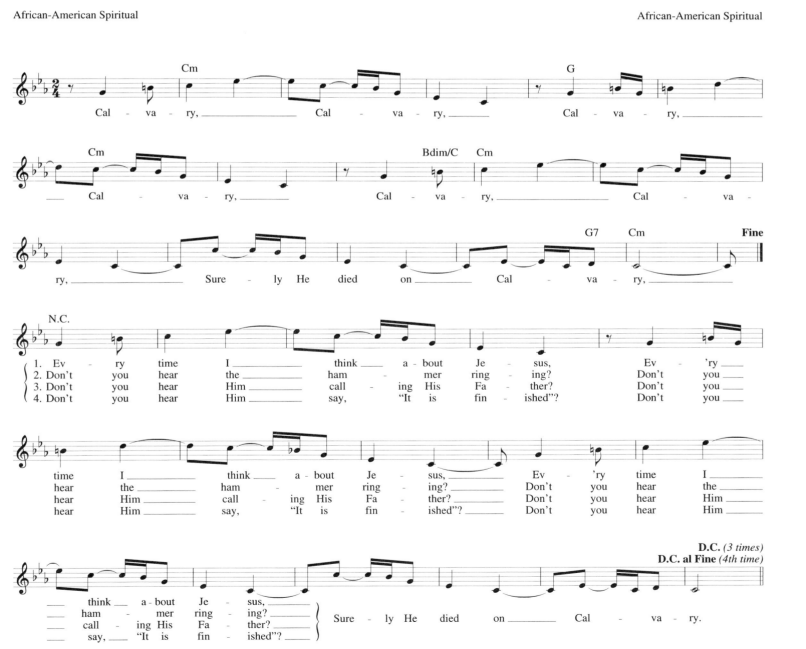

Cal - va - ry, _____ Cal - va - ry, _____ Cal - va - ry, _____

Cal - va - ry, _____ Cal - va - ry, _____ Cal - va -

ry, _____ Sure - ly He died on _____ Cal - va - ry, _____

1. Ev - ry time I _____ think _____ a - bout Je - sus, Ev - 'ry _____
2. Don't you hear the _____ ham - mer ring - ing? Don't you _____
3. Don't you hear Him _____ call - ing His Fa - ther? Don't you _____
4. Don't you hear Him _____ say, "It is fin - ished"? Don't you _____

time I _____ think _____ a - bout Je - sus, _____ Ev - 'ry time I _____
hear the _____ ham - mer ring - ing? _____ Don't you hear Him _____
hear Him _____ call - ing His Fa - ther? _____ Don't you hear Him _____
hear Him _____ say, "It is fin - ished"? _____ Don't you hear Him _____

D.C. (3 times)
D.C. al Fine (4th time)

_____ think _____ a - bout Je - sus, _____
_____ ham - mer ring - ing? _____
_____ call - ing His Fa - ther? _____   Sure - ly He died on _____ Cal - va - ry.
_____ say, _____ "It is fin - ished"? _____

CAST THY BURDEN UPON THE LORD

CAST THY BURDEN

words based on
Psalms 55:22, 16:8

music by
Felix Mendelssohn, from *Elijah*

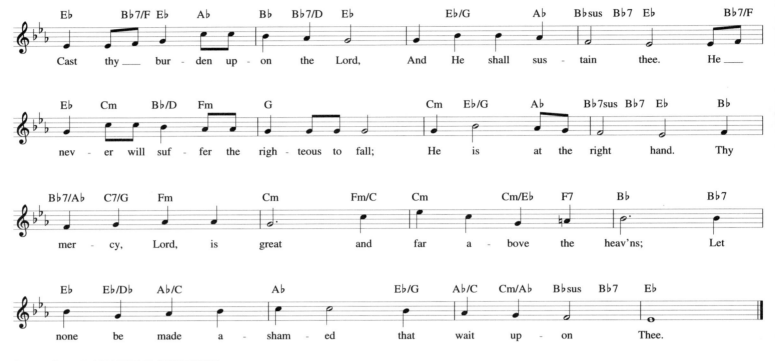

Cast thy ___ bur - den up - on the Lord, And He shall sus - tain thee. He ___ nev - er will suf - fer the righ - teous to fall; He is at the right hand. Thy mer - cy, Lord, is great and far a - bove the heav'ns; Let none be made a - sham - ed that wait up - on Thee.

CHANNELS ONLY

CHANNELS

words by
Mary E. Maxwell (1837-1915)

music by
Ada R. Gibbs (1865-1905)

1. How I praise Thee, pre - cious Sav - ior, That Thy love laid hold of me; Thou hast
2. Emp - tied that Thou should - est fill me, A clean ves - sel in Thy hand; With no
3. Je - sus, fill now with Thy Spir - it Hearts that full sur - ren - der know; That the

saved and cleansed and filled me That I might Thy chan - nel be. } Chan - nels
pow'r but as Thou giv - est Gra - cious - ly with each com - mand.
streams of liv - ing wa - ter From our in - ner man may flow.

on - ly, bless - ed Mas - ter, But with all Thy won - drous pow'r Flow - ing

through us, Thou canst use us Ev - 'ry day and ev - 'ry hour.

CHIEF OF SINNERS THOUGH I BE

words by
William McComb (1793-c. 1870)

GETHSEMANE
music by
Richard Redhead (1820-1901)

1. Chief of sin - ners though I be, Je - sus shed his blood for me,
2. Oh, the height of Je - sus' love! High - er than the heav'ns a - bove,
3. On - ly Je - sus can im - part Balm to heal the wound - ed heart,
4. Chief of sin - ners though I be, Christ is All in All to me;
5. O my Sav - ior, help af - ford By Your Spir - it and Your Word!

Died that I might live on high, Lives that I might nev - er die.
Deep - er than the depths of sea, Last - ing as e - ter - ni - ty.
Peace that flows from sin for - giv'n, Joy that lifts the soul to heav'n,
All my wants to Him are known, All my sor - rows are His own.
When my way - ward heart would stray, Keep me in the nar - row way;

As the branch is to the vine, I am His, and He is mine.
Love that found me won - drous thought Found me when I sought Him not.
Faith and hope to walk with God In the way that E - noch trod.
He sus - tains the hid - den life Safe with Him from earth - ly strife.
Grace in time of need sup - ply While I live and when I die.

Copyright © 2000 by HAL LEONARD CORPORATION

A CHILD OF THE KING

words by
Harriet E. Buell, 1877

BINGHAMTON
music by
John B. Sumner, 1877

1. My Fa - ther is rich in hous - es and lands; He hold - eth the
2. My Fa - ther's own Son, the Sav - ior of men, Once wan - dered o'er
3. I once was an out - cast strang - er on earth, A sin - ner by
4. A tent or a cot - tage why should I care? They're build - ing a

wealth of the world in His hands! Of ru - bies and dia - monds, of sil - ver and
earth as the poor - est of them! But now He is reign - ing for - ev - er on
choice and an al - ien by birth! But I've been a - dopt - ed; my name's writ - ten
pal - ace for me o - ver there! Tho' ex - iled from home,__ yet still I may

gold, His cof - fers are full He has rich - es un - told! I'm a child of the
high, And will give me a home in__ heav'n by and by.
down. I'm heir to a man - sion, a__ robe and a crown!
sing: "All glo - ry to God, I'm a child of the King!"

King! A child of the King! With Je - sus, my Sav - ior, I'm a child of the King!

Copyright © 2000 by HAL LEONARD CORPORATION

CHRIST AROSE
(Low in the Grave He Lay)

words by
Robert Lowry (1826-1899)

music by
Robert Lowry (1826-1899)

1. Low in the grave He lay, Je - sus my Sav - ior!
2. Vain - ly they watch His bed, Je - sus my Sav - ior!
3. Death can - not keep his prey, Je - sus my Sav - ior!

Wait - ing the com - ing day, Je - sus my Lord!
Vain - ly they seal the dead, Je - sus my Lord!
He tore the bars a - way, Je - sus my Lord!

Refrain

Up from the grave He a - rose, With a might - y tri - umph o'er His foes; He a -
rose a Vic - tor from the dark do - main, And He lives for - ev - er with His saints to reign, He a -
rose! He a - rose! Hal - le - lu - jah! Christ a - rose!

CHRIST FOR THE WORLD WE SING

ITALIAN HYMN
music by
Felice de Giardini, 1769

words by
Samuel Wolcott, 1869

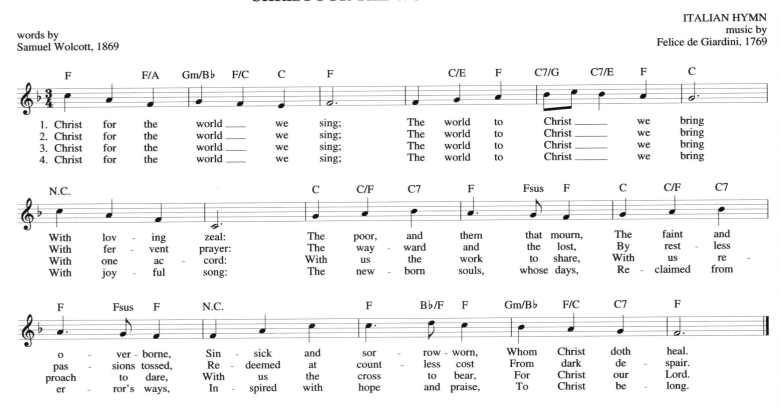

1. Christ for the world we sing; The world to Christ we bring
2. Christ for the world we sing; The world to Christ we bring
3. Christ for the world we sing; The world to Christ we bring
4. Christ for the world we sing; The world to Christ we bring

With lov - ing zeal: The poor, and them that mourn, The faint and
With fer - vent prayer: The way - ward and the lost, By rest - less
With one ac - cord: With us the work to share, With us re -
With joy - ful song: The new - born souls, whose days, Re - claimed from

o - ver-borne, Sin - sick and sor - row - worn, Whom Christ doth heal.
pas - sions tossed, Re - deemed at count - less cost, From dark de - spair.
proach to dare, With us the cross to bear, For Christ our Lord.
er - ror's ways, In - spired with hope and praise, To Christ be - long.

CHRIST, FROM WHOM ALL BLESSINGS FLOW

words by
Charles Wesley, 1740

CANTERBURY
music adapt. from
Orlando Gibbons, 1623

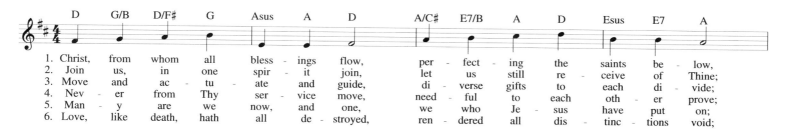

1. Christ, from whom all bless - ings flow, per - fect - ing the saints be - low,
2. Join us, in one spir - it join, let us still re - ceive of Thine,
3. Move and ac - tu - ate and guide, di - verse gifts to each di - vide;
4. Nev - er from Thy ser - vice move, need - ful to each oth - er prove;
5. Man - y are we now, and one, we who Je - sus have put on;
6. Love, like death, hath all de - stroyed, ren - dered all dis - tinc - tions void;

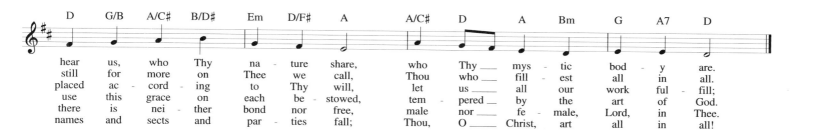

hear us, who Thy na - ture share, who Thy mys - tic bod - y are.
still for more on Thee we call, Thou who fill - est all in all.
placed ac - cord - ing to Thy will, let us all our work ful - fill;
use this grace on each be - stowed, tem - pered by the art of God.
there is nei - ther bond nor free, male nor fe - male, Lord, in Thee.
names and sects and par - ties fall; Thou, O Christ, art all in all!

CHRIST IS MADE THE SURE FOUNDATION

words from
Angularis fundamentum, 6th or 7th century
tr. by J.M. Neale (1818-1866)

LAUDA ANIMA
music by
J. Goss (1800-1880)

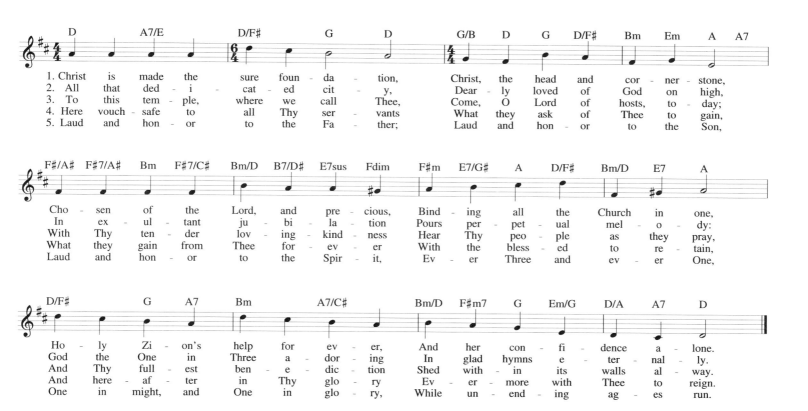

1. Christ is made the sure foun - da - tion, Christ, the head and cor - ner - stone,
2. All that ded - i - cat - ed cit - y, Dear - ly loved of God on high,
3. To this tem - ple, where we call Thee, Come, O Lord of hosts, to - day;
4. Here vouch - safe to all Thy ser - vants What they ask of Thee to gain;
5. Laud and hon - or to the Fa - ther; Laud and hon - or to the Son,

Cho - sen of the Lord, and pre - cious, Bind - ing all the Church in one,
In ex - ul - tant ju - bi - la - tion Pours per - pet - ual mel - o - dy:
With Thy ten - der lov - ing - kind - ness Hear Thy peo - ple as they pray,
What they gain from Thee for ev - er With the bless - ed to re - tain,
Laud and hon - or to the Spir - it, Ev - er Three and ev - er One,

Ho - ly Zi - on's help for ev - er, And her con - fi - dence a - lone.
God the One in Three a - dor - ing In glad hymns e - ter - nal - ly.
And Thy full - est ben - e - dic - tion Shed with - in its walls al - way.
And here - af - ter in Thy glo - ry Ev - er - more with Thee to reign.
One in might, and One in glo - ry, While un - end - ing ag - es run.

A CHARGE TO KEEP I HAVE

BOYLSTON
music by
Lowell Mason, 1832

words by
Charles Wesley, 1762

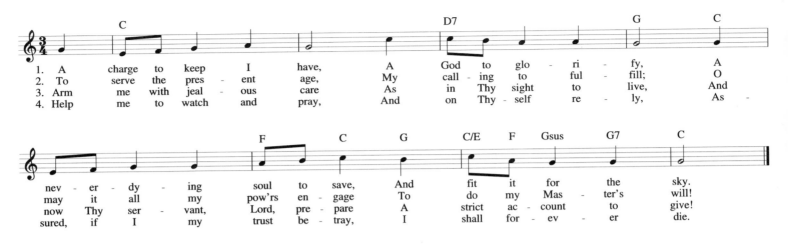

CHRIST JESUS LAY IN DEATH'S STRONG BANDS

CHRIST LAG IN TODESBANDEN
music from
Geistliche Gesangbüchlein, 1524

words by
Martin Luther, 1524
tr. by Richard Massie, 1854

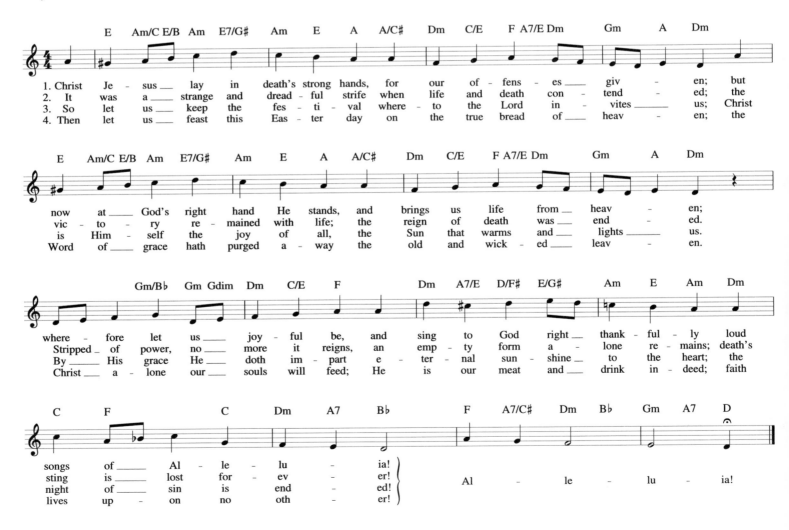

CHRIST IS MADE THE SURE FOUNDATION

Latin text, 7th century
tr. by John M. Neale (1818-1866)

REGENT SQUARE
music by
Henry T. Smart (1813-1879)

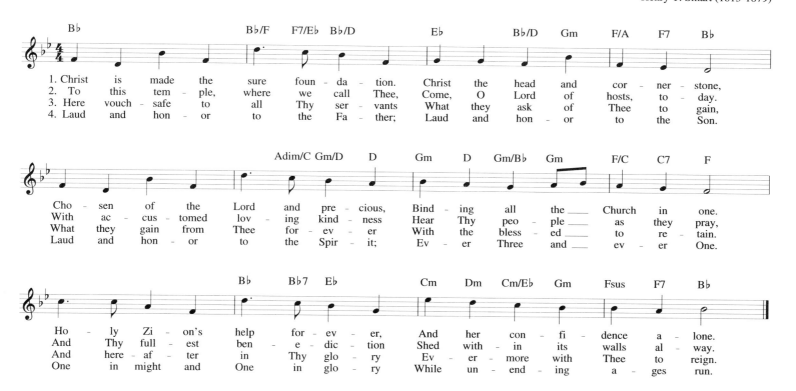

1. Christ is made the sure foun - da - tion. Christ the head and cor - ner - stone,
2. To this tem - ple, where we call Thee, Come, O Lord of hosts, to - day.
3. Here vouch - safe to all Thy ser - vants What they ask of Thee to gain,
4. Laud and hon - or to the Fa - ther; Laud and hon - or to the Son.

Cho - sen of the Lord and pre - cious, Bind - ing all the ___ Church in one.
With ac - cus - tomed lov - ing kind - ness Hear Thy peo - ple ___ as they pray,
What they gain from Thee for - ev - er With the bless - ed ___ to re - tain.
Laud and hon - or to the Spir - it; Ev - er Three and ___ ev - er One.

Ho - ly Zi - on's help for - ev - er, And her con - fi - dence a - lone.
And Thy full - est ben - e - dic - tion Shed with - in its walls al - way.
And here - af - ter in Thy glo - ry Ev - er - more with Thee to reign.
One in might and One in glo - ry While un - end - ing a - ges run.

CHRIST OF THE UPWARD WAY

words by
Walter J. Mathams, c. 1915

SURSUM CORDA
music by
George Lomas (1834-1884)

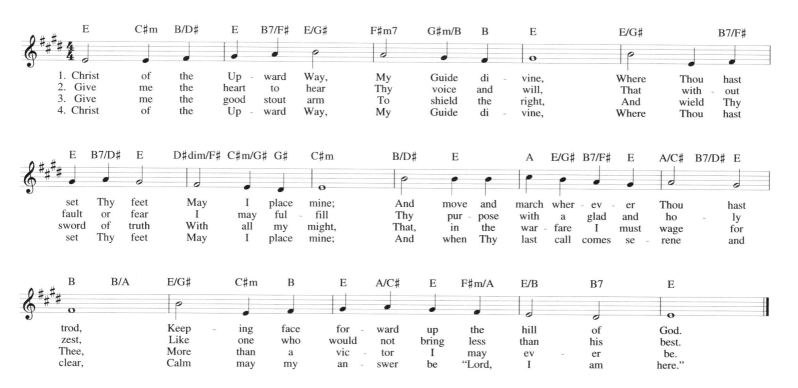

1. Christ of the Up - ward Way, My Guide di - vine, Where Thou hast
2. Give me the heart to hear Thy voice and will, That with - out
3. Give me the good stout arm To shield the right, And wield Thy
4. Christ of the Up - ward Way, My Guide di - vine, Where Thou hast

set Thy feet May I place mine; And move and march wher - ev - er Thou hast
fault or fear I may ful - fill Thy pur - pose with a glad and ho - ly
sword of truth With all my might, That, in the war - fare I must wage for
set Thy feet May I place mine; And when Thy last call comes se - rene and

trod, Keep - ing face for - ward up the hill of God.
zest, Like one who would not bring less than his best.
Thee, More than a vic - tor I may ev - er be.
clear, Calm may my an - swer be "Lord, I am here."

CHRIST RECEIVETH SINFUL MEN

words by
Erdmann Neumeister (1671-1756)
tr. by Emma F. Bevan (1827-1909)

NEUMEISTER
music by
James McGranahan (1840-1907)

1. Sin - ners Je - sus will re - ceive: Sound this word of grace to all Who the
2. Come, and He will give you rest; Trust Him, for His Word is plain; He will
3. Now my heart con - demns me not, Pure be - fore the law I stand; He Who
4. Christ re - ceiv - eth sin - ful men, E - ven me with all my sin; Purged from

heav'n - ly path - ways leave, All who lin - ger, all who fall. Sing __ it
take the sin - ful - est, Christ re - ceiv - eth sin - ful men.
cleansed me from all spot, Sat - is - fied its last de - mand.
ev - 'ry spot and stain, Heav'n with Him I en - ter in.

o'er __ and o'er __ a - gain; __ Christ __ re - ceiv - eth sin - ful men; __ Make __ the

mes - sage clear __ and plain: __ Christ re - ceiv - eth sin - ful men. __

CHRIST RETURNETH

words by
H.L. Turner, 19th century

music by
James McGranahan (1840-1907)

1. It may be at morn, when the day is a - wak - ing, When
2. It may be at mid - day, it may be at twi - light, It
3. O joy! O de - light! should we go with - out dy - ing, No

sun - light thru dark - ness and shad - ow is break - ing, That Je - sus will
may be, per - chance, that the black - ness of mid - night Will burst in - to
sick - ness, no sad - ness, no dread and no cry - ing— Caught up thru the

come in the full - ness of glo - ry To re - ceive from the world __ His own.
light in the blaze of His glo - ry, When __ Je - sus re - ceives __ His own.
clouds with our Lord in - to glo - ry, When __ Je - sus re - ceives __ His own.

O Lord Je - sus, how long, how long Ere we shout the glad song: Christ re -

turn - eth! Hal - le - lu - jah! Hal - le - lu - jah, A - men! Hal - le - lu - jah, A - men!

CHRIST, THE LIFE OF ALL THE LIVING

words by
E.C. Homburg (1605-1681)
tr. by C. Winkworth (1827-1878)

JESU, MEINES LEBENS LEBEN
music from
Kirchengesangbuch, Darmstadt, 1687

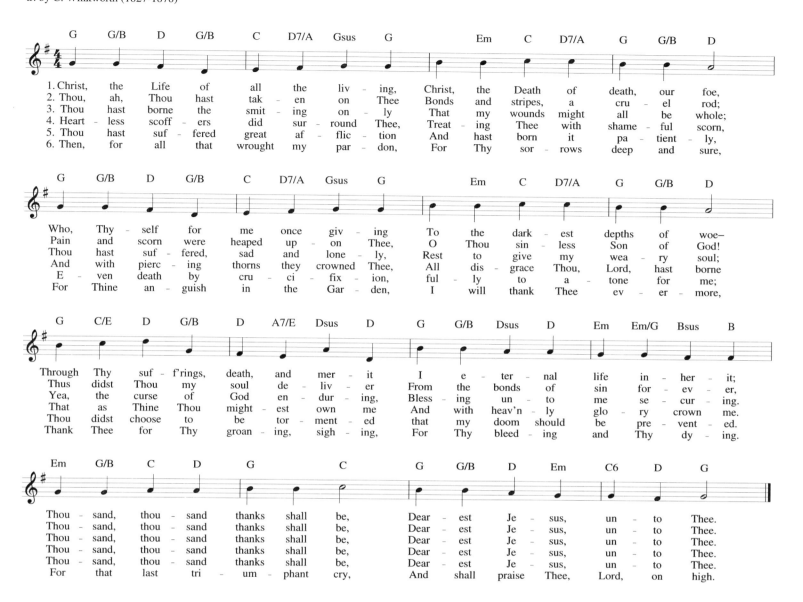

CHRIST THE LORD IS RISEN AGAIN

words by
Michael Weisse (c. 1480-1534)
tr. by Catherine Winkworth, 1858

ESSEX
music by
Thomas Clark

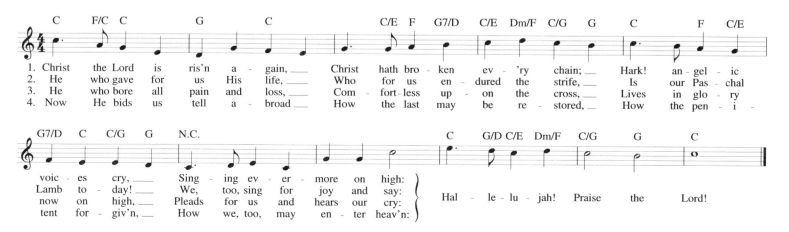

CHRIST THE LORD IS RISEN TODAY

EASTER HYMN

words by
Charles Wesley, 1739

music from
Lyra Davidica, London, 1708

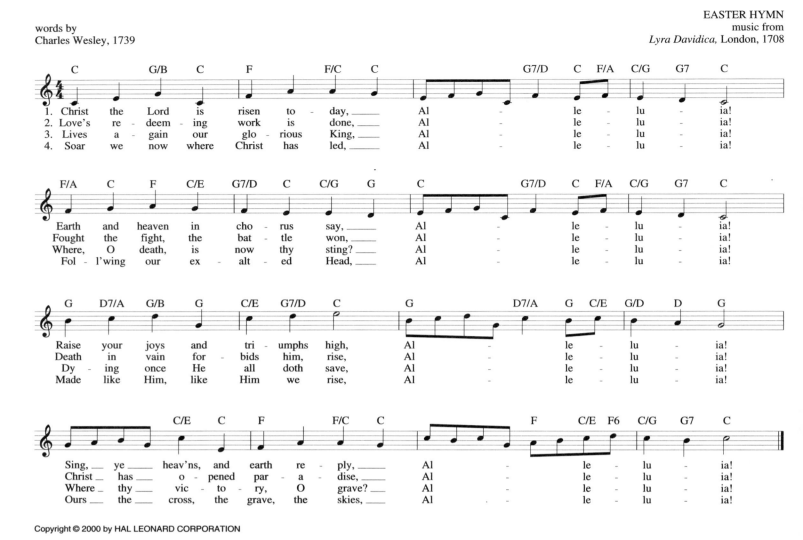

1. Christ the Lord is risen to - day, _____ Al - le - lu - ia!
2. Love's re - deem - ing work is done, _____ Al - le - lu - ia!
3. Lives a - gain our glo - rious King, _____ Al - le - lu - ia!
4. Soar we now where Christ has led, _____ Al - le - lu - ia!

Earth and heaven in cho - rus say, _____ Al - le - lu - ia!
Fought the fight, the bat - tle won, _____ Al - le - lu - ia!
Where, O death, is now thy sting? _____ Al - le - lu - ia!
Fol - l'wing our ex - alt - ed Head, _____ Al - le - lu - ia!

Raise your joys and tri - umphs high, Al - le - lu - ia!
Death in vain for - bids him, rise, Al - le - lu - ia!
Dy - ing once He all doth save, Al - le - lu - ia!
Made like Him, like Him we rise, Al - le - lu - ia!

Sing, ye _____ heav'ns, and earth re - ply, _____ Al - le - lu - ia!
Christ _ has _____ o - pened par - a - dise, _____ Al - le - lu - ia!
Where thy _____ vic - to - ry, O grave? _____ Al - le - lu - ia!
Ours _____ the _____ cross, the grave, the skies, _____ Al - le - lu - ia!

CHRIST THE LORD IS RISEN TODAY

LLANFAIR

words by
Charles Wesley (1707-1788)

music by
Robert Williams (1781-1821)

1. Christ the Lord is ris'n to - day, Al - le - lu - ia! All on earth with
2. Lives a - gain our glo - rious _ King; Al - le - lu - ia! Where, O death, is
3. Love's re - deem - ing work is _ done, Al - le - lu - ia! Fought the fight, the
4. Soar we now where Christ has _ led, Al - le - lu - ia! Fol - l'wing our ex -

an - gels _____ say, Al - le - lu - ia! Raise your joys and tri - umphs _ high,
now your _ sting? Al - le - lu - ia! Once He died our souls _ to _ save,
bat - tle _____ won. Al - le - lu - ia! Death in vain for - bids _ Him _ rise;
alt - ed _____ Head; Al - le - lu - ia. Made like Him, like Him _ we _____ rise,

Al - le - lu - ia! Sing, O heav'ns, and earth re - ply, Al - le - lu - ia!
Al - le - lu - ia! Where your vic - to - ry, O _ grave? Al - le - lu - ia!
Al - le - lu - ia! Christ has o - pened par - a - dise. Al - le - lu - ia!
Al - le - lu - ia! Ours the cross, the grave, the _ skies. Al - le - lu - ia!

CHRIST, WE DO ALL ADORE THEE

words from
Adoramus Te
English version by Theodore Baker

ADORE THEE
music by
Theodore Dubois
from *The Seven Last Words of Christ*

CHRIST, WHOSE GLORY FILLS THE SKIES

words by
Charles Wesley, 1740

LUX PRIMA
music by
Charles F. Gounod, 1872

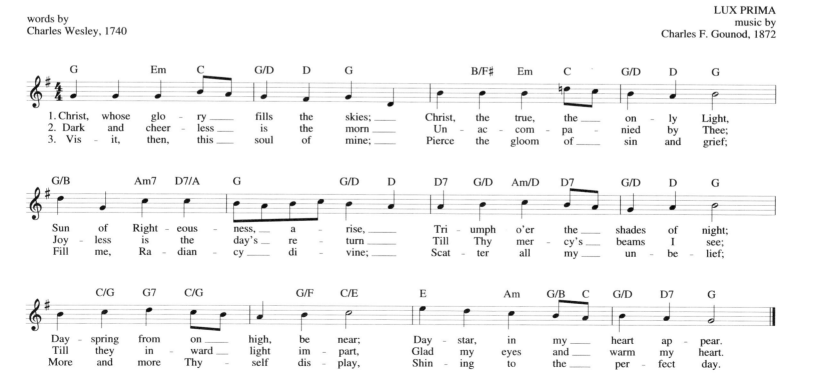

CHRIST, WHOSE GLORY FILLS THE SKIES

words by
Charles Wesley, 1740

RATISBON
music from
Freylinghausen's *Gesangbuch*, 1704
adapted in Werner's *Choralbuch*, 1815

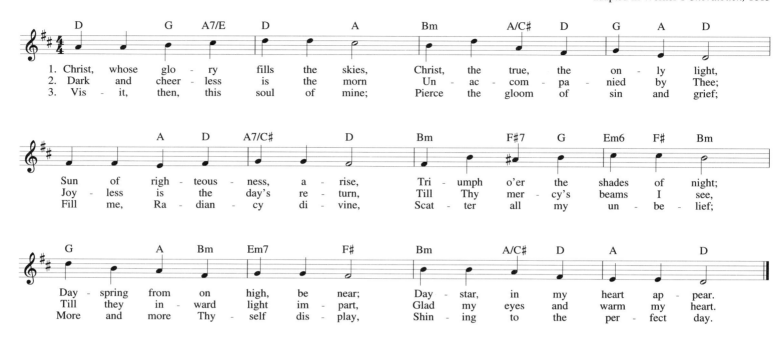

CHURCH IN THE WILDWOOD

words by
Dr. William S. Pitts, 1865

CHURCH IN THE VALLEY
music by
Dr. William S. Pitts, 1865

CHRIST THE LORD IS RISEN TODAY

words by
Charles Wesley (1707-1788)

ORIENTIS PARTIBUS
music by
Pierre de Corbeille (d. 1221)

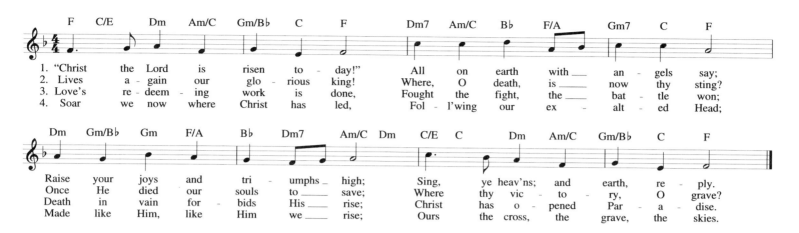

1. "Christ the Lord is risen to - day!" All on earth with ___ an - gels say;
2. Lives a - gain our glo - rious king! Where, O death, is ___ now thy sting?
3. Love's re - deem - ing work is done, Fought the fight, the ___ bat - tle won;
4. Soar we now where Christ has led, Fol - l'wing our ex - alt - ed Head;

Raise your joys and tri - umphs ___ high; Sing, ye heav'ns; and earth, re - ply.
Once He died our souls to ___ save; Where thy vic - to - ry, O grave?
Death in vain for - bids His ___ rise; Christ has o - pened Par - a - dise.
Made like Him, like Him we ___ rise; Ours the cross, the grave, the skies.

THE CHURCH'S ONE FOUNDATION

words by
Samuel John Stone (1839-1900)

AURELIA
music by
Samuel Sebastian Wesley (1810-1876)

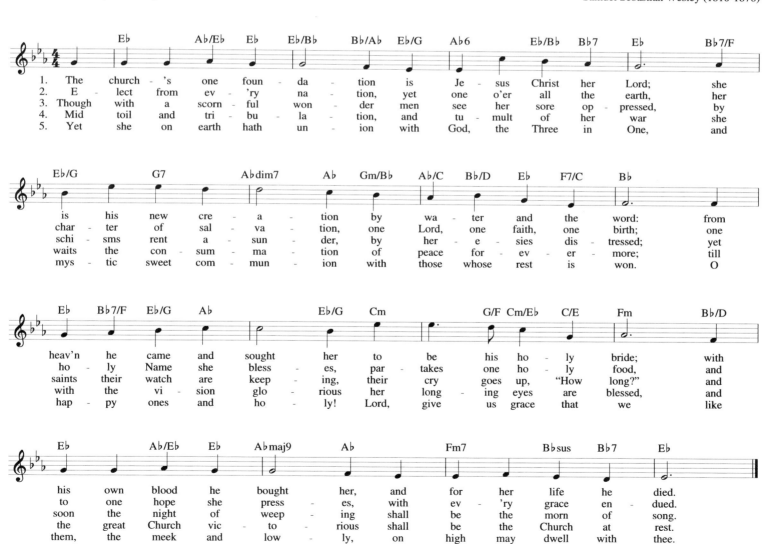

1. The church - 's one foun - da - tion is Je - sus Christ her Lord; she
2. E - lect from ev - 'ry na - tion, yet one o'er all the earth, her
3. Though with a scorn - ful won - der men see her sore op - pressed, by
4. Mid toil and tri - bu - la - tion, and tu - mult of her war she
5. Yet she on earth hath un - ion with God, the Three in One, and

is his new cre - a - tion by wa - ter and the word: from
char - ter of sal - va - tion, one Lord, one faith, one birth; one
schi - sms rent a - sun - der, by her e - sies dis - tressed; yet
waits the con - sum - ma - tion of peace for ev - er - more; till
mys - tic sweet com - mun - ion with those whose rest is won. O

heav'n he came and sought her to be his ho - ly bride; with
ho - ly Name she bless - es, par - takes one ho - ly food, and
saints their watch are keep - ing, their cry goes up, "How long?" and
with the vi - sion glo - rious her long - ing eyes are blessed, and
hap - py ones and ho - ly! Lord, give us grace that we like

his own blood he bought her, and for her life he died.
to one hope she press - es, with ev - 'ry grace en - dued.
soon the night of weep - ing shall be the morn of song.
the great Church vic - to - rious shall be the Church at rest.
them, the meek and low - ly, on high may dwell with thee.

CLEANSE ME

ELLERS
music by
Edward J. Hopkins

words by
J. Edwin Orr
based on Psalm 139:23

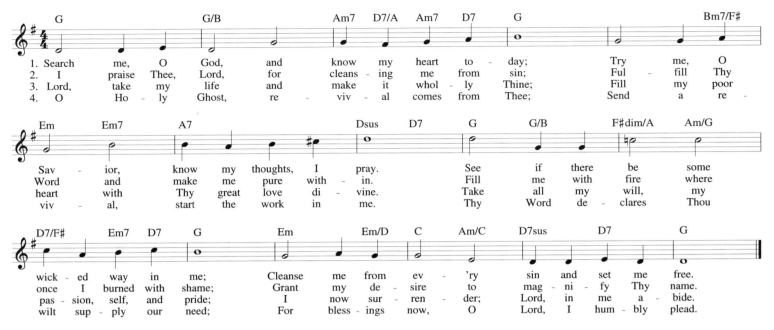

1. Search me, O God, and know my heart to - day; Try me, O
2. I praise Thee, Lord, for cleans - ing me from sin; Ful - fill Thy
3. Lord, take my life and make it whol - ly Thine; Fill my poor
4. O Ho - ly Ghost, re - viv - al comes from Thee; Send a re -

Sav - ior, know my thoughts, I pray. See if there be some
Word and make me pure with - in. Fill me with fire some - where
heart with Thy great love di - vine. Take all my will, my
viv - al, start the work in me. Thy Word de - clares Thou

wick - ed way in me; Cleanse me from ev - 'ry sin and set me free.
once I burned with shame; Grant my de - sire to mag - ni - fy Thy name.
pas - sion, self, and pride; I now sur - ren - der; Lord, in me a - bide.
wilt sup - ply our need; For bless - ings now, O Lord, I hum - bly plead.

Copyright © 2000 by HAL LEONARD CORPORATION

CLEANSE ME

MAORI
Traditional Maori melody

words by
J. Edwin Orr
based on Psalm 139:23

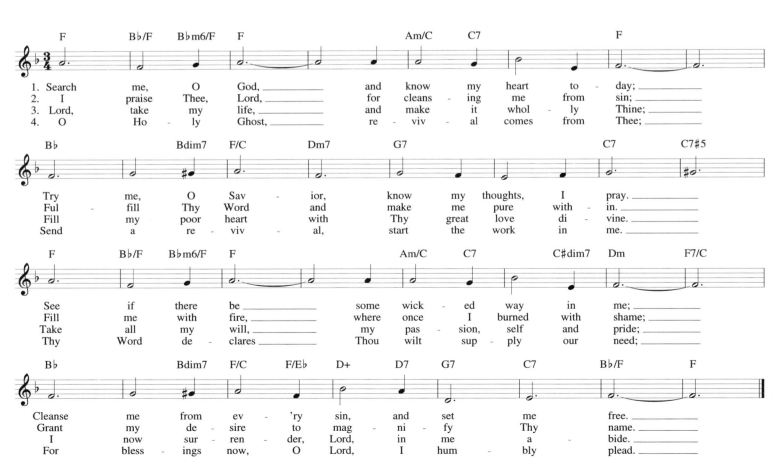

1. Search me, O God, and know my heart to - day;
2. I praise Thee, Lord, for cleans - ing me from sin;
3. Lord, take my life, and make it whol - ly Thine;
4. O Ho - ly Ghost, re - viv - al comes from Thee;

Try me, O Sav - ior, know my thoughts, I pray.
Ful - fill Thy Word and make me pure with - in.
Fill my poor heart with Thy great love di - vine.
Send a re - viv - al, start the work in me.

See if there be some wick - ed way in me;
Fill me with fire, where once I burned with shame;
Take all my will, my pas - sion, self, and pride;
Thy Word de - clares Thou wilt sup - ply our need;

Cleanse me from ev - 'ry sin, and set me free.
Grant my de - sire to mag - ni - fy Thy name.
I now sur - ren - der, Lord, in me a - bide.
For bless - ings now, O Lord, I hum - bly plead.

Copyright © 2000 by HAL LEONARD CORPORATION

THE CLEANSING WAVE

words by
Phoebe Palmer (1807-1874)

KNAPP
music by
Phoebe Palmer Knapp (1839-1908)

CLOSE TO THEE

words by
Fanny J. Crosby (1820-1915)

music by
Silas J. Vail (1818-1884)

COME AND DINE

WIDMEYER

words by
C.B. Widmeyer, 1907

music by
C.B. Widmeyer, 1907

1. Je - sus has a ta - ble spread Where the saints of God are fed; He in - vites His cho - sen peo - ple, "Come and
2. The dis - ci - ples came to land, Thus o - bey - ing Christ's com-mand; For the Mas - ter called to them, "O come and
3. Soon the Lamb will take His bride To be ev - er at His side; All the hosts of heav - en will as - sem - bled

dine." With His man - na He doth feed And sup - plies our ev - 'ry need. O 'tis
dine." There they found their hearts' de - sire— Bread and fish up - on the fire; Thus He
be. O 'twill be a glo - rious sight— All the saints in spot - less white; And with

sweet to sup with Je - sus all the time!
sat - is - fies the hun - gry ev - 'ry time.
Je - sus they will feast e - ter - nal - ly.

Refrain

"Come and dine," the Mas - ter call - eth, "come and

dine." You may feast at Je - sus' ta - ble all the time. He who

fed the mul - ti - tude, turned the wa - ter in - to wine, To the hun - gry call - eth now, "Come and dine."

COME, AND LET US SWEETLY JOIN

CANTERBURY

words by
Charles Wesley, 1740

music adapt. from
Orlando Gibbons, 1623

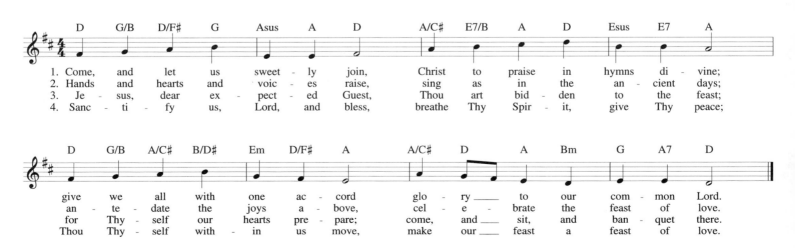

1. Come, and let us sweet - ly join, Christ to praise in hymns di - vine;
2. Hands and hearts and voic - es raise, sing as in the an - cient days;
3. Je - sus, dear ex - pect - ed Guest, Thou art bid - den to the feast;
4. Sanc - ti - fy us, Lord, and bless, breathe Thy Spir - it, give Thy peace;

give we all with one ac - cord glo - ry to our com - mon Lord.
an - te - date the joys a - bove, cel - e - brate the feast of love.
for Thy - self our hearts pre - pare; come, and sit, and ban - quet there.
Thou Thy - self with - in us move, make our feast a feast of love.

COME, CHRISTIANS, JOIN TO SING

words by
Christian H. Bateman, 1843

MADRID
Traditional Spanish melody

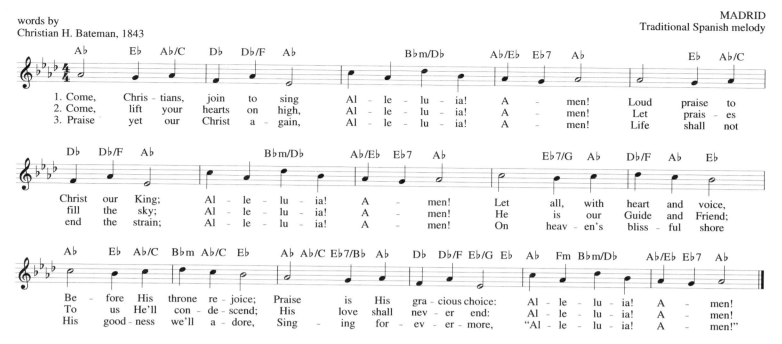

1. Come, Chris - tians, join to sing Al - le - lu - ia! A - men! Loud praise to
2. Come, lift your hearts on high, Al - le - lu - ia! A - men! Let prais - es
3. Praise yet our Christ a - gain, Al - le - lu - ia! A - men! Life shall not

Christ our King; Al - le - lu - ia! A - men! Let all, with heart and voice,
fill the sky; Al - le - lu - ia! A - men! He is our Guide and Friend;
end the strain; Al - le - lu - ia! A - men! On heav - en's bliss - ful shore

Be - fore His throne re - joice; Praise is His gra - cious choice: Al - le - lu - ia! A - men!
To us He'll con - de - scend; His love shall nev - er end: Al - le - lu - ia! A - men!
His good - ness we'll a - dore, Sing - ing for - ev - er - more, "Al - le - lu - ia! A - men!"

COME, DEAREST LORD, DESCEND AND DWELL

words by
Isaac Watts, 1709

FEDERAL STREET
music by
Henry K. Oliver, 1832

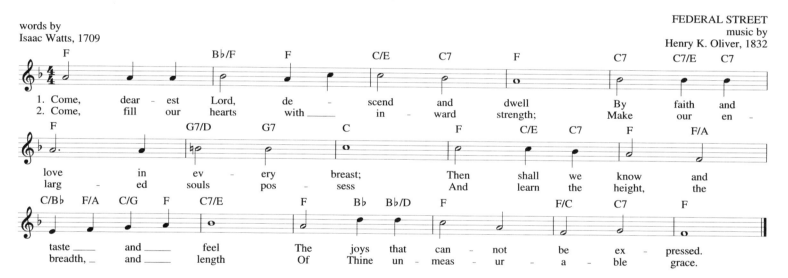

1. Come, dear - est Lord, de - scend and dwell By faith and
2. Come, fill our hearts with in - ward strength; Make our en -

love in ev - ery breast; Then shall we know and
larg - ed souls pos - sess And learn the height, and the

taste and feel The joys that can - not be ex - pressed.
breadth, and length Of Thine un - meas - ur - a - ble grace.

COME, HOLY GHOST, OUR HEARTS INSPIRE

words by
Charles Wesley, 1740

WINCHESTER OLD
music from
Est's *The Whole Booke of Psalmes,* 1592

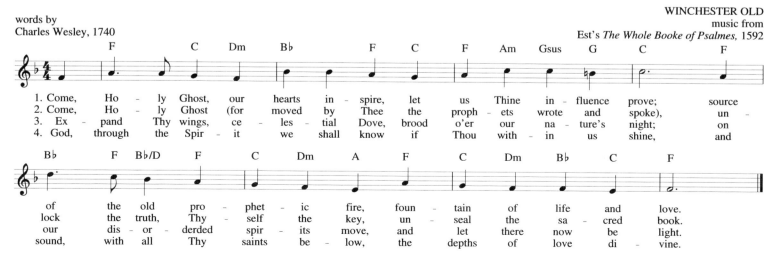

1. Come, Ho - ly Ghost, our hearts in - spire, let us Thine in - fluence prove; source
2. Come, Ho - ly Ghost (for moved by Thee the proph - ets wrote and spoke), un
3. Ex - pand Thy wings, ce - les - tial Dove, brood o'er our na - ture's night; on
4. God, through the Spir - it we shall know if Thou with - in us shine, and

of the old pro - phet - ic fire, foun - tain of life and love.
lock the truth, Thy - self the key, un - seal the sa - cred book.
our dis - or - derded spir - its move, and let there now be light.
sound, with all Thy saints be - low, the depths of love di - vine.

"COME, FOLLOW ME," THE SAVIOR SPAKE

MACH'S MIT MIR, GOTT
music by
Bartholomäus Gesius (c. 1555-1613)

words by
Johann Scheffler (1624-1677)
tr. by Charles W. Schaeffer (1813-1896)

1. "Come, fol-low Me," the Sav-ior spake, "All in My way a-bid-ing;
2. "I am the Light; I light the way, A god-ly life dis-play-ing;
3. "My heart a-bounds in low-li-ness, My soul with love is glow-ing,
4. "I teach you how to shun and flee What harms your soul's sal-va-tion.
5. "Who seeks to find his soul's wel-fare With-out Me, he shall lose it;
6. Then let us fol-low Christ, our Lord, And take the cross ap-point-ed;

De-ny your-selves, the world for-sake, O-bey My call and guid-ing.
I bid you walk as in the day; I keep your feet from stray-ing.
And gra-cious words My lips ex-press, With meek-ness o-ver-flow-ing.
Your heart from ev-'ry guile to free, From sin and its temp-ta-tion.
But who to lose it may ap-pear, In God shall in-tro-duce it.
And, firm-ly cling-ing to His Word, In suf-f'ring be un-daunt-ed.

O bear the cross, what-e'er be-tide, Take My ex-am-ple for your guide.
I am the Way, and well I show How you must so-journ here be-low.
My heart, My mind, My strength, My all, To God I yield, on Him I call.
I am the Ref-uge of the soul And lead you to your heav'n-ly goal.
Who bears no cross nor fal-lows hard De-serves not Me nor My re-ward."
For who bears not the bat-tle's strain The crown of life shall not ob-tain.

COME, GRACIOUS SPIRIT, HEAVENLY DOVE

WAREHAM
music by
William Knapp (1698-1768)

words by
Simon Browne (1680-1732)

1. Come, gra-cious Spir-it, heav'n-ly dove, With light and
2. To us the light of truth dis-play, And make us
3. Lead us to ho-li-ness, the road Which we must
4. Lead us to God, our fi-nal rest, To be with

com-fort from a-bove. Be Thou our guard-ian,
know and choose Thy way. Plant ho-ly fear in
take to dwell with God. Lead us to Christ, the
Him for-ev-er blest. Lead us to heav'n, its

Thou our guide; O'er ev-'ry thought and step pre-side.
ev-'ry heart, That we from God may ne'er de-part.
Liv-ing Way, Nor let us from His pas-tures stray.
bliss to share Full-ness of joy for-ev-er there.

COME, HOLY GHOST, OUR SOULS INSPIRE

words attr. to
Rhabanus Maurus (776-856)
tr. by John Cosin (1594-1672)

VENI, CREATOR SPIRITUS
Sarum plainsong, mode VIII

1. Come, Ho - ly Ghost, our souls in - spire, And light - en with cel - es - tial fire;
2. Thy bless - ed unc - tion from a - bove Is com - fort, life, and fire of love.
3. A - noint and cheer our soil - ed face With the a - bun - dance of Thy grace.
4. Teach us to know the Fa - ther, Son, And Thee, of both, to be but one;

Thou the a - noint - ing Spir - it art, Who dost Thy sev'n - fold gifts im - part.
En - a - ble with per - pet - ual light The dull - ness of our blind - ed sight.
Keep far our foes; give peace at home; Where Thou art guide, no ill can come.
That through the a - ges all a - long Thy praise may be our end - less song!

5. Praise to Thine e - ter - nal mer - it, Fa - ther Son, and Ho - ly Spir - it. A - men.

COME, HOLY SPIRIT, DOVE DIVINE

words by
Adoniram Judson, 1832

MARYTON
music by
H. Percy Smith, 1874

1. Come, Ho - ly Spir - it, Dove di - vine, On these bap - tis - mal wa - ters shine,
2. We love Thy name, we love Thy laws, And joy - ful - ly em - brace Thy cause;
3. We sink be - neath the wa - ter's face, And thank Thee for Thy sav - ing grace;
4. And as we rise with Thee to live, O let the Ho - ly Spir - it give

And teach our hearts, in high - est strain, To praise the Lamb for sin - ners slain.
We love Thy cross, the shame, the pain, O Lamb of God for sin - ners slain.
We die to sin and seek a grave With Thee, be - neath the yield - ing wave.
The seal - ing unc - tion from a - bove, The joy of life, the fire of love.

COME, HOLY SPIRIT, HEAVENLY DOVE

words by
Isaac Watts (1674-1748)

ST. AGNES
music by
John Bacchus Dykes (1823-1876)

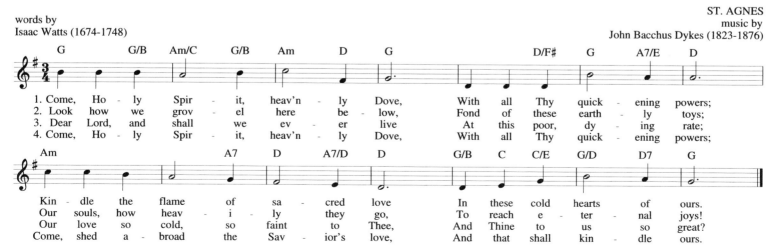

1. Come, Ho - ly Spir - it, heav'n - ly Dove, With all Thy quick - ening powers;
2. Look how we grov - el here be - low, Fond of these earth - ly toys;
3. Dear Lord, and shall we ev - er live At this poor, dy - ing rate;
4. Come, Ho - ly Spir - it, heav'n - ly Dove, With all Thy quick - ening powers;

Kin - dle the flame of sa - cred love In these cold hearts of ours.
Our souls, how heav - i - ly they go, To reach e - ter - nal joys!
Our love so cold, so faint to Thee, And Thine to us so great?
Come, shed a - broad the Sav - ior's love, And that shall kin - dle ours.

COME, LET US JOIN OUR CHEERFUL SONGS

words by
Isaac Watts (1674-1748)

NUN DANKET ALL' UND BRINGET EHR'
music by
Johann Crüger (1598-1662)

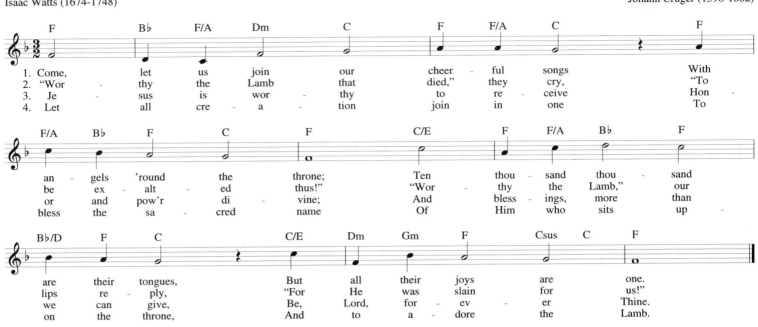

1. Come, let us join our cheer - ful songs With
2. "Wor - thy the Lamb that died," they cry, "To
3. Je - sus is wor - thy to re - ceive Hon
4. Let all cre - a - tion join in one To

an - gels 'round the throne; Ten thou - sand thou - sand
be ex - alt - ed thus!" "Wor - thy the Lamb," our
or and pow'r di - vine; And bless - ings, more than
bless the sa - cred name Of Him who sits up -

are their tongues, But all their joys are one.
lips re - ply, "For He was slain for us!"
we can give, Be, Lord, for - ev - er Thine.
on the throne, And to a - dore the Lamb.

COME, LET US JOIN OUR FRIENDS ABOVE

words by
Charles Wesley, 1759

FOREST GREEN
Traditional English melody
arr. by Ralph Vaughan Williams, 1906

1. Come, let us join our friends a - bove who have ob - tained the prize, and
2. One fam - i - ly we dwell in Him, one church a - bove, be - neath, though
3. Ten thou - sand to their end - less home this sol - emn mo - ment fly, and
4. Our spir - its too shall quick - ly join, like theirs with glo - ry crowned, and

on the ea - gle wings of love to joys ce - les - tial rise. Let
now di - vid - ed by the stream, the nar - row stream of death; one
we are to the mar - gin come, and we ex - pect to die. E'en
shout to see our Cap - tain's sign, to hear His trum - pet sound. O

saints on earth u - nite to sing with those to glo - ry gone, for
ar - my of the liv - ing God, to His com - mand we bow; part
now by faith we join our hands with those that went be - fore, and
that we now might grasp our Guide! O that the word were given! Come,

all the ser - vants of our King in earth and heaven are one.
of His host have crossed the flood, and part are cross - ing now.
greet the blood - be - sprin - kled bands on the e - ter - nal shore.
Lord of Hosts, the waves di - vide, and land us all in heaven.

COME, HOLY GHOST, CREATOR BLEST

words attr. to
Rhabanus Maurus (776-856)
tr. by Edward Caswall (1814-1878)

KOMM, GOTT SCHÖPFER
music based on *Veni Creator Spiritus*
Sarum plainsong, c. 9th century

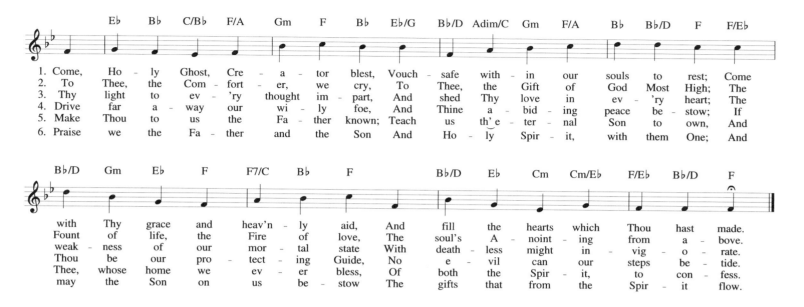

1. Come, Ho-ly Ghost, Cre-a-tor blest, Vouch-safe with-in our souls to rest; Come
2. To Thee, the Com-fort-er, we cry, To Thee, the Gift of God Most High; The
3. Thy light to ev-'ry thought im-part, And shed Thy love in ev-'ry heart; The
4. Drive far a-way our wi-ly foe, And Thine a-bid-ing peace be-stow; If
5. Make Thou to us the Fa-ther known; Teach us th' e-ter-nal Son to own, And
6. Praise we the Fa-ther and the Son And Ho-ly Spir-it, with them One; And

with Thy grace and heav'n-ly aid, And fill the hearts which Thou hast made.
Fount of life, the Fire of love, The soul's A-noint-ing from a-bove.
weak-ness of our mor-tal state With death-less might in-vig-o-rate.
Thou be our pro-tect-ing Guide, No e-vil can our steps be-tide.
Thee, whose home we ev-er bless, Of both the Spir-it, to con-fess.
may the Son on us be-stow The gifts that from the Spir-it flow.

COME, LET US USE THE GRACE DIVINE

words by
Charles Wesley, 1762

KINGSFOLD
Traditional English melody
arr. by Ralph Vaughan Williams, 1906

1. Come, let us use the grace di-vine, and all with one ac-cord, in
2. The cov-enant we this mo-ment make be ev-er kept in mind; we
3. Thee, Fa-ther, Son, and Ho-ly Ghost, let all our hearts re-ceive, pres

a per-pet-ual cov-'nant join our-selves to Christ the Lord; give
will no more our God for-sake, or cast these words be-hind. We
ent with Thy ce-les-tial host the peace-ful an-swer give; to each

up our-selves, thru Je-sus' power, His name to glo-ri-fy; and
nev-er will throw off the fear of God who hears our vow; and
cov-e-nant the blood ap-ply which takes our sins a-way, and

prom-ise, in this sa-cred hour, for God to live and die.
if Thou art well-pleased to hear, come down and meet us now.
reg-is-ter our names on high and keep us to that day!

COME, MY WAY, MY TRUTH, MY LIFE

THE CALL

words by
George Herbert, 1633

music by
Ralph Vaughan Williams, 1911

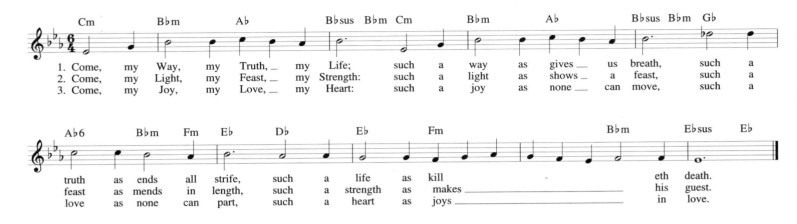

1. Come, my Way, my Truth, my Life; such a way as gives us breath, such a truth as ends all strife, such a life as kill eth death.
2. Come, my Light, my Feast, my Strength: such a light as shows a feast, such a feast as mends in length, such a strength as makes his guest.
3. Come, my Joy, my Love, my Heart: such a joy as none can move, such a love as none can part, such a heart as joys in love.

COME, O THOU TRAVELER UNKNOWN

VERNON
Traditional melody

words by
Charles Wesley (1707-1788)

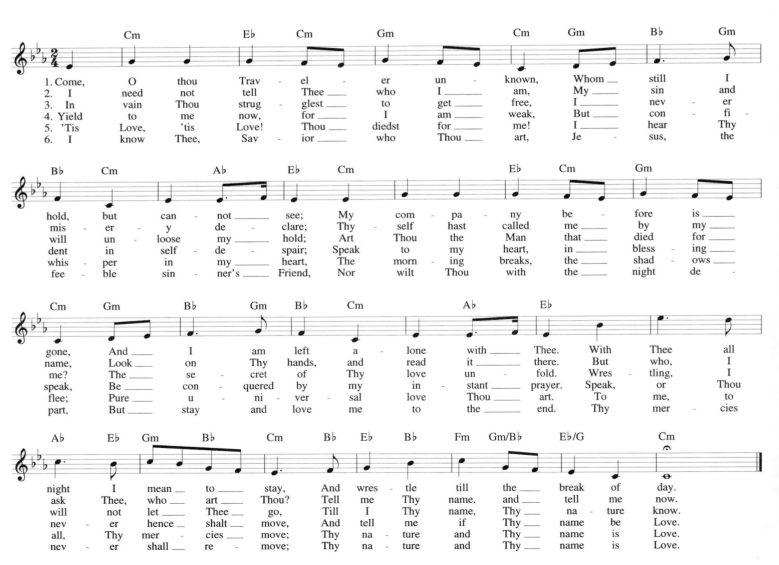

1. Come, O thou Trav-el-er un-known, Whom still I hold, but can-not see; My com-pa-ny be-fore is gone, And I am left a-lone with Thee. With Thee all night I mean to stay, And wres-tle till the break of day.
2. I need not tell Thee who I am, My sin and mis-er-y de-clare; Thy-self hast called me by my name, Look on Thy hands, and read it there. But who, I ask Thee, who art Thou? Tell me Thy name, and tell me now.
3. In vain Thou strug-glest to get free, I nev-er will un-loose my hold; Art Thou the Man that died for me? The se-cret of Thy love un-fold. Wres-tling, I will not let Thee go, Till I Thy name, Thy na-ture know.
4. Yield to me now, for I am weak, But con-fi-dent in self-de-spair; Speak to my heart, in bless-ing speak, Be con-quered by my in-stant prayer. Speak, or Thou nev-er hence shalt move, And tell me if Thy name be Love.
5. 'Tis Love, 'tis Love! Thou diedst for me! I hear Thy whis-per in my heart, The morn-ing breaks, the shad-ows flee; Pure u-ni-ver-sal love Thou art. To me, to all, Thy mer-cies move; Thy na-ture and Thy name is Love.
6. I know Thee, Sav-ior who Thou art, Je-sus, the fee-ble sin-ner's Friend, Nor wilt Thou with the night de-part, But stay and love me to the end. Thy mer-cies nev-er shall re-move; Thy na-ture and Thy name is Love.

COME SING, YE CHOIRS EXULTANT

Latin text by
Adam of St. Victor, c. 1170
tr. by Jackson Mason (1833-1889)

ACH GOTT, VOM HIMMELREICHE
music by
Michael Praetorius (1571-1621)

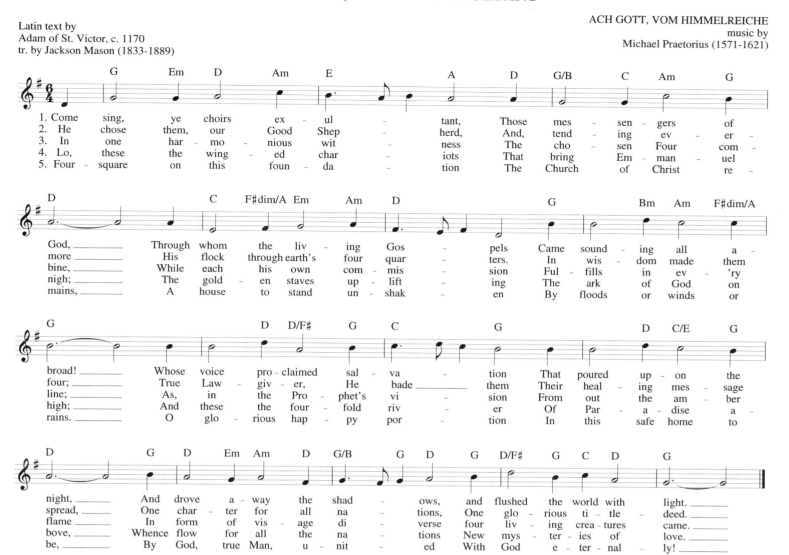

COME, SINNERS, TO THE GOSPEL FEAST

words by
Charles Wesley (1707-1788)

HEBRON
music by
Lowell Mason (1792-1872)

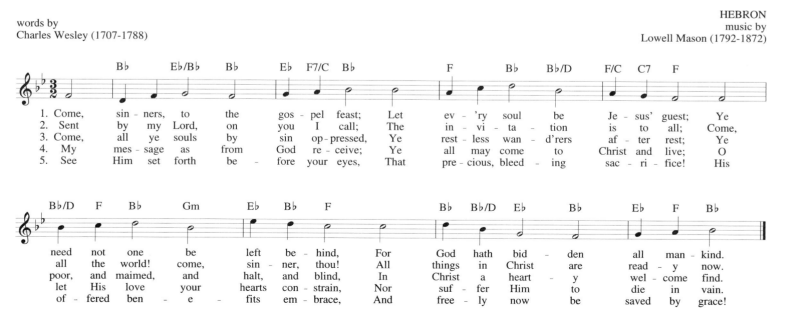

COME, THOU FOUNT OF EVERY BLESSING

NETTLETON
music from
John Wyeth's *Repository of Sacred Music, Part Second*, 1813

words by
Robert Robinson, 1758

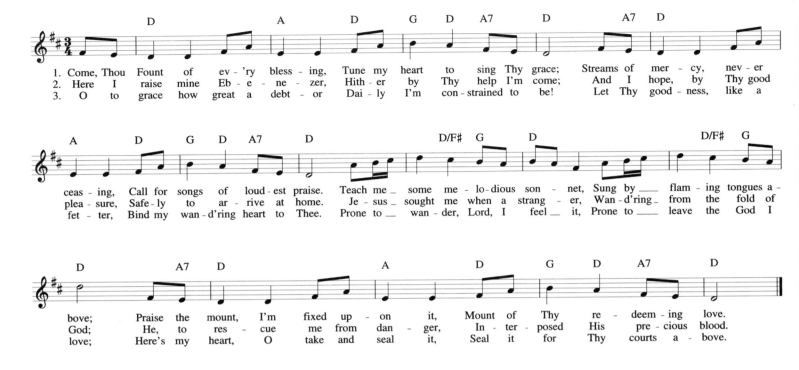

1. Come, Thou Fount of ev-'ry bless-ing, Tune my heart to sing Thy grace; Streams of mer-cy, nev-er
2. Here I raise mine Eb-e-ne-zer, Hith-er by Thy help I'm come; And I hope, by Thy good
3. O to grace how great a debt-or Dai-ly I'm con-strained to be! Let Thy good-ness, like a

ceas-ing, Call for songs of loud-est praise. Teach me some me-lo-dious son-net, Sung by flam-ing tongues a-
plea-sure, Safe-ly to ar-rive at home. Je-sus sought me when a strang-er, Wan-d'ring from the fold of
fet-ter, Bind my wan-d'ring heart to Thee. Prone to wan-der, Lord, I feel it, Prone to leave the God I

bove; Praise the mount, I'm fixed up-on it, Mount of Thy re-deem-ing love.
God; He, to res-cue me from dan-ger, In-ter-posed His pre-cious blood.
love; Here's my heart, O take and seal it, Seal it for Thy courts a-bove.

COME, THOU FOUNT OF EVERY BLESSING

WARRENTON
music from
The Sacred Harp, 1844

words by
Robert Robinson (1735-1790)

1. Come, Thou Fount of ev-'ry bless-ing, Tune my heart to
2. Here I raise mine Eb-en-e-zer– Hith-er by Thy
3. O to grace how great a debt-or Dai-ly I'm con

sing Thy grace; Streams of mer-cy, nev-er ceas-ing,
help I'm come; And I hope, by Thy good pleas-ure,
strained to be! Let Thy good-ness, like a fet-ter,

Call for songs of loud-est praise. }
Safe-ly to ar-rive at home. } I am bound for the king-dom, Will you
Bind my wan-d'ring heart to Thee. }

go to glo-ry with me? Hal-le-lu-jah, praise the Lord!

COME, THOU ALMIGHTY KING

Author unknown, c. 1757

ITALIAN HYMN
music by
Felice de Giardini (1716-1796)

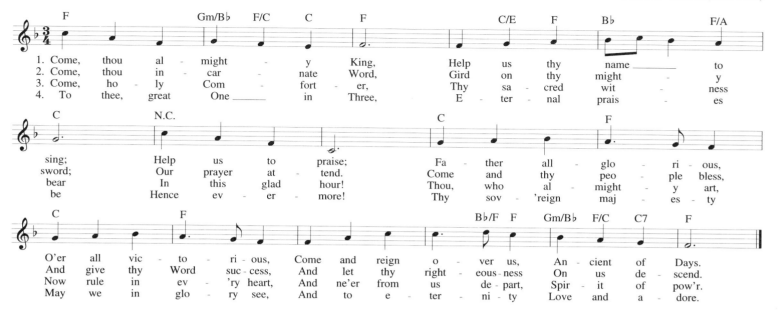

1. Come, thou al - might - y King, Help us thy name __ to sing; Help us to praise; Fa - ther all - glo - ri - ous, O'er all vic - to - ri - ous, Come and reign o - ver us, An - cient of Days.
2. Come, thou in - car - nate Word, Gird on thy might - y sword; Our prayer at - tend. Come and thy peo - ple bless, And give thy Word suc - cess, And let thy right - eous - ness On us de - scend.
3. Come, ho - ly Com - fort - er, Thy sa - cred wit - ness bear In this glad hour! Thou, who al - might - y art, Now rule in ev - 'ry heart, And ne'er from us de - part, Spir - it of pow'r.
4. To thee, great One __ in Three, E - ter - nal prais - es be Hence ev - er - more! Thy sov - 'reign maj - es - ty May we in glo - ry see, And to e - ter - ni - ty Love and a - dore.

COME, THOU LONG-EXPECTED JESUS

words by
Charles Wesley, 1744

HYFRYDOL
music by
Rowland Hugh Prichard, 1831

1. Come, Thou long - ex - pect - ed Je - sus, Born to set Thy peo - ple free; From our fears __ and sins re - lease __ us; Let us find our rest __ in Thee. Is - rael's strength __ and con - so - la - tion, Hope of ev - 'ry na - tion, Joy of ev - 'ry long - ing heart.
2. Born Thy peo - ple to de - liv - er, Born a child and yet __ a King, Born to reign __ in us for - ev - er, Now Thy gra - cious king - dom bring. By Thine own __ e - ter - nal Spir - it Rule in all __ our hearts __ a - lone; By __ Thine all - suf - fi - cient mer - it Raise us to __ Thy glo - rious throne.

COME, THOU LONG-EXPECTED JESUS

words by
Charles Wesley (1707-1788)

STUTTGART
music by
C.F. Witt (1660-1716)
from *Psalmodia Sacra*, Gotha, 1715

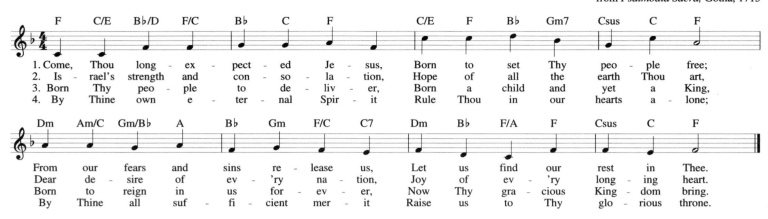

1. Come, Thou long - ex - pect - ed Je - sus, Born to set Thy peo - ple free;
2. Is - rael's strength and con - so - la - tion, Hope of all the earth Thou art,
3. Born Thy peo - ple to de - liv - er, Born a child and yet a King,
4. By Thine own e - ter - nal Spir - it Rule Thou in our hearts a - lone;

From our fears and sins re - lease us, Let us find our rest in Thee.
Dear de - sire of ev - 'ry na - tion, Joy of ev - 'ry long - ing heart.
Born to reign in us for - ev - er, Now Thy gra - cious King - dom bring.
By Thine all suf - fi - cient mer - it Raise us to Thy glo - rious throne.

COME TO CALVARY'S HOLY MOUNTAIN

words by
James Montgomery (1771-1854)

HOLY MOUNTAIN
music by
Ludwig M. Lindeman (1812-1887)

1. Come to Cal - v'ry's ho - ly moun - tain, sin - ners ru - ined by the fall;
2. Come in pov - er - ty and mean - ness, come de - filed, with - out, with - in;
3. Come in sor - row and con - tri - tion, wound - ed im - po - tent, and blind;
4. All who drink shall live for - ev - er- 'tis a soul - re - new - ing flood;

here a pure and heal - ing foun - tain flows to you, to me, to all,
from in - fec - tion and un - clean - ness, from the lep - ro - sy of sin,
here the guilt - y free re - mis - sion, here the trou - bled peace may find:
God is faith - ful, God will nev - er break his cov - e - nant of blood,

in a full, per - pet - ual tide, o - pened when our Sav - ior died.
wash your robes and make them white: you shall walk with God in light.
health this foun - tain will re - store; all who drink shall thirst no more.
signed when our Re - deem - er died, sealed when He was glo - ri - fied.

COME, WE THAT LOVE THE LORD

words by
Isaac Watts (1674-1748)

ST. THOMAS
music by
Aaron Williams (1731-1776)

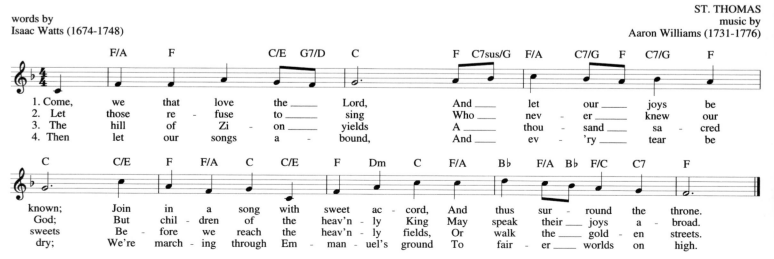

1. Come, we that love the Lord, And let our joys be
2. Let those re - fuse to sing Who nev - er knew our
3. The hill of Zi - on yields A thou - sand sa - cred
4. Then let our songs a - bound, And ev - 'ry tear be

known; Join in a song with sweet ac - cord, And thus sur - round the throne.
God; But chil - dren of the heav'n - ly King May speak their joys a - broad.
sweets Be - fore we reach the heav'n - ly fields, Or walk the gold - en streets.
dry; We're march - ing through Em - man - uel's ground To fair - er worlds on high.

COME, YE DISCONSOLATE

words by
Thomas Moore (v.1, 2)
and Thomas Hastings (v.3)

CONSOLATOR
music by
Samuel Webbe, (1740-1816)

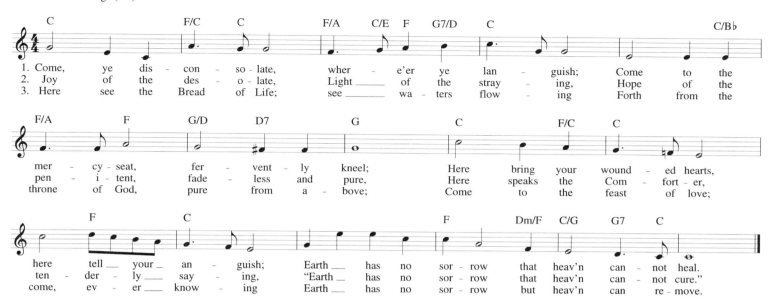

1. Come, ye dis - con - so - late, wher - e'er ye lan - guish; Come to the
2. Joy of the des - o - late, Light ___ of the stray - ing, Hope of the
3. Here see the Bread of Life; see ___ wa - ters flow - ing Forth from the

mer - cy - seat, fer - vent - ly kneel; Here bring your wound - ed hearts,
pen - i - tent, fade - less and pure, Here speaks the Com - fort - er,
throne of God, pure from a - bove; Come to the feast of love;

here tell ___ your ___ an - guish; Earth ___ has no sor - row that heav'n can - not heal.
ten - der - ly ___ say - ing, "Earth ___ has no sor - row that heav'n can - not cure."
come, ev - er ___ know - ing Earth ___ has no sor - row but heav'n can re - move.

COME, YE FAITHFUL, RAISE THE STRAIN

words by
John of Damascus (c. 675-c. 749)
tr. by John Mason Neale (1818-1866)

GAUDEAMUS PARITER
music by
Johann Horn (c. 1495-1547)

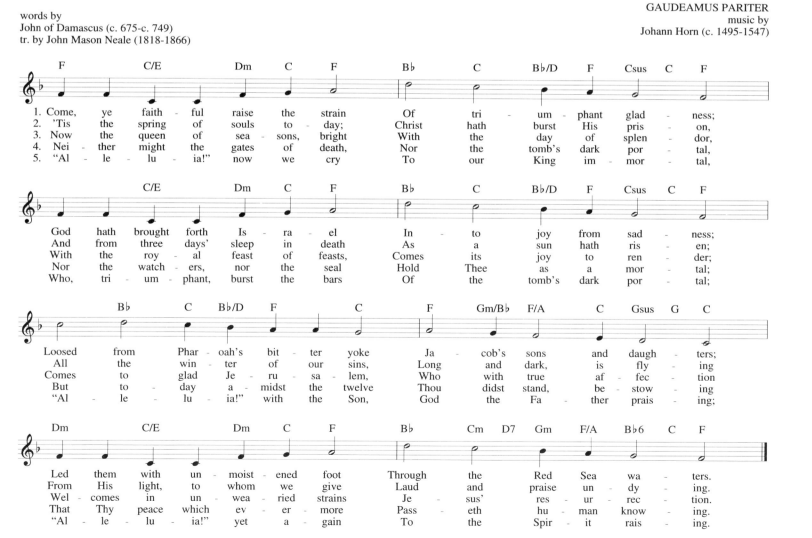

1. Come, ye faith - ful raise the strain Of tri - um - phant glad - ness;
2. 'Tis the spring of souls to - day; Christ hath burst His pris - on,
3. Now the queen of sea - sons, bright With the day of splen - dor,
4. Nei - ther might the gates of death, Nor the tomb's dark por - tal,
5. "Al - le - lu - ia!" now we cry To our King im - mor - tal,

God hath brought forth Is - ra - el In - to joy from sad - ness;
And from three days' sleep in death As a sun hath ris - en,
With the roy - al feast of feasts, Comes its joy to ren - der;
Nor the watch - ers, nor the seal Hold Thee as a mor - tal;
Who, tri - um - phant, burst the bars Of the tomb's dark por - tal;

Loosed from Phar - oah's bit - ter yoke Ja - cob's sons and daugh - ters;
All the win - ter of our sins, Long and dark, is fly - ing
Comes to glad Je - ru - sa - lem, Who with true af - fec - tion
But to - day a - midst the twelve Thou didst stand, be - stow - ing
"Al - le - lu - ia!" with the Son, God the Fa - ther prais - ing;

Led them with un - moist - ened foot Through the Red Sea wa - ters.
From His light, to whom we give Laud and praise un - dy - ing.
Wel - comes in un - wea - ried strains Je - sus' res - ur - rec - tion.
That Thy peace which ev - er - more Pass - eth hu - man know - ing.
"Al - le - lu - ia!" yet a - gain To the Spir - it rais - ing.

COME WITH US, O BLESSED JESUS

JESU, JOY OF MAN'S DESIRING
music by
Johann Schop (1600-1665)

words by
John H. Hopkins, Jr. (1820-1891)

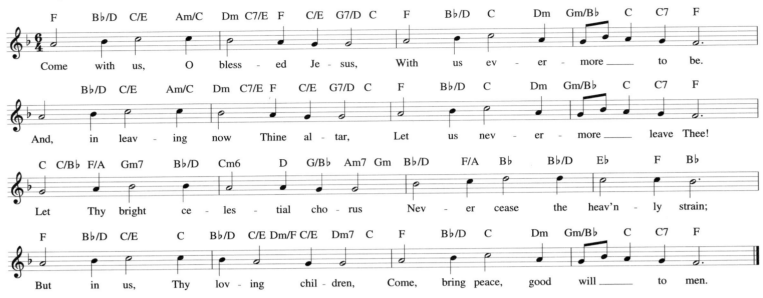

Come with us, O bless-ed Je-sus, With us ev-er-more ___ to be.

And, in leav-ing now Thine al-tar, Let us nev-er-more ___ leave Thee!

Let Thy bright ce-les-tial cho-rus Nev-er cease the heav'n-ly strain;

But in us, Thy lov-ing chil-dren, Come, bring peace, good will ___ to men.

COME, YE FAITHFUL, RAISE THE STRAIN

ST. KEVIN
music by
Arthur Seymour Sullivan (1842-1900)

words by
John of Damascus, 8th century
tr. by John Mason Neale (1818-1866)

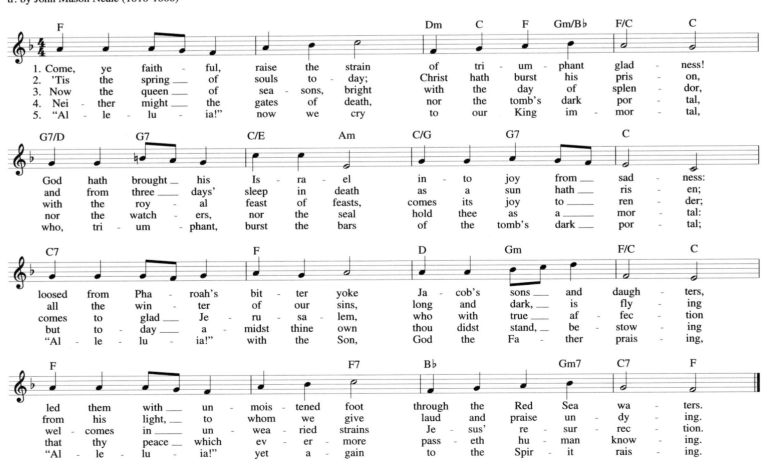

1. Come, ye faith-ful, raise the strain of tri-um-phant glad-ness!
2. 'Tis the spring of souls to day; Christ hath burst his pris-on,
3. Now the queen of sea-sons, bright with the day of splen-dor,
4. Nei-ther might the gates of death, nor the tomb's dark por-tal,
5. "Al-le-lu-ia!" now we cry to our King im-mor-tal,

God hath brought his Is-ra-el in-to joy from sad-ness:
and from three days' sleep in death as a sun hath ris-en;
with the roy-al feast of feasts, comes its joy to ren-der;
nor the watch-ers, nor the seal hold thee as a mor-tal;
who, tri-um-phant, burst the bars of the tomb's dark por-tal;

loosed from Pha-roah's bit-ter yoke Ja-cob's sons and daugh-ters,
all the win-ter of our sins, long and dark, is fly-ing
comes to glad Je-ru-sa-lem, who with true af-fec-tion
but to day a-midst thine own thou didst stand, be-stow-ing
"Al-le-lu-ia!" with the Son, God the Fa-ther prais-ing,

led them with un-mois-tened foot through the Red Sea wa-ters.
from his light, to whom we give laud and praise un-dy-ing.
wel-comes in un-wea-ried strains Je-sus' re-sur-rec-tion.
that thy peace which ev-er-more pass-eth hu-man know-ing.
"Al-le-lu-ia!" yet a-gain to the Spir-it rais-ing.

COME, YE SINNERS, POOR AND NEEDY

words by
Joseph Hart (1712-1768)

RESTORATION
music from
Walker's *Southern Harmony*, 1835

1. Come, ye sin - ners, ____ poor and need - y, Weak and wound - ed, ____ sick and sore;
2. Come, ye thirst - y, ____ come, and wel - come, God's free boun - ty ____ glo - ri - fy;
3. Come, ye wea - ry, ____ heav - y la - den, Lost and ru - ined ____ by the fall;
4. Let not con - science ____ make you lin - ger, Nor of fit - ness ____ fond - ly dream;

Je - sus read - y stands to save ____ you, Full of pit - y, ____ love, and pow'r.
True be - lief ____ and true re - pen - tance, Ev - 'ry grace ____ that ____ brings you nigh.
If you tar - ry till you're bet - ter, You will nev - er ____ come at all.
All the fit - ness He re - quir - eth Is to feel ____ your need of Him.

I will a - rise and ____ go to Je - sus, He will em - brace me ____ in His arms;

In the arms ____ of my dear Sav - ior, O there are ____ ten ____ thou - sand charms.

Copyright © 2000 by HAL LEONARD CORPORATION

COME, YE THANKFUL PEOPLE, COME

words by
Henry Alford (1810-1871)

ST. GEORGE'S WINDSOR
music by
George Job Elvey (1816-1893)

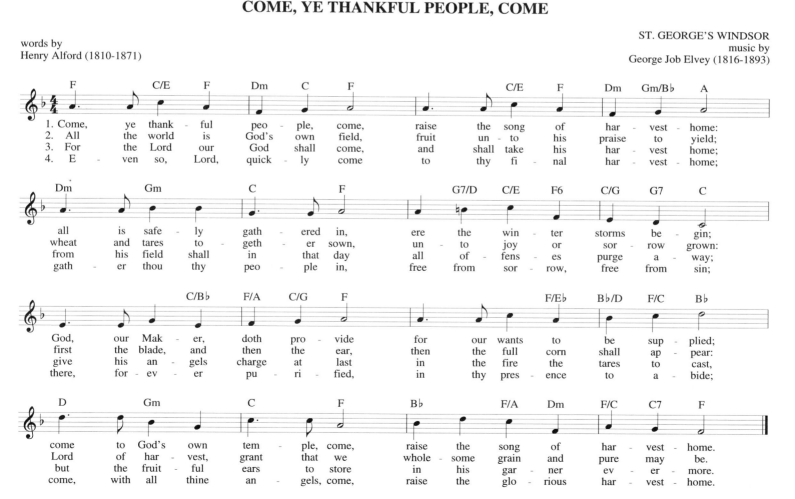

1. Come, ye thank - ful peo - ple, come, raise the song of har - vest - home:
2. All the world is God's own field, fruit un - to his praise to yield;
3. For the Lord our God shall come, and shall take his har - vest home;
4. E - ven so, Lord, quick - ly come to thy fi - nal har - vest - home;

all is safe - ly gath - ered in, ere the win - ter storms be - gin;
wheat and tares to - geth - er sown, un - to joy or sor - row grown:
from his field shall in that day all of - fens - es purge a - way;
gath - er thou thy peo - ple in, free from sor - row, free from sin;

God, our Mak - er, doth pro - vide for our wants to be sup - plied;
first the blade, and then the ear, then the full corn shall ap - pear:
give his an - gels charge at last in the fire the tares to cast,
there, for - ev - er pu - ri - fied, in thy pres - ence to a - bide;

come to God's own tem - ple, come, raise the song of har - vest - home.
Lord of har - vest, grant that we whole - some grain and pure may be.
but the fruit - ful ears to store in his gar - ner ev - er - more.
come, with all thine an - gels, come, raise the glo - rious har - vest - home.

Copyright © 2000 by HAL LEONARD CORPORATION

COME, YE THAT KNOW AND FEAR THE LORD

WARWICK
music by
Samuel Stanley (1767-1822)

words by
George Burder (1752-1832)

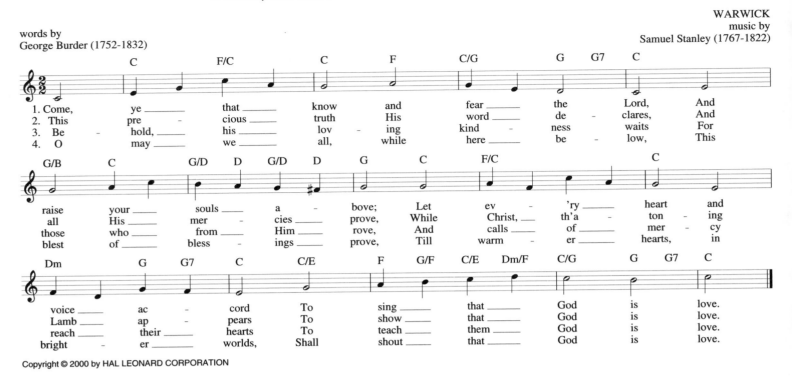

1. Come, ye that know and fear the Lord, And raise your souls a - bove; Let ev - 'ry heart and voice ac - cord, To sing that God is love.
2. This pre - cious truth His word de - clares, And all His mer - cies prove, While Christ, th'a - ton - ing Lamb ap - pears, To show that God is love.
3. Be - hold, his lov - ing kind - ness waits For those who from Him rove, And calls of ten - der mer - cy reach their hearts, To teach them that God is love.
4. O may we all, while here be - low, This blest of bless - ings prove, Till warm - er hearts, in bright - er worlds, Shall shout that God is love.

THE COMFORTER HAS COME

COMFORTER
music by
William J. Kirkpatrick, 1890

words by
Frank Bottome, 1890

1. O spread the ti - dings 'round, wher - ev - er man is found, Wher - ev - er hu - man hearts and hu - man woes a - bound. Let ev - 'ry Chris - tian tongue pro - claim the joy - ful sound: The Com - fort - er has
2. The long, long night is past; the morn - ing breaks at last; And hushed the dread - ed wail and fu - ry of the blast, As o'er the gold - en hills the day ad - vanc - es fast! The Com - fort - er has
3. Lo, the great King of kings, with heal - ing in His wings, To ev - 'ry cap - tive soul a full de - liv - 'rance brings; And thro' the va - cant cells the song of tri - umph rings: The Com - fort - er has
4. O bound - less love di - vine! How shall this tongue of mine To won - d'ring mor - tals tell the match - less grace di - vine— That I, a child of hell, should in His im - age shine? The Com - fort - er has

Refrain

come! come! come! come! The Com - fort - er has come! The Com - fort - er has come! The Ho - ly Ghost from heav'n, the Fa - ther's prom - ise giv'n, O spread the ti - dings 'round, wher - ev - er man is found: The Com - fort - er has come!

CONSTANTLY ABIDING

words by
Anne S. Murphy, 1908

music by
Anne S. Murphy, 1908

1. There's a peace in my heart that the world nev-er gave, A peace it can-
2. All the world seemed to sing of a Sav-ior and King, When peace sweet-ly
3. This treas-ure I have in a tem-ple of clay, While here on His

not take a-way; Though the tri-als of life may sur-round like a
came to my heart; Trou-bles all fled a-way and my night turned to
foot-stool I roam: But He's com-ing to take me some glo-ri-ous

cloud, I've a peace that has come there to stay! Con-stant-ly a-
day, Bless-ed Je-sus, how glo-rious Thou art!
day, O-ver there to my heav-en-ly home!

bid-ing, Je-sus is mine; Con-stant-ly a-

bid-ing, Rap-ture di-vine! He nev-er leaves me lone-ly,

Whis-pers, O so kind: "I will nev-er leave thee," Je-sus is mine.

COUNT YOUR BLESSINGS

words by
Johnson Oatman, Jr. (1856-1922)

BLESSINGS
music by
Edwin O. Excell (1851-1921)

1. When up-on life's bil-lows you are tem-pest tossed, When you are dis-cour-aged, think-ing all is lost,
2. Are you ev-er bur-dened with a load of care? Does the cross seem heav-y you are called to bear?
3. When you look at oth-ers with their lands and gold, Think that Christ has prom-ised you His wealth un-told.
4. So a-mid the con-flict, wheth-er great or small, Do not be dis-cour-aged; God is o-ver all.

Count your man-y bless-ings; name them one by one, And it will sur-prise you what the Lord hath done.
Count your man-y bless-ings; ev-'ry doubt will fly, And you will be sing-ing as the days go by.
Count your man-y bless-ings; mon-ey can-not buy Your re-ward in heav-en nor your home on high.
Count your man-y bless-ings; an-gels will at-tend, Help and com-fort give you to your jour-ney's end.

Count your bless-ings, name them one by one; Count your bless-ings, see what God hath done.

Count your bless-ings, name them one by one; Count your man-y bless-ings, see what God hath done.

COMMIT WHATEVER GRIEVES THEE

HERZLICH TUT MICH VERLANGEN
music by
Hans Leo Hassler (1564-1612)

words by
Paul Gerhardt (1607-1676)
translators unknown

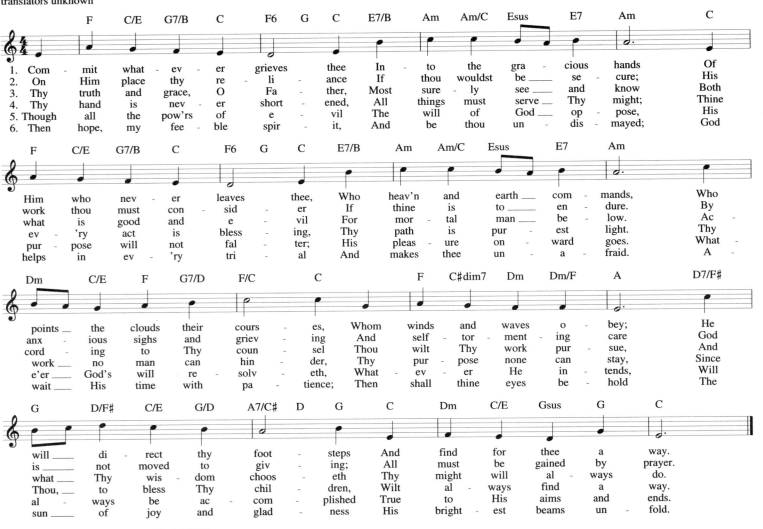

1. Com - mit what - ev - er grieves thee In - to the gra - cious hands Of
2. On Him place thy re - li - ance If thou wouldst be __ se - cure; His
3. Thy truth and grace, O Fa - ther, Most sure - ly see __ and know Both
4. Thy hand is nev - er short - ened, All things must serve __ Thy might; Thine
5. Though all the pow'rs of e - vil The will of God __ op - pose, His
6. Then hope, my fee - ble spir - it, And be thou un - dis - mayed; God

Him who nev - er leaves thee, Who heav'n and earth __ com - mands, Who
work thou must con - sid - er If thine is to __ en - dure. By
what is good and e - vil For mor - tal man __ be - low. Ac
ev - 'ry act is bless - ing, Thy path is pur - est light. Thy
pur - pose will not fal - ter; His pleas - ure on - ward goes. What -
helps in ev - 'ry tri - al And makes thee un - a - fraid. A

points __ the clouds their cours - es, Whom winds and waves o - bey; He
anx - ious sighs and griev - ing And self - tor - ment - ing care God
cord - ing to Thy coun - sel, Thou wilt Thy work pur - sue, And
work __ no man can hin - der, Thy pur - pose none can stay, Since
e'er __ God's will re - solv - eth, What - ev - er He in - tends, Will
wait __ His time with pa - tience; Then shall thine eyes be - hold The

will __ di - rect thy foot - steps And find for thee a way.
is __ not moved to giv - ing; All must be gained by prayer.
what __ Thy wis - dom choos - eth, Thy might will al - ways do.
Thou, __ to bless Thy chil - dren, Wilt al - ways find a way.
al - ways be ac - com - plished; True to His aims and ends.
sun __ of joy and glad - ness His bright - est beams un - fold.

COVERED BY THE BLOOD

words by
Nellie Edwards, 20th century

music by
Ran C. Story, 20th century

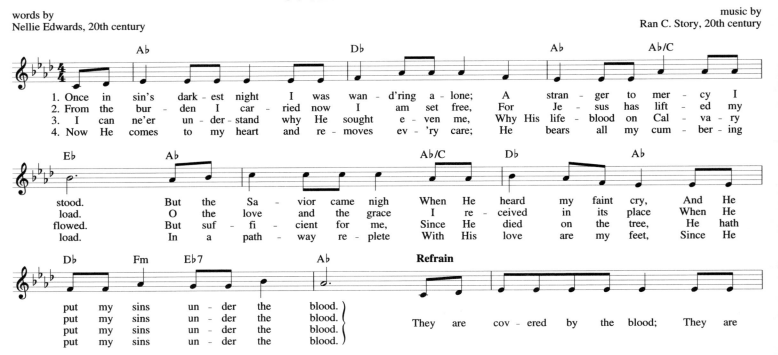

1. Once in sin's dark - est night I was wan - d'ring a - lone; A stran - ger to mer - cy I
2. From the bur - den I car - ried now I am set free, For Je - sus has lift - ed my
3. I can ne'er un - der - stand why He sought e - ven me, Why His life - blood on Cal - va - ry
4. Now He comes to my heart and re - moves ev - 'ry care; He bears all my cum - ber - ing

stood. But the Sa - vior came nigh When He heard my faint cry, And He
load. O the love and the grace I re - ceived in its place When He
flowed. But suf - fi - cient for me, Since He died on the tree, He hath
load. In a path - way re - plete With His love are my feet, Since He

put my sins un - der the blood.)
put my sins un - der the blood.)
put my sins un - der the blood.)
put my sins un - der the blood.)

Refrain

They are cov - ered by the blood; They are

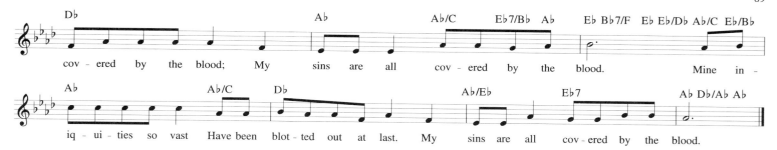

CREATOR SPIRIT, BY WHOSE AID

words attr. to
Rhabanus Maurus (778-856)
tr. by John Dryden (1631-1700)

SURREY
music by
Henry Carey (c. 1690-1743)

CROSS OF JESUS, CROSS OF SORROW

words by
William J.S. Simpson (1860-1952)

CROSS OF JESUS
music by
John Stainer (1840-1901)

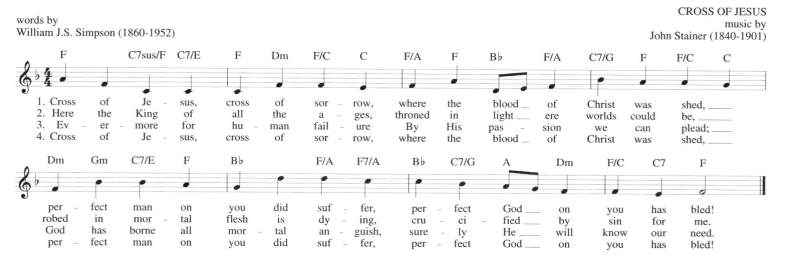

CREATOR SPIRIT, BY WHOSE AID

words attr. to
Rhabanus Maurus (778-856)
tr. by John Dryden (1631-1700)

ALL EHR UND LOB
music from
Kirchengesangbuch, Strassburg, 1541

1. Cre - a - tor Spir - it, by whose aid The world's foun - da - tions first were laid.
2. O Source of un - cre - a - ted light, The Fa - ther's prom - ised Par - a - clete,
3. Plen - teous of grace, de - scend from high, Rich in the sev'n - fold en - er - gy;
4. Im - mor - tal hon - or, end - less fame, At - tend the al - might - y Fa - ther's name;

Come, vis - it ev - 'ry hum - ble mind; Come, pour Thy joys on hu - man - kind;
Thrice ho - ly fount, thrice ho - ly fire, Our hearts with heav'n - ly love in - spire;
Make us e - ter - nal truths re - ceive And prac - tice all that we be - lieve;
The Sav - ior Son be glo - ri - fied, Who for lost man's re - demp - tion died;

From sin and sor - row set us free, And make Thy tem - ples fit ___ for Thee.
Come, and Thy sa - cred unc - tion bring To sanc - ti - fy us while ___ we sing.
Give us Thy - self, that we may see The Fa - ther and the Son ___ by Thee.
And e - qual ad - o - ra - tion be, E - ter - nal Par - a - clete, ___ to Thee.

CROWN HIM WITH MANY CROWNS

words by Matthew Bridges (1800-1894), v. 1,2,4,5
and Godfrey Thring (1823-1903), v. 3

DIADEMATA
music by
George Job Elvey (1816-1893)

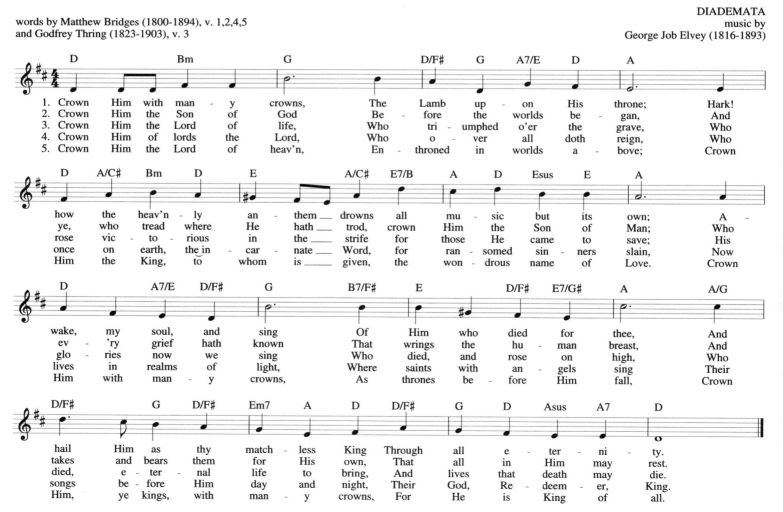

1. Crown Him with man - y crowns, The Lamb up - on His throne; Hark!
2. Crown Him the Son of God Be - fore the worlds be - gan, And
3. Crown Him the Lord of life, Who tri - umphed o'er the grave, Who
4. Crown Him of lords the Lord, Who o - ver all doth reign, Who
5. Crown Him the Lord of heav'n, En - throned in worlds a - bove; Crown

how the heav'n - ly an - them ___ drowns all mu - sic but its own; A
ye, who tread where He hath ___ trod, crown Him the Son of Man; Who
rose vic - to - rious in the ___ strife for those He came to save; His
once on earth, the in - car - nate ___ Word, for ran - somed sin - ners slain, Now
Him the King, to whom is ___ given, the won - drous name of Love. Crown

wake, my soul, and sing Of Him who died for thee, And
ev - 'ry grief hath known That wrings the hu - man breast, And
glo - ries now we sing Who died, and rose on high, Who
lives in realms of light, Where saints with an - gels sing Their
Him with man - y crowns, As saints thrones be - fore Him fall, Their

hail Him as thy match - less King Through all e - ter - ni - ty.
takes and bears them for His own, That all in Him may rest.
died, e - ter - nal life to bring, And lives that death may die.
songs be - fore Him day and night, Their God, Re - deem - er, King.
Him, ye kings, with man - y crowns, For He is King of all.

DAY BY DAY

words by
Carolina Sandell Bergh (1832-1903)
tr. by Andrew L. Skoog

BLOTT EN DAG
music by
Oscar Ahnfelt (1813-1882)

THE DAY IS PAST AND OVER

Greek text, c. 6th century
tr. by John Mason Neale, 1853

DU FRIEDENSFÜRST, HERR JESU CHRIST
music by
Bartholomaus Gesius, 1601

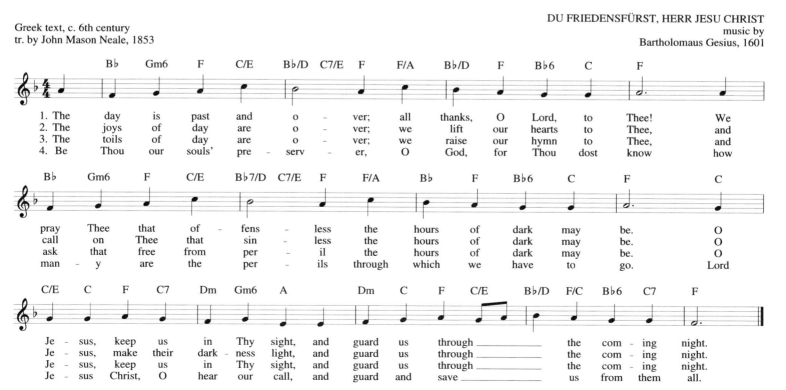

THE DAY IS SURELY DRAWING NEAR

ES IST GEWISSLICH
music by
J. Klug, *Geistliche Lieder*, Wittenberg, 1535

words by
Bartholomäus Ringwaldt (1532-1599)
tr. by Philip A. Peter (1832-1919)

1. The day is sure - ly draw - ing near When God's Son, the A - noint - ed,
2. A trum - pet loud shall then re - sound And all the earth be shak - en.
3. A book is o - pened then to all, A rec - ord tru - ly tell - ing
4. Then woe to those who scorned the Lord And sought but car - nal pleas - ures,
5. O Je - sus, who my debt didst pay And for my sin wast smit - ten,
6. O Je - sus Christ, do not de - lay, But has - ten our sal - va - tion;

Shall with great maj - es - ty ap - pear As Judge of all ap - point - ed.
Then all who in their graves are found Shall from their sleep a - wak - en;
What each hath done, both great and small, When he on earth was dwell - ing;
Who here de - spised His pre - cious Word And loved their earth - ly treas - ures!
With in the Book of Life, O may My name be al - so writ - ten!
We of - ten trem - ble on our way In fear and trib - u - la - tion.

All mirth and laugh - ter then shall cease When flames on flames will still in - crease,
But all that live shall in that hour By the Al - might - y's bound - less pow'r
And ev - 'ry heart be clear - ly seen, And all be known as they have been
With shame and trem - bling they will stand And at the Judg - e's stern com - mand
I will not doubt; I trust in Thee, From Sa - tan Thou hast made me free
Then hear us when we cry to Thee; Come, might - y Judge, and make us free

As Scrip - ture tru - ly teach - eth.
Be changed at His com - mand - ing.
In thoughts and words and ac - tions.
To Sa - tan be de - liv - ered.
And from all con - dem - na - tion.
From ev - 'ry e - vil! A - men.

DAY IS DYING IN THE WEST

CHAUTAUQUA
music by
William F. Sherwin (1826-1888)

words by
Mary A. Lathbury (1841-1913)

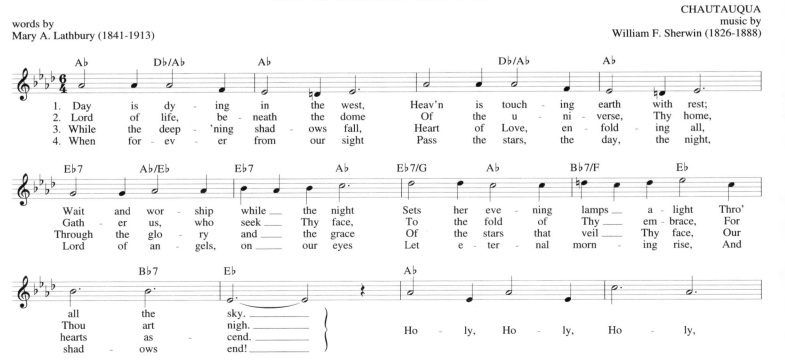

1. Day is dy - ing in the west, Heav'n is touch - ing earth with rest;
2. Lord of life, be - neath the dome Of the u - ni - verse, Thy home,
3. While the deep 'ning shad - ows fall, Heart of Love, en - fold - ing all,
4. When for - ev - er from our sight Pass the stars, the day, the night,

Wait and wor - ship while the night Sets her eve - ning lamps a - light Thro'
Gath - er us, who seek Thy face, To the fold of Thy em - brace, For
Through the glo - ry and the grace Of the stars that veil Thy face, Our
Lord of an - gels, on our eyes Let e - ter - nal morn - ing rise, And

all the sky. Ho - ly, Ho - ly, Ho - ly,
Thou art nigh.
hearts as - cend.
shad - ows end!

THE DAY OF RESURRECTION

words by
John of Damascus (c. 675-749)
tr. by John Mason Neale, 1862

LANCASHIRE
music by
Henry Thomas Smart, c. 1835

1. The day of res - ur - rec - tion! Earth, tell it out a - broad; The Pass - o - ver of
2. Our hearts be pure from e - vil, That we may see a - right The Lord in rays e -
3. Now let the heavens be joy - ful, Let earth the song be - gin, Let the round world keep

glad - ness, The Pass - o - ver of God. From death to life e - ter - nal, From
ter - nal Of res - ur - rec - tion light; And, lis - tening to His ac - cents, May
tri - umph, And all that is there - in; Let all things seen and un - seen Their

this world to the sky, _____ Our Christ hath brought us o - ver With hymns of vic - to - ry.
hear, so calm and plain, _____ His own "All hail!" and, hear - ing, May raise the vic - tor strain.
notes of glad - ness blend, _____ For Christ the Lord is ris - en, Our joy that hath no end.

THE DAY OF RESURRECTION

words by
John of Damascus (c. 675-749)
tr. by John Mason Neale, 1862

ROTTERDAM
music by
Berthold Tours (1838-1897)

1. The day of res - ur - rec - tion! Earth, tell it out a - broad; The
2. Our hearts be pure from e - vil, That we may see a - right The
3. Now let the heav'ns be joy - ful! Let earth her song be - gin! Let

pass - o - ver of glad - ness, The pass - o - ver of God, From
Lord in rays e - ter - nal Of res - ur - rec - tion light; And
the round world keep tri - umph, And all that is there - in! Let

death to life e - ter - nal, From earth un - to the sky, Our
lis - t'ning to His ac - cents, May hear, so calm and plain, His
all things seen and un - seen Their notes in glad - ness blend, For

Christ hath brought us o - ver With hymns of _____ vic - to - ry.
own "All hail!" and hear - ing, May raise the _____ vic - tor strain.
Christ the Lord hath ris - en, Our joy that _____ hath no end.

THE DAY THOU GAVEST, LORD, IS ENDED

words by
John Ellerton, 1870

ST. CLEMENT
music by
Clement Cotterill Scholefield, 1874

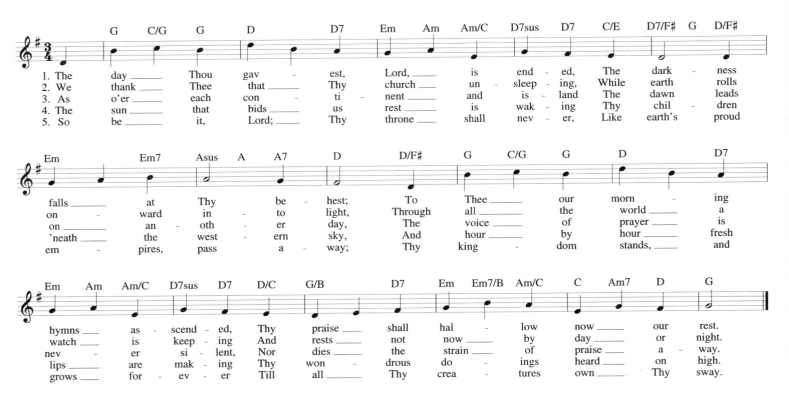

DEAR LORD AND FATHER OF MANKIND

words by
John Greenleaf Whittier, 1872

REST
music by
Frederick Charles Maker, 1887

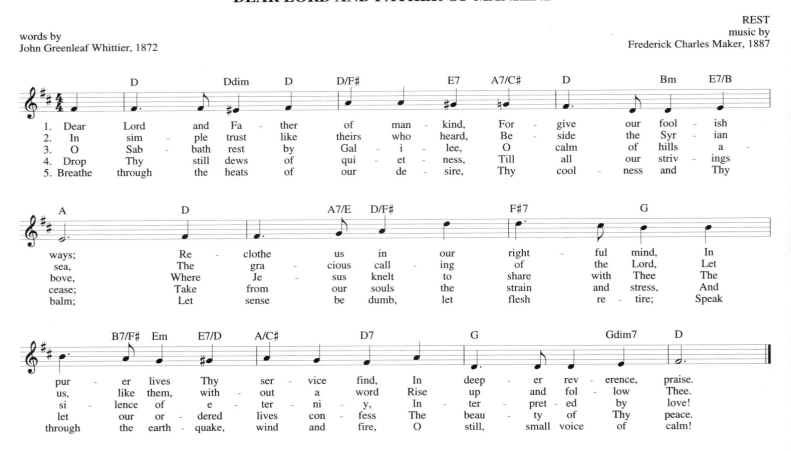

DEAREST JESUS, WE ARE HERE

LIEBSTER JESU, WIR SIND HIER

words by
B. Schmolck (1672-1737)
tr. by C. Winkworth (1827-1878)

music by
J.R. Ahle (1625-1673)

1. Dear - est Je - sus, we are here, Glad - ly Thy com - mand o - bey - ing;
2. Yea, Thy Word is clear and plain, And we would o - bey it du - ly:
3. There - fore hast - en we to Thee, In our arms this in - fant bear - ing;
4. Wash it, Je - sus, in Thy blood, From the sin - stain of its na - ture;
5. Gra - cious Head, Thy mem - ber own; Shep - herd, take Thy lamb and feed it.
6. Now in - to Thy heart we pour Prayers that from our hearts pro - ceed - ed.

With this child we now draw near In ac - cord with Thine own say - ing
"He who is not born a - gain, Heart and life re - new - ing tru - ly,
Let us here Thy glo - ry see, Let this child, Thy mer - cy shar - ing,
Let it rise from out this flood Clothed in Thee, a new - born crea - ture;
Prince of Peace, make here Thy throne; Way of Life, to heav - en lead it.
Our pe - ti - tion heav'n - ward soar; May our warm de - sires be heed - ed!

That to Thee it shall be giv - en As a child and heir of heav - en.
Born of wa - ter and the Spir - it, Can My king - dom not in - her - it."
In Thine arms be shield - ed ev - er, Thine on earth and Thine for - ev - er.
May it, washed as Thou hast bid - den, In Thine in - no - cence be hid - den.
Pre - cious Vine, let noth - ing sev - er From Thy side this branch for - ev - er.
Write the name we now have giv - en, Write it in the book of heav - en.

DECK THYSELF, MY SOUL, WITH GLADNESS

SCHMÜCKE DICH

words by
Johann Franck, 1649
tr. by Catherine Winkworth, 1863

music by
Johann Crüger, 1653

1. Deck thy - self, my soul, with glad - ness, leave the gloom - y haunts of sad - ness.
2. Sun, who all my life dost bright - en; Light, who dost my soul en - light - en;
3. Je - sus, bread of life, I pray Thee, let me glad - ly here o - bey Thee;

Come in - to the day - light's splen - dor; there with joy thy prais - es ren - der
Joy, the best that an - y know - eth, Fount, whence all my be - ing flow - eth;
nev - er to my hurt in - vit - ed, be Thy love with love re - quit - ed.

un - to Christ, whose grace un - bound - ed hath this won - drous ban - quet found - ed.
at Thy feet I cry, my Mak - er, let me be a fit par - ta - ker
From this ban - quet let me meas - ure, Lord, how vast and deep its treas - ure;

High o'er all the heavens He reign - eth, yet to dwell with Thee he deign - eth.
of this bless - ed food from heav - en, for our good, Thy glo - ry giv - en.
through the gifts Thou here dost give me, as Thy guest in Heaven re - ceive me.

DEAR JESUS, IN WHOSE LIFE I SEE

words by
John Hunter, 1889

HURSLEY
music from
Katholisches Gesangbuch, 1774
adapt. from *Metrical Psalter, 1855*

1. Dear Je - sus, in _____ whose life _____ I see all that I
would, _____ but fail _____ to be, let Thy clear light for -
ev - er shine, to shame and guide this life _____ of mine.

2. Though what I dream _____ and what _____ I do in my weak
days _____ are al - ways two, help me, op - pressed by
things un - done, O Thou whose deeds and dreams _____ were one!

DEEPER AND DEEPER

words by
Oswald J. Smith, 1914

music by
Oswald J. Smith, 1914

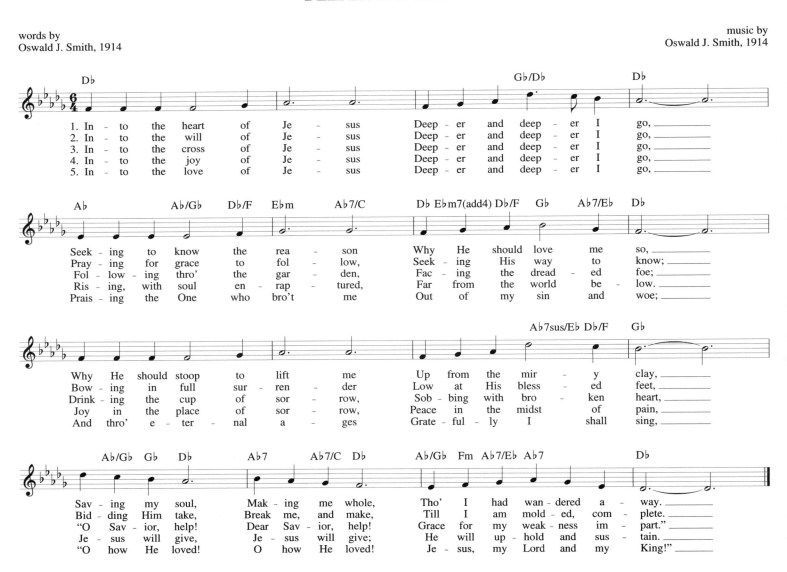

1. In - to the heart of Je - sus Deep - er and deep - er I go, _____
2. In - to the will of Je - sus Deep - er and deep - er I go, _____
3. In - to the cross of Je - sus Deep - er and deep - er I go, _____
4. In - to the joy of Je - sus Deep - er and deep - er I go, _____
5. In - to the love of Je - sus Deep - er and deep - er I go, _____

Seek - ing to know the rea - son Why He should love me so, _____
Pray - ing for grace to fol - low, Seek - ing His way to know; _____
Fol - low - ing thro' the gar - den, Fac - ing the dread - ed foe; _____
Ris - ing, with soul en - rap - tured, Far from the world be - low. _____
Prais - ing the One who bro't me Out of my sin and woe; _____

Why He should stoop to lift me Up from the mir - y clay, _____
Bow - ing in full sur - ren - der Low at His bless - ed feet, _____
Drink - ing the cup of sor - row, Sob - bing with bro - ken heart, _____
Joy in the place of sor - row, Peace in the midst of pain, _____
And thro' e - ter - nal a - ges Grate - ful - ly I shall sing, _____

Sav - ing my soul, Mak - ing me whole, Tho' I had wan - dered a - way. _____
Bid - ding Him take, Break me, and make, Till I am mold - ed, com - plete. _____
"O Sav - ior, help! Dear Sav - ior, help! Grace for my weak - ness im - part." _____
Je - sus will give, Je - sus will give; He will up - hold and sus - tain. _____
"O how He loved! O how He loved! Je - sus, my Lord and my King!" _____

DEEPER, DEEPER

words by
Charles P. Jones, 1900

music by
Charles P. Jones, 1900

DOES JESUS CARE?

words by
Frank E. Graeff, 1901

MY SAVIOR CARES
music by
J. Lincoln Hall, 1901

DEPTH OF MERCY

CANTERBURY
music adapt. from
Orlando Gibbons, 1623

words by
Charles Wesley, 1740

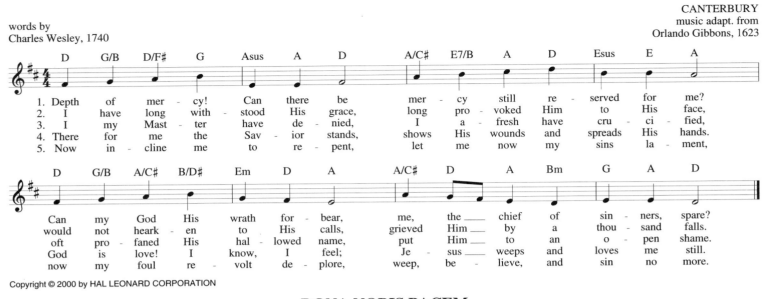

1. Depth of mer - cy! Can there be mer - cy still re - served for me?
2. I have long with - stood His grace, long pro - voked Him to His face,
3. I my Mast - er have de - nied, I a - fresh have cru - ci - fied,
4. There for me the Sav - ior stands, shows His wounds and spreads His hands.
5. Now in - cline me to re - pent, let me now my sins la - ment,

Can my God His wrath for - bear, me, the ___ chief of sin - ners, spare?
would not heark - en to His calls, grieved Him ___ by a thou - sand falls.
oft pro - faned His hal - lowed name, put Him ___ to an o - pen shame.
God is love! I know, I feel! Je - sus ___ weeps and loves me still.
now my foul re - volt de - plore, weep, be - lieve, and sin no more.

DONA NOBIS PACEM

Traditional Latin text

Traditional music

* ① Do - na no - bis pa - cem, pa - cem. Do - na ___ no - bis pa - cem.

② Do - na no - bis pa - cem. Do - na no - bis pa - cem.

③ Do - na no - bis ___ pa - cem. Do - na no - bis pa - cem.

*May be sung as a round.

DOWN AT THE CROSS
(Glory to His Name)

GLORY TO HIS NAME
music by
John H. Stockton, 1878

words by
Elisha A. Hoffman, 1878

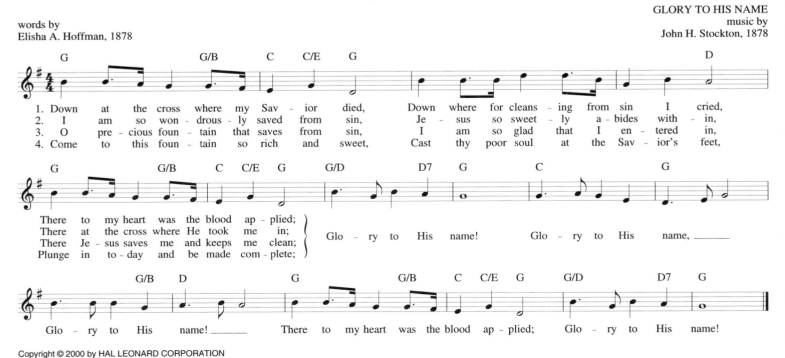

1. Down at the cross where my Sav - ior died, Down where for cleans - ing from sin I cried,
2. I am so won - drous - ly saved from sin, Je - sus so sweet - ly a - bides with - in,
3. O pre - cious foun - tain that saves from sin, I am so glad that I en - tered in,
4. Come to this foun - tain so rich and sweet, Cast thy poor soul at the Sav - ior's feet,

There to my heart was the blood ap - plied;)
There at the cross where He took me in;)
There Je - sus saves me and keeps me clean;) Glo - ry to His name! Glo - ry to His name, ___
Plunge in to - day and be made com - plete;)

Glo - ry to His name! ___ There to my heart was the blood ap - plied; Glo - ry to His name!

DOWN BY THE RIVERSIDE

Traditional Spiritual

WAR NO MORE
Traditional Spiritual

1. Gon - na lay down my bur - den __
2. Gon - na lay down my sword and shield
3. Gon - na try on my long white robe

Down by the riv - er - side, __

Down by the riv - er - side, __ Down by the riv - er - side. __

Gon - na
Gon - na
Gon - na

lay down my bur - den __
lay down my sword and shield
try on my long white robe

Down by the riv - er - side __ And stud - y __

war no more. I ain't gon - na stud - y war __ no more, Ain't gon - na

stud - y war __ no more, Ain't gon - na stud - y war no more.

I ain't gon - na stud - y war __ no more, Ain't gon - na stud - y war __ no

more, Ain't gon - na stud - y __ war no more. __

DRAW NIGH AND TAKE THE BODY OF THE LORD

Latin text, 7th century
tr. by John M. Neale (1818-1866)

COENA DOMINI
music by
Arthur S. Sullivan (1842-1900)

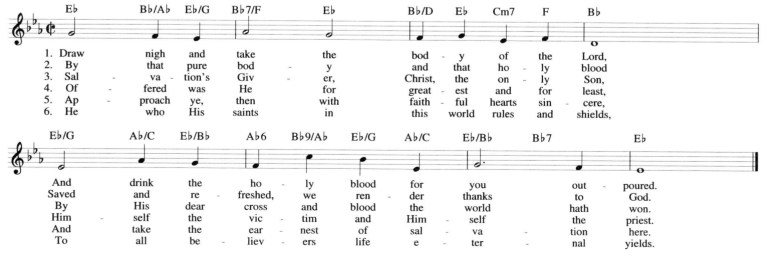

1. Draw nigh and take the bod - y of the Lord,
2. By that pure bod - y and that ho - ly blood
3. Sal - va - tion's Giv - er, Christ, the on - ly Son,
4. Of - fered was He for great - est and for least,
5. Ap - proach ye, then with faith - ful hearts sin - cere,
6. He who His saints in this world rules and shields,

And drink the ho - ly blood for you out - poured.
Saved and re - freshed, we ren - der thanks to God.
By His dear cross and blood the world hath won.
Him - self the vic - tim and Him - self the priest.
And take the ear - nest of sal - va - tion here.
To all be - liev - ers life e - ter - nal yields.

DOWN IN THE VALLEY

LEND A HAND
music by
Leonard Daugherty, 1922

words by
Mary Barrett, 1922

1. Are you dwell - ing in the sun - light? Is your path with ros - es strewn? Do you
2. Is your day one round of pleas - ure, From the morn till set of sun? Know you
3. Sweet it is to dwell in sun - light, Where the shad - ows nev - er rise, Where the

walk with buoy - ant glad - ness In the steps that you have hewn? Have you
not of pain or sor - row? Are your vic - to - ries all won? Lend a
balm - y, waft - ing breez - es Kiss the blue, o'er - hang - ing skies; But there's

reached the top of * Pis - gah, Climb - ing al - ways firm and true? } Don't for -
hand to help your broth - er, Who is strug - gling hard and true, }
al - ways in the shad - ow Some poor mor - tal, brave and true, }

get that in the val - ley There is some - one need - ing you. Lend a

hand _____ to help a broth - er Who is striv - ing hard and true, Don't for -

get _____ that in the val - ley There is some - one need - ing you.

* Pisgah: mountain from which Moses viewed the Promised Land

THE DUTEOUS DAY NOW CLOSETH

O WELT, ICH MUSS DICH LASSEN
music attr. to
Heinrich Isaac (c.1450-1517)

words by
Paul Gerhardt (1607-1676)
tr. by Robert Seymour Bridges (1844-1930), et al.

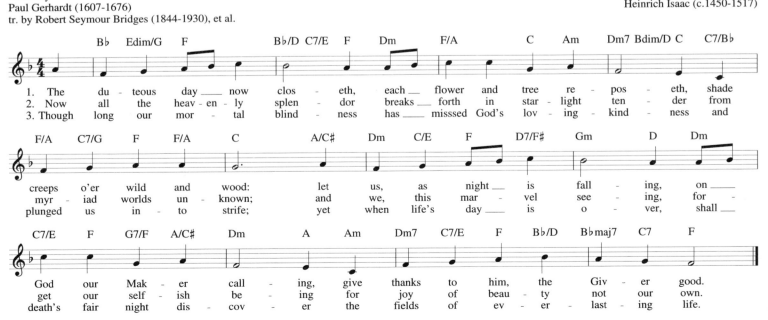

1. The du - teous day _____ now clos - eth, each _____ flower and tree re - pos - eth, shade
2. Now all the heav - en - ly splen - dor breaks _____ forth in star - light ten - der from
3. Though long our mor - tal blind - ness has _____ misssed God's lov - ing - kind - ness and

creeps o'er wild and wood: let us, as night _____ is fall - ing, on _____
myr - iad worlds un - known; and we, this mar - vel see - ing, for -
plunged us in - to strife; yet when life's day _____ is o - ver, shall _____

God our Mak - er call - ing, give thanks to him, the Giv - er good.
get our self - ish be - ing, for joy of beau - ty not our own.
death's fair night dis - cov - er the joy of ev - er - last - ing life.

DWELLING IN BEULAH LAND

words by
C. Austin Miles, 1911

BEULAH LAND
music by
C. Austin Miles, 1911

THE EARTH, WITH ALL THAT DWELL THEREIN

words from
The Psalter, 1912
based on Psalm 24

CAITHNESS
music from
Scottish Psalter, 1635

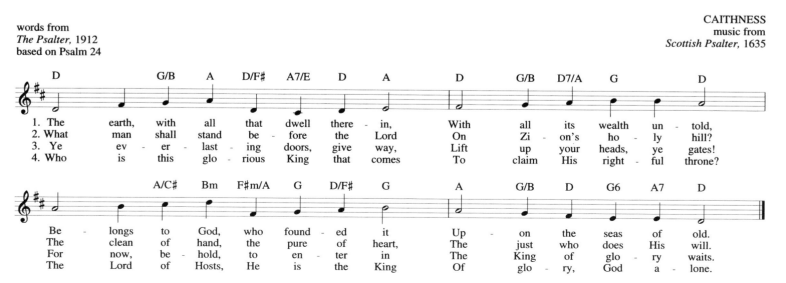

THE EASTERN GATE

EASTERN GATE
music by
Isaiah G. Martin, 1905

words by
Isaiah G. Martin, 1905

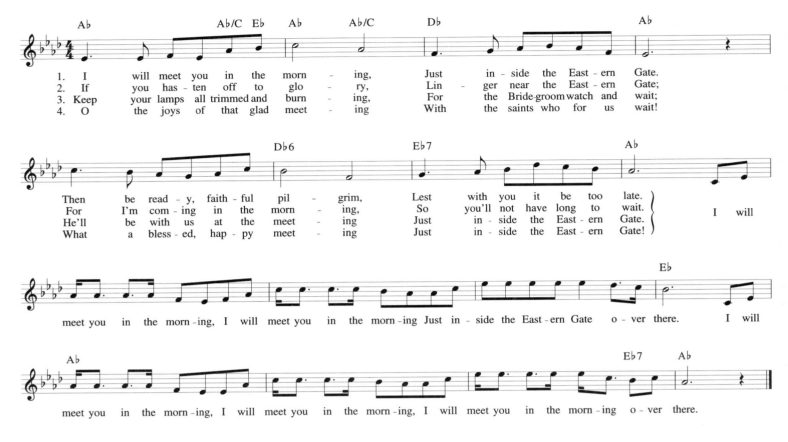

1. I will meet you in the morn - ing, Just in - side the East - ern Gate.
2. If you has - ten off to glo - ry, Lin - ger near the East - ern Gate;
3. Keep your lamps all trimmed and burn - ing, For the Bride-groom watch and wait;
4. O the joys of that glad meet - ing With the saints who for us wait!

Then be read - y, faith - ful pil - grim, Lest with you it be too late.
For I'm com - ing in the morn - ing, So you'll not have long to wait.
He'll be with us at the meet - ing Just in - side the East - ern Gate.
What a bless - ed, hap - py meet - ing Just in - side the East - ern Gate!

I will meet you in the morn - ing, I will meet you in the morn - ing Just in - side the East - ern Gate o - ver there. I will

meet you in the morn - ing, I will meet you in the morn - ing, I will meet you in the morn - ing o - ver there.

ETERNAL FATHER, STRONG TO SAVE

MELITA
music by
John Bacchus Dykes (1823-1876)

words by
William Whiting (1825-1878)

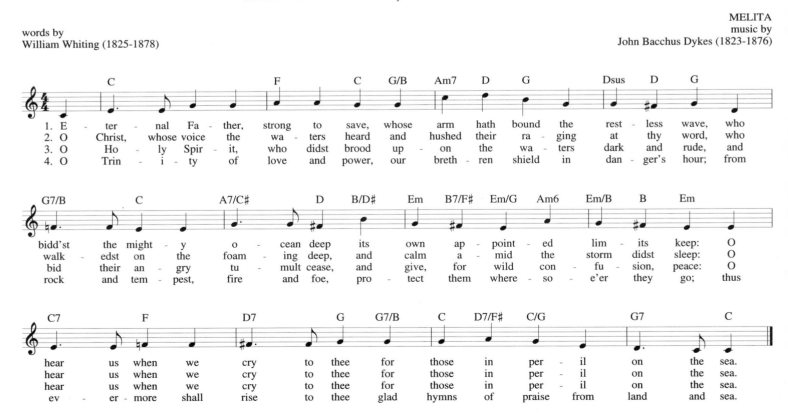

1. E - ter - nal Fa - ther, strong to save, whose arm hath bound the rest - less wave, who
2. O Christ, whose voice the wa - ters heard and hushed their ra - ging at thy word, who
3. O Ho - ly Spir - it, who didst brood up - on the wa - ters dark and rude, and
4. O Trin - i - ty of love and power, our breth - ren shield in dan - ger's hour; from

bidd'st the might - y o - cean deep its own ap - point - ed lim - its keep: O
walk - edst on the foam - ing deep, and calm a - mid the storm didst sleep: O
bid their an - gry tu - mult cease, and give, for wild con - fu - sion, peace: O
rock and tem - pest, fire and foe, pro - tect them where - so - e'er they go; thus

hear us when we cry to thee for those in per - il on the sea.
hear us when we cry to thee for those in per - il on the sea.
hear us when we cry to thee for those in per - il on the sea.
ev - er - more shall rise to thee glad hymns of praise from land and sea.

ETERNAL RULER OF THE CEASELESS ROUND

words by
John W. Chadwick (1840-1904)

SONG 1
music by
Orlando Gibbons (1583-1625)

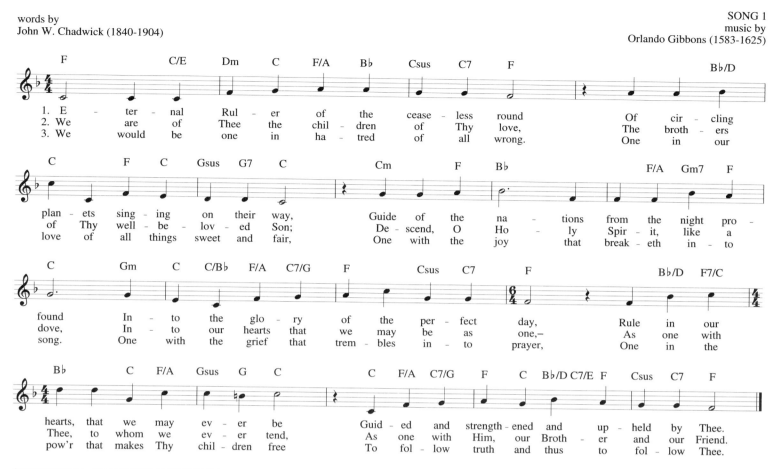

1. E - ter - nal Rul - er of the cease - less round Of cir - cling
2. We are of Thee the chil - dren of Thy love, The broth - ers
3. We would be one in ha - tred of all wrong. One in our

plan - ets sing - ing on their way, Guide of the na - tions from the night pro -
of Thy well - be - lov - ed Son; De - scend, O Ho - ly Spir - it, like a
love of all things sweet and fair, One with the joy that break - eth in - to

found In - to the glo - ry of the per - fect day, Rule in our
dove, In - to our hearts that we may be as one,— As one with
song. One with the grief that trem - bles in - to prayer, One in with the

hearts, that we may ev - er be Guid - ed and strength - ened and up - held by Thee.
Thee, to whom we ev - er tend, As one with Him, our Broth - er and our Friend.
pow'r that makes Thy chil - dren free To fol - low truth and thus to fol - low Thee.

EVERY BRIDGE IS BURNED BEHIND ME

words by
Johnson Oatman, Jr. (1856-1922)

EVERY BRIDGE
music by
George C. Hugg (1848-1907)

1. Since I start - ed out to find Thee, Since I to the cross did flee,
2. Thou didst hear my plea so kind - ly; Thou didst grant me so much grace.
3. Cares of life per - plex and grind me, Yet I keep the nar - row way.
4. All in All I ev - er find Thee, Sav - ior, Lov - er, Broth - er, Friend.

Ev - 'ry bridge is burned be - hind me; I will nev - er turn from Thee.
Ev - 'ry bridge is burned be - hind me; I will ne'er my steps re - trace.
Ev - 'ry bridge is burned be - hind me; I from Thee will nev - er stray.
Ev - 'ry bridge is burned be - hind me; I will serve Thee to the end.

Refrain

Strength - en all the ties that bind me Clos - er, clos - er, Lord, to Thee.

Ev - 'ry bridge is burned be - hind me; Thine I ev - er - more will be.

EVERY TIME I FEEL THE SPIRIT

EVERY TIME
Traditional Spiritual

Traditional Spiritual

FACE TO FACE

words by
Carrie E. Breck, 1898
based on I Corinthians 13:12

music by
Grant C. Tullar, 1898

FAIREST LORD JESUS

words from
Münster Gesangbuch, 1677 (v. 1-3)
v. 4 by Joseph A. Seiss (1823-1904)

CRUSADERS' HYMN
music from
Schlesische Volkslieder, 1842

1. Fair - est Lord Je - sus, Ru - ler of all na - ture,
2. Fair are the mea - dows, Fair - er still the wood - lands,
3. Fair is the sun - shine, Fair - er still the moon - light,
4. Beau - ti - ful Sav - ior! Lord ____ of the na - tions!

O Thou of God and ____ man the Son;
Robed in the bloom - ing ____ garb of spring:
And all the twin - kling, ____ star - ry host:
Son of ____ God and ____ Son of Man!

Thee will I cher - ish, Thee will I hon - or, Thou,
Je - sus is fair - er, Je - sus is pur - er, Who
Je - sus shines bright - er, Je - sus shines pur - er, Than
Glo - ry and hon - or, Praise, ad - o - ra - tion, Now

my soul's glo - ry, joy, and crown.
makes the woe - ful heart to sing.
all the an - gels heav'n can boast.
and for - ev - er - more be Thine!

FAIREST LORD JESUS

words from
Münster Gesangbuch, 1677 (v. 1-3)
v. 4 by Joseph A. Seiss (1823-1904)

SCHÖNSTER HERR JESU (II)
music from
Münster Gesangbuch, 1677

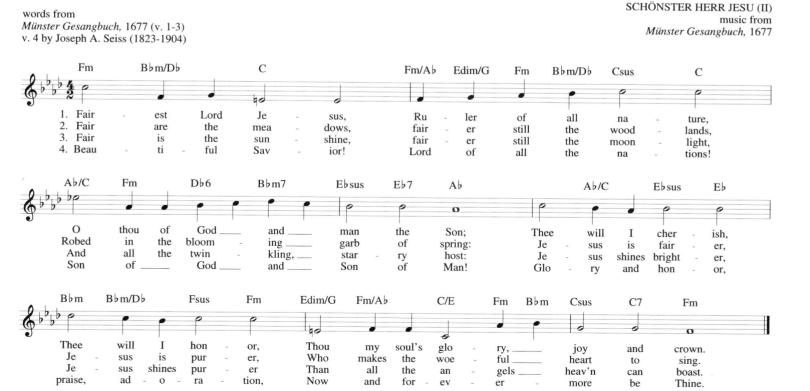

1. Fair - est Lord Je - sus, Ru - ler of all na - ture,
2. Fair are the mea - dows, fair - er still the wood - lands,
3. Fair is the sun - shine, fair - er still the moon - light,
4. Beau - ti - ful Sav - ior! Lord of all the na - tions!

O thou of God ____ and ____ man the Son;
Robed in the bloom - ing ____ garb of spring:
And all the twin - kling, ____ star - ry host:
Son of ____ God ____ and ____ Son of Man!

Thee will I cher - ish,
Je - sus is fair - er,
Je - sus shines bright - er,
Glo - ry and hon - or,

Thee will I hon - or, Thou my soul's glo - ry, ____ joy and crown.
Je - sus is pur - er, Who makes the woe - ful heart to sing.
Je - sus shines pur - er, Than all the an - gels ____ heav'n can boast.
praise, ad - o - ra - tion, Now and for - ev - er - more be Thine.

FAITH IS THE VICTORY

words by
John H. Yates, 1891

SANKEY
music by
Ira D. Sankey, 1891

1. En - camped a - long the hills of light, Ye Chris - tian sol - diers, rise, _____ And
2. His ban - ner o - ver us is love, Our sword the Word of God; _____ We
3. On ev - 'ry hand the foe we find Drawn up in dread ar - ray; _____ Let
4. To him that o - ver - comes the foe, White rai - ment shall be giv'n; _____ Be -

press the bat - tle ere the night Shall veil the glow - ing skies. _____ A
tread the road the saints a - bove With shouts of tri - umph trod. _____ By
tents of ease be left be - hind, And on - ward to the fray; _____ Sal -
fore the an - gels he shall know His name con - fessed in heav'n. _____ Then

gainst the foe in vales be - low Let all our strength be hurled; _____ Faith
faith they, like a whirl - wind's breath, Swept on o'er ev - 'ry field; _____ The
va - tion's hel - met on each head, With truth all girt a - bout, _____ The
on - ward from the hills of light, Our hearts with love a - flame, _____ We'll

is the vic - to - ry, we know, That o - ver - comes the world. _____ Faith
faith by which they con - quered death Is still our shin - ing shield. _____ faith
earth shall trem - ble 'neath our tread, And ech - o with our shout. _____ earth
van - quish all the hosts of night, In Je - sus' con - quering name. _____ van -

Refrain

Faith _____ is the vic - to - ry! Faith _____ is the vic - to - ry!

O, glo - ri - ous vic - to - ry, That o - ver - comes the world. _____

FAITH OF OUR FATHERS

ST. CATHERINE
music by
Henri F. Hemy (1818-1888)

words by
Frederick William Faber (1814-1863)

1. Faith of our fa - thers! liv - ing still in spite of dun - geon,
2. Faith of our fa - thers! faith _____ and prayer shall win all na - tions
3. Faith of our fa - thers! we _____ will love both friend and foe in

fire _____ and sword: O how our hearts _____ beat high _____ with joy,
un - to thee; and through the truth _____ that comes _____ from God,
all _____ our strife: and preach thee, too, _____ as love _____ knows how,

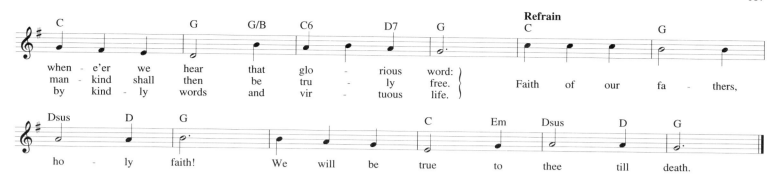

FATHER OF MERCIES, IN THY WORD

words by
Anne Steele, 1760

DETROIT
music from
The Sacred Harp, Philadelphia, 1844

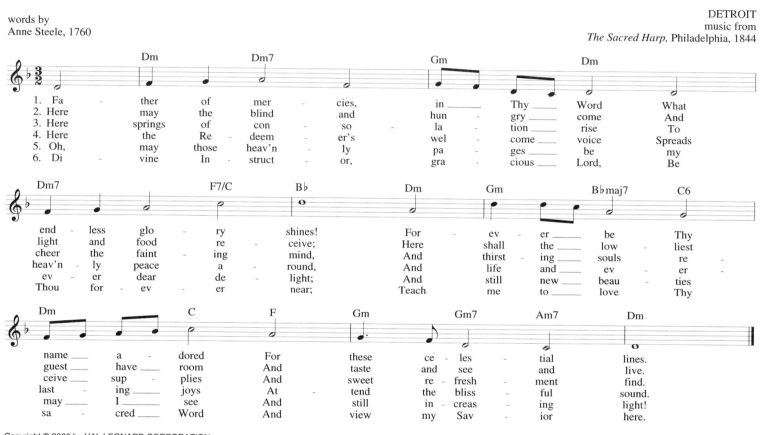

FIGHT THE GOOD FIGHT

words by
John Samuel Bewley Monsell, 1863

DUKE STREET
music by
John Hatton (c.1710-1793)

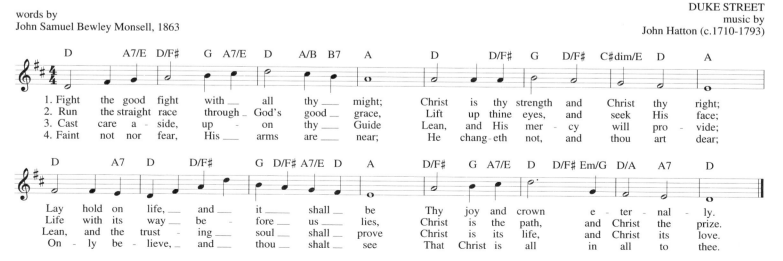

FIGHT THE GOOD FIGHT

words by
John S.B. Monsell (1811-1875)

MENDON
music from
The Methodist Harmonist, New York, 1821

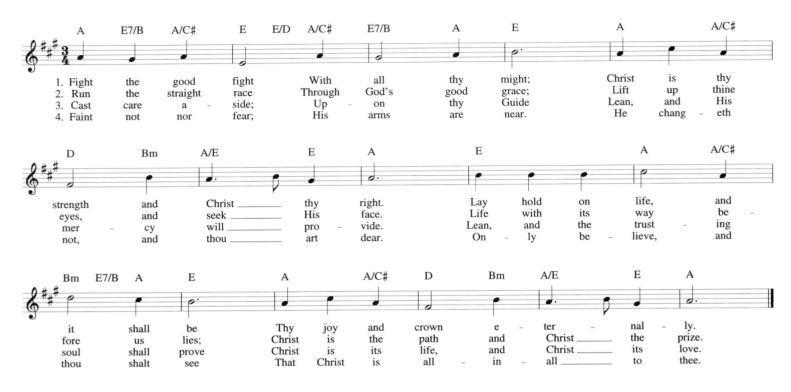

1. Fight the good fight With all thy might; Christ is thy
2. Run the straight race Through God's good grace; Lift up thine
3. Cast care a - side; Up - on thy Guide Lean, and His
4. Faint not nor fear; His arms are near. He chang - eth

strength and Christ ____ thy right. Lay hold on life, and
eyes, and seek ____ His face. Life with its way be -
mer - cy will ____ pro - vide. Lean, and the trust - ing
not, and thou ____ art dear. On - ly be - lieve, and

it shall be Thy joy and crown e - ter - nal - ly.
fore us lies; Christ is the path and Christ ____ the prize.
soul shall prove Christ is its life, and Christ ____ its love.
thou shalt see That Christ is all — in — all ____ to thee.

FILL ME NOW

words by
Elwood H. Stokes, 1879

music by
John R. Sweney, 1879

1. Hov - er o'er me, Ho - ly Spir - it, Bathe my trem - bling heart and brow;
2. Thou canst fill me, gra - cious Spir - it, Though I can - not tell Thee how;
3. I am weak - ness, full of weak - ness, At Thy sa - cred feet I bow;
4. Cleanse and com - fort, bless and save me, Bathe, O bathe my heart and brow;

Fill me with Thy hal - lowed pres - ence, Come, O come and fill me now.
But I need Thee, great - ly need Thee, Come, O come and fill me now.
Blest, di - vine, e - ter - nal Spir - it, Fill with pow'r, and fill me now.
Thou art com - fort - ing and sav - ing, Thou art sweet - ly fill - ing now.

Refrain

Fill me now, fill me now, Je - sus, come and fill me now;

Fill me with Thy hal - lowed pres - ence Come, O come and fill me now.

FATHER, WE PRAISE THEE

words attributed to
Gregory the Great (540-604)
tr. by Percy Dearmer, 1906

CHRISTE SANCTORUM
music from
Paris *Antiphoner,* 1681

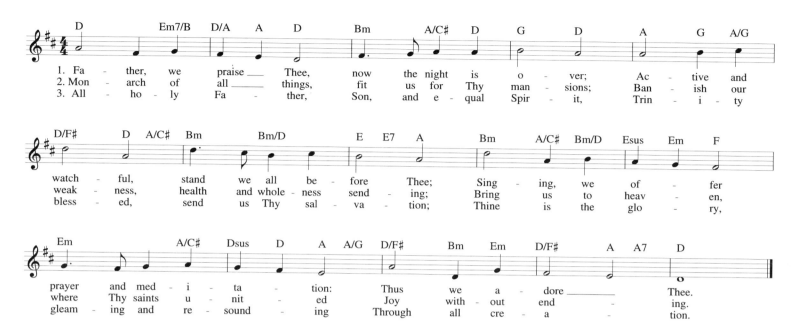

1. Fa - ther, we praise ___ Thee, now the night is o - ver; Ac - tive and
2. Mon - arch of all ___ things, fit us for Thy man - sions; Ban - ish our
3. All - ho - ly Fa - ther, Son, and e - qual Spir - it, Trin - i - ty

watch - ful, stand we all be - fore Thee; Sing - ing, we of - fer
weak - ness, health and whole - ness send - ing; Bring us to heav - en,
bless - ed, send us Thy sal - va - tion; Thine is the glo - ry,

prayer and med - i - ta - tion: Thus we a - dore ___ Thee.
where Thy saints u - nit - ed Joy with - out end ___ ing.
gleam - ing and re - sound - ing Through all cre - a - tion.

FILL THOU MY LIFE, O LORD, MY GOD

words by
Horatius Bonar, 1866

RICHMOND
music by
Thomas Haweis, 1792

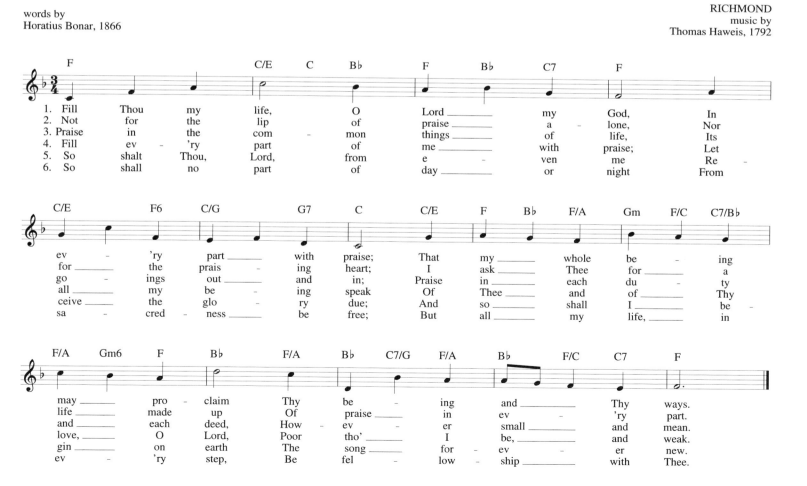

1. Fill Thou my life, O Lord ___ my God, In
2. Not for the lip of praise ___ a - lone, Nor
3. Praise in the com - mon things ___ of life, Its
4. Fill ev - 'ry part of me ___ with praise; Let
5. So shalt Thou, Lord, from e - ven me Re -
6. So shall no part of day ___ or night From

ev - 'ry part ___ with praise; That my ___ whole be - ing
for ___ the prais - ing heart; I ask ___ Thee for a
go - ings out ___ and in; Praise in ___ each du - ty
all ___ my be - ing speak Of Thee ___ and so shall I ___ Thy
ceive ___ the glo - ry due; And so ___ shall my life, ___ be
sa - cred - ness ___ be free; But all ___ my life, ___ in

may ___ pro - claim Thy be - ing and ___ Thy ways.
life ___ made up Of praise ___ in ev - 'ry part.
and ___ each deed, How ev - er small ___ and mean.
love, ___ O Lord, Poor tho' I be, ___ and weak.
gin ___ on earth The song ___ for - ev - er new.
ev - 'ry step, Be fel - low - ship ___ with Thee.

THE FIRST NOEL

Traditional English carol, 17th century

music from
W. Sandys' *Christmas Carols,* 1833

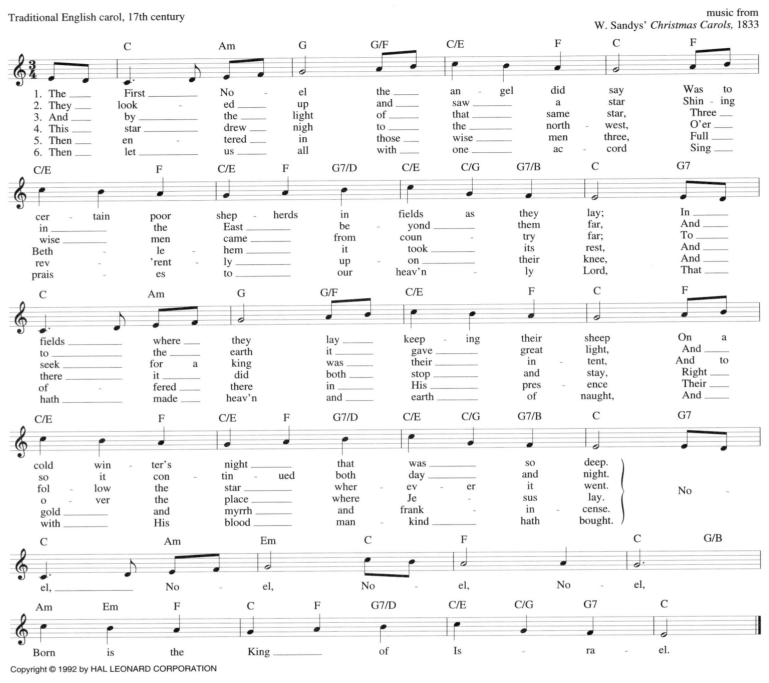

FIX ME, JESUS

African-American Spiritual

African-American Spiritual

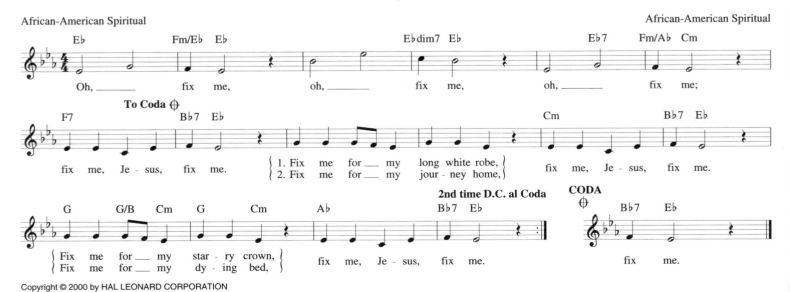

FOLLOW ON

words by
William O. Cushing (1823-1902)

music by
Robert Lowry (1826-1899)

FOOTSTEPS OF JESUS

words by
Mary B.C. Slade (1826-1882)

FOOTSTEPS
music by
Asa B. Everett (1828-1875)

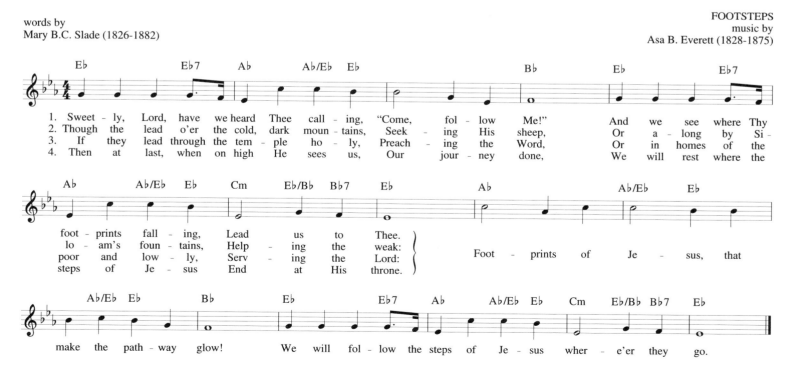

FOR ALL THE BLESSINGS OF THE YEAR

OLDBRIDGE
music by
Robert N. Quaile

words by
Albert H. Hutchinson

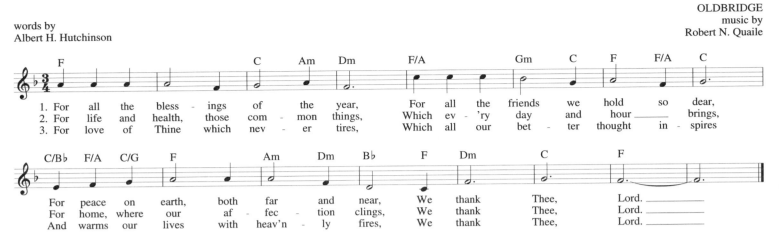

1. For all the bless - ings of the year, For all the friends we hold so dear,
2. For life and health, those com - mon things, Which ev - 'ry day and hour _____ brings,
3. For love of Thine which nev - er tires, Which all our bet - ter thought in - spires

For peace on earth, both far and near, We thank Thee, Lord. _____
For home, where our af - fec - tion clings, We thank Thee, Lord. _____
And warms our lives with heav'n - ly fires, We thank Thee, Lord. _____

Copyright © 2000 by HAL LEONARD CORPORATION

FOR ALL THY SAINTS, O LORD

FESTAL SONG
music by
William H. Walter (1825-1893)

words by
Richard Mant (1776-1848)

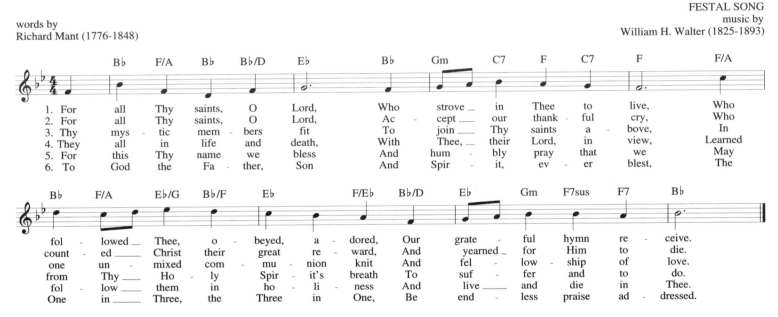

1. For all Thy saints, O Lord, Who strove ___ in Thee to live, Who
2. For all Thy saints, O Lord, Ac - cept ___ our thank - ful cry, Who
3. Thy mys - tic mem - bers fit To join ___ Thy saints a - bove, In
4. They all in life and death, With Thee, ___ their Lord, in view, Learned
5. For this Thy name we bless And hum - bly pray that we May
6. To God the Fa - ther, Son And Spir - it, ev - er blest, The

fol - lowed ___ Thee, o - beyed, a - dored, Our grate - ful hymn re - ceive.
count - ed _____ Christ their great re - ward, And yearned ___ for Him to die.
one un - mixed com - mu - nion knit And fel - low - ship of love.
from Thy ___ Ho - ly Spir - it's breath To suf - fer and to do.
fol - low them in ho - li - ness And live _____ and die in Thee.
One in _____ Three, the Three in One, Be end - less praise ad - dressed.

Copyright © 2000 by HAL LEONARD CORPORATION

FOR ALL THY SAINTS, O LORD

ST. GEORGE
music by
Henry John Gauntlett (1805-1876)

words by
Richard Mant (1776-1848)

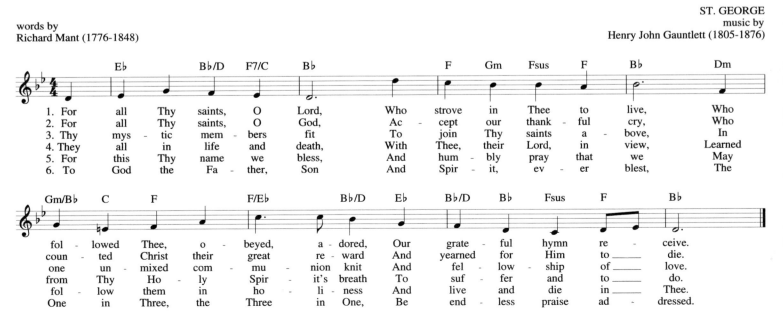

1. For all Thy saints, O Lord, Who strove in Thee to live, Who
2. For all Thy saints, O God, Ac - cept our thank - ful cry, Who
3. Thy mys - tic mem - bers fit To join Thy saints a - bove, In
4. They all in life and death, With Thee, their Lord, in view, Learned
5. For this Thy name we bless, And hum - bly pray that we May
6. To God the Fa - ther, Son And Spir - it, ev - er blest, The

fol - lowed Thee, o - beyed, a - dored, Our grate - ful hymn re - ceive.
coun - ted Christ their great re - ward, And yearned for Him to ___ die.
one un - mixed com - mu - nion knit And fel - low - ship of ___ love.
from Thy Ho - ly Spir - it's breath To suf - fer and to ___ do.
fol - low them in ho - li - ness And live and die in ___ Thee.
One in Three, the Three in One, Be end - less praise ad - dressed.

Copyright © 2000 by HAL LEONARD CORPORATION

FOR ALL THE SAINTS

SINE NOMINE
music by
Ralph Vaughan Williams, 1906

words by
William W. How, 1864

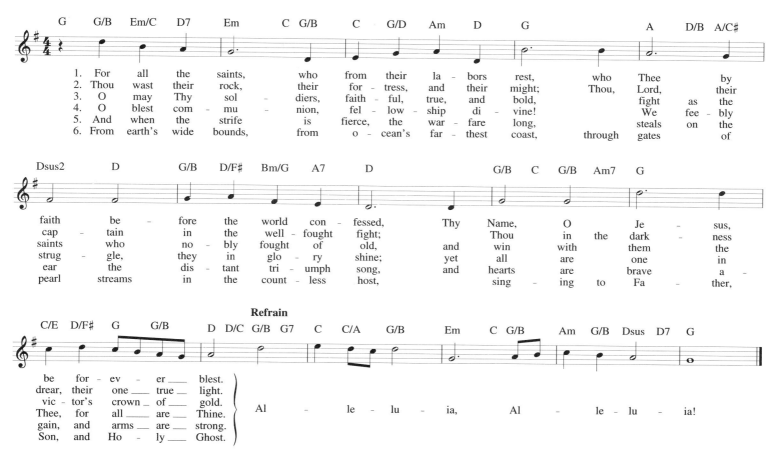

1. For all the saints, who from their la - bors rest, who Thee by
2. Thou wast their rock, their for - tress, and their might; who Thou, Lord, their
3. O may Thy sol - diers, faith - ful, true, and bold, We fight as the
4. O blest com - mu - nion, fel - low - ship di - vine! We fee - bly
5. And when the strife is fierce, the war - fare long, steals on the
6. From earth's wide bounds, from o - cean's far - thest coast, through gates of

faith be - fore the world con - fessed, Thy Name, O Je - sus,
cap - tain in the well - fought fight; Thou in the dark - ness
saints who no - bly fought of old, and win with them the
strug - gle, they in glo - ry shine; yet all are one in
ear the dis - tant tri - umph song, and hearts are brave a -
pearl streams in the count - less host, sing - ing to Fa - ther,

Refrain

be for - ev - er ___ blest.
drear, their one ___ true ___ light.
vic - tor's crown ___ of ___ gold.
Thee, for all ___ are ___ Thine.
gain, and arms ___ are ___ strong.
Son, and Ho - ly ___ Ghost.

Al - le - lu - ia, Al - le - lu - ia!

FOR THE BEAUTY OF THE EARTH

DIX
music by
Conrad Kocher, 1838

words by
Folliot S. Pierpoint, 1864

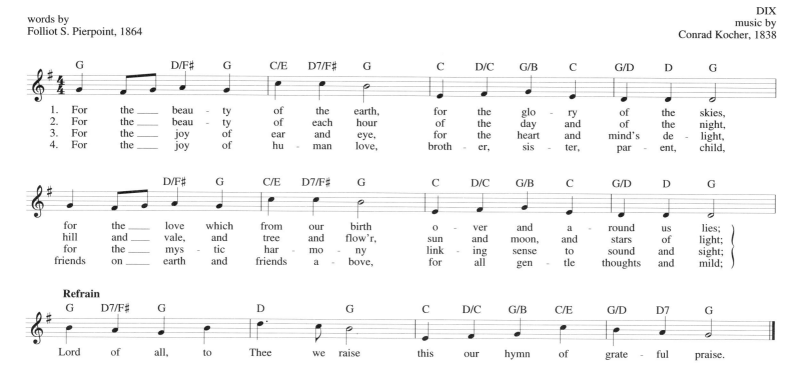

1. For the ___ beau - ty of the earth, for the glo - ry of the skies,
2. For the ___ beau - ty of each hour, of the day and of the night,
3. For the ___ joy of ear and eye, for the heart and mind's de - light,
4. For the ___ joy of hu - man love, broth - er, sis - ter, par - ent, child,

for the ___ love which from our birth o - ver and a - round us lies;
hill and ___ vale, and tree and flow'r, sun and moon, and stars of light;
for the ___ mys - tic har - mo - ny link - ing sense to sound and sight;
friends on ___ earth and friends a - bove, for all gen - tle thoughts and mild;

Refrain

Lord of all, to Thee we raise this our hymn of grate - ful praise.

FORTH IN THY NAME, O LORD, I GO

SONG 34

words by
Charles Wesley (1707-1788)

music by
Orlando Gibbons (1583-1625)

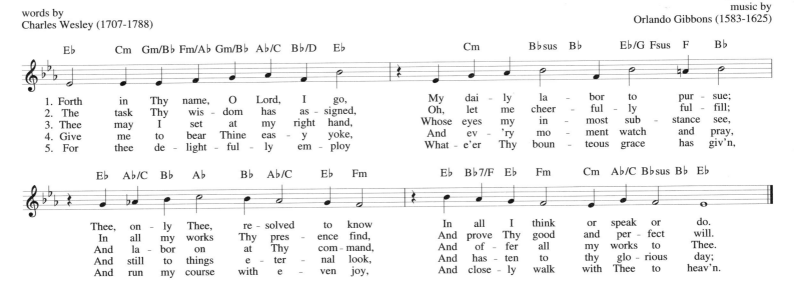

1. Forth in Thy name, O Lord, I go, My dai - ly la - bor to pur - sue;
2. The task Thy wis - dom has as - signed, Oh, let me cheer - ful - ly ful - fill;
3. Thee may I set at my right hand, Whose eyes my in - most sub - stance see,
4. Give me to bear Thine eas - y yoke, And ev - 'ry mo - ment watch and pray,
5. For thee de - light - ful - ly em - ploy What - e'er Thy boun - teous grace has giv'n,

Thee, on - ly Thee, re - solved to know In all I think or speak or do.
In all my works Thy pres - ence find, And prove Thy good and per - fect will.
And la - bor on at Thy com - mand, And of - fer all my works to Thee.
And still to things e - ter - nal look, And has - ten to thy glo - rious day;
And run my course with e - ven joy, And close - ly walk with Thee to heav'n.

FORTY DAYS AND FORTY NIGHTS

HEINLEIN
music attributed to
Martin Herbst (1654-1681)

words by
George H. Smyttan (1822-1870) and F. Pott

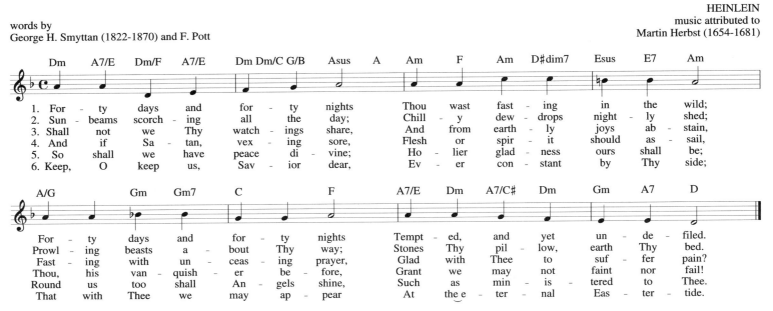

1. For - ty days and for - ty nights Thou wast fast - ing in the wild;
2. Sun - beams scorch - ing all the day; Chill - y dew - drops night - ly shed;
3. Shall not we Thy watch - ings share, And from earth - ly joys ab - stain,
4. And if Sa - tan, vex - ing sore, Flesh or spir - it should as - sail,
5. So shall we have peace di - vine; Ho - lier glad - ness ours shall be;
6. Keep, O keep us, Sav - ior dear, Ev - er con - stant by Thy side;

For - ty days and for - ty nights Tempt - ed, and yet un - de - filed.
Prowl - ing beasts a - bout Thy way; Stones Thy pil - low, earth Thy bed.
Fast - ing with un - ceas - ing prayer, Glad with Thee to suf - fer pain?
Thou, his van - quish - er be - fore, Grant we may not faint nor fail!
Round us too shall An - gels shine, Such as min - is - tered to Thee.
That with Thee we may ap - pear At the e - ter - nal Eas - ter - tide.

FORWARD THROUGH THE AGES

ST. GERTRUDE
music by
Arthur S. Sullivan, 1871

words by
Frederick Lucian Hosmer, 1908

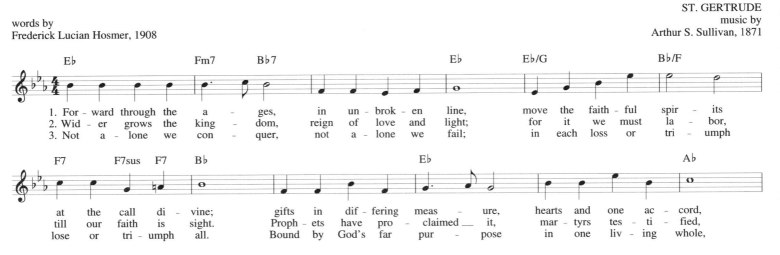

1. For - ward through the a - ges, in un - brok - en line, move the faith - ful spir - its
2. Wid - er grows the king - dom, reign of love and light; for it we must la - bor,
3. Not a - lone we con - quer, not a - lone we fail; in each loss or tri - umph

at the call di - vine; gifts in dif - fering meas - ure, hearts and one ac - cord,
till our faith is sight. Proph - ets have pro - claimed it, mar - tyrs tes - ti - fied,
lose or tri - umph all. Bound by God's far pur - pose in one liv - ing whole,

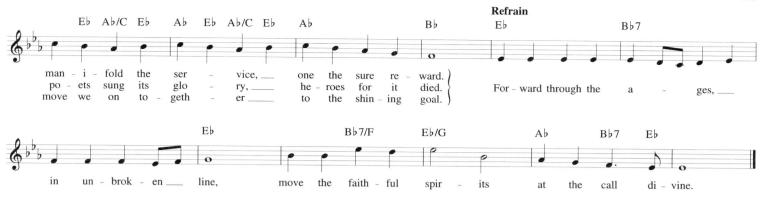

FRIENDSHIP WITH JESUS

words by
Joseph C. Ludgate, 1898

music arr. from
Stephen Foster (1826-1864)

FROM ALL THAT DWELL BELOW THE SKIES

OLD HUNDREDTH

words by
Isaac Watts (1674-1748)

music by
Louis Bourgeois (c. 1510-1561)

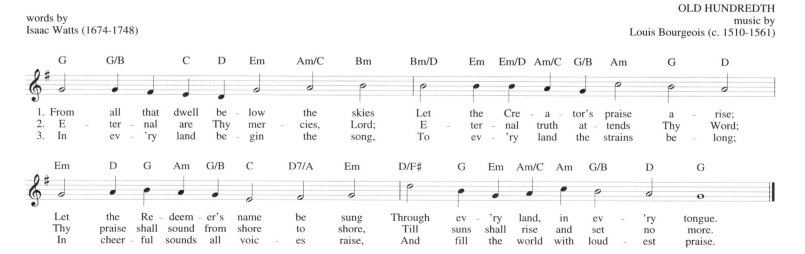

FROM ALL THAT DWELL BELOW THE SKIES

DUKE STREET
music by
John Hatton (c. 1710-1793)

words by
Isaac Watts (1674-1748)

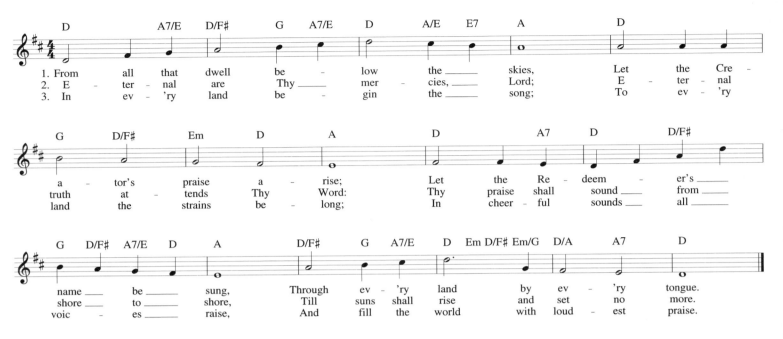

1. From all that dwell be - low the _____ skies, Let the Cre - a - tor's praise a - rise; Let the Re - deem - er's _____ name _____ be _____ sung, Through ev - 'ry land by ev - 'ry tongue.
2. E - ter - nal are Thy _____ mer - cies, _____ Lord; E - ter - nal truth at - tends Thy Word: Let Thy praise shall sound _____ from _____ shore _____ to _____ shore, Till suns shall rise and set no more.
3. In ev - 'ry land be - gin the _____ song; To ev - 'ry land the strains be - long; In cheer - ful sounds _____ all _____ voic - es _____ raise, And fill the world with loud - est praise.

FROM ALL THAT DWELL BELOW THE SKIES

LASST UNS ERFREUEN
music from
Geistliche Kirchengesäng, 1623

words by
Isaac Watts (1674-1748)

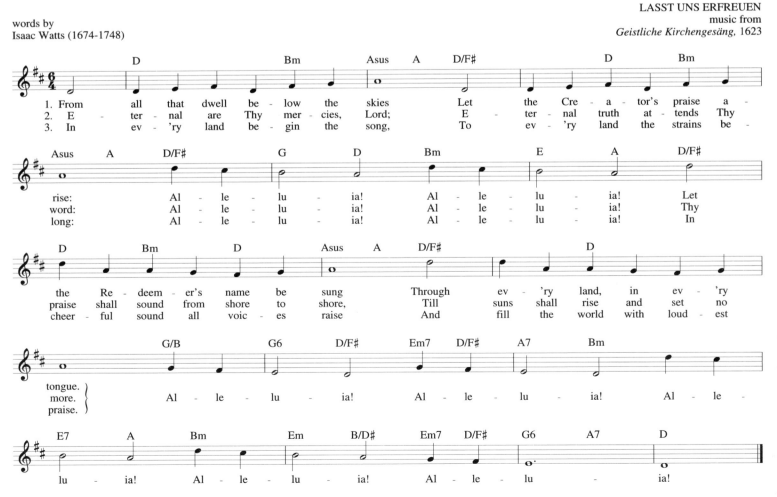

1. From all that dwell be - low the skies Let the Cre - a - tor's praise a - rise: Al - le - lu - ia! Al - le - lu - ia! Let the Re - deem - er's name be sung Through ev - 'ry land, in ev - 'ry tongue. Al - le - lu - ia! Al - le - lu - ia! Al - le - lu - ia!
2. E - ter - nal are Thy mer - cies, Lord; E - ter - nal truth at - tends Thy word: Al - le - lu - ia! Al - le - lu - ia! Thy praise shall sound from shore to shore, Till suns shall rise and set no more. Al - le - lu - ia!
3. In ev - 'ry land be - gin the song, To ev - 'ry land the strains be - long: Al - le - lu - ia! Al - le - lu - ia! In cheer - ful sound all voic - es raise And fill the world with loud - est praise. Al - le - lu - ia!

FROM EVERY STORMY WIND THAT BLOWS

words by
Hugh Stowell, 1828

RETREAT
music by
Thomas Hastings, 1842

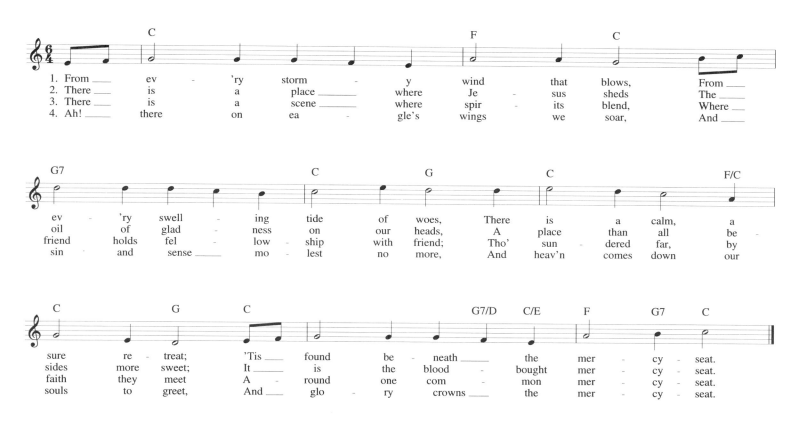

1. From ___ ev - 'ry storm - y wind that blows, From ___
2. There ___ is a place ___ where Je - sus sheds The ___
3. There ___ is a scene ___ where spir - its blend, Where ___
4. Ah! ___ there on ea - gle's wings we soar, And ___

ev - 'ry swell - ing tide of woes, There is a calm, a
oil of glad - ness tide on our heads, A place than all be -
friend holds fel - low - ship with friend; Tho' sun - dered far, by
sin and sense ___ mo - lest no more, And heav'n comes down our

sure re - treat; 'Tis ___ found be - neath ___ the mer - cy - seat.
sides more sweet; It ___ is the blood - bought mer - cy - seat.
faith they meet A - round one com - mon mer - cy - seat.
souls to greet, And ___ glo - ry crowns ___ the mer - cy - seat.

GENTLE JESUS, MEEK AND MILD

words by
Charles Wesley (1707-1788)

SEYMOUR
music by
Carl Maria von Weber (1786-1826)

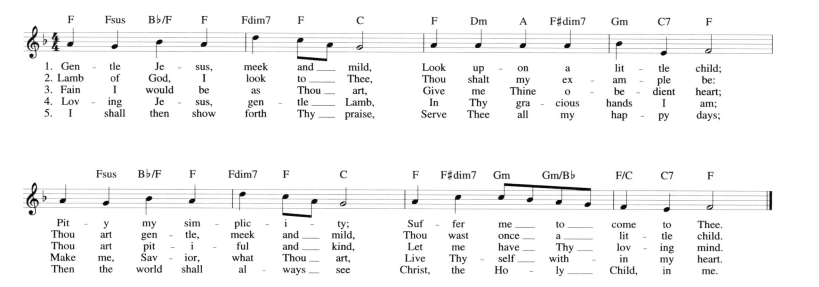

1. Gen - tle Je - sus, meek and ___ mild, Look up - on a lit - tle child;
2. Lamb of God, I look to ___ Thee, Thou shalt my ex - am - ple be:
3. Fain I would be as Thou ___ art, Give me Thine o - be - dient heart;
4. Lov - ing Je - sus, gen - tle ___ Lamb, In Thy gra - cious hands I am;
5. I shall then show forth Thy ___ praise, Serve Thee all my hap - py days;

Pit - y my sim - plic - i - ty; Suf - fer me ___ to ___ come to Thee.
Thou art gen - tle, meek and ___ mild, Thou wast once ___ a lit - tle child.
Thou art pit - i - ful and ___ kind, Let me have ___ Thy ___ lov - ing mind.
Make me, Sav - ior, what Thou ___ art, Live Thy - self ___ with - in my heart.
Then the world shall al - ways ___ see Christ, the Ho - ly ___ Child, in me.

GIVE ME JESUS

words by
Fanny J. Crosby, 1879

music by
John R. Sweney, 1879

1. Take the world, but give me Je - sus, All its joys are but a
2. Take the world, but give me Je - sus, Sweet - est com - fort of my
3. Take the world, but give me Je - sus, Let me view His con - stant
4. Take the world, but give me Je - sus, In His cross my trust shall

name; But His love a - bid - eth ev - er, Thru e - ter - nal years the
soul; With my Sav - ior watch - ing o'er me, I can sing though bil - lows
smile; Then through - out my pil - grim jour - ney Light will cheer me all the
be; Till, with clear - er, bright - er vi - sion, Face to face my Lord I

Refrain

same.
roll.
while.
see.

O the height and depth of mer - cy! O the length and breadth of

love! O the full - ness of re - demp - tion, Pledge of end - less life a - bove!

GIVE ME THE FAITH WHICH CAN REMOVE

SURREY

words by
Charles Wesley, 1749

music by
Henry Carey, c. 1732

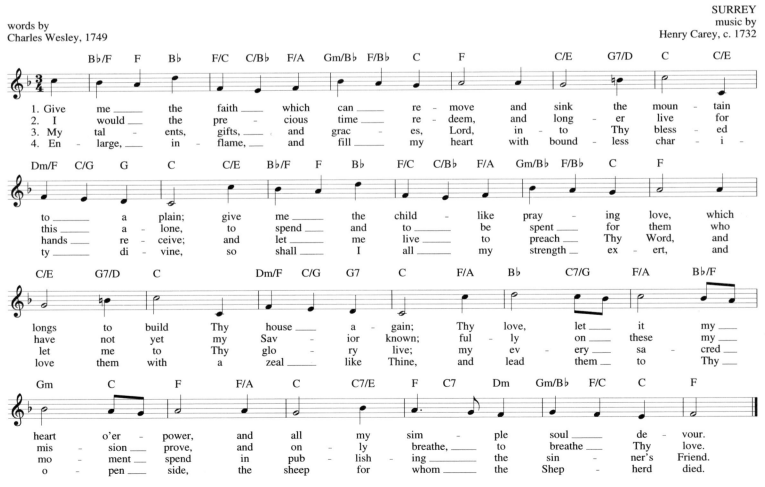

1. Give me the faith which can re - move and sink the moun - tain
2. I would the pre - cious time re - deem, and long - er live for
3. My tal - ents, gifts, and grac - es, Lord, in - to Thy bless - ed
4. En - large, in - flame, and fill my heart with bound - less char - i -

to a plain; give me the child - like pray - ing love, which
this a - lone, to spend and to be spent for them who
hands re - ceive; and let me live to preach Thy Word, and
ty di - vine, so shall I all my strength ex - ert, and

longs to build Thy house a - gain; Thy love, let it my
have not yet my Sav - ior known; ful - ly on these my
let me to Thy glo - ry live; my ev - ery sa - cred
love them with a zeal like Thine, and lead them to Thy

heart o'er - power, and all my sim - ple soul de - vour.
mis - sion prove, and on - ly breathe, to breathe Thy love.
mo - ment spend in pub - lish - ing the sin - ner's Friend.
o - pen side, the sheep for whom the Shep - herd died.

GIVE HIM THE GLORY

words by
Elisha A. Hoffman, 1893

GLORY
music by
Elisha A. Hoffman, 1893

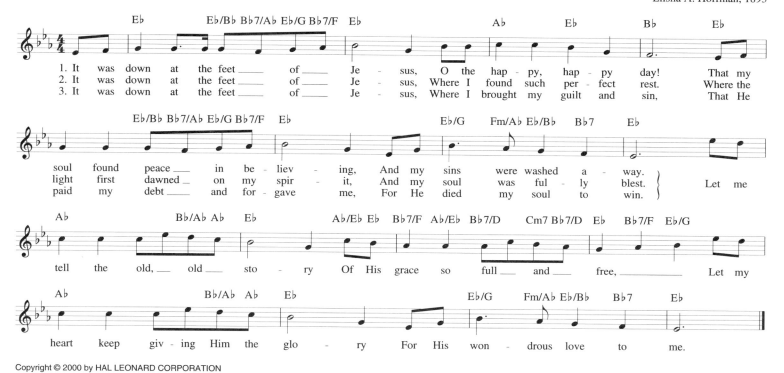

1. It was down at the feet ___ of ___ Je - sus, O the hap - py, hap - py day! That my
2. It was down at the feet ___ of ___ Je - sus, Where I found such per - fect rest. Where the
3. It was down at the feet ___ of ___ Je - sus, Where I brought my guilt and sin, That He

soul found peace ___ in be - liev - ing, And my sins were washed a - way.
light first dawned ___ on my spir - it, And my soul was ful - ly blest.
paid my debt ___ and for - gave me, For He died my soul to win.

Let me

tell the old, ___ old ___ sto - ry Of His grace so full ___ and ___ free, ___ Let my

heart keep giv - ing Him the glo - ry For His won - drous love to me.

GIVE ME THY HEART

words by
Eliza E. Hewitt, 1898

BOURNE
music by
William J. Kirkpatrick, 1898

1. "Give Me thy heart," says the Fa - ther a - bove. No gift so pre - cious to
2. "Give Me thy heart," says the Sav - ior of men, Call - ing in mer - cy a -
3. "Give Me thy heart," says the Spir - it di - vine. "All that thou hast, to My

Him as our love. Soft - ly He whis - pers, wher - ev - er thou art,
gain and a - gain. "Turn now from sin, and from e - vil de - part.
keep - ing re - sign. Grace more a - bound - ing is Mine to im - part.

Refrain

"Grate - ful - ly trust Me, and give Me thy heart.
Have I not died for thee? Give Me thy heart.
Make full sur - ren - der and give Me thy heart.

Give Me thy heart. Give Me thy

heart." Hear the soft whis - per, wher - ev - er thou art. From this dark world He would

draw thee a - part, Speak - ing so ten - der - ly, "Give Me thy heart."

GIVE OF YOUR BEST TO THE MASTER

BARNARD

words by
Howard B. Grose (1851-1939)

music by
Charlotte A. Barnard (1830-1869)

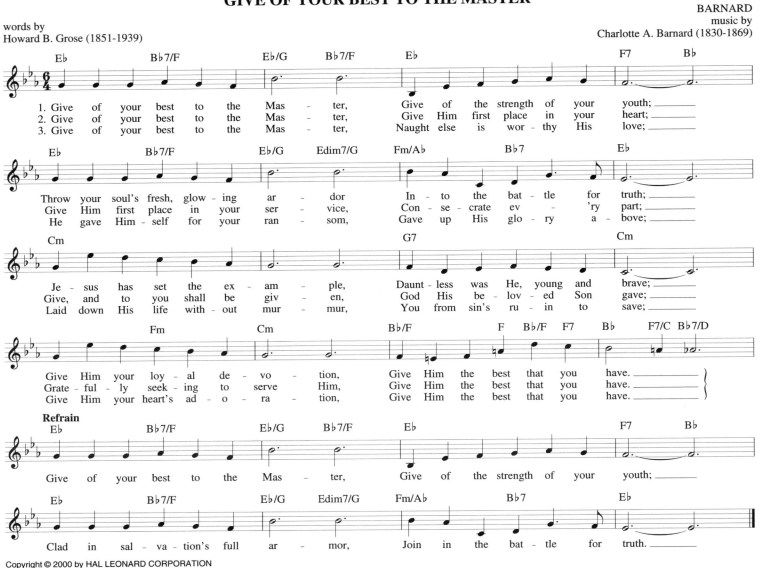

GIVE REST, O CHRIST

KONTAKION
Kievan chant from
Eastern Orthodox Memorial Service

words from
Eastern Orthodox Memorial Service
tr. by W.J. Birkbeck

when Thou cre - at - edst me, say - ing, "Dust Thou art, and un - to dust shalt __ thou re - turn."

All __ we go down __ to the dust; and, weep - ing o'er the grave, we make our song:

al - le - lu - ya, al - le - lu - ya, al - le - lu - ya.

D.C. al Fine

GIVE TO OUR GOD IMMORTAL PRAISE

words by
Isaac Watts (1674-1748)

DUKE STREET
music attr. to
John Hatton (d.1793)

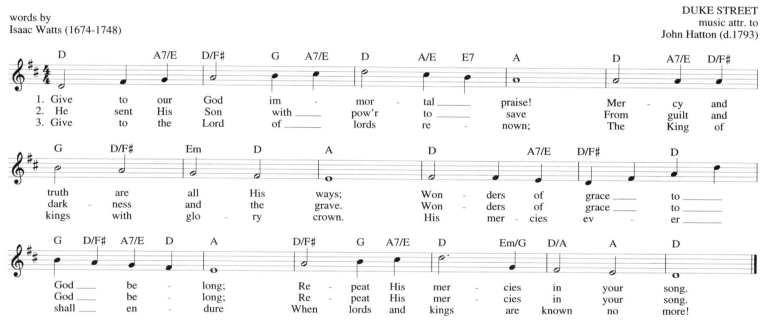

1. Give to our God im - mor - tal __ praise! Mer - cy and
2. He sent His Son with __ pow'r to save From guilt and
3. Give to the Lord of __ lords re - nown; The King of

truth are all His ways; Won - ders of grace ____ to _____
dark - ness and the grave. Won - ders of grace ____ to _____
kings with glo - ry crown. His mer - cies ev - er _____

God ____ be - long; Re - peat His mer - cies in your song.
God ____ be - long; Re - peat His mer - cies in your song.
shall ____ en - dure When lords and kings are known no more!

GIVE TO THE WINDS THY FEARS

words by
Paul Gerhardt, 1656
tr. by John Wesley, 1739

ST. BRIDE
music by
Samuel Howard, 1762

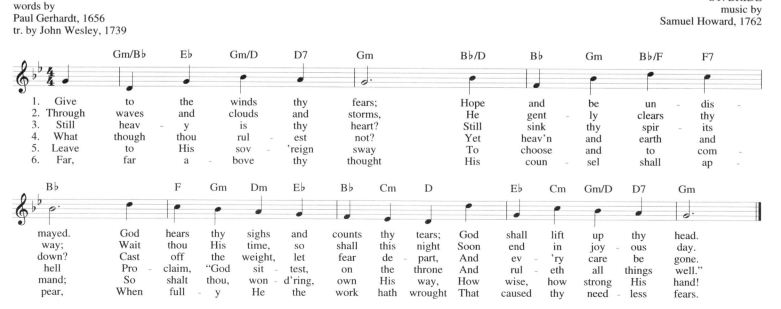

1. Give to the winds thy fears; Hope and be un - dis -
2. Through waves and clouds and storms, He gent - ly clears thy
3. Still heav - y is thy heart? Still sink thy spir - its
4. What though thou rul - est not? Yet heav'n and earth and
5. Leave to His sov - 'reign sway To choose and to com -
6. Far, far a - bove thy thought His coun - sel shall ap -

mayed. God hears thy sighs and counts thy tears; God shall lift up thy head.
way; Wait thou His time, so shall this night Soon end in joy - ous day.
down? Cast off the weight, let fear de - part, And ev - 'ry care be gone.
hell Pro - claim, "God sit - test, on the throne And rul - eth all things well."
mand; So shalt thou, won - d'ring, own His way, How wise, how strong His hand!
pear, When full - y He the work hath wrought That caused thy need - less fears.

GLORIA PATRI
(Glory Be to the Father)

Traditional words

GREATOREX
music by
Henry W. Greatorex, 1851

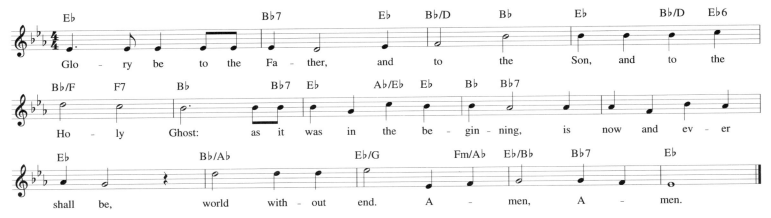

GLORIA PATRI
(Glory Be to the Father)

Traditional words

MEINEKE
music by
Christoph Meineke, 1844

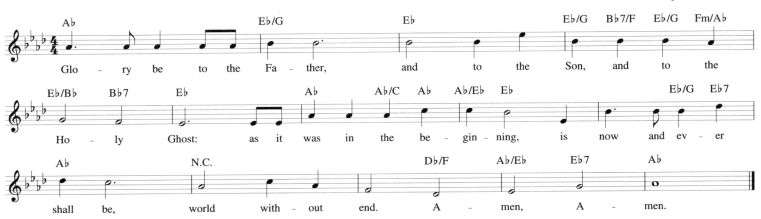

A GLORIOUS CHURCH

words by
Ralph E. Hudson (1843-1901)

music by
Ralph E. Hudson (1843-1901)

GLORIOUS FREEDOM

words by
Haldor Lillenas, 1917

music by
Alfred Judson, 1917

GLORIOUS THINGS OF THEE ARE SPOKEN

words by
John Newton (1725-1807)

AUSTRIAN HYMN
music by
Franz Joseph Haydn (1732-1809)

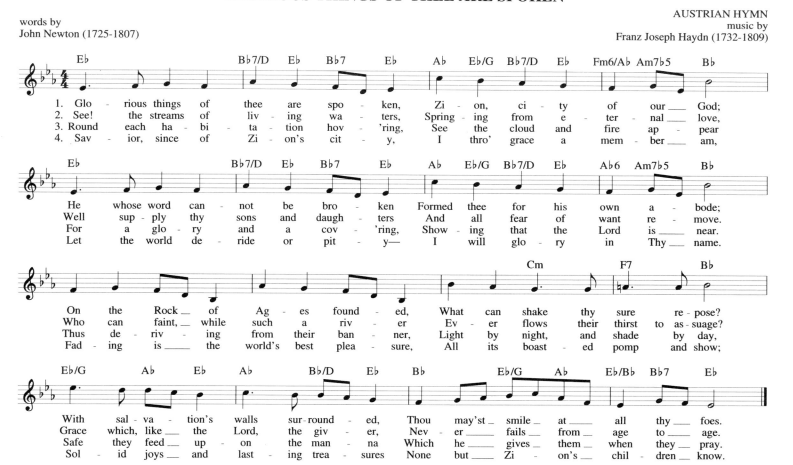

GLORY BE TO GOD THE FATHER

CWM RHONDDA
music by
John Hughes, 1907

words by
Horatius Bonar, 1866

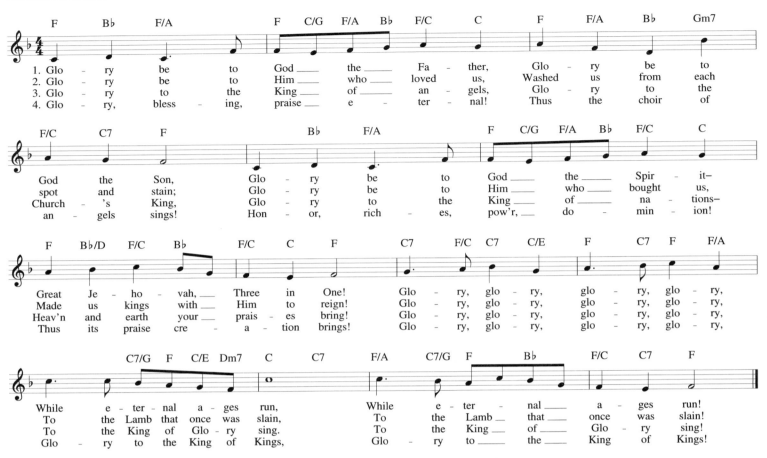

GLORY BE TO GOD THE FATHER

WORCESTER
music by
Walter G. Whinfield (1865-1919)

words by
Horatius Bonar (1808-1889)

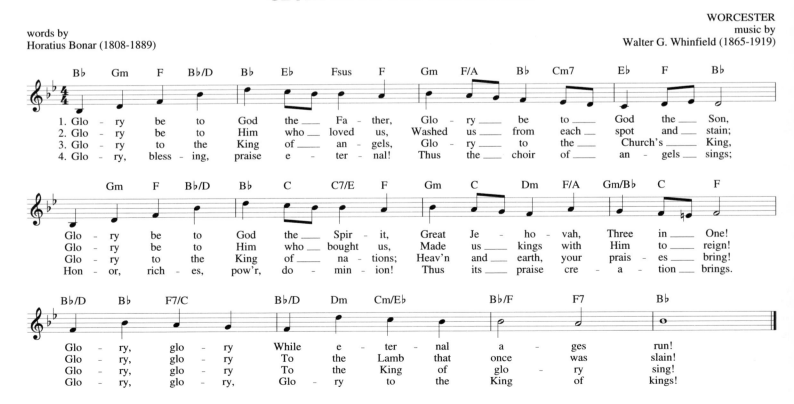

GLORY BE TO JESUS

Italian text, 18th century
tr. by Edward Caswall (1814-1878)

WEM IN LEIDENSTAGEN
music by
Friedrich Filitz (1804-1876)

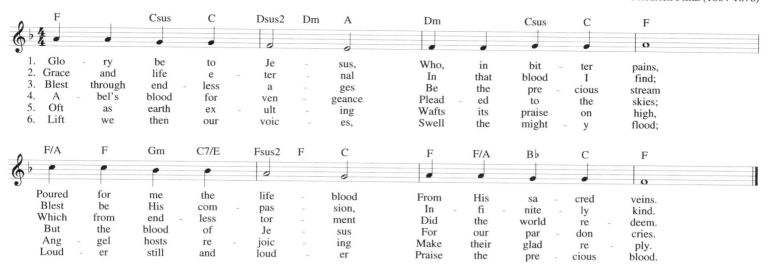

1. Glo - ry be to Je - sus, Who, in bit - ter pains,
2. Grace and life e - ter - nal In that blood I find;
3. Blest through end - less a - ges Be the pre - cious stream;
4. A - bel's blood for ven - geance Plead - ed to the skies;
5. Oft as earth ex - ult - ing Wafts its praise on high,
6. Lift we then our voic - es, Swell the might - y flood;

Poured for me the life - blood From His sa - cred veins.
Blest be His com - pas - sion, In - fi - nite - ly kind.
Which from end - less tor - ment Did the world re - deem.
But the blood of Je - sus For our par - don cries.
Ang - gel hosts re - joic - ing Make their glad re - ply.
Loud - er still and loud - er Praise the pre - cious blood.

GO FORWARD, CHRISTIAN SOLDIER

words by
Laurence Tuttiett (1825-1895)

LANCASHIRE
music by
Henry Thomas Smart (1813-1879)

1. Go for - ward, Christ - ian sol - dier, be - neath his ban - ner true; the Lord him - self, thy
2. Go for - ward, Christ - ian sol - dier, fear not the se - cret foe; far more o'er thee are
3. Go for - ward, Christ - ian sol - dier, nor dream of peace - ful rest, till Sa - tan's host is
4. Go for - ward, Christ - ian sol - dier, fear not the gath - er - ing night; the Lord has been thy

Lead - er, shall all thy foes sub - due. His love fore - tells thy tri - als; he
watch - ing than hu - man eyes can know; trust on - ly Christ, thy Cap - tain; cease
van - quished and heaven is all pos - sessed; till Christ him - self shall call thee to
shel - ter; the Lord will be thy light. When morn his face re - veal - eth thy

knows thine hour - ly need; he can with bread of heav - en thy faint - ing spir - it feed.
not to watch and pray; heed not the treach - 'rous voic - es that lure thy soul a - stray.
lay thine ar - mor by, and wear in end - less glo - ry the crown of vic - to - ry.
dan - gers all are past: O pray that faith and vir - tue may keep thee to the last!

GOD IS SO GOOD

Traditional words

Traditional music

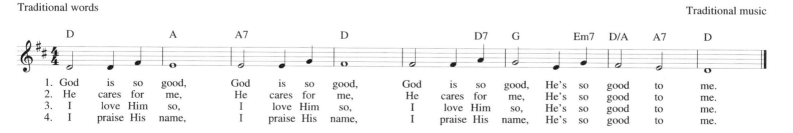

1. God is so good, God is so good, God is so good, He's so good to me.
2. He cares for me, He cares for me, He cares for me, He's so good to me.
3. I love Him so, I love Him so, I love Him so, He's so good to me.
4. I praise His name, I praise His name, I praise His name, He's so good to me.

GO, TELL IT ON THE MOUNTAIN

GO TELL IT
African-American Spiritual

African-American Spiritual
verses by John W. Work, Jr., 1907

GO TO DARK GETHSEMANE

GETHSEMANE
music by
Richard Redhead (1820-1901)

words by
James Montgomery (1771-1854)

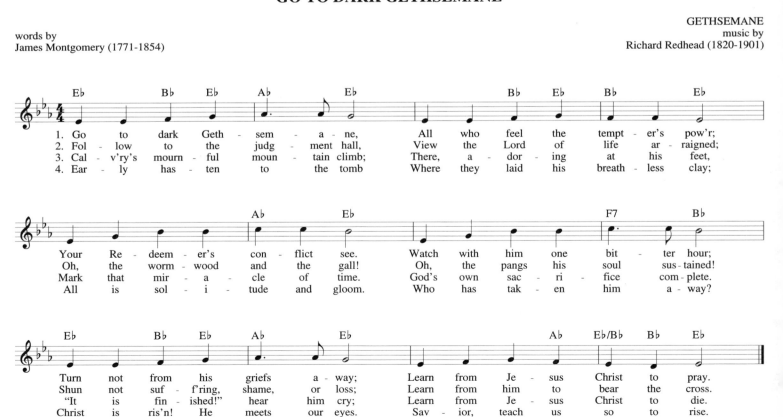

GOD BE WITH YOU TILL WE MEET AGAIN

words by
Jeremiah E. Rankin, 1880

GOD BE WITH YOU
music by
William G. Tomer, 1880

1. God be with you till we meet a - gain; By His coun - sels guide, up - hold you,
2. God be with you till we meet a - gain; 'Neath His wings pro - tect - ing hide you,
3. God be with you till we meet a - gain; When life's per - ils thick con - found you,
4. God be with you till we meet a - gain; Keep love's ban - ner float - ing o'er you,

With His sheep se - cure - ly fold you;
Dai - ly man - na still pro - vide you;
Put His arms un - fail - ing round you;
Smite death's threat - ening wave be - fore you;

God be with you till we meet a - gain. Till we

meet, _____ till we meet, _____ Till we meet at Je - sus' ___ feet, Till we

meet, _____ till we meet, _____ God be with you till we meet a - gain.

GOD BE WITH YOU TILL WE MEET AGAIN

words by
Jeremiah E. Rankin, 1880

RANDOLPH
music by
Ralph Vaughan Williams, 1906

1. God be with you till we meet a - gain; by His coun - sels guide, up - hold you,
2. God be with you till we meet a - gain; 'neath His wings se - cure - ly ____ hide you,
3. God be with you till we meet a - gain; when life's per - ils thick con - found you,
4. God be with you till we meet a - gain; keep love's ban - ner float - ing ____ o'er you,

with His sheep se - cure - ly ____ fold you; God be with you till we meet a - gain;
dai - ly man - na still pro - vide you; God be with you till we meet a - gain;
put His arms un - fail - ing ____ 'round you; God be with you till we meet a - gain;
smite death's threat - 'ning wave be - fore you; God be with you till we meet a - gain;

GOD IS MY STRONG SALVATION

words by
James Montgomery, 1822

CHRISTUS, DER IST MEIN LEBEN
music by
Melchior Vulpius, 1609

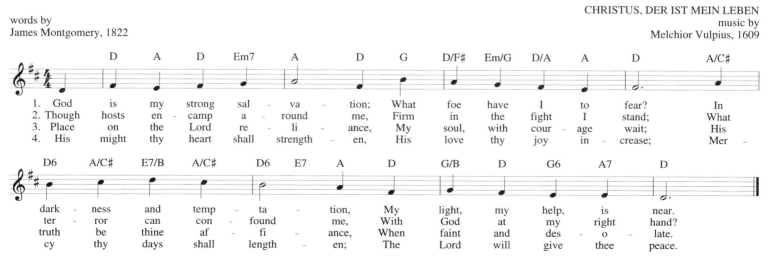

1. God is my strong sal - va - tion; What foe have I to fear? In
2. Though hosts en - camp a - round me, Firm in the fight I stand; What
3. Place on the Lord re - li - ance, My soul, with cour - age wait; His
4. His might thy heart shall strength - en, His love thy joy in - crease; Mer -

dark - ness and temp - ta - tion, My light, my help, is near.
ter - ror can con - found me, With God at my right hand?
truth be thine af - fi - ance, When faint and des - o - late.
cy thy days shall length - en; The Lord will give thee peace.

GOD IS OUR REFUGE AND OUR STRENGTH

Author unknown
words based on Psalm 46

WINCHESTER OLD
music from
Este's *Psalmes*, 1592

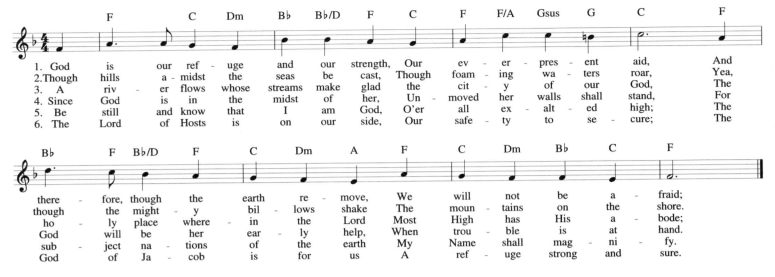

1. God is our ref - uge and our strength, Our ev - er - pres - ent aid, And
2. Though hills a - midst the seas be cast, Though foam - ing wa - ters roar, Yea,
3. A riv - er flows whose streams make glad the cit - y of our God, The
4. Since God is in the midst of her, Un - moved her walls shall stand, For
5. Be still and know that I am God, O'er all ex - alt - ed high; The
6. The Lord of Hosts is on our side, Our safe - ty to se - cure; The

there - fore, though the earth re - move, We will not be a - fraid;
though the might - y bil - lows shake The moun - tains on the shore.
ho - ly place where - in the Lord Most High has His a - bode;
God will be her ear - ly help, When trou - ble is at hand.
sub - ject na - tions of the earth My Name shall mag - ni - fy.
God of Ja - cob is for us A ref - uge strong and sure.

GOD IS THE REFUGE OF HIS SAINTS

words by
Isaac Watts, 1719

WARD
music by
Lowell Mason, 1830

1. God is the ref - uge of His saints, When storms of sharp dis - tress in - vade;
2. Loud may the troub - led o - cean roar, In sa - cred peace our souls a - bide,
3. There is a stream, whose gen - tle flow Sup - plies the cit - y of our God,
4. That sa - cred stream, that ho - ly Word, Our grief al - lays, our fear con - trols;

Ere we can of - fer our com - plaints, Be - hold Him pres - ent with His aid.
While ev - 'ry na - tion, ev - 'ry shore, Trem - bles and dreads the swell - ing tide.
Life, love, and joy still glid - ing thro', And wa - t'rin' our di - vine a - bode.
Sweet peace Thy prom - is - es af - ford, And give new strength to faint - ing souls.

GOD LOVED THE WORLD

Author unknown, 1791
tr. by August Crull (1846-1923)

ST. CRISPIN
music by
Melchior Vulpius (c. 1560-1615)

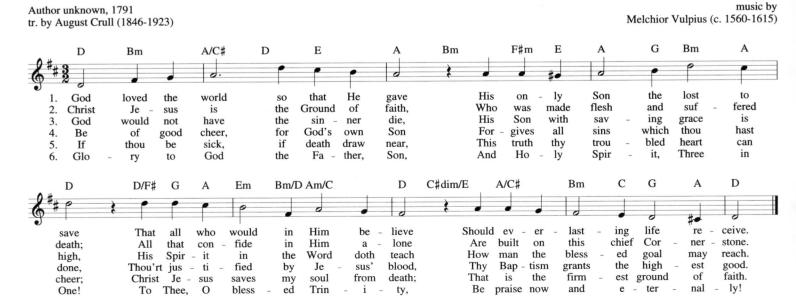

1. God loved the world so that He gave His on - ly Son the lost to
2. Christ Je - sus is the Ground of faith, Who was made flesh and suf - fered
3. God would not have the sin - ner die, His Son with sav - ing grace is
4. Be of good cheer, for God's own Son For - gives all sins which thou hast
5. If thou be sick, if death draw near, This truth thy trou - bled heart can
6. Glo - ry to God the Fa - ther, Son, And Ho - ly Spir - it, Three in

save That all who would in Him be - lieve Should ev - er - last - ing life re - ceive.
death; All that con - fide in Him a - lone Are built on this chief Cor - ner - stone.
high, His Spir - it in the Word doth teach How man the bless - ed goal may reach.
done, Thou'rt jus - ti - fied by Je - sus' blood, Thy Bap - tism grants the high - est good.
cheer; Christ Je - sus saves my soul from death; That is the firm - est ground of faith.
One! To Thee, O bless - ed Trin - i - ty, Be praise now and e - ter - nal - ly!

GOD LEADS US ALONG

words by
G.A. Young

GOD LEADS US
music by
G.A. Young

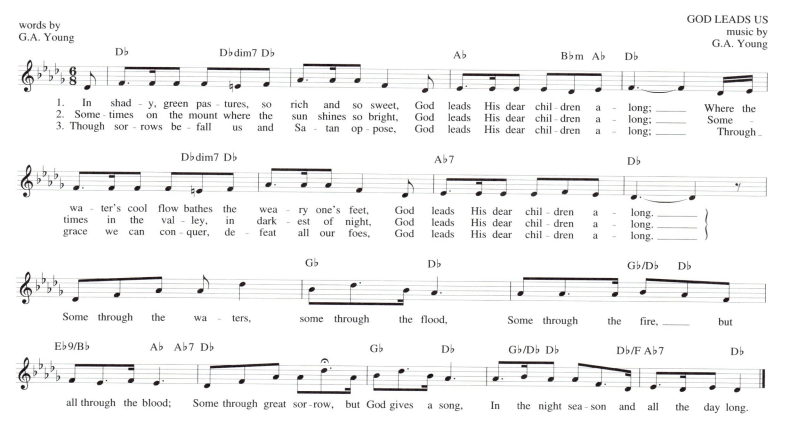

THE GOD OF ABRAHAM PRAISE

words by Thomas Olivers, c. 1770
based on Hebrew *Yigdal* of Daniel Ben Judah

LEONI
Traditional Hebrew melody
adapted by Meyer Lyon, c. 1770

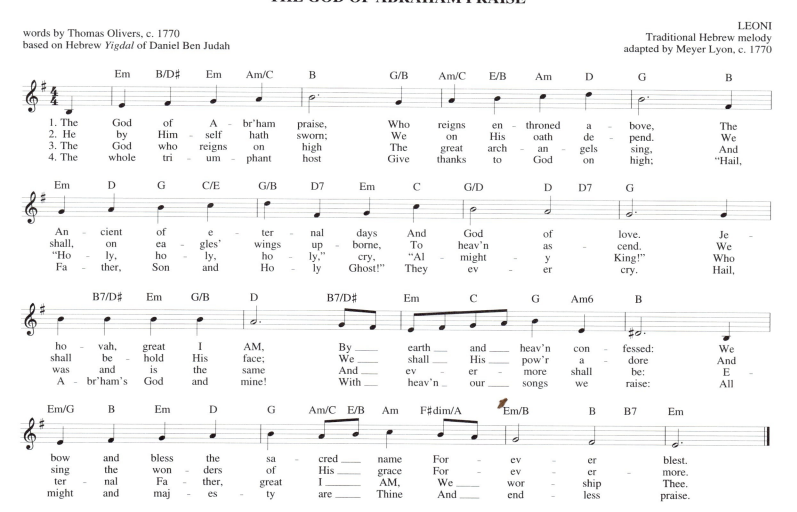

GOD MOVES IN A MYSTERIOUS WAY

LONDON NEW
music from
Scottish Psalter, 1635

words by
William Cowper (1731-1800)

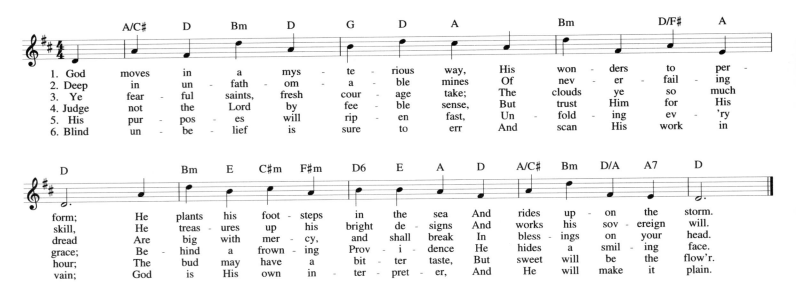

1. God moves in a mys - te - rious way, His won - ders to per - form;
2. Deep in un - fath - om - a - ble mines Of nev - er - fail - ing skill,
3. Ye fear - ful saints, fresh cour - age take; The clouds ye so much dread
4. Judge not the Lord by fee - ble sense, But trust Him for His grace;
5. His pur - pos - es will rip - en fast, Un - fold - ing ev - 'ry hour;
6. Blind un - be - lief is sure to err And scan His work in vain;

He plants his foot - steps in the sea And rides up - on the storm.
He treas - ures up his bright de - signs And works his sov - ereign will.
Are big with mer - cy, and shall break In bless - ings on your head.
Be - hind a frown - ing Prov - i - dence He hides a smil - ing face.
The bud may have a bit - ter taste, But sweet will be the flow'r.
God is His own in - ter - pret - er, And He will make it plain.

GOD OF GRACE AND GOD OF GLORY

CWM RHONDDA
music by
John Hughes

words by
Harry Emerson Fosdick

1. God of grace and God of glo - ry, On Thy peo - ple
2. Lo! the hosts of e - vil round us Scorn Thy Christ, as -
3. Cure Thy chil - dren's war - ring mad - ness; Bend our pride to
4. Set our feet on loft - y plac - es, Gird our lives that

pour Thy power; Crown Thine an - cient Church - 's sto - ry,
sail His ways! From Thine the fears that long have bound us,
Thy con - trol; Shame our wan - ton, self - ish glad - ness,
they may be Ar - mored with all Christ - like grac - es

Bring her bud to glo - rious flower. Grant us wis - dom, Grant us cour - age,
Free our hearts to faith and praise. Grant us wis - dom, Grant us cour - age,
Rich in things and poor in soul. Grant us wis - dom, Grant us cour - age,
In the fight to set men free. Grant us wis - dom, Grant us cour - age,

For the fac - ing of this hour, For the fac - ing of this hour.
For the liv - ing of these days, For the liv - ing of these days.
Lest we miss Thy king-dom's goal, Lest we miss Thy king - dom's goal.
That we fail not man nor Thee, That we fail not man nor Thee.

GOD OF MY LIFE

words by
Philip Doddridge (1702-1751)

WARD
Traditional Scottish Melody
arr. by Lowell Mason (1792-1872)

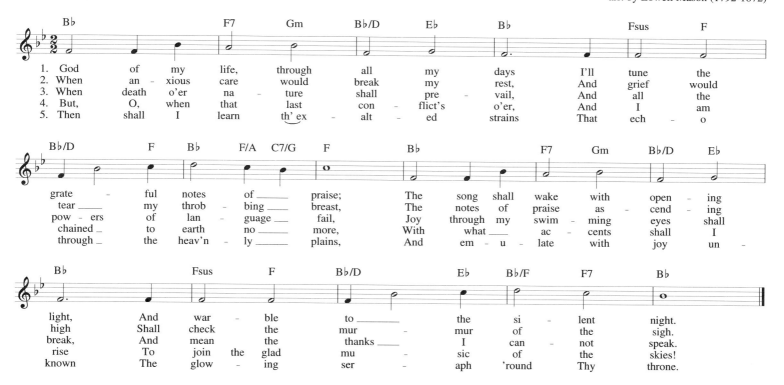

1. God of my life, through all my days I'll tune the
2. When an - xious care would break my rest, And grief would
3. When death o'er na - ture shall pre - vail, And all the
4. But, O, when that last con - flict's o'er, And I am
5. Then shall I learn th' ex - alt - ed strains That ech - o

grate - ful notes of _____ praise; The song shall wake with open - ing
tear _____ my throb - bing _____ breast, The notes of praise as - cend - ing
pow - ers of lan - guage _____ fail, Joy through my swim - ming eyes shall
chained to earth no _____ more, With what _____ ac - cents shall I
through _____ the heav'n - ly plains, And em - u - late with joy un -

light, And war - ble to _____ the si - lent night.
high Shall check the mur - mur of the sigh.
break, And mean the thanks _____ I can - not speak.
rise To join the glad mu - sic of the skies!
known The glow - ing ser - aph 'round Thy throne.

GOD OF OUR FATHERS

words by
Daniel Crane Roberts (1841-1907)

NATIONAL HYMN
music by
George William Warren (1828-1902)

Trumpets, before each stanza

1. God of our fa - thers,
2. Thy love di - vine hath
3. From war's a - larms, from
4. Re - fresh thy peo - ple

whose al - might - y hand leads forth in beau - ty all the star - ry
led us in the past, in this free land by thee our lot is
dead - ly pes - ti - lence, be thy strong arm our ev - er sure de -
on their toil - some way, lead us from night to nev - er - end - ing

band of shin - ing worlds in splen - dor through the skies,
cast; be thou our ru - ler, guard - ian, guide, and stay,
fense; thy true re - li - gion in our hearts in - crease,
day; fill all our lives with love and grace di - vine,

our grate - ful songs be - fore thy throne a - rise.
thy word our law, thy paths our cho - sen way.
thy boun - teous good - ness nour - ish us in peace.
and glo - ry, laud, and praise be ev - er thine.

GOD, OUR FATHER, WE ADORE THEE

BEECHER
music by
John Zundel

words by George W. Frazier (v.1, 2, 4)
and Alfred S. Loizeaux (v.3)

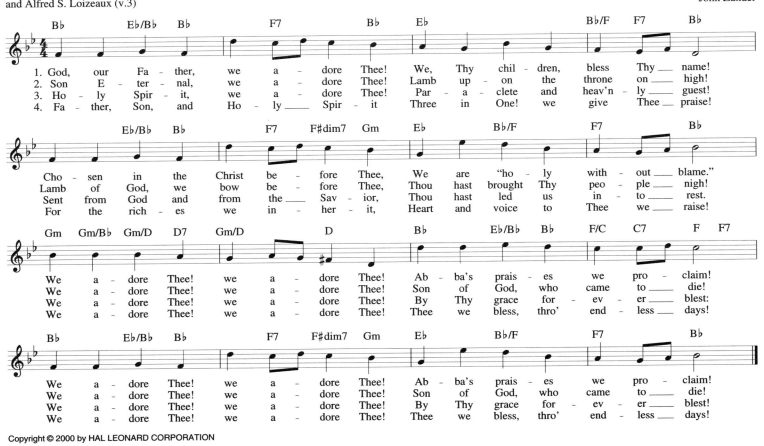

1. God, our Fa - ther, we a - dore Thee! We, Thy chil - dren, bless Thy __ name!
2. Son E - ter - nal, we a - dore Thee! Lamb up - on the throne on __ high!
3. Ho - ly Spir - it, we a - dore Thee! Par - a - clete and heav'n - ly __ guest!
4. Fa - ther, Son, and Ho - ly __ Spir - it Three in One! we give Thee __ praise!

Cho - sen in the Christ be - fore Thee, We are "ho - ly with - out __ blame."
Lamb of God, we bow be - fore Thee, Thou hast brought Thy peo - ple __ nigh!
Sent from God and from the __ Sav - ior, Thou hast led us in - to __ rest.
For the rich - es we in - her - it, Heart and voice to Thee we __ raise!

We a - dore Thee! we a - dore Thee! Ab - ba's prais - es we pro - claim!
We a - dore Thee! we a - dore Thee! Son of God, who came to __ die!
We a - dore Thee! we a - dore Thee! By Thy grace for - ev - er __ blest:
We a - dore Thee! we a - dore Thee! Thee we bless, thro' end - less __ days!

We a - dore Thee! we a - dore Thee! Ab - ba's prais - es we pro - claim!
We a - dore Thee! we a - dore Thee! Son of God, who came to __ die!
We a - dore Thee! we a - dore Thee! By Thy grace for - ev - er __ blest!
We a - dore Thee! we a - dore Thee! Thee we bless, thro' end - less __ days!

GOD SO LOVED THE WORLD

STAINER
music by
John Stainer (1840-1901)

words based on
John 3:16, 17

God so loved the world, __ God so loved the

world, __ that He gave His on - ly be - got - ten Son, that

who - so be - liev - eth, be - liev - eth in Him should not per - ish,

should not per - ish but have ev - er - last - ing life. For God

sent not His Son in - to the world to con - demn the world. God sent not His Son in - to the

To Coda

D.C. al Coda

world to con - demn the world, But that the world through Him might be sav - ed.

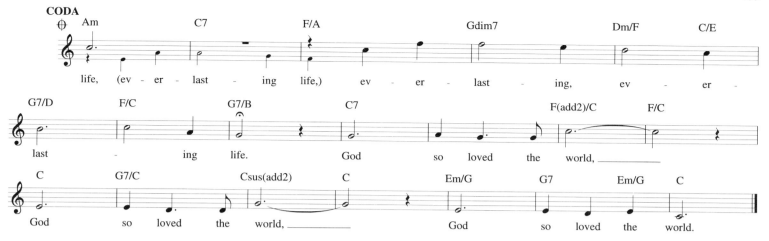

GOD, THAT MADEST EARTH AND HEAVEN

words by Reginald Heber, 1827 (v.1)
and Frederick Lucian Hosmer, 1912 (v.2)

AR HYD Y NOS
Traditional Welsh melody

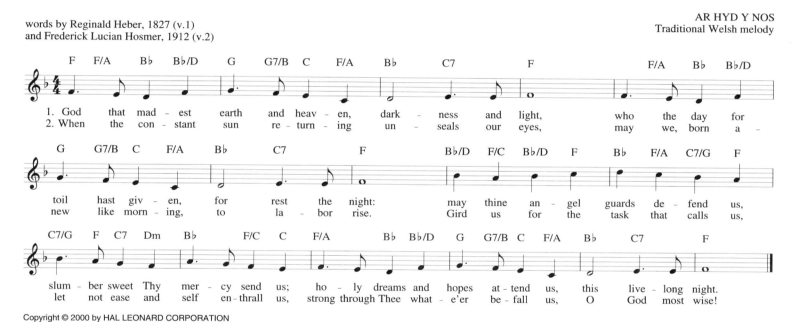

GOD WILL TAKE CARE OF YOU

words by
Civilla D. Martin, 1904

GOD CARES
music by
W. Stillman Martin, 1904

GOD THE OMNIPOTENT!

RUSSIAN HYMN
music by
Alexis T. Lvov, 1833

words by
Henry F. Chorley, 1842
and John Ellerton, 1870

1. God the Om - ni - po - tent! King, who or - dain - est Thun - der Thy clar - ion, the light - ning Thy sword; Show forth Thy pit - y on high _____ where Thou reign - est, Give to us peace in our time, O Lord.
2. God the All - mer - ci - ful! earth hath for - sak - en The ways of bless - ed - ness, slight - ed Thy Word; Bid not Thy wrath in its ter - rors a - wak - en; Give to us peace in our time, O Lord.
3. God the All - right - eous One! man hath de - fied Thee; Yet to e - ter - ni - ty stand - eth Thy Word, False - hood and wrong shall not tar - ry be - side Thee; Give to us peace in our time, O Lord.
4. God thee All - wise! by the fire of Thy Chas - tening, Earth shall to free - dom and truth be re - stored; Through the thick dark - ness Thy king - dom is has - tening; Thou wilt give peace in Thy time, O Lord.
5. So shall Thy chil - dren with thank - ful de - vo - tion, Praise Him who saved them from per - il and sword, Sing - ing in cho - rus from o - cean to o - cean, Peace to the na - tions, and praise to the Lord.

GOOD CHRISTIAN MEN, REJOICE

IN DULCI JUBILO
14th century German melody

14th century Latin text
tr. by John Mason Neale (1818-1866)

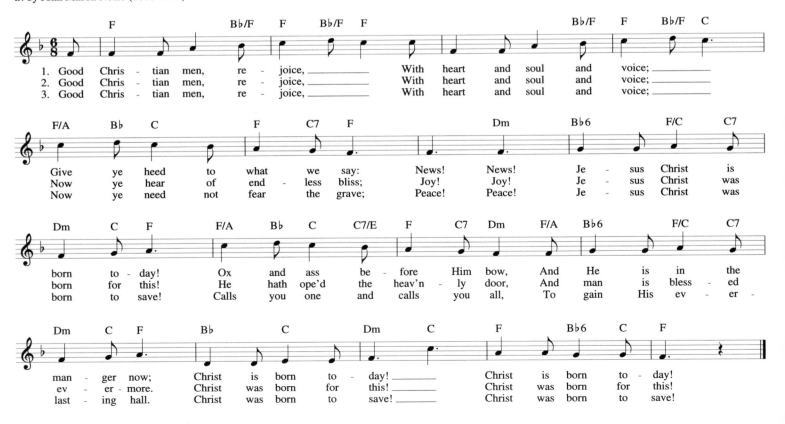

1. Good Chris - tian men, re - joice, _____ With heart and soul and voice; _____ Give ye heed to what we say: News! News! Je - sus Christ is born to - day! Ox and ass be - fore Him bow, And He is in the man - ger now; Christ is born to - day! _____
2. Good Chris - tian men, re - joice, _____ With heart and soul and voice; _____ Now ye hear of end - less bliss; Joy! Joy! Je - sus Christ was born for this! He hath ope'd the heav'n - ly door, And man is bless - ed ev - er - more. Christ was born for this! _____
3. Good Chris - tian men, re - joice, _____ With heart and soul and voice; _____ Now ye need not fear the grave; Peace! Peace! Je - sus Christ was born to save! Calls you one and calls you all, To gain His ev - er - last - ing hall. Christ was born to save! _____

GOD'S WORD IS OUR GREAT HERITAGE

words by
Nikolai F.S. Grundtvig, 1817
tr. by Ole G. Belsheim, 1909

REUTER
music by
Friedrich O. Reuter, 1916

God's Word is our great her-i-tage And shall be ours for-ev-er; To spread its light from age to age Shall be our chief en-deav-or. Through life it guides our way; In death it is our stay. Lord, grant, while worlds en-dure, We keep its teach-ings pure Through-out all gen-er-a-tions.

GRACE GREATER THAN OUR SIN

words by
Daniel B. Towner, 1910

MOODY
music by
Julia H. Johnston, 1910

1. Mar-vel-ous grace of our lov-ing Lord, Grace that ex-ceeds our
2. Sin and de-spair, like the sea-waves cold, Threat-en the soul with
3. Dark is the stain that we can-not hide; What can a-vail to
4. Mar-vel-ous, in-fi-nite, match-less grace, Free-ly be-stowed on

sin and our guilt! Yon-der on Cal-va-ry's mount out-poured,
in-fi-nite loss; Grace that is great-er, yes, grace un-told,
wash it a-way? Look! there is flow-ing a crim-son tide;
all who be-lieve! You that are long-ing to see His face,

There where the blood of the Lamb was spilt.
Points to the ref-uge, the might-y cross.
Whit-er than snow you may be to-day.
Will you this mo-ment His grace re-ceive?

Refrain

Grace grace,
(Mar-vel-ous grace,

God's in-fi-nite grace, Grace that will par-don and cleanse with-in, Grace,
in-fi-nite grace,) (Mar-vel-ous

grace, God's in-fi-nite grace, Grace that is great-er than all our sin!
grace, in-fi-nite grace,)

GRACE! 'TIS A CHARMING SOUND

v. 1, 3 by Philip Doddridge (1702-1751)
v. 2, 4, 5 by Augustus M. Toplady (1740-1778)

SILVER STREET
music by
Ira D. Sankey (1840-1908)

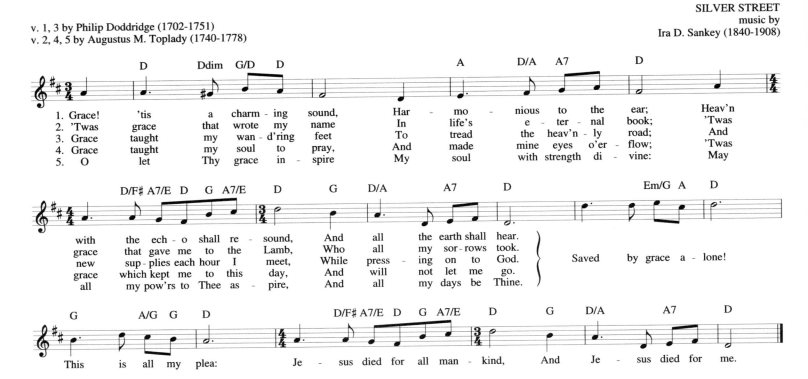

THE GREAT PHYSICIAN

words by
Rev. William Hunter, 1842

music arr. by
Rev. J.H. Stockton (1813-1877)

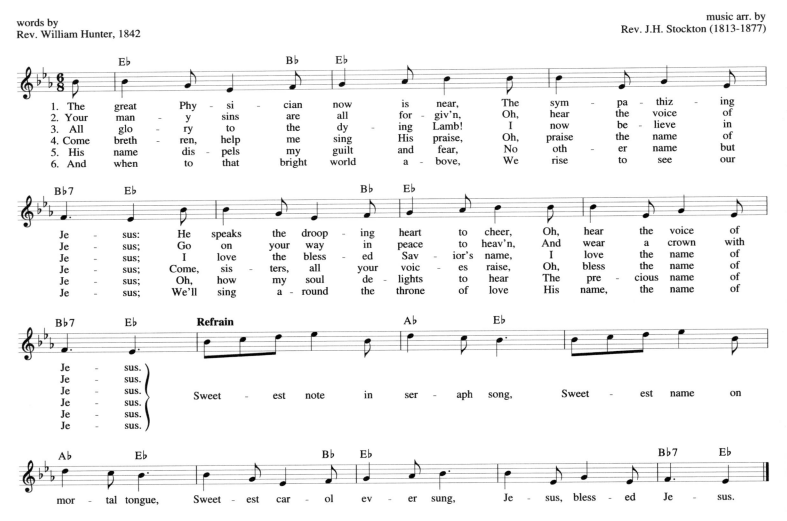

GREAT GOD, WE SING THAT MIGHTY HAND

words by
Philip Doddridge (1702-1751)
from Orton's *Hymns Founded on Various Texts,* 1755

WAREHAM
music by
William Knapp, 1738

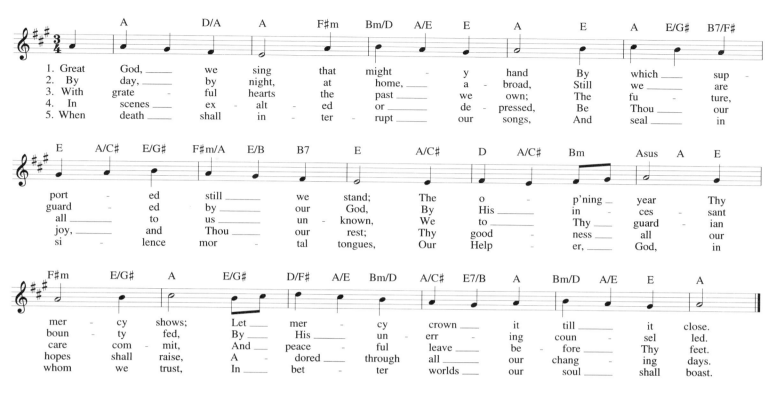

1. Great God, we sing that might - y hand By which sup -
2. By day, by night, at home, a - broad, Still we are
3. With grate - ful hearts the past we own; The fu - ture,
4. In scenes ex - alt - ed or de - pressed, Be Thou our
5. When death shall in - ter - rupt our songs, And seal

port - ed still we stand; The o - p'ning year Thy
guard - ed by our God, By His in - ces - sant
all to us un - known, We to Thy guard - ian
joy, and Thou our rest; Thy good - ness all our
si - lence mor - tal tongues, Our Help - er, God, in

mer - cy shows; Let mer - cy crown it till it close.
boun - ty fed, By His un - err - ing coun - sel led.
care com - mit, And peace - ful leave be - fore Thy feet.
hopes shall raise, A - dored through all our chang - ing days.
whom we trust, In bet - ter worlds our soul shall boast.

GUIDE ME, O THOU GREAT JEHOVAH

words by
William Williams, 1745
v. 1 tr. by Peter Williams, 1771
v. 2,3 tr. by William Williams, 1772

CWM RHONDDA
music by
John Hughes, 1907

1. Guide me, O Thou great Je - ho - vah, Pil - grim through this bar - ren land;
2. O - pen now the crys - tal foun - tain, Whence the heal - ing stream doth flow;
3. When I tread the verge of Jor - dan, Bid my anx - ious fears sub - side;

I am weak, but Thou art might - y; Hold me with Thy pow'r - ful hand;
Let the fire and cloud - y pil - lar Lead me all my jour - ney through;
Death of death, and hell's de - struc - tion, Land me safe on Ca - naan's side;

Bread of heav - en, bread of heav - en, Feed me till I want no
Strong de - liv - 'rer, strong de - liv - 'rer, Be Thou still my strength and
Songs of prais - es, songs of prais - es I will ev - er give to

more, Feed me till I want no more.
shield, Be Thou still my strength and shield.
Thee, I will ev - er give to Thee.

GUIDE ME, O THOU GREAT JEHOVAH

ZION
music by
Thomas Hastings, 1830

words by
W. Williams, 1745

1. Guide me, O Thou great Je - ho - vah, Pil - grim thru this bar - ren
2. O - pen now the crys - tal foun - tain, Whence the heal - ing wa - ters
3. When I tread the verge of Jor - dan, Bid my anx - ious fears sub -

land; I am weak, but Thou art might - y, Hold me
flow; Let the fier - y, the cloud - y pil - lar, Lead me
side; Bear me thru the swell - ing cur - rent, Land me

with Thy pow'r - ful hand; Bread of heav - en, Feed me till I want no
all my jour - ney thru; Strong De - liv - 'rer, Be Thou still my strength and
safe on Ca - naan's side; Songs of prais - es I will ev - er give to

more: Bread of heav - en, Feed me till I want no more.
shield: Strong De - liv - 'rer, Be Thou still my strength and shield.
Thee; Songs of prais - es I will ev - er give to Thee.

GUIDE MY FEET

African-American Spiritual

African-American Spiritual

1. Guide my feet Guide my
2. Hold my hand Hold my
3. Stand by me Stand by
4. I'm Your child I'm Your
5. Search my heart Search my

while I run this race,

feet
hand
me   while I run this race,
child
heart

Guide my feet
Hold my hand
Stand by me   while I run this
I'm Your child
Search my heart

race, For I don't want to run this race in vain!

HAIL, HOLY QUEEN ENTHRONED ABOVE

words from
Salve, Regina, mater misericordia, c. 1080
tr. in *Roman Hymnal*, 1884

SALVE REGINA COELITUM
music from
Choralmelodien zum Heiligen Gasänge, 1808

HAIL THE DAY THAT SEES HIM RISE

words by
Charles Wesley, 1739

LLANFAIR
music by
Robert Williams, 1817

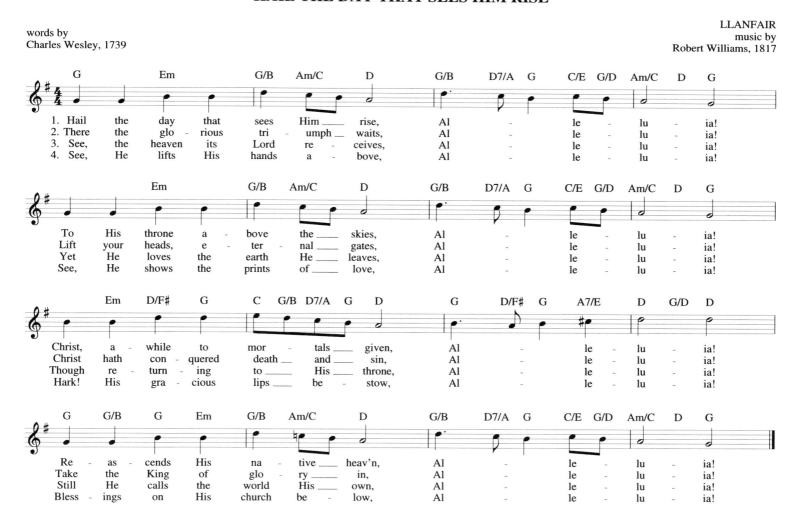

HAIL THE DAY THAT SEES HIM RISE

ORIENTIS PARTIBUS

words by
Charles Wesley (1707-1788)

music by
Pierre de Corbeille (d. 1221)

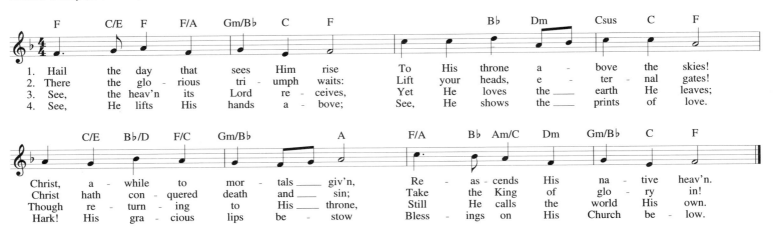

1. Hail the day that sees Him rise To His throne a - bove the skies!
2. There the glo - rious tri - umph waits: Lift your heads, e - ter - nal gates!
3. See, the heav'n its Lord re - ceives, Yet He loves the earth He leaves;
4. See, He lifts His hands a - bove; See, He shows the prints of love.

Christ, a - while to mor - tals giv'n, Re - as - cends His na - tive heav'n.
Christ hath con - quered death and sin; Take the King of glo - ry in!
Though re - turn - ing to His throne, Still He calls the world His own.
Hark! His gra - cious lips be - stow Bless - ings on His Church be - low.

HAIL, THOU ONCE DESPISED JESUS

IN BABILONE

words by John Bakewell (1721-1819)
and Martin Madan (1726-1790)

music from
Oude en Nieuwe Hollantse Boerenlities en Contradanseu, 1710

1. Hail, Thou once de - spis - ed Je - sus! Hail, Thou Gal - i -
2. Pas - chal Lamb, by God ap - point - ed, All our sins on
3. Je - sus, hail, en - throned in glo - ry, There for - ev - er
4. Wor - ship, hon - or, pow'r, and bless - ing Thou art wor - thy

le - an King! Thou didst suf - fer to re - lease us;
Thee were laid; By al - might - y love a - noint - ed,
to a - bide! All the heav'n - ly hosts a - dore Thee,
to re - ceive Loud - est prais - es with - out ceas - ing,

Thou didst free sal - va - tion bring. Hail Thou u - ni -
Thou hast full a - tone - ment made. Ev - 'ry sin may
Seat - ed at Thy Fa - ther's side. Hail Thou u - ni -
Meet it is for us to give. Help, ye bright an -

ver - sal Sav - ior, Who hast borne our sin and shame! By whose mer - its
be for - giv - en Through the vir - tue of Thy blood; O - pen is the
Thou art plead - ing; There Thou dost our place pre - pare, Ev - er for us
gel - ic spir - its, Bring your sweet - est, no - blest lays; Help to sing our

we find fa - vor, Life is giv - en through Thy name.
gate of heav - en, Peace is made 'twixt man and God.
in - ter - ced - ing, Till in glo - ry we ap - pear.
Sav - ior's mer - its, Help to chant Im - man - uel's praise!

HAIL, THOU ONCE DESPISED JESUS

words by John Bakewell (1721-1819)
and Martin Madan (1726-1790)

AUTUMN
music by
Francois H. Barthélémon (1741-1808)

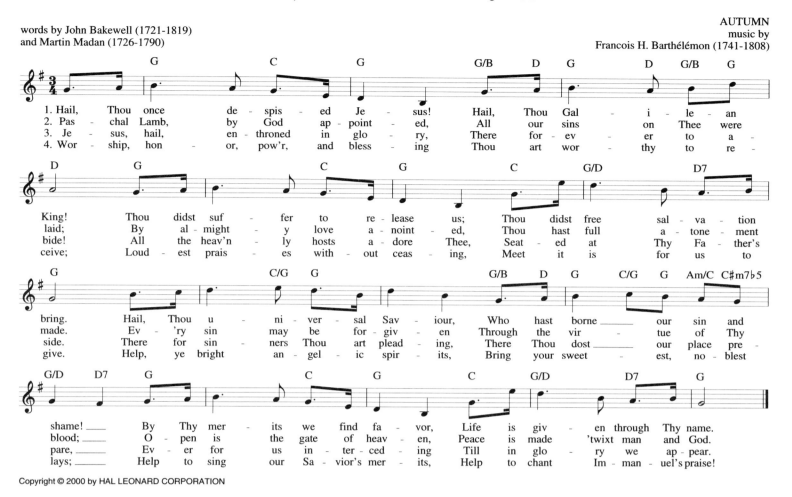

1. Hail, Thou once de - spis - ed Je - sus! Hail, Thou Gal - i - le - an
2. Pas - chal Lamb, by God ap - point - ed, All our sins on Thee were
3. Je - sus, hail, en - throned in glo - ry, There for ev - er to a -
4. Wor - ship, hon - or, pow'r, and bless - ing Thou art wor - thy to re -

King! Thou didst suf - fer to re - lease us; Thou didst free sal - va - tion
laid; By al - might - y love a - noint - ed, Thou hast full a - tone - ment
bide! All the heav'n - ly hosts a - dore Thee, Seat - ed at Thy Fa - ther's
ceive; Loud - est prais - es with - out ceas - ing, Meet it is for us to

bring. Hail, Thou u - ni - ver - sal Sav - iour, Who hast borne our sin and
made. Ev - 'ry sin may be for - giv - en, Through the vir - tue of Thy
side. There for sin - ners Thou art plead - ing, There Thou dost our place pre -
give. Help, ye bright an - gel - ic spir - its, Bring your sweet - est, no - blest

shame! By Thy mer - its we find fa - vor, Life is giv - en through Thy name.
blood; O - pen is the gate of heav - en, Peace is made 'twixt man and God.
pare, Ev - er for us in - ter - ced - ing Till in glo - ry we ap - pear.
lays; Help to sing our Sa - vior's mer - its, Help to chant Im - man - uel's praise!

HAIL TO THE LORD'S ANOINTED

words by
James Montgomery, 1821

ELLACOMBE
music from
Gesangbuch der Herzogl, Württemburg, 1784

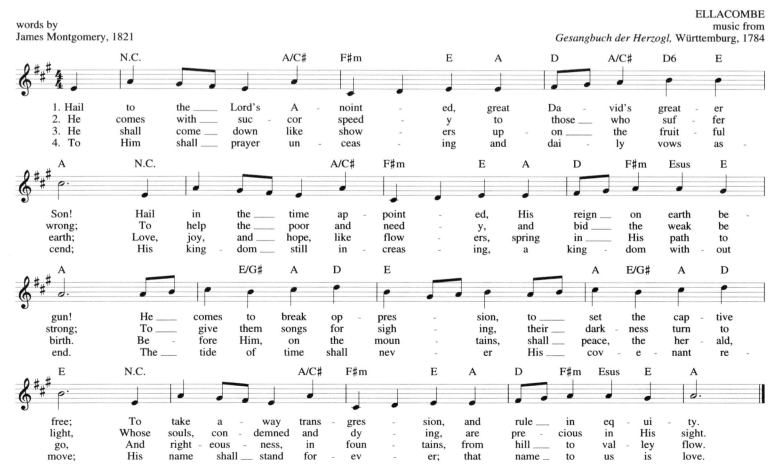

1. Hail to the Lord's A - noint - ed, great Da - vid's great - er
2. He comes with suc - cor speed - y to those who suf - fer
3. He shall come down like show - ers up - on the fruit - ful
4. To Him shall prayer un - ceas - ing and dai - ly vows as -

Son! Hail in the time ap - point - ed, His reign on earth be -
wrong; To help the poor and need - y, and bid the weak be
earth; Love, joy, and hope, like flow - ers, spring in His path to
cend; His king - dom still in - creas - ing, a king - dom with - out

gun! He comes to break op - pres - sion, to set the cap - tive
strong; To give them songs for sigh - ing, their dark - ness turn to
birth. Be - fore Him, on the moun - tains, shall peace, the her - ald,
end. The tide of time shall nev - er His cov - e - nant re -

free; To take a - way trans - gres - sion, and rule in eq - ui - ty.
light, Whose souls, con - demned and dy - ing, are pre - cious in His sight.
go, And right - eous - ness, in foun - tains, from hill to val - ley flow.
move; His name shall stand for ev - er; that name to us is love.

HAIL TO THE LORD'S ANOINTED

ES FLOG EIN KLEINS WALDVÖGELEIN
German folk song

words by
James Montgomery (1771-1854)
para. of Psalm 72

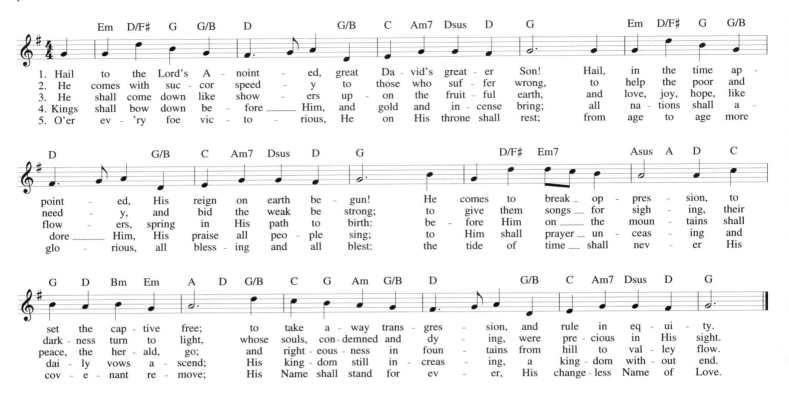

1. Hail to the Lord's A - noint - ed, great Da - vid's great - er Son! Hail, in the time ap -
2. He comes with suc - cor speed - y to those who suf - fer wrong, to help the poor and
3. He shall come down like show - ers up - on the fruit - ful earth, and love, joy, hope, like
4. Kings shall bow down be - fore Him, and gold and in - cense bring; all na - tions shall a -
5. O'er ev - 'ry foe vic - to - rious, He on His throne shall rest; from age to age more

point - ed, His reign on earth be - gun! He comes to break op - pres - sion, to
need - y, and bid the weak be strong; to give them songs for sigh - ing, their
flow - ers, spring in His path to birth: be - fore Him on the moun - tains shall
dore Him, His praise all peo - ple sing; to Him shall prayer un - ceas - ing and
glo - rious, all bless - ing and all blest: the tide of time shall nev - er His

set the cap - tive free; to take a - way trans - gres - sion, and rule in eq - ui - ty.
dark - ness turn to light, whose souls, con - demned and dy - ing, were pre - cious in His sight.
peace, the her - ald, go; and right - eous - ness in foun - tains from hill to val - ley flow.
dai - ly vows a - scend; His king - dom still in - creas - ing, a king - dom with - out end.
cov - e - nant re - move; His Name shall stand for ev - er, His change - less Name of Love.

HALLELUJAH! AMEN!

words by
Henrietta E. Blair, 19th century

Composer unknown
arr. by William J. Kirkpatrick (1838-1921)

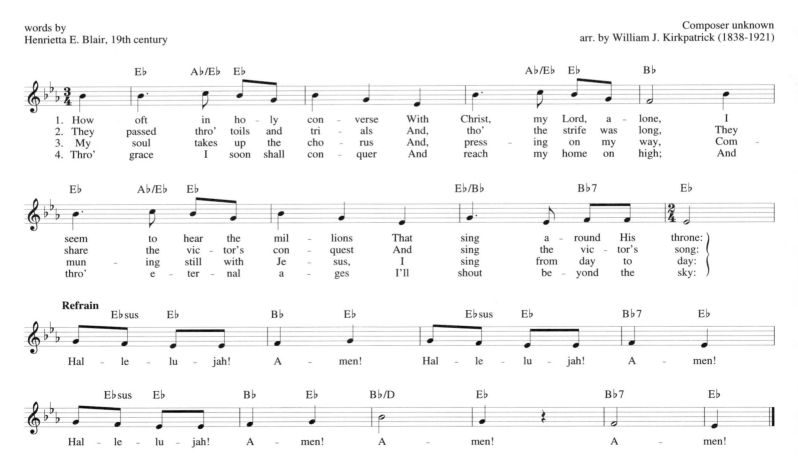

1. How oft in ho - ly con - verse With Christ, my Lord, a - lone, I
2. They passed thro' toils and tri - als And, tho' the strife was long, They
3. My soul takes up the cho - rus And, press - ing on my way, Com -
4. Thro' grace I soon shall con - quer And reach my home on high; And

seem to hear the mil - lions That sing a - round His throne:
share the vic - tor's con - quest And sing the vic - tor's song:
mun - ing still with Je - sus, I sing from day to day:
thro' e - ter - nal a - ges I'll shout be - yond the sky:

Refrain

Hal - le - lu - jah! A - men! Hal - le - lu - jah! A - men!

Hal - le - lu - jah! A - men! A - men! A - men!

HALLELUJAH, PRAISE JEHOVAH

words by
William J. Kirkpatrick, 1893

AINOS
music by
William J. Kirkpatrick, 1893

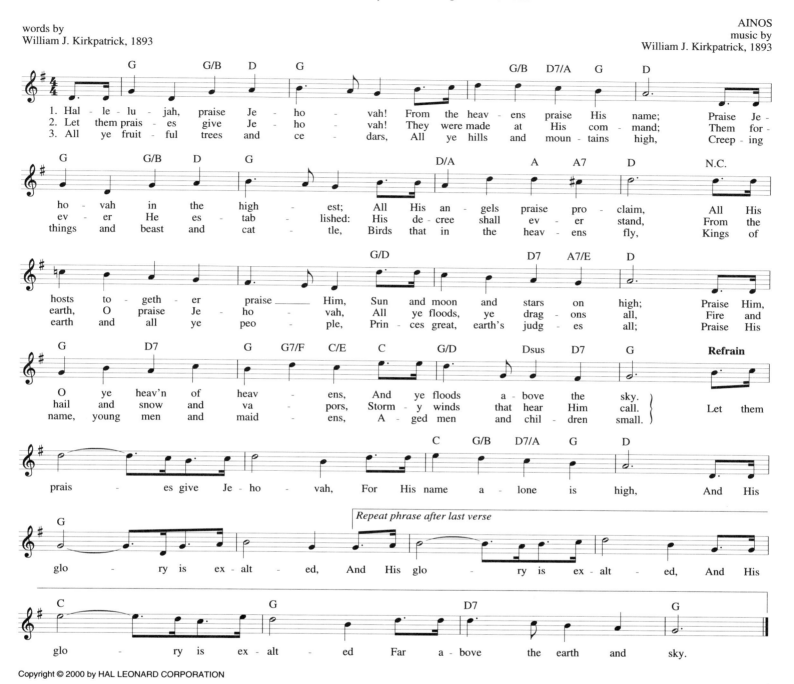

HAPPY THE HOME WHEN GOD IS THERE

words by
Henry Ware, Jr. (1794-1843)

ST. AGNES
music by
John B. Dykes (1823-1876)

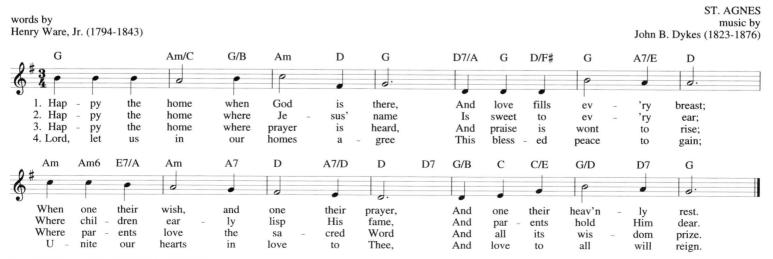

HALLELUJAH, WHAT A SAVIOR!

MAN OF SORROWS

words by
Philip P. Bliss (1838-1876)

music by
Philip P. Bliss (1838-1876)

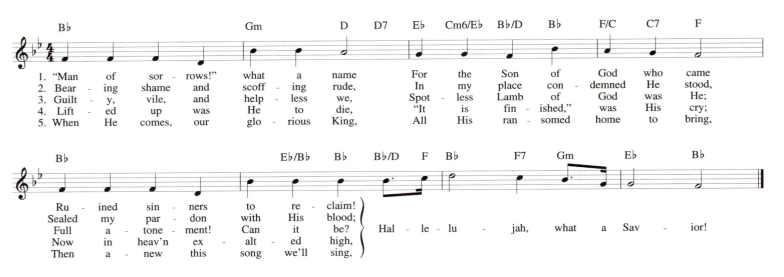

1. "Man of sor - rows!" what a name For the Son of God who came
2. Bear - ing shame and scoff - ing rude, In my place con - demned He stood;
3. Guilt - y, vile, and help - less we, Spot - less Lamb of God was He;
4. Lift - ed up was He to die, "It is fin - ished," was His cry;
5. When He comes, our glo - rious King, All His ran - somed home to bring,

Ru - ined sin - ners to re - claim!
Sealed my par - don with His blood;
Full a - tone - ment! Can it be?   } Hal - le - lu - jah, what a Sav - ior!
Now in heav'n ex - alt - ed high,
Then a - new this song we'll sing,

HARK! THE HERALD ANGELS SING

MENDELSSOHN

words by
Charles Wesley, 1739
alt. by George Whitefield, 1753

music by
Felix Mendelssohn, 1840
arr. by William H. Cummings, 1856

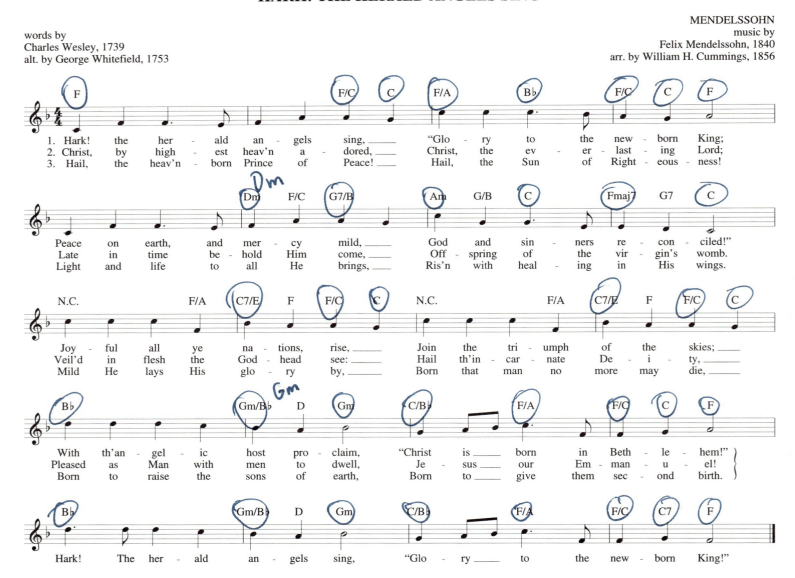

1. Hark! the her - ald an - gels sing, "Glo - ry to the new - born King;
2. Christ, by high - est heav'n a - dored, Christ, the ev - er - last - ing Lord;
3. Hail, the heav'n - born Prince of Peace! Hail, the Sun of Right - eous - ness!

Peace on earth, and mer - cy mild, God and sin - ners re - con - ciled!"
Late in time be - hold Him come, Off - spring of the vir - gin's womb.
Light and life to all He brings, Ris'n with heal - ing in His wings.

Joy - ful all ye na - tions, rise, Join the tri - umph of the skies;
Veil'd in flesh the God - head see: Hail th'in - car - nate De - i - ty,
Mild He lays His glo - ry by, Born that man no more may die,

With th'an - gel - ic host pro - claim, "Christ is born in Beth - le - hem!" }
Pleased as Man with men to dwell, Je - sus our Em - man - u - el!   }
Born to raise the sons of earth, Born to give them sec - ond birth.   }

Hark! The her - ald an - gels sing, "Glo - ry to the new - born King!"

HARK! TEN THOUSAND HARPS

words by
Thomas Kelly (1769-1854)

HARWELL
music by
Lowell Mason (1792-1872)

HARK! THE SOUND OF HOLY VOICES

words by
Christopher Wordsworth (1807-1885)

MOULTRIE
music by
Gerard Francis Cobb (1838-1904)

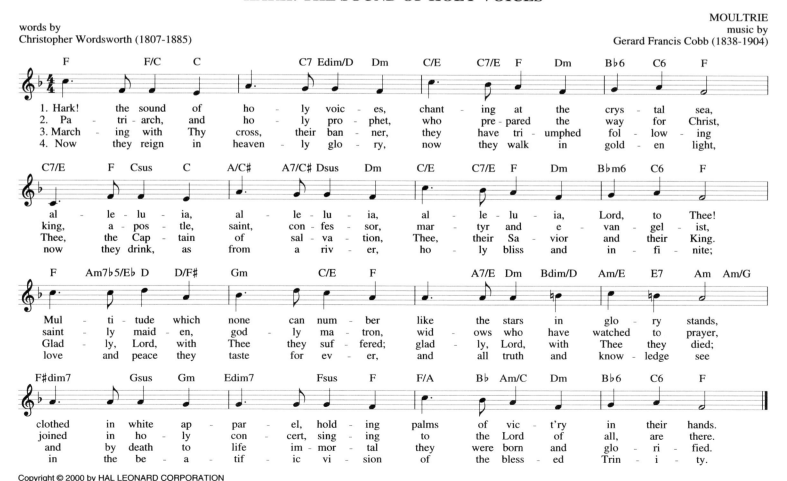

HARK! THE VOICE OF JESUS CRYING

ELLESDIE

words by
Daniel March, 1868 (v.1,2,4)
Author unknown (v.3)

music by
Wolfgang Amadeus Mozart (1756-1791)
arr. by Hubert P. Main (1839-1925)

1. Hark! the voice of Je-sus cry-ing, "Who will go and work to-day?
2. If you can-not speak like an-gels, If you can-not preach like Paul,
3. If you can-not be a watch-man, Stand-ing high on Zi-on's walls,
4. Let none hear you i-dly say-ing, "There is noth-ing I can do,"

Fields are white, and har-vests wait-ing, Who will bear the sheaves a-way?"
You can tell the love of Je-sus, You can say He died for all.
Point-ing out the path to heav-en, Of-f'ring life and peace to all,
While the souls of men are dy-ing And the Mas-ter calls for you.

Loud and long the Mas-ter call-eth, Rich re-ward He of-fers thee;
If you can-not rouse the wick-ed With the Judg-ment's dread a-larms,
With your prayers and with your boun-ties You can do what God de-mands;
Take the task He gives you glad-ly, Let His work your pleas-ure be;

Who will an-swer, glad-ly say-ing, "Here am I, send me, send me"?
You can lead the lit-tle chil-dren To the Sav-ior's wait-ing arms.
You can be like faith-ful Aar-on, Hold-ing up the proph-et's hands.
An-swer quick-ly when He call-eth, "Here am I, send me, send me!"

HARK! THE VOICE OF JESUS CRYING

GALILEAN

words by
Daniel March, 1868 (v.1,2,4)
Author unknown (v.3)

music by
Joseph Barnby, 1883

1. Hark! the voice of Je-sus cry-ing, "Who will go and work to-day?
2. If you can-not speak like an-gels, If you can-not preach like Paul,
3. If you can-not be a watch-man, Stand-ing high on Zi-on's wall,
4. Let none hear you i-dly say-ing, "There is noth-ing I can do,"

Fields are white and har-vests wait-ing, Who will bear the sheaves a-way?"
You can tell the love of Je-sus, You can say He died for all.
Point-ing out the path to heav-en, Of-f'ring life and peace to all,
While the souls of men are dy-ing And the Mas-ter calls for you.

Loud and long the Mas-ter call-eth, Rich re-ward He of-fers thee;
If you can-not rouse the wick-ed With the Judg-ment's dread a-larms,
With your prayers and with your boun-ties You can do what God de-mands;
Take the task He gives you glad-ly, Let His work your pleas-ure be;

Who will an-swer, glad-ly say-ing, "Here am I, send me, send me"?
You can lead the lit-tle chil-dren To the Sav-ior's wait-ing arms.
You can be like faith-ful Aar-on, Hold-ing up the proph-et's hands.
An-swer quick-ly when He call-eth, "Here am I, send me, send me!"

HAVE THINE OWN WAY, LORD

words by
Adelaide A. Pollard, 1902

POLLARD
music by
George C. Stebbins, 1907

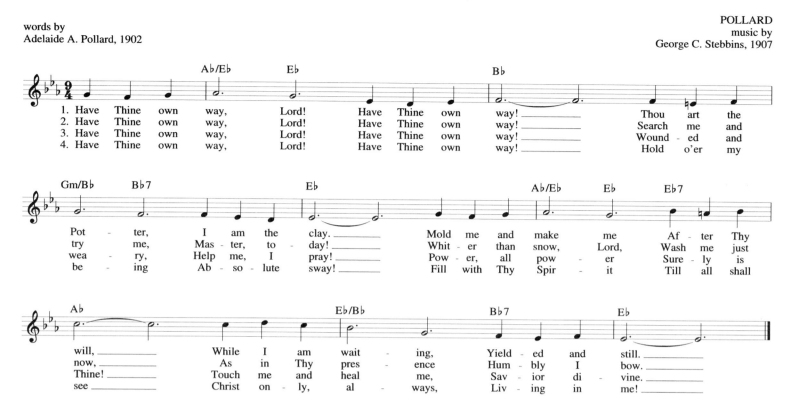

1. Have Thine own way, Lord! Have Thine own way! Thou art the Pot-ter, I am the clay. Mold me and make me Af-ter Thy will, While I am wait-ing, Yield-ed and still.
2. Have Thine own way, Lord! Have Thine own way! Search me and try me, Mas-ter, to-day! Whit-er than snow, Lord, Wash me just now, As in Thy pres-ence Hum-bly I bow.
3. Have Thine own way, Lord! Have Thine own way! Wound-ed and wea-ry, Help me, I pray! Pow-er, all pow-er Sure-ly is Thine! Touch me and heal me, Sav-ior di-vine!
4. Have Thine own way, Lord! Have Thine own way! Hold o'er my be-ing Ab-so-lute sway! Fill with Thy Spir-it Till all shall see Christ on-ly, al-ways, Liv-ing in me!

HAVE YOU ANY ROOM FOR JESUS

Author unknown
adapted by
Daniel W. Whittle (1840-1901)

ANY ROOM
music by
C.C. Williams, 19th century

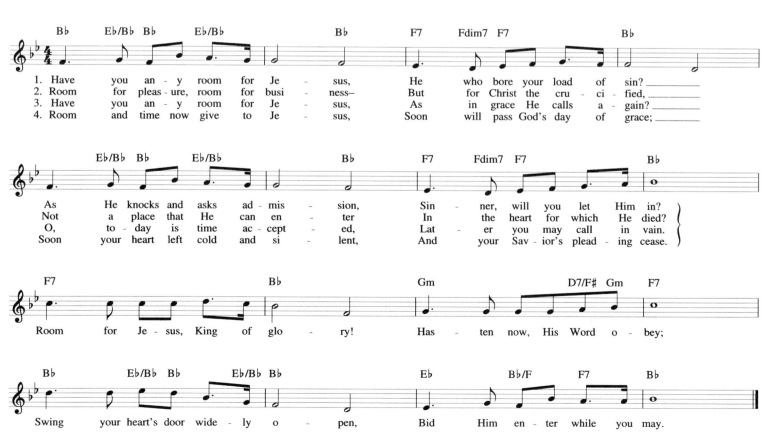

1. Have you an-y room for Je-sus, He who bore your load of sin? As He knocks and asks ad-mis-sion, Sin-ner, will you let Him in?
2. Room for pleas-ure, room for busi-ness– But for Christ the cru-ci-fied, Not a place that He can en-ter In the heart for which He died?
3. Have you an-y room for Je-sus, As in grace He calls a-gain? O, to-day is time ac-cept-ed, Lat-er you may call in vain.
4. Room and time now give to Je-sus, Soon will pass God's day of grace; Soon your heart left cold and si-lent, And your Sav-ior's plead-ing cease.

Room for Je-sus, King of glo-ry! Has-ten now, His Word o-bey; Swing your heart's door wide-ly o-pen, Bid Him en-ter while you may.

THE HAVEN OF REST

HAVEN OF REST
music by
George D. Moore, 1890

words by
Henry L. Gilmour, 1890

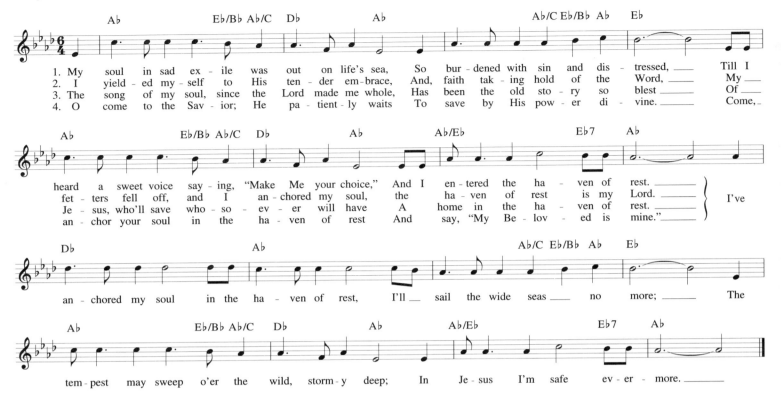

1. My soul in sad ex-ile was out on life's sea, So bur-dened with sin and dis-tressed, ___ Till I
2. I yield-ed my-self to His ten-der em-brace, And, faith tak-ing hold of the Word, ___ My
3. The song of my soul, since the Lord made me whole, Has been the old sto-ry so blest ___ Of
4. O come to the Sav-ior; He pa-tient-ly waits To save by His pow-er di-vine. ___ Come,

heard a sweet voice say-ing, "Make Me your choice," And I en-tered the ha-ven of rest. ___
fet-ters fell off, and I an-chored my soul, the ha-ven of rest is my Lord. ___
Je-sus, who'll save who-so-ev-er will have A home in the ha-ven of rest. ___
an-chor your soul in the ha-ven of rest And say, "My Be-lov-ed is mine." ___

I've

an-chored my soul in the ha-ven of rest, I'll ___ sail the wide seas ___ no more; ___ The

tem-pest may sweep o'er the wild, storm-y deep; In Je-sus I'm safe ev-er-more. ___

HE AROSE

Traditional Spiritual

Traditional Spiritual

1. They cru-ci-fied my Sav-ior and nailed Him to the cross, They cru-ci-fied my Sav-ior and
2. And Jo-seph begged His bod-y and laid it in the tomb, And Jo-seph begged His bod-y and
3. Sister Mar-y, she came run-ning, a look-ing for my Lord, Sister Mar-y she came run-ning, a
4. An an-gel came from heav-en and rolled the stone a-way, An an-gel came from heav-en and

nailed Him to the cross, cross, ___ And the Lord will bear my spir-it home.
laid it in the tomb, tomb, ___ And the Lord will bear my spir-it home.
look-ing for my Lord, Lord, ___ And the Lord will bear my spir-it home.
rolled the stone a-way, way, ___ And the Lord will bear my spir-it home.

He

Refrain

'rose, He 'rose, He 'rose ___ from the dead, He 'rose, He 'rose, He

'rose ___ from the dead, He dead, ___ And the Lord shall bear my spir-it home.

HAVE MERCY, LORD, ON ME

words by Nahum Tate (1652-1715)
and Nicholas Brady (1659-1726)

SOUTHWELL
music from
Damon's *Psalmes,* 1579

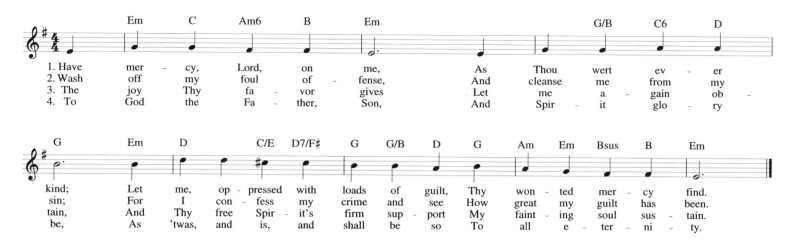

1. Have mer - cy, Lord, on me, As Thou wert ev - er
2. Wash off my foul of - fense, And cleanse me from my
3. The joy Thy fa - vor gives, Let me a - gain ob -
4. To God the Fa - ther, Son, And Spir - it glo - ry

kind; Let me, op - pressed with loads of guilt, Thy won - ted mer - cy find.
sin; For I con - fess my crime and see How great my guilt has been.
tain, And Thy free Spir - it's firm sup - port My faint - ing soul sus - tain.
be, As 'twas, and is, and shall be so To all e - ter - ni - ty.

HE BROUGHT ME OUT

words by Henry J. Zelley, 1898 (verses)
and Henry L. Gilmour, 1898 (refrain)

music by
Henry L. Gilmour, 1898

1. My heart was dis - tressed 'neath Je - ho - vah's dread frown, And low in the pit where my
2. He placed me up - on the strong rock by His side. My steps were es - tab - lished, and
3. He gave me a song: 'twas a new song of praise. By day and by night its sweet
4. I'll sing of His won - der - ful mer - cy to me; I'll praise Him till all men His

sins dragged me down, I cried to the Lord from the deep mir - y clay, Who
here I'll a - bide. No dan - ger of fall - ing while here I re - main, But
notes I will raise. My heart's o - ver - flow - ing; I'm hap - py and free. I'll
good - ness shall see. I'll sing of sal - va - tion at home and a - broad, Till

ten - der - ly bro't me out to gol - den day.
stand by His grace un - til the crown I gain.
praise my Re - deem - er, who has res - cued me.
man - y shall hear the truth and trust in God.

Refrain

He bro't me out of the

mir - y clay; He set my feet on the Rock to stay. _____

He puts a song in my soul to - day— A song of praise, hal - le - lu - jah!

HE HIDETH MY SOUL

KIRKPATRICK

words by
Fanny J. Crosby (1820-1915)

music by
William J. Kirkpatrick (1838-1921)

1. A won - der - ful Sav - ior is Je - sus my Lord, A
2. A won - der - ful Sav - ior is Je - sus my Lord, He
3. With num - ber - less bless - ings each mo - ment He crowns; And,
4. When clothed in His bright - ness, trans - port - ed I rise To

won - der - ful Sav - ior to me; He hid - eth my soul in the
tak - eth my bur - den a - way. He hold - eth me up, and I
filled with His full - ness di - vine, I sing in my rap - ture, "O
meet Him in clouds of the sky; His per - fect sal - va - tion, His

cleft of the rock, Where riv - ers of pleas - ure I see. He
shall not be moved; He giv - eth me strength as my day. He
glo - ry to God For such a Re - deem - er as mine!" He
won - der - ful love I'll shout with the mil - lions on high! He

hid - eth my soul in the cleft of the rock That shad - ows a dry, thirst - y

land; He hid - eth my life in the depths of His love And

cov - ers me there with His hand, And cov - ers me there with His hand.

HE IS ABLE TO DELIVER THEE

DELIVERANCE

words by
William A. Ogden, 1887

music by
William A. Ogden, 1887

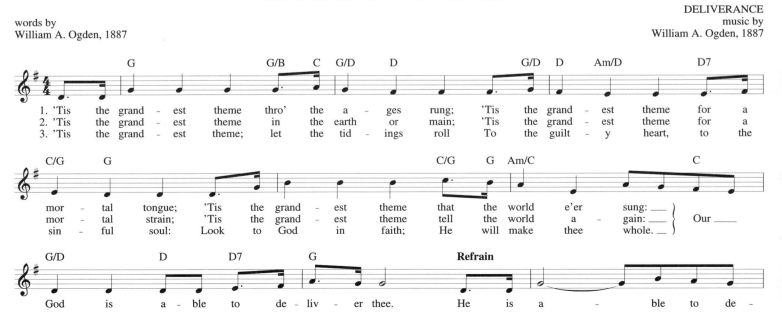

1. 'Tis the grand - est theme thro' the a - ges rung; 'Tis the grand - est theme for a
2. 'Tis the grand - est theme in the earth or main; 'Tis the grand - est theme for a
3. 'Tis the grand - est theme; let the tid - ings roll To the guilt - y heart, to the

mor - tal tongue; 'Tis the grand - est theme that the world e'er sung: Our
mor - tal strain; 'Tis the grand - est theme tell the world a - gain: Our
sin - ful soul: Look to God in faith; He will make thee whole.

God is a - ble to de - liv - er thee. He is a - ble to de -

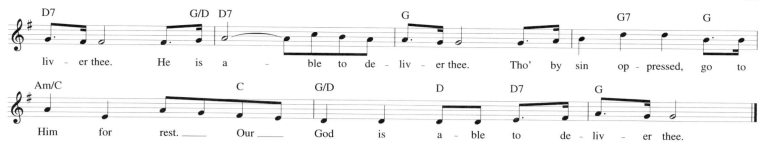

liv- er thee. He is a - ble to de - liv- er thee. Tho' by sin op - pressed, go to

Him for rest.___ Our ___ God is a - ble to de - liv - er thee.

HE IS ARISEN! GLORIOUS WORD!

words by
B.K. Boye (1791-1853)
tr. by G.A.T. Rygh (1860-1942)

WIE SCHÖN LEUCHTET
music by
P. Nicolai (1556-1608)

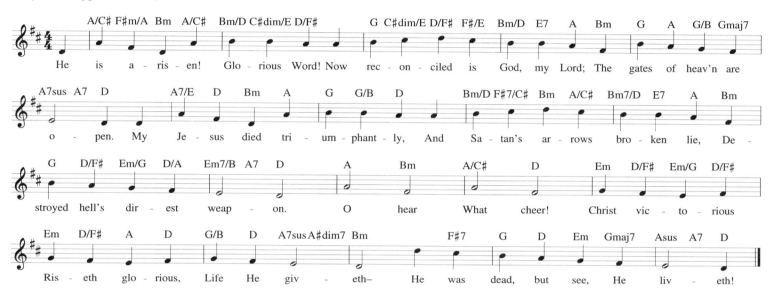

He is a - ris- en! Glo - rious Word! Now rec - on - ciled is God, my Lord; The gates of heav'n are

o - pen. My Je- sus died tri - um- phant- ly, And Sa - tan's ar - rows bro - ken lie, De -

stroyed hell's dir - est weap - on. O hear What cheer! Christ vic - to - rious

Ris - eth glo - rious, Life He giv - eth– He was dead, but see, He liv - eth!

HE IS KING OF KINGS

African-American Spiritual

HE IS KING
African-American Spiritual

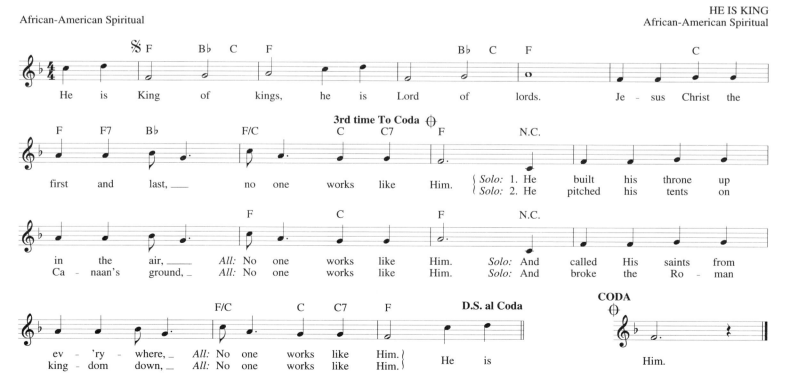

He is King of kings, he is Lord of lords. Je - sus Christ the

first and last, ___ no one works like Him.
Solo: 1. He built his throne up
Solo: 2. He pitched his tents on

in the air, ___ All: No one works like Him. Solo: And called His saints from
Ca - naan's ground, _ All: No one works like Him. Solo: And broke the Ro - man

ev - 'ry - where, _ All: No one works like Him.} He is
king - dom down, _ All: No one works like Him.}

CODA
Him.

3rd time To Coda

D.S. al Coda

HE IS COMING AGAIN

DIAPASON
music from
The Diapason, 1860

Traditional words

O, ___ Je - sus is ___ com - ing, He is com - ing a - gain. He is com - ing in ___

glo - ry, But we do not know when. Com - ing, com - ing, com - ing a - gain.

*may be sung as a round

HE IS SO PRECIOUS TO ME

PRECIOUS TO ME
music by
Charles H. Gabriel, 1902

words by
Charles H. Gabriel, 1902

1. So pre - cious is Je - sus, my Sav - ior, my King; His
2. He stood at my heart's door 'mid sun - shine and rain, And
3. I stand on the moun - tain of bless - ing at last No
4. I praise Him be - cause He ap - point - ed a place Where

praise all the day long with rap - ture I sing. To Him in my
pa - tient - ly wait - ed with an en - trance to gain. What shame that so
cloud in the heav - ens a shad - ow to cast. His smile is up -
some - day, thro' faith in His won - der - ful grace, I know I shall

weak - ness for strength I can cling, For He is so pre - cious to
long He en - treat - ed in vain, For He is so pre - cious to
on me; the val - ley is past, For He is so pre - cious to
see Him, shall look on His face, For He is so pre - cious to

Refrain

me. ___
me. ___
me. ___ For He is so pre - cious to me; ___ For
me. ___

He is so pre - cious to me. ___ 'Tis heav - en be - low, my Re -

deem - er to know, For He is so pre - cious to me. ___

HE IS RISEN, HE IS RISEN

words by
Mrs. Cecil Frances Alexander (1818-1895)

UNSER HERRSCHER
music by
Joachim Neander (1650-1680)

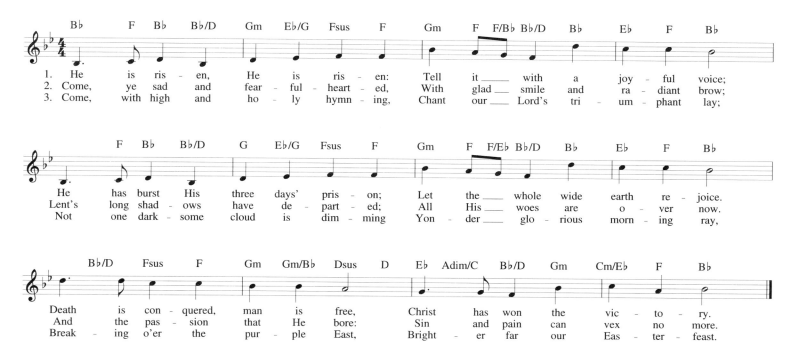

1. He is ris - en, He is ris - en: Tell it ___ with a joy - ful voice;
2. Come, ye sad and fear - ful - heart - ed, With glad ___ smile and ra - diant brow;
3. Come, with high and ho - ly hymn - ing, Chant our ___ Lord's tri - um - phant lay;

He has burst His three days' pris - on; Let the ___ whole wide earth re - joice.
Lent's long shad - ows have de - part - ed; All His ___ woes are o - ver now.
Not one dark - some cloud is dim - ming Yon - der ___ glo - rious morn - ing ray,

Death is con - quered, man is free, Christ has won the vic - to - ry.
And the pas - sion that He bore; Sin and pain can vex no more.
Break - ing o'er the pur - ple East, Bright - er far our Eas - ter - feast.

HE KEEPS ME SINGING

words by
Luther B. Bridgers, 1910

SWEETEST NAME
music by
Luther B. Bridgers, 1910

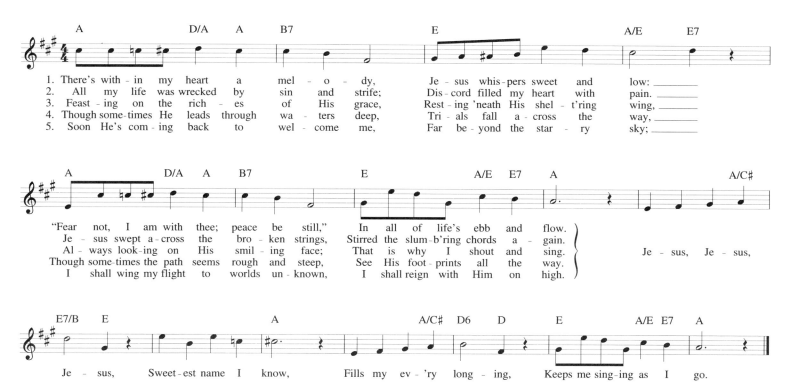

1. There's with - in my heart a mel - o - dy, Je - sus whis-pers sweet and low: ___
2. All my life was wrecked by sin and strife; Dis - cord filled my heart with pain. ___
3. Feast - ing on the rich - es of His grace, Rest - ing 'neath His shel - t'ring wing, ___
4. Though some-times He leads through wa - ters deep, Tri - als fall a - cross the way, ___
5. Soon He's com - ing back to wel - come me, Far be - yond the star - ry sky; ___

"Fear not, I am with thee; peace be still," In all of life's ebb and flow.
Je - sus swept a - cross the bro - ken strings, Stirred the slum-b'ring chords a - gain.
Al - ways look - ing on His smil - ing face, That is why I shout and sing.
Though some-times the path seems rough and steep, See His foot - prints all the way.
I shall wing my flight to worlds un - known, I shall reign with Him on high.

Je - sus, Je - sus,

Je - sus, Sweet-est name I know, Fills my ev - 'ry long - ing, Keeps me sing-ing as I go.

HE LEADETH ME

words by
Joseph H. Gilmore (1834-1918)

music by
William B. Bradbury (1816-1868)

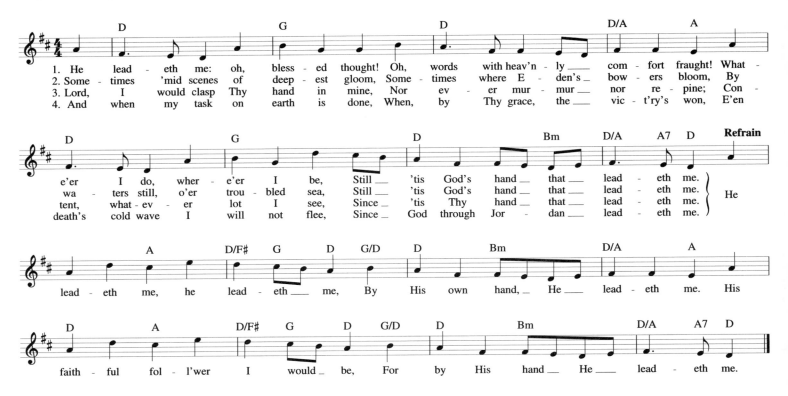

1. He lead - eth me: oh, bless - ed thought! Oh, words with heav'n - ly ___ com - fort fraught! What
2. Some - times 'mid scenes of deep - est gloom, Some - times where E - den's bow - ers bloom, By
3. Lord, I would clasp Thy hand in mine, Nor ev - er mur - mur ___ nor re - pine; Con -
4. And when my task on earth is done, When, by Thy grace, the ___ vic - t'ry's won, E'en

e'er I do, wher - e'er I be, Still ___ 'tis God's hand ___ that ___ lead - eth me.
wa - ters still, o'er trou - bled sea, Still ___ 'tis God's hand ___ that ___ lead - eth me.
tent, what - ev - er lot I see, Since ___ 'tis Thy hand ___ that ___ lead - eth me.
death's cold wave I will not flee, Since ___ God through Jor - dan ___ lead - eth me.

Refrain

He lead - eth me, he lead - eth ___ me, By His own hand, ___ He ___ lead - eth me. His

faith - ful fol - l'wer I would ___ be, For by His hand ___ He ___ lead - eth me.

HE LIFTED ME

words by
Charles H. Gabriel, 1905

music by
Charles H. Gabriel, 1905

1. In lov - ing kind - ness Je - sus came My soul in mer - cy to re - claim, And
2. He called me long be - fore I heard, Be - fore my sin - ful heart was stirred, But
3. His brow was pierced with man - y a thorn, His hands by cru - el nails were torn, When
4. Now on a high - er plane I dwell, And with my soul I know 'tis well; Yet

from the depths of sin and shame Thro' grace He lift - ed me. ___
when I took Him at His word, For - giv'n He lift - ed me. ___
from my guilt and grief, for - lorn, In love He lift - ed me. ___
how or why, I can - not tell, He should have lift - ed me. ___

Refrain

From

sink - ing sand He lift - ed me, With ten - der hand He lift - ed me, From

shades of night to plains of light, O praise His name, He lift - ed me!

HE LOVES ME

words by Isaac Watts, 1707 (verses)
Author of refrain unknown

Composer unknown

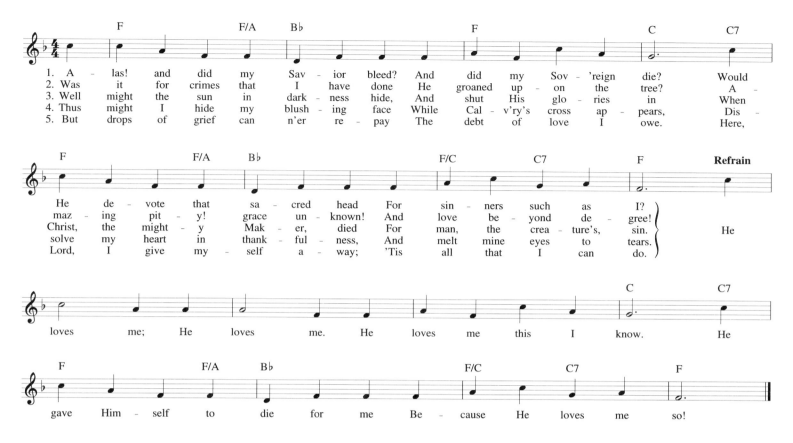

1. A - las! and did my Sav - ior bleed? And did my Sov - 'reign die? Would
2. Was it for crimes that I have done He groaned up - on the tree? A
3. Well might the sun in dark - ness hide, And shut His glo - ries in When
4. Thus might I hide my blush - ing face While Cal - v'ry's cross ap - pears, Dis -
5. But drops of grief can n'er re - pay The debt of love I owe. Here,

He de - vote that sa - cred head For sin - ners such as I?
maz - ing pit - y! grace un - known! And love be - yond de - gree!
Christ, the might - y Mak - er, died For man, the crea - ture's, sin.
solve my heart in thank - ful - ness, And melt mine eyes to tears.
Lord, I give my - self a - way; 'Tis all that I can do.

He

Refrain

loves me; He loves me. He loves me this I know. He

gave Him - self to die for me Be - cause He loves me so!

Copyright © 2000 by HAL LEONARD CORPORATION

HE NEVER SAID A MUMBALIN' WORD

African-American Spiritual

African-American Spiritual

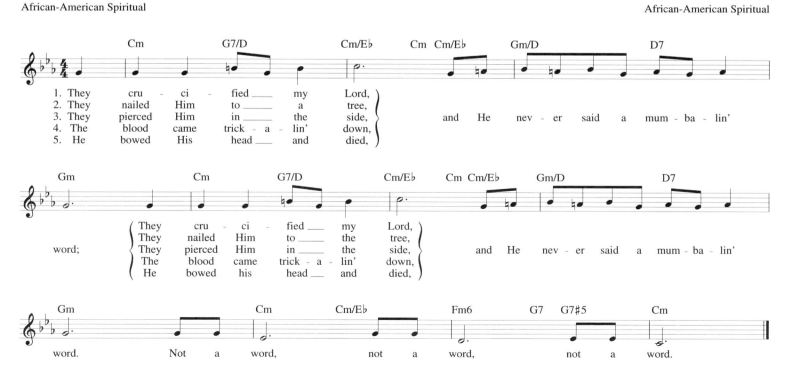

1. They cru - ci - fied ___ my Lord,
2. They nailed Him to ___ a tree,
3. They pierced Him in ___ the side,
4. The blood came trick - a - lin' down,
5. He bowed His head ___ and died,

and He nev - er said a mum - ba - lin'

word;

They cru - ci - fied ___ my Lord,
They nailed Him to ___ the tree,
They pierced Him in ___ the side,
The blood came trick - a - lin' down,
He bowed his head ___ and died,

and He nev - er said a mum - ba - lin'

word. Not a word, not a word, not a word.

Copyright © 2000 by HAL LEONARD CORPORATION

HE PAID A DEBT

American Folk Text

American Folk Melody

1. He paid a debt He did not owe, ___ I owed a debt I could not pay.
2. He paid that debt at Cal-va-ry, ___ He cleansed my soul and set me free,
3. One day He's com-ing back for me ___ To live with Him e-ter-nal-ly,

___ I need-ed some-one to wash my sins a-way. ___
___ I'm glad that Je-sus did all my sins e-rase; ___
___ Won't it be glo-ry to see Him on that day! ___

___ And now I sing a brand new song: ___ }
___ I now can sing a brand new song: ___ } "A-maz-ing Grace." All day
___ I then will sing a brand new song: ___ }

long. Christ Je-sus paid the debt that I could nev-er pay. ___

HE RANSOMED ME

words by
Julia H. Johnson, 1916

music by
J.W. Henderson, 1916

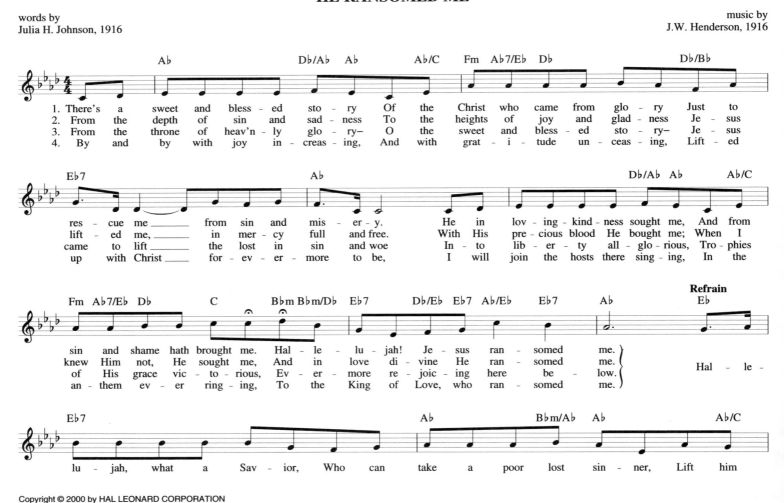

1. There's a sweet and bless-ed sto-ry Of the Christ who came from glo-ry Just to
2. From the depth of sin and sad-ness To the heights of joy and glad-ness Je-sus
3. From the throne of heav'n-ly glo-ry— O the sweet and bless-ed sto-ry— Je-sus
4. By and by with joy in-creas-ing, And with grat-i-tude un-ceas-ing, Lift-ed

res-cue me ___ from sin and mis-er-y. He in lov-ing-kind-ness sought me, And from
lift-ed me, ___ in mer-cy full and free. With His pre-cious blood He bought me; When I
came to lift ___ the lost in sin and woe. In-to lib-er-ty all-glo-rious, Tro-phies
up with Christ ___ for-ev-er-more to be, I will join the hosts there sing-ing, In the

sin and shame hath brought me. Hal-le-lu-jah! Je-sus ran-somed me. }
knew Him not, He sought me, And in love di-vine He ran-somed me. } Hal-le-
of His grace vic-to-rious, Ev-er-more re-joic-ing here be-low. }

lu-jah, what a Sav-ior, Who can take a poor lost sin-ner, Lift him

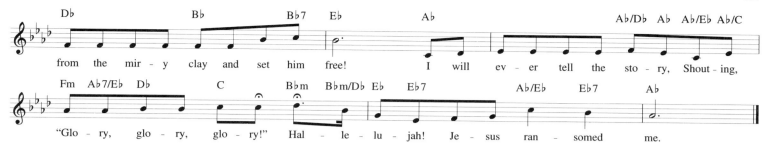

from the mir-y clay and set him free! I will ev-er tell the sto-ry, Shout-ing,

"Glo-ry, glo-ry, glo-ry!" Hal-le-lu-jah! Je-sus ran-somed me.

HE ROLLED THE SEA AWAY

words by
Henry J. Zelley, 1896

GILMOUR
music by
Henry L. Gilmour, 1896

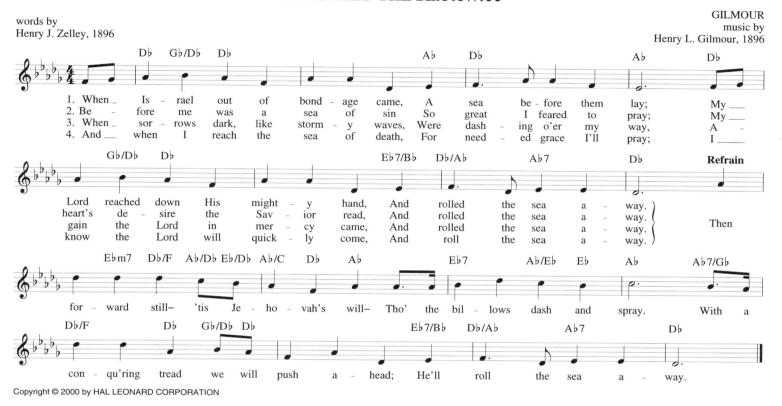

1. When Is-rael out of bond-age came, A sea be-fore them lay; My
2. Be-fore me was a sea of sin So great I feared to pray; My
3. When sor-rows dark, like storm-y waves, Were dash-ing o'er my way, A-
4. And when I reach the sea of death, For need-ed grace I'll pray; I

Lord reached down His might-y hand, And rolled the sea a-way.
heart's de-sire His the Sav-ior read, And rolled the sea a-way.
gain the Lord in mer-cy came, And rolled the sea a-way.
know the Lord will quick-ly come, And roll the sea a-way.

Refrain

Then

for-ward still—'tis Je-ho-vah's will—Tho' the bil-lows dash and spray. With a

con-qu'ring tread we will push a-head; He'll roll the sea a-way.

HE'S A WONDERFUL SAVIOR TO ME

words by
Virgil P. Brock, 1918

WONDERFUL SAVIOR
music by
Blanche Kerr Brock, 1918

1. I was lost in sin but Je-sus res-cued me,
2. He's a Friend so true, so pa-tient and so kind,
3. Dear-er grows the love of Je-sus day by day,

He's a won-der-ful Sav-ior to

me;
I was bound by fear but Je-sus set me free,
Ev-'ry-thing I need in Him I al-ways find,
Sweet-er is His grace while press-ing on my way,

He's a won-der-ful Sav-ior to

me. For He's a won-der-ful Sav-ior to me, He's a won-der-ful Sav-ior to

me; I was lost in sin, but Je-sus took me in, He's a won-der-ful Sav-ior to me.

HE THE PEARLY GATES WILL OPEN

PEARLY GATES

words by
Fredrick A. Blom
tr. by Nathaniel Carlson

music by
Elsie Ahlwén

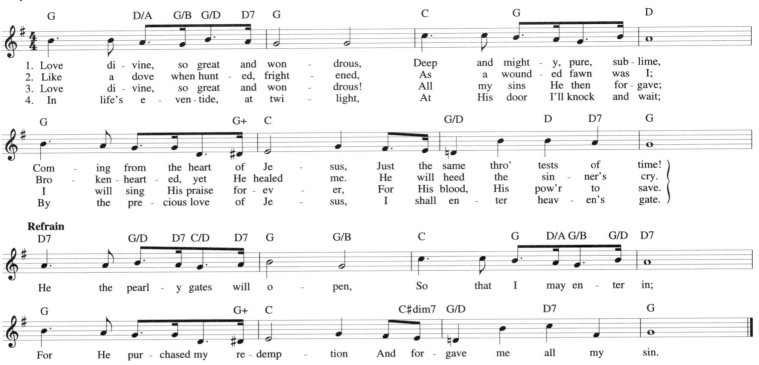

1. Love di - vine, so great and won - drous, Deep and might - y, pure, sub - lime,
2. Like a dove when hunt - ed, fright - ened, As a wound - ed fawn was I;
3. Love di - vine, so great and won - drous! All my sins He then for - gave;
4. In life's e - ven - tide, at twi - light, At His door I'll knock and wait;

Com - ing from the heart of Je - sus, Just the same thro' tests of time!
Bro - ken - heart - ed, yet He healed me. He will heed the sin - ner's cry.
I will sing His praise for - ev - er, For His blood, His pow'r to save.
By the pre - cious love of Je - sus, I shall en - ter heav - en's gate.

Refrain

He the pearl - y gates will o - pen, So that I may en - ter in;

For He pur - chased my re - demp - tion And for - gave me all my sin.

HE TOOK MY SINS AWAY

words by
Margaret J. Harris, 1903

music by
Margaret J. Harris, 1903

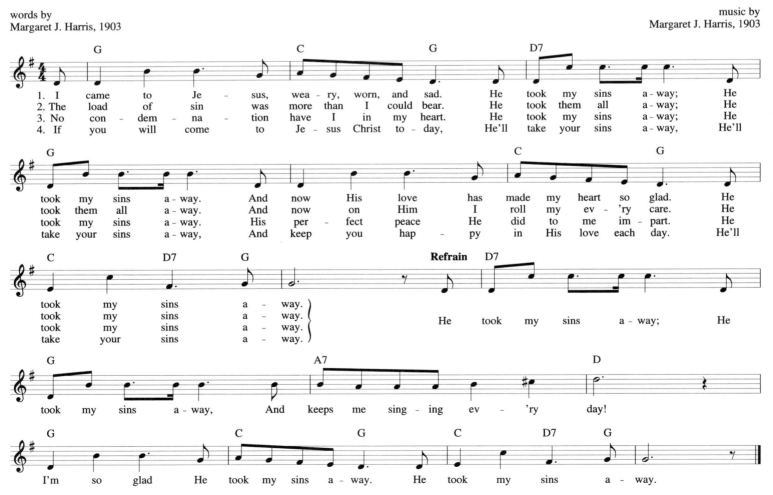

1. I came to Je - sus, wea - ry, worn, and sad. He took my sins a - way; He
2. The load of sin was more than I could bear. He took them all a - way; He
3. No con - dem - na - tion have I in my heart. He took my sins a - way; He
4. If you will come to Je - sus Christ to - day, He'll take your sins a - way, He'll

took my sins a - way. And now His love has made my heart so glad. He
took them all a - way. And now on Him I roll my ev - 'ry care. He
took my sins a - way. His per - fect peace He did to me im - part. He
take your sins a - way, And keep you hap - py in His love each day. He'll

took my sins a - way. }
took my sins a - way. }
took my sins a - way. }
take your sins a - way. }

Refrain

He took my sins a - way; He

took my sins a - way, And keeps me sing - ing ev - 'ry day!

I'm so glad He took my sins a - way. He took my sins a - way.

HE'S EVERYTHING TO ME

words by
Kate Byron, 1907

music by
Hampton H. Sewell, 1907

1. In sin I once had wan-dered, All wea-ry, sad, and lone,____ Till Je-sus thro' His mer-cy A-dopt-ed me His own.____ E'er since I learned to trust Him, His grace doth make me free,____ And now I feel His par-don. He's ev-'ry-thing to me.____
2. In sin no more I'll wan-der; He's Pi-lot, Friend, and Guide.____ He brings me joy and sing-ing; His Spir-it doth a-bide.____ A bless-ed, lov-ing Sav-ior, The Lamb of Cal-va-ry! He pur-chased my re-demp-tion. He's ev-'ry-thing to me.____
3. No long-er will I stray from His ten-der, lov-ing care;____ Like Him to be my pur-pose, my aim, my con-stant prayer.____ And when He bids me wel-come Thro'-out e-ter-ni-ty,____ I'll praise His name for-ev-er. He's ev-'ry-thing to me.____

He's ev-'ry-thing to me;____ From sin He sets me free____ His peace and love my por-tion____ thro' all e-ter-ni-ty!____ He's ev-'ry-thing to me,____ More than I dreamed could be.____ O praise His name for-ev-er! He's ev-'ry-thing to me.____

THE HEAD THAT ONCE WAS CROWNED WITH THORNS

ST. MAGNUS

words by
Thomas Kelly (1769-1855)

music by
Jeremiah Clarke (c. 1669-1707)

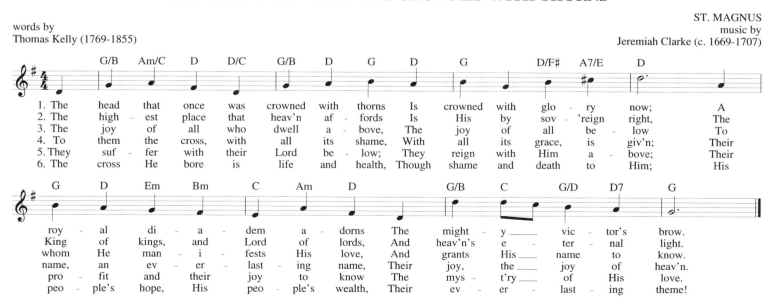

1. The head that once was crowned with thorns Is crowned with glo-ry now; A roy-al di-a-dem a-dorns The might-y vic-tor's brow.
2. The high-est place that heav'n af-fords Is His by sov-'reign right, The King of kings, and Lord of lords, And heav'n's e-ter-nal light.
3. The joy of all who dwell a-bove, The joy of all be-low To whom He man-i-fests His love, And grants His name to know.
4. To them the cross, with all its shame, With all its grace, is giv'n; Their name, an ev-er-last-ing name, Their joy, the joy of heav'n.
5. They suf-fer with their Lord be-low; They reign with Him a-bove; Their pro-fit and their joy to know The mys-t'ry of His love.
6. The cross He bore is life and health, Though shame and death to Him; His peo-ple's hope, His peo-ple's wealth, Their ev-er-last-ing theme!

HE'S GOT THE WHOLE WORLD IN HIS HANDS

WHOLE WORLD
Traditional Spiritual

Traditional Spiritual

He's got the whole world _ is His hands, _ He's got the whole wide world _ in His hands, _ He's got the

whole world _ in His hands, _ He's got the whole world in His hands.

1. He's got the
2. He's got
3. He's got

lit - tle ti - ny ba - by in His hands, _ He's got the lit - tle ti - ny ba - by
you and me, _ broth - er, in His hands, _ He's got you and me, _ sis - ter,
ev - 'ry - bod - y here _ in His hands, _ He's got ev - 'ry - bod - y here _

in His hands, _ He's got the lit - tle ti - ny ba - by in His hands, _
in His hands, _ He's got you and me, _ broth - er, in His hands, _ He's got the
in His hands, _ He's got ev - 'ry - bod - y here _ in His hands, _

1, 2
whole world in His hands. He's got the hands.
3
He's got the

CODA
hands.

D.S. al Coda

Copyright © 2000 by HAL LEONARD CORPORATION

HEAR WHAT GOD THE LORD HATH SPOKEN

CRUCIFER
music by
Henry Smart (1813-1879)

words by
William Cowper (1731-1800)

1. Hear what God the Lord hath spo - ken: O my peo - ple, faith and _ few, Com - fort -
2. There, like streams that feed the gar - den, Pleas - ures with - out end shall _ flow; For the
3. Ye no more your suns de - scend - ing, Wan - ing moons no more shall _ see; But, your

less, af - flict - ed, bro - ken, Fair a - bodes I build for you; Scenes of
Lord, your faith re - ward - ing, All His boun - ty shall be - stow. Still in
griefs for - ev - er end - ing, Find e - ter - nal noon in me: God shall

heart - felt trib - u - la - tion Shall no more per - plex your ways; You shall
un - dis - turbed pos - ses - sion, Peace and right - eous - ness shall reign; Nev - er
rise and, shin - ing o'er you, Change to day the gloom of night; He, the

name your walls "Sal - va - tion," And your gates shall all be "Praise."
shall you feel op - pres - sion, Hear the voice of war a - gain.
Lord, shall be your glo - ry, God your ev - er - last - ing light.

Copyright © 2000 by HAL LEONARD CORPORATION

HEAR OUR PRAYER, O LORD

words based on
Psalm 143:1

WHELPTON
music by
George Whelpton

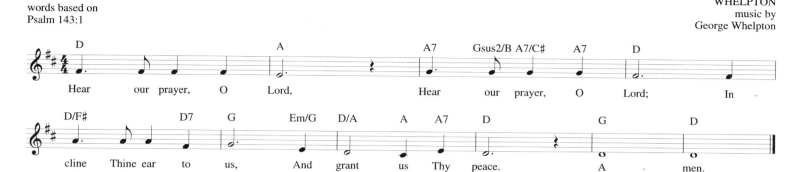

Hear our prayer, O Lord, Hear our prayer, O Lord; In-cline Thine ear to us, And grant us Thy peace. A - men.

HEAVEN

Traditional words

REWARD
Traditional music

1. A robe of white, and pure de - light, With love and beau - ty ev - 'ry - where; A
2. E - tern - al days, un - end - ing praise, The Sav - ior's smile, His words, "well done!" There
3. The bat - tle done, the vic - t'ry won, And heav - en's bliss e - nough re - ward; My

crown of gold and joys un - told Are mine when I get there.
is no night for God is light, No need of moon or sun.
voice I'll raise in end - less praise To Je - sus Christ my Lord.

HEAVENLY SUNLIGHT

words by
H.J. Zelley, 1899

SUNLIGHT
music by
G.H. Cook, 1899

1. Walk - ing in sun - light all of my jour - ney; O - ver the moun - tains, thru the deep
2. Shad - ows a - round me, shad - ows a - bove me, Nev - er con - ceal my Sav - ior and
3. In the bright sun - light, ev - er re - joic - ing, Press - ing my way to man - sions a -

vale; Je - sus has said, "I'll nev - er for - sake thee," Prom - ise di - vine that nev - er can
Guide; He is the light, in Him is no dark - ness, Ev - er I'm walk - ing close to His
bove; Sing - ing His prais - es, glad - ly I'm walk - ing, Walk - ing in sun - light, sun - light of

Refrain

fail.
side. }
love. }

Heav - en - ly sun - light, heav - en - ly sun - light, Flood - ing my soul with glo - ry di -

vine; ___ Hal - le - lu - jah! I am re - joic - ing, Sing - ing His prais - es, Je - sus is mine.

THE HEAVENS DECLARE THY GLORY, LORD

UXBRIDGE

words by
Isaac Watts, 1719
based on Psalm 19

music by
Lowell Mason, 1830

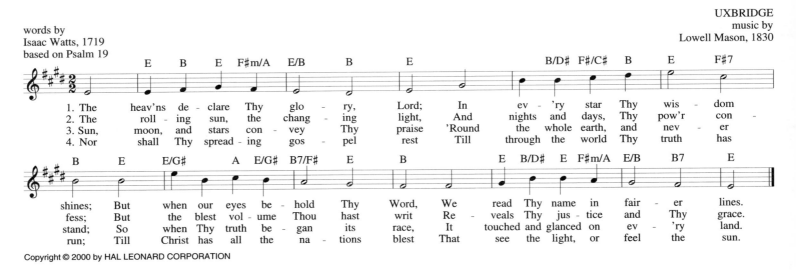

1. The heav'ns de-clare Thy glo-ry, Lord; In ev-'ry star Thy wis-dom
2. The roll-ing sun, the chang-ing light, And nights and days, Thy pow'r con-
3. Sun, moon, and stars con-vey Thy praise 'Round the whole earth, and nev-er
4. Nor shall Thy spread-ing gos-pel rest Till through the world Thy truth has

shines; But when our eyes be-hold Thy Word, We read Thy name in fair-er lines.
fess; But the blest vol-ume Thou hast writ Re-veals Thy jus-tice and Thy grace.
stand; So when Thy truth be-gan its race, It touched and glanced on ev-'ry land.
run; Till Christ has all the na-tions blest That see the light, or feel the sun.

HERALDS OF CHRIST

NATIONAL HYMN

words by
Laura S. Copenhaver, 1915

music by
George W. Warren, 1894

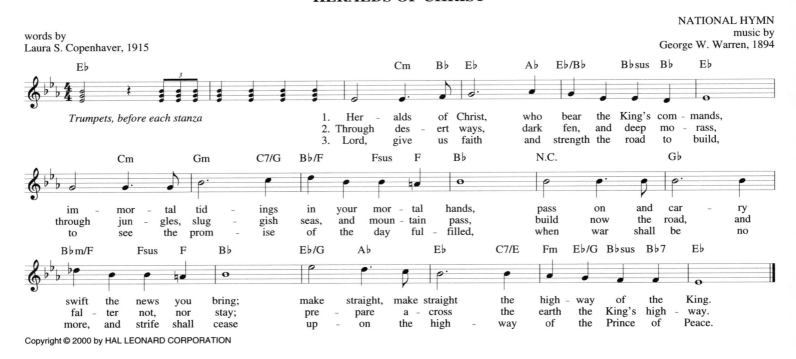

Trumpets, before each stanza

1. Her-alds of Christ, who bear the King's com-mands,
2. Through des-ert ways, dark fen, and deep mo-rass,
3. Lord, give us faith and strength the road to build,

im-mor-tal tid-ings in your mor-tal hands, pass on and car-ry
through jun-gles, slug-gish seas, and moun-tain pass, build now the road, and
to see the prom-ise of the day ful-filled, when war shall be no

swift the news you bring; make straight, make straight the high-way of the King.
fal-ter not, nor stay; pre-pare a-cross the earth the King's high-way.
more, and strife shall cease up-on the high-way of the Prince of Peace.

HERE AT THY TABLE, LORD

BREAD OF LIFE

words by
May P. Hoyt, 19th century

music by
William F. Sherwin, 1877

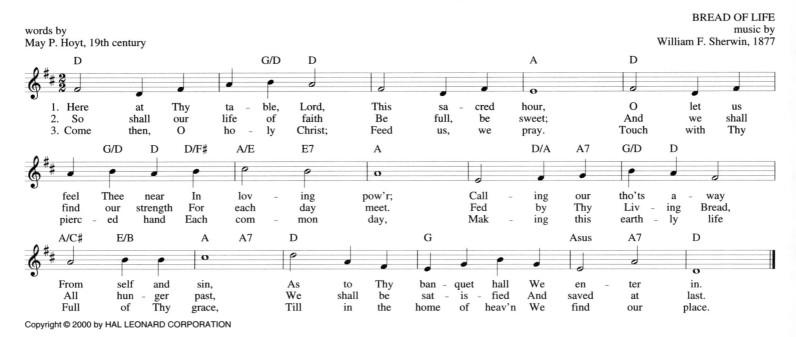

1. Here at Thy ta-ble, Lord, This sa-cred hour, O let us
2. So shall our life of faith Be full, be sweet; And we shall
3. Come then, O ho-ly Christ; Feed us, we pray. Touch with Thy

feel Thee near In lov-ing pow'r; Call-ing our tho'ts a-way
find our strength For each day meet. Fed by Thy Liv-ing Bread,
pierc-ed hand Each com-mon day, Mak-ing this earth-ly life

From self and sin, As to Thy ban-quet hall We en-ter in.
All hun-ger past, We shall be sat-is-fied And saved at last.
Full of Thy grace, Till in the home of heav'n We find our place.

HERE, O MY LORD, I SEE THEE FACE TO FACE

words by
Horatius Bonar (1808-1889)

FARLEY CASTLE
music attr. to
Henry Lawes (1596-1662)

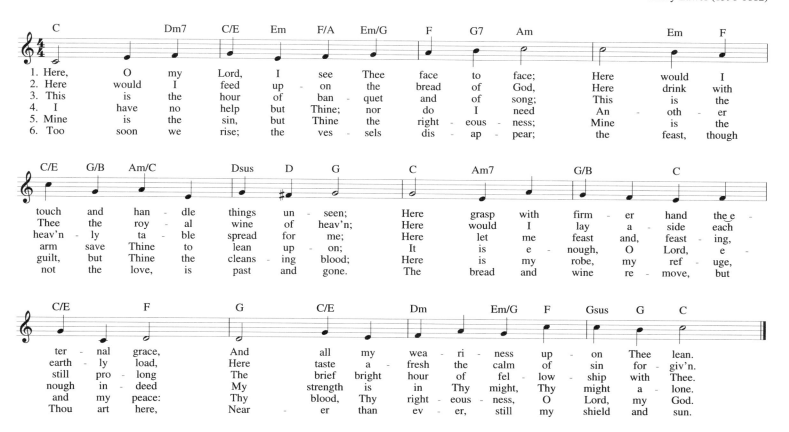

HERE, O MY LORD, I SEE THEE FACE TO FACE

words by
Horatius Bonar (1808-1889)

PENITENTIA
music by
Edward Dearle (1806-1891)

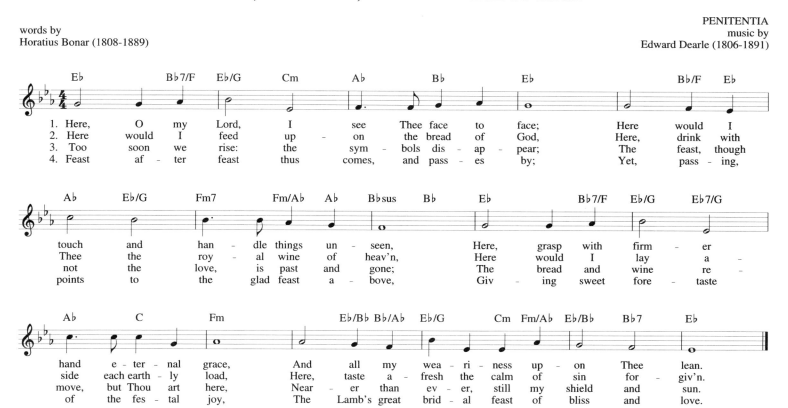

HIDDEN PEACE

words by
John S. Brown, 1899

music by
L.O. Brown, 1899

HIDING IN THEE

words by
William O. Cushing, 1876

music by
Ira D. Sankey, 1877

HIS EYE IS ON THE SPARROW

words by
Civilla D. Martin, 1905

SPARRO
music by
Charles H. Gabriel, 1905

1. Why should I feel dis - cour - aged? ____ Why should the shad - ows come? ____
2. "Let not your heart be trou - bled," ____ His ten - der words I hear;
3. When - ev - er I am tempt - ed, ____ When - ev - er clouds a - rise, ____

Why should my heart be lone - ly ____ And long for heav'n and home When
And rest - ing on His good - ness, ____ I lose my doubt and fear. ____ Though
When songs give place to sigh - ing, ____ When hope with - in me dies, ____ I

Je - sus is ____ my por - tion? ____ My con - stant Friend ___ is He: ____
by the path ___ He lead - eth ____ But one step I ____ may see: ____ His
draw the clos - er to Him; From care He sets ___ me free: ____

eye is on ____ the spar - row, ____ And I know He watch - es me. ____ His

eye is on the spar - row, ____ And I know He watch - es me. ____ I

sing be - cause I'm hap - py, I sing be - cause I'm free; ____ For His

eye is on the spar - row, ____ And I know He watch - es me. ____

HOLY BIBLE, BOOK DIVINE

words by
John Burton (1773-1822)

ALETTA
music by
William B. Bradbury (1816-1868)

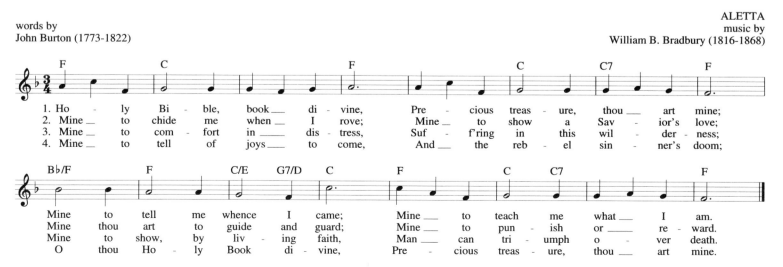

1. Ho - ly Bi - ble, book ___ di - vine, Pre - cious treas - ure, thou ___ art mine;
2. Mine ___ to chide me when ___ I rove; Mine ___ to show a Sav - ior's love;
3. Mine ___ to com - fort in ____ dis - tress, Suf - f'ring in this wil - der - ness;
4. Mine ___ to tell of joys ___ to come, And ___ the reb - el sin - ner's doom;

Mine to tell me whence I came; Mine ___ to teach me what ___ I am.
Mine thou art to guide and guard; Mine ___ to pun - ish or re - ward.
Mine to show, by liv - ing faith, Man ___ can tri - umph o - ver death.
O thou Ho - ly Book di - vine, Pre - cious treas - ure, thou ___ art mine.

HIGHER GROUND

music by
Charles H. Gabriel, 1898

, Jr. (1856-1922)

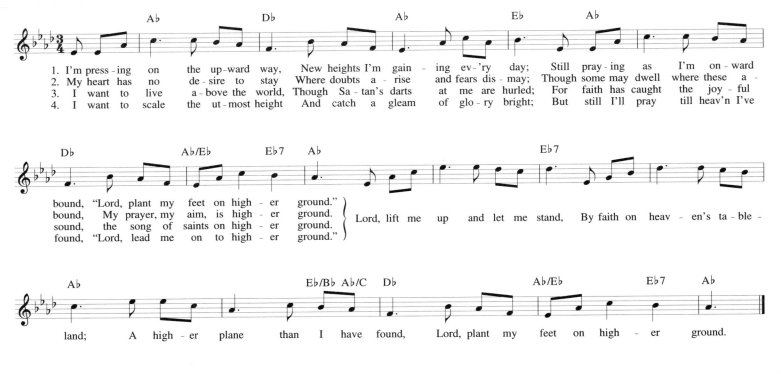

1. I'm press-ing on the up-ward way, New heights I'm gain-ing ev-'ry day; Still pray-ing as I'm on-ward
2. My heart has no de-sire to stay Where doubts a-rise and fears dis-may; Though some may dwell where these a-
3. I want to live a-bove the world, Though Sa-tan's darts at me are hurled; For faith has caught the joy-ful
4. I want to scale the ut-most height And catch a gleam of glo-ry bright; But still I'll pray till heav'n I've

bound, "Lord, plant my feet on high-er ground." }
bound, My prayer, my aim, is high-er ground. } Lord, lift me up and let me stand, By faith on heav-en's ta-ble-
sound, the song of saints on high-er ground. }
found, "Lord, lead me on to high-er ground." }

land; A high-er plane than I have found, Lord, plant my feet on high-er ground.

HIS GRACE ABOUNDETH MORE

words by
Kate Ulmer, 1899

music by
William J. Kirkpatrick, 1899

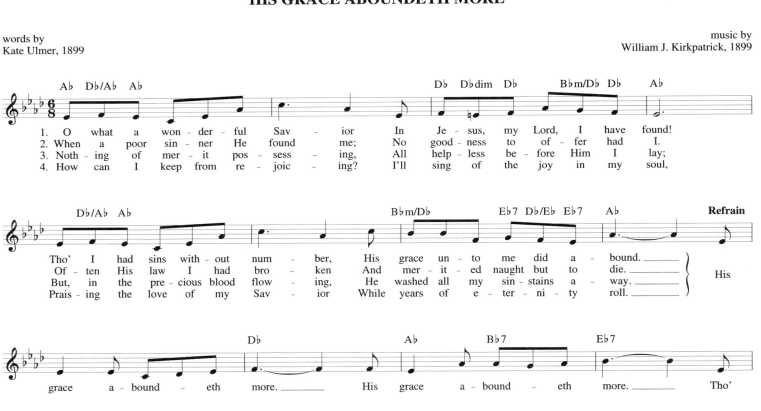

1. O what a won-der-ful Sav-ior In Je-sus, my Lord, I have found!
2. When a poor sin-ner He found me; No good-ness to of-fer had I.
3. Noth-ing of mer-it pos-sess-ing, All help-less be-fore Him I lay;
4. How can I keep from re-joic-ing? I'll sing of the joy in my soul,

Tho' I had sins with-out num-ber, His grace un-to me did a-bound. }
Of-ten His law I had bro-ken And mer-it-ed naught but to die. } His
But, in the pre-cious blood flow-ing, He washed all my sin-stains a-way. }
Prais-ing the love of my Sav-ior While years of e-ter-ni-ty roll. }

grace a-bound-eth more. His grace a-bound-eth more. Tho'

sin a-bound-eth in my heart, His grace a-bound-eth more.

HIS WAY WITH THEE

words by
Cyrus S. Nusbaum, 1898

NUSBAUM
music by
Cyrus S. Nusbaum, 1898

F   Fsus   F   F/C   C   F/C   C7   C   F/C   C7

1. Would you live for Je - sus, and be al - ways pure and good? Would you walk with Him with -
2. Would you have Him make you free, and fol - low at His call? Would you know the peace that
3. Would you in His king - dom find a place of con - stant rest? Would you prove Him true in

F   Fsus   F   Gm/Bb   D7/A   Gm

in the nar - row road? Would you have Him bear your bur - den, car - ry all your load?
comes by giv - ing all? Would you have Him save you, so that you need nev - er fall?
prov - i - den - tial test? Would you in His ser - vice la - bor al - ways at your best?

C   F/C   C7   F   **Refrain**   C   C7   F

Let Him have His way with thee. }
Let Him have His way with thee. } His pow'r can make you what you ought to be. His
Let Him have His way with thee. }

C   C7   F   C   F   F7

blood can cleanse your heart and make you free. His love can fill your soul, and

Bb   F/C   C7   F/C   Bb/C   F/C   C7   F

you will see 'Twas best for Him to have His way with thee.

HIS YOKE IS EASY

words by
Ralph E. Hudson, 1885

music by
Ralph E. Hudson, 1885

Bb   Eb/Bb   Bb   Eb   Bb   Eb   Bb

1. The Lord is my Shep - herd; I shall not want. He mak - eth me down to
2. My soul cri - eth out: "Re - store me a - gain, And give me the strength to
3. Yea, tho' I should walk the val - ley of death, Yet why should I fear from

F   F7   Bb   Eb   Bb/F   F   F7   Bb   **Refrain**

lie ___ In pas - tures green. He lead - eth me The qui - et wa - ters by. ___ }
take ___ The nar - row path of right - eous - ness, E'en for His own name's sake." ___ } His
ill? ___ For Thou art with me, and Thy rod And staff me com - fort still. ___ }

Eb   Bb   Bb/F   F7   Bb   F7   Bb

yoke is eas - y; His bur - den is light. I've found it so; I've found it so. He

Eb   Bb   Eb   Gm   F   F7   Bb

lead - eth me by day and by night Where liv - ing wa - ters flow. ___

HOLD THE FORT

words by
Philip P. Bliss (1838-1876)

music by
Philip P. Bliss (1838-1876)

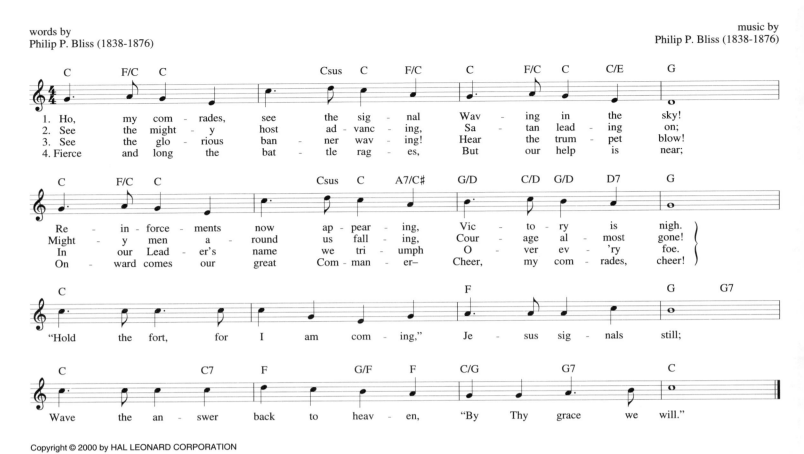

1. Ho, my com - rades, see the sig - nal Wav - ing in the sky!
2. See the might - y host ad - vanc - ing, Sa - tan lead - ing on;
3. See the glo - rious ban - ner wav - ing! Hear the trum - pet blow!
4. Fierce and long the bat - tle rag - es, But our help is near;

Re - in - force - ments now ap - pear - ing, Vic - to - ry is nigh.
Might - y men a - round us fall - ing, Cour - age al - most gone!
In our Lead - er's name we tri - umph O - ver ev - 'ry foe.
On - ward comes our great Com - man - er— Cheer, my com - rades, cheer!

"Hold the fort, for I am com - ing," Je - sus sig - nals still;

Wave the an - swer back to heav - en, "By Thy grace we will."

HOLD TO GOD'S UNCHANGING HAND

GOD'S UNCHANGING HAND

words by
Jennie Wilson

music by
F.L. Eiland

1. Time is filled with swift tran - si - tion, ___ Naught of earth un - moved can stand,
2. Trust in Him who will not leave you, ___ What - so - ev - er years may bring;
3. Cov - et not this world's vain rich - es, ___ That so rap - id - ly de - cay;
4. When your jour - ney is com - plet - ed, ___ If to God you have been true;

Build your hopes on things e - ter - nal, Hold to God's un - chang - ing hand!
If by earth - ly friends for - sak - en, Still more close - ly to Him cling!
Seek to gain the heav'n - ly treas - ures, They will nev - er pass a - way!
Fair and bright the home in glo - ry Your en - rap - tured soul will view!

Hold to God's un - chang - ing hand! Hold to God's un - chang - ing hand!

Build your hopes on things e - ter - nal, Hold to God's un - chang - ing hand!

HOLINESS UNTO THE LORD

words by
Lelia N. Morris, 1900

music by
Lelia N. Morris, 1900

1. "Called un-to ho-li-ness," Church of our God, Pur-chase of Je-sus, re-
2. "Called un-to ho-li-ness," chil-dren of light, Walk-ing with Je-sus in
3. "Called un-to ho-li-ness," praise His dear name! This bless-ed se-cret to
4. "Called un-to ho-li-ness," bride of the Lamb, Wait-ing the Bride-groom's re-

deemed by His blood; Called from the world and its i-dols to flee,
gar-ments of white; Rai-ment un-sul-lied, nor tar-nished with sin;
faith now made plain: Not our own righ-teous-ness, but Christ with-in,
turn-ing a-gain! Lift up your heads, for the day draw-eth near

Called from the bond-age of sin to be free.
God's Ho-ly Spir-it a-bid-ing with-in.
Liv-ing, and reign-ing, and sav-ing from sin.
When in His beau-ty the King shall ap-pear!

Refrain
"Ho-li-ness un-to the Lord" is our

watch-word and song; "Ho-li-ness un-to the Lord" as we're march-ing a-long.

Sing it, shout it, loud and long: "Ho-li-ness un-to the Lord" now and for-ev-er.

HOLY FATHER, GREAT CREATOR

REGENT SQUARE

words by
Alexander Viets Griswold (1766-1843)

music by
Henry Thomas Smart (1813-1879)

1. Ho-ly Fa-ther, great Cre-a-tor, Source of mer-cy, love, and peace,
2. Ho-ly Je-sus, Lord of glo-ry, Whom an-gel-ic hosts pro-claim,
3. Ho-ly Spir-it, Sanc-ti-fi-er, Come with unc-tion from a-bove,
4. God the Lord, through ev-'ry na-tion Let Thy won-drous mer-cies shine.

Look up-on the Me-di-a-tor, clothe us with His right-eous-ness;
While we hear Thy won-drous sto-ry, Meet and wor-ship in Thy name,
Raise our hearts to rap-tures high-er, Fill them with the Sav-ior's love.
In the song of Thy sal-va-tion Ev-'ry tongue and race com-bine.

Heav'n-ly Fa-ther, heav'n-ly Fa-ther, Through the Sav-ior hear and bless.
Dear Re-deem-er, dear Re-deem-er, In our hearts Thy peace pro-claim.
Source of com-fort, source of com-fort, Cheer us with the Sav-ior's love.
Great Je-ho-vah, great Je-ho-vah, Form our hearts and make them Thine.

HOLY GOD, WE PRAISE THY NAME

words from *Katholisches Gesangbuch*, Vienna, c. 1774
attr. to Ignaz Franz (1719-1790)
tr. by Clarence Walworth (1820-1900)

GROSSER GOTT
music from
Katholisches Gesangbuch, Vienna, c. 1774

1. Ho-ly God, we praise Thy name! Lord of all, we
2. Hark! the loud ce-les-tial hymn An-gel choirs a-
3. Ho-ly Fa-ther, Ho-ly Son, Ho-ly Spir-it,

bow be-fore Thee; All on earth Thy scep-ter claim,
bove are rais-ing; Cher-u-bim and Ser-a-phim
Three we name Thee, While in es-sence on-ly One,

All in heav'n a-bove a-dore thee; In-fi-nite Thy vast do-
In un-ceas-ing cho-rus prais-ing, Fill the heav'ns with sweet ac-
Un-di-vid-ed God we claim Thee, And a-dor-ing bend the

Last 8 measures optional

main, Ev-er-last-ing is Thy reign. In-fi-nite Thy
cord: Ho-ly, ho-ly, ho-ly Lord! Fill the heav'ns with
knee, While we own the mys-ter-y. And a-dor-ing

vast do-main, Ev-er-last-ing is Thy reign.
sweet ac-cord: Ho-ly, ho-ly, ho-ly Lord!
bend the knee, While we own the mys-ter-y.

HOLY IS THE LORD

Traditional words

music by
Franz Schubert (1797-1828)

Ho-ly, ho-ly, ho-ly, Ho-ly is the Lord.

To Coda

Ho-ly, ho-ly, ho-ly, Ho-ly is the Lord.

Ho-ly is the Fa-ther, Ho-ly is the Son,

D.C. al Coda   **CODA**

Ho-ly is the Spir-it; Bless-ed Three in One.   Lord.

HOLY, HOLY, HOLY! LORD GOD ALMIGHTY

words by
Reginald Heber (1783-1826)

NICAEA
music by
John B. Dykes (1823-1876)

HOLY SPIRIT, LIGHT DIVINE

words by
Andrew Reed, 1817

MERCY
music by
Louis M. Gottschalk, 1854
arr. by Edwin P. Parker, 1888

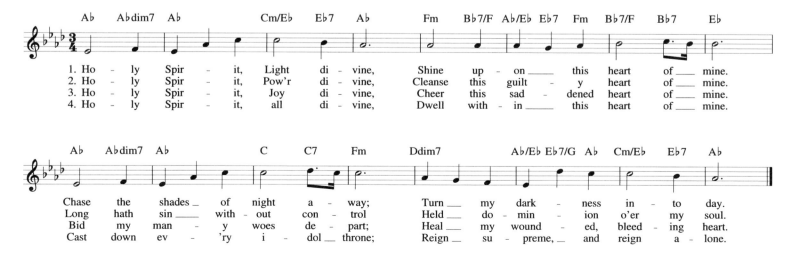

172

HOLY SPIRIT, TRUTH DIVINE

SONG 13

words by
Samuel Longfellow, 1864

music by
Orlando Gibbons, 1623

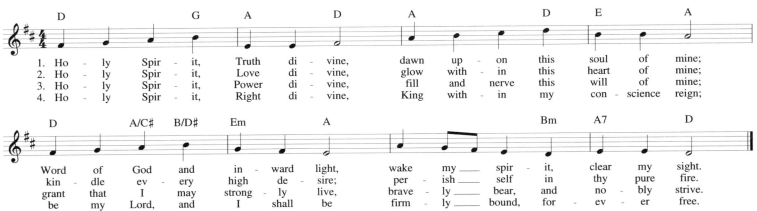

1. Ho - ly Spir - it, Truth di - vine, dawn up - on this soul of mine;
2. Ho - ly Spir - it, Love di - vine, glow with - in this heart of mine;
3. Ho - ly Spir - it, Power di - vine, fill and nerve this will of mine;
4. Ho - ly Spir - it, Right di - vine, King with - in my con - science reign;

Word of God and in - ward light, wake my spir - it, clear my sight.
kin - dle ev - ery high de - sire; per - ish self in thy pure fire.
grant that I may strong - ly live, brave - ly bear, and no - bly strive.
be my Lord, and I shall be firm - ly bound, for - ev - er free.

HOSANNA TO THE LIVING LORD

HOSANNA

words by
Reginald Heber (1783-1826)

music by
John Bacchus Dykes (1823-1876)

1. Ho - san - na to the liv - ing Lord! Ho - san - na to th' in -
2. Ho - san - na, Lord, Thine an - gels cry; Ho - san - na, Lord, Thy
3. O Sav - ior, with pro - tect - ing care A - bide in this Thy
4. But, chief - est, in our cleans - ed breast, E - ter - nal, bid Thy
5. So in the last and dread - ful day, When earth and heav'n shall

car - nate Word! To Christ, Cre - a - tor, Sav - ior, King, let earth, let heav'n, ho -
saints re - ply; A - bove, be - neath us, and a - round, both dead and liv - ing
house of prayer, Where we Thy part - ing prom - ise claim, As - sem - bled in Thy
Spir - it rest; And make our se - cret soul to be a tem - ple pure and
melt a - way, Thy flock, re - deemed from sin - ful stain, shall swell the sound of

san - na sing! }
swell the sound: }
sa - cred name. } Ho - san - na, Lord! Ho - san - na in the high - est!
wor - thy Thee. }
praise a - gain. }

HOSANNA, LOUD HOSANNA

ELLACOMBE

words by
Jennette Threlfall, 1873

music from
Gesangbuch der Herzogl, Württemberg, 1784

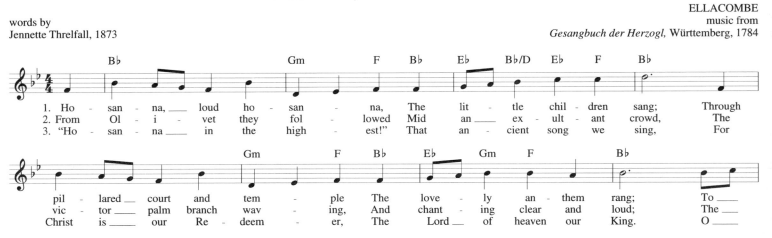

1. Ho - san - na, loud ho - san - na, The lit - tle chil - dren sang; Through
2. From Ol - i - vet they fol - lowed Mid an ex - ult - ant crowd, The
3. "Ho - san - na in the high - est!" That an - cient song we sing, For

pil - lared court and tem - ple The love - ly an - them rang; To
vic - tor palm branch wav - ing, And chant - ing clear and loud; The
Christ is our Re - deem - er, The Lord of heaven our King. O

Je- sus, who had blessed _____ them Close _____ fold - ed to his breast, The
Lord of men and an - gels Rode _____ on in low - ly state, Nor
may we ev - er praise _____ him With _____ heart and life and voice, And

chil - dren _____ sang their prais - es, The sim - plest and the best.
scorned that _____ lit - tle chil - dren Should on _____ his bid - ding wait.
in his _____ bliss - ful pres - ence E - ter - nal - ly re - joice.

HOW CAN A SINNER KNOW

words by
Charles Wesley (1707-1788)

GERAR
music by
Lowell Mason (1792-1872)

1. How can a sin - ner know His sins _____ on
2. What we have felt and seen With con - fi -
3. We who in Christ be - lieve That He _____ for
4. Ex - ults our ris - ing soul, Dis - bur - dened
5. His love sur - pass - ing far The love _____ of
6. Strong - er than death or hell The sa - cred

earth _____ for - giv'n? How can my gra - cious
dence _____ we tell; And pub - lish to the
us _____ hath died, We all _____ His un - known
of _____ her load, And swells un - ut - ter -
all _____ be - neath We find _____ with - in _____ our
pow'r _____ we prove; And, con - querors of _____ the

Sav - ior show _____ My name _____ in - scribed _____ in heav'n?
sons _____ of men _____ The signs _____ in - fal - li - ble.
peace _____ re - ceive, _____ And feel _____ His blood _____ ap - plied.
a - bly full _____ Of glo - ry and _____ of God.
hearts, _____ and dare _____ The point - less darts _____ of death.
world, _____ we dwell _____ In heav'n, _____ who dwell _____ in love.

HOW SWEET THE NAME OF JESUS SOUNDS

words by
John Newton (1725-1807)

ORTONVILLE
music by
Thomas Hastings (1784-1872)

1. How sweet the name of Je - sus sounds In a be - liev - er's ear! _____ It
2. It makes the wound - ed spir - it whole, And calms the trou - bled breast; _____ 'Tis
3. Dear name! the rock on which I build, My shield and hid - ing place; _____ My
4. Je - sus, my shep - herd, broth - er, friend, My proph - et, priest, and king, _____ My

soothes his sor - rows, heals his wounds, And drives a - way his fear, _____ And drives a - way his fear.
man - na to the hun - gry soul, And to the wea - ry, rest, And to the wea - ry, rest.
nev - er - fail - ing treas - ure, filled With bound - less stores of grace! _____ With bound - less stores of grace! _____
Lord, my life, my way, my end, Ac - cept the praise I bring, _____ Ac - cept the praise I bring. _____

HOW FIRM A FOUNDATION

words from
John Rippon's *Selection of Hymns*, 1787

ADESTE FIDELES
music from
John F. Wade's *Cantus Diversi*, 1751

1. How firm a foun - da - tion, ye saints ___ of the Lord, ___ Is laid for your
2. "Fear not, I am with thee; O be ___ not dis - mayed, ___ For I am thy
3. "When through fier - y tri - als thy path - way shall lie, ___ My grace, all - suf -
4. "The soul that on Je - sus hath leaned ___ for re - pose ___ I will not, I

faith ___ in His ex - cel - lent Word! What more can He say than to
God, ___ and will still give thee aid; I'll strength - en thee, help thee, and
fi - cient, shall be thy sup - ply; The flame shall not hurt thee, I
will ___ not de - sert to his foes; That soul, though all hell should en -

you ___ He hath said, ___ To you ___ who for ref - uge to Je - sus have fled? ___ To
cause ___ thee to stand, ___ Up - held ___ by My right - eous, om - nip - o - tent hand, ___ Up
on - ly de - sign ___ Thy dross ___ to con - sume, and thy gold ___ to re - fine, ___ Thy
deav - or to shake, ___ I'll nev - er, no, nev - er, no, nev - er for - sake! ___ I'll

you ___ who for ref - uge to Je - sus have fled?
held ___ by My right - eous, om - nip - o - tent hand."
dross ___ to con - sume, and thy gold to re - fine."
nev - er, no, nev - er, no, nev - er for - sake!"

HOW RICH THY BOUNTY, KING OF KINGS

words by
Philip Doddridge (1702-1751)

ST. GABRIEL
music by
Henry W. Greatorex (1813-1858)

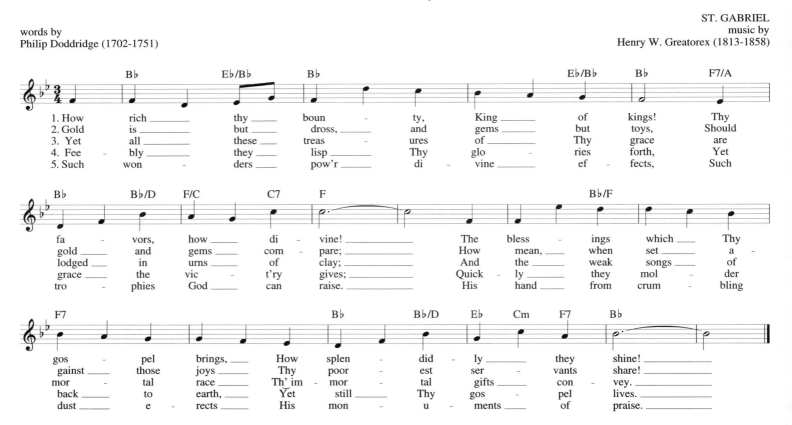

1. How rich ___ thy ___ boun - ty, King ___ of kings! Thy
2. Gold is ___ but ___ dross, ___ and gems ___ but toys, Should
3. Yet all ___ these ___ treas - ures of ___ Thy grace are
4. Fee - bly they ___ lisp ___ Thy glo - ries forth, Yet
5. Such won - ders ___ pow'r ___ di - vine ___ ef - fects, Such

fa - vors, how ___ di - vine! ___ The bless - ings which ___ Thy
gold ___ and gems ___ com - pare; ___ How mean, ___ when set ___ a
lodged in urns ___ of clay; ___ And the ___ weak songs ___ of
grace ___ the vic - t'ry gives; ___ Quick - ly ___ they mol - der
tro - phies God ___ can raise. ___ His hand ___ from crum - bling

gos - pel brings, ___ How splen - did - ly ___ they shine! ___
gainst ___ those joys ___ Thy poor - est ser - vants share! ___
mor - tal race ___ Th' im - mor - tal gifts ___ con - vey. ___
back ___ to earth, ___ Yet still ___ Thy gos - pel lives. ___
dust ___ e - rects ___ His mon - u - ments ___ of praise.

HOW FIRM A FOUNDATION

words by
John Rippon (1751-1836)
from *A Selection of Hymns,* 1787

FOUNDATION
Early American melody

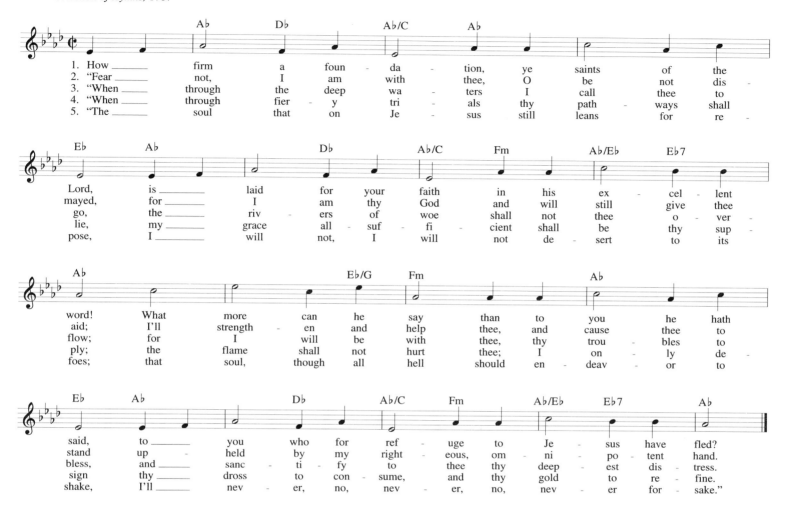

HOW SWEET THE NAME OF JESUS SOUNDS

words by
John Newton (1725-1807)

ST. PETER
music by
Alexander R. Reinagle (1799-1877)

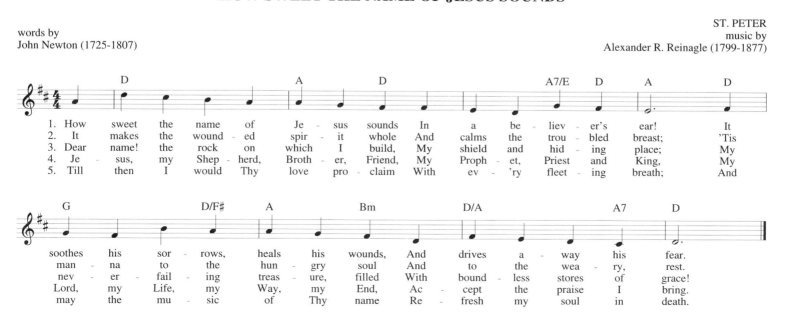

HOW THE FIRE FELL

FIRE FELL
music by
Miriam E. Oatman, 1905

words by
Johnson Oatman, Jr., 1905

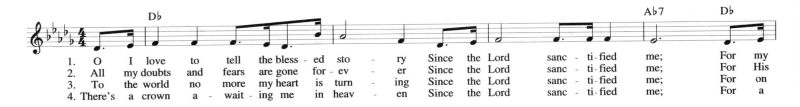

1. O I love to tell the bless-ed sto - ry Since the Lord sanc - ti-fied me; For my
2. All my doubts and fears are gone for-ev - er Since the Lord sanc - ti-fied me; For His
3. To the world no more my heart is turn - ing Since the Lord sanc - ti-fied me; For on
4. There's a crown a - wait-ing me in heav - en Since the Lord sanc - ti-fied me; For a

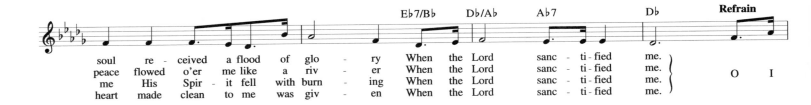

soul re - ceived a flood of glo - ry When the Lord sanc - ti-fied me.
peace flowed o'er me like a riv - er When the Lord sanc - ti-fied me.
me His Spir - it fell with burn - ing When the Lord sanc - ti-fied me.
heart made clean to me was giv - en When the Lord sanc - ti-fied me.

Refrain

O I

nev - er shall for - get how the fire fell, How the fire ___ fell, how the fire ___ fell. O I

nev - er shall for - get how the fire fell When the Lord sanc - ti-fied me.

HOW WONDROUS AND GREAT THY WORKS

OLD 104TH
music from
The Whole Booke of Psalmes, 1621

words by
Henry Ustick Onderdonk (1759-1858)

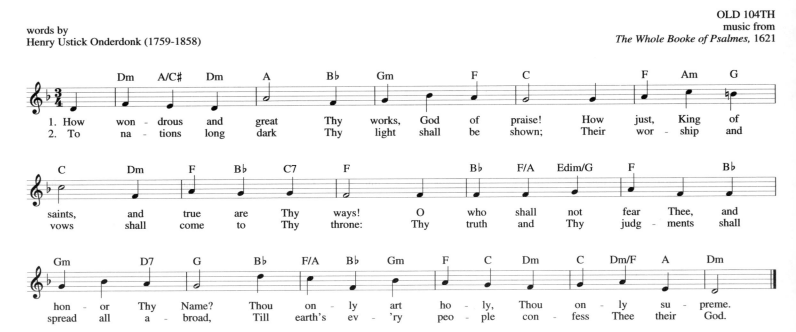

1. How won - drous and great Thy works, God of praise! How just, King of
2. To na - tions long dark Thy light shall be shown; Their wor - ship and

saints, and true are Thy ways! O who shall not fear Thee, and
vows shall come to Thy throne: Thy truth and Thy judg - ments shall

hon - or Thy Name? Thou on - ly art ho - ly, Thou on - ly su - preme.
spread all a - broad, Till earth's ev - 'ry peo - ple con - fess Thee their God.

I AM COMING, LORD

I HEAR THY VOICE

words by
Louis Hartsough, 1872

music by
Louis Hartsough, 1872

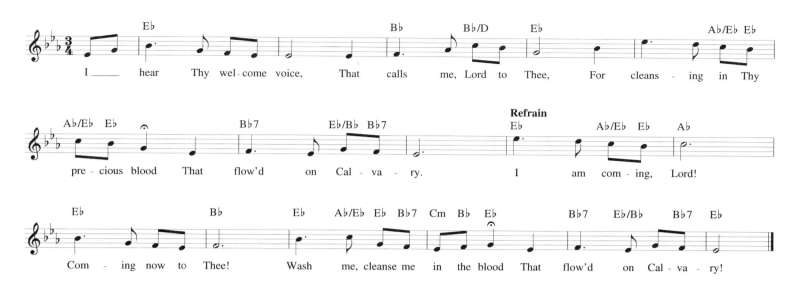

I _____ hear Thy wel-come voice, That calls me, Lord to Thee, For cleans - ing in Thy pre - cious blood That flow'd on Cal - va - ry.

Refrain

I am com - ing, Lord! Com - ing now to Thee! Wash me, cleanse me in the blood That flow'd on Cal - va - ry!

I AM HIS AND HE IS MINE

EVERLASTING LOVE

words by
George W. Robinson, 1890

music by
James Mountain, 1890

1. Loved with ev - er - last - ing love, Led by grace that love to know; Gra - cious
2. Heav'n a - bove is soft - er blue; Earth a - round is sweet - er green. Some - thing
3. Things that once were wild a - larms Can - not now dis - turb my rest. Closed in
4. His for - ev - er, on - ly His; Who the Lord and me shall part? Ah, with

Spir - it from a - bove, Thou hast taught me it is so. O this full and per - fect
lives in ev - 'ry hue Christ - less eyes have nev - er seen. Birds with glad - der songs o'er -
ev - er - last - ing arms, Pil - lowed on the lov - ing breast— O to lie for - ev - er
what a rest of bliss Christ can fill the lov - ing heart! Heav'n and earth may fade and

peace! O this trans - port all di - vine! In a love which can - not cease, I am
flow; Flow'rs with deep - er beau - ties shine, Since I know, as now I know, I am
here, Doubt and care and self re - sign While He whis - pers in my ear, I am
flee; First - born light in gloom de - cline. But while God and I shall be, I am

His and He is mine. In a love which can - not cease, I am His and He is mine.
His and He is mine. Since I know, as now I know, I am His and He is mine.
His and He is mine. While He whis - pers in my ear, I am His and He is mine.
His and He is mine. But while God and I shall be, I am His and He is mine.

I AM RESOLVED

RESOLUTION
music by
James H. Fillmore, 1896

words by
Palmer Hartsough, 1896

1. I am re-solved no long-er to lin-ger, Charmed by the world's de-light;
2. I am re-solved to go to the Sav-ior, Leav-ing my sin and strife.
3. I am re-solved to fol-low the Sav-ior, Faith-ful and true each day.
4. I am re-solved to en-ter the King-dom, Leav-ing the paths of sin.
5. I am re-solved, and who will go with me? Come, friends with-out de-lay.

Things that are high-er, things that are no-bler— These have al-lured my sight.
He is the true One; He is the just One; He hath the words of life.
Heed what He say-eth, do what He will-eth; He is the Liv-ing Way.
Friends may op-pose me, foes may be-set me; Still will I en-ter in.
Taught by the Bi-ble, led by the Spir-it, We'll walk the heav'n-ly way.

Refrain

I will has-ten to Him, Has-ten so glad and free.

Je-sus, Great-est, High-est, I will __ come to Thee.

I AM THINE, O LORD

I AM THINE
music by
William H. Doane (1832-1915)

words by
Fanny J. Crosby (1820-1915)

1. I am Thine, O Lord; I have heard Thy voice, And it told Thy love to __ me. But I long to rise in the
2. Con-se-crate me now to Thy ser-vice, Lord, By the pow'r of grace di-vine. Let my soul look up with a
3. O the pure de-light of a sin-gle hour That be-fore Thy throne I __ spend, When I kneel in prayer and with
4. There are depths of love that I can-not know Till I cross the nar-row __ sea; There are heights of joy that I

arms of faith, And be clos-er drawn to Thee.
stead-fast hope, And my will be lost in Thine.
Thee, my God, I com-mune as friend with friend!
may not reach Till I rest in peace with Thee.

Draw me near-er, near-er, bless-ed Lord, To the

cross where Thou hast died. Draw me near-er, near-er, near-er, bless-ed Lord, To Thy pre-cious, bleed-ing side.

I AM TRUSTING THEE, LORD JESUS

words by
F.R. Havergal (1836-1879)

STEPHANOS
music by
H.W. Baker (1821-1877)

1. I am trust - ing Thee, Lord Je - sus, Trust - ing on - ly Thee,
2. I am trust - ing Thee for par - don; At Thy feet I bow,
3. I am trust - ing Thee for cleans - ing In the crim - son flood,
4. I am trust - ing Thee to guide me; Thou a - lone shalt lead,
5. I am trust - ing Thee for pow - er; Thine can nev - er fail.
6. I am trust - ing Thee, Lord Je - sus; Nev - er let me fall.

Trust - ing ____ Thee for full sal - va - tion, Great and free.
For Thy ____ grace and ten - der ____ mer - cy Trust - ing now.
Trust - ing ____ Thee to make me ____ ho - ly By Thy blood.
Ev - 'ry ____ day and hour sup - ply - ing All my need.
Words which ____ Thou Thy - self shalt ____ give me Must pre - vail.
I am ____ trust - ing Thee for - ev - er And for all.

I BELONG TO THE KING

words by
Ida Reed Smith, 1896

CLIFTON
music by
Lincoln Hall, 1896

1. I be - long to the King; I'm a child of His love. I shall dwell in His
2. I be - long to the King, and He loves me I know, For His mer - cy and
3. I be - long to the King, and His prom - ise is sure— That we all shall be

pal - ace so fair, _____ For He tells of its bliss in yon heav - en a - bove, And His
kind - ness so free _____ Are un - ceas - ing - ly mine where - so - ev - er I go, And my
gath - ered at last _____ In His king - dom a - bove, by life's wa - ters so pure, When this

chil - dren in splen - dor shall share. _____ I be - long to the King; I'm a child of His
Ref - uge un - fail - ing is He. _____
life with its tri - als is past. _____

love, And He nev - er for - sak - eth His own. _____ He will call me some -

day to His pal - ace a - bove; I shall dwell by His glo - ri - fied throne. _____

I AM REDEEMED

PRICELESS

words by
James M. Gray (1851-1935)

music by
Daniel B. Towner (1850-1919)

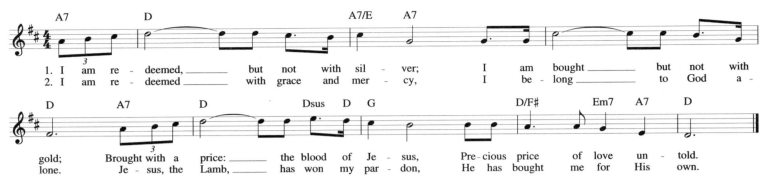

1. I am re-deemed, _____ but not with sil - ver; I am bought _____ but not with
2. I am re-deemed _____ with grace and mer - cy, I be-long _____ to God a -

gold; Brought with a price: _____ the blood of Je - sus, Pre-cious price of love un - told.
lone. Je - sus, the Lamb, _____ has won my par - don, He has bought me for His own.

I BIND UNTO MYSELF TODAY

ST. PATRICK'S BREASTPLATE
Traditional Irish melody

words attr. to
St. Patrick (c. 372-466)
para. by Cecil F. Alexander (1823-1895)

I bind un-to _____ my - self _____ to - day The strong _____ name

of _____ the Trin - i - ty By in - vo - ca - tion

of the same, _____ The _ Three in _ One _____ and One in Three. I

bind this day _____ to me _____ for - ev - er, By
bind un - to _____ my - self _____ to - day _____ The
bind un - to _____ my - self _____ to - day _____ The
bind un - to _____ my - self _____ the name, _____ The

pow - er of faith, _____ Christ's in - car - na - tion, His
vir - tues of _____ the star - lit heav - en, The
pow - er of God _____ to hold and lead, _____ His
strong _____ name of _____ the Trin - i - ty. _____ By

bap - tism _____ in _____ the Jor - dan Riv - er, His _____
glo - rious _____ sun's _____ life - giv - ing ray, _____ The _____
eye _____ to _____ watch, _____ His might to stay, _____ His _____
in - vo - ca - tion of the same, _____ The _____

cross of _____ death _____ for my sal - va - tion, His
white - ness _____ of _____ the moon at e - ven, The
ear to _____ heark - en to my need, _____ The
Three in _____ One _____ and One in Three, _____ Of

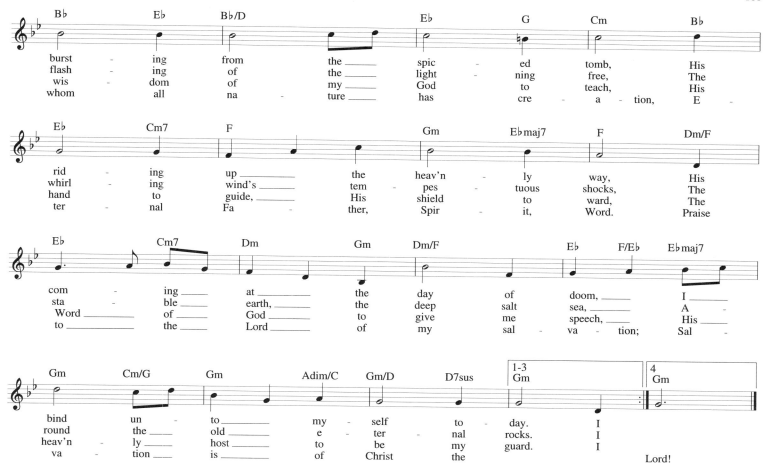

burst - ing from the _____ spic - ed tomb, His
flash - ing of the _____ light - ning free, The
wis - dom of my _____ God to teach, His
whom all na - ture _____ has cre - a - tion, E -

rid - ing up _____ the heav'n - ly way, His
whirl - ing wind's _____ the tem - pes - tuous shocks, The
hand to guide, _____ His shield to ward, The
ter - nal Fa - ther, Spir - it, Word. Praise

com - ing _____ at _____ the day of doom, _____ I _____
sta - ble _____ of _____ earth, the deep salt sea, _____ A -
Word _____ of _____ God _____ to give me speech, _____ His _____
to the _____ Lord _____ of my sal - va - tion; Sal -

bind un - to _____ my - self to - day. I
round the _____ old _____ e - ter - nal rocks. I
heav'n - ly _____ host to be my guard. I
va - tion _____ is _____ of Christ the Lord!

I FEEL LIKE TRAVELING ON

words by
William Hunter (1811-1877)

TRAVELING ON
Composer unknown

1. My _____ heav - en - ly home _____ is _____ bright and fair, } I feel like tra - vel - ing on. { No _____
2. Its _____ glit - t'ring tow - ers the _____ sun out - shine, That _____
3. Let _____ oth - ers seek _____ a _____ home be - low, Which _____
4. The _____ Lord _____ has been _____ so _____ good to me, Un -

pain or death _____ can _____ en - ter there, } I feel like _____ tra - vel - ing on. Yes, I
heav'n - ly man - sion _____ shall be mine,
flames de - vour _____ or _____ waves o'er - flow,
til that bless - ed _____ home I see,

feel like tra - vel - ing on. I feel like tra - vel - ing on. My _____

heav - en - ly home _____ is _____ bright and fair, I feel like _____ tra - vel - ing on.

I CALL ON THEE, LORD JESUS CHRIST

ICH RUF ZU DIR
music from
Geistliche Lieder, 1533

words by
Miles Coverdale (1487-1568)

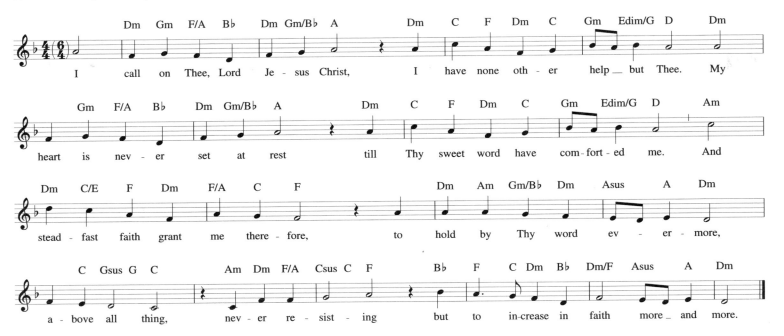

I GAVE MY LIFE FOR THEE

KENOSIS
music by
Philip P. Bliss, 1873

words by
Frances Ridley Havergal, 1859

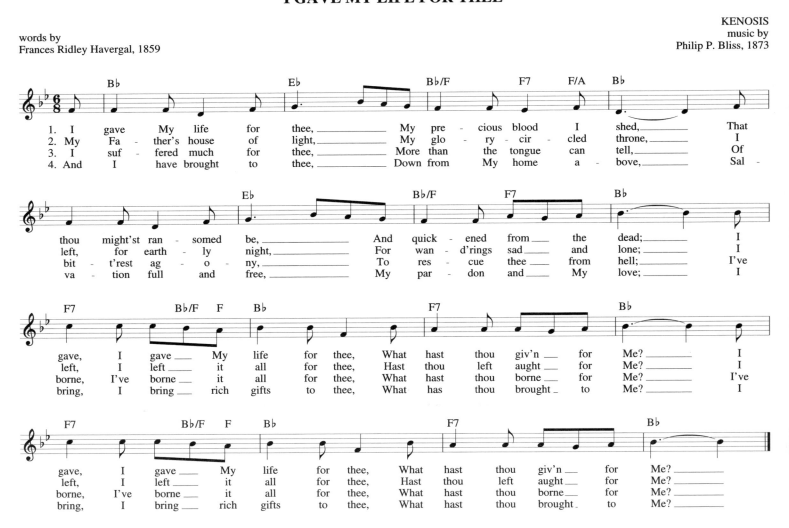

I GREET THEE, WHO MY SURE REDEEMER ART

OLD 124TH
music from
Genevan Psalter, 1551

words attr. to
John Calvin (1509-1564)
as in *French Psalter,* Strassburg, 1545
tr. by Elizabeth Lee Smith, 1868

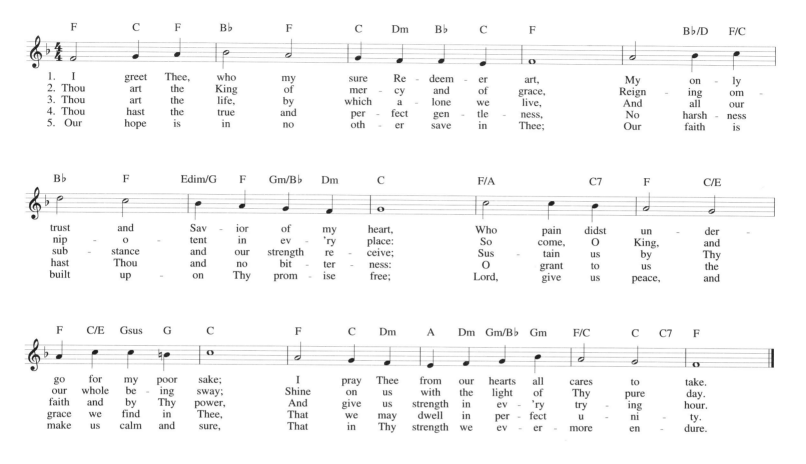

I HAVE DECIDED TO FOLLOW JESUS

Author unknown

ASSAM
Folk melody from India

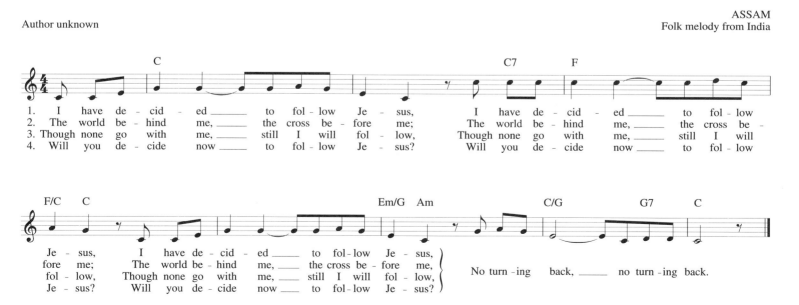

I HEARD THE VOICE OF JESUS SAY

VOX DILECTI

words by
Horatius Bonar (1808-1889)

music by
John B. Dykes (1823-1876)

Copyright © 2000 by HAL LEONARD CORPORATION

I KNOW A FOUNT

words by
Oliver Cooke

music by
Oliver Cooke

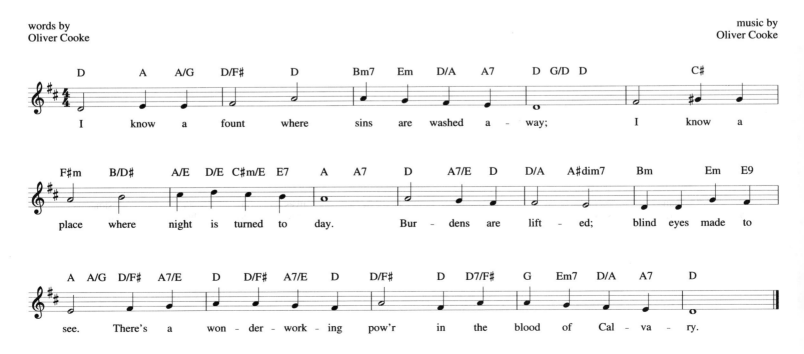

Copyright © 2000 by HAL LEONARD CORPORATION

I KNOW GOD'S PROMISE IS TRUE

words by
Lelia N. Morris, 1899

GOD'S PROMISE IS TRUE
music by
Lelia N. Morris, 1899

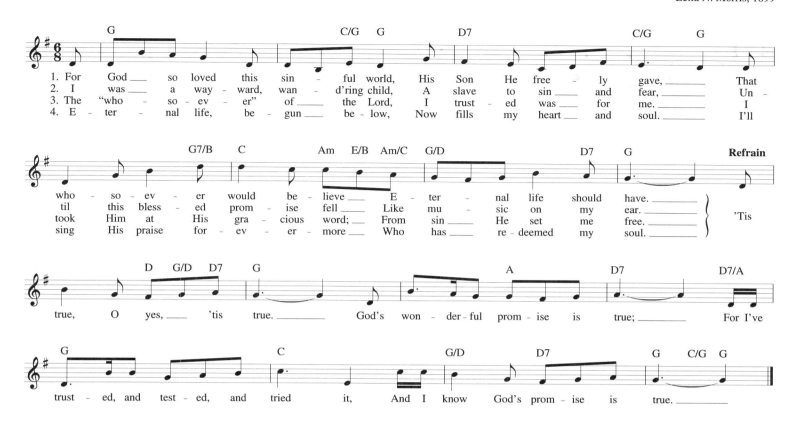

1. For God so loved this sin - ful world, His Son He free - ly gave, That
2. I was a way - ward, wan - d'ring child, A slave to sin and fear, Un -
3. The "who - so - ev - er" of the Lord, I trust - ed was for me. I
4. E - ter - nal life, be - gun be - low, Now fills my heart and soul. I'll

who - so - ev - er would be - lieve E - ter - nal life should have. 'Tis
til this bless - ed prom - ise fell Like mu - sic on my ear.
took Him at His gra - cious word; From sin He set me free.
sing His praise for - ev - er - more Who has re - deemed my soul.

true, O yes, 'tis true. God's won - der - ful prom - ise is true; For I've

trust - ed, and test - ed, and tried it, And I know God's prom - ise is true.

I KNOW THAT MY REDEEMER LIVES

words by
Samuel Medley (1738-1799)

DUKE STREET
music by
John Hatton (c.1710-1793)

1. I know that my Re - deem - er lives; What joy the
2. He lives, to bless me with His love; He lives, to
3. He lives, and grants me dai - ly breath; He lives, and
4. He lives, all glo - ry to His name; He lives, my

blest as - sur - ance gives! He lives, He lives, who
plead for me a - bove; He lives, my hun - gry
I shall con - quer death; He lives, my man - sion
Sav - ior, still the same; What joy the blest as -

once was dead; He lives, my ev - er - last - ing Head!
soul to feed; He lives, to help in time of need.
to pre - pare; He lives, to bring me safe - ly there.
sur - ance gives; I know that my Re - deem - er lives!

I KNOW THAT MY REDEEMER LIVES

words by
Fred A. Fillmore, 1917

FILLMORE
music by
Fred A. Fillmore, 1917

I KNOW THAT MY REDEEMER LIVETH

words by
Jessie Brown Pounds (1861-1921)

HANNAH
music by
James H. Fillmore (1849-1936)

I KNOW WHOM I HAVE BELIEVED

words by
Daniel W. Whittle, 1883
based on II Timothy 1:12

EL NATHAN
music by
James McGranahan, 1883

1. I know not why God's won-drous grace To me He hath made known, Nor
2. I know not how this sav-ing faith To me He did im-part, Nor
3. I know not how the Spir-it moves, Con-vinc-ing men of sin, Re-
4. I know not what of good or ill May be re-served for me, Of
5. I know not when my Lord may come, At night or noon-day fair, Nor

why, un-wor-thy, Christ in love Re-deemed me for His own.
how be-liev-ing in His Word Wro't peace with-in my heart.
veal-ing Je-sus thro' the Word, Cre-at-ing faith in Him.
wea-ry ways or gold-en days Be-fore His face I see.
if I'll walk the vale with Him, Or meet Him, in the air.

But I

know whom I have be-liev-ed, And am per-suad-ed that He is

a-ble To keep that which I've com-mit-ted Un-to Him a-gainst that day.

I LAY MY SINS ON JESUS

words by
Horatius Bonar, 1843

CRUCIFIX
Traditional Greek melody
adapt. in Sullivan's *Church Hymns,* 1874

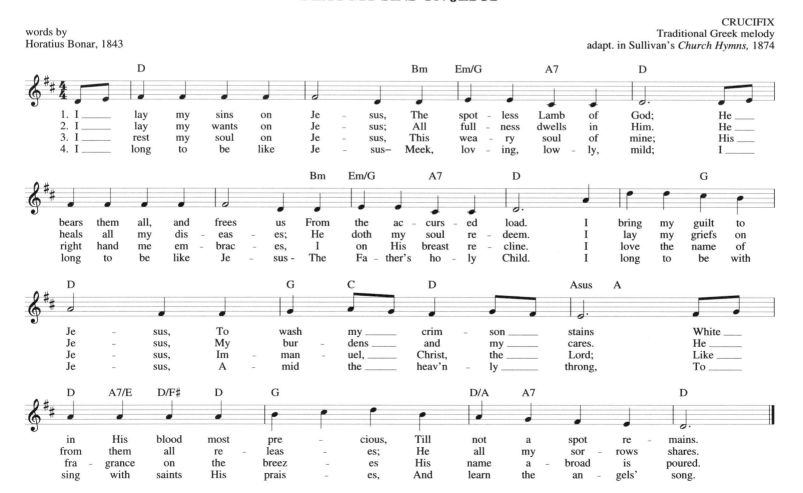

1. I lay my sins on Je-sus, The spot-less Lamb of God; He
2. I lay my wants on Je-sus; All full-ness dwells in Him. He
3. I rest my soul on Je-sus, This wea-ry soul of mine; His
4. I long to be like Je-sus— Meek, lov-ing, low-ly, mild; I

bears them all, and frees us From the ac-curs-ed load. I bring my guilt to
heals all my dis-eas-es; He doth my soul re-deem. I lay my griefs on
right hand me em-brac-es, I on His breast re-cline. I love the name of
long to be like Je-sus— The Fa-ther's ho-ly Child. I long to be with

Je-sus, To wash my crim-son stains White
Je-sus, My bur-dens and my cares. He
Je-sus, Im-man-uel, Christ, the Lord; Like
Je-sus, A-mid the heav'n-ly throng, To

in His blood most pre-cious, Till not a spot re-mains.
from them all re-leas-es; He all my sor-rows shares.
fra-grance on the breez-es His name a-broad is poured.
sing with saints His prais-es, And learn the an-gels' song.

I LAY MY SINS ON JESUS

MUNICH
music from
Neu-vermehrtes Gesangbuch, Meiningen, 1693

words by
Horatius Bonar (1808-1889)

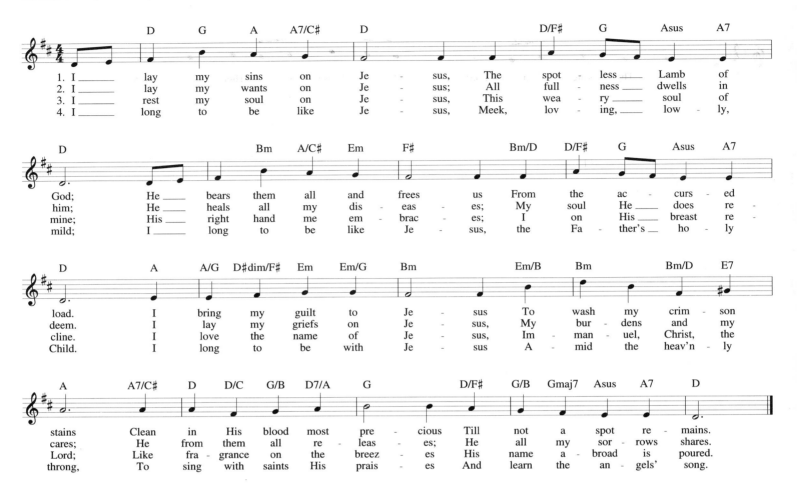

1. I _____ lay my sins on Je - sus, The spot - less _____ Lamb of
2. I _____ lay my wants on Je - sus; All full - ness _____ dwells in
3. I _____ rest my soul on Je - sus, This wea - ry _____ soul of
4. I _____ long to be like Je - sus, Meek, lov - ing, _____ low - ly,

God; He _____ bears them all and frees us From the ac - curs - ed
him; He _____ heals all my dis - eas - es; My soul He _____ does re -
mine; His _____ right hand me em - brac - es; I on His _____ breast re -
mild; I _____ long to be like Je - sus, the Fa - ther's _____ ho - ly

load. I bring my guilt to Je - sus To wash my crim - son
deem. I lay my griefs on Je - sus, My bur - dens and my
cline. I love the name of Je - sus, Im - man - uel, Christ, the
Child. I long to be with Je - sus A - mid the heav'n - ly

stains Clean in His blood most pre - cious Till not a spot re - mains.
cares; He from them all re - leas - es; He all my sor - rows shares.
Lord; Like fra - grance on the breez - es His name a - broad is poured.
throng, To sing with saints His prais - es And learn the an - gels' song.

I LOVE THE LORD, WHO HEARD MY CRY

words by
Isaac Watts, 1719

African-American Spiritual

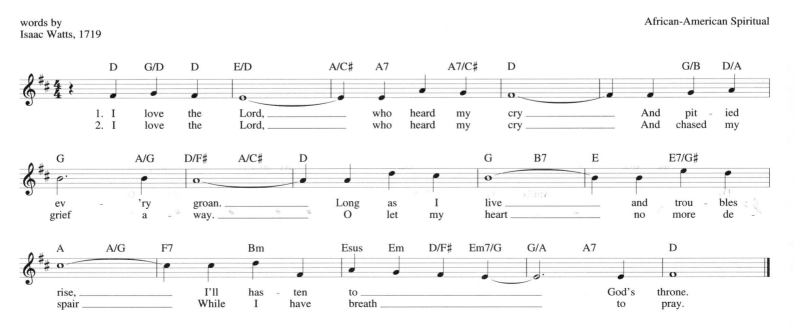

1. I love the Lord, _____ who heard my cry _____ And pit - ied
2. I love the Lord, _____ who heard my cry _____ And chased my

ev - 'ry groan. _____ Long as I live _____ and trou - bles
grief a - way. _____ O let my heart _____ no more de -

rise, _____ I'll has - ten to _____ God's throne.
spair _____ While I have breath _____ to pray.

I LOVE THY KINGDOM, LORD

words by
Timothy Dwight, 1800

ST. THOMAS
music from
The Universal Psalmodist, 1763
adapt. by Aaron Williams, 1770

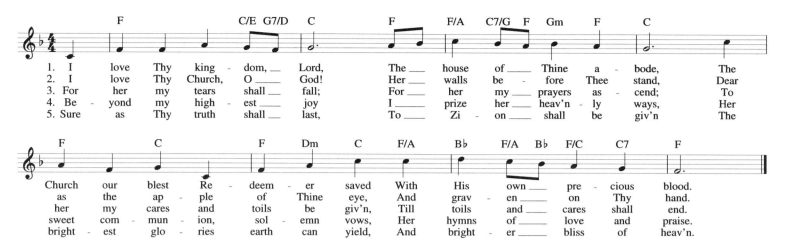

1. I love Thy king - dom, __ Lord, The __ house of __ Thine a - bode, The __
2. I love Thy Church, O __ God! Her __ walls be - fore Thee stand, Dear
3. For her my tears shall __ fall; For __ her my __ prayers as - cend; To
4. Be - yond my high - est __ joy I __ prize her __ heav'n - ly ways, Her
5. Sure as Thy truth shall __ last, To __ Zi - on __ shall be giv'n The

Church our blest Re - deem - er saved With His own __ pre - cious blood.
as the ap - ple of Thine eye, And grav - en __ on Thy hand.
her my cares and toils be giv'n, Till toils and __ cares shall end.
sweet com - mun - ion, sol - emn vows, Her hymns of __ love and praise.
bright - est glo - ries earth can yield, And bright - er __ bliss of heav'n.

I LOVE TO TELL THE STORY

words by
A. Catherine Hankey (1834-1911)

HANKEY
music by
William G. Fischer (1835-1912)

1. I love to tell the sto - ry of un - seen things a - bove, Of
2. I love to tell the sto - ry, more won - der - ful it seems Than
3. I love to tell the sto - ry 'tis pleas - ant to __ re - peat What
4. I love to tell the sto - ry, for those who know __ it best Seem

Je - sus and His glo - ry, of __ Je - sus and __ His love; I
all the gold - en fan - cies of __ all our gold - en dreams; I
seems, each time I tell it, more __ won - der - ful - ly sweet; I
hun - ger - ing and thirst - ing to __ hear it like __ the rest; And

love to tell the sto - ry be - cause I know 'tis __ true, It
love to tell the sto - ry, it did so much for __ me, And
love to tell the sto - ry, for some have nev - er __ heard The
when in scenes of glo - ry I sing the new, new __ song, 'Twill

sat - is - fies my long - ings as noth - ing else can do.
that is just the rea - son I tell it now to thee.
mes - sage of sal - va - tion from God's own ho - ly Word.
be the old, old sto - ry that I have loved so long.

Refrain

I love to tell the sto - ry! 'Twill be my theme in glo - ry To

tell the old, __ old sto - ry Of Je - sus and His love.

I LOVE THEE

words by
Jeremiah Ingalls' *Christian Harmony*, 1805

music from
Jeremiah Ingalls' *Christian Harmony*, 1805

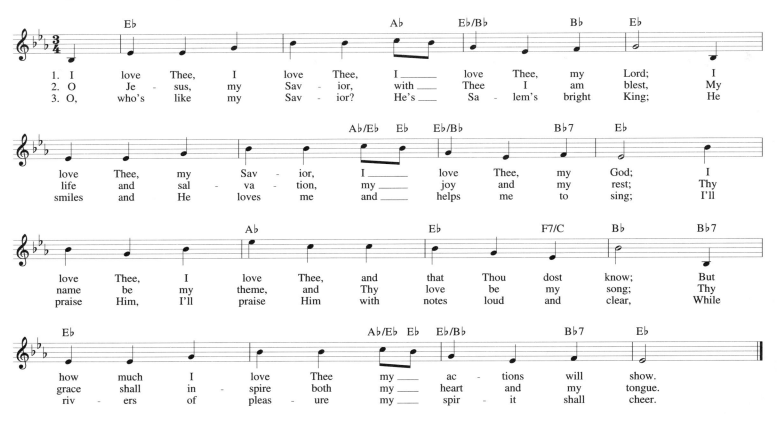

1. I love Thee, I love Thee, I ___ love Thee, my Lord; I love Thee, my Sav - ior, I ___ love Thee, my God; I love Thee, I love Thee, and that Thou dost know; But how much I love Thee my ___ ac - tions will show.
2. O Je - sus, my love Sav - ior, with ___ Thee I am blest, My life Thee and my sal - va - tion, my ___ joy and my rest; Thy name be my theme, and Thy love be my song; Thy grace shall in - spire both my ___ heart and my tongue.
3. O, who's like my Sav - ior? He's ___ Sa - lem's bright King; He smiles and He loves me and ___ helps me to sing; I'll praise Him, I'll praise Him with notes loud and clear, While riv - ers of pleas - ure my ___ spir - it shall cheer.

I MUST TELL JESUS

ORWIGSBURG

words by
Elisha A. Hoffman, 1894

music by
Elisha A. Hoffman, 1894

1. I must tell Je - sus all of my tri - als; I can - not bear these bur - dens a - lone. In my dis - tress He kind - ly will help me; He ev - er loves and cares for His own. I must tell Je - sus! I must tell Je - sus! I can - not bear my bur - dens a - lone; I must tell Je - sus! I must tell Je - sus! Je - sus can help me, Je - sus a - lone.
2. I must tell Je - sus all of my trou - bles; He is a kind, com - pas - sion - ate Friend. If I but ask Him, He will de - liv - er, Make of my trou - bles quick - ly an end.
3. O how the world to e - vil al - lures me! O how my heart is tempt - ed to sin! I must tell Je - sus, and He will help me O - ver the world the vic - t'ry to win.

I NEED THEE EVERY HOUR

words by
Annie S. Hawks, 1872 (verses)
Refrain by Robert Lowry (1826-1899)

NEED
music by
Robert Lowry (1826-1899)

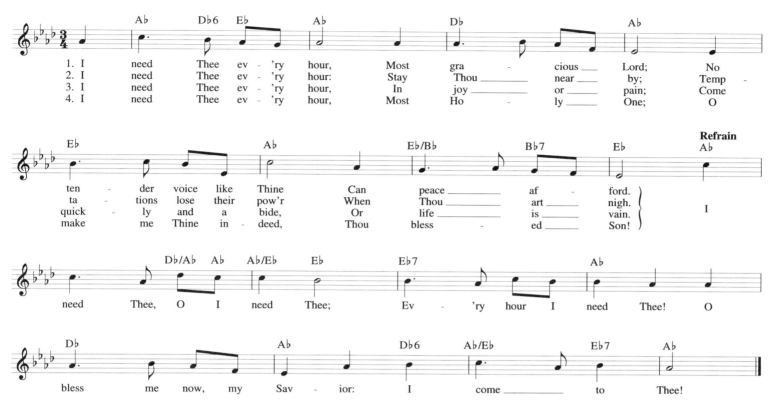

1. I need Thee ev-'ry hour, Most gra - cious Lord; No
2. I need Thee ev-'ry hour: Stay Thou near by; Temp -
3. I need Thee ev-'ry hour, In joy or pain; Come
4. I need Thee ev-'ry hour, Most Ho - ly One; O

ten - der voice like Thine Can peace af - ford.
ta - tions lose their pow'r When Thou art nigh.
quick - ly and a - bide, Or life is vain.
make me Thine in - deed, Thou bless - ed Son!

Refrain

I need Thee, O I need Thee; Ev - 'ry hour I need Thee! O

bless me now, my Sav - ior: I come to Thee!

Copyright © 2000 by HAL LEONARD CORPORATION

I SHALL KNOW HIM

words by
Fanny J. Crosby (1820-1915)

SAVIOR FIRST
music by
John R. Sweney (1837-1899)

1. When my life work is end - ed, and I cross the swell - ing tide, When the
2. O the soul - thrill - ing rap - ture when I view His bless - ed face, And the
3. Thru the gates to the cit - y in a robe of spot - less white, He will

bright and glo - rious morn - ing I shall see;
lus - ter of His kind - ly beam - ing eye;
lead me where no tears shall ev - er fall;

I shall know my Re - deem - er when I
How my full heart will praise Him for the
In the glad song of a - ges I shall

reach the oth - er side, And His smile will be the first to wel - come me.
mer - cy, love, and grace, That pre - pares me for a man - sion in the sky.
min - gle with de - light; But I long to meet my Sav - ior first of all.

I shall

know Him, I shall know Him, As re - deemed by His side I shall stand; I shall

know Him, I shall know Him By the print of the nails in His hand.

Copyright © 2000 by HAL LEONARD CORPORATION

I SHALL NOT BE MOVED

words by
Edward H. Boatner

American Folk melody

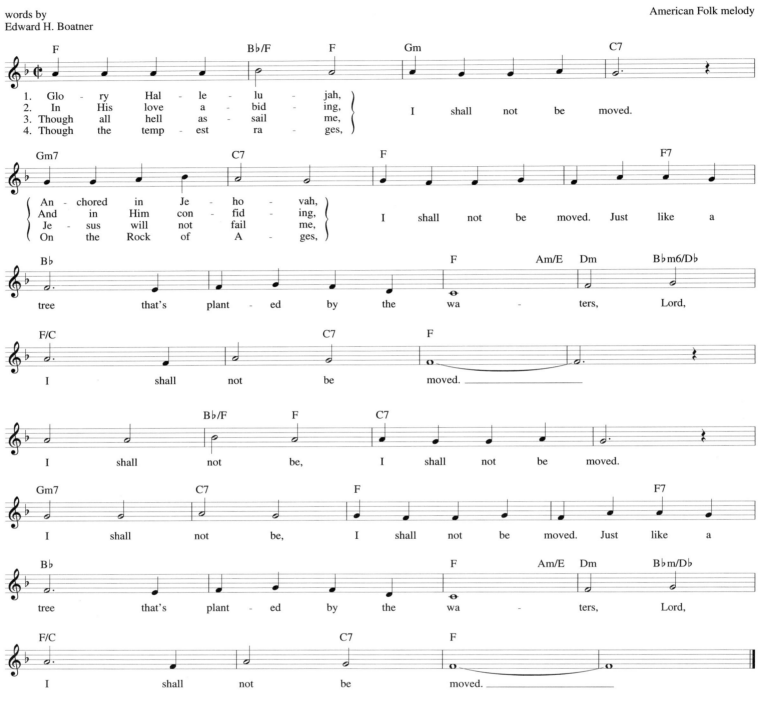

I SING THE MIGHTY POWER OF GOD

words by
Isaac Watts, 1715

ELLACOMBE
music from
Gesangbuch der Herzogl, Württemberg, 1784

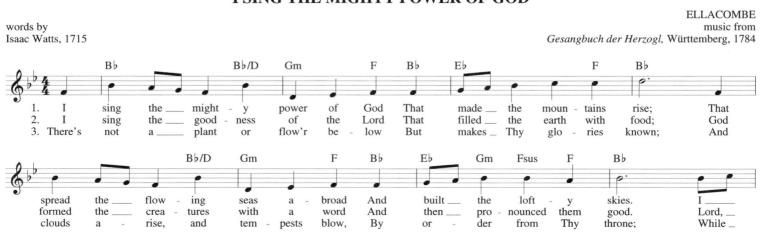

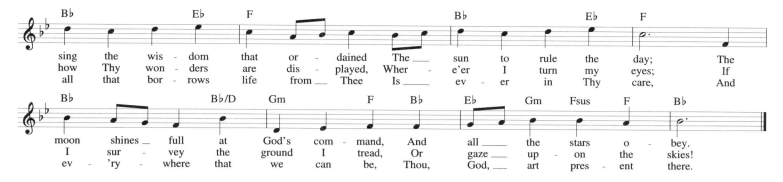

Bb   Eb   F   Bb   Eb   F

sing the wis - dom that or - dained The __ sun to rule the day; The
how Thy won - ders are dis - played, Wher e'er I turn my eyes; If
all that bor - rows life from __ Thee Is __ ev - er in Thy care, And

Bb   Bb/D Gm   F Bb   Eb   Gm Fsus F Bb

moon shines __ full at God's com - mand, And all __ the stars o - bey.
I sur - vey the ground I tread, Or gaze __ up - on the skies!
ev - 'ry - where that we can be, Thou, God, __ art pres - ent there.

I SING THE MIGHTY POWER OF GOD

words by
Isaac Watts, 1715

FOREST GREEN
Traditional English melody
arr. by Ralph Vaughan Williams, 1906

1. I sing the might - y pow'r of __ God, that made the __ moun - tains rise, that
2. I sing the good - ness of __ the __ Lord, who filled the __ earth with food, that who
3. There's not a plant or flower be - low, but makes Thy __ glo - ries known, and

spread the flow - ing seas __ a - broad, and built the __ loft - y skies. I __
formed the crea - tures thru __ the __ Word, and then pro - nounced them good. Lord, __
clouds a - rise, and tem - pests __ blow, by or - der __ from Thy throne; while __

sing the wis - dom __ that __ or - dained the sun to rule the day; the
how Thy won - ders __ are __ dis - played, wher - e'er I turn my eye, if
all that bor - rows __ life __ from __ Thee is ev - er in my care; and

moon shines full at God's __ com - mand, and all the __ stars o - bey.
I sur - vey the ground __ I tread, or gaze up - on the sky.
ev - ery - where that we __ can be, Thou, God, art __ pres - ent there.

I TO THE HILLS WILL LIFT MY EYES

Author unknown
words based on Psalm 121

DUNDEE
music from
Scottish Psalter, 1615

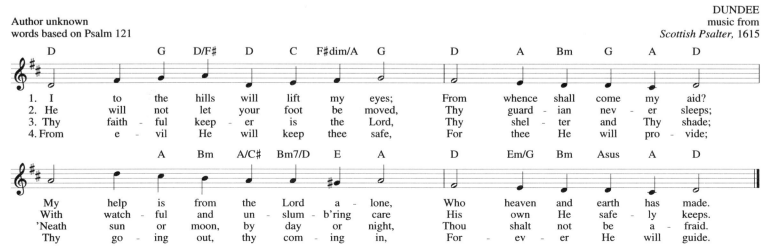

1. I to the hills will lift my eyes; From whence shall come my aid?
2. He will not let your foot be moved, Thy guard - ian nev - er sleeps;
3. Thy faith - ful keep - er is the Lord, Thy shel - ter and Thy shade;
4. From e - vil He will keep thee safe, For thee He will pro - vide;

My help is from the Lord a - lone, Who heaven and earth has made.
With watch - ful and un - slum - b'ring care His own He safe - ly keeps.
'Neath sun or moon, by day or night, Thou shalt not be a - fraid.
Thy go - ing out, thy com - ing in, For - ev - er He will guide.

I SING THE MIGHTY POWER OF GOD

words by
Isaac Watts, 1715

MOZART (I)
music attr. to
Wolfgang A. Mozart (1756-1791)

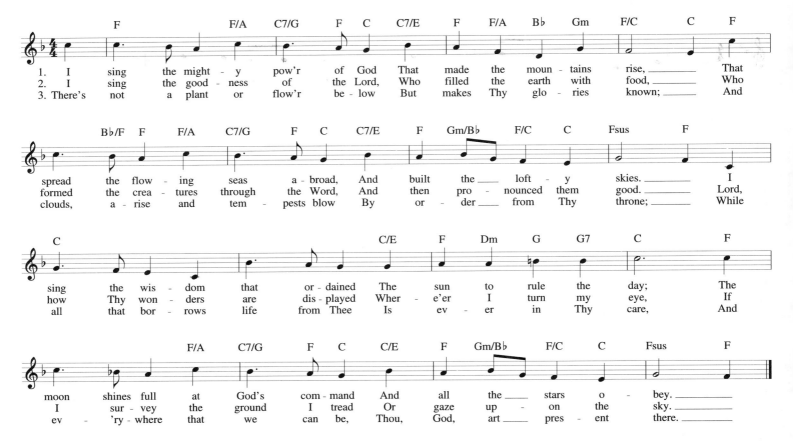

I SOUGHT THE LORD

Author unknown, c. 1890

PEACE
music by
George W. Chadwick, 1890

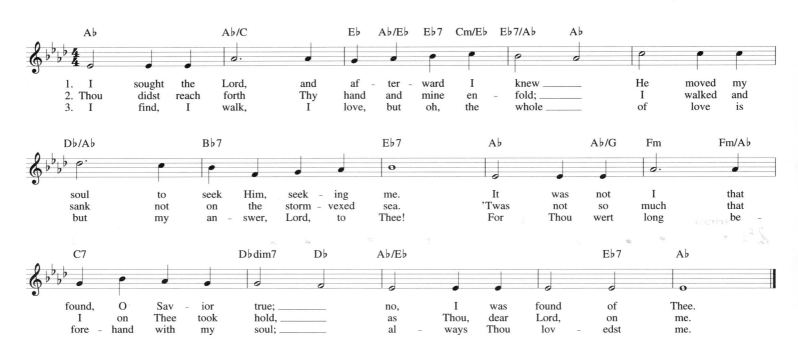

I STAND AMAZED IN THE PRESENCE
(My Savior's Love)

words by
Charles H. Gabriel, 1905

MY SAVIOR'S LOVE
music by
Charles H. Gabriel, 1905

1. I stand a - mazed in the pres - ence Of Je - sus the Naz - a - rene, And
2. For me it was in the gar - den He prayed, "Not My will, but Thine." And
3. In pit - y an - gels be - held Him, And came from the world of light To
4. He took my sins and my sor - rows, He made them His ver - y own; He
5. When with the ran - somed in glo - ry His face I at last shall see, 'Twill

won - der how He could love me, A sin - ner, con - demned, un - clean.
had no tears for His own griefs, But sweat - drops of blood for mine.
com - fort Him in the sor - rows He bore for my soul that night.
bore the bur - den to Cal - v'ry, And suf - fered and died a - lone.
be my joy through the a - ges To sing of His love for me.

How mar - vel - ous! How won - der - ful! And my song shall ev - er be:

How mar - vel - ous! How won - der - ful Is my __ Sav - ior's love for me!

I SURRENDER ALL

words by
Judson W. Van De Venter (1855-1939)

SURRENDER
music by
Winfield S. Weeden (1847-1908)

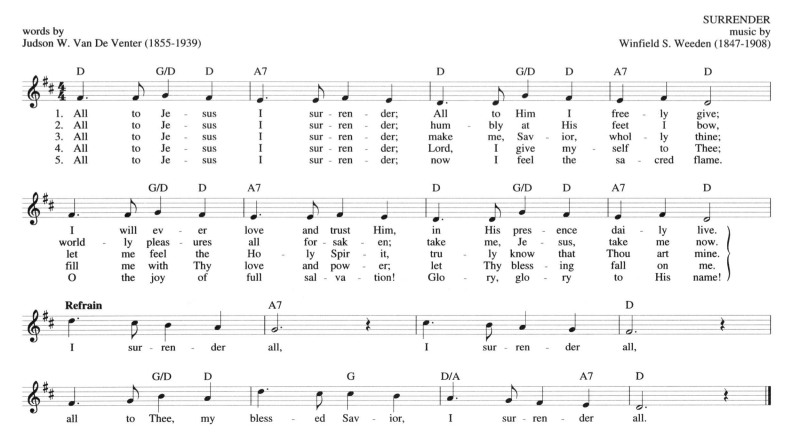

1. All to Je - sus I sur - ren - der; All to Him I free - ly give;
2. All to Je - sus I sur - ren - der; hum - bly at His feet I bow,
3. All to Je - sus I sur - ren - der; make me, Sav - ior, whol - ly thine;
4. All to Je - sus I sur - ren - der; Lord, I give my - self to Thee;
5. All to Je - sus I sur - ren - der; now I feel the sa - cred flame.

I will ev - er love and trust Him, in His pres - ence dai - ly live.
world - ly pleas - ures all for - sak - en; take me, Je - sus, take me now.
let me feel the Ho - ly Spir - it, tru - ly know that Thou art mine.
fill me with Thy love and pow - er; let Thy bless - ing fall on me.
O the joy of full sal - va - tion! Glo - ry, glo - ry to His name!

Refrain

I sur - ren - der all, I sur - ren - der all,

all to Thee, my bless - ed Sav - ior, I sur - ren - der all.

I WANT A PRINCIPLE WITHIN

GERALD

words by
Charles Wesley, 1749

music by
Louis Spohr, 1834
adapted by James Stimpson (1820-1886)

1. I want a prin-ci-ple with-in of watch-ful, god-ly fear, _____ a
2. From Thee that I no more may stray, no more Thy good-ness grieve, _____ grant
3. Al-might-y God of truth and love, to me Thy power im-part; _____ the

sen-si-bil-i-ty of sin, a pain to feel it near. _____ I
me the fil-ial awe, I pray, the ten-der con-science give. _____ Quick
moun-tain from my soul re-move, the hard-ness from my heart. _____ O

want the first _____ ap-proach to feel of pride of _____ wrong de-sire, _____ to
as the ap-ple of an eye, O God, my _____ con-science make; _____ a-
may the least _____ o-mis-sion pain my re-a-wak-ened soul, _____ and

catch the wan-dering of my will, and quench the kin-dling fire. _____
wake my soul when sin is nigh, and keep it still a-wake. _____
drive me to that blood a-gain, which makes the wound-ed whole. _____

I WILL PRAISE HIM

words by
Margaret J. Harris, 1898

music by
Margaret J. Harris, 1898

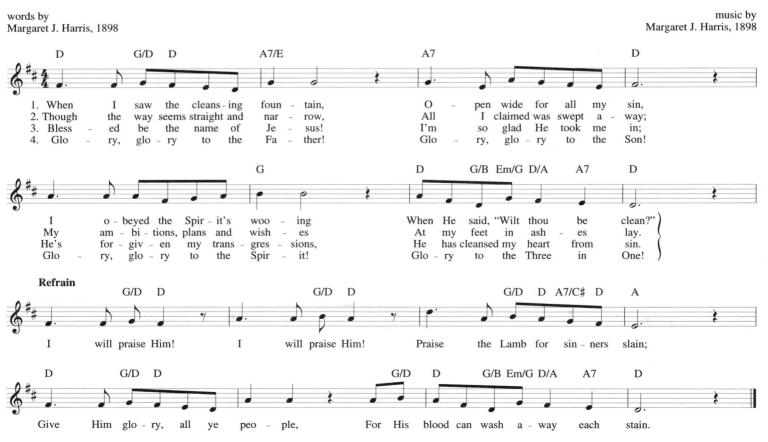

1. When I saw the cleans-ing foun-tain, O-pen wide for all my sin,
2. Though the way seems straight and nar-row, All I claimed was swept a-way;
3. Bless-ed be the name of Je-sus! I'm so glad He took me in;
4. Glo-ry, glo-ry to the Fa-ther! Glo-ry, glo-ry to the Son!

I o-beyed the Spir-it's woo-ing When He said, "Wilt thou be clean?"
My am-bi-tions, plans and wish-es At my feet in ash-es lay.
He's for-giv-en my trans-gres-sions, He has cleansed my heart from sin.
Glo-ry, glo-ry to the Spir-it! Glo-ry to the Three in One!

Refrain

I will praise Him! I will praise Him! Praise the Lamb for sin-ners slain;

Give Him glo-ry, all ye peo-ple, For His blood can wash a-way each stain.

I WANT JESUS TO WALK WITH ME

African-American Spiritual

SOJOURNER
African-American Spiritual

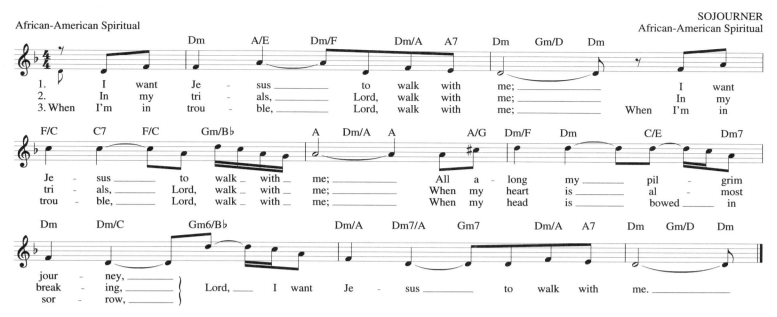

1. I want Je - sus __ to walk with me; __ I want
2. In my tri - als, __ Lord, walk with me; __ In my
3. When I'm in trou - ble, __ Lord, walk with me; __ When I'm in

Je - sus __ to walk with __ me; __ All a - long my __ pil - grim
tri - als, __ Lord, walk with __ me; __ When my heart is al - most
trou - ble, __ Lord, walk with __ me; __ When my head is bowed __ in

jour - ney, __ Lord, __ I want Je - sus __ to walk with me. __
break - ing, __
sor - row,

I WILL BLESS THEE, O LORD

words by
Esther Watanabe

I WILL BLESS THEE
music by
Esther Watanabe

I will bless Thee, O Lord. __ I will bless Thee, O
hands lift - ed up, __ And my mouth filled with

Lord. __ With a heart of thanks - giv - ing, __ I will
praise,

bless Thee, O Lord. __ With my Lord. __

I'LL BE SO GLAD WHEN JESUS COMES

Traditional words

GLAD
Traditional music

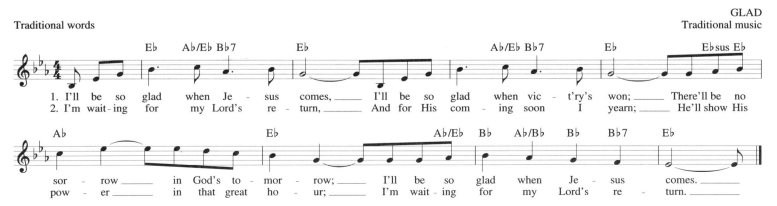

1. I'll be so glad when Je - sus comes, __ I'll be so glad when vic - t'ry's won; __ There'll be no
2. I'm wait - ing for my Lord's re - turn, __ And for His com - ing soon I yearn; __ He'll show His

sor - row __ in God's to - mor - row; __ I'll be so glad when Je - sus comes.
pow - er __ in that great ho - ur; __ I'm wait - ing for my Lord's re - turn.

I WILL REMEMBER THEE

words by
James Montgomery (1771-1854)

MANOAH
music from
Henry W. Greatorex's
Collection of Church Music, 1851

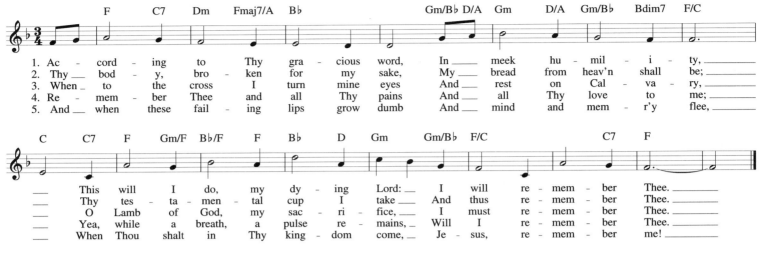

1. Ac - cord - ing to Thy gra - cious word, In ___ meek hu - mil - i - ty, ___
2. Thy ___ bod - y, bro - ken for my sake, My ___ bread from heav'n shall be; ___
3. When ___ to the cross I turn mine eyes And ___ rest on Cal - va - ry, ___
4. Re - mem - ber Thee and all Thy pains And ___ all Thy love to me; ___
5. And ___ when these fail - ing lips grow dumb And ___ mind and mem - r'y flee, ___

___ This will I do, my dy - ing Lord: ___ I will re - mem - ber Thee. ___
___ Thy tes - ta - men - tal cup I take ___ And thus re - mem - ber Thee. ___
___ O Lamb of God, my sac - ri - fice, I must re - mem - ber Thee. ___
___ Yea, while a breath, a pulse re - mains, ___ Will I re - mem - ber Thee. ___
___ When Thou shalt in Thy king - dom come, ___ Je - sus, re - mem - ber me! ___

I WILL SING OF THE MERCIES OF THE LORD

words based on
Psalm 89:1

I WILL SING
music by
James H. Fillmore (1849-1936)

I will sing of the mer - cies of the Lord for - ev - er, I will sing, I will

sing. I will sing of the mer - cies of the Lord for - ev - er, I will

sing of the mer - cies of the Lord. With my mouth ___ will I make known Thy

faith - ful - ness, Thy faith - ful-ness; With my mouth ___ I will make known Thy

faith - ful-ness to all gen - er - a - tions. I will sing of the mer - cies of the

Lord for - ev - er, I will sing, I will sing. I will sing of the mer - cies of the

Lord for - ev - er, I will sing of the mer - cies of the Lord.

I WILL SING OF MY REDEEMER

words by
Philip P. Bliss (1838-1876)

MY REDEEMER
music by
James McGranahan (1840-1907)

I WILL SING THE WONDROUS STORY

words by
Francis H. Rowley, 1886

WONDROUS STORY
music by
Peter P. Bilhorn, 1886

I WOULD BE LIKE JESUS

SPRING HILL
music by
Bentley D. Ackley

words by
James Rowe

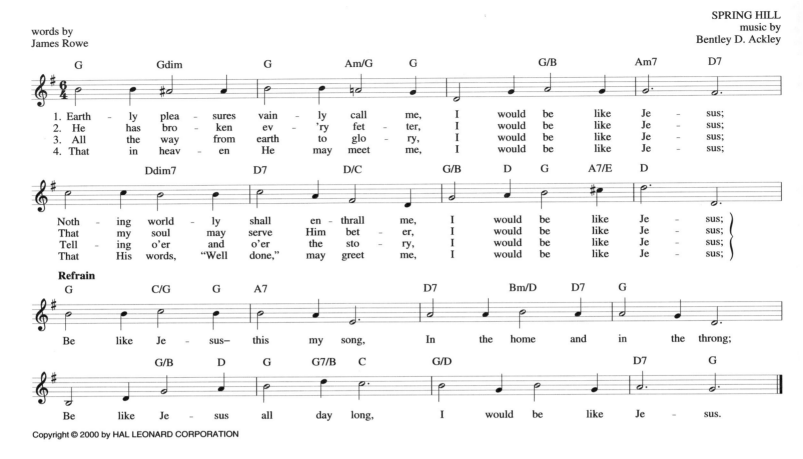

I WOULD BE TRUE

PEEK
music by
Joseph Y. Peek (1843-1911)

words by
Howard A. Walter (1883-1918)

I WOULD NOT BE DENIED

words by
Charles P. Jones, c. 1900

NOT DENIED
music by
Charles P. Jones, c. 1900

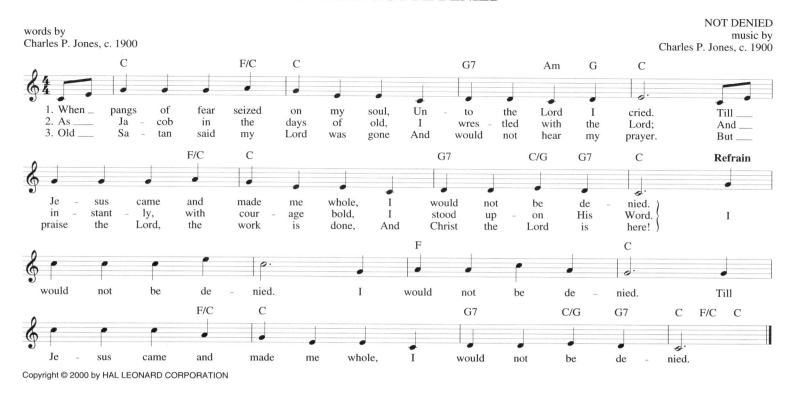

I'LL GO WHERE YOU WANT ME TO GO

words by
Mary Brown (v.1), 1894
and Charles E. Prior (v.2,3), 1894

I'LL GO
music by
Carrie E. Rounsefell, 1894

I'LL LIVE FOR HIM

words by
Ralph E. Hudson, 1882

DUNBAR
music by
C.R. Dunbar, 1882

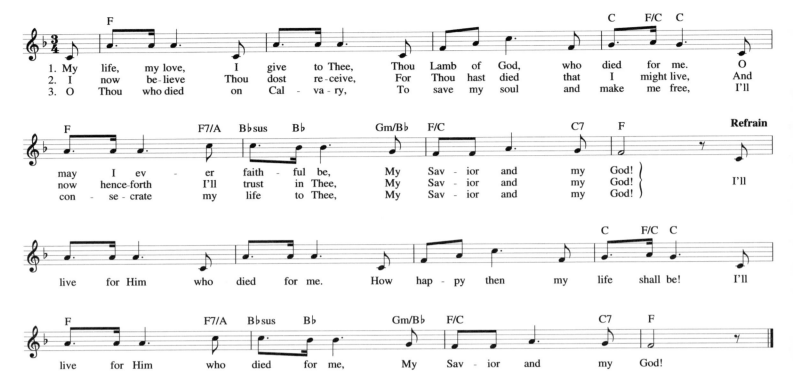

I'LL PRAISE MY MAKER WHILE I'VE BREATH

words by
Isaac Watts (1674-1748)
alt. by John Wesley (1703-1791)
based on Psalm 146

OLD 113TH
music attr. to
Mattaeus Greiter, 1525

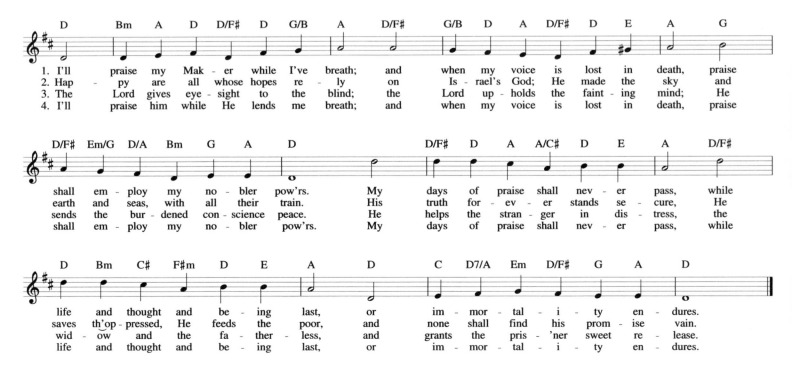

I'M GONNA SING WHEN THE SPIRIT SAYS SING

African-American Spiritual

I'M GONNA SING
African-American Spiritual

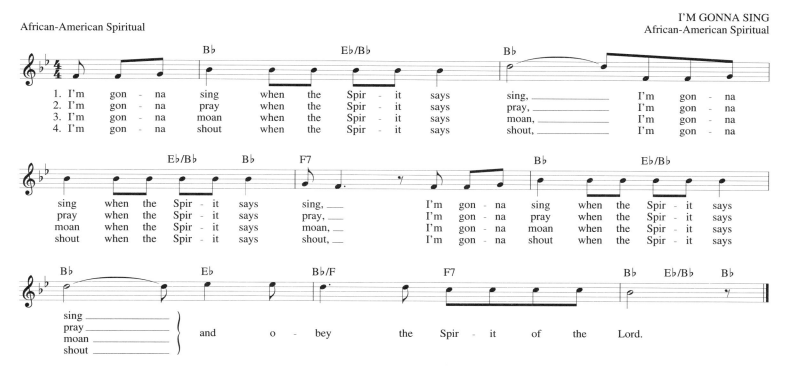

1. I'm gon - na sing when the Spir - it says sing, _____ I'm gon - na
2. I'm gon - na pray when the Spir - it says pray, _____ I'm gon - na
3. I'm gon - na moan when the Spir - it says moan, _____ I'm gon - na
4. I'm gon - na shout when the Spir - it says shout, _____ I'm gon - na

sing when the Spir - it says sing, ___ I'm gon - na sing when the Spir - it says
pray when the Spir - it says pray, ___ I'm gon - na pray when the Spir - it says
moan when the Spir - it says moan, ___ I'm gon - na moan when the Spir - it says
shout when the Spir - it says shout, ___ I'm gon - na shout when the Spir - it says

sing _____
pray _____ and o - bey the Spir - it of the Lord.
moan _____
shout _____

I'VE ANCHORED IN JESUS

words by
Lewis E. Jones, 1901

ANCHORED IN JESUS

music by
Lewis E. Jones, 1901

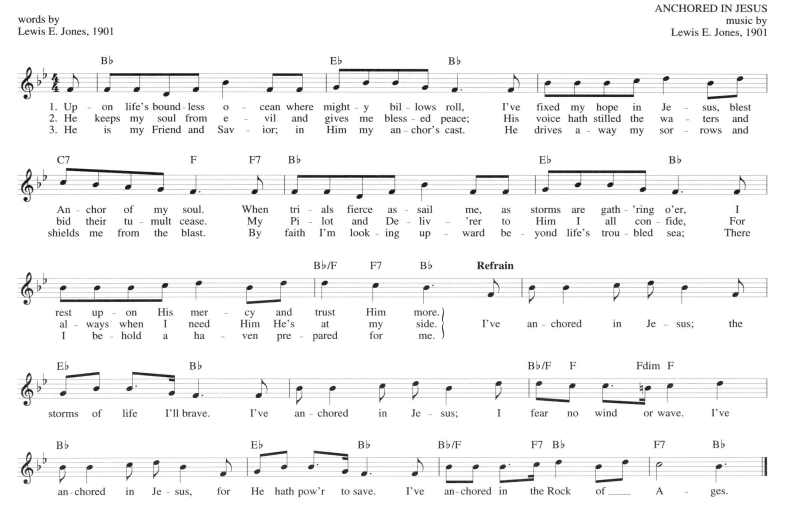

1. Up - on life's bound - less o - cean where might - y bil - lows roll, I've fixed my hope in Je - sus, blest
2. He keeps my soul from e - vil and gives me bless - ed peace; His voice hath stilled the wa - ters and
3. He is my Friend and Sav - ior; in Him my an - chor's cast. He drives a - way my sor - rows and

An - chor of my soul. When tri - als fierce as - sail me, as storms are gath - 'ring o'er, I
bid their tu - mult cease. My Pi - lot and De - liv - 'rer to Him I all con - fide, For
shields me from the blast. By faith I'm look - ing up - ward be - yond life's trou - bled sea; There

rest up - on His mer - cy and trust Him more.
al - ways when I need Him He's at my side. I've an - chored in Je - sus; the
I be - hold a ha - ven pre - pared for me.

storms of life I'll brave. I've an - chored in Je - sus; I fear no wind or wave. I've

an - chored in Je - sus, for He hath pow'r to save. I've an - chored in the Rock of ___ A - ges.

I'VE FOUND A FRIEND, O SUCH A FRIEND!

CONSTANCE

words by
James G. Small (1817-1888)

music by
Arthur Sullivan (1842-1900)

I'VE FOUND A FRIEND, O SUCH A FRIEND!

FRIEND

words by
James G. Small (1817-1888)

music by
George C. Stebbins (1846-1945)

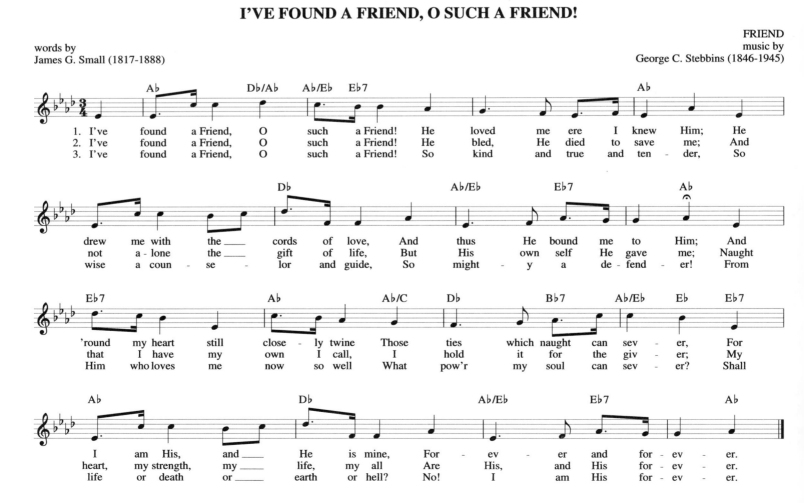

I'LL WALK WITH HIM ALWAYS

Traditional words

ALWAYS
Traditional music

The Lord is my ___ Shep - herd, I'll walk with Him al - ways. He leads by still ___ wa - ters; I'll walk with Him al - ways. Al - ways, al - ways, I'll walk with Him al - ways. Al - ways, al - ways, I'll walk with Him al - ways.

May be sung as a round.

IF GOD HIMSELF BE FOR ME

IST GOTT FÜR MICH
music by
D. Spaiser, *24 Geystliche Lieder,* Augsburg, 1609

words by
Paul Gerhardt, 1656
tr. based on Richard Massie, 1857

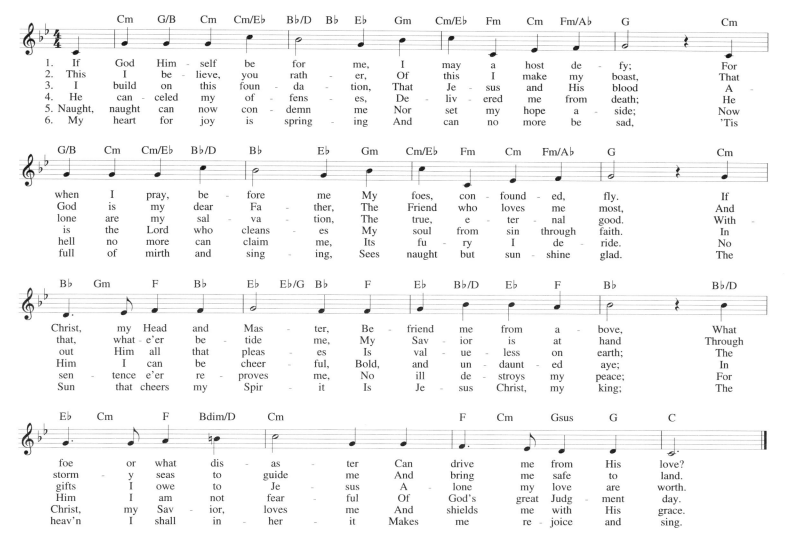

1. If God Him - self be for me, I may a host de - fy; For when I pray, be - fore me My foes, con - found - ed, fly. If Christ, my Head and Mas - ter, Be - friend me from a - bove, What foe or what dis - as - ter Can drive me from His love?

2. This I be - lieve, you rath - er, Of this I make my boast, That God is my dear Fa - ther, The Friend who loves me most, And that, what - e'er be - tide me, My Sav - ior is at hand, Through storm - y seas to guide me And bring me safe to land.

3. I build on this foun - da - tion, That Je - sus and His blood A - lone are my sal - va - tion, The true, e - ter - nal good. With - out Him all that pleas - es Is val - ue - less on earth; The gifts I owe to Je - sus A - lone my love are worth.

4. He can - celed my of - fens - es, De - liv - ered me from death; He is the Lord who cleans - es My soul from sin through faith. In Him I can be cheer - ful, Bold, and un - daunt - ed aye; Of God's great Judg - ment Day.

5. Naught, naught can now con - demn me Nor set my hope a - side; Now hell no more can claim me, Its fu - ry I de - ride. No sen - tence e'er re - proves me, No ill de - stroys my peace; For Christ, my Sav - ior, loves me And shields me with His grace.

6. My heart for joy is spring - ing And can no more be sad, 'Tis full of mirth and sing - ing, Sees naught but sun - shine glad. The Sun that cheers my Spir - it Is Je - sus Christ, my king; The heav'n I shall in - her - it Makes me re - joice and sing.

206

I'VE GOT PEACE LIKE A RIVER

PEACE LIKE A RIVER
Traditional music

Traditional words

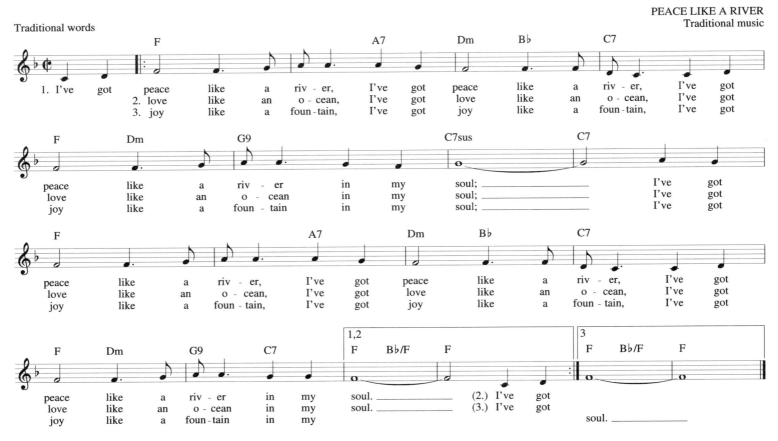

IF THOU BUT SUFFER GOD TO GUIDE THEE

NEUMARK

words by
Georg Neumark, 1657
tr. by Catherine Winkworth, 1863

music by
Georg Neumark, 1657

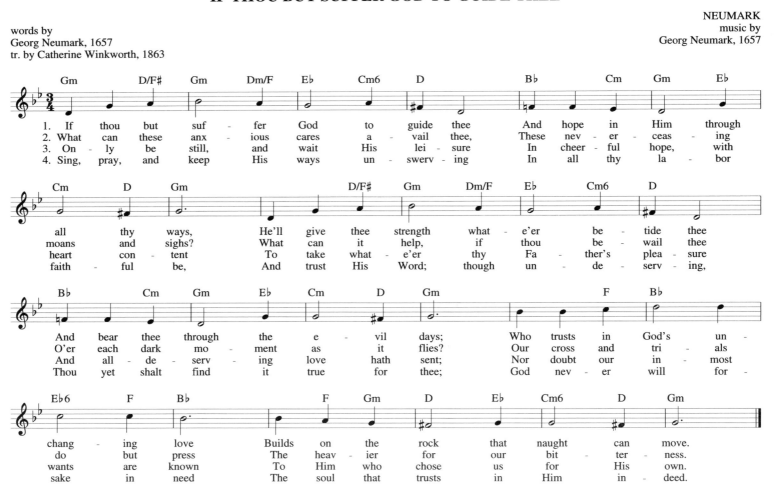

IF JESUS GOES WITH ME

words by
C. Austin Miles, 1908

IF JESUS GOES
music by
C. Arthur Miles, 1908

1. It may be in the val - ley, where count - less dan - gers hide; ___ It
2. It may be I must car - ry the bless - ed word of life ___ A -
3. But if it be my por - tion to bear my cross at home, ___ While
4. It is not mine to ques - tion the judg - ments of my Lord; ___ It

may be in the sun - shine that I in peace a - bide. ___ But
cross the burn - ing des - erts to those in sin - ful strife; ___ And
oth - ers bear their bur - dens be - yond the bil - lows' foam, ___ I'll
is but mine to fol - low the lead - ings of His Word. ___ But

this one thing I know ___ if it be dark or fair, ___ If
tho' it be my lot ___ to bear my col - ors there, ___ If
prove my faith in Him, ___ con - fess His judg - ments fair; ___ And
if to go or stay, ___ or wheth - er here or there, ___ I'll

Je - sus is with me, ___ I'll go an - y - where! ___
Je - sus goes with me, ___ I'll go an - y - where! ___
if He stays with me, ___ I'll stay an - y - where! ___
be, with my Sav - ior, ___ con - tent an - y - where! ___

Refrain
If Je - sus goes with me, I'll

go an - y - where! ___ 'Tis heav - en to me, wher - e'er I may be, if He is

there! ___ I count it a priv - i - lege here ___ His cross to

bear. ___ If Je - sus goes with me, I'll go ___ an - y - where!

IN ALL MY VAST CONCERNS WITH THEE

words by
Isaac Watts (1674-1748)

DOWNS
music by
Lowell Mason (1792-1872)

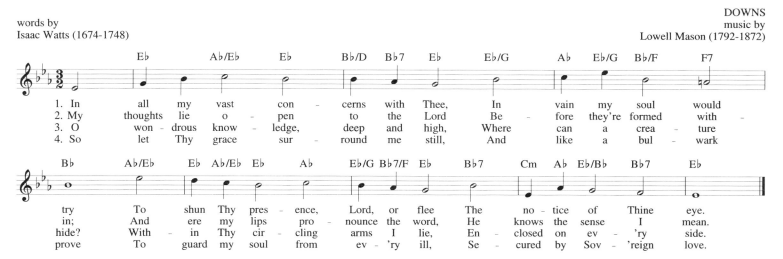

1. In all my vast con - cerns with Thee, In vain my soul would
2. My thoughts lie o - pen to the Lord, Be - fore they're formed with -
3. O won - drous know - ledge, deep and high, Where can a crea - ture
4. So let Thy grace sur - round me still, And like a bul - wark

try To shun Thy pres - ence, Lord, or flee The no - tice of Thine eye.
in; And ere my lips pro - nounce the word, He knows the sense I mean.
hide? With - in Thy cir - cling arms I lie, En - closed on ev - 'ry side.
prove To guard my soul from ev - 'ry ill, Se - cured by Sov - 'reign love.

IMMORTAL, INVISIBLE

words by
Walter Chalmers Smith (1824-1908)

ST. DENIO
Traditional Welsh melody
from John Roberts' *Canaidau y Cyssegr*, 1839

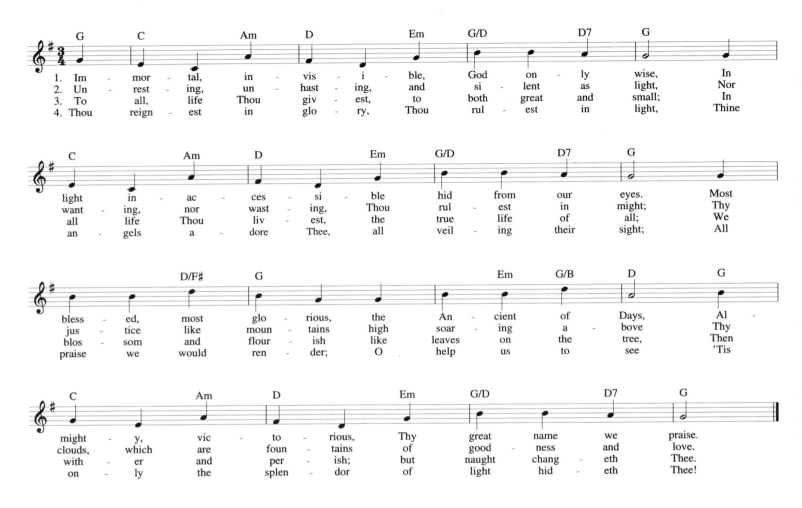

1. Im - mor - tal, in - vis - i - ble, God on - ly wise, In
2. Un - rest - ing, un - hast - ing, and si - lent as light, Nor
3. To all, life Thou giv - est, to both great and small; In
4. Thou reign - est in glo - ry, Thou rul - est in light, Thine

light in - ac - ces - si - ble hid from our eyes. Most
want - ing, nor wast - ing, Thou rul - est in might; Thy
all life Thou liv - est, the true life of all; We
an - gels a - dore Thee, all veil - ing their sight; All

bless - ed, most glo - rious, the An - cient of Days, Al -
jus - tice like moun - tains high soar - ing a - bove Thy
blos - som and flour - ish like leaves on the tree, Then
praise we would ren - der; O help us to see 'Tis

might - y, vic - to - rious, Thy great name we praise.
clouds, which are foun - tains of good - ness and love.
with - er and per - ish; but naught chang - eth Thee.
on - ly the splen - dor of light hid - eth Thee!

Copyright © 2000 by HAL LEONARD CORPORATION

IN CHRIST THERE IS NO EAST OR WEST

words by
John Oxenham, 1908

McKEE
African-American melody

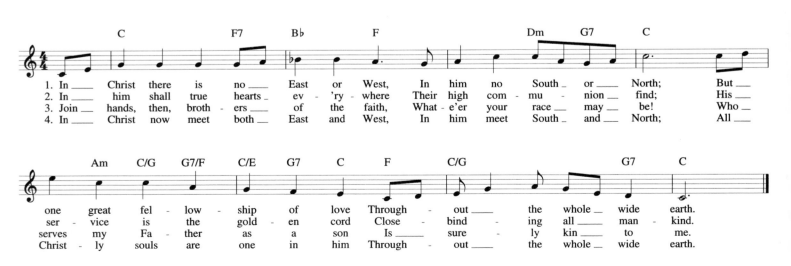

1. In Christ there is no East or West, In him no South or North;
2. In him shall true hearts ev - 'ry - where Their high com - mu - nion find;
3. Join hands, then, broth - ers of the faith, What - e'er your race may be!
4. In Christ now meet both East and West, In him meet South and North;

one great fel - low - ship of love Through - out the whole wide earth.
ser - vice is the gold - en cord Close bind - ing all man - kind.
serves my Fa - ther as a son Is sure - ly kin to me.
Christ - ly souls are one in him Through - out the whole wide earth.

Copyright © 2000 by HAL LEONARD CORPORATION

IN CHRIST THERE IS NO EAST OR WEST

words by
John Oxenham, 1908

ST. PETER
music by
Alexander Robert Reinagle, 1836

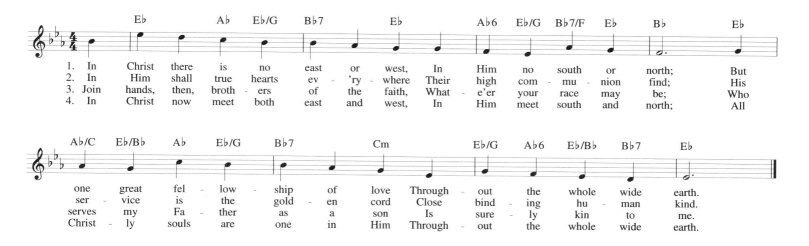

1. In Christ there is no east or west, In Him no south or north; But
2. In Him shall true hearts ev - 'ry - where Their high com - mu - nion find; His
3. Join hands, then, broth - ers of the faith, What - e'er your race may be; Who
4. In Christ now meet both east and west, In Him meet south and north; All

one great fel - low - ship of love Through - out the whole wide earth.
ser - vice is the gold - en cord Close bind - ing hu - man kind.
serves my Fa - ther as a son Is sure - ly kin to me.
Christ - ly souls are one in Him Through - out the whole wide earth.

IN HEAVEN ABOVE

words by
Laurentius L. Laurinus
rev. by John Astrom
tr. by William Maccall (1812-1888)

HAUGE
Norwegian Folk melody

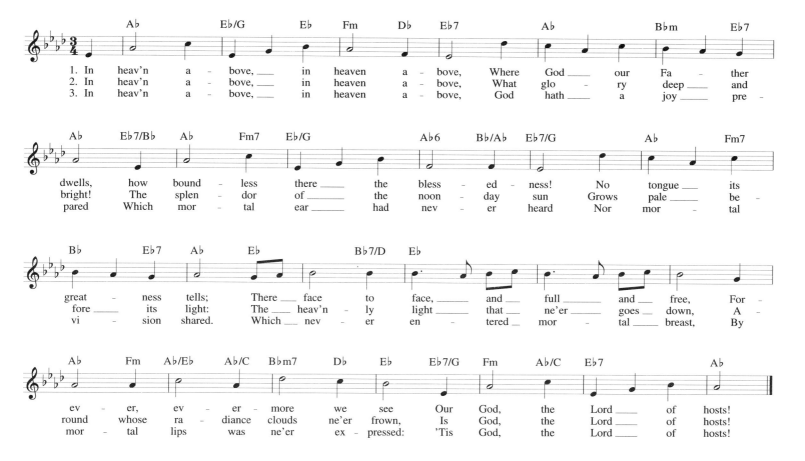

1. In heav'n a - bove, in heaven a - bove, Where God our Fa - ther
2. In heav'n a - bove, in heaven a - bove, What glo - ry deep and
3. In heav'n a - bove, in heaven a - bove, God hath a joy pre -

dwells, how bound - less there the bless - ed - ness! No tongue its
bright! The splen - dor of the noon - day sun Grows pale be -
pared Which mor - tal ear had nev - er heard Nor mor - tal

great - ness tells; There face to face, and full and free, For -
fore its light: The heav'n - ly light that ne'er goes down, A -
vi - sion shared. Which nev - er en - tered mor - tal breast, By

ev - er, ev - er - more we see Our God, the Lord of hosts!
round whose ra - diance clouds ne'er frown, Is God, the Lord of hosts!
mor - tal lips was ne'er ex - pressed: 'Tis God, the Lord of hosts!

IN HEAVENLY LOVE ABIDING

AURELIA
music by
Samuel S. Wesley, 1864

words by
Anna L. Waring, 1850

IN THE CROSS OF CHRIST I GLORY

RATHBUN
music by
Ithamar Conkey, 1849

words by
John Bowring, 1825

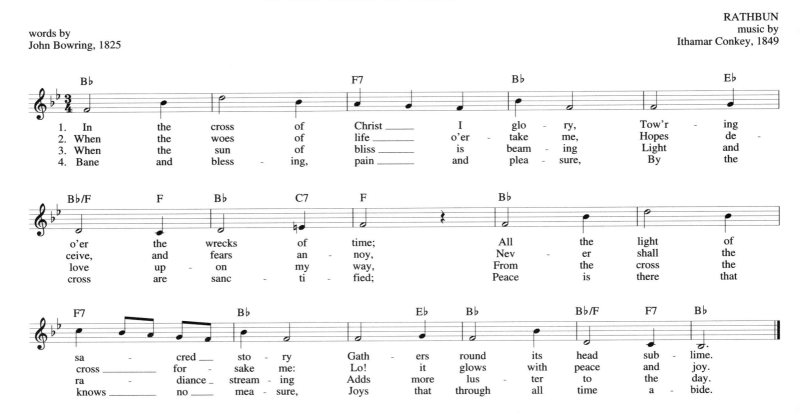

IN THE GARDEN

words by
C. Austin Miles, 1912

GARDEN
music by
C. Austin Miles, 1912

1. I come to the gar-den a-lone _____ while the dew is still on the ros-es. And the
2. He speaks and the sound of His voice _____ is so sweet the birds stop their sing-ing. And the
3. I'd stay in the gar-den with Him, _____ though the night a-round me be fall-ing. But He

voice I hear fall-ing on my ear, the Son of God dis-clos-es.
mel-o-dy that He gave to me with-in my heart is ring-ing. } And He
bids me go; thru the voice of woe, His voice to me is call-ing.

walks with me and He talks with me, and He tells me I am His own. _____ And the

joy we share as we tar-ry there, none oth-er has ev-er _____ known. _____

IN THE HOUR OF TRIAL

words by
James Montgomery (1771-1854)
alt. by Frances A. Hutton (1811-1877)

PENITENCE
music by
Spencer Lane (1843-1903)

1. In the hour of tri-al, Je-sus, plead for me;
2. With for-bid-den plea-sures Would this vain world charm,
3. Should Thy mer-cy send me Sor-row, toil, and woe,
4. When my last hour com-eth, Fraught with strife and pain,

Lest by base de-ni-al, I de-part from Thee.
Or its sor-did trea-sures Spread to work me harm;
Or should pain at-tend me On my path be-low,
When my dust re-turn-eth To the dust a-gain,

When Thou see'st me wa-ver, With a look re-call, _____
Bring to my re-mem-brance Sad Geth-sem-a-ne, _____
Grant that I may nev-er Fail Thy hand to see: _____
On Thy truth re-ly-ing, Through that mor-tal strife: _____

Nor for fear or fa-vor Suf-fer me to fall.
Or, in dark-er sem-blance, Cross-crowned Cal-va-ry.
Grant that I may ev-er Cast my care on Thee.
Je-sus, take me, dy-ing, To e-ter-nal life.

IN THE NEW JERUSALEM

words by
C.B. Widmeyer, 1911

music by
C.B. Widmeyer, 1911

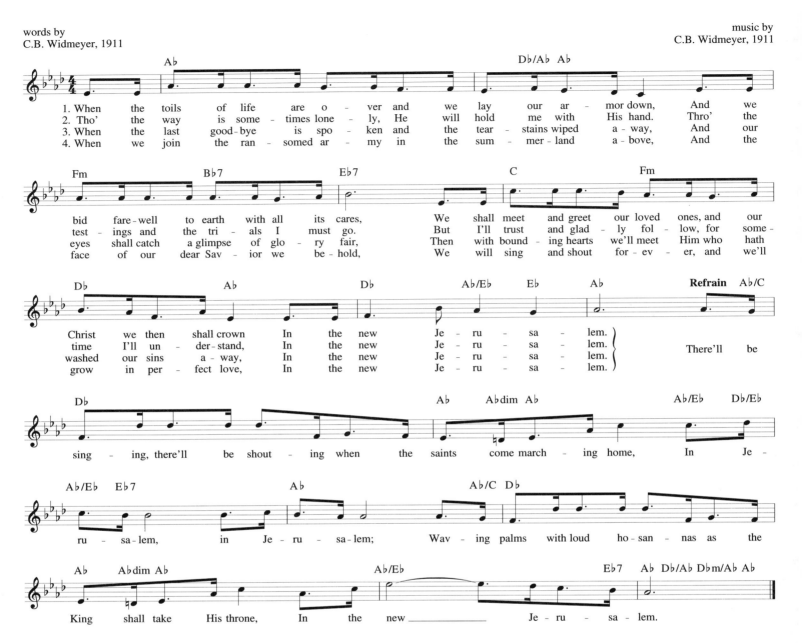

1. When the toils of life are o - ver and we lay our ar - mor down, And we
2. Tho' the way is some - times lone - ly, He will hold me with His hand. And Thro' the
3. When the last good-bye is spo - ken and the tear - stains wiped a - way, And our
4. When we join the ran - somed ar - my in the sum - mer - land a - bove, And the

bid fare-well to earth with all its cares, We shall meet and greet our loved ones, and our
test - ings and the tri - als I must go. But I'll trust and glad - ly fol - low, for some-
eyes shall catch a glimpse of glo - ry fair, Then with bound - ing hearts we'll meet Him who hath
face of our dear Sav - ior we be - hold, We will sing and shout for - ev - er, and we'll

Christ we then shall crown In the new Je - ru - sa - lem.
time I'll un - der-stand, In the new Je - ru - sa - lem.
washed our sins a - way, In the new Je - ru - sa - lem.
grow in per - fect love, In the new Je - ru - sa - lem.

Refrain There'll be

sing - ing, there'll be shout - ing when the saints come march - ing home, In Je -

ru - sa-lem, in Je - ru - sa-lem; Wav - ing palms with loud ho - san - nas as the

King shall take His throne, In the new _____ Je - ru - sa - lem.

IN THE SERVICE OF THE KING

SERVICE OF THE KING

words by
Alfred H. Ackley, 1912

music by
Bentley D. Ackley, 1912

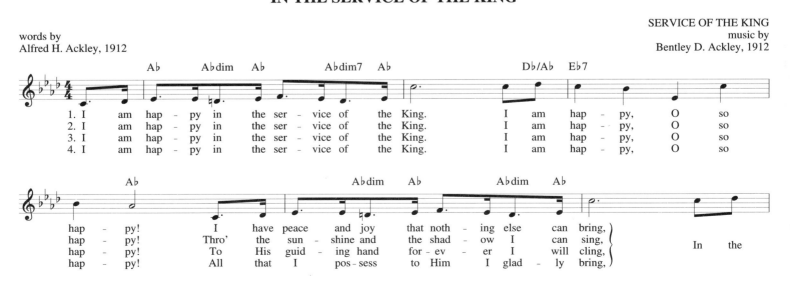

1. I am hap - py in the ser - vice of the King. I am hap - py, O so
2. I am hap - py in the ser - vice of the King. I am hap - py, O so
3. I am hap - py in the ser - vice of the King. I am hap - py, O so
4. I am hap - py in the ser - vice of the King. I am hap - py, O so

hap - py! I have peace and joy that noth - ing else can bring, In the
hap - py! Thro' the sun - shine and the shad - ow I can sing,
hap - py! To His guid - ing hand for - ev - er I will cling,
hap - py! All that I pos - sess to Him I glad - ly bring,

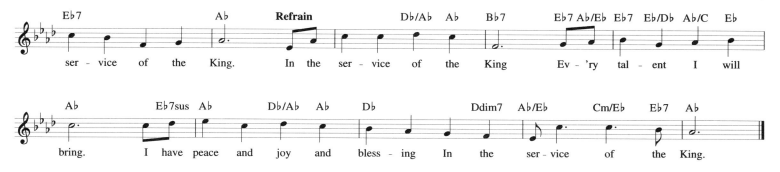

ser - vice of the King. In the ser - vice of the King Ev - 'ry tal - ent I will

bring. I have peace and joy and bless - ing In the ser - vice of the King.

IN THEE IS GLADNESS

IN DIR IST FREUDE

words by
Johann Lindemann, 1598
tr. by Catherine Winkworth, 1858

music by
Giovanni Giacomo Gastoldi, 1593

1. In Thee is glad - ness, a - mid all sad - ness, Je - sus, sun - shine
2. If God be ours, we fear no pow - ers, not of earth or

of my heart. By Thee are giv - en the gifts of heav - en, Thou the
sin or death. God sees and bless - es in worst dis - tress - es, and can

true Re - deem - er art. Our souls Thou mak - est, our bonds Thou
change them in a breath. Where - fore the sto - ry tell of God's

break - est; who trusts Thee sure - ly hath built se - cure - ly, and stands for - ev - er.
glo - ry with heart and voic - es; all heaven re - joic - es, sing - ing for - ev - er.

Al - le - lu - ia! Our hearts are pin - ing to see Thy shin - ing: dy - ing or
Al - le - lu - ia! We shout for glad - ness, tri - umph o'er sad - ness, lov - ing and

liv - ing, to Thee are cleav - ing; naught ran us sev - er. Al - le - lu - ia!
prais - ing, voic - es still rais - ing glad hymns for - ev - er. Al - le - lu - ia!

IN THEE, LORD, HAVE I PUT MY TRUST

IN DICH HAB' ICH GEHOFFET
music from
Sunderreiter's *Himmlische Harfen,* 1573

words by
Adam Reusner, 1533
tr. by Catherine Winkworth, 1863

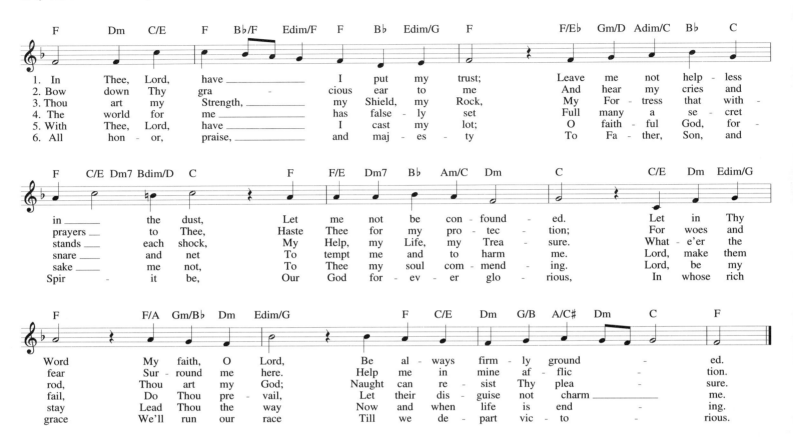

1. In Thee, Lord, have ____ I put my trust; Leave me not help - less in ____ the dust, Let me not be con - found - ed. Let in Thy Word My faith, O Lord, Be al - ways firm - ly ground - ed.
2. Bow down Thy gra - cious ear to me And hear my cries and prayers ____ to Thee, Haste Thee for my pro - tec - tion; For woes and fear Sur - round me here. Help me in mine af - flic - tion.
3. Thou art my Strength, ____ my Shield, my Rock, My For - tress that with - stands ____ each shock, My Help, my Life, my Trea - sure. What - e'er the rod, Thou art my God; Naught can re - sist Thy plea - sure.
4. The world for me ____ has false - ly set Full many a se - cret snare ____ and net To tempt me and to harm me. Lord, make them fail, Do Thou pre - vail, Let their dis - guise not charm ____ me.
5. With Thee, Lord, have ____ I cast my lot; O faith - ful God, for - sake ____ me not, To Thee my soul com - mend - ing. Lord, be my stay Lead Thou the way Now and when life is end - ing.
6. All hon - or, praise, ____ and maj - es - ty To Fa - ther, Son, and Spir - it be, Our God for - ev - er glo - rious, In whose rich grace We'll run our race Till we de - part vic - to - rious.

Copyright © 2000 by HAL LEONARD CORPORATION

IN THY CLEFT, O ROCK OF AGES

HIDE THOU ME
music by
Robert Lowry (1826-1899)

words by
Fanny J. Crosby (1820-1915)

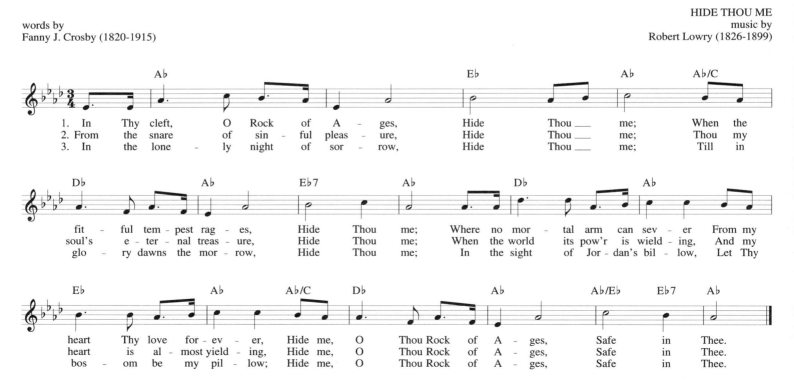

1. In Thy cleft, O Rock of A - ges, Hide Thou ____ me; When the fit - ful tem - pest rag - es, Hide Thou me; Where no mor - tal arm can sev - er From my heart Thy love for - ev - er, Hide me, O Thou Rock of A - ges, Safe in Thee.
2. From the snare of sin - ful pleas - ure, Hide Thou ____ me; When Thou my soul's e - ter - nal treas - ure, Hide Thou me; When the world its pow'r is wield - ing, And my heart is al - most yield - ing, Hide me, O Thou Rock of A - ges, Safe in Thee.
3. In the lone - ly night of sor - row, Hide Thou ____ me; Till in glo - ry dawns the mor - row, Hide Thou me; In the sight of Jor - dan's bil - low, Let Thy bos - om be my pil - low; Hide me, O Thou Rock of A - ges, Safe in Thee.

Copyright © 2000 by HAL LEONARD CORPORATION

INFANT HOLY, INFANT LOWLY

Traditional Polish carol
para. by Edith M.G. Reed

W ZLOBIE LEZY
Traditional Polish melody

IS IT FOR ME?

words by
Frances R. Havergal, 1871

O'KANE
music by
Tullius C. O'Kane, 1871

IS IT THE CROWNING DAY

words by
George Walker Whitcomb, 20th century

CROWNING DAY
music by
Charles H. Marsh (1886-1956)

1. Je - sus may come to - day, _____ Glad day! Glad day! And I would see my
2. I may go home to - day, _____ Glad day! Glad day! Seem - eth I hear their
3. Faith - ful I'll be to - day, _____ Glad day! Glad day! And I will free - ly

Friend; _____ Dan - gers and trou - bles would end _____ If Je - sus should come to -
song; _____ Hail to the ra - di - ant throng! _____ If I should go home to -
tell _____ Why I should love Him so well, _____ For He is my all to -

day. _____ Glad day! Glad day! Is it the crown - ing
day. _____
day. _____

day? _____ I'll live for to - day, nor anx - ious be, Je - sus my Lord I

soon shall see; Glad day! Glad day! Is it the crown - ing day? _____

IS THY HEART RIGHT WITH GOD?

words by
Elisha A. Hoffman (1839-1929)

IS THY HEART RIGHT?
music by
Elisha A. Hoffman (1839-1929)

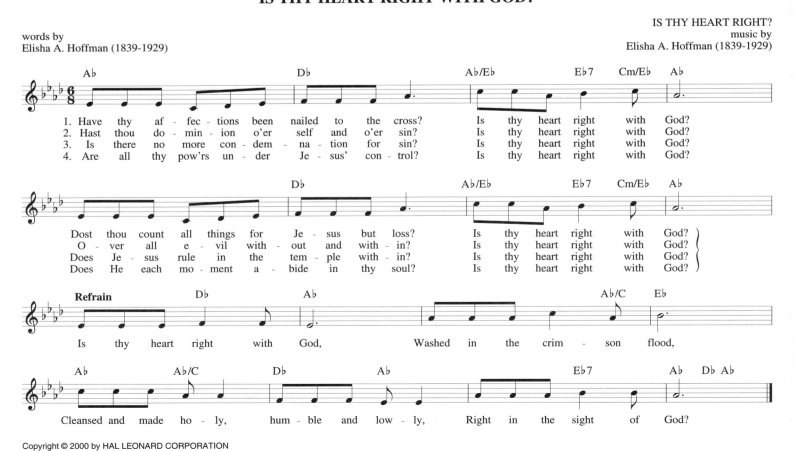

1. Have thy af - fec - tions been nailed to the cross? Is thy heart right with God?
2. Hast thou do - min - ion o'er self and o'er sin? Is thy heart right with God?
3. Is there no more con - dem - na - tion for sin? Is thy heart right with God?
4. Are all thy pow'rs un - der Je - sus' con - trol? Is thy heart right with God?

Dost thou count all things for Je - sus but loss? Is thy heart right with God?
O - ver all e - vil with - out and with - in? Is thy heart right with God?
Does Je - sus rule in the tem - ple with - in? Is thy heart right with God?
Does He each mo - ment a - bide in thy soul? Is thy heart right with God?

Refrain

Is thy heart right with God, Washed in the crim - son flood,

Cleansed and made ho - ly, hum - ble and low - ly, Right in the sight of God?

IT CAME UPON THE MIDNIGHT CLEAR

CAROL

words by
Edmund Hamilton Sears (1810-1876)

music by
Richard Storrs Willis (1819-1900)

IS YOUR ALL ON THE ALTAR?

HOFFMAN

words by
Elisha A. Hoffman, 1905

music by
Elisha A. Hoffman, 1905

1. You have longed for sweet peace, and for faith to in-crease, And have ear-nest-ly,
2. Would you walk with the Lord in the light of His Word, And have peace and con-
3. Oh, we nev-er can know what the Lord will be-stow Of the bless-ings for
4. Who can tell all the love He will send from a-bove, And how hap-py our

fer-vent-ly prayed; But you can-not have rest or be per-fect-ly blest, Un-til
tent-ment al-way? You must do His sweet will to be free from all ill, On the
which we have prayed, Till our bod-y and soul He doth ful-ly con-trol, And our
hearts will be made, Of the fel-low-ship sweet we shall share at His feet, When our

all on the al-tar is laid.
al-tar your all you must lay.
all on the al-tar is laid.
all on the al-tar is laid.

Refrain Is your all on the al-tar of

sac-ri-fice laid? Your heart, does the Spir-it con-trol? You can on-ly be

blest and have peace and sweet rest, As you yield Him your bod-y and soul.

IT CLEANSETH ME

words by
F.L. Snyder, 1899

music by
A.F. Meyers, 1899

1. There is a stream that flows from Cal-va-ry, A crim-son tide so
2. Its sav-ing vir-tues ev-er are the same. It cleans-eth still, and
3. No oth-er foun-tain can for sin a-tone But Je-sus' blood— O

deep and wide. It wash-es whit-er than the pur-est snow; It
al-ways will. Poor sin-ners who will seek the Sav-ior's face Shall
pre-cious flood! And who-so-ev-er will may plunge there-in, And

cleans-eth me, I know.
know His won-drous grace.
be made free from sin.

Refrain Hal-le-lu-jah! 'tis His blood that cleans-eth me; 'Tis His

grace that makes me free. And, my broth-er, 'tis for thee. O hal-le-lu-jah! 'tis sal-

va-tion full and free; And it cleans-eth, yes, it cleans-eth me.

IT IS GLORY JUST TO WALK WITH HIM

GLORY JUST TO WALK

words by
Avis B. Christiansen, 1918

music by
Haldor Lillenas, 1918

1. It is glo - ry just to walk with Him whose blood has ran - somed me; It is
2. It is glo - ry when the shad - ows fall to know that He is near. O what
3. 'Twill be glo - ry when I walk with Him on heav - en's gold - en shore, Nev - er

rap - ture for my soul each day. It is joy di - vine to feel Him near wher -
joy to sim - ply trust and pray! It is glo - ry to a - bide in Him when
from His side a - gain to stray. 'Twill be glo - ry, won - drous glo - ry with the

e'er my path may be. Bless the Lord, it's glo - ry all the way!
skies a - bove are clear. Yes, with Him, it's glo - ry all the way! It is
Sav - ior ev - er - more, Ev - er - last - ing glo - ry all the way!

glo - ry just to walk with Him. It is glo - ry just to walk with Him. He will

guide my steps a - right Thro' the vale and o'er the height. It is glo - ry just to walk with Him.

IT IS GOOD TO SING THY PRAISES

ELLESDIE

words from *The Psalter,* 1912
based on Psalm 92

music from Leavitt's *The Christian Lyre,* 1831
attr. to Wolfgang A. Mozart
arr. by Hubert P. Main, c. 1868

1. It is good to sing Thy prais - es And to thank Thee, O Most High—
2. Thou hast filled my heart with glad - ness Thro' the works Thy hands have wrought.
3. But the good shall live be - fore Thee, Plant - ed in Thy dwell - ing place—

Show - ing forth Thy lov - ing - kind - ness When the morn - ing lights the sky.
Thou hast made my life vic - to - rious; Great Thy works and deep Thy thought.
Fruit - ful trees and ev - er ver - dant, Nour - ished by Thy bound - less grace.

It is good, when night is fall - ing, Of Thy faith - ful - ness to tell,
Thou, O Lord, on high ex - alt - ed, Reign - est ev - er - more in might.
In His good - ness to the right - eous, God His right - eous - ness dis - plays.

While, with sweet me - lo - dious prais - es, Songs of ad - o - ra - tion swell.
All Thy en - e - mies shall per - ish— Sin be ban - ished from Thy sight.
God, my Rock, my Strength, my Ref - uge— Just and true are all His ways.

IT IS MINE

words by
Elisha A. Hoffman (1839-1929)

music by
William Edie Marks, 20th century

1. God's a - bid - ing peace is in my soul to - day. Yes, I feel it now; yes, I
2. He has wrought in me a sweet and per - fect rest; In my rap - tured heart I can
3. He has giv - en me a nev - er - fail - ing joy. O, I have it now! O, I
4. O, the love of God is com - fort - ing my soul, For His love is mine— yes, His

feel it now. He has tak - en all my doubts and fears a - way, Tho' I can - not tell you
feel it now. He each pass - ing mo - ment keeps me saved and blest, Floods with light my heart and
have it now! To His praise I will my ran - somed pow'rs em - ploy, And re - new my grate - ful
love is mine. Waves of joy and glad - ness o'er my spir - it roll, Thrill - ing me with life di -

Refrain

how.
brow.
vow.
vine.

It is mine, mine; bless - ed be His name! He has giv - en peace, per - fect

peace to me. It is mine, mine; bless - ed be His name—Mine for all e - ter - ni - ty!

Copyright © 2000 by HAL LEONARD CORPORATION

IT IS TRULY WONDERFUL

TRULY WONDERFUL

words by
Barney E. Warren, 1897

music by
Barney E. Warren, 1897

1. He par - doned my trans - gres - sions; He sanc - ti - fied my soul. He
2. He keeps me ev - 'ry mo - ment By trust - ing in His grace. 'Tis
3. He brings me thro' af - flic - tion; He leaves me not a - lone. He's
4. He pros - pers and pro - tects me; His bless - ings ev - er flow. He
5. There's not a sin - gle bless - ing Which we re - ceive on earth That

hon - ors my con - fes - sions Since by His blood I'm whole.
thro' His blest a - tone - ment That I may see His face.
with me in temp - ta - tion; He keeps me for His own.
fills me with His glo - ry; He makes me white as snow.
does not come from heav - en, The source of our new birth.

It is

Refrain

tru - ly won - der - ful what the Lord has done! It is tru - ly won - der - ful! It is

tru - ly won - der - ful what the Lord has done! Glo - ry to His name!

Copyright © 2000 by HAL LEONARD CORPORATION

IT IS WELL WITH MY SOUL

VILLE DU HAVRE

words by
Horatio G. Spafford (1828-1888)

music by
Philip P. Bliss (1838-1876)

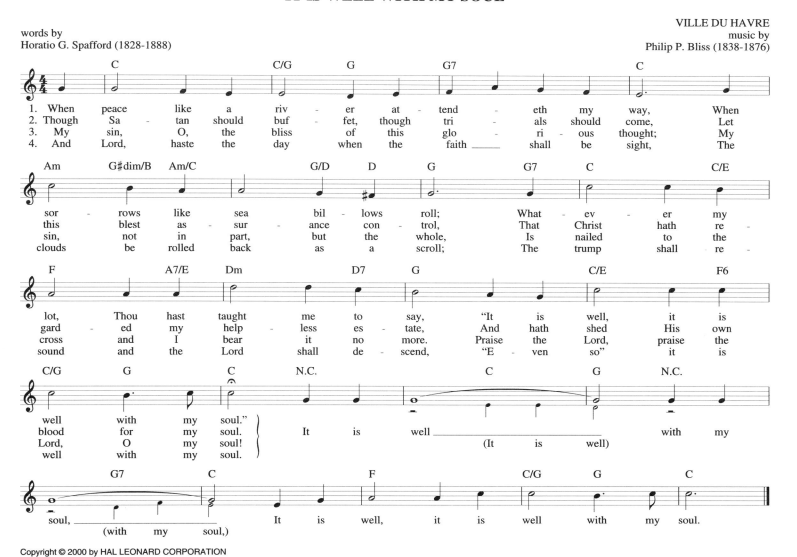

IVORY PALACES

words by
Henry Barraclough, 1915

music by
Henry Barraclough, 1915

IT'S JUST LIKE HIS GREAT LOVE

words by
Edna R. Worrell, 1903

HIS GREAT LOVE
music by
Clarence B. Strouse, 1903

JERUSALEM, MY HAPPY HOME

words attr. to
Joseph Bromehead (1747-1826)

ST. PETER
music by
Alexander R. Reinagle, 1836

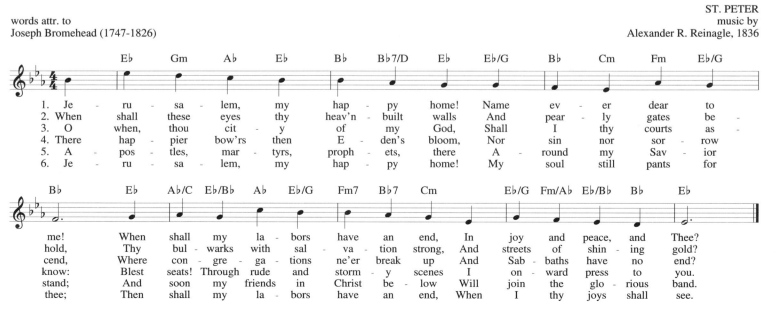

JERUSALEM THE GOLDEN

words by
Bernard of Cluny, c. 1145
tr. by John Mason Neale, 1851

EWING
music by
Alexander Ewing, 1853

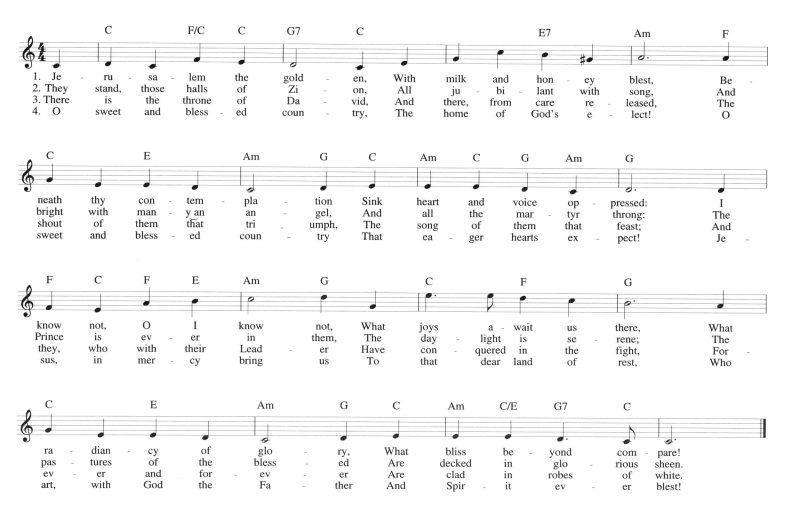

1. Je - ru - sa - lem the gold - en, With milk and hon - ey blest, Be
2. They stand, those halls of Zi - on, All ju - bi - lant with song, And
3. There is the throne of Da - vid, And there, from care re - leased, The
4. O sweet and bless - ed coun - try, The home of God's e - lect! O

neath thy con - tem - pla - tion Sink heart and voice op - pressed: I
bright with man - y an an - gel, And all the mar - tyr throng: The
shout of them that tri - umph, The song of them that feast; And
sweet and bless - ed coun - try That ea - ger hearts ex - pect! Je -

know not, O I know not, What joys a - wait us there, What
Prince is ev - er in them, The day - light is se - rene; The
they, who with their Lead - er Have con - quered in the fight, For -
sus, in mer - cy bring us To that dear land of rest, Who

ra - dian - cy of glo - ry, What bliss be - yond com - pare!
pas - tures of the bless - ed Are decked in glo - rious sheen.
ev - er and for - ev - er Are clad in robes of white.
art, with God the Fa - ther And Spir - it ev - er blest!

JESUS BIDS US SHINE

words by
Anna B. Warner (1820-1915)

music by
Edwin O. Excell (1851-1921)

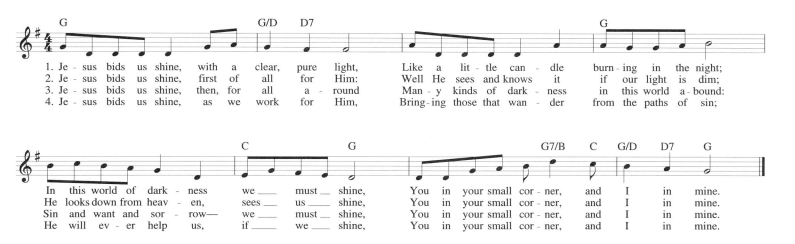

1. Je - sus bids us shine, with a clear, pure light, Like a lit - tle can - dle burn - ing in the night;
2. Je - sus bids us shine, first of all for Him: Well He sees and knows it if our light is dim;
3. Je - sus bids us shine, then, for all a - round Man - y kinds of dark - ness in this world a - bound:
4. Je - sus bids us shine, as we work for Him, Bring - ing those that wan - der from the paths of sin;

In this world of dark - ness we must shine, You in your small cor - ner, and I in mine.
He looks down from heav - en, sees us shine, You in your small cor - ner, and I in mine.
Sin and want and sor - row— we must shine, You in your small cor - ner, and I in mine.
He will ev - er help us, if we shine, You in your small cor - ner, and I in mine.

JESUS CALLS US O'ER THE TUMULT

GALILEE
music by
William H. Jude, 1874

words by
Cecil Frances Alexander, 1852

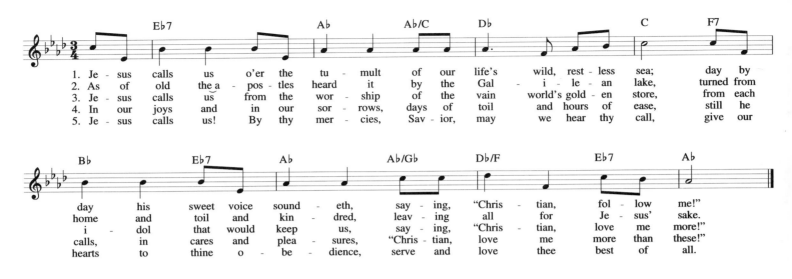

					Eb7							Ab	Ab/C	Db			C	F7	

1. Je - sus calls us o'er the tu - mult of our life's wild, rest - less sea; day by
2. As of old the a - pos - tles heard it by the Gal - i - le - an lake, turned from
3. Je - sus calls us from the wor - ship of the vain world's gold - en store, from each
4. In our joys and in our sor - rows, days of toil and hours of ease, still he
5. Je - sus calls us! By thy mer - cies, Sav - ior, may we hear thy call, give our

Bb Eb7 Ab Ab/Gb Db/F Eb7 Ab

day his sweet voice sound - eth, say - ing, "Chris - tian, fol - low me!"
home and toil and kin - dred, leav - ing all, for Je - sus' sake.
i - dol that would keep us, say - ing, "Chris - tian, love me more!"
calls, in cares and plea - sures, "Chris - tian, love me more than these!"
hearts to thine o - be - dience, serve and love thee best of all.

Copyright © 2000 by HAL LEONARD CORPORATION

JESUS CHRIST IS RISEN TODAY

EASTER HYMN
music from
Lyra Davidica, 1708

words from
Lyra Davidica, 1708 (v. 1-3)
v. 4 by Charles Wesley, 1740

C G/B C F/A F F/C G C G7/D C F/A C/G G7 C

1. Je - sus Christ is risen to - day, ____ Al - le - lu - ia!
2. Hymns of praise then let us sing, ____ Al - le - lu - ia!
3. But the pains which He en - dured, ____ Al - le - lu - ia!
4. Sing we to our God a - bove, ____ Al - le - lu - ia!

F/A C F C/E Dm7 C/E C/G G C G7/D C F/A C/G G7 C

Our tri - um - phant ho - ly day, ____ Al - le - lu - ia!
Un - to Christ, our heav'n - ly King, ____ Al - le - lu - ia!
Our sal - va - tion have pro - cured; ____ Al - le - lu - ia!
Praise e - ter - nal as God's love; ____ Al - le - lu - ia!

G D7/A G/B G C/E G7/D C G D7/A G C/E G/D D7 G

Who did once up - on the cross, Al - le - lu - ia!
Who en - dured the cross and grave. Al - le - lu - ia!
Now a - bove the sky, He's King, Al - le - lu - ia!
Praise our God, ye heav'n - ly host, Al - le - lu - ia!

G/F C/E C F/A F F/C C F C/G G7 C

Suf - fer ____ to re - deem our loss. ____ Al - le - lu - ia!
Sin - ners ____ to re - deem and save. ____ Al - le - lu - ia!
Where ____ the ____ an - gels ev - er sing. ____ Al - le - lu - ia!
Fa - ther, ____ Son, and Ho - ly Ghost. ____ Al - le - lu - ia!

Copyright © 2000 by HAL LEONARD CORPORATION

JESUS CHRIST IS RISEN TODAY

words by
Lyra Davidica, 1708 (v. 1-3)
v. 4 by Charles Wesley, 1740

LLANFAIR
music by
Robert Williams (1781-1821)

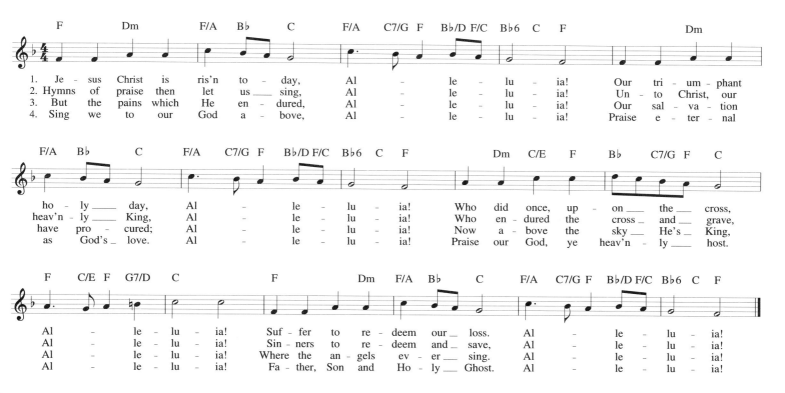

1. Je - sus Christ is ris'n to - day, Al - le - lu - ia! Our tri - um - phant
2. Hymns of praise then let us ___ sing, Al - le - lu - ia! Un - to Christ, our
3. But the pains which He en - dured, Al - le - lu - ia! Our sal - va - tion
4. Sing we to our God a - bove, Al - le - lu - ia! Praise e - ter - nal

ho - ly ___ day, Al - le - lu - ia! Who did once, up - on ___ the ___ cross,
heav'n - ly ___ King, Al - le - lu - ia! Who en - dured the cross ___ and ___ grave,
have pro - cured; Al - le - lu - ia! Now a - bove the sky ___ He's ___ King,
as God's ___ love. Al - le - lu - ia! Praise our God, ye heav'n - ly ___ host.

Al - le - lu - ia! Suf - fer to re - deem our ___ loss. Al - le - lu - ia!
Al - le - lu - ia! Sin - ners to re - deem and ___ save, Al - le - lu - ia!
Al - le - lu - ia! Where the an - gels ev - er ___ sing. Al - le - lu - ia!
Al - le - lu - ia! Fa - ther, Son and Ho - ly ___ Ghost. Al - le - lu - ia!

JESUS CHRIST, MY SURE DEFENSE

Author unknown, 1653
tr. based on Catherine Winkworth, 1863

JESUS, MEINE ZUVERSICHT
music by
Johann Crüger, 1653

1. Je - sus Christ, my sure De - fense And my Sav - ior, ev - er
2. Je - sus, my Re - deem - er, lives; I, too, un - to life shall
3. Nay, too close - ly am I bound Un - to Him by hope for -
4. I am flesh and must re - turn Un - to dust, where I am

liv - eth; Know - ing this, my con - fi - dence Rests up - on the hope it
wak - en. End - less joy my Sav - ior gives; Shall my cour - age, then, be
ev - er; Faith's strong hand the Rock hath found, Grasped it, and will leave it
tak - en; But by faith I now dis - cern That from death I shall a -

giv - eth Though the night of death be fraught Still with man - y an anx - ious thought.
shak - en? Shall I fear, or could the Head Rise and leave His mem - bers dead?
nev - er; E - ven death now can - not part From its Lord the trust - ing heart.
wak - en With my Sav - ior to a - bide In His glo - ry, at His side.

JESUS, I AM RESTING, RESTING

words by
Jean S. Pigott (1845-1882)

TRANQUILITY
music by
James Mountain (1844-1933)

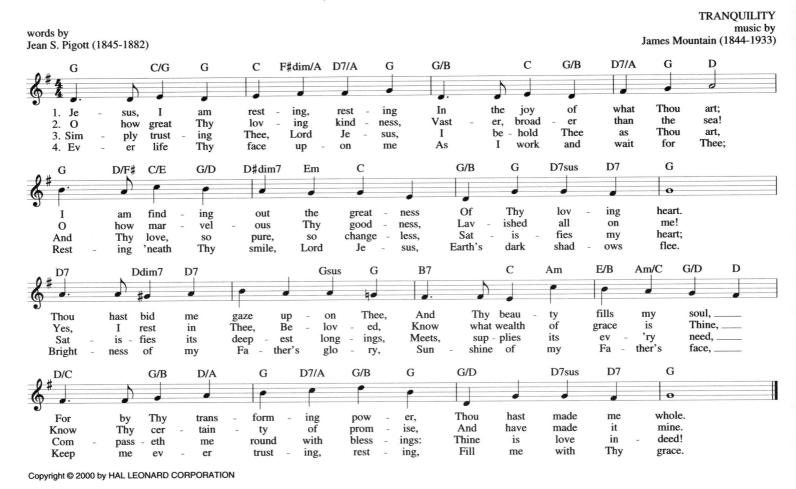

JESUS, I COME

words by
William T. Sleeper, 1887

music by
George C. Stebbins, 1887

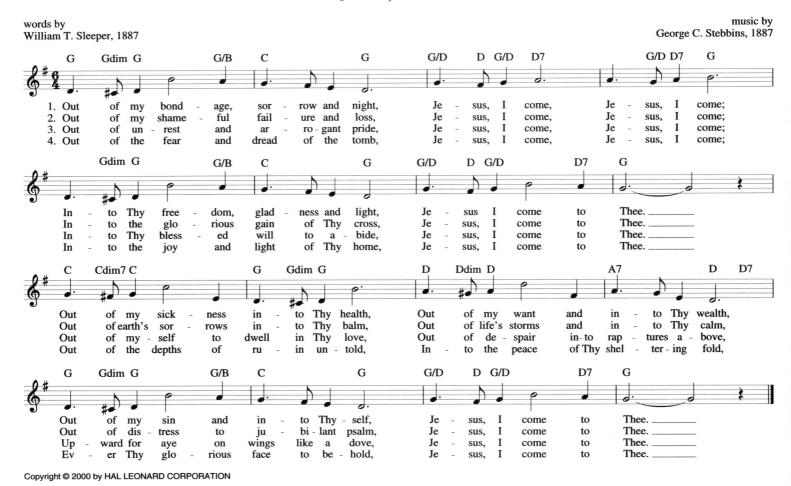

JESUS, I MY CROSS HAVE TAKEN

words by
Henry F. Lyte, 1824

ELLESDIE
music from
Leavitt's *The Christian Lyre,* 1831
attr. to Wolfgang Amadeus Mozart
arr. by Hubert P. Main, c. 1868

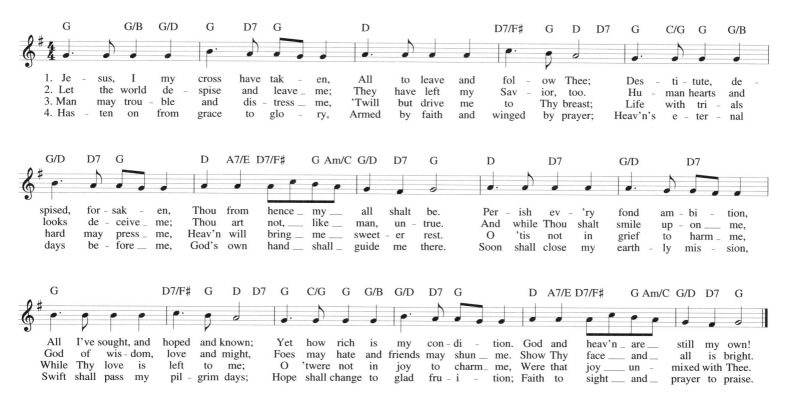

1. Je - sus, I my cross have tak - en, All to leave and fol - ow Thee; Des - ti - tute, de -
2. Let the world de - spise and leave _ me; They have left my Sav - ior, too. Hu - man hearts and
3. Man may trou - ble and dis - tress _ me, 'Twill but drive me to Thy breast; Life with tri - als
4. Has - ten on from grace to glo - ry, Armed by faith and winged by prayer; Heav'n's e - ter - nal

spised, for - sak - en, Thou from hence _ my _ all shalt be. Per - ish ev - 'ry fond am - bi - tion,
looks de - ceive _ me; Thou art not, _ like _ man, un - true. And while Thou shalt smile up - on _ me,
hard may press _ me, Heav'n will bring _ me _ sweet - er rest. O 'tis not in grief to harm _ me,
days be - fore _ me, God's own hand _ shall _ guide me there. Soon shall close my earth - ly mis - sion,

All I've sought, and hoped and known; Yet how rich is my con - di - tion. God and heav'n _ are _ still my own!
God of wis - dom, love and might, Foes may hate and friends may shun _ me. Show Thy face _ and _ all is bright.
While Thy love is left to me; O 'twere not in joy to charm _ me, Were that joy _ un - mixed with Thee.
Swift shall pass my pil - grim days; Hope shall change to glad fru - i - tion; Faith to sight _ and _ prayer to praise.

JESUS, IN THY DYING WOES

words by
Thomas B. Pollock (1836-1896)

ACK, VAD ÄR DOCK LIVET HÄR
music from
Koralpsalmboken, Stockholm, 1697

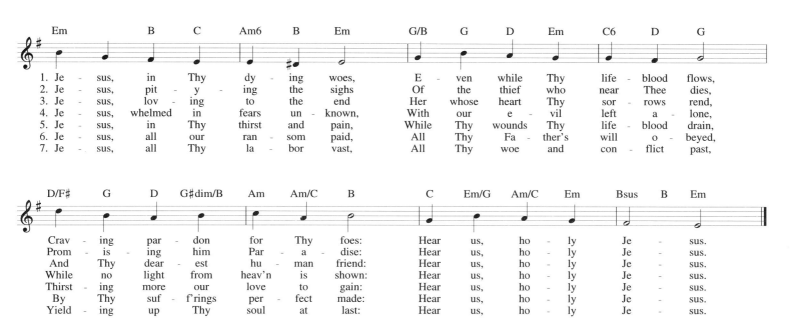

1. Je - sus, in Thy dy - ing woes, E - ven while Thy life - blood flows,
2. Je - sus, pit - y - ing the sighs Of the thief who near Thee dies,
3. Je - sus, lov - ing to the end Her whose heart Thy sor - rows rend,
4. Je - sus, whelmed in fears un - known, With our e - vil left a - lone,
5. Je - sus, in Thy thirst and pain, While Thy wounds Thy life - blood drain,
6. Je - sus, all our ran - som paid, All Thy Fa - ther's will o - beyed,
7. Je - sus, all Thy la - bor vast, All Thy woe and con - flict past,

Crav - ing par - don for Thy foes: Hear us, ho - ly Je - sus.
Prom - is - ing him Par - a - dise: Hear us, ho - ly Je - sus.
And Thy dear - est hu - man friend: Hear us, ho - ly Je - sus.
While no light from heav'n is shown: Hear us, ho - ly Je - sus.
Thirst - ing more our love to gain: Hear us, ho - ly Je - sus.
By Thy suf - f'rings per - fect made: Hear us, ho - ly Je - sus.
Yield - ing up Thy soul at last: Hear us, ho - ly Je - sus.

JESUS, I WILL PONDER NOW

JESU KREUZ, LEIDEN UND PEIN

words by
Sigismund von Birken (1626-1681)
tr. by August Crull (1846-1923)

music by
Melchior Vulpius (c. 1560-1615)

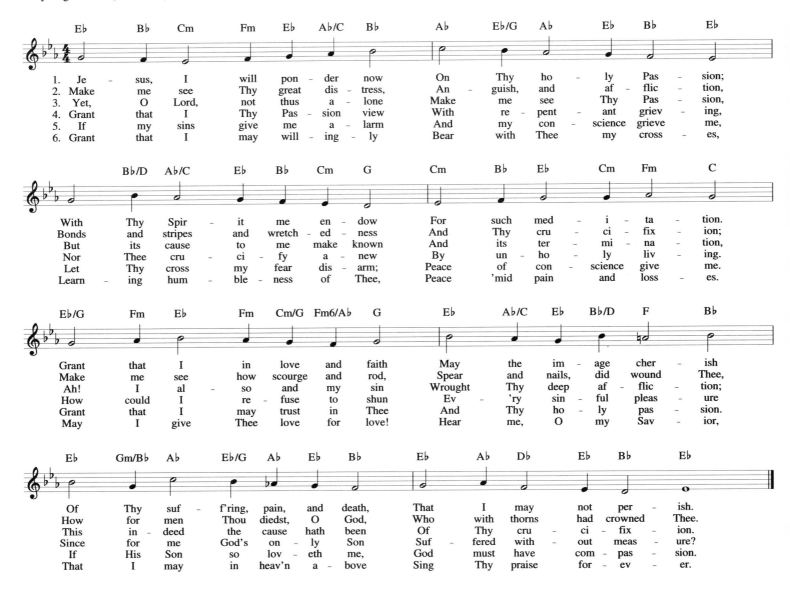

1. Je - sus, I will pon - der now On Thy ho - ly Pas - sion;
2. Make me see Thy great dis - tress, An - guish, and af - flic - tion,
3. Yet, O Lord, not thus a - lone Make me see Thy Pas - sion,
4. Grant that I Thy Pas - sion view With re - pent - ant griev - ing,
5. If my sins give me a - larm And my con - science grieve me,
6. Grant that I may will - ing - ly Bear with Thee my cross - es,

With Thy Spir - it me en - dow For such med - i - ta - tion.
Bonds and stripes and wretch - ed - ness And Thy cru - ci - fix - ion;
But its cause to me make known And its ter - mi - na - tion,
Nor Thee cru - ci - fy a - new By un - ho - ly liv - ing.
Let Thy cross my fear dis - arm; Peace of con - science give me.
Learn - ing hum - ble - ness of Thee, Peace 'mid pain and loss - es.

Grant that I in love and faith May the im - age cher - ish
Make me see how scourge and rod, Spear and nails, did wound Thee,
Ah! I al - so and my sin Wrought Thy deep af - flic - tion;
How could I re - fuse to shun Ev - 'ry sin - ful pleas - ure
Grant that I may trust in Thee And Thy ho - ly pas - sion.
May I give Thee love for love! Hear me, O my Sav - ior,

Of Thy suf - f'ring, pain, and death, That I may not per - ish.
How for men Thou diedst, O God, Who with thorns had crowned Thee.
This in - deed the cause hath been Of Thy cru - ci - fix - ion?
Since for me God's on - ly Son Suf - fered with - out meas - ure?
If His Son so lov - eth me, God must have com - pas - sion.
That I may in heav'n a - bove Sing Thy praise for - ev - er.

JESUS IS ALL THE WORLD TO ME

ELIZABETH

words by
Will L. Thompson (1847-1909)

music by
Will L. Thompson (1847-1909)

1. Je - sus is all the world to me, My life, my joy, my
2. Je - sus is all the world to me, My Friend in tri - als
3. Je - sus is all the world to me, And true to Him I'll
4. Je - sus is all the world to me, I want no bet - ter

all; _____ He is my strength from day to day, With - He -
sore; _____ I go to Him for bless - ings, and When
be; _____ O how could I this Friend de - ny When
friend; _____ I trust Him now, I'll trust Him when Life's

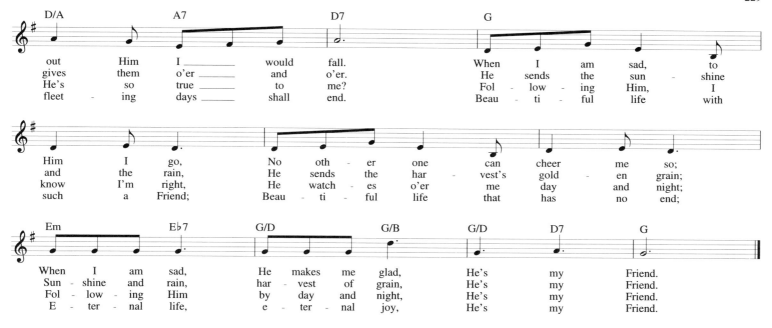

JESUS IS THE SWEETEST NAME I KNOW

words by
Lela Long, 20th century

SWEETEST NAME

music by
Lela Long, 20th century

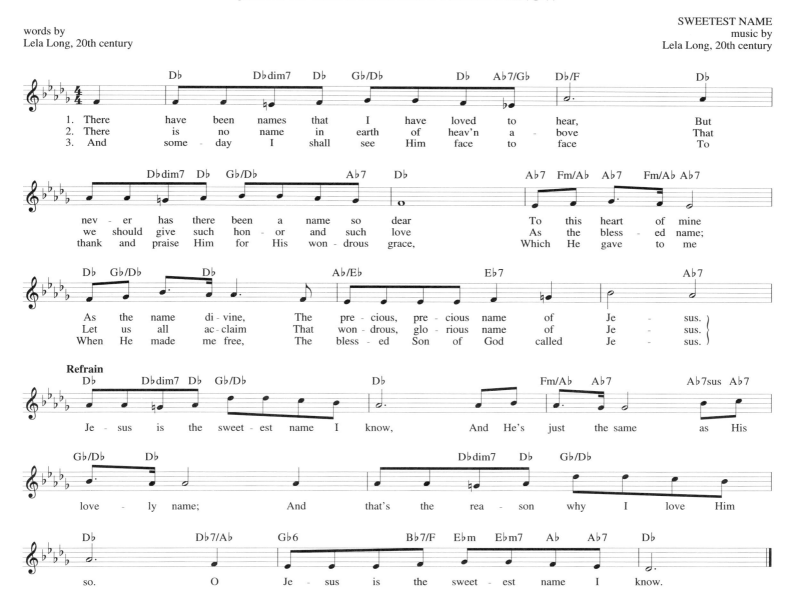

JESUS IS TENDERLY CALLING

CALLING TODAY

words by
Fanny J. Crosby, 1883

music by
George C. Stebbins, 1883

1. Je - sus is ten - der - ly call - ing thee home — Call - ing to - day, call - ing to - day;
2. Je - sus is call - ing the wea - ry to rest — Call - ing to - day, call - ing to - day;
3. Je - sus is wait - ing, O come to Him now — Wait - ing to - day, wait - ing to - day;
4. Je - sus is plead - ing, O list to His voice — Hear Him to - day, hear Him to - day;

Why from the sun - shine of love wilt thou roam Far - ther and far - ther a - way?
Bring Him thy bur - den and thou shalt be blest — He will not turn thee a - way.
Come with thy sins, at His feet low - ly bow — Come, and no long - er de - lay.
Those who be - lieve on His name shall re - joice — Quick - ly a - rise and a - way.

Call - ing to - day, Call - ing to - day,

Je - sus is call - ing, Is ten - der - ly call - ing to - day.

JESUS, KEEP ME NEAR THE CROSS

NEAR THE CROSS

words by
Fanny J. Crosby (1820-1915)

music by
William H. Doane (1832-1915)

1. Je - sus, keep me near the cross, There a pre - cious
2. Near the cross, a trem - bling soul, Love and mer - cy
3. Near the cross! O Lamb of God, Bring its scenes be -
4. Near the cross I'll watch and wait, Hop - ing, trust - ing

foun - tain, Free to all, a heal - ing stream,
found me; There the Bright and Morn - ing Star
fore me; Help me walk from day to day
ev - er, Till I reach the gold - en strand

Flows from Cal - v'ry's moun - tain.
Sheds its beams a - round me. In the cross,
With its shad - ows o'er me.
Just be - yond the riv - er.

in the cross Be my glo - ry ev - er,

Till my rap - tured soul shall find Rest be - yond the riv - er.

JESUS LIVES! THE VICTORY'S WON!

words by
Christian F. Gellert (1715-1769)
tr. by Frances E. Cox (1812-1897)

JESUS, MEINE ZUVERSICHT
music by
Johann Crüger (1598-1662)

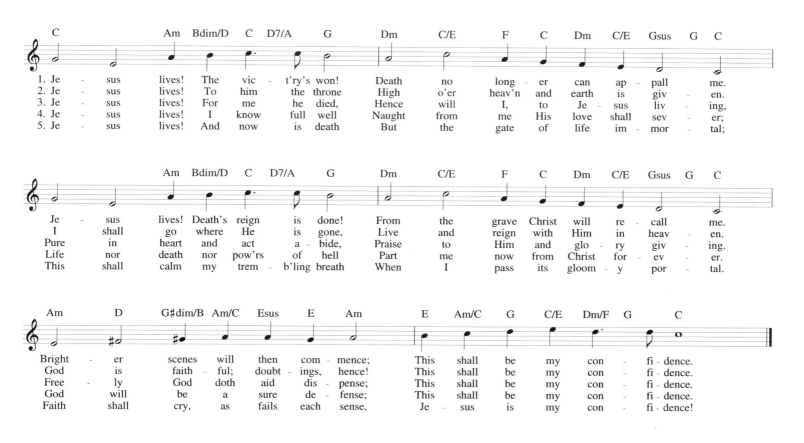

JESUS, LORD, WE LOOK TO THEE

words by
Charles Wesley, 1749

SAVANNAH
music from
Foundery Collection, 1742

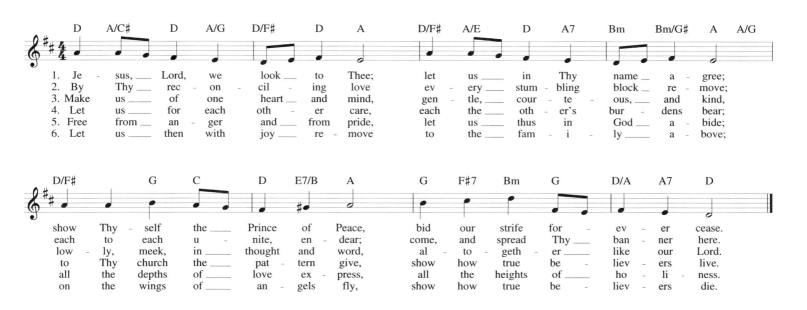

JESUS, LOVER OF MY SOUL

ABERYSTWYTH

words by
Charles Wesley (1707-1788)

music by
Joseph Parry (1841-1903)

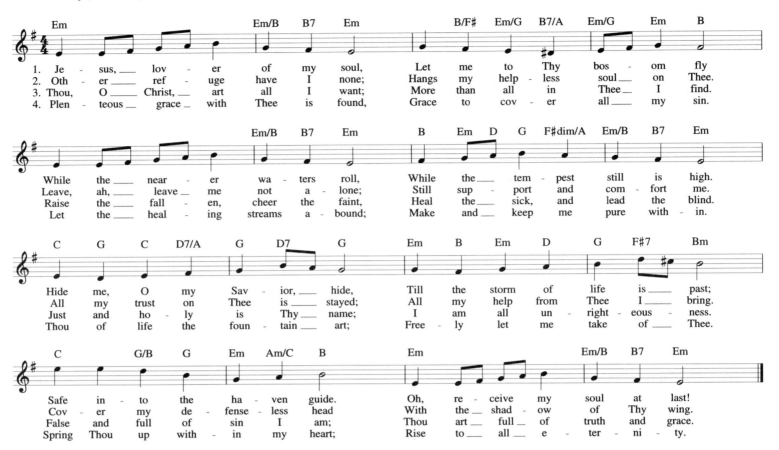

1. Je - sus, lov - er of my soul, Let me to Thy bos - om fly
2. Oth - er ref - uge have I none; Hangs my help - less soul on Thee.
3. Thou, O Christ, art all I want; More than all in Thee I find.
4. Plen - teous grace with Thee is found, Grace to cov - er all my sin.

While the near - er wa - ters roll, While the tem - pest still is high.
Leave, ah, leave me not a - lone; Still sup - port and com - fort me.
Raise the fall - en, cheer the faint, Heal the sick, and lead the blind.
Let the heal - ing streams a - bound; Make and keep me pure with - in.

Hide me, O my Sav - ior, hide, Till the storm of life is past;
All my trust on Thee is stayed; All my help from Thee I bring.
Just and ho - ly is Thy name; I am all un - right - eous - ness.
Thou of life the foun - tain art; Free - ly let me take of Thee.

Safe in - to the ha - ven guide. Oh, re - ceive my soul at last!
Cov - er my de - fense - less head With the shad - ow of Thy wing.
False and full of sin I am; Thou art full of truth and grace.
Spring Thou up with - in my heart; Rise to all e - ter - ni - ty.

JESUS LOVES EVEN ME

GLADNESS

words by
Philip P. Bliss, 1870

music by
Philip P. Bliss, 1870

1. I am so glad that our Fa - ther in heav'n Tells of His love in the Book He has giv'n.
2. Tho' I for - get Him and wan - der a - way, Still He doth love me wher - ev - er I stray.
3. O if there's on - ly one song I can sing When in His beau - ty I see the great King,

Won - der - ful things in the Bi - ble I see; This is the dear - est, that Je - sus loves me.
Back to His dear, lov - ing arms would I flee When I re - mem - ber that Je - sus loves me.
This shall my song in e - ter - ni - ty be; "O what a won - der that Je - sus loves me!"

Refrain

I am so glad that Je - sus loves me, Je - sus loves me, Je - sus loves me!

I am so glad that Je - sus loves me, Je - sus loves e - ven me!

JESUS, LOVER OF MY SOUL

words by
Charles Wesley (1707-1788)

MARTYN
music by
Simeon B. Marsh (1798-1875)

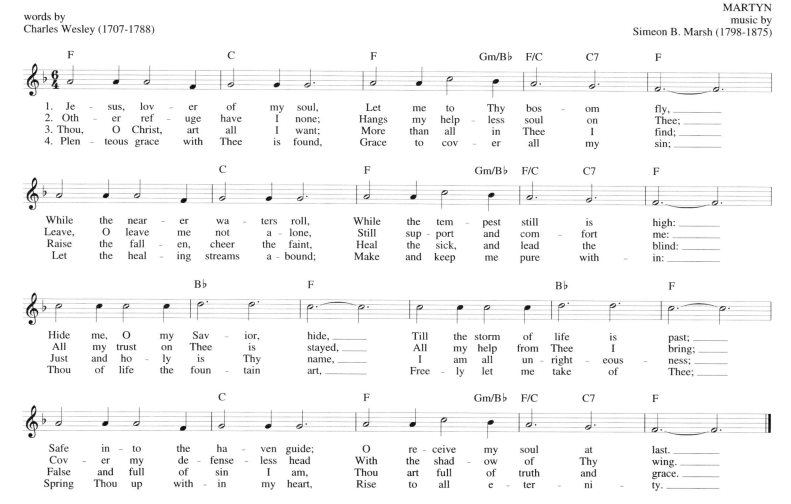

1. Je - sus, lov - er of my soul, Let me to Thy bos - om fly, _____
2. Oth - er ref - uge have I none; Hangs my help - less soul on Thee; _____
3. Thou, O Christ, art all I want; More than all in Thee I find; _____
4. Plen - teous grace with Thee is found, Grace to cov - er all my sin; _____

While the near - er wa - ters roll, While the tem - pest still is high: _____
Leave, O leave me not a - lone, Still sup - port and com - fort me: _____
Raise the fall - en, cheer the faint, Heal the sick, and lead the blind: _____
Let the heal - ing streams a - bound; Make and keep me pure with - in: _____

Hide me, O my Sav - ior, hide, _____ Till the storm of life is past; _____
All my trust on Thee is stayed, _____ All my help from Thee I bring; _____
Just and ho - ly is Thy name, _____ I am all un - right - eous - ness; _____
Thou of life the foun - tain art, _____ Free - ly let me take of Thee; _____

Safe in - to the ha - ven guide; O re - ceive my soul at last. _____
Cov - er my de - fense - less head With the shad - ow of Thy wing. _____
False and full of sin I am, Thou art full of truth and grace. _____
Spring Thou up with - in my heart, Rise to all e - ter - ni - ty. _____

JESUS LOVES ME

words by
Anna B. Warner (1820-1915)

CHINA
music by
William B. Bradbury (1816-1868)

1. Je - sus loves me! this I know, For the Bi - ble tells me so;
2. Je - sus loves me! He who died Heav - en's gates to o - pen wide!
3. Je - sus loves me! loves me still, Tho' I'm ver - y weak and ill;
4. Je - sus loves me! He will stay Close be - side me all the way;

Lit - tle ones to Him be - long; They are weak, but He is strong.
He will wash a - way my sin, Let His lit - tle child come in.
From His shin - ing throne on high, Comes to watch me where I lie.
If I love Him, when I die He will take me home on high.

Refrain

Yes, Je - sus loves me, Yes, Je - sus loves me,

Yes, Je - sus loves me, The Bi - ble tells me so.

JESUS LOVES THE LITTLE CHILDREN

CHILDREN

words by
Rev. C.H. Woolston (1856-1927)

music by
George F. Root (1820-1895)

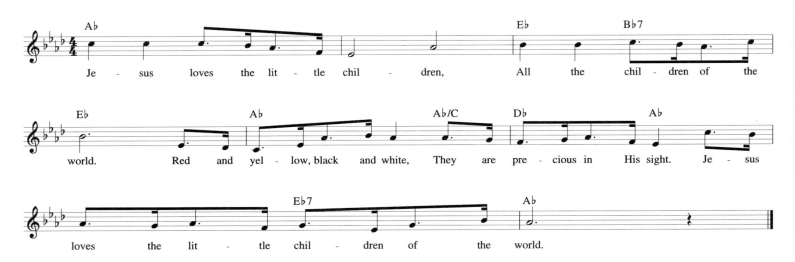

Je - sus loves the lit - tle chil - dren, All the chil - dren of the world. Red and yel - low, black and white, They are pre - cious in His sight. Je - sus loves the lit - tle chil - dren of the world.

JESUS, MY STRENGTH, MY HOPE

DIADEMATA

words by
Charles Wesley, 1742

music by
George J. Elvey, 1868

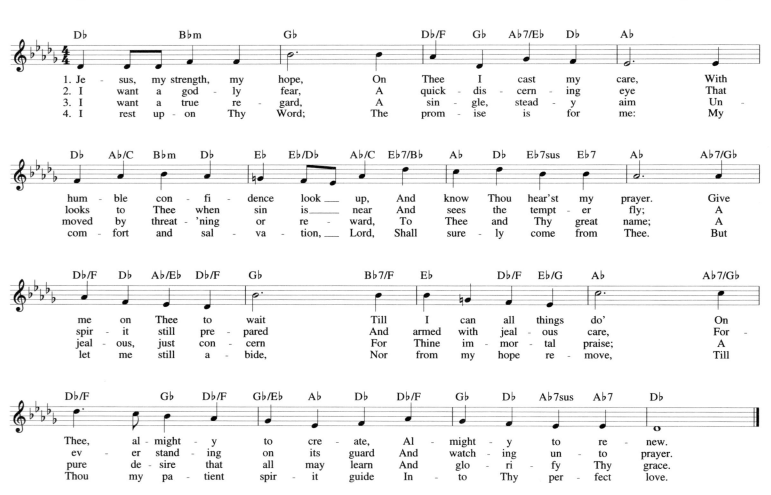

1. Je - sus, my strength, my hope, On Thee I cast my care, With
2. I want a god - ly fear, A quick - dis - cern - ing eye, That
3. I want a true re - gard, A sin - gle, stead - y aim, Un -
4. I rest up - on Thy Word; The prom - ise is for me: My

hum - ble con - fi - dence look __ up, And know Thou hear'st my prayer. Give
looks to Thee when sin is __ near And sees the tempt - er fly; A
moved by threat - 'ning or re - ward, To Thee and Thy great name; A
com - fort and sal - va - tion, __ Lord, Shall sure - ly come from Thee. But

me on Thee to wait Till I can all things do' On
spir - it still pre - pared And armed with jeal - ous care, For -
jeal - ous, just con - cern For Thine im - mor - tal praise; A
let me still a - bide, Nor from my hope re - move, Till

Thee, al - might - y to cre - ate, Al - might - y to re - new.
ev - er stand - ing on its guard And watch - ing un - to prayer.
pure de - sire that all may learn And glo - ri - fy Thy grace.
Thou my pa - tient spir - it guide In - to Thy per - fect love.

JESUS! NAME OF WONDROUS LOVE

GOTT SEI DANK
music by
J.A. Freylinghausen,
Geistreiches Gesang-Buch, Halle, 1704

words by
William W. How (1823-1897)

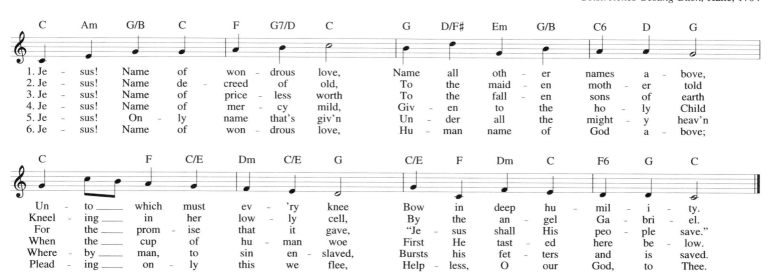

1. Je - sus!	Name of	won - drous love,	Name all oth - er names a - bove,
2. Je - sus!	Name de - creed of old,	To the maid - en moth - er told
3. Je - sus!	Name of price - less worth	To the fall - en sons of earth
4. Je - sus!	Name of mer - cy mild,	Giv - en to the ho - ly Child
5. Je - sus!	On - ly name that's giv'n	Un - der all the might - y heav'n
6. Je - sus!	Name of won - drous love,	Hu - man name of God a - bove;

Un - to ___ which must ev - 'ry knee Bow in deep hu - mil - i - ty.
Kneel - ing ___ in her low - ly cell, By the an - gel Ga - bri - el.
For the ___ prom - ise that it gave, "Je - sus shall His peo - ple save."
When the ___ cup of hu - man woe First He tast - ed here be - low.
Where - by ___ man, to sin en - slaved, Bursts his fet - ters and is saved.
Plead - ing ___ on - ly this we flee, Help - less, O our God, to Thee.

JESUS, PRICELESS TREASURE

JESU, MEINE FREUDE
music by
Johann Crüger, 1653

words by
Johann Franck, 1650
tr. by Catherine Winkworth, 1863

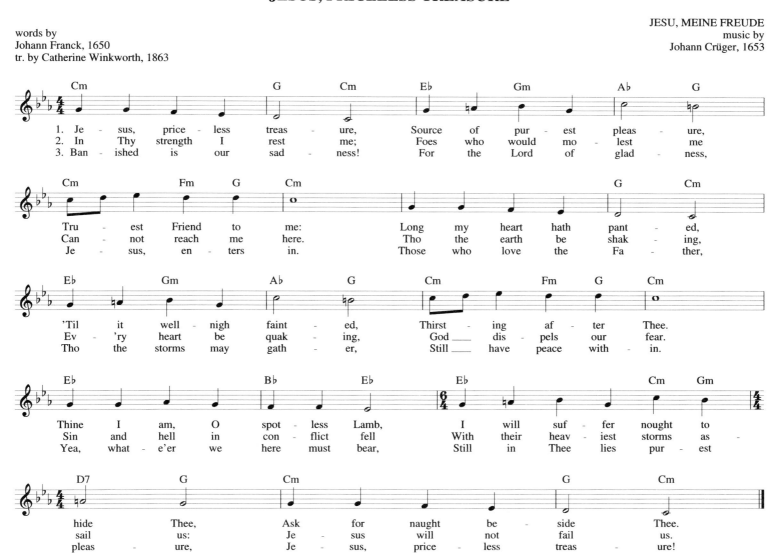

1. Je - sus, price - less treas - ure, Source of pur - est pleas - ure,
2. In Thy strength I rest me; Foes who would mo - lest me
3. Ban - ished is our sad - ness! For the Lord of glad - ness,

Tru - est Friend to me: Long my heart hath pant - ed,
Can - not reach me here. Tho' my the earth be shak - ing,
Je - sus, en - ters in. Those who love the Fa - ther,

'Til it well - nigh faint - ed, Thirst - ing af - ter Thee.
Ev - 'ry heart be quak - ing, God ___ dis - pels our fear.
Tho' the storms may gath - er, Still ___ have peace with - in.

Thine I am, O spot - less Lamb, I will suf - fer nought to
Sin and hell in con - flict fell With their heav - iest storms as
Yea, what - e'er we here must bear, Still in Thee lies pur - est

hide Thee, Ask for naught be - side Thee.
sail us: Je - sus will not fail us.
pleas - ure, Je - sus, price - less treas - ure!

JESUS PAID IT ALL

ALL TO CHRIST

words by
Elvina M. Hall (1820-1889)

music by
John T. Grape (1835-1915)

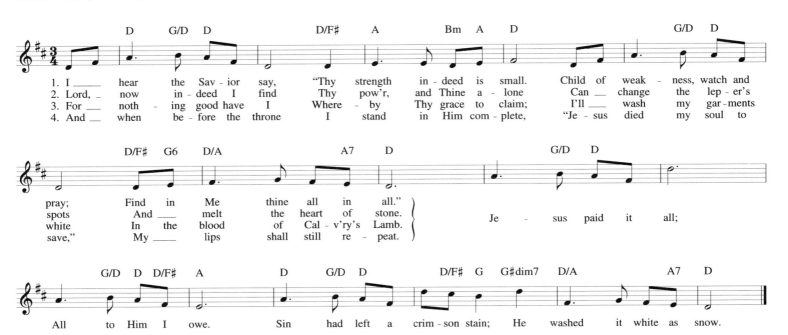

1. I ___ hear the Sav - ior say, "Thy strength in - deed is small. Child of weak - ness, watch and
2. Lord, _ now in - deed I find Thy pow'r, and Thine a - lone Can change the lep - er's
3. For ___ noth - ing good have I Where - by Thy grace to claim; I'll ___ wash my gar - ments
4. And ___ when be - fore the throne I stand in Him com - plete, "Je - sus died my soul to

pray; Find in Me thine all in all." } Je - sus paid it all;
spots And ___ melt the heart of stone. }
white In the blood of Cal - v'ry's Lamb. }
save," My ___ lips shall still re - peat. }

All to Him I owe. Sin had left a crim - son stain; He washed it white as snow.

Copyright © 2000 by HAL LEONARD CORPORATION

JESUS, REFUGE OF THE WEARY

O DU LIEBE MEINER LIEBE

words by
Girolamo Savonarola (1452-1498)
tr. by J.F. Wilde (1826-1896)

music from
Erbaulicher Musikalischer Christenschatz, Basel, 1745

1. Je - sus, Ref - uge of the wea - ry, Blest Re - deem - er, whom we love,
2. Do we pass that cross un - heed - ing, Breath - ing no re - pen - tant vow,
3. Je - sus, may our hearts be burn - ing With more fer - vent love for Thee!

Foun - tain in life's des - ert drea - ry, Sav - ior from the world a - bove,
Though we see Thee wound - ed, bleed - ing, See Thy thorn - en - cir - cled brow?
May our eyes be ev - er turn - ing To Thy cross of ag - o - ny,

O how oft Thine eyes, of - fend - ed, Gaze up - on the sin - ner's fall!
Yet Thy sin - less death hath brought us Life e - ter - nal, peace, and rest,
Till in glo - ry, part - ed nev - er From the bless - ed Sav - ior's side,

Yet, up - on the cross ex - tend - ed, Thou didst bear the pain of all.
On - ly what Thy grace hath taught us Calms the sin - ner's storm - y breast.
Grav - en in our hearts for - ev - er, Dwell the cross, the Cru - ci - fied!

Copyright © 2000 by HAL LEONARD CORPORATION

JESUS, REFUGE OF THE WEARY

WETTERLING

words by
Girolamo Savonarola (1454-1498)
tr. by Jane Francesca Wilde (1826-1896)

music by
Hampus Wetterling (1830-1870)

1. Je - sus, Ref - uge of the wea - ry, Blest Re - deem - er, whom we love, Foun - tain
2. Do we pass that cross un - heed - ing, Breath - ing no re - pent - ant vow, Though we
3. Je - sus, may our hearts be burn - ing With more fer - vent love for Thee! May our

in life's des - ert drear - y. Sav - ior from the world a - bove: O how
see Thee wound - ed, bleed - ing, See Thy thorn - en - cir - cled brow? Yet Thy
eyes be ev - er turn - ing To Thy cross of ag - o - ny, Till in

oft Thine eyes, of - fend - ed, Gaze up - on the sin - ner's fall! Yet, up -
sin - less death hath brought _ us Life e - ter - nal, peace, and rest; On - ly
glo - ry, part - ed nev - er From the bless - ed Sav - ior's side, Grav - en

on the cross ex - tend - ed, Thou didst bear the pain of all.
what Thy grace hath taught _ us Calms the sin - ner's storm - y breast.
in our hearts for - ev - er, Dwell the cross, the Cru - ci - fied!

JESUS SAVES

words by
Priscilla J. Owens (1829-1907)

music by
William J. Kirkpatrick (1838-1921)

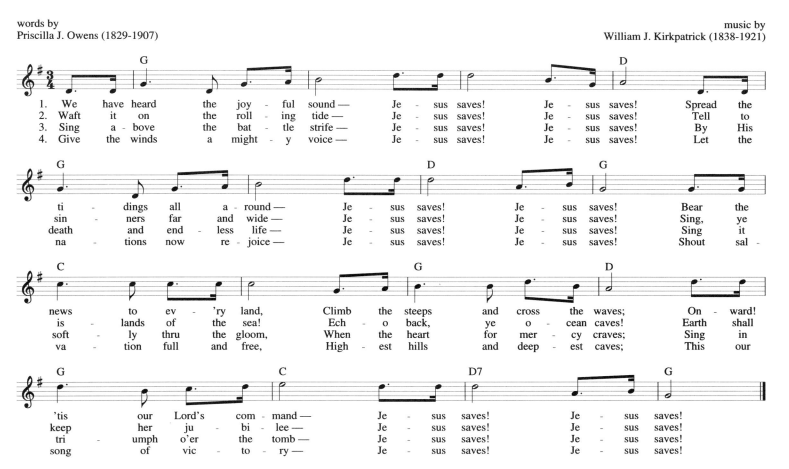

1. We have heard the joy - ful sound — Je - sus saves! Je - sus saves! Spread the
2. Waft it on the roll - ing tide — Je - sus saves! Je - sus saves! Tell to
3. Sing a - bove the bat - tle strife — Je - sus saves! Je - sus saves! By His
4. Give the winds a might - y voice — Je - sus saves! Je - sus saves! Let the

ti - dings all a - round — Je - sus saves! Je - sus saves! Bear the
sin - ners far and wide — Je - sus saves! Je - sus saves! Sing, ye
death and end - less life — Je - sus saves! Je - sus saves! Sing it
na - tions now re - joice — Je - sus saves! Je - sus saves! Shout sal -

news to ev - 'ry land, Climb the steeps and cross the waves; On - ward!
is - lands of the sea! Ech - o back, ye o - cean caves! Earth shall
soft - ly thru the gloom, When the heart for mer - cy craves; Sing in
va - tion full and free, High - est hills and deep - est caves; This our

'tis our Lord's com - mand — Je - sus saves! Je - sus saves!
keep her ju - bi - lee — Je - sus saves! Je - sus saves!
tri - umph o'er the tomb — Je - sus saves! Je - sus saves!
song of vic - to - ry — Je - sus saves! Je - sus saves!

JESUS, SAVIOR, PILOT ME

PILOT
music by
John E. Gould (1822-1875)

words by
Edward Hopper (1816-1888)

1. Je - sus, Sav - ior, pi - lot me o - ver life's tem - pes - tuous
2. As a moth - er stills ___ her child, Thou canst hush the o - cean
3. When at last I near ___ the shore, and the fear - ful break - ers

sea; un - known waves be - fore me roll, hid - ing rock and treach - 'rous shoal. Chart and
wild; bois - terous waves o - bey Thy will, when Thou sayest to them, "Be still!" Won - drous
roar 'twixt me and the peace - ful rest, then, while lean - ing on Thy breast, may I

com - pass came ___ from Thee; Je - sus, Sav - ior, pi - lot me.
sov - 'reign of ___ the sea, Je - sus, Sav - ior, pi - lot me.
hear Thee say ___ to me, "Fear not, I will pi - lot thee."

Copyright © 2000 by HAL LEONARD CORPORATION

JESUS SHALL REIGN

DUKE STREET
music attr. to
John Hatton (c. 1710-1793)

words by
Isaac Watts (1674-1748)

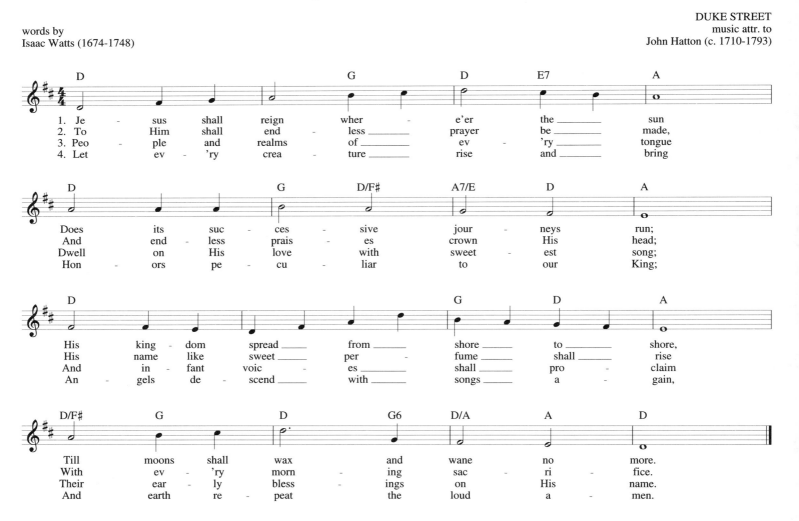

1. Je - sus shall reign wher - e'er the ___ sun
2. To Him shall end - less ___ prayer be ___ made,
3. Peo - ple and realms of ___ ev - 'ry ___ tongue
4. Let ev - 'ry crea - ture ___ rise and ___ bring

Does its suc - ces - sive jour - neys run;
And end - less prais - es crown His head;
Dwell on His love with sweet - est song;
Hon - ors pe - cu - liar to our King;

His king - dom spread ___ from ___ shore ___ to ___ shore,
His name like sweet ___ per ___ fume ___ shall ___ rise
And in - fant voic - es ___ shall ___ pro - claim
An - gels de - scend ___ with ___ songs ___ a - gain,

Till moons shall wax and wane no more.
With ev - 'ry morn - ing sac - ri - fice.
Their ear - ly bless - ings on His name.
And earth re - peat the loud a - men.

Copyright © 2000 by HAL LEONARD CORPORATION

JESUS, STILL LEAD ON

words by
Nicolaus L. von Zinzendorf (1700-1760)
tr. by Jane L. Borthwick (1813-1897)

SEELENBRÄUTIGAM
music by
Adam Drese (1620-1701)

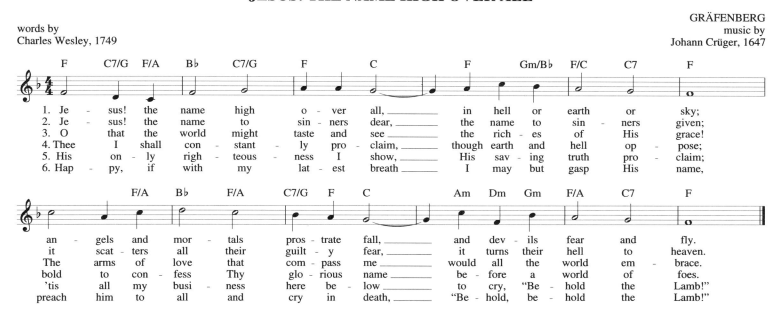

1. Je - sus, still lead on, Till our rest is won; And al - though the way be cheer - less,
2. If the way be drear, If the foe be near, Let not faith - less fears o'er - take us;
3. When we seek re - lief From a long - felt grief; When temp - ta - tions come al - lur - ing,
4. Je - sus, still lead on, Till our rest be won; Heav'n - ly Lead - er, still di - rect us,

We will fol - low, calm and fear - less; Guide us by Thy hand To our Fa - ther - land!
Let not faith and hope for - sake us; For, through man - y a foe, To our home we go!
Make us pa - tient and en - dur - ing; Show us that bright shore Where we weep no more!
Still sup - port, con - sole, pro - tect us, Till we safe - ly stand In our Fa - ther - land!

JESUS! THE NAME HIGH OVER ALL

words by
Charles Wesley, 1749

GRÄFENBERG
music by
Johann Crüger, 1647

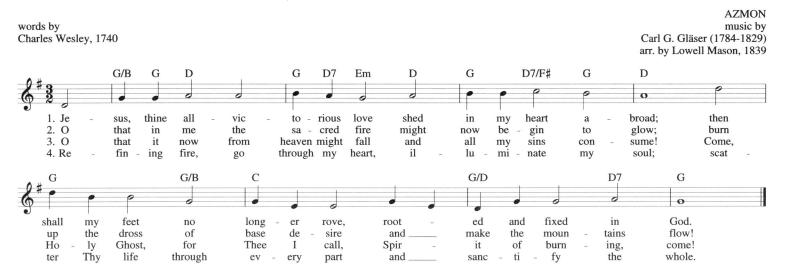

1. Je - sus! the name high o - ver all, _____ in hell or earth or sky;
2. Je - sus! the name to sin - ners dear, _____ the name to sin - ners given;
3. O that the world might taste and see _____ the rich - es of His grace!
4. Thee I shall con - stant - ly pro - claim, _____ though earth and hell op - pose;
5. His on - ly righ - teous - ness I show, _____ His sav - ing truth pro - claim;
6. Hap - py, if with my lat - est breath _____ I may but gasp His name,

an - gels and mor - tals pros - trate fall, _____ and dev - ils fear and fly.
it scat - ters all their guilt - y fear, _____ it turns their hell to heaven.
The arms of love that com - pass me _____ would all the world em - brace.
bold to con - fess Thy glo - rious name _____ be - fore a world of foes.
'tis all my busi - ness here be - low _____ to cry, "Be - hold the Lamb!"
preach him to all and cry in death, _____ "Be - hold, be - hold the Lamb!"

JESUS, THINE ALL-VICTORIOUS LOVE

words by
Charles Wesley, 1740

AZMON
music by
Carl G. Gläser (1784-1829)
arr. by Lowell Mason, 1839

1. Je - sus, thine all - vic - to - rious love shed in my heart a - broad; then
2. O that in me the sa - cred fire might now be - gin to glow; burn
3. O that it now from heaven might fall and all my sins con - sume! Come,
4. Re - fin - ing fire, go through my heart, il - lu - mi - nate my soul; scat -

shall my feet no long - er rove, root - ed and fixed in God.
up the dross of base de - sire and _____ make the moun - tains flow!
Ho - ly Ghost, for Thee I call, Spir - it of burn - ing, come!
ter Thy life through ev - ery part and _____ sanc - ti - fy the whole.

JESUS, THE VERY THOUGHT OF THEE

ST. AGNES
music by
John Bacchus Dykes, 1866

words attr. to
Bernard of Clairvaux (1091-1153)
tr. by Edward Caswall, 1849

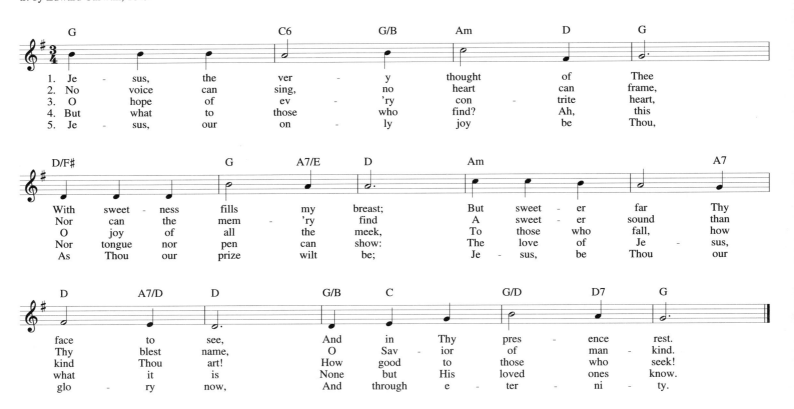

JESUS, THOU EVERLASTING KING

TRURO
music by
Charles Burney

words by
Isaac Watts (1674-1748)

JESUS, THOU JOY OF LOVING HEARTS

words attr. to
Bernard of Clairvaux (1091-1153)
tr. by Ray Palmer, 1858

QUEBEC
music by
Henry Baker, 1854

1. Je - sus, Thou joy of lov - ing hearts, Thou fount of life, Thou light of all,
2. Thy truth un - changed hath ev - er stood; Thou sav - est those that on Thee call,
3. We taste Thee, O Thou liv - ing bread, And long to feast up - on Thee still;
4. Our rest - less spir - its yearn for Thee, Wher - e'er our change - ful lot is cast,
5. O Je - sus ev - er with us stay, Make all our mo - ments calm and bright;

From the best bliss that earth im - parts We turn, un - filled, __ to heed Thy call.
To them that seek Thee Thou art good, To them that find __ Thee, all in all.
We drink of Thee, the foun - tain - head, And thirst our souls __ from Thee to fill.
Glad when Thy gra - cious smile we see, Blest when our faith __ can hold Thee fast.
O chase the night of sin a - way, Shed o'er the world __ Thy ho - ly light.

JESUS, THY BLOOD AND RIGHTEOUSNESS

words by
Ludwig von Zinzendorf (1700-1760)
tr. by John Wesley (1703-1791)

GERMANY
music from
William Gardiner's *Sacred Melodies*, 1815

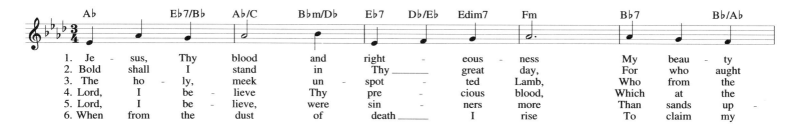

1. Je - sus, Thy blood and right - eous - ness My beau - ty
2. Bold shall I stand in Thy __ great day, For who aught
3. The ho - ly, meek un - spot - ted Lamb, Who from the
4. Lord, I be - lieve Thy pre - cious blood, Which at the
5. Lord, I be - lieve, were sin - ners more Than sands up -
6. When from the dust of death __ I rise To claim my

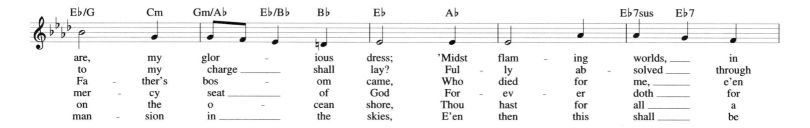

are, my glor - ious dress; 'Midst flam - ing worlds, __ in
to my charge __ shall lay? Ful - ly ab - solved __ through
Fa - ther's bos - om came, Who died for me, __ e'en
mer - cy seat __ of God For ev - er doth __ for
on the o - cean shore, Thou hast for all __ a
man - sion in __ the skies, E'en then this shall __ be

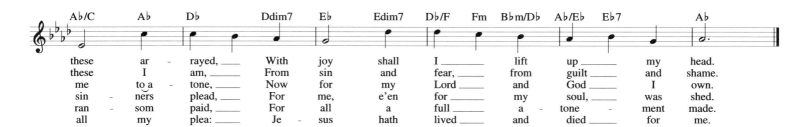

these ar - rayed, __ With joy shall I __ lift up __ my head.
these I am, __ From sin and fear, __ from guilt __ and shame.
me to a - tone, Now for my Lord __ and God __ I own.
sin - ners plead, __ For me, e'en for __ my soul, __ was shed.
ran - som paid, __ For all a full a - tone - ment made.
all my plea: __ Je - sus hath lived __ and died for me.

JESUS, THY BLOOD AND RIGHTEOUSNESS

ST. CRISPIN
music by
George Job Elvey, 1862

words by
Ludwig von Zinzendorf, 1739
tr. by John Wesley, 1740

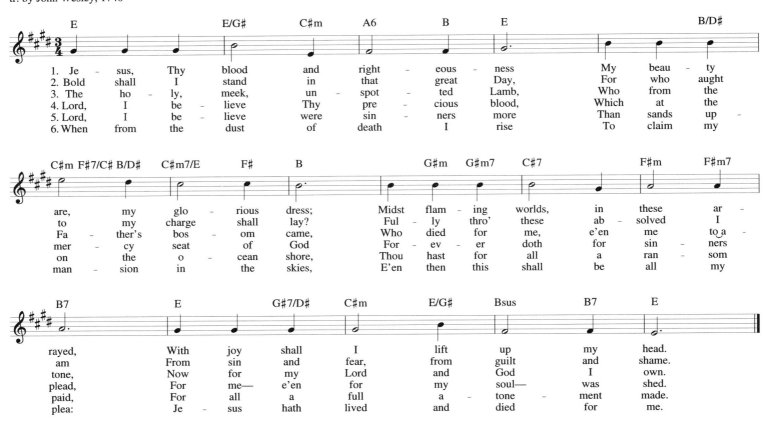

1. Je - sus, Thy blood and right - eous - ness My beau - ty who aught
2. Bold shall I stand in that great Day, For who from the
3. The ho - ly, meek, un - spot - ted Lamb, Who at the
4. Lord, I be - lieve Thy pre - cious blood, Which at the
5. Lord, I be - lieve were sin - ners more Than sands up -
6. When from the dust of death I rise To claim my

are, my glo - rious dress; Midst flam - ing worlds, in these ar -
to my charge shall lay? Ful - ly thro' these in ab - solved I
Fa - ther's bos - om came, Who died for me, e'en me to a
mer - cy seat of God For ev - er doth for sin - ners
on the o - cean shore, Thou hast for all a ran - som
man - sion in the skies, E'en then this shall be all my

rayed, With joy shall I lift up my head.
am, From sin and fear, from guilt and shame.
tone, Now for my Lord and God I own.
plead, For me— e'en for my soul— was shed.
paid, For all a full a - tone - ment made.
plea: Je - sus hath lived and died for me.

Copyright © 2000 by HAL LEONARD CORPORATION

JESUS, THY BOUNDLESS LOVE TO ME

ST. CATHERINE
music by
Henri F. Hemy, 1864
arr. by James G. Walton, 1874

words by
Paul Gerhardt, 1653
tr. by John Wesley, 1739

1. Je - sus, Thy bound - less love to me No thought can reach, no tongue de - clare;
2. O grant that noth - ing in my soul May dwell, but Thy pure love a - lone;
3. O Love, how gra - cious is Thy ray! All fear be - fore Thy pres - ence flies.
4. In suf - f'ring be Thy love my peace; In weak - ness be Thy love my pow'r.

O knit my thank - ful heart to Thee And reign with - out a ri - val there.
O may Thy love pos - sess me whole My joy, my treas - ure, and my crown.
Care, an - guish, sor - row melt a - way Wher - e'er Thy heal - ing beams a - rise.
And when the storms of life shall cease, Je - sus, in that im - por - tant hour,

Thine whol - ly, Thine a - lone I am; Be Thou a - lone my con - stant flame.
All cold - ness from my heart re - move; My ev - 'ry act, word, thought, be love.
O Je - sus, noth - ing may I see, Noth - ing de - sire or seek but Thee!
In death as life, be Thou my Guide, And save me, who for me hast died!

Copyright © 2000 by HAL LEONARD CORPORATION

JESUS, UNITED BY THY GRACE

ST. AGNES
music by
John Dykes, 1866

words by
Charles Wesley, 1742

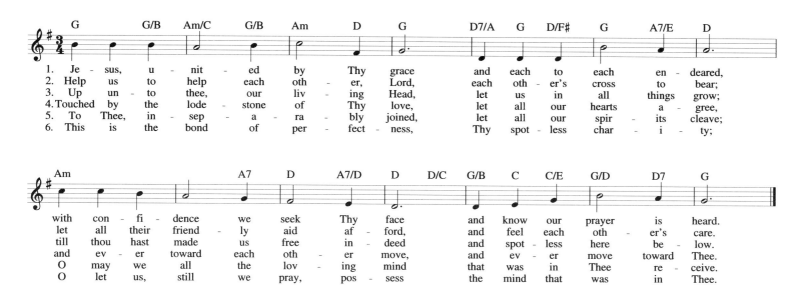

1. Je - sus, u - nit - ed by Thy grace and each to each en - deared,
2. Help us to help each oth - er, Lord, each oth - er's cross to bear;
3. Up un - to thee, our liv - ing Head, let us in all things grow;
4. Touched by the lode - stone of Thy love, let all our hearts a - gree,
5. To Thee, in - sep - a - ra - bly joined, let all our spir - its cleave;
6. This is the bond of per - fect - ness, Thy spot - less char - i - ty;

with con - fi - dence we seek Thy face and know our prayer is heard.
let all their friend - ly aid af - ford, and feel each oth - er's care.
till thou hast made us free in - deed and spot - less here be - low.
and ev - er toward each oth - er move, and ev - er move toward Thee.
O may we all the lov - ing mind that was in Thee re - ceive.
O let us, still we pray, pos - sess the mind that was in Thee.

JESUS! WHAT A FRIEND TO SINNERS

HYFRYDOL
music by
Rowland H. Prichard, 1830

words by
J. Wilbur Chapman, 1910

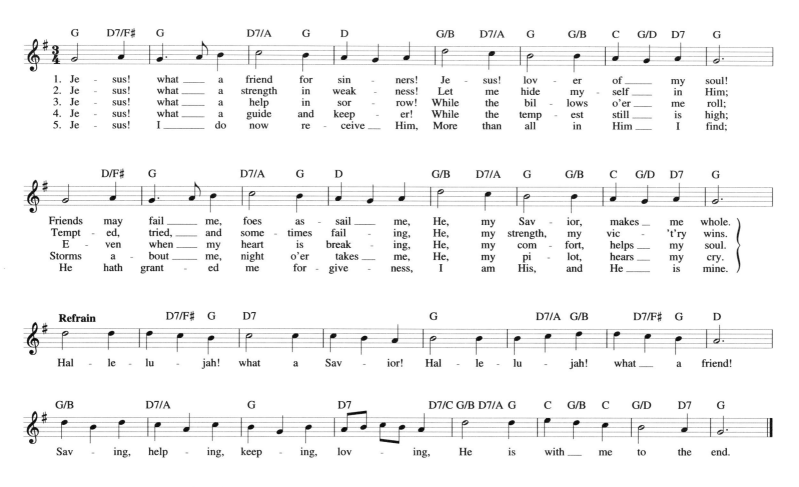

1. Je - sus! what a friend for sin - ners! Je - sus! lov - er of my soul!
2. Je - sus! what a strength in weak - ness! Let me hide my - self in Him;
3. Je - sus! what a help in sor - row! While the bil - lows o'er me roll;
4. Je - sus! what a guide and keep - er! While the temp - est still is high;
5. Je - sus! I do now re - ceive Him, More than all in Him I find;

Friends may fail me, foes as - sail me, He, my Sav - ior, makes me whole.
Tempt - ed, tried, and some - times fail - ing, He, my strength, my vic - 't'ry wins.
E - ven when my heart is break - ing, He, my com - fort, helps my soul.
Storms a - bout me, night o'er takes me, He, my pi - lot, hears my cry.
He hath grant - ed me for - give - ness, I am His, and He is mine.

Refrain

Hal - le - lu - jah! what a Sav - ior! Hal - le - lu - jah! what a friend!

Sav - ing, help - ing, keep - ing, lov - ing, He is with me to the end.

JESUS WALKED THIS LONESOME VALLEY

LONESOME VALLEY
Traditional Spiritual

Traditional Spiritual

1. Je - sus walked _____ this lone-some val - ley. He had to walk _____ it by Him - self. O,
2. We must walk _____ this lone-some val - ley. We have to walk _____ it by our - selves. O,
3. You must go _____ and stand your tri - al. You have to stand _____ it by your - self. O,

no-bod - y else _____ could walk it for Him. He had to walk it by _____ Him - self.
no-bod - y else _____ can walk it for us. We have to walk it by _____ our - selves.
no-bod - y else _____ can stand it for you. You have to stand it by _____ your - self.

JESUS, WHERE'ER THY PEOPLE MEET

MALVERN
music by
Lowell Mason (1792-1872)

words by
William Cowper (1731-1800)

1. Je - sus, wher - e'er Thy peo - ple _____ meet, There they be -
2. For Thou, with - in no walls _____ con - fined, Dost dwell with
3. Great Shep - herd of Thy cho - sen _____ few, Thy for - mer
4. Here may we prove the pow - er of _____ prayer To strength - en

hold Thy mer - cy _____ seat; Wher - e'er they seek Thee Thou _____ art _____
those of hum - ble _____ mind; Such ev - er bring Thee where _____ they _____
mer - cies here _____ re - new; Here, to our wait - ing hearts, _____ pro -
faith and sweet - en _____ care; To teach our faint de - sires _____ to _____

found, And ev - 'ry place is hal - lowed _____ ground.
come, And go - ing, take Thee to _____ their _____ home.
claim The sweet - ness of, Thy sav - ing _____ name.
rise, And bring all heav'n be - fore _____ our _____ eyes.

JOYFUL, JOYFUL, WE ADORE THEE

HYMN TO JOY
music by
Ludwig van Beethoven (1770-1827)
from *Ninth Symphony*
adapt. by Edward Hodges (1796-1867)

words by
Henry van Dyke, 1907

1. Joy - ful, joy - ful, we a - dore Thee God of glo - ry, Lord of love;
2. All Thy works with joy sur - round Thee, Earth and heaven re - flect Thy rays,
3. Thou art giv - ing and for - giv - ing, Ev - er bless - ing, ev - er blest,
4. Mor - tals, join the hap - py cho - rus Which the morn - ing stars be - gan;

Hearts un - fold like flow'rs be - fore Thee, O - p'ning to the sun a - bove.
Stars and an - gels sing a - round Thee, Cen - ter of un - bro - ken praise!
Well - spring of the joy of liv - ing, O - cean depth of hap - py rest!
Fa - ther love is reign - ing o'er us, Broth - er love binds man to man.

JUST A CLOSER WALK WITH THEE

Traditional words

CLOSER WALK
Traditional music

1. I am weak but Thou art strong. Je - sus, keep me from all wrong. ___ I'll be sat - is - fied as
2. Thro' this world of toil and snares, If I fal - ter, Lord, who cares? ___ Who with me my bur - den
3. When my fee - ble life is o'er, Time for me will be no more. ___ Guide me gen - tly, safe - ly

long ___ as I walk, let me walk close to Thee.
shares? ___ None but Thee, dear _ Lord, none but Thee. } Just a clos - er walk with Thee,
o'er ___ to Thy king - dom _ shore, to Thy shore. }

Grant it, Je - sus, is my plea. ___ Dai - ly walk - ing close to Thee, ___ Let it be, dear Lord, let it be.

Copyright © 2000 by HAL LEONARD CORPORATION

JUST AS I AM

DUNSTAN
music by
Joseph Barnby (1838-1896)

words by
Charlotte Elliott (1789-1871)

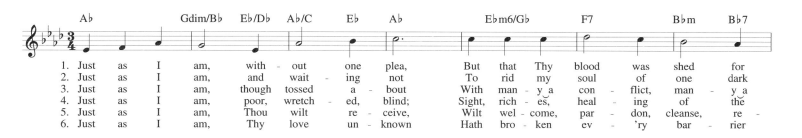

1. Just as I am, with - out one plea, But that Thy blood was shed for
2. Just as I am, and wait - ing not To rid my soul of one dark
3. Just as I am, though tossed a - bout With man - y a con - flict, man - y a
4. Just as I am, poor, wretch - ed, blind; Sight, rich - es, heal - ing of the
5. Just as I am, Thou wilt re - ceive, Wilt wel - come, par - don, cleanse, re -
6. Just as I am, Thy love un - known Hath bro - ken ev - 'ry bar - rier

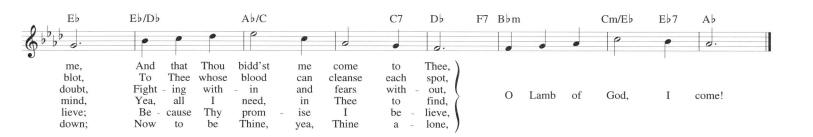

me, And that Thou bidd'st me come to Thee,
blot, To Thee whose blood can cleanse each spot,
doubt, Fight - ing with - in and fears with - out, } O Lamb of God, I come!
mind, Yea, all I need, in Thee to find,
lieve; Be - cause Thy prom - ise I be - lieve,
down; Now to be Thine, yea, Thine a - lone, }

Copyright © 2000 by HAL LEONARD CORPORATION

JUST AS I AM

WOODWORTH

words by
Charlotte Elliott, 1834

music by
William B. Bradbury, 1849

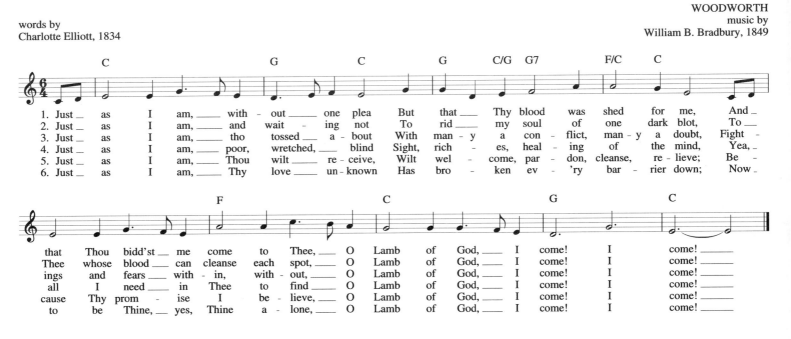

1. Just as I am, without one plea But that Thy blood was shed for me, And that Thou bidd'st me come to Thee, O Lamb of God, I come! I come!
2. Just as I am, and waiting not To rid my soul of one dark blot, To Thee whose blood can cleanse each spot, O Lamb of God, I come! I come!
3. Just as I am, tho tossed about With many a conflict, many a doubt, Fightings and fears within, without, O Lamb of God, I come! I come!
4. Just as I am, poor, wretched, blind Sight, riches, healing of the mind, Yea, all I need in Thee to find O Lamb of God, I come! I come!
5. Just as I am, Thou wilt receive, Wilt welcome, pardon, cleanse, relieve; Because Thy promise I believe, O Lamb of God, I come! I come!
6. Just as I am, Thy love unknown Has broken ev'ry barrier down; Now to be Thine, yes, Thine alone, O Lamb of God, I come! I come!

JUST OVER IN THE GLORYLAND

GLORYLAND

words by
James W. Acuff

music by
Emmett S. Dean

1. I've a home prepared where the saints abide, Just over in the gloryland; And I long to be by my Savior's side, Just over in the gloryland.
2. I am on my way to those mansions fair, Just over in the gloryland; There to sing God's praise and His glory share, Just over in the gloryland.
3. What a joyful thought that my Lord I'll see, Just over in the gloryland; And with kindred saved, there forever be, Just over in the gloryland.
4. With the blood-washed throng I will shout and sing, Just over in the gloryland; Glad hosannas to Christ, the Lord and King, Just over in the gloryland.

Just over in the gloryland I'll join the happy angel band, just over in the gloryland; Just over in the gloryland, There with the mighty host I'll stand Just over in the gloryland.

THE KING OF LOVE MY SHEPHERD IS

words by
Henry Williams Baker, 1868

DOMINUS REGIT ME
music by
John Bacchus Dykes, 1868

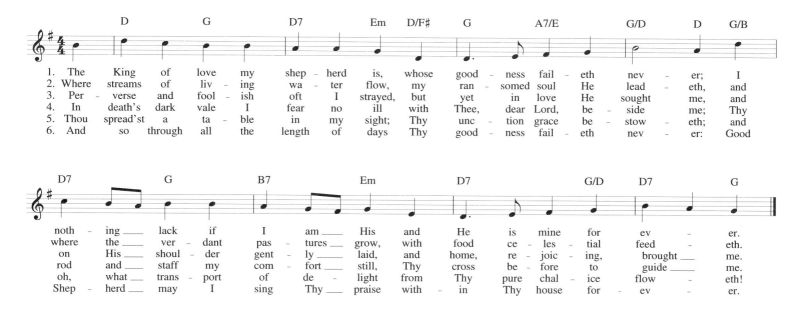

THE KING OF LOVE MY SHEPHERD IS

words by
Henry W. Baker (1821-1877)

ST. COLUMBA
Traditional Irish melody

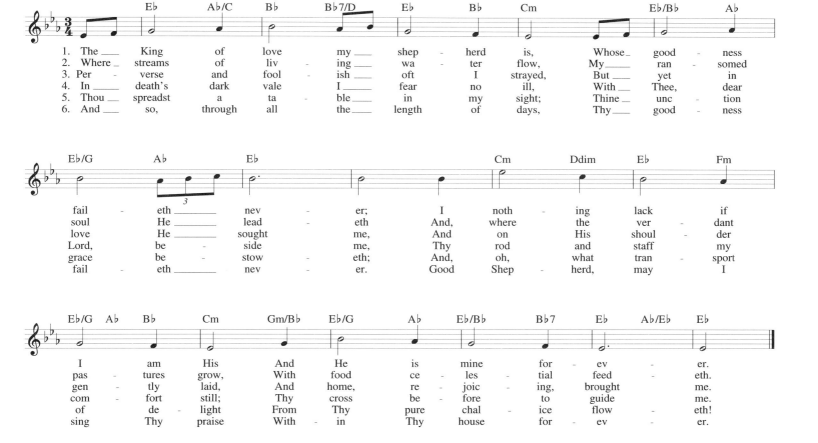

KUM BA YAH

Traditional Spiritual

Traditional Spiritual

LAMP OF OUR FEET, WHEREBY WE TRACE

NUN DANKET ALL' UND BRINGET EHR'
music attributed to
Johann Crüger (1598-1662)

words by
Bernard Barton (1784-1849)

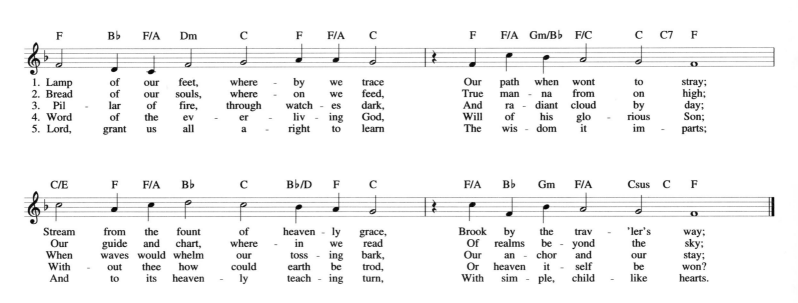

LEAD ME, LORD

words based on
Psalm 5:8, 4:8

LEAD ME, LORD
music by
Samuel Sebastian Wesley, 1861

Lead me, Lord, lead me in Thy right-eous-ness; make Thy way plain be-fore my face.

For it is Thou, Lord, Thou, __ Lord __ on - ly, that mak-est me dwell in _____ safe - ty.

LEAD ME TO CALVARY

words by
Jennie Evelyn Hussey, 1921

DUNCANNON
music by
William J. Kirkpatrick, 1921

1. King of my life I crown Thee now, Thine shall the glo - ry be; Lest I for - get Thy
2. Show me the tomb where Thou wast laid, Ten - der - ly mourned and wept; An - gels in robes of
3. Let me, like Mar - y, through the gloom, Come with a gift to Thee; Show to me now the
4. May I be will - ing, Lord, to bear Dai - ly my cross for Thee; E - ven Thy cup of

Refrain

thorn - crowned brow; Lead me to Cal - va - ry.
light ar - rayed Guard - ed Thee whilst Thou slept. } Lest I for - get Geth - sem - a - ne;
emp - ty tomb, Lead me to Cal - va - ry.
grief to share, Thou hast borne all for me.

Lest I for - get Thine ag - o - ny; Lest I for - get Thy love for me, Lead me to Cal - va - ry.

LEAD ON, O KING ETERNAL

words by
Ernest W. Shurtleff, 1888

LANCASHIRE
music by
Henry T. Smart, c. 1835

1. Lead on, O King E - ter - nal, The day of march has come; Hence - forth in fields of
2. Lead on, O King E - ter - nal, Till sin's fierce war shall cease, And ho - li - ness shall
3. Lead on, O King E - ter - nal, We fol - low, not with fears; For glad - ness breaks like

con - quest Thy tents shall be our home. Through days of prep - a - ra - tion Thy
whis - per The sweet A - men of peace; For not with swords loud crash - ing, Nor
morn - ing Wher - e'er Thy face ap - pears; Thy cross is lift - ed o'er _____ us; We

grace has made us strong, _____ And now, O King E - ter - nal, We lift our bat - tle song.
roll of stir - ring drums, _____ With deeds of love and mer - cy The heav'n - ly king - dom comes.
jour - ney in its light; _____ The crown a - waits the con - quest; Lead on, O God of might.

LEAD ON, O KING ETERNAL

words by
Ernest W. Shurtleff, 1888

LLANGLOFFAN
Welsh folk melody
from Evans' *Hymnau a Thonau*, 1865

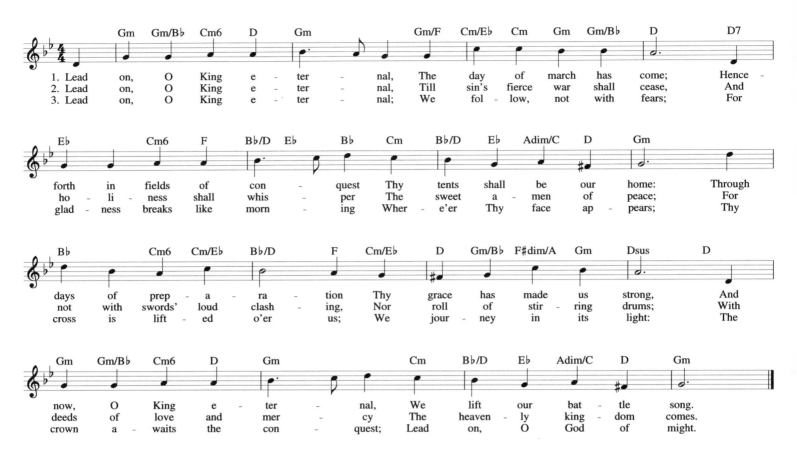

1. Lead on, O King e - ter - nal, The day of march has come; Hence -
2. Lead on, O King e - ter - nal, Till sin's fierce war shall cease, And
3. Lead on, O King e - ter - nal; We fol - low, not with fears; For

forth in fields of con - quest Thy tents shall be our home: Through
ho - li - ness shall whis - per The sweet a - men of peace; For
glad - ness breaks like morn - ing Wher - e'er Thy face ap - pears; Thy

days of prep - a - ra - tion Thy grace has made us strong, And
not with swords' loud clash - ing, Nor roll of stir - ring drums; With
cross is lift - ed o'er us; We jour - ney in its light: The

now, O King e - ter - nal, We lift our bat - tle song.
deeds of love and mer - cy The heaven - ly king - dom comes.
crown a - waits the con - quest; Lead on, O God of might.

LEAD US, HEAVENLY FATHER, LEAD US

words by
James Edmeston (1791-1867)

DULCE CARMEN
music from
An Essay on the Church Plain Chant, 1782

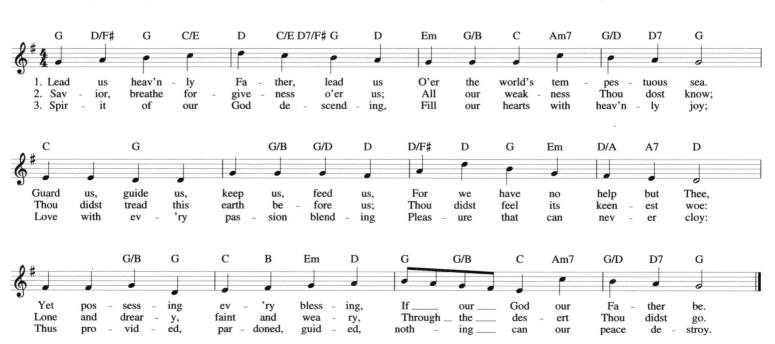

1. Lead us heav'n - ly Fa - ther, lead us O'er the world's tem - pes - tuous sea.
2. Sav - ior, breathe for - give - ness o'er us; All our weak - ness Thou dost know;
3. Spir - it of our God de - scend - ing, Fill our hearts with heav'n - ly joy;

Guard us, guide us, keep us, feed us, For we have no help but Thee,
Thou didst tread this earth be - fore us; Thou didst feel its keen - est woe:
Love with ev - 'ry pas - sion blend - ing Pleas - ure that can nev - er cloy:

Yet pos - sess - ing ev - 'ry bless - ing, If our God our Fa - ther be.
Lone and drear - y, faint and wea - ry, Through the des - ert Thou didst go.
Thus pro - vid - ed, par - doned, guid - ed, noth - ing can our peace de - stroy.

LEAD US, O FATHER, IN THE PATHS OF PEACE

words by
William H. Burleigh (1812-1871)

BURLEIGH
music by
Joseph Barnby (1838-1896)

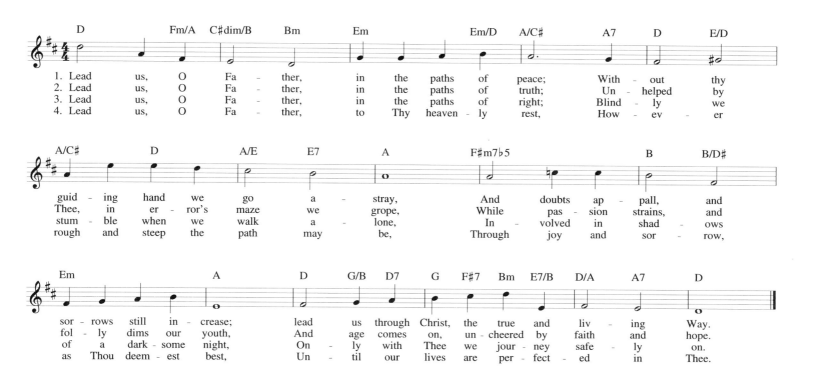

LEANING ON THE EVERLASTING ARMS

words by
Elisha A. Hoffman, 1887

SHOWALTER
music by
Anthony J. Showalter, 1887

LEAVE IT THERE

words by
Charles Albert Tindley, c. 1906

music by
Charles Albert Tindley, c. 1906
arr. by Charles A. Tindley, Jr., 1916

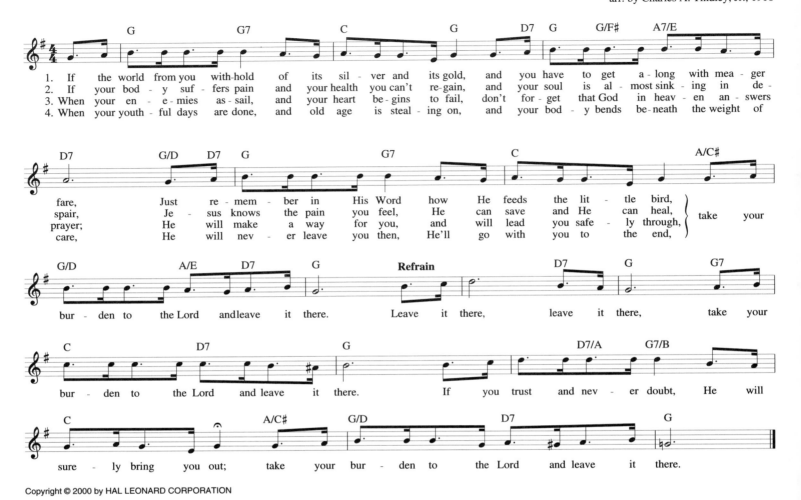

1. If the world from you with-hold of its sil - ver and its gold, and you have to get a - long with mea - ger
2. If your bod - y suf - fers pain and your health you can't re - gain, and your soul is al - most sink - ing in de -
3. When your en - e - mies as - sail, and your heart be - gins to fail, don't for - get that God in heav - en an - swers
4. When your youth - ful days are done, and old age is steal - ing on, and your bod - y bends be - neath the weight of

fare, Just re - mem - ber in His Word how He feeds the lit - tle bird,
spair, Je - sus knows the pain you feel, He can save and He can heal,
prayer; He will make a way for you, and will lead you safe - ly through,
care, He will nev - er leave you then, He'll go with you to the end,

take your bur - den to the Lord and leave it there. Leave it there, leave it there, take your

bur - den to the Lord and leave it there. If you trust and nev - er doubt, He will

sure - ly bring you out; take your bur - den to the Lord and leave it there.

Copyright © 2000 by HAL LEONARD CORPORATION

LET ALL MORTAL FLESH KEEP SILENCE

words from
The Liturgy of St. James, 4th century
tr. by Gerard Moultrie, 1864

PICARDY
Traditional French melody, 17th century

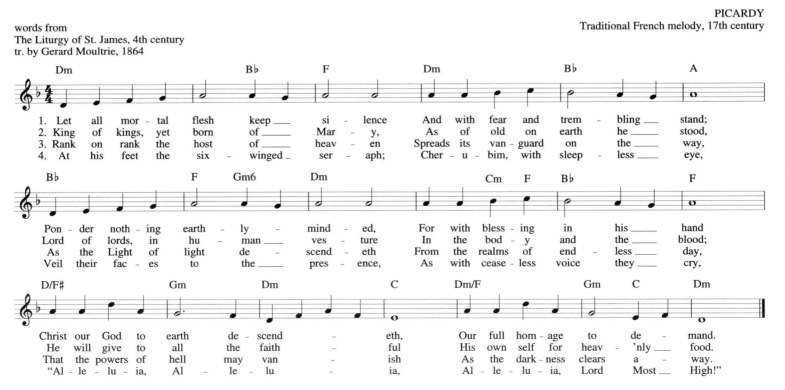

1. Let all mor - tal flesh keep __ si - lence And with fear and trem - bling __ stand;
2. King of kings, yet born of __ Mar - y, As of old on earth he __ stood,
3. Rank on rank the host of __ heav - en Spreads its van - guard on the __ way,
4. At his feet the six - winged __ ser - aph; Cher - u - bim, with sleep - less __ eye,

Pon - der noth - ing earth - ly - mind - ed, For with bless - ing in his __ hand
Lord of lords, in hu - man __ ves - ture In the bod - y and the __ blood;
As the Light of light de - scend - eth From the realms of end - less __ day,
Veil their fac - es to the __ pres - ence, As with cease - less voice they __ cry,

Christ our God to earth de - scend - eth, Our full hom - age to de - mand.
He will give to all the faith - ful His own self for heav - 'nly __ food.
That the powers of hell may van - ish As the dark - ness clears a - way.
"Al - le - lu - ia, Al - le - lu - ia, Al - le - lu - ia, Lord Most __ High!"

Copyright © 2000 by HAL LEONARD CORPORATION

LET ALL THE PEOPLE PRAISE THEE

words by
Lelia N. Morris, 1906

PEOPLE PRAISE
music by
Lelia N. Morris, 1906

LET ALL TOGETHER PRAISE OUR GOD

LOBT GOTT, IHR CHRISTEN

words by
Nikolaus Herman (c. 1480-1561)
tr. by Arthur Tozer Russell (1806-1874)

music by
Nikolaus Herman (c. 1480-1561)

LET ALL ON EARTH THEIR VOICES RAISE

ARIEL

words by
Isaac Watts (1674-1748)

music arr. by
Lowell Mason (1792-1872)

1. Let all on earth their voi - ces raise, To sing the great Je - ho - vah's
2. He framed the globe, He built the sky; He made the shin - ing worlds on
3. Come the great day, the glo - rious hour, When earth shall feel His sav - ing

praise, And bless his ho - ly name: His glo - ry let the hea - then know, His
high, And reigns in glo - ry there: His beams are maj - es - ty and light; His
pow'r, All na - tions fear His name: Then shall the race of man con - fess The

won - ders to the na - tions show, His sav - ing grace pro - claim, His sav - ing grace pro - claim.
beau - ties, how di - vine - ly bright! His dwell - ing place how fair, His dwell - ing place how fair!
beau - ty of His ho - li - ness, His sav - ing grace pro - claim, His sav - ing grace pro - claim.

LET JESUS COME INTO YOUR HEART

McCONNELSVILLE

words by
Lelia N. Morris (1862-1929)

music by
Lelia N. Morris (1862-1929)

1. If you are tired of the load of your sin, } Let Je - sus come in - to your heart;
2. If there's a tem - pest your voice can - not still, }
3. If you would join the glad songs of the blest, }

If you de - sire a new life to be - gin, } Let Je - sus come in - to your heart.
If there's a void this world nev - er can fill, }
If you would en - ter the man - sions of rest, }

Just now, your doubt - ings give o'er; Just now, re - ject Him no more;

Just now, throw o - pen the door; Let Je - sus come in - to your heart.

LET ME BE THINE FOREVER

LOB GOTT GETROST MIT SINGEN
music from
Musika Deutsch, Nürnberg, 1532

words by
Nikolaus Selnecker (1532-1592), v.1
v.2,3 from *Gesangbuch,* Rudolstadt, 1688
tr. by Matthias Loy (1828-1915)

LET SAINTS ON EARTH IN CONCERT SING

DUNDEE
music from
Scottish Psalter, 1615

words by
Charles Wesley (1707-1788)

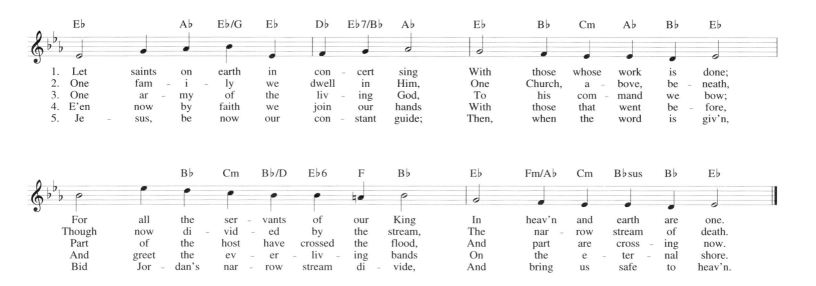

LET THE LOWER LIGHTS BE BURNING

LOWER LIGHTS
words by
Philip P. Bliss (1838-1876)

music by
Philip P. Bliss (1838-1876)

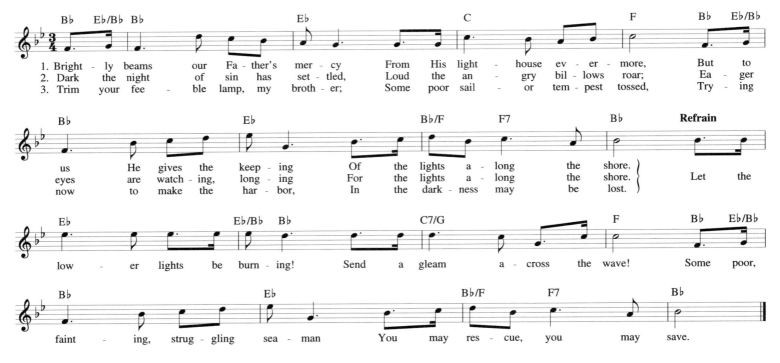

LET THE WHOLE CREATION CRY

LLANFAIR
words by
Stopford A. Brooke, 1881
based on Psalm 148

music by
Robert Williams, 1817

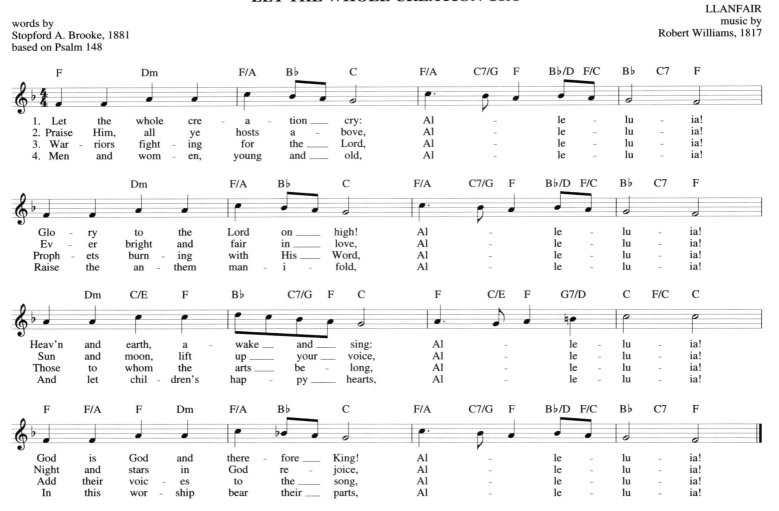

LET THE WHOLE CREATION CRY

words by
Stopford A. Brooke, 1881

SALZBURG
music by
Jacob Hintze, 1678
As in *Hymns Ancient and Modern,* 1861

1. Let the whole cre - a - tion cry, "Glo - ry to the Lord on high."
2. Men and wom - en, young and old, Raise the an - them man - i - fold;

Heaven and earth, a - wake and sing, "God is our e - ter - nal King."
Join with chil - dren's songs of praise, Wor - ship God through length of days.

Praise God, all ___ ye hosts a - bove, Ev - er shin - ing forth in love;
From the north ___ to south - ern pole Let the might - y cho - rus roll:

Sun and moon, up - lift your voice; Night and stars, in God re - joice!
"Ho - ly, ho - ly, ho - ly One, Glo - ry be to God a - lone!"

LET THY BLOOD IN MERCY POURED

words by
John Brownlie (1859-1925)

JESUS, MEINE ZUVERSICHT
music by
Johann Crüger (1598-1662)

1. Let Thy Blood in mer - cy poured, let Thy gra - cious Bo - dy bro - ken,
2. Thou didst die that I might live; bless - ed Lord, Thou cam'st to save me,
3. By the thorns that crowned Thy brow, by the spear wound and the nail - ing,
4. Wilt Thou own the gift I bring? All my pen - i - tence I give Thee;

be to me, O gra - cious Lord, of Thy bound - less love the to - ken.
all that love of God could give Je - sus by His sor - rows gave me.
by the pain and death, I now claim, O Christ, Thy love un - fail - ing.
Thou art my ex - alt - ed King, of Thy match - less love for - give me.

Refrain

Thou didst give Thy - self for me, now I give my - self to Thee.

LET US BREAK BREAD TOGETHER

LET US BREAK BREAD
Traditional Spiritual

Traditional Spiritual

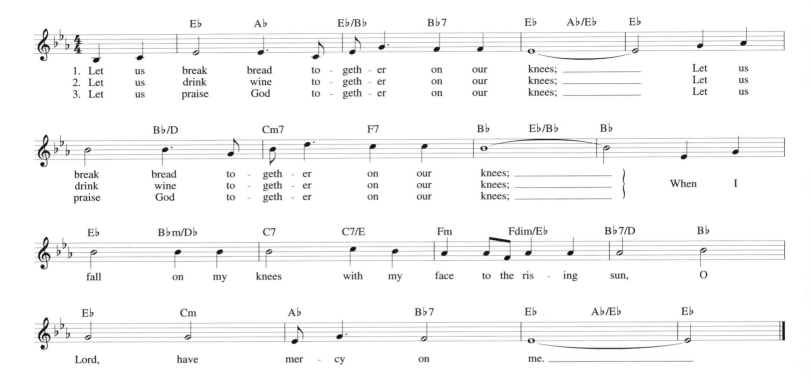

LET US NOW OUR VOICES RAISE

GAUDEAMUS PARITER
music from
Medieval [German or] Bohemian Carol Melody, 1544

words by
Joseph the Hymnographer, 9th century
tr. by John Mason Neale (1818-1866)

LET US PLEAD FOR FAITH ALONE

words by
Charles Wesley, 1740

SAVANNAH
music from
Foundery Collection, 1742

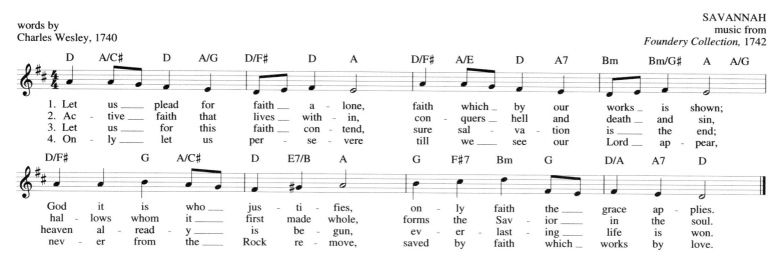

LET US WITH A GLADSOME MIND

words by
John Milton (1608-1674)

MONKLAND
music from
Freylinghausen's *Geistreiches Gesangbuch,* 1704

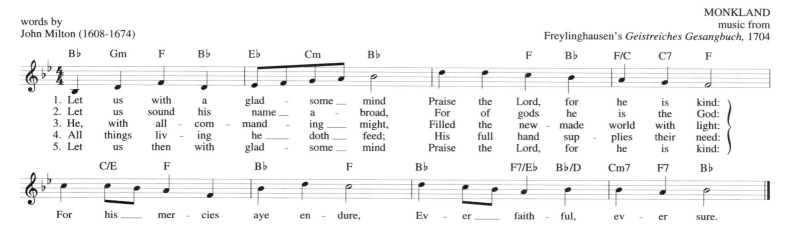

LIFT UP YOUR HEADS, YE MIGHTY GATES

words by
Georg Weissel, 1642
tr. by Catherine Winkworth, 1855

TRURO
music by
Thomas Williams, 1789

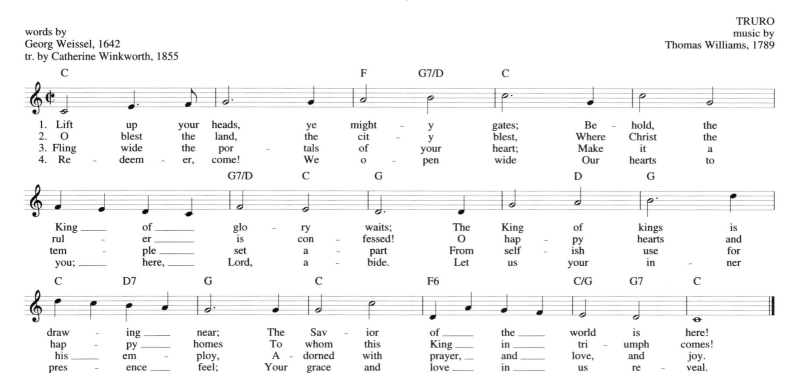

LIFE'S RAILWAY TO HEAVEN

words by
M.E. Abbey

music by
Charles D. Tillman

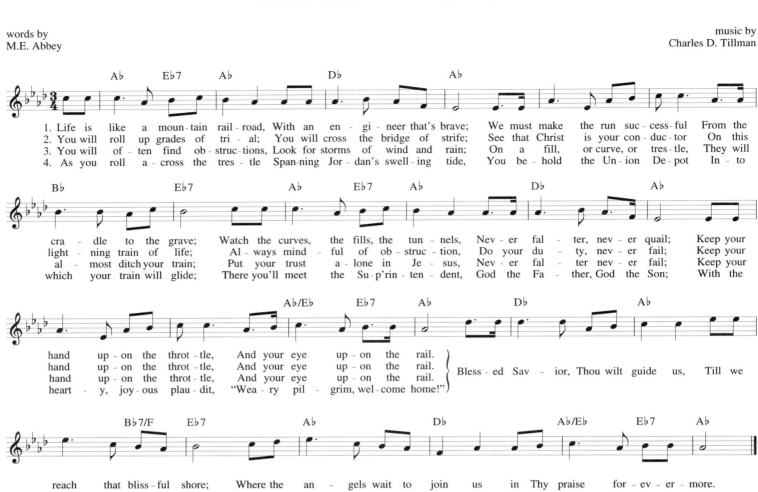

1. Life is like a moun-tain rail-road, With an en - gi - neer that's brave; We must make the run suc-cess-ful From the
2. You will roll up grades of tri - al; You will cross the bridge of strife; See that Christ is your con - duc - tor On this
3. You will of - ten find ob-struc-tions, Look for storms of wind and rain; On a fill, or curve, or tres - tle, They will
4. As you roll a - cross the tres - tle Span-ning Jor - dan's swell-ing tide, You be - hold the Un - ion De - pot In - to

cra - dle to the grave; Watch the curves, the fills, the tun - nels, Nev - er fal - ter, nev - er quail; Keep your
light - ning train of life; Al - ways mind - ful of ob-struc-tion, Do your du - ty, nev - er fail; Keep your
al - most ditch your train; Put your trust a - lone in Je - sus, Nev - er fal - ter nev - er fail; Keep your
which your train will glide; There you'll meet the Su-p'rin-ten-dent, God the Fa - ther, God the Son; With the

hand up - on the throt - tle, And your eye up - on the rail. }
hand up - on the throt - tle, And your eye up - on the rail. } Bless - ed Sav - ior, Thou wilt guide us, Till we
hand up - on the throt - tle, And your eye up - on the rail. }
heart - y, joy - ous plau - dit, "Wea - ry pil - grim, wel - come home!" }

reach that bliss - ful shore; Where the an - gels wait to join us in Thy praise for - ev - er - more.

LIGHT'S ABODE, CELESTIAL SALEM

RHUDDLAN
Traditional Welsh melody

Latin text by
Thomas a Kempis (d. 1471)
tr. by John Mason Neale (1818-1866)

1. Light's a - bode, ce - les - tial Sa - lem, Vi - sion dear whence peace doth spring;
2. There for ev - er and for ev - er Al - le - lu - ya is out - poured;
3. There no cloud nor pass - ing va - pour Dims the bright - ness of the air;
4. O how glo - rious and re - splen - dent, Fra - gile bod - y, shalt thou be,
5. Now with glad - ness, now with cour - age, Bear the bur - den on thee laid,
6. Laud and hon - our to the Fa - ther, Laud and hon - our to the Son,

Bright - er than the heart can fan - cy, Man - sion of the high - est King;
For un - end - ing, for un - bro - ken Is the feast - day of the Lord;
End - less noon - day, glo - rious noon - day, From the Sun of suns is there;
When en - dued with so much beau - ty, Full of health, and strong, and free,
That here - af - ter these thy la - bours May with end - less gifts be paid,
Laud and hon - our to the Spir - it, Ev - er Three and ev - er One.

O, how glo - rious are the prais - es Which of thee the proph - ets sing!
All is pure and all is ho - ly That with - in thy walls is stored.
There no night brings rest from la - bour, There un - known are toil and care.
Full of vig - our, full of pleas - ure That shall last e - ter - nal - ly!
And in ev - er - last - ing glo - ry Thou with joy may'st be ar - rayed.
Con - sub - stan - tial, co - e - ter - nal, While un - end - ing ag - es run.

THE LIGHT OF THE WORLD IS JESUS

LIGHT OF THE WORLD

words by
Philip P. Bliss, 1875

music by
Philip P. Bliss, 1875

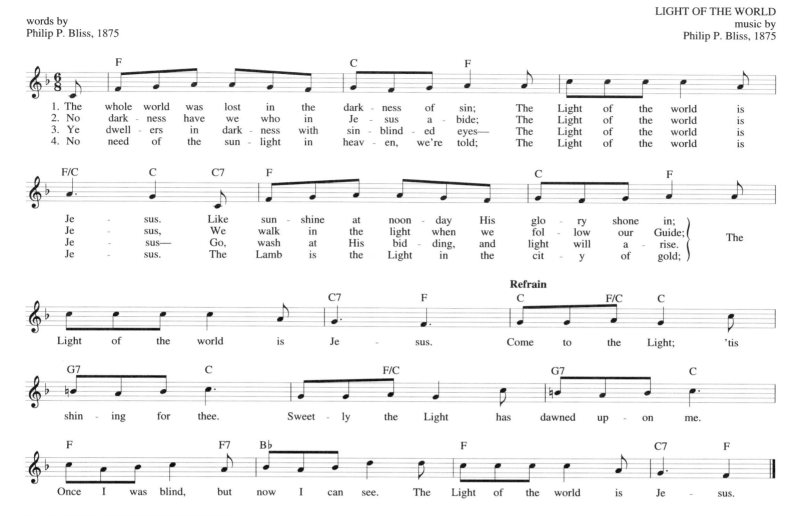

1. The whole world was lost in the dark-ness of sin; The Light of the world is
2. No dark-ness have we who in Je-sus a-bide; The Light of the world is
3. Ye dwell-ers in dark-ness with sin-blind-ed eyes— The Light of the world is
4. No need of the sun-light in heav-en, we're told; The Light of the world is

Je - sus. Like sun-shine at noon-day His glo-ry shone in;
Je - sus, We walk in the light when we fol-low our Guide;
Je - sus— Go, wash at His bid-ding, and light will a-rise.
Je - sus. The Lamb is the Light in the cit-y of gold;

The

Refrain

Light of the world is Je - sus. Come to the Light; 'tis

shin-ing for thee. Sweet-ly the Light has dawned up-on me.

Once I was blind, but now I can see. The Light of the world is Je - sus.

LIKE A RIVER GLORIOUS

WYE VALLEY

words by
Frances R. Havergal, 1874

music by
James Mountain, 1876

1. Like a riv-er glo-rious Is God's per-fect peace, O-ver all vic-to-rious
2. Hid-den in the hol-low Of His bless-ed hand, Nev-er foe can fol-low,
3. Ev-'ry joy or tri-al Fall-eth from a-bove, Traced up-on our di-al

In its bright in-crease. Per-fect, yet it flow-erth Full-er ev-'ry day;
Nev-er trai-tor stand. Not a surge of wor-ry, Not a shade of care,
By the Sun of Love. We may trust Him ful-ly All for us to do;

Per-fect, yet it grow-eth Deep-er all the way.
Not a blast of hur-ry Touch the Spir-it there.
They who trust Him whol-ly Find Him whol-ly true.

Refrain Stayed up-on Je-ho-vah,

Hearts are ful-ly blest. Find-ing, as He prom-ised, Per-fect peace and rest.

THE LILY OF THE VALLEY

SALVATIONIST
music by
William S. Hays (1837-1907)

(1838-1882)

1. I have found a friend in Je - sus, He's ev - 'ry - thing to me, He's the
2. He all my griefs has tak - en and all my sor - rows borne, In temp -
3. He will nev - er, nev - er leave me nor yet for - sake me here, While I

fair - est of ten thou - sand to my soul. The Lil - y of the Val - ley, in
ta - tion He's my strong and might - y tow'r. I have all for Him for - sak - en and
live by faith and do His bless - ed will. A wall of fire a - bout me, I've

Him a - lone I see All I need to cleanse and make me ful - ly whole. In
all my i - dols torn From my heart, and now He keeps me by His pow'r. Though
noth - ing now to fear; With His man - na He my hun - gry soul shall fill. Then

sor - row He's my com - fort, in trou - ble He's my stay, He tells me ev - 'ry care on Him to
all the world for - sake me and Sa - tan tempt me sore, Through Je - sus I shall safe - ly reach the
sweep - ing up to glo - ry I'll see His bless - ed face Where riv - ers of de - light shall ev - er

roll.
goal. } He's the Lil - y of the Val - ley, the Bright and Morn-ing Star, He's the fair - est of ten thou-sand to my soul.
roll.

Copyright © 2000 by HAL LEONARD CORPORATION

LITTLE IS MUCH WHEN GOD IS IN IT

words by Mrs. F.W. Suffield
and Dwight Brock

LITTLE IS MUCH
music by
Mrs. F.W. Suffield

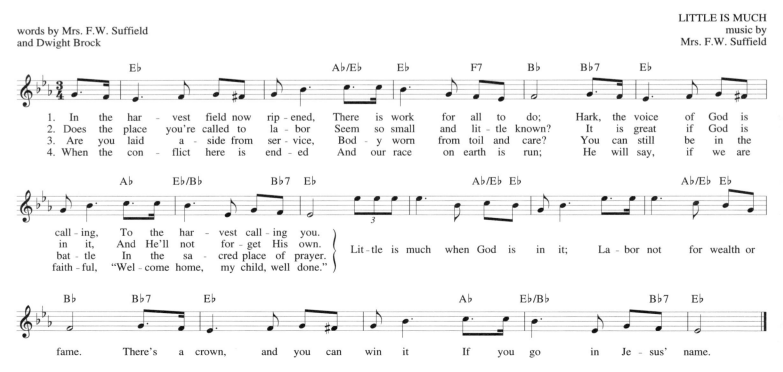

1. In the har - vest field now rip - ened, There is work for all to do; Hark, the voice of God is
2. Does the place you're called to la - bor Seem so small and lit - tle known? It is great if God is
3. Are you laid a - side from ser - vice, Bod - y worn from toil and care? You can still be in the
4. When the con - flict here is end - ed And our race on earth is run; He will say, if we are

call - ing, To the har - vest call - ing you.
in it, And He'll not for - get His own.
bat - tle In the sa - cred place of prayer. } Lit - tle is much when God is in it; La - bor not for wealth or
faith - ful, "Wel - come home, my child, well done."

fame. There's a crown, and you can win it If you go in Je - sus' name.

Copyright © 2000 by HAL LEONARD CORPORATION

LIVING FOR JESUS

LIVING

words by
Thomas O. Chisholm, 1917

music by
C. Harold Lowden, 1917

1. Liv - ing for Je - sus a life that is true, Striv - ing to please Him in
2. Liv - ing for Je - sus who died in my place, Bear - ing on Cal - v'ry my
3. Liv - ing for Je - sus wher - ev - er I am, Do - ing each du - ty in
4. Liv - ing for Je - sus thru earth's lit - tle while, My dear - est treas - ure, the

all that I do; Yield - ing al - le - giance, glad - heart - ed and free,
sin and dis - grace; Such love con - strains me to an - swer His call,
His ho - ly name; Will - ing to suf - fer af - flic - tion and loss,
light of His smile; See - ing the lost ones He died to re - deem,

This is the path - way of bless - ing for me.
Fol - low His lead - ing and give Him my all.
Tak - ing each tri - al as part of my cross.
Bring - ing the wea - ry to find rest in Him.

O Je - sus, Lord and

Sav - ior, I give my - self to Thee; For Thou, in Thy a - tone - ment, Didst

give Thy - self for me; I own no oth - er Mas - ter, My heart shall be Thy

throne; My life I give, hence - forth to live, O Christ, for Thee a - lone.

LIVING FOR JESUS

words by
Charles F. Weigle, 1903

music by
Charles F. Weigle, 1903

1. Liv - ing for Je - sus O what peace! Riv - ers of pleas - ure nev - er
2. Liv - ing for Je - sus O what rest! Pleas - ing my Sav - ior, I am
3. Liv - ing for Je - sus ev - 'ry - where, All of my bur - dens He doth
4. Liv - ing for Je - sus till at last In - to His glo - ry I have

cease. Tri - als may come, yet I'll not fear. Liv - ing for Je - sus, He is
blest. On - ly to live for Him a - lone, Do - ing His will till life is
bear. Friends may for - sake me; He'll be true. Trust - ing in Him, He'll guide me
passed; There to be - hold Him on His throne, Hear from His lips, "My child, well

near.
done!
through.
done!"

Help me to serve Thee more and more. Help me to praise Thee o'er and

o'er; Live in Thy pres - ence day by day, Nev - er to turn from Thee a - way.

LO, HE COMES WITH CLOUDS DESCENDING

HELMSLEY
Traditional English melody, 18th century

words by
Charles Wesley, 1758

1. Lo, He comes with clouds descending, once for favored sinners slain; thousand, thousand saints attending, swell the triumph of His train. Hallelujah! Hallelujah! Hallelujah! God appears on earth to reign.
2. Every eye shall now behold Him, robed in dreadful majesty; those who set at naught and sold Him, pierced and nailed Him to the tree, deeply wailing, deeply wailing, deeply wailing, shall the true Messiah see.
3. The dear tokens of His passion still His dazzling body bears cause of endless exultation to His ransomed worshipers; with what rapture, with what rapture, with what rapture, gaze we on those glorious scars!
4. Yea, Amen! Let all adore Thee, high on Thy eternal throne; Savior, take the power and glory, claim the kingdom for Thine own. Hallelujah! Hallelujah! Hallelujah! Everlasting God, come down!

LO, WHAT A CLOUD OF WITNESSES

ST. FULBERT
music by
Henry John Gauntlett (1805-1876)

words from
Translations and Paraphrases, 1745
para. of Hebrews 12:1-3

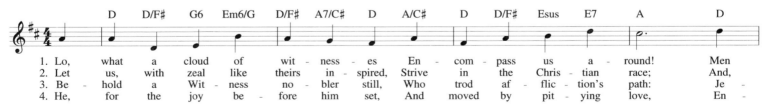

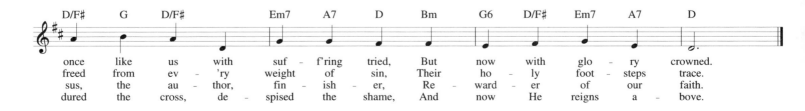

1. Lo, what a cloud of witnesses Encompass us around! Men once like us with suff'ring tried, But now with glory crowned.
2. Let us, with zeal like theirs inspired, Strive in the Christian race; And, freed from ev'ry weight of sin, Their holy footsteps trace.
3. Behold a Witness nobler still, Who trod affliction's path: Jesus, the author, finisher, Rewarder of our faith.
4. He, for the joy before him set, And moved by pitying love, Endured the cross, despised the shame, And now He reigns above.

LO, HOW A ROSE E'RE BLOOMING

15th century German carol
tr. by Theodore Baker, 1894

ES IST EIN' ROS'
music from
Alte Catholische Geistliche Kirchengesäng, Cologne, 1599

1. Lo, how a rose e'er bloom - ing From ten - der _____ stem hath
2. I - sa - iah 'twas fore - told it, The Rose I _____ have in

sprung! Of Jes - se's lin - eage com - ing As men of _____
mind, With Ma - ry we be - hold it, The Vir - gin _____

_____ old have sung. It came, a flow'r - et bright, A -
_____ Moth - er kind. To show God's love a - right. She

mid the cold of win - ter, When half spent _____ was the night.
bore to men a Sav - ior, When half spent _____ was the night.

LOOK AND LIVE

words by
William A. Ogden (1841-1897)

music by
William A. Ogden (1841-1897)

1. I've a mes - sage from the Lord, Hal - le - lu - jah! The mes - sage un - to you I
2. I've a mes - sage full of love, Hal - le - lu - jah! A mes - sage from the Lord for
3. Life is of - fered un - to you, Hal - le - lu - jah! E - ter - nal life your soul shall

give; 'Tis re - cord - ed in His Word, Hal - le - lu - jah! It is on - ly that you look and
you; 'Tis a mes - sage from a - bove, Hal - le - lu - jah! Je - sus said it and I know it's
have, If you'll on - ly look to Him, Hal - le - lu - jah! Look to Je - sus, who a - lone can

live.)
true. }
save.)

Look and live, _____ O will you live, Look to Je - sus now and

live; 'Tis re - cord - ed in His Word, Hal - le - lu - jah! It is on - ly that you look and live.

LOOK, YE SAINTS, THE SIGHT IS GLORIOUS

BRYN CALFARIA

words by
Thomas Kelly (1769-1855)

music by
William Owen (1814-1893)

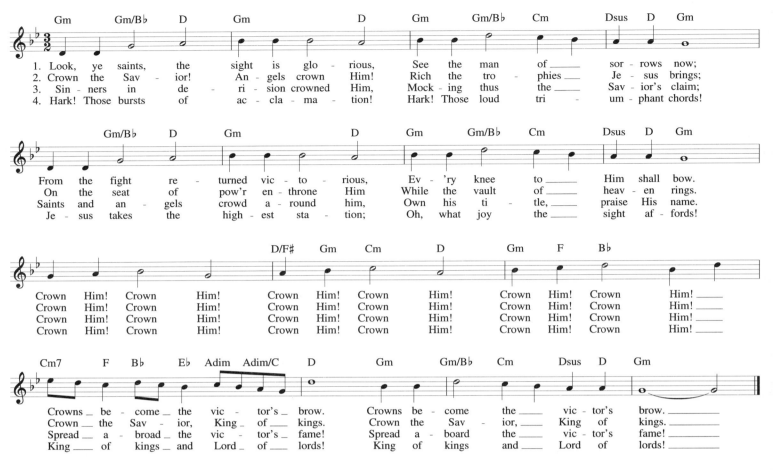

1. Look, ye saints, the sight is glorious, See the man of _____ sorrows now;
2. Crown the Savior! Angels crown Him! Rich the trophies _____ Jesus brings;
3. Sinners in derision crowned Him, Mocking thus the _____ Savior's claim;
4. Hark! Those bursts of acclamation! Hark! Those loud triumphant chords!

From the fight returned victorious, Ev'ry knee to _____ Him shall bow.
On the seat of pow'r enthrone Him, While the vault of _____ heaven rings.
Saints and angels crowd around him, Own his title, _____ praise His name.
Jesus takes the highest station; Oh, what joy the _____ sight affords!

Crown Him! Crown Him! Crown Him! Crown Him! Crown Him! Crown Him! _____
Crown Him! Crown Him! Crown Him! Crown Him! Crown Him! Crown Him! _____
Crown Him! Crown Him! Crown Him! Crown Him! Crown Him! Crown Him! _____
Crown Him! Crown Him! Crown Him! Crown Him! Crown Him! Crown Him! _____

Crowns become the victor's brow. Crowns become the _____ victor's brow.
Crown the Savior, King of kings. Crown the Savior, _____ King of kings.
Spread abroad the victor's fame! Spread aboard the _____ victor's fame!
King of kings and Lord of lords! King of kings and _____ Lord of lords!

LOOK, YE SAINTS, THE SIGHT IS GLORIOUS

CORONAE

words by
Thomas Kelly (1769-1855)

music by
William H. Monk (1823-1889)

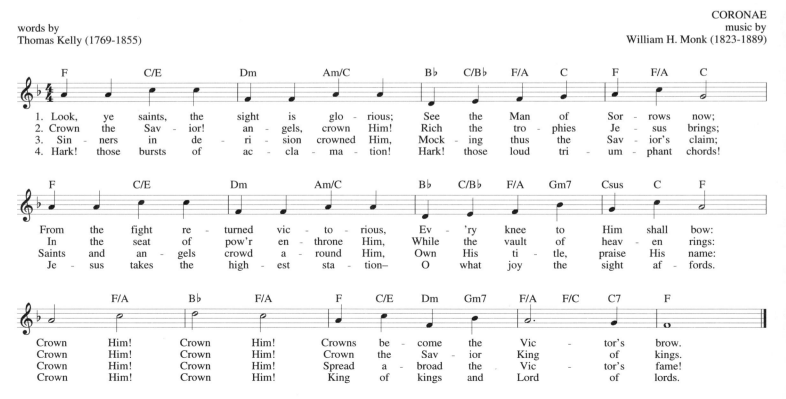

1. Look, ye saints, the sight is glorious; See the Man of Sorrows now;
2. Crown the Savior! angels, crown Him! Rich the trophies Jesus brings;
3. Sinners in derision crowned Him, Mocking thus the Savior's claim;
4. Hark! those bursts of acclamation! Hark! those loud triumphant chords!

From the fight returned victorious, Ev'ry knee to Him shall bow:
In the seat of pow'r enthrone Him, While the vault of heaven rings.
Saints and angels crowd around Him, Own His title, praise His name:
Jesus takes the highest station— O what joy the sight affords.

Crown Him! Crown Him! Crowns become the Victor's brow.
Crown Him! Crown Him! Crown the Savior King of kings.
Crown Him! Crown Him! Spread abroad the Victor's fame!
Crown Him! Crown Him! King of kings and Lord of lords.

THE LORD ASCENDETH UP ON HIGH

ACH HERR, DU ALLERHÖCHSTER GOTT

words by
Arthur T. Russell (1806-1874)

music by
Michael Praetorius (1571-1621)

THE LORD JEHOVAH REIGNS

DARWALL'S 148TH

words by
Isaac Watts, 1709

music by
John Darwall, 1770

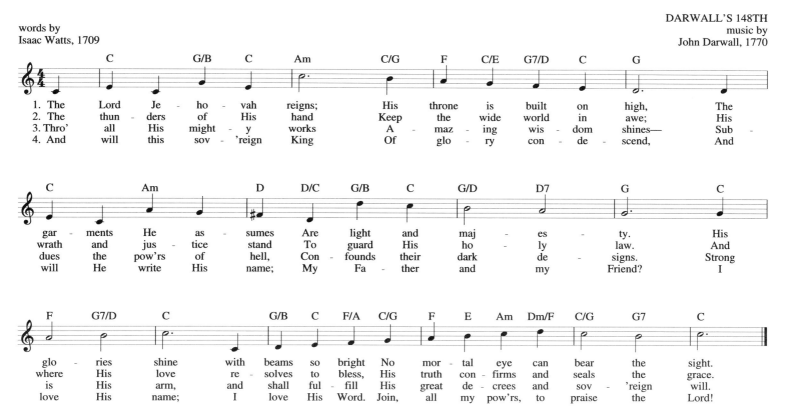

THE LORD IS IN HIS HOLY TEMPLE

QUAM DILECTA
music by
George F. Root (1820-1895)

words based on
Habakkuk 2:20

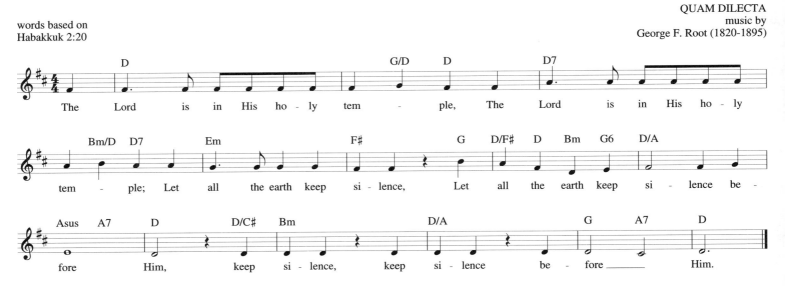

The Lord is in His ho-ly tem - ple, The Lord is in His ho-ly
tem - ple; Let all the earth keep si - lence, Let all the earth keep si - lence be-
fore Him, keep si - lence, keep si - lence be - fore _____ Him.

LORD JESUS CHRIST, BE PRESENT NOW

HERR JESU CHRIST, DICH ZU UNS WEND
music from
Cantionale Germanicum, Gochsheim, 1628

words from
Lutherische Hand-Büchlein, 2nd Ed., Altenburg, 1648
tr. by C. Winkworth (1827-1878)

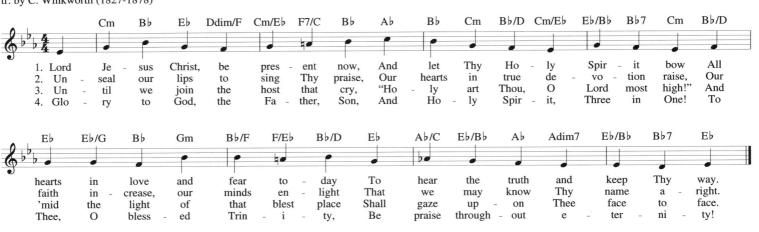

1. Lord Je - sus Christ, be pres - ent now, And let Thy Ho - ly Spir - it bow All
2. Un - seal our lips to sing Thy praise, Our hearts in true de - vo - tion raise, Our
3. Un - til we join the host that cry, "Ho - ly art Thou, O Lord most high!" And
4. Glo - ry to God, the Fa - ther, Son, And Ho - ly Spir - it, Three in One! To

hearts in love and fear to - day To hear the truth and keep Thy way.
faith in - crease, our minds en - light That we may know Thy name a - right.
'mid the light of that blest place Shall gaze up - on Thee face to face.
Thee, O bless - ed Trin - i - ty, Be praise through - out e - ter - ni - ty!

LORD JESUS CHRIST, OUR LORD MOST DEAR

VOM HIMMEL HOCH
music from
Schumann's *Geistliche Lieder,* 1539

words by
Heinrich von Laufenberg, 1429
tr. by Catherine Winkworth, 1869

1. Lord Je - sus Christ, our Lord most dear, As thou wast once an ___ in - fant here, So
2. As in Thy heav'n - ly king - dom, Lord, All things o - bey Thy ___ sa - cred word, Do
3. Their watch let an - gels round him keep Wher - e'er he be, a - wake, a - sleep; Thy

give this child ___ of thine, ___ we pray, Thy grace and bless - ing ___ day ___ by day.
Thou Thy might - y suc - cour give, And shield this child by ___ morn and eve.
ho - ly Cross ___ not let ___ him bear, That he Thy crown with ___ Saints may wear.

LORD JESUS CHRIST, WE HUMBLY PRAY

words by
Henry E. Jacobs (1844-1932)

GRACE CHURCH
music by
Ignaz J. Pleyel (1757-1831)

1. Lord Je - sus Christ, we hum - bly pray That we may feast on Thee to - day; Be - neath these forms of bread and wine En - rich us with Thy grace _____ di - vine.
2. The chas - tened peace of sin for - giv'n, The fil - ial joy of heirs to heav'n, Grant as we share this won - drous food, Thy bro - ken bod - y we re - ceive, And all we are to Thee we give.
3. Our trem - bling hearts cleave to Thy Word. All Thou hast said Thou dost af - ford; All Thy love pro - claim till Thou shalt come, To bring Thy scat - tered loved ones home.
4. One bread, one cup, one bod - y, we, U - nit - ed by our life in Thee, That each may be Thy wel - comed guest When Thou shalt spread Thy heav'n - ly feast.
5. Lord Je - sus Christ, we hum - bly pray: Oh, keep us stead - fast to that day,

LORD JESUS, THINK ON ME

words by
Synesius of Cyrene (c. 375-430)
tr. by Allen W. Chatfield (1808-1896)

SOUTHWELL
music from
William Damon's *Psalms*, 1579

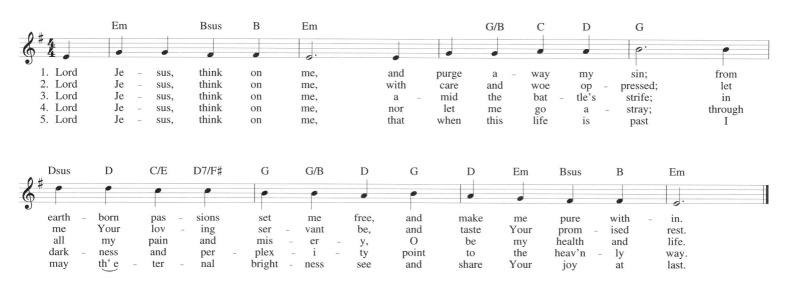

1. Lord Je - sus, think on me, and purge a - way my sin; from earth - born pas - sions set me free, and make me pure with - in.
2. Lord Je - sus, think on me, with care and woe op - pressed; let me Your lov - ing ser - vant be, and taste Your prom - ised rest.
3. Lord Je - sus, think on me, a - mid the bat - tle's strife; in all my pain and mis - er - y, O be my health and life.
4. Lord Je - sus, think on me, nor let me go a - stray; through dark - ness and per - plex - i - ty point to the heav'n - ly way.
5. Lord Je - sus, think on me, that when this life is past I may th' e - ter - nal bright - ness see and share Your joy at last.

LORD, BE THY WORD MY RULE

QUAM DILECTA
music by
Henry Lascelles Jenner (1820-1898)

words by
Christopher Wordsworth (1807-1885)

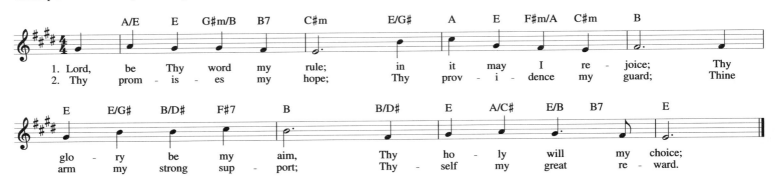

1. Lord, be Thy word my rule; in it may I re - joice; Thy
2. Thy prom - is - es my hope; Thy prov - i - dence my guard; Thine

glo - ry be my aim, Thy ho - ly will my choice;
arm my strong sup - port; Thy - self my will great re - ward.

LORD, ENTHRONED IN HEAVENLY SPLENDOR

BRYN CALFARIA
music by
William Owen (1814-1893)

words by
George H. Bourne (1840-1925)

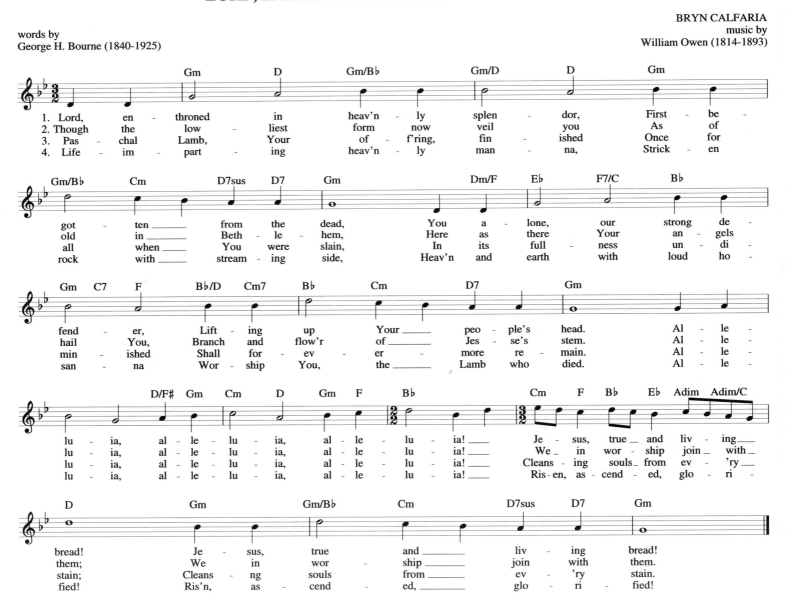

1. Lord, en - throned in heav'n - ly splen - dor, First - be -
2. Though the low - liest form now veil you, As of
3. Pas - chal Lamb, Your of - f'ring, fin - ished Once for
4. Life - im - part - ing heav'n - ly man - na, Strick - en

got - ten from the dead, You a - lone, our strong de -
old in Beth - le - hem, Here as there Your an - gels
all when You were slain, In its full - ness un - di -
rock with stream - ing side, Heav'n and earth with loud ho -

fend - er, Lift - ing up Your peo - ple's head. Al - le -
hail You, Branch and flow'r of Jes - se's stem. Al - le -
min - ished Shall for - ev - er - more re - main. Al - le -
san - na Wor - ship You, the Lamb who died. Al - le -

lu - ia, al - le - lu - ia, al - le - lu - ia! Je - sus, true and liv - ing
lu - ia, al - le - lu - ia, al - le - lu - ia! We in wor - ship join with
lu - ia, al - le - lu - ia, al - le - lu - ia! Cleans - ing souls from ev - 'ry
lu - ia, al - le - lu - ia, al - le - lu - ia! Ris - en, as - cend - ed, glo - ri -

bread! Je - sus, true and liv - ing bread!
them; We in wor - ship join with them.
stain; Cleans - ng souls from ev - 'ry stain.
fied! Ris'n, as - cend - ed, glo - ri - fied!

LORD, DISMISS US WITH THY BLESSING

SICILIAN MARINERS
Sicilian melody
as in *The European Magazine and London Review,* 1792

words attributed to
John Fawcett, 1773

1. Lord, dis-miss us with Thy bless-ing; fill our hearts with joy and peace;
2. Thanks we give and a-dor-a-tion fill for Thy Gos-pel's joy-ful sound:
3. So that when Thy love shall call us, Sa-vior, from the world a-way,

let us each, Thy love pos-sess-ing, tri-umph in re-deem-ing grace:
may the fruits of Thy sal-va-tion in our hearts and lives a-bound:
fear of death shall not ap-pall us, glad Thy sum-mons to o-bey.

O re-fresh us, O re-fresh us, trav-'ling through this wil-der-ness.
ev-er faith-ful, ev-er faith-ful to Thy truth may we be found;
May we ev-er, may we ev-er reign with Thee in end-less day.

LORD, FOR TOMORROW AND ITS NEEDS

VINCENT
music by
Horatio R. Palmer (1834-1917)

words by
Sybil F. Partridge

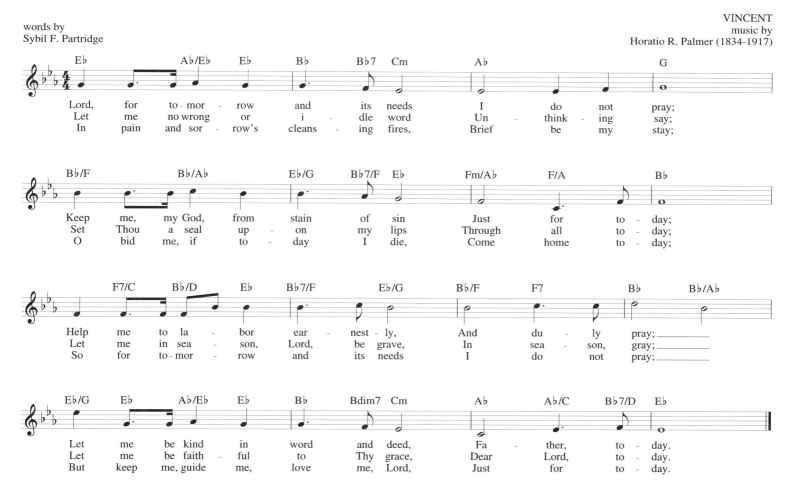

Lord, for to-mor-row and its needs I do not pray;
Let me no wrong or i-dle word Un-think-ing say;
In pain and sor-row's cleans-ing fires, Brief be my stay;

Keep me, my God, from stain of sin Just for to-day;
Set Thou a seal up-on my lips Through all to-day;
O bid me, if to-day I die, Come home to-day;

Help me to la-bor ear-nest-ly, And du-ly pray;
Let me in sea-son, Lord, be grave, In sea-son, gray;
So for to-mor-row and its needs I do not pray;

Let me be kind in word and deed, Fa-ther, to-day.
Let me be faith-ful to Thy grace, Dear Lord, to-day.
But keep me, guide me, love me, Lord, Just for to-day.

LORD, I WANT TO BE A CHRISTIAN

I WANT TO BE A CHRISTIAN
Traditional Spiritual

Traditional Spiritual

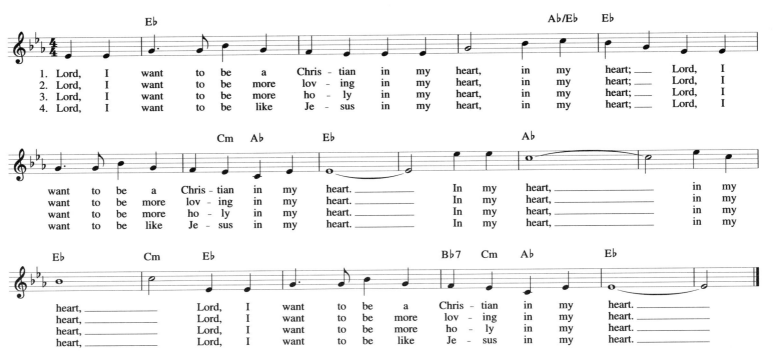

LORD, I'M COMING HOME

COMING HOME
music by
William J. Kirkpatrick (1838-1921)

words by
William J. Kirkpatrick (1838-1921)

LORD, FROM THE DEPTHS TO THEE I CRY

words from
Scottish Psalter, 1650
based on Psalm 130

SONG 67
music by
Orlando Gibbons (1583-1625)

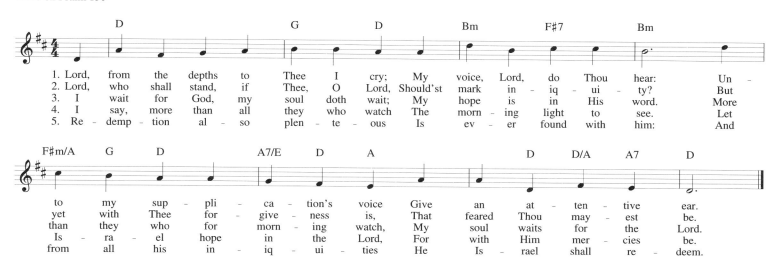

1. Lord, from the depths to Thee I cry; My voice, Lord, do Thou hear: Un-
2. Lord, who shall stand, if Thee, O Lord, Should'st mark in - iq - ui - ty? But
3. I wait for God, my soul doth wait; My hope is in His word. More
4. I say, more than all they who watch The morn - ing light to see. Let
5. Re - demp - tion al - so plen - te - ous Is ev - er found with him: And

to my sup - pli - ca - tion's voice Give an at - ten - tive ear.
yet with Thee for - give - ness is, That feared Thou may - est be.
than they who for morn - ing watch, My soul waits for the Lord.
Is - ra - el hope in the Lord, For with Him mer - cies be.
from all his in - iq - ui - ties He Is - rael shall re - deem.

LORD, IF AT THY COMMAND

words by
Charles Wesley (1707-1788)

SWABIA
music by
Johann M. Spiess (1715-1772)

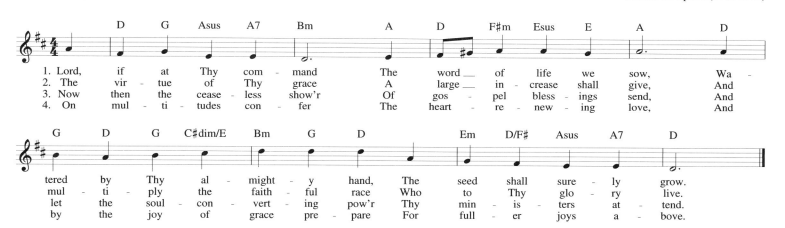

1. Lord, if at Thy com - mand The word __ of life we sow, Wa -
2. The vir - tue of Thy grace A large __ in - crease shall give, And
3. Now then the cease - less show'r Of gos - pel bless - ings send, And
4. On mul - ti - tudes con - fer The heart - re - new - ing love, And

tered by Thy al - might - y hand, The seed shall sure - ly grow.
mul - ti - ply the faith - ful race Who to Thy glo - ry live.
let the soul - con - vert - ing pow'r Thy min - is - ters at - tend.
by the joy of grace pre - pare For full - er joys a - bove.

LORD, KEEP US STEADFAST IN THY WORD

words by
Martin Luther (1483-1546)
tr. by C. Winkworth (1827-1878)

ERHALT UNS, HERR
music by
J. Klug, *Geistliche Lieder,* Wittenberg, 1543

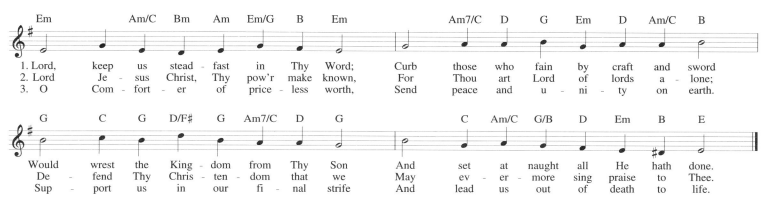

1. Lord, keep us stead - fast in Thy Word; Curb those who fain by craft and sword
2. Lord Je - sus Christ, Thy pow'r make known, For Thou art Lord of lords a - lone;
3. O Com - fort - er of price - less worth, Send peace and u - ni - ty on earth.

Would wrest the King - dom from Thy Son And set at naught all He hath done.
De - fend Thy Chris - ten - dom that we May ev - er - more sing praise to Thee.
Sup - port us in our fi - nal strife And lead us out of death to life.

LORD, LAY SOME SOUL UPON MY HEART

IRA

words by
Leon Tucker, 19th century

music by
Ira D. Sankey (1840-1908)

Lord, lay some soul up - on my heart And love that soul through me; _____ And

may I al - ways do my part To win that soul for Thee. _____

LORD, MAKE US MORE HOLY

African-American Spiritual

African-American Spiritual

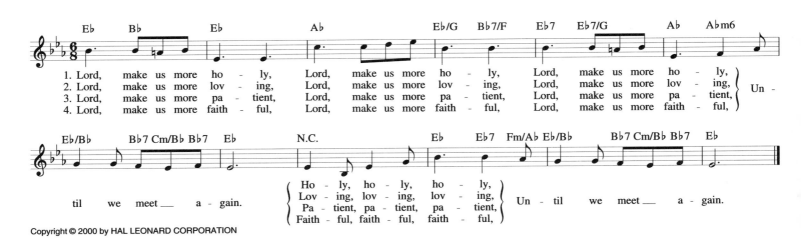

1. Lord, make us more ho - ly, Lord, make us more ho - ly, Lord, make us more ho - ly, Un -
2. Lord, make us more lov - ing, Lord, make us more lov - ing, Lord, make us more lov - ing,
3. Lord, make us more pa - tient, Lord, make us more pa - tient, Lord, make us more pa - tient,
4. Lord, make us more faith - ful, Lord, make us more faith - ful, Lord, make us more faith - ful,

til we meet _____ a - gain.

Ho - ly, ho - ly, ho - ly,
Lov - ing, lov - ing, lov - ing,
Pa - tient, pa - tient, pa - tient,
Faith - ful, faith - ful, faith - ful,

Un - til we meet _____ a - gain.

LORD OF ALL BEING, THRONED AFAR

MENDON

words by
Oliver Wendell Holmes (1809-1894)

music from
Methodist Harmonist, 1821

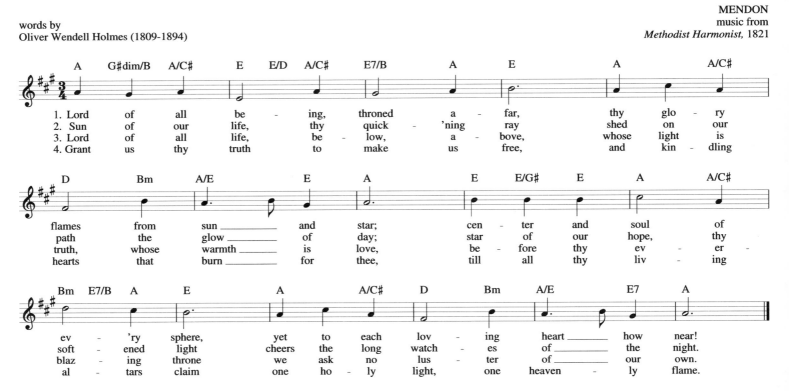

1. Lord of all be - ing, throned a - far, thy glo - ry
2. Sun of our life, thy quick - 'ning ray shed on our
3. Lord of all life, be - low, a - bove, whose light is
4. Grant us thy truth to make us free, and kin - dling

flames from sun _____ and star; cen - ter and soul of
path the glow _____ of day; star of our hope, thy
truth, whose warmth _____ is love, be - fore thy ev - er
hearts that burn _____ for thee, till all thy liv - ing

ev - 'ry sphere, yet to each lov - ing heart _____ how near!
soft - ened light cheers the long watch - es of _____ the night.
blaz - ing throne we ask no lus - ter of _____ our own.
al - tars claim one ho - ly light, one heaven - ly flame.

LORD OF GLORY, WHO HAST BOUGHT US

words by
E.S. Alderson (1818-1889)

HYFRYDOL
music by
R.H. Prichard (1811-1887)

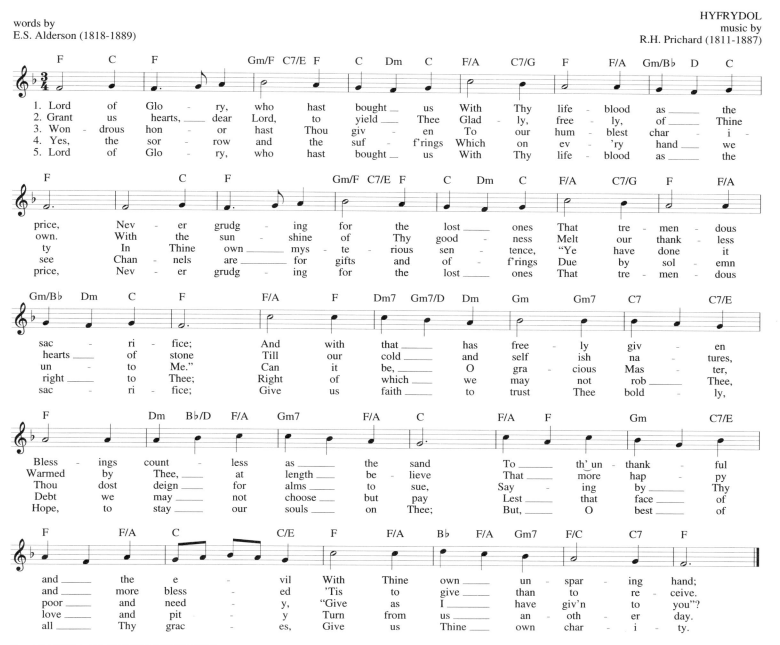

1. Lord of Glory, who hast bought us With Thy life-blood as the price, Never grudging for the lost ones That tremendous sacrifice; And with that has freely given Blessings countless as the sand To th' unthankful and the evil With Thine own unsparing hand;

2. Grant us hearts, dear Lord, to yield Thee Gladly, freely, of Thine own. With the sunshine of Thy goodness Melt our thankless hearts of stone Till our cold and selfish natures, Warmed by Thee, at length believe That more happy by Thy dost deign for alms to sue, Saying by Thy more blessed 'Tis to give than to receive.

3. Wondrous honor hast Thou given To our humblest charity In Thine own mysterious sentence, "Ye have done it unto Me." Can it be, O gracious Master, That Thou deignest for alms to sue, Saying by Thy poor and needy, "Give as I have giv'n to you"? Turn from us Thine own charity.

4. Yes, the sorrow and the suff'rings Which on ev'ry hand we see Channels are for gifts and off'rings Due by solemn right to Thee; Right of which we may not rob Thee, Debt we may not choose but pay Lest that face of love and pity Turn from us another day.

5. Lord of Glory, who hast bought us With Thy life-blood as the price, Never grudging for the lost ones That tremendous sacrifice; Give us faith to trust Thee boldly, Hope, to stay our souls on Thee; But, O best of all Thy graces, Give us Thine own charity.

LORD, OUR LORD, THY GLORIOUS NAME

Author unknown
words based on Psalm 8

GOTT SEI DANK
music from
Freylinghausen's *Geistreiches Gesangbuch,* 1704

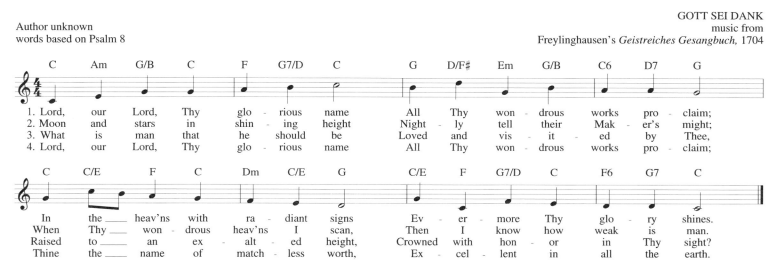

1. Lord, our Lord, Thy glorious name All Thy wondrous works proclaim; In the heav'ns with radiant signs Evermore Thy glory shines.

2. Moon and stars in shining height Nightly tell their Maker's might; When Thy wondrous heav'ns I scan, Then I know how weak is man.

3. What is man that he should be Loved and visited by Thee, Raised to an exalted height, Crowned with honor in Thy sight?

4. Lord, our Lord, Thy glorious name All Thy wondrous works proclaim; Thine the name of matchless worth, Excellent in all the earth.

LORD, SPEAK TO ME

words by
Frances Ridley Havergal, 1872

CANONBURY
music adapt. from
Robert Schumann, 1839

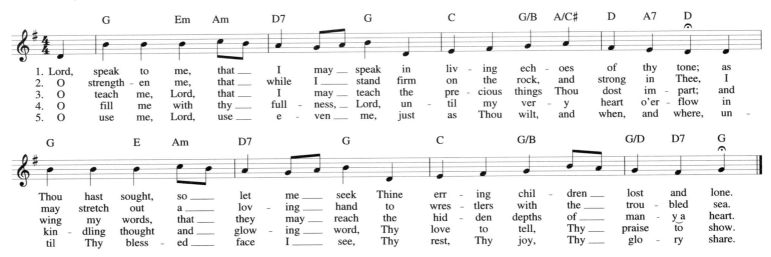

Copyright © 2000 by HAL LEONARD CORPORATION

LORD, TEACH US HOW TO PRAY ARIGHT

words by
James Montgomery (1771-1854)

DOMINE, CLAMAVI
music by
J.H. Knecht (1752-1817)

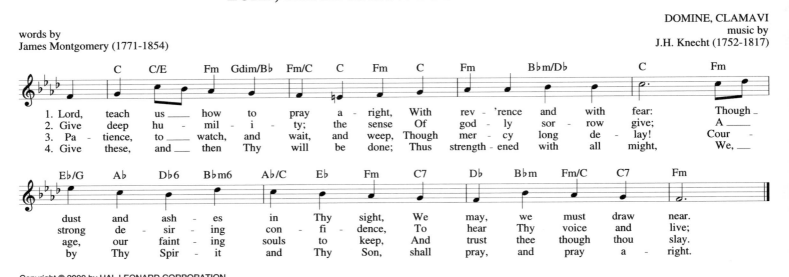

Copyright © 2000 by HAL LEONARD CORPORATION

LORD, TEACH US HOW TO PRAY ARIGHT

words by
James Montgomery (1771-1854)

SONG 67
music by
Orlando Gibbons (1583-1625)

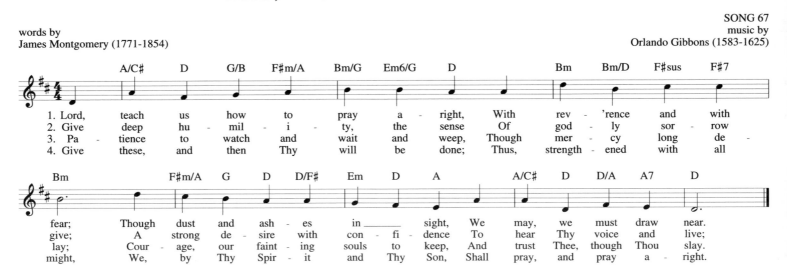

Copyright © 2000 by HAL LEONARD CORPORATION

LORD, THEE I LOVE WITH ALL MY HEART

words by
Martin M. Schalling (1532-1608)
tr. by Catherine Winkworth (1827-1878)

HERZLICH LIEB HAB ICH DICH, O HERR
music from
Zwey Bücher... Tabulatur, Strassburg, 1577

1. Lord, Thee I love with all my heart; I pray Thee, ne'er from me de-part;
2. Yea, Lord, 'twas Thy rich boun-ty gave My bod-y, soul, and all I have
3. Lord, let at last Thine an-gels come, To A-bram's bos-om bear me home,

With ten-der mer-cies cheer me. Earth has no plea-sure I would share,
In this poor life of la-bor. Lord, grant that I in ev-'ry place
That I may die un-fear-ing; And in its nar-row cham-ber keep

Yea, heav'n it-self were void and bare If Thou, Lord, wert not near
May glo-ri-fy Thy lav-ish grace And serve and help my neigh-
My bod-y safe in peace-ful sleep Un-til Thy re-ap-pear-

me. And should my heart for sor-row break, My trust in Thee no one could shake.
bor. Let no false doc-trine me be-guile; Let Sa-tan not my soul de-file.
ing. And then from death a-wak-en me That these mine eyes with joy may see,

Thou art the Por-tion I have sought; Thy pre-cious blood my soul has bought. Lord
Give strength and pa-tience un-to me To bear my cross and fol-low Thee. Lord
O Son of God, Thy glo-rious face, My Sav-ior and my Fount of grace. Lord

Je-sus Christ, My God and Lord, my God and Lord, For-sake me not! I trust Thy Word.
Je-sus Christ, My God and Lord, my God and Lord, In death Thy com-fort still af-ford.
Je-sus Christ, My prayer at-tend, my prayer at-tend, And I will praise Thee with-out end.

LORD, WHO THROUGHOUT THESE FORTY DAYS

words by
Claudia Frances Hernaman (1838-1898)

ST. FLAVIAN
music from
Day's *Psalter,* 1562

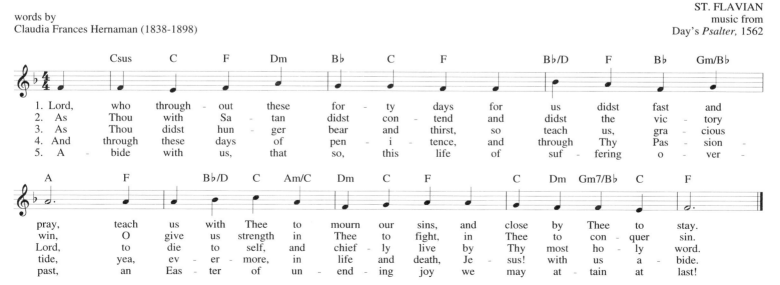

1. Lord, who through-out these for-ty days for us didst fast and
2. As Thou with Sa-tan didst con-tend and didst the vic-tory
3. As Thou didst hun-ger bear and thirst, so teach us, gra-cious
4. And through these days of pen-i-tence, and through Thy Pas-sion
5. A-bide with us, that so, this life of suf-fering o-ver

pray, teach us with Thee to mourn our sins, and close by Thee to stay.
win, O give us strength in Thee to fight, in Thee to con-quer sin.
Lord, to die to self, and chief-ly live by Thy most ho-ly word.
tide, yea, ev-er-more, in life and death, Je-sus! with us a-bide.
past, an Eas-ter of un-end-ing joy we may at-tain at last!

THE LORD WILL COME AND NOT BE SLOW

ST. STEPHEN
music by
William Jones (1726-1800)

words by
John Milton (1608-1674)

1. The Lord will come and ___ not be slow, His ___ foot - steps ___ can - not
2. Truth from the earth, like ___ to a flower, Shall ___ bud and ___ blos - som
3. Rise, God, judge Thou the ___ earth in might, This ___ wick - ed ___ earth re -
4. The na - tions all whom ___ Thou hast made Shall ___ come, and ___ all shall
5. For great Thou art, and ___ won - ders great By ___ Thy strong ___ hand are

err; Be - fore Him right - eous - ness shall ___ go, His roy - al ___ har - bin - ger.
then; And jus - tice, from her heaven - ly ___ bower, Look down on ___ mor - tal men.
dress; For Thou art He who shalt by ___ right The na - tions ___ all pos - sess.
frame To bow them low be - fore Thee, ___ Lord, And glo - ri - fy Thy Name.
done: Thou in Thy ev - er - last - ing ___ seat Re - main - est ___ God a - lone.

LORD, WITH GLOWING HEART I'D PRAISE THEE

PLEADING SAVIOR
music by
J. Leavitt, *Christian Lyre*, 1831

words by
Francis Scott Key (1779-1843)

1. Lord, with ___ glow - ing ___ heart I'd praise Thee For the ___ bliss Thy ___
2. Praise, my ___ soul, the ___ God that sought thee, Wretch - ed wan - d'rer,
3. Lord, my ___ spir - its ___ ar - dent feel - ings Vain - ly ___ would my ___

love be - stows, For the ___ par - d'ning ___ grace that saves me, And the ___ peace that ___
far a - stray; Found thee ___ lost, and ___ kind - ly brought thee From the ___ paths of ___
lips ex - press. Low be - fore Thy ___ foot - stool kneel - ing, Deign Thy ___ sup - pli - ant's

from it flows. Help, O ___ God, my weak en - deav - or;
death a - way. Praise, with ___ love's de - vout - est ___ feel - ing,
prayer to bless; Let Thy ___ grace, my soul's chief ___ treas - ure,

This dull soul to rap - ture ___ raise; Thou must ___ light the ___
Him who ___ saw thy guil - born ___ fear And, the ___ light of ___
Love's pure ___ flame with - in me ___ raise; And, since ___ words can ___

flame, or nev - er Can my ___ love be ___ warmed to praise.
hope re - veal - ing, Bade the ___ blood - stained ___ cross ap - pear.
nev - er meas - ure, Let my ___ life show ___ forth Thy praise!

THE LORD'S MY SHEPHERD, I'LL NOT WANT

BELMONT
music by
William Gardiner (1770-1853)

words from
Scottish Psalter, 1650
based on Psalm 23

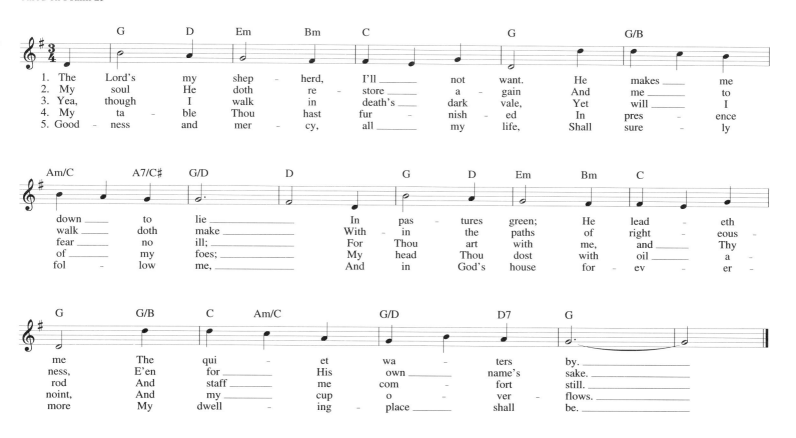

1. The Lord's my shep - herd, I'll _____ not want. He makes _____ me
2. My soul He doth re - store _____ a - gain And me _____ to
3. Yea, though I walk in death's _____ dark vale, Yet will _____ I
4. My ta - ble Thou hast fur - nish - ed In pres - ence
5. Good - ness and mer - cy, all _____ my life, Shall sure - ly

down _____ to lie _____ In pas - tures green; He lead - eth
walk _____ doth make _____ With - in the paths of right - eous -
fear _____ no ill; _____ For Thou art with me, and _____ Thy
of _____ my foes; _____ My head Thou dost with oil _____ a -
fol - low me, _____ And in God's house for - ev - er -

me The qui - et wa - ters by. _____
ness, E'en for _____ His own _____ name's sake. _____
rod And staff _____ me com - fort still. _____
noint, And my _____ cup o - ver - flows. _____
more My dwell - ing - place _____ shall be. _____

THE LORD'S MY SHEPHERD, I'LL NOT WANT

CRIMOND
music by
Jessie S. Irvine (1836-1887)

words from
Scottish Psalter, 1650
based on Psalm 23

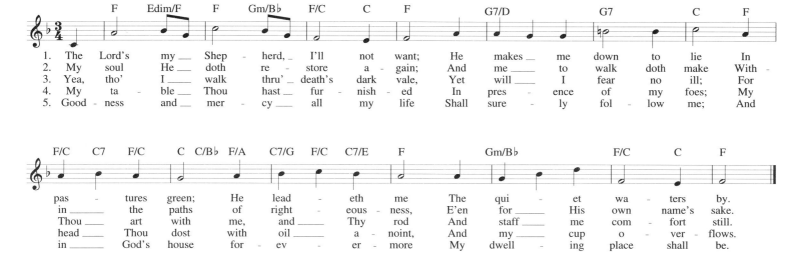

1. The Lord's my _____ Shep - herd, I'll not want; He makes _____ me down to lie In
2. My soul He doth re - store thru' death's a - gain; And me _____ to walk doth make With -
3. Yea, tho' I walk thru' death's dark vale, Yet will _____ I fear no ill; For
4. My ta - ble _____ Thou hast _____ fur - nish - ed In pres - ence of my foes; My
5. Good - ness and _____ mer - cy _____ all my life Shall sure - ly fol - low me; And

pas - tures green; He lead - eth me The qui - et wa - ters by.
in _____ the paths of right - eous - ness, E'en for _____ His own _____ name's sake.
Thou _____ art with me, and _____ Thy rod And staff _____ me com - fort still.
head _____ Thou dost with oil _____ a - noint, And my _____ cup o - ver - flows.
in _____ God's house for - ev - er - more My dwell - ing - place shall be.

LOVE DIVINE, ALL LOVES EXCELLING

BEECHER

words by
Charles Wesley, 1747

music by
John Zundel, 1870

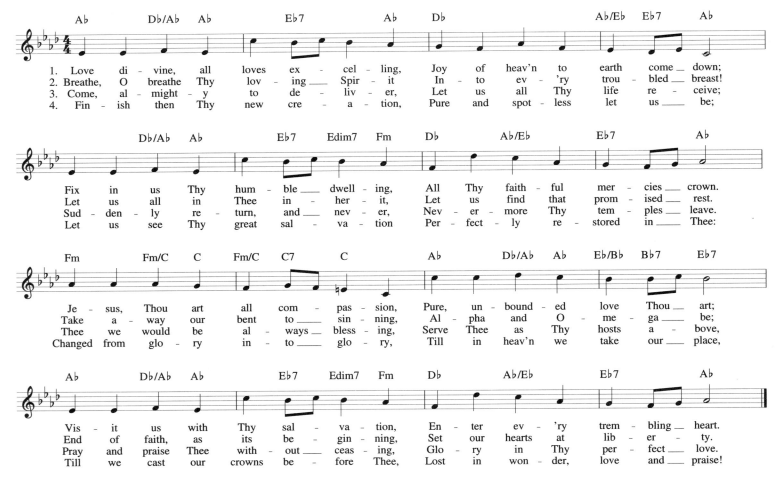

1. Love di - vine, all loves ex - cel - ling, Joy of heav'n to earth come __ down;
2. Breathe, O breathe Thy lov - ing __ Spir - it In - to ev - 'ry trou - bled __ breast!
3. Come, al - might - y to de - liv - er, Let us all Thy life re - ceive;
4. Fin - ish then Thy new cre - a - tion, Pure and spot - less let us __ be;

Fix in us Thy hum - ble __ dwell - ing, All Thy faith - ful mer - cies __ crown.
Let us all in Thee in - her - it, Let us find that prom - ised __ rest.
Sud - den - ly re - turn, and __ nev - er, Nev - er - more Thy tem - ples __ leave.
Let us see Thy great sal - va - tion Per - fect - ly re - stored in __ Thee:

Je - sus, Thou art all com - pas - sion, Pure, un - bound - ed love Thou __ art;
Take a - way our bent to __ sin - ning, Al - pha and O - me - ga __ be;
Thee we would be al - ways __ bless - ing, Serve Thee as Thy hosts a - bove,
Changed from glo - ry in - to __ glo - ry, Till in heav'n we take our __ place,

Vis - it us with Thy sal - va - tion, En - ter ev - 'ry trem - bling __ heart.
End of faith, as its be - gin - ning, Set our hearts at lib - er - ty.
Pray and praise Thee with - out __ ceas - ing, Glo - ry in Thy per - fect __ love.
Till we cast our crowns be - fore Thee, Lost in won - der, love and __ praise!

LOVE DIVINE, ALL LOVES EXCELLING

HYFRYDOL

words by
Charles Wesley, 1747

music by
Rowland Hugh Prichard, 1831

1. Love di - vine, _____ all loves ex - cel - ling, Joy of heaven, to
2. Breathe, O breathe _____ Thy lov - ing Spir - it In - to ev - 'ry
3. Come, Al - might - y to de - liv - er, Let us all Thy
4. Fin - ish, then, _____ Thy new cre - a - tion; Pure and spot - less

earth _____ come down, Fix in us _____ Thy hum - ble dwell - ing,
trou - bled breast! Let us all _____ in Thee in - her - it,
life _____ re - ceive; Sun - den - ly _____ re - turn, and nev - er,
let _____ us be; Let us see _____ Thy great sal - va - tion

All Thy faith - ful mer - cies crown! Je - sus, Thou __ art all com -
Let us find the prom - ised rest; Take a - way __ the love of
Nev - er - more Thy tem - ples leave. Thee we would __ be al - ways
Per - fect - ly re - stored in Thee; Changed from glo - ry in - to

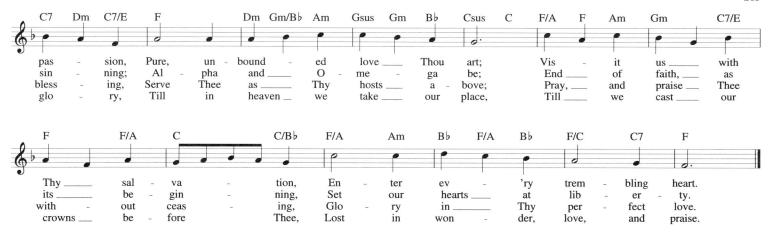

pas - sion, Pure, un - bound - ed love ___ Thou art; Vis - it us ___ with
sin - ning; Al - pha and ___ O - me - ga be; End ___ of faith, ___ as
bless - ing, Serve Thee as ___ Thy hosts ___ a - bove; Pray, ___ and praise ___ Thee
glo - ry, Till in heaven ___ we take ___ our place, Till ___ we cast ___ our

Thy ___ sal - va - tion, En - ter ev - 'ry trem - bling heart.
its ___ be - gin - ning, Set our hearts ___ at lib - er - ty.
with - out ceas - ing, Glo - ry in ___ Thy per - fect love.
crowns ___ be - fore Thee, Lost in won - der, love, and praise.

LOVE LIFTED ME

SAFETY

words by
James Rowe, 1912

music by
Howard E. Smith, 1912

1. I was sink - ing deep in sin, far from the peace - ful shore, ___ Ver - y deep - ly
2. All my heart to Him I give, ev - er to Him I'll cling, ___ In His bless - ed
3. Souls in dan - ger, look a - bove; Je - sus com - plete - ly saves. ___ He will lift you

stained with - in, sink - ing to rise no more. ___ But the Mas - ter of the sea
pres - ence live, ev - er His prais - es sing. ___ Love so might - y and so true
by His love out of the an - gry waves; ___ He's the Mas - ter of the sea,

heard my de - spair - ing cry, ___ From the wa - ters lift - ed me; now safe am I.
mer - its my soul's best songs; ___ Faith - ful lov - ing serv - ice, too, to Him be - longs.
bil - lows His will o - bey. ___ He your Sav - ior wants to be; be saved to - day.

Love lift - ed me! ___ Love lift - ed me! ___ When noth - ing

else could help, love lift - ed me. Love lift - ed me!

Love lift - ed me! ___ When noth - ing else could help, Love lift - ed me.

THE LOVE OF GOD

LOVE OF GOD

words by Frederick M. Lehman, 1917 (v. 1,2)
and Meir Ben Isaac Nehorai, 1050 (v. 3)

music by
Frederick M. Lehman, 1917

1. The love of God is great-er far _____ Than tongue or pen can ev-er tell; It goes be-
2. When years of time shall pass a-way _____ And earth-ly thrones and king-doms fall, When men, who
3. Could we with ink the o-cean fill, _____ And were the skies of parch-ment made, Were ev-'ry

yond the high-est star _____ And reach-es to the low-est hell. The guilt-y pair, bowed down with
here re-fuse to pray, _____ On rocks and hills and moun-tains call; God's love so sure shall still en-
stalk on earth a quill, _____ And ev-'ry man a scribe by trade; To write the love of God a-

care, _____ God gave His Son _____ to win; His err-ing child He rec-on-ciled _____ And par-doned
dure, _____ All mea-sure-less _____ and strong. Re-deem-ing grace to Ad-am's race, _____ The saints' and
bove _____ Would drain the o-cean dry; Nor could the scroll con-tain the whole, _ Though stretched from

from _____ his sin.) O love of God, how rich and pure! _____ How mea-sure-less _____ and
an - gels' song.)
sky _____ to sky.)

strong! It shall for-ev-er-more en-dure, _____ The saints' and an - gels' song.

Copyright © 2000 by HAL LEONARD CORPORATION

MAJESTIC SWEETNESS SITS ENTHRONED

ORTONVILLE

words by
Samuel Stennett (1727-1795)

music by
Thomas Hastings (1784-1872)

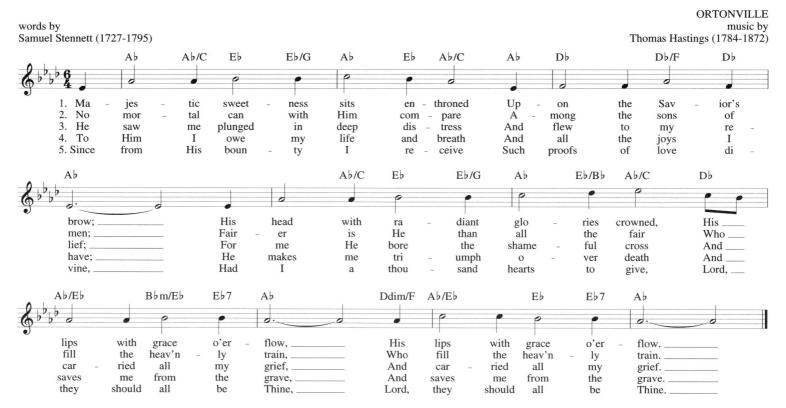

1. Ma - jes - tic sweet - ness sits en - throned Up - on the Sav - ior's
2. No mor - tal can with Him com - pare A - mong the sons of
3. He saw me plunged in deep dis - tress And flew to my re -
4. To Him I owe my life and breath And all the joys I
5. Since from His boun - ty I re - ceive Such proofs of love di -

brow; _____ His head with ra - diant glo - ries crowned, His _____
men; _____ Fair - er is He than all the fair Who _____
lief; _____ For me He bore the shame - ful cross And _____
have; _____ He makes me tri - umph o - ver death And _____
vine, _____ Had I a thou - sand hearts to give, Lord, _____

lips with grace o'er - flow, _____ His lips with grace o'er - flow. _____
fill the heav'n - ly train, _____ Who fill the heav'n - ly train. _____
car - ried all my grief, _____ And car - ried all my grief. _____
saves me from the grave, _____ And saves me from the grave. _____
they should all be Thine, _____ Lord, they should all be Thine.

Copyright © 2000 by HAL LEONARD CORPORATION

MAKE ME A CAPTIVE, LORD

DIADEMATA

words by
George Matheson, 1890

music by
George J. Elvey, 1868

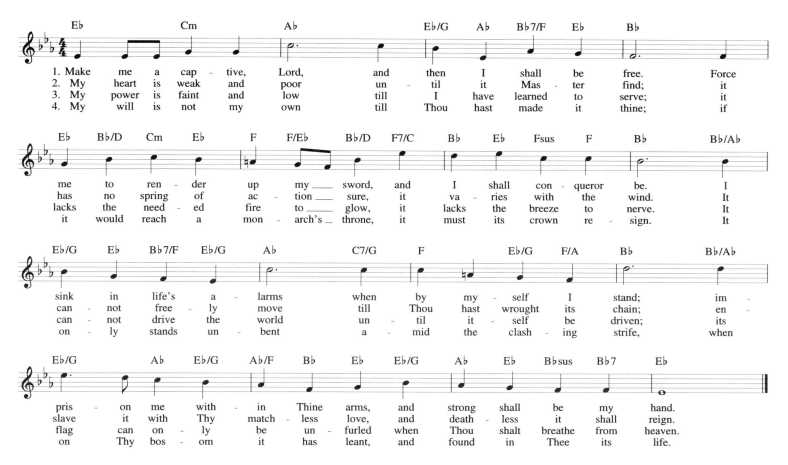

1. Make me a cap - tive, Lord, and then I shall be free. Force
2. My heart is weak and poor un - til it Mas - ter find; it
3. My power is faint and low till I have learned to serve; it
4. My will is not my own till Thou hast made it thine; if

me to ren - der up my ___ sword, and I shall con - queror be. I
has no spring of ac - tion ___ sure, it va - ries with the wind. It
lacks the need - ed fire to ___ glow, it lacks the breeze to nerve. It
it would reach a mon - arch's ___ throne, it must its crown re - sign. It

sink in life's a - larms when by my - self I stand; im -
can - not free - ly move till Thou hast wrought its chain; en -
can - not drive the world un - til it - self be driven; its
on - ly stands un - bent a - mid the clash - ing strife, when

pris - on me with - in Thine arms, and strong shall be my hand.
slave it with Thy match - less love, and death - less it shall reign.
flag can on - ly be un - furled when Thou shalt breathe from heaven.
on Thy bos - om it has leant, and found in Thee its life.

Copyright © 2000 by HAL LEONARD CORPORATION

MAKER, IN WHOM WE LIVE

DIADEMATA

words by
Charles Wesley, 1747

music by
George J. Elvey, 1868

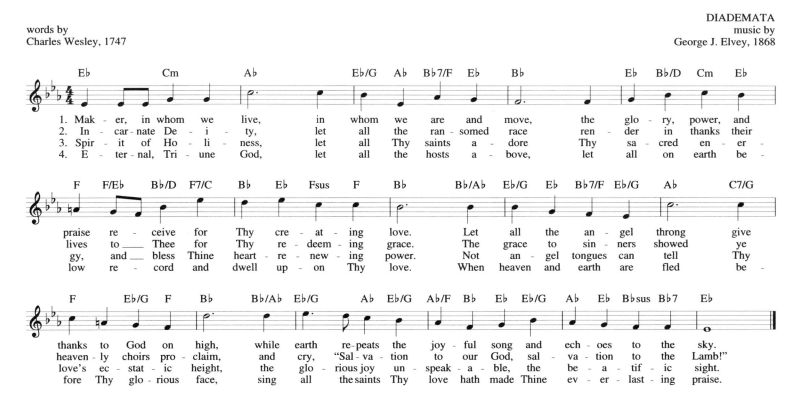

1. Mak - er, in whom we live, in whom we are and move, the glo - ry, power, and
2. In - car - nate De - i - ty, let all the ran - somed race ren - der in thanks their
3. Spir - it of Ho - li - ness, let all Thy saints a - dore Thy sa - cred en - er -
4. E - ter - nal, Tri - une God, let all the hosts a - bove, let all on earth be -

praise re - ceive for Thy cre - at - ing love. Let all the an - gel throng give
lives to ___ Thee for Thy re - deem - ing grace. The grace to sin - ners showed ye
gy, and ___ bless Thine heart - re - new - ing power. Not an - gel tongues can tell Thy
low re - cord and dwell up - on Thy love. When heaven and earth are fled be -

thanks to God on high, while earth re - peats the joy - ful song and ech - oes to the sky.
heaven - ly choirs pro - claim, and cry, "Sal - va - tion to our God, sal - va - tion to the Lamb!"
love's ec - stat - ic height, the glo - rious joy un - speak - a - ble, the be - a - tif - ic sight.
fore Thy glo - rious face, sing all the saints Thy love hath made Thine ev - er - last - ing praise.

Copyright © 2000 by HAL LEONARD CORPORATION

MAKE ME A CHANNEL OF BLESSING

EUCLID

words by
Harper G. Smyth (1873-1945)

music by
Harper G. Smyth (1873-1945)

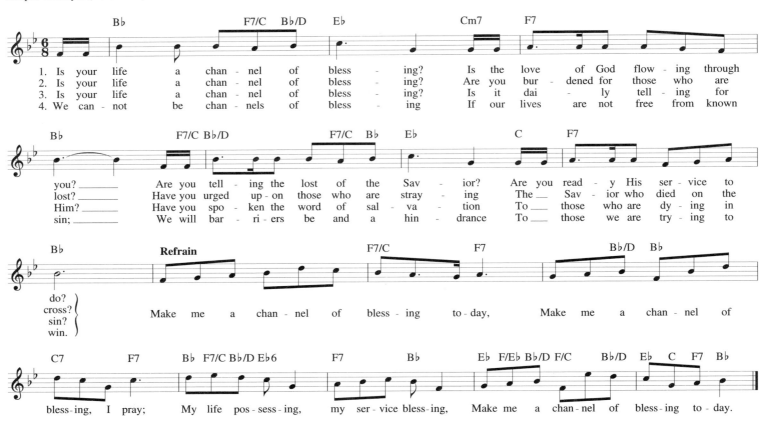

MASTER, THE TEMPEST IS RAGING

PEACE BE STILL

words by
Mary A. Baker (1831-1921)

music by
Horatio R. Palmer (1834-1907)

winds and the waves shall o - bey Thy will, Peace _____ be still!

Wheth - er the wrath of the storm - tossed sea, Or de - mons, or men, or what - ev - er it be, No

wa - ter can swal - low the ship where lies The Mas - ter of o - cean and earth and skies; They

all shall sweet - ly o - bey Thy will; Peace, be still! Peace, be still! They

all shall sweet - ly o - bey Thy will; Peace, peace, be still!

MAY GOD BESTOW ON US HIS GRACE

ES WOLLE UNS GOTT GENÄDIG SEIN
music from
Deutsch Kirchenamt, Strassburg, 1525

words by
Martin Luther (1483-1546)
tr. by R. Massie (1800-1887)

1. May God be - stow on us _____ His grace, With bless - ings rich pro -
2. Thine o - ver all shall be _____ the praise And thanks of ev - 'ry
3. O let the peo - ple praise _____ Thy worth, In all good works in -

vide _____ us, And may the bright - ness of _____ His
na - tion, And all the world with joy _____ shall
creas - ing; The land shall plen - teous fruit _____ bring

face To life e - ter - nal guide _____ us That we His sav - ing health may
raise The voice of ex - ul - ta - tion; For Thou shalt judge the earth, O
forth, Thy Word is rich in bless - ing. May God the Fa - ther, God the

know, His gra - cious will and pleas - ure, And al - so to the hea - then
Lord, Nor suf - fer sin to flour - ish. Thy peo - ple's pas - ture is Thy
Son, And God the Spir - it bless us! Let all the world praise Him a -

show Christ's rich - es with - out meas - ure And un - to God con - vert _____ them.
Word, Their souls to feed and nour - ish, In right - eous paths to keep _____ them.
lone; Let sol - emn awe pos - sess us. Now let our hearts say A - men.

288

MAY THE GRACE OF CHRIST OUR SAVIOR

SARDIS

words by
John Newton (1725-1807)

music by
Ludwig van Beethoven (1770-1827)

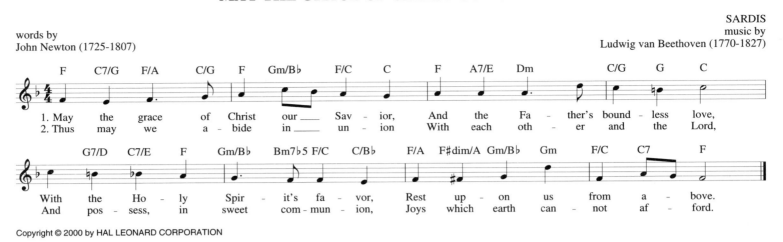

1. May the grace of Christ our ___ Sav – ior, And the Fa – ther's bound – less love,
2. Thus may we a – bide in ___ un – ion With each oth – er and the Lord,

With the Ho – ly Spir – it's fa – vor, Rest up – on us from a – bove.
And pos – sess, in sweet com – mun – ion, Joys which earth can – not af – ford.

Copyright © 2000 by HAL LEONARD CORPORATION

MAY THE GRACE OF CHRIST OUR SAVIOR

STUTTGART

words by
John Newton (1725-1807)

music by
Christian F. Witt (1660-1716)

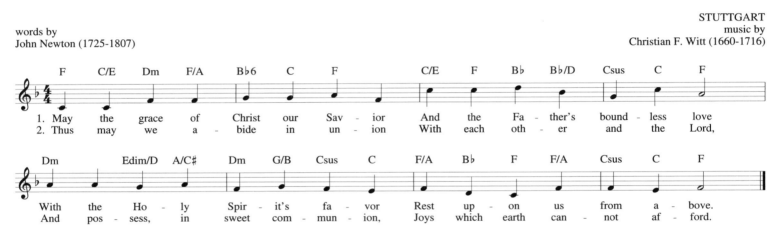

1. May the grace of Christ our Sav – ior And the Fa – ther's bound – less love
2. Thus may we a – bide in un – ion With each oth – er and the Lord,

With the Ho – ly Spir – it's fa – vor Rest up – on us from a – bove.
And pos – sess, in sweet com – mun – ion, Joys which earth can – not af – ford.

Copyright © 2000 by HAL LEONARD CORPORATION

MAY WE THY PRECEPTS, LORD, FULFILL

MERIBAH

words by
Edward Osler (1798-1863)

music by
Lowell Mason (1792-1872)

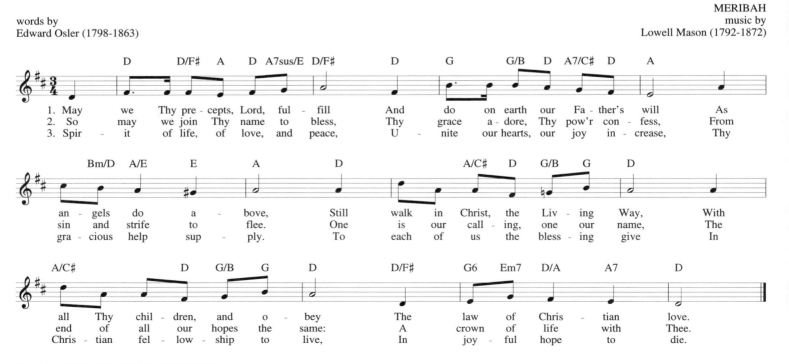

1. May we Thy pre – cepts, Lord, ful – fill And do on earth our Fa – ther's will As
2. So may we join Thy name to bless, Thy grace a – dore, Thy pow'r con – fess, From
3. Spir – it of life, of love, and peace, U – nite our hearts, our joy in – crease, Thy

an – gels do a – bove, Still walk in Christ, the Liv – ing Way, With
sin and strife to flee. One is our call – ing, one our name, The
gra – cious help sup – ply. To each of us the bless – ing give In

all Thy chil – dren, and o – bey The law of Chris – tian love.
end of all our hopes the same: A crown of life with Thee.
Chris – tian fel – low – ship to live, In joy – ful hope to die.

Copyright © 2000 by HAL LEONARD CORPORATION

A MIGHTY FORTRESS IS OUR GOD

words by
Martin Luther, 1529
tr. by Frederick H. Hedge, 1852
based on Psalm 46

EIN' FESTE BURG
music by
Martin Luther, 1529

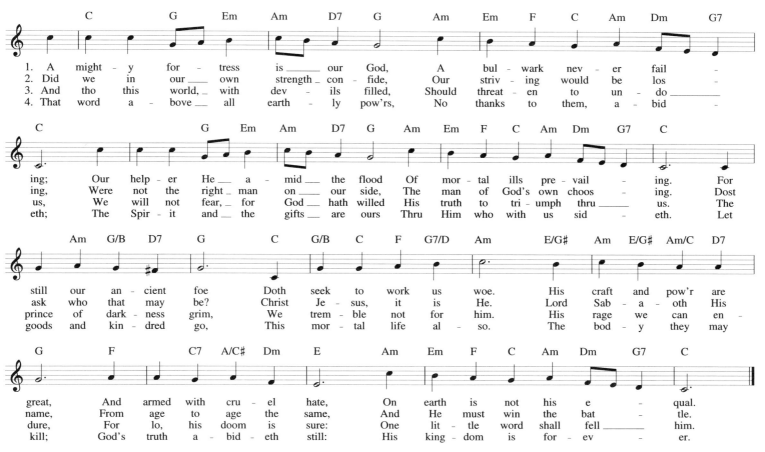

MORE ABOUT JESUS

words by
Eliza E. Hewitt, 1887

SWENEY
music by
John R. Sweney, 1887

MOMENT BY MOMENT

WHITTLE

words by
Daniel W. Whittle, 1893

music by
Mary Whittle Moody, 1893

MORE LOVE TO THEE

words by
Elizabeth Payson Prentiss, 1856

music by
William H. Doane, 1870

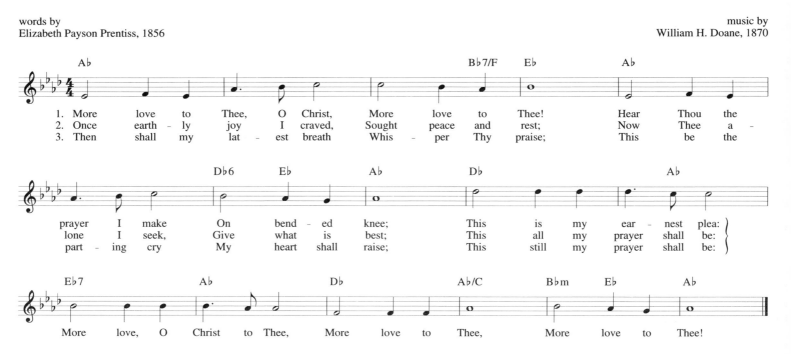

MUST JESUS BEAR THE CROSS ALONE

MAITLAND

words by
Thomas Shepherd (1665-1739)

music by
George N. Allen (1812-1877)

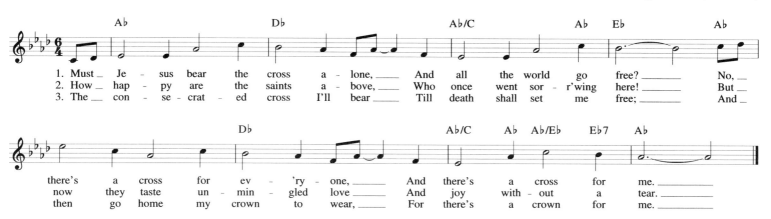

1. Must Je - sus bear the cross a - lone, _____ And all the world go free? _____ No, _____
2. How hap - py are the saints a - bove, _____ Who once went sor - r'wing here! _____ But
3. The con - se - crat - ed cross I'll bear _____ Till death shall set me free; _____ And _____

there's a cross for ev - 'ry - one, _____ And there's a cross for me. _____
now they taste un - min - gled love _____ And joy with - out a tear. _____
then go home my crown to wear, _____ For there's a crown for me. _____

MY ANCHOR HOLDS

words by
W.C. Martin, 1902

music by
Daniel B. Towner, 1902

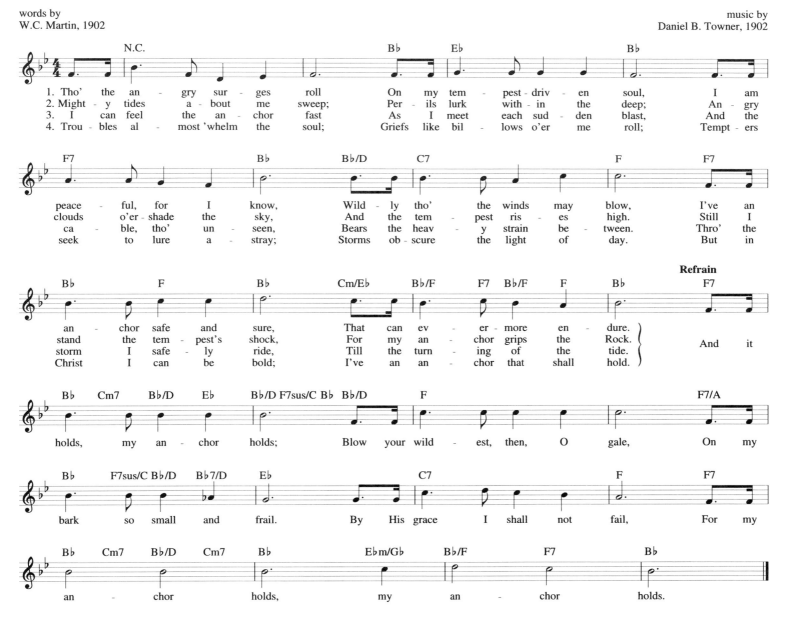

1. Tho' the an - gry sur - ges roll On my tem - pest-driv - en soul, I am
2. Might - y tides a - bout me sweep; Per - ils lurk with - in the deep; An - gry
3. I can feel the an - chor fast As I meet each sud - den blast, And the
4. Trou - bles al - most 'whelm the soul; Griefs like bil - lows o'er me roll; Tempt - ers

peace - ful, for I know, Wild - ly tho' the winds may blow, I've an
clouds o'er - shade the sky, And the tem - pest ris - es high. Still I
ca - ble, tho' un - seen, Bears the heav - y strain be - tween. Thro' the
seek to lure a - stray; Storms ob - scure the light of day. But in

an - chor safe and sure, That can ev - er - more en - dure. }
stand the tem - pest's shock, For my an - chor grips the Rock. }
storm I safe - ly ride, Till the turn - ing of the tide. }
Christ I can be bold; I've an an - chor that shall hold. }

Refrain

And it

holds, my an - chor holds; Blow your wild - est, then, O gale, On my

bark so small and frail. By His grace I shall not fail, For my

an - chor holds, my an - chor holds.

MY BURDENS ROLLED AWAY

words by
Minnie A. Steele, 1908

music by
Minnie A. Steele, 1908

MY COUNTRY, 'TIS OF THEE

words by
Samuel F. Smith (1808-1895)

AMERICA
music from
Thesaurus Musicus, 1744

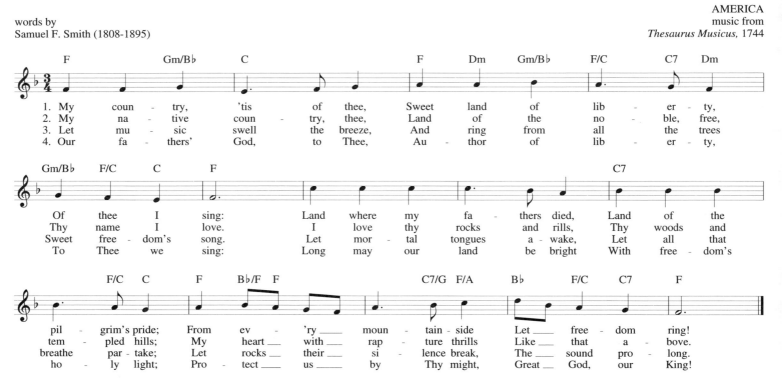

MY FAITH HAS FOUND A RESTING PLACE

words by
Lidie H. Edmunds, c. 1891

LANDAS
music by
André Grétry (1741-1831)
arr. by William J. Kirkpatrick (1838-1921)

1. My faith has found a rest - ing place Not in de - vice or creed: I
2. E - nough for me that Je - sus saves This ends my fear and doubt; A
3. My heart is lean - ing on the Word The writ - ten Word of God: Sal -
4. My great Phy - si - cian heals the sick The lost He came to save; For

trust the Ev - er - liv - ing One, His wounds for me shall plead.
sin - ful soul I come to Him, He'll nev - er cast me out.
va - tion by my Sav - ior's name, Sal - va - tion thru His blood.
me His pre - cious blood He shed, For me His life He gave.

Refrain

I need no oth - er ar - gu - ment, I need no oth - er plea; _____ It

is e - nough that Je - sus died, And that He died for me.

MY FAITH LOOKS UP TO THEE

words by
Ray Palmer, 1830

OLIVET
music by
Lowell Mason, 1831

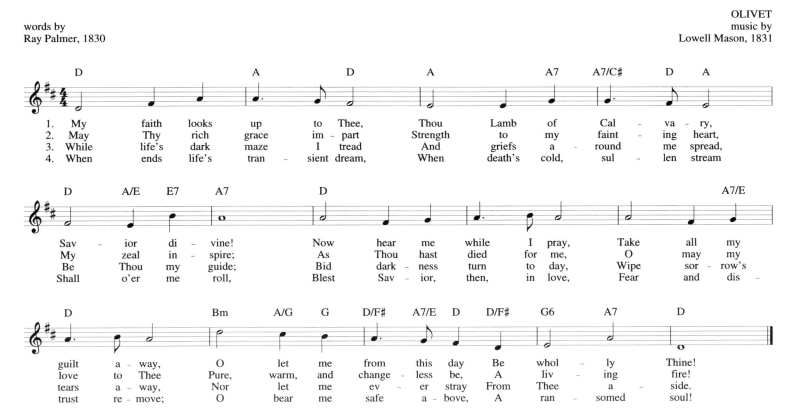

1. My faith looks up to Thee, Thou Lamb of Cal - va - ry,
2. May Thy rich grace im - part Strength to my faint - ing heart,
3. While life's dark maze I tread And griefs a - round me spread,
4. When ends life's tran - sient dream, When death's cold, sul - len stream

Sav - ior di - vine! Now hear me while I pray, Take all my
My zeal in - spire; As Thou hast died for me, O may my
Be Thou my guide; Bid dark - ness turn to day, Wipe sor - row's
Shall o'er me roll, Blest Sav - ior, then, in love, Fear and dis -

guilt a - way, O let me from this day Be whol - ly Thine!
love to Thee, Pure, warm, and change - less be, A liv - ing fire!
tears a - way, Nor let me ev - er stray From Thee a - side.
trust re - move; O bear me safe a - bove, A ran - somed soul!

MY GOD, AND IS THY TABLE SPREAD

ROCKINGHAM

words by
Philip Doddridge (1702-1751)

music from
Second Supplement to Psalms in Miniature, c. 1788
adapt. by Edward Miller (1731-1807)

MY GOD, HOW WONDERFUL THOU ART

DUNDEE

words by
Frederick W. Faber (1814-1863)

music from
Psalter, Edinburgh, 1615

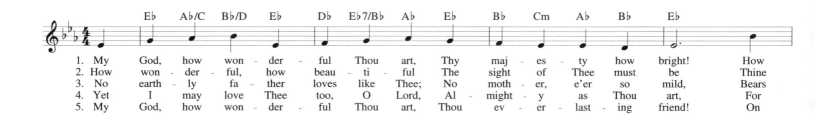

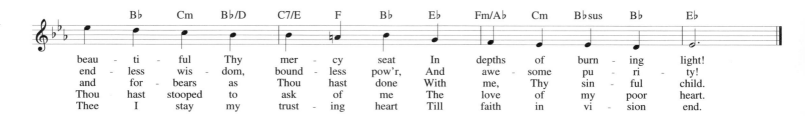

MY HOPE IS BUILT ON NOTHING LESS

words by
Edward Mote (1797-1874)

MELITA
music by
John B. Dykes (1823-1876)

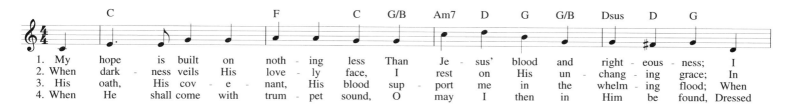

MY HOPE IS BUILT ON NOTHING LESS

words by
Edward Mote, c. 1834

SOLID ROCK
music by
William B. Bradbury, 1863

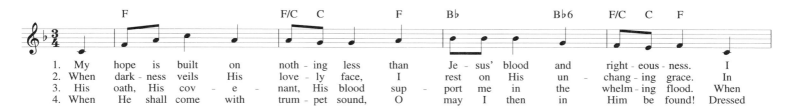

MY GOD, I LOVE THEE

Latin text, 17th century
tr. by Edward Caswall, 1849

WINCHESTER OLD
music from
Est's *The Whole Booke of Psalmes,* 1592

1. My God, I love Thee, not be - cause I hope for heaven there - by, nor
2. Thou, O my Je - sus, Thou didst me up - on the cross em - brace; for
3. Then why, O bless - ed Je - sus Christ, should I not love Thee well? Not
4. Not with the hope of gain - ing aught, not seek - ing a re - ward, but
5. So would I love Thee, dear - est Lord, and in Thy praise will sing; be

yet be - cause, if I love not, I must for - ev - er die.
me didst bear if the nails and spear and man - i - fold dis - grace.
for the sake of win - ning heaven, nor of es - cap - ing hell.
as Thy - self hast lov - ed me, O ev - er - last - ing Lord.
cause Thou art my lov - ing God and my e - ter - nal King.

MY JESUS, I LOVE THEE

words by
William R. Featherston (1846-1873)

GORDON
music by
Adoniram J. Gordon (1836-1895)

1. My Je - sus, I love Thee, I know Thou art mine; For
2. I love Thee be - cause Thou hast first lov - ed me, And
3. I'll love Thee in life, I will love Thee in death, And
4. In man - sions of glo - ry and end - less de - light, I'll

Thee all the fol - lies of sin I re - sign; My
pur - chased my par - don on Cal - va - ry's tree; I
praise Thee as long as Thou lend - est me breath; And
ev - er a - dore Thee in heav - en so bright; I'll

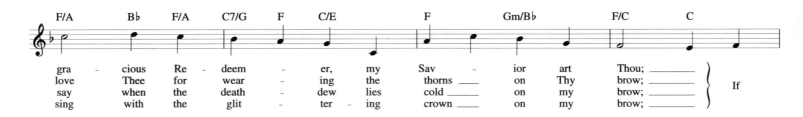

gra - cious Re - deem - er, my Sav - ior art Thou; ⎫
love Thee for wear - ing the thorns on Thy brow; ⎪ If
say when the death - dew lies cold on my brow; ⎪
sing with the glit - ter - ing crown on my brow; ⎭

ev - er I loved Thee, my Je - sus, 'tis now.

MY LORD, WHAT A MORNING

African-American Spiritual

STARS FALL
African-American Spiritual

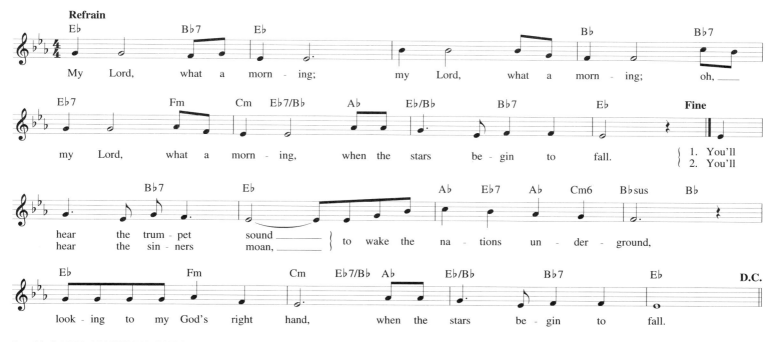

Copyright © 2000 by HAL LEONARD CORPORATION

MY SAVIOR FIRST OF ALL

words by
Fanny J. Crosby (1820-1915)

I SHALL KNOW HIM
music by
John R. Sweney (1837-1899)

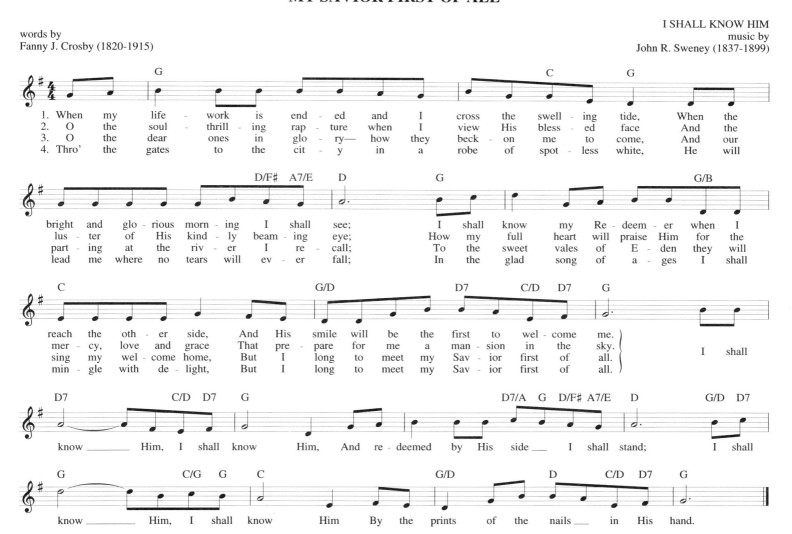

Copyright © 2000 by HAL LEONARD CORPORATION

MY SHEPHERD IS THE LORD

HEBRON
music by
Lowell Mason (1792-1872)

Author unknown
based on Psalm 23

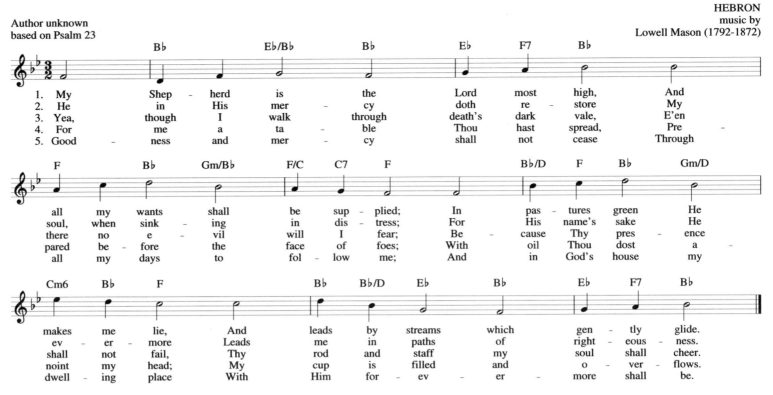

1. My Shep-herd is the Lord most high, And all my wants shall be sup-plied; In pas-tures green He makes me lie, And leads by streams which gen-tly glide.
2. He in His mer-cy doth re-store My soul, when sink-ing in dis-tress; For His name's sake He Leads me in paths of right-eous-ness.
3. Yea, though I walk through death's dark vale, My E'en there no e-vil will I fear; Be-cause Thy pres-ence shall not fail, Thy rod and staff my soul shall cheer.
4. For me a ta-ble Thou hast spread, Pre-pared be-fore the face of foes; With oil Thou dost a-noint my head; My cup is filled and o-ver-flows.
5. Good-ness and mer-cy shall not cease Through all my days to fol-low me; And in God's house a dwell-ing place With Him for-ev-er-more shall be.

Copyright © 2000 by HAL LEONARD CORPORATION

MY SHEPHERD WILL SUPPLY MY NEED

RESIGNATION
music from
Walker's *Southern Harmony*, 1835

words by
Isaac Watts (1674-1748)
para. of Psalm 23

1. My Shep-herd will sup-ply my need; Je-ho-vah is His name; In pas-tures fresh He makes me feed, Be-side the liv-ing stream. He brings my wan-d'ring spir-it back, When I for-sake His ways; And leads me for His mer-cy's sake, In paths of truth and grace.
2. When I walk through the shades of death Thy pres-ence is my stay; One word of thy sup-port-ing breath Drives all my fears a-way. Thy hand, in sight of all my foes, Doth still my ta-ble spread; My cup with bless-ings o-ver-flows, Thy oil a-noints my head.
3. The sure pro-vi-sions of my God At-tend me all my days; O may thy House be mine a-bode, And all my work be praise. There would I find a set-tled rest, While oth-ers go and come; No more a strang-er, or a guest, But like a child at home.

Copyright © 2000 by HAL LEONARD CORPORATION

MY SONG FOREVER SHALL RECORD

words from
The Psalter, 1912
based on Psalm 89

ST. PETERSBURG
music by
Dimitri S. Bortniansky, 1825

1. My song for - ev - er shall _____ re - cord The ten - der mer - cies
2. Al - might - y God, Thy loft - y throne Has jus - tice for its
3. The swell - ing sea o - beys _____ Thy will, Its an - gry waves Thy
4. With bless - ing is the na - tion crowned Whose peo - ple know the

of _____ the Lord; Thy faith - ful - ness will I _____ pro - claim, And
cor - ner - stone, And shin - ing bright be - fore _____ Thy face Are
voice _____ can still; The heav'ns and earth, by right _____ di - vine, The
joy - ful sound; They in the light, O Lord, _____ shall live, The

ev - 'ry age shall know _____ Thy name. I sing of mer - cies
truth _____ and love and bound - less grace. The heav'ns shall join in
world _____ and all there - in, _____ are Thine; The whole cre - a - tion's
light _____ Thy face and fa - vor give. Their fame and might to

that _____ en - dure, _____ For - ev - er build - ed firm and sure.
glad _____ ac - cord _____ To praise _____ Thy won - drous works, O Lord.
won - drous frame _____ Pro - claims _____ its Mak - er's glo - rious name.
Thee _____ be - long, _____ For in _____ Thy fa - vor they are strong.

MY SOUL, REPEAT HIS PRAISE

words by
Isaac Watts (1674-1748)

BEN RHYDDING
music by
Alexander R. Reinagle (1799-1877)

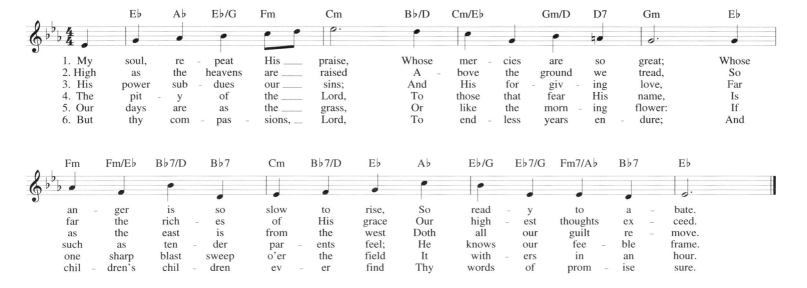

1. My soul, re - peat His _____ praise, Whose mer - cies are so great; Whose
2. High as the heavens are _____ raised A - bove the ground we tread, So
3. His power sub - dues our _____ sins; And His for - giv - ing love, Far
4. The pit - y of the _____ Lord, To those that fear His name, Is
5. Our days are as the _____ grass, Or like the morn - ing flower: If
6. But thy com - pas - sions, _____ Lord, To end - less years en - dure; And

an - ger is so slow to rise, So read - y to a - bate.
far the rich - es of His grace Our high - est thoughts ex - ceed.
as the east is from the west Doth all our guilt re - move.
such as ten - der par - ents feel; He knows our fee - ble frame.
one sharp blast sweep o'er the field It with - ers in an hour.
chil - dren's chil - dren ev - er find Thy words of prom - ise sure.

MY SONG IS LOVE UNKNOWN

RHOSYMEDRE

words by
Samuel Crossman (c. 1624-1683)

music by
John P. Edwards (1806-1885)

MY SOUL IS FILLED WITH GLORY

FILLED WITH GLORY

words by
J.M. Harris, 1905

music by
J.M. Harris, 1905

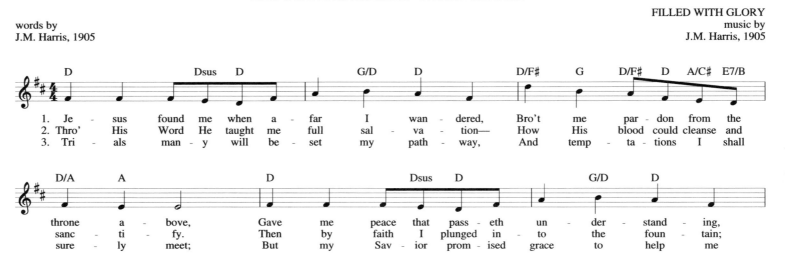

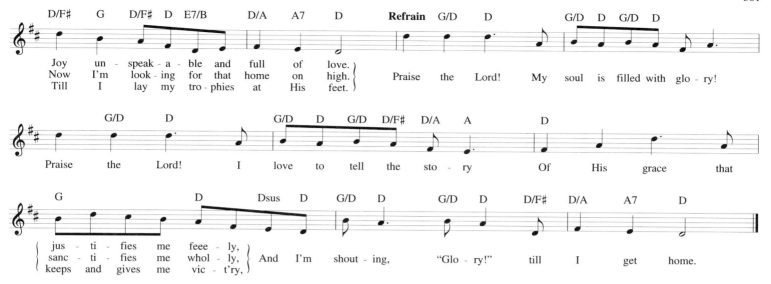

Joy un-speak-a-ble and full of love.
Now I'm look-ing for that home on high.
Till I lay my tro-phies at His feet.

Praise the Lord! My soul is filled with glo-ry!

Praise the Lord! I love to tell the sto-ry Of His grace that

jus-ti-fies me feee-ly,
sanc-ti-fies me whol-ly,
keeps and gives me vic-t'ry,

And I'm shout-ing, "Glo-ry!" till I get home.

MY SOUL, NOW BLESS THY MAKER

words by
Johann Gramann (1487-1541)
tr. by Catherine Winkworth (1827-1878)

NUN LOB, MEIN SEEL
music from
Concentus Novi, Augsburg, 1540

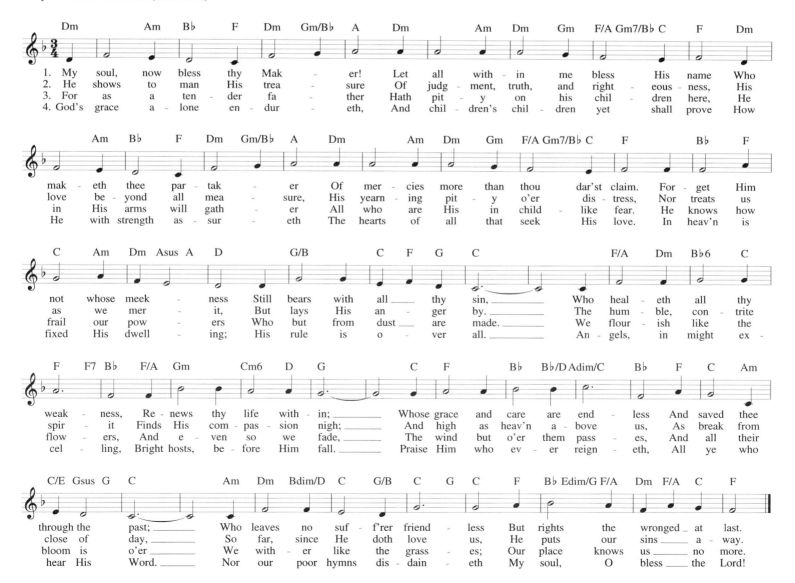

1. My soul, now bless thy Mak — er! Let all with-in me bless His name Who
2. He shows to man His trea — sure Of judg-ment, truth, and right-eous-ness, His
3. For as a ten-der fa — ther Hath pit-y on his chil-dren here, He
4. God's grace a-lone en-dur — eth, And chil-dren's chil-dren yet shall prove How

mak — eth thee par-tak — er Of mer-cies more than thou dar'st claim. For-get Him
love be-yond all mea — sure, His yearn-ing pit-y o'er dis-tress, Nor treats us
in His arms will gath — er All who are His in child-like fear. He knows how
He with strength as-sur — eth The hearts of all that seek His love. In heav'n is

not whose meek — ness Still bears with all ___ thy sin, ___ Who heal-eth all thy
as we mer — it, But lays His an-ger by. ___ The hum-ble, con-trite
frail our pow — ers Who but from dust are made. ___ We flour-ish like the
fixed His dwell — ing; His rule is o-ver all. ___ An-gels, in might ex-

weak — ness, Re-news thy life with-in; ___ Whose grace and care are end-less And saved thee
spir — it Finds His com-pas-sion nigh; ___ And high as heav'n a-bove us, As break from
flow — ers, And e-ven so we fade, ___ The wind but o'er them pass-es, And all their
cel — ling, Bright hosts, be-fore Him fall. ___ Praise Him who ev-er reign-eth, All ye who

through the past; ___ Who leaves no suf-f'rer friend-less But rights the wronged ___ at last.
close of day, ___ So far, since He doth love us, He puts our sins ___ a-way.
bloom is o'er ___ We with-er like the grass-es; Our place knows us ___ no more.
hear His Word. ___ Nor our poor hymns dis-dain-eth My soul, O bless ___ the Lord!

NEAR TO THE HEART OF GOD

McAFEE
music by
Cleland B. McAfee, 1901

words by
Cleland B. McAfee, 1901

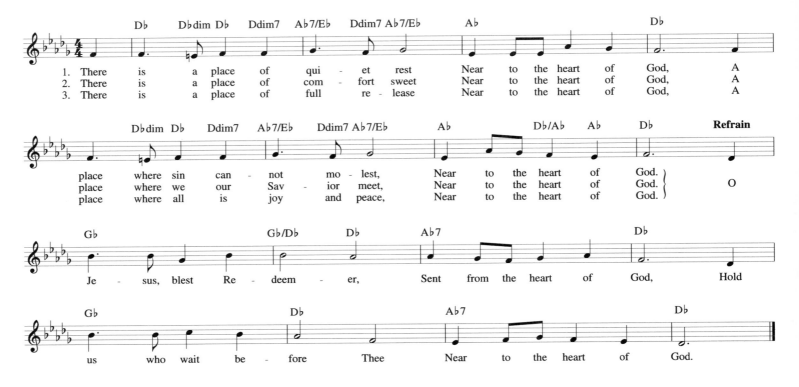

NEARER, MY GOD, TO THEE

BETHANY
music by
Lowell Mason (1792-1872)

words by
Sarah F. Adams (1805-1848)
based on Genesis 28:10-22

NATURE WITH OPEN VOLUME STANDS

words by
Isaac Watts (1674-1748)

ELTHAM
music by
Nathaniel Gawthorn, 18th century

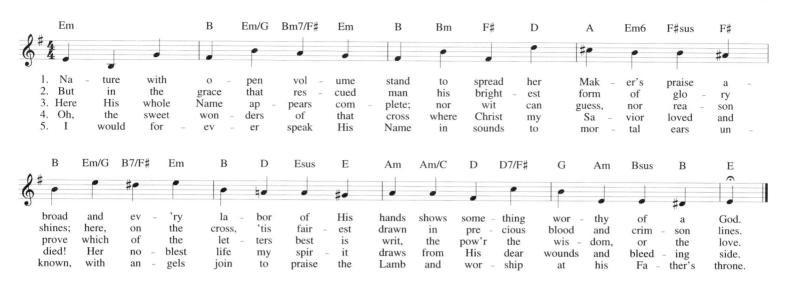

1. Na - ture with o - pen vol - ume stand to spread her Mak - er's praise a -
2. But in the grace that res - cued man his bright - est form of glo - ry
3. Here His whole Name ap - pears com - plete; nor wit can guess, nor rea - son
4. Oh, the sweet won - ders of that cross where Christ my Sa - vior loved and
5. I would for - ev - er speak His Name in sounds to mor - tal ears un -

broad and ev - 'ry la - bor of His hands shows some - thing wor - thy of a God.
shines; here, on the cross, 'tis fair - est drawn in pre - cious blood and crim - son lines.
prove which of the let - ters best is writ, the pow'r the wis - dom, or the love.
died! Her no - blest life my spir - it draws from His dear wounds and bleed - ing side.
known, with an - gels join to praise the Lamb and wor - ship at his Fa - ther's throne.

NEARER, STILL NEARER

words by
Lelia N. Morris, 1898

MORRIS
music by
Lelia N. Morris, 1898

1. Near - er, still near - er, close to Thy heart, Draw me, my
2. Near - er, still near - er, noth - ing I bring, Naught as an
3. Near - er, still near - er, Lord, to be Thine! Sin, with its
4. Near - er, still near - er, while life shall last, Till safe in

Sav - ior— so pre - cious Thou art! Fold me, O fold me
of - f'ring to Je - sus, my King— On - ly my sin - ful,
fol - lies, I glad - ly re - sign, All of its plea - sures,
glo - ry my an - chor is cast; Through end - less a - ges

close to Thy breast. Shel - ter me safe in that ha - ven of
now con - trite heart. Grant me the cleans - ing Thy blood doth im -
pomp and its pride. Give me but Je - sus, my Lord, cru - ci -
ev - er to be Near - er, my Sav - ior, still near - er to

rest; Shel - ter me safe in that ha - ven of rest.
part; Grant me the cleans - ing Thy blood doth im - part.
fied; Give me but Je - sus, my Lord, cru - ci - fied.
Thee; Near - er, my Sav - ior, still near - er to Thee.

NEW EVERY MORNING IS THE LOVE

KEDRON
music attributed to
Elkanah Kelsay Dare (1782-1826)

words by
John Keble (1792-1866)

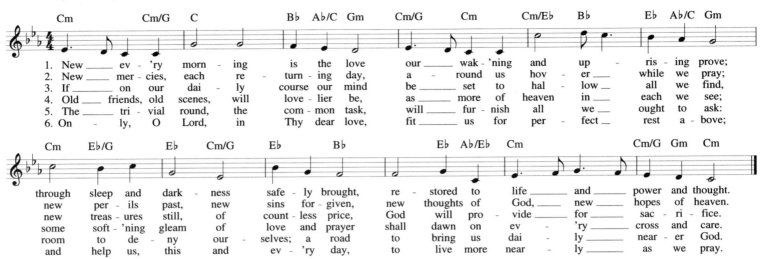

1. New ev - 'ry morn - ing is the love our wak - 'ning and up - ris - ing prove;
2. New mer - cies, each re - turn - ing day, a - round us hov - er while we pray;
3. If on our dai - ly course our mind be set to hal - low all we find,
4. Old friends, old scenes, will love - lier be, as more of heaven in each we see;
5. The tri - vial round, the com - mon task, will fur - nish all we ought to ask:
6. On - ly, O Lord, in Thy dear love, fit us for per - fect rest a - bove;

through sleep and dark - ness safe - ly brought, re - stored to life and power and thought.
new per - ils past, new sins for - given, new thoughts of God, new hopes of heaven.
new treas - ures still, of count - less price, God will pro - vide for sac - ri - fice.
some soft - 'ning gleam of love and prayer shall dawn on ev - 'ry cross and care.
room to de - ny our - selves; a road to bring us dai - ly near - er God.
and help us, this and ev - 'ry day, to live more near - ly as we pray.

A NEW NAME IN GLORY

NEW NAME
music by
C. Austin Miles, 1910

words by
C. Austin Miles, 1910

1. I was once a sin - ner, but I came, Par - don to re - ceive from my
2. I was hum - bly kneel - ing at the cross, Fear - ing naught but God's an - gry
3. In the Book 'tis writ - ten, "Saved by grace." O, the joy that came to my

Lord. This was free - ly giv - en, and I found That He al - ways kept His
frown, When the heav - ens o - pened and I saw That my name was writ - ten
soul! Now I am for - giv - en, and I know By the blood I am made

word.
down. There's a new name writ - ten down in glo - ry, And it's
whole.

mine, O yes, it's mine! And the white - robed an - gels sing the sto - ry, "A

sin - ner has come home." For there's a new name writ - ten down in

glo - ry, And it's mine, O yes, it's mine! With my

sins for - giv - en I am bound for heav - en, Nev - er - more to roam.

NO, NOT ONE!

words by
Johnson Oatman, Jr. (1856-1922)

music by
George C. Hugg (1848-1907)

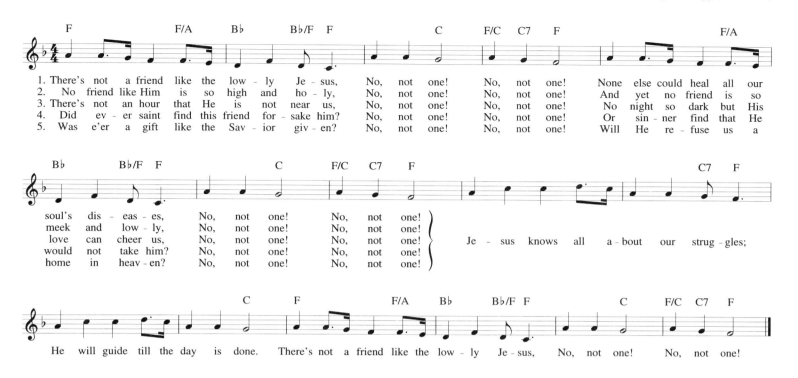

NOTHING BETWEEN

words by
Charles Albert Tindley, c. 1906

music by
Charles Albert Tindley, c. 1906

NOTHING BUT THE BLOOD

PLAINFIELD
music by
Robert Lowry, 1876

Robert Lowry, 1876

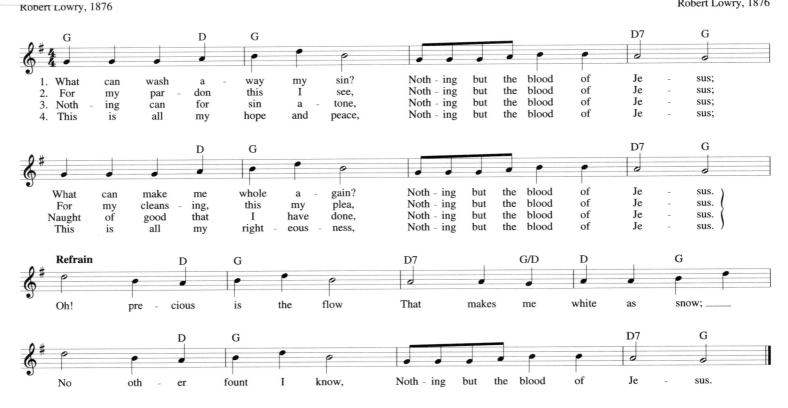

NOW ISRAEL MAY SAY

OLD 124TH
music from
Genevan Psalter, 1551

words from
The Psalter, 1912
based on Psalm 124

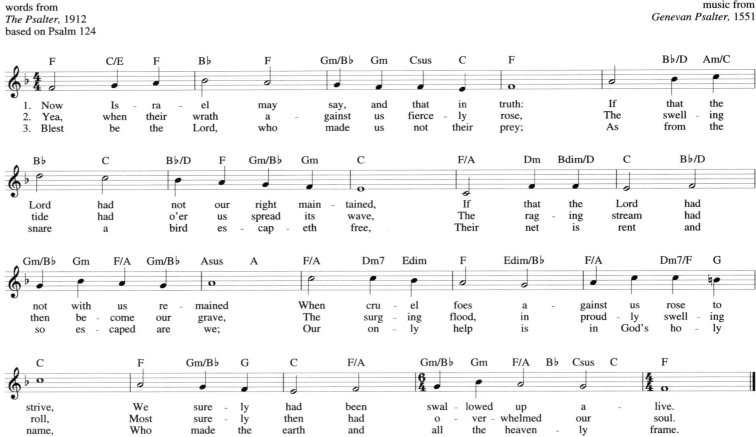

NOW, ON LAND AND SEA DESCENDING

words by
Samuel Longfellow, 1859

VESPER HYMN
music attributed to
Dimitri S. Bortniansky (1751-1825)
from Stevenson's *A Selection of Popular National Airs*, 1818

NOW THANK WE ALL OUR GOD

words by
Martin Rinkart, c. 1636
tr. by Catherine Winkworth, 1858

NUN DANKET ALLE GOTT
music by
Johann Crüger, 1648

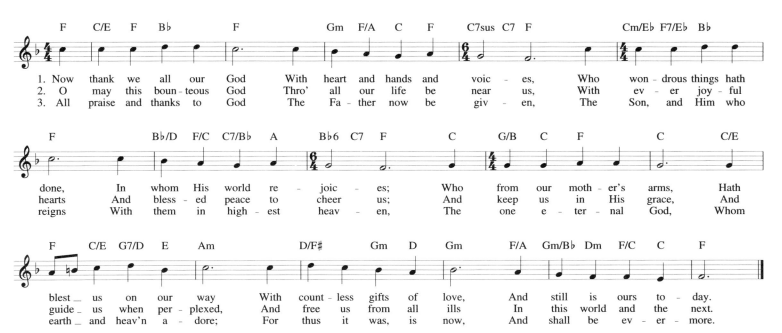

NOT SO IN HASTE, MY HEART

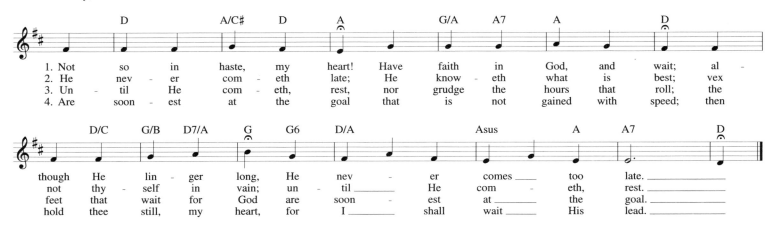

DOLOMITE CHANT
Traditional Austrian melody

words by
Bradford Torrey, c. 1875

1. Not so in haste, my heart! Have faith in God, and wait; al -
2. He nev - er com - eth late; He know - eth what is best; vex
3. Un - til He com - eth, rest, nor grudge the hours that roll; the
4. Are soon - est at the goal that is not gained with speed; then

though He lin - ger long, He nev - er comes too late.
not thy - self in vain; un - til He com - eth, rest.
feet that wait for God are soon - est at the goal.
hold thee still, my heart, for I shall wait His lead.

NOW THE DAY IS OVER

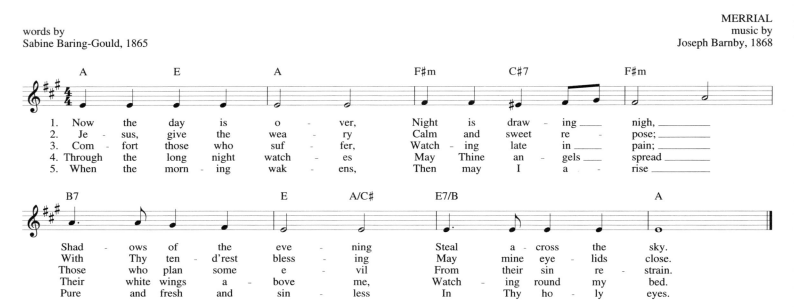

MERRIAL
music by
Joseph Barnby, 1868

words by
Sabine Baring-Gould, 1865

1. Now the day is o - ver, Night is draw - ing nigh,
2. Je - sus, give the wea - ry Calm and sweet re - pose;
3. Com - fort those who suf - fer, Watch - ing late in pain;
4. Through the long night watch - es May Thine an - gels spread
5. When the morn - ing wak - ens, Then may I a - rise

Shad - ows of the eve - ning Steal a - cross the sky.
With Thy ten - d'rest bless - ing May mine eye - lids close.
Those who plan some e - vil From their sin re - strain.
Their white wings a - bove me, Watch - ing round my bed.
Pure and fresh and sin - less In Thy ho - ly eyes.

NOW TO THE KING OF HEAVEN

ST. JOHN
music from
The Parish Choir, 1851

words by Isaac Watts (1674-1748)
and Philip Doddridge (1702-1751)

Now to the King of heav'n Your cheer - ful voic - es raise; To
Him be glo - ry giv'n, Pow'r, maj - es - ty and praise; Wide as he reigns His
name be sung By ev - 'ry tongue in end - less strains.

O BLEST THE HOUSE, WHATE'ER BEFALL

words by
C.C.L. von Pfeil (1712-1784)
v. 1, 2, 4, 5 tr. by C. Winkworth (1827-1878)
v. 3 tr. in *Evangelical Lutheran Hymnal,* Columbus, Ohio, 1880

WO GOTT ZUM HAUS
music by
J. Klug, *Geistliche Lieder,* Wittenberg, 1535

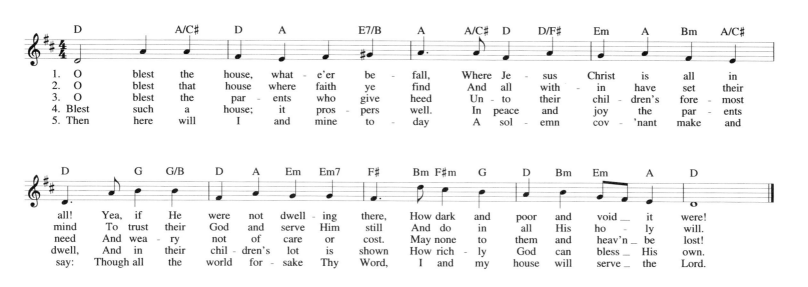

1. O blest the house, what - e'er be - fall, Where Je - sus Christ is all in
2. O blest that house where faith ye find, And all with - in have set their
3. O blest the par - ents who give heed Un - to their chil - dren's fore - most
4. Blest such a house; it pros - pers well. In peace and joy the par - ents
5. Then here will I and mine to - day A sol - emn cov - 'nant make and

all! Yea, if He were not dwell - ing there, How dark and poor and void __ it were!
mind To trust their God and serve Him still, And do in all His ho - ly will.
need And wea - ry not of care or cost, May none to them and heav'n __ be lost!
dwell, And in their chil - dren's lot is shown How rich - ly God can bless __ His own.
say: Though all the world for - sake Thy Word, I and my house will serve __ the Lord.

O BROTHER MAN, FOLD TO THY HEART

words by
John Greenleaf Whittier (1807-1892)

WELWYN
music by
Alfred Scott-Gatty (1847-1918)

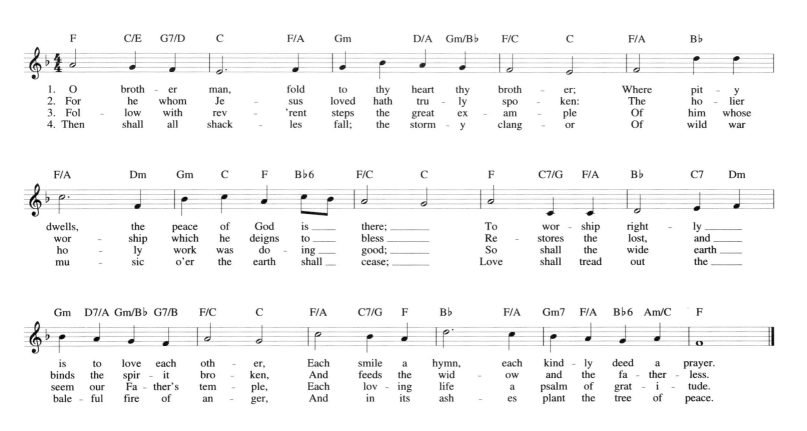

1. O broth - er man, fold to thy heart thy broth - er; Where pit - y
2. For he whom Je - sus loved hath tru - ly spo - ken: The ho - lier
3. Fol - low with rev - 'rent steps the great ex - am - ple Of him whose
4. Then shall all shack - les fall; the storm - y clang - or Of wild war

dwells, the peace of God is __ there; __ To wor - ship right - ly __
wor - ship which he deigns to __ bless __ Re - stores the lost, and __
ho - ly work was do - ing __ good; __ So shall the wide earth __
mu - sic o'er the earth shall __ cease; __ Love shall tread out the __

is to love each oth - er, Each smile a hymn, each kind - ly deed a prayer.
binds the spir - it bro - ken, And feeds the wid - ow and the fa - ther - less.
seem our Fa - ther's tem - ple, Each lov - ing life a psalm of grat - i - tude.
bale - ful fire of an - ger, And in its ash - es plant the tree of peace.

O BLESS THE LORD, MY SOUL!

ST. THOMAS

words by
James Montgomery (1771-1854)
para. of Psalm 103:1-5

music by
Aaron Williams (1731-1776)

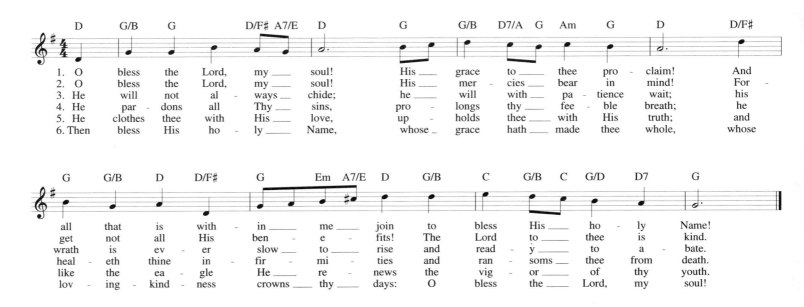

1. O bless the Lord, my ___ soul! His ___ grace to ___ thee pro - claim! And
2. O bless the Lord, my ___ soul! His ___ mer - cies ___ bear in mind! For -
3. He will not al - ways ___ chide; he ___ will with pa - tience wait; his
4. He par - dons all Thy ___ sins, pro - longs thy ___ fee - ble breath; he
5. He clothes thee with His ___ love, up - holds thee ___ with His truth; and
6. Then bless His ho - ly ___ Name, whose ___ grace hath ___ made thee whole, whose

all that is with - in ___ me ___ join to bless His ___ ho - ly Name!
get not all His ben - e - fits! The Lord to ___ thee is kind.
wrath is ev - er slow to ___ rise and read - y ___ to a - bate.
heal - eth thine in - fir - mi - ties and ran - soms ___ thee from death.
like the ea - gle He ___ re - news the vig - or ___ of thy youth.
lov - ing - kind - ness crowns ___ thy ___ days: O bless the ___ Lord, my soul!

O BREATH OF LIFE

DET AR ETT FAST ORD

words by
Bessie Porter Head, c.1914

music by
Joel Blomquist, 1877

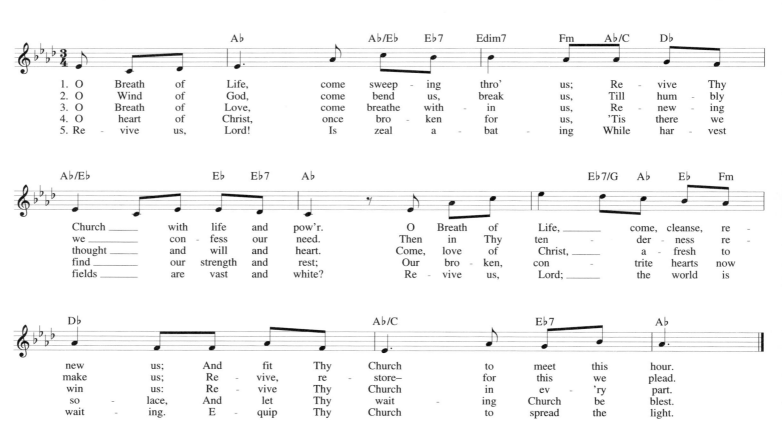

1. O Breath of Life, come sweep - ing thro' us; Re - vive Thy
2. O Wind of God, come bend us, break us, Till hum - bly
3. O Breath of Love, come breathe with - in us, Re - new - ing
4. O heart of Christ, once bro - ken for us, 'Tis there we
5. Re - vive us, Lord! Is zeal a - bat - ing While har - vest

Church ___ with life and pow'r. O Breath of Life, ___ come, cleanse, re -
we ___ con - fess our need. Then in Thy ten - der - ness re -
thought ___ and will and heart. Come, love of Christ, ___ a - fresh to
find ___ our strength and rest; Our bro - ken, con - trite hearts now
fields ___ are vast and white? Re - vive us, Lord; ___ the world is

new us; And fit Thy Church to meet this hour.
make us; Re - vive, re - store– for this we plead.
win us: Re - vive Thy Church in ev - 'ry part.
so - lace, And let Thy Church wait - ing Church be blest.
wait - ing. E - quip Thy Church to spread the light.

O CHRIST, OUR HOPE

Latin text, c. 8th century
tr. by John Chandler (1806-1876)

LOBT GOTT, IHR CHRISTEN
music by
Nikolaus Herman (c. 1480-1561)

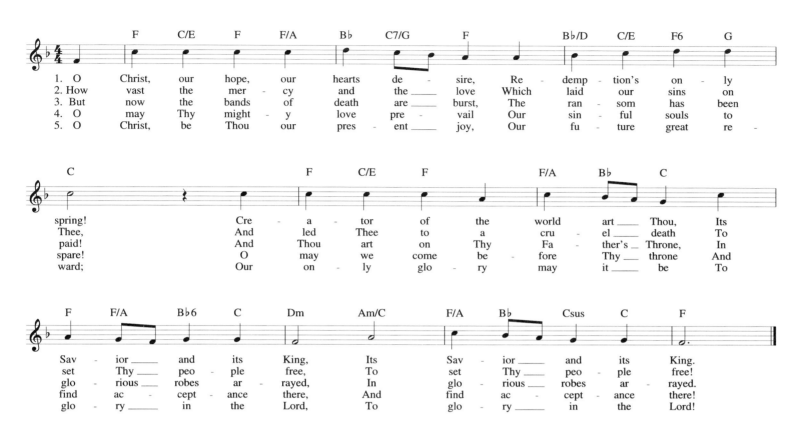

O CHRIST, OUR TRUE AND ONLY LIGHT

words from
Johann Heermann (1584-1647)
tr. by Catherine Winkworth, 1858

O JESU CHRISTE, WAHRES LICHT
music from
Gesang-Buch, Nürnberg, 1676

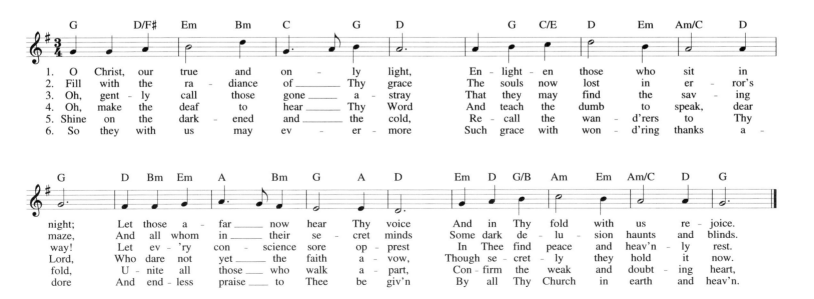

O CHRIST, THOU LAMB OF GOD

Traditional German text, 1528

CHRISTE DU LAMM GOTTES
music from
Kirchenordnung, Braunschweig, 1528

O CHRIST, WHO ART THE LIGHT AND DAY

Author unknown
tr. by W.J. Copeland (1804-1885)

CHRISTE, DER DU BIST TAG UND LICHT
Latin melody, c. 600

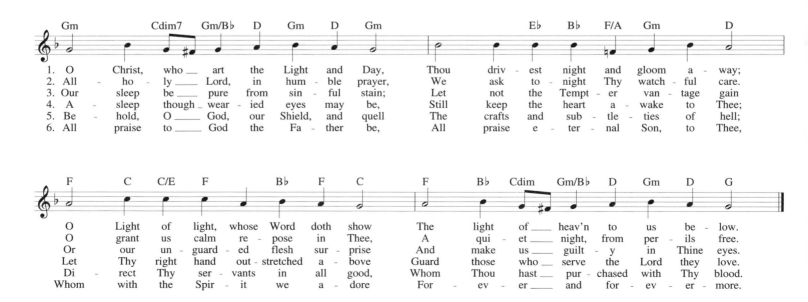

O COME, ALL YE FAITHFUL

ADESTE FIDELIS

words by
John Francis Wade (1711-1786)
tr. by Frederick Oakley (1802-1880)

music by
John Francis Wade (1711-1786)

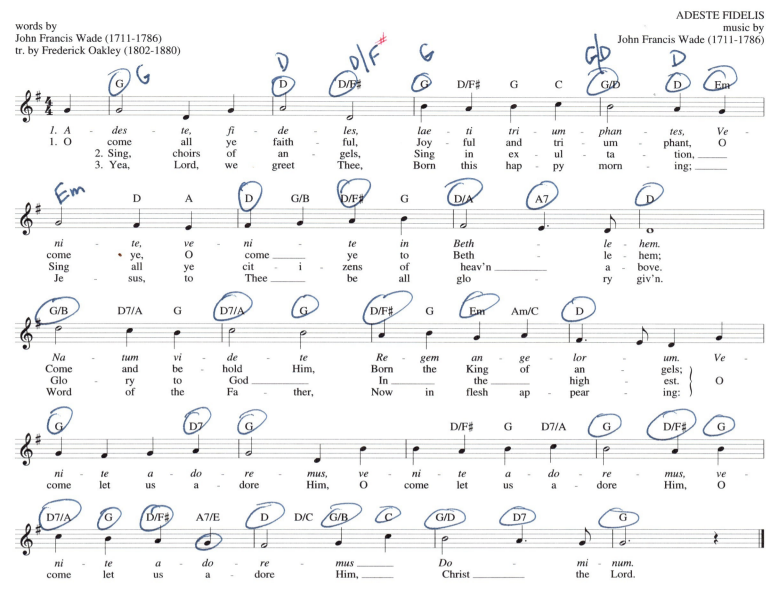

1. A - des - te, fi - de - les, lae - ti tri - um - phan - tes, Ve -
1. O come all ye faith - ful, Joy - ful and tri - um - phant, O
2. Sing, choirs of an - gels, Sing in ex - ul - ta - tion, _____
3. Yea, Lord, we greet Thee, Born this hap - py morn - ing; _____

ni - te, ve - ni - te in Beth - le - hem.
come ye, O come _____ ye to Beth - le - hem;
Sing all ye cit - i - zens of heav'n _____ a - bove.
Je - sus, to Thee _____ be all glo - ry giv'n.

Na - tum vi - de - te Re - gem an - ge - lor - um. Ve -
Come and be - hold Him, Born the King of an - gels;
Glo - ry to God _____ In _____ the _____ high - est. } O
Word of the Fa - ther, Now in flesh ap - pear - ing: }

ni - te a - do - re - mus, ve - ni - te a - do - re - mus, ve -
come let us a - dore Him, O come let us a - dore Him, O

ni - te a - do - re mus _____ Do - mi - num.
come let us a - dore Him, _____ Christ _____ the Lord.

Copyright © 1992 by HAL LEONARD CORPORATION

O COME AND DWELL IN ME

ST. MICHAEL

words by
Charles Wesley, 1762

music from
Genevan Psalter, 1551
adapt. by William Crotch, 1836

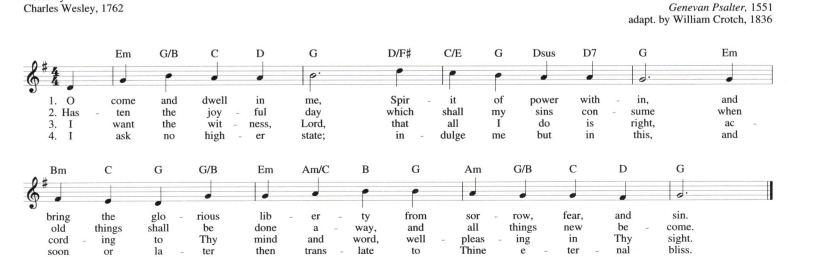

1. O come and dwell in me, Spir - it of power with - in, and
2. Has - ten the joy - ful day which shall my sins con - sume, when
3. I want the wit - ness, Lord, that all I do is right, ac -
4. I ask no high - er state; in - dulge me but in this, and

bring the glo - rious lib - er - ty from sor - row, fear, and sin.
old things shall be done a - way, and all things new be - come.
cord - ing to Thy mind and word, well - pleas - ing in Thy sight.
soon or la - ter then trans - late to Thine e - ter - nal bliss.

Copyright © 2000 by HAL LEONARD CORPORATION

O COME AND MOURN WITH ME AWHILE

ST. CROSS

words by
Frederick W. Faber (1814-1863)

music by
John Bacchus Dykes (1823-1876)

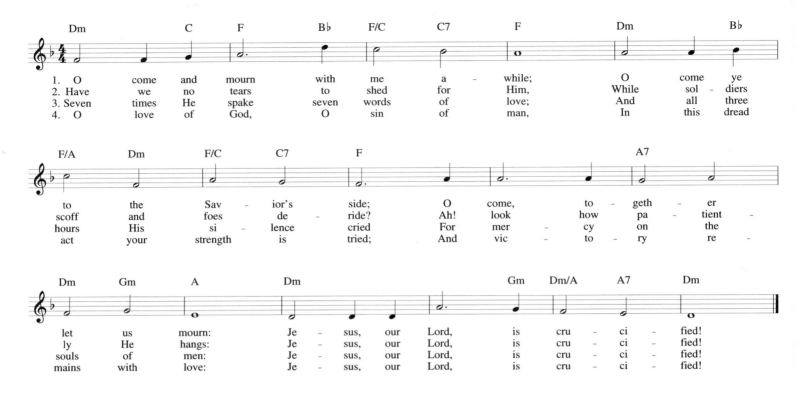

1. O come and mourn with me a - while; O come ye
2. Have we no tears to shed for Him, While sol - diers
3. Seven times He spake seven words of love; And all three
4. O love of God, O sin of man, In this dread

to the Sav - ior's side; O come, to - geth - er
scoff and foes de - ride? Ah! look how pa - tient -
hours His si - lence cried; For mer - cy on the
act your strength is tried; And vic - to - ry re -

let us mourn: Je - sus, our Lord, is cru - ci - fied!
ly He hangs: Je - sus, our Lord, is cru - ci - fied!
souls of men: Je - sus, our Lord, is cru - ci - fied!
mains with love: Je - sus, our Lord, is cru - ci - fied!

O COME, O COME, EMMANUEL

VENI EMMANUEL
15th century French melody
adapt. by Thomas Helmore, 1854

Traditional Latin text
v. 1,2 tr. by John M. Neale, 1851
v. 3,4 tr. by Henry S. Coffin, 1916

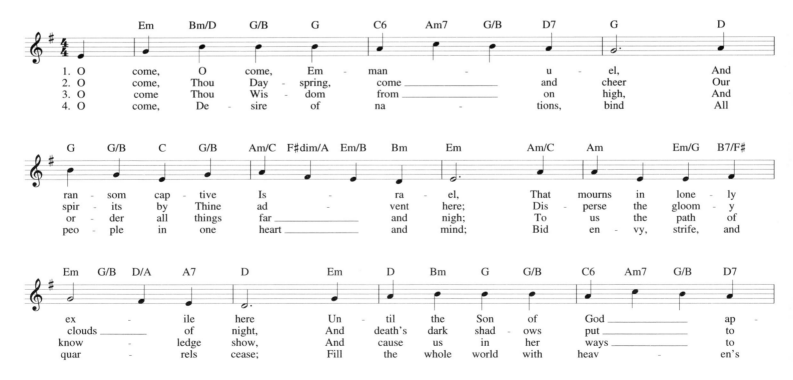

1. O come, O come, Em - man - u - el, And
2. O come, Thou Day - spring, come and cheer Our
3. O come Thou Wis - dom from on high, And
4. O come, De - sire of na - tions, bind All

ran - som cap - tive Is - ra - el, That mourns in lone - ly
spir - its by Thine ad - vent here; Dis - perse the gloom - y
or - der all things far and nigh; To us the path of
peo - ple in one heart and mind; Bid en - vy, strife, and

ex - ile here; Un - til the Son of God ap -
clouds of night, And death's dark shad - ows put to
know - ledge show, And cause us in her ways to
quar - rels cease; Fill the whole world with heav - en's

O COULD I SPEAK THE MATCHLESS WORTH

ARIEL
arr. by Lowell Mason (1792-1872)

words by
Samuel Medley (1738-1799)

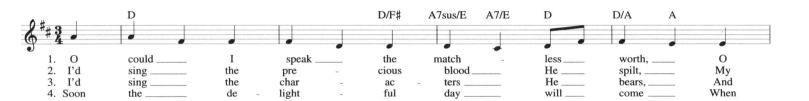

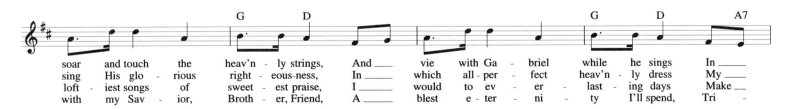

O DAY OF REST AND GLADNESS

ELLACOMBE

words by
Christopher Wordsworth (1807-1885)

music from
Gesangbuch der Herzogl. Hofkapelle, Wittenberg, 1784

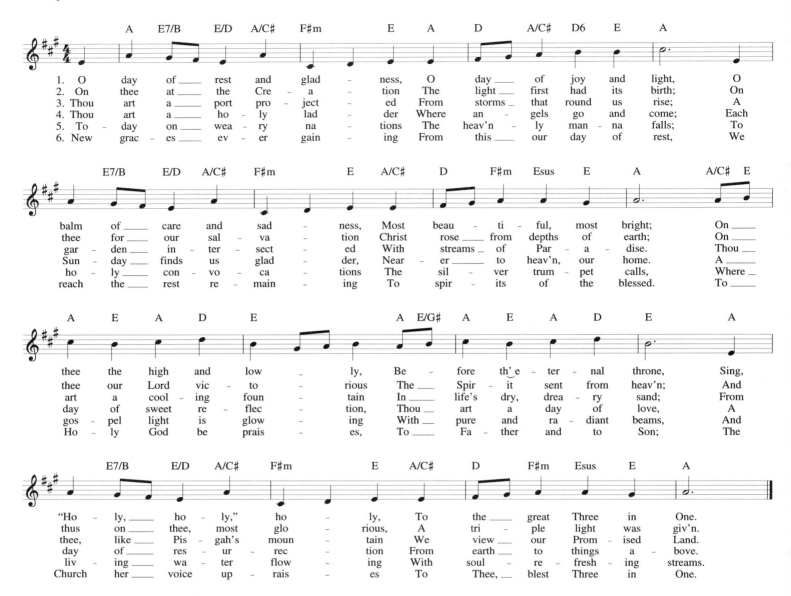

1. O day of ____ rest and glad - ness, O day ____ of joy and light, O
2. On thee at ____ the Cre - a - tion The light ____ first had its birth; On
3. Thou art a ____ port pro - ject - ed From storms ____ that round us rise; A
4. Thou art a ____ ho - ly lad - der Where an - gels go and come; Each
5. To - day on ____ wea - ry na - tions The heav'n - ly man - na falls; To
6. New grac - es ____ ev - er gain - ing From this ____ our day of rest, We

balm of ____ care and sad - ness, Most beau - ti - ful, most bright; On ____
thee for ____ our sal - va - tion Christ rose ____ from depths of earth; On ____
gar - den in - ter - sect - ed With streams ____ of Par - a - dise. Thou ____
Sun - day ____ finds us glad - der, Near - er ____ to heav'n, our home. A ____
ho - ly ____ con - vo - ca - tions The sil - ver trum - pet calls, Where ____
reach the ____ rest re - main - ing To spir - its of the blessed. To ____

thee the high and low - ly, Be - fore th' e - ter - nal throne, Sing,
thee our Lord vic - to - rious The ____ Spir - it sent from heav'n; And
art a cool - ing foun - tain In ____ life's dry, drea - ry sand; From
day of sweet re - flec - tion, Thou ____ art a day of love, A
gos - pel light is glow - ing With ____ pure and ra - diant beams, And
Ho - ly God be prais - es, To ____ Fa - ther and to Son; The

"Ho - ly, ____ ho - ly," ho - ly, To the ____ great Three in One.
thus on ____ thee, most glo - rious, A tri - ple light was giv'n.
thee, like ____ Pis - gah's moun - tain We view ____ our Prom - ised Land.
day of ____ res - ur - rec - tion From earth ____ to things a - bove.
liv - ing ____ wa - ter flow - ing With soul - re - fresh - ing streams.
Church her ____ voice up - rais - es To Thee, ____ blest Three in One.

O DAY OF REST AND GLADNESS

MENDEBRAS

words by
Christopher Wordsworth, 1862

Traditional German melody
arr. by Lowell Mason, 1839

1. O ____ day of rest ____ and ____ glad - ness,
2. On ____ thee, at the ____ Cre - a - tion,
3. New ____ gra - ces ev - er ____ gain - ing

O ____ day of joy ____ and ____ light,
The ____ light first had ____ its ____ birth;
From ____ this our day ____ of ____ rest,

O ____ balm of care ____ and ____ sad - ness,
On ____ thee, for our ____ sal - va - tion,
We ____ reach the rest ____ re - main - ing

Most ____ beau - ti - ful, ____ most
Christ ____ rose from depths ____ of
To ____ spir - its of ____ the

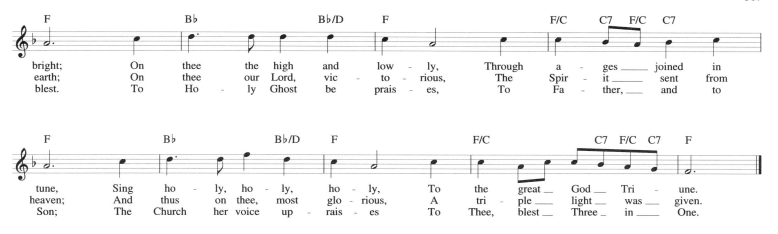

O FATHER, ALL-CREATING

words by
John Ellerton (1826-1893)

AURELIA
music by
Samuel S. Wesley (1810-1876)

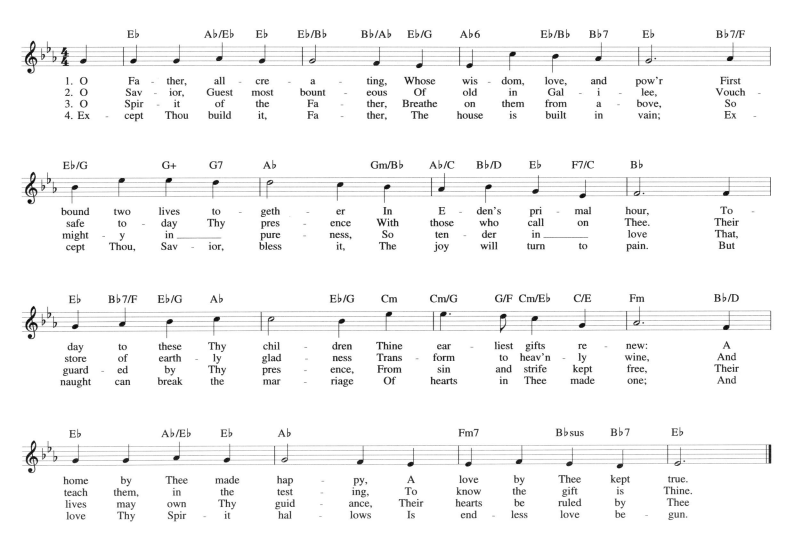

O FOOD TO PILGRIMS GIVEN

words from
Maintzich Gesangbuch, 1661
tr. by John Athelstan Laurie Riley, 1906

O WELT, ICH MUSS DICH LASSEN
Traditional German melody, 15th century
adapt. by Heinrich Isaac, 1539

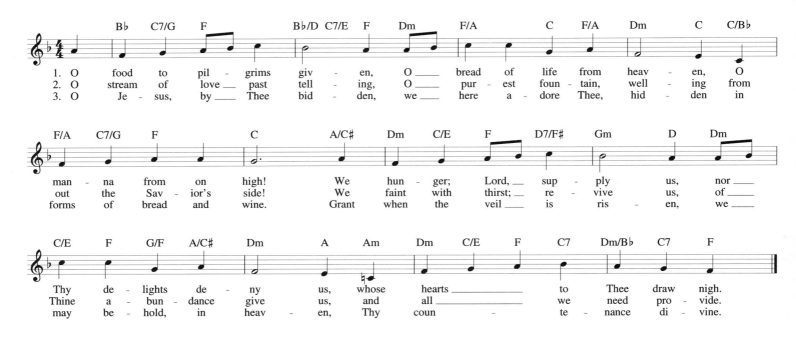

1. O food to pil - grims giv - en, O ___ bread of life from heav - en, O
2. O stream of love ___ past tell - ing, O ___ pur - est foun - tain, well - ing from
3. O Je - sus, by ___ Thee bid - den, we ___ here a - dore Thee, hid - den in

man - na from on high! We hun - ger; Lord, ___ sup - ply us, nor ___
out the Sav - ior's side! We faint with thirst; ___ re - vive us, of ___
forms of bread and wine. Grant when the veil ___ is ris - en, we ___

Thy de - lights de - ny us, whose hearts ___ to Thee draw nigh.
Thine a - bun - dance give us, and all ___ we need pro - vide.
may be - hold, in heav - en, Thy coun - te - nance di - vine.

O FOR A CLOSER WALK WITH GOD

words by
William Cowper (1731-1800)

ZERAH
music by
Lowell Mason (1792-1872)

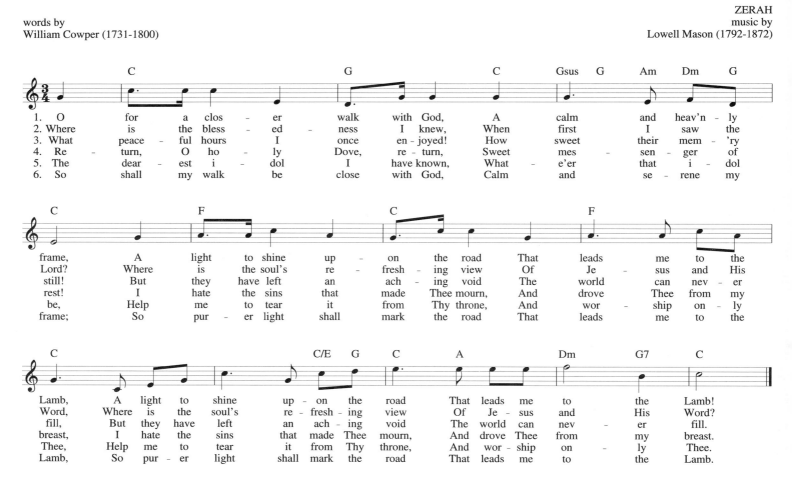

1. O for a clos - er walk with God, A calm and heav'n - ly
2. Where is the bless - ed ness I knew, When first I saw the
3. What peace - ful hours I once en - joyed! How sweet their mem - 'ry
4. Re - turn, O ho - ly Dove, re - turn, Sweet mes - sen - ger of
5. The dear - est i - dol I have known, What - e'er that i - dol
6. So shall my walk be close with God, Calm and se - rene my

frame, A light to shine up - on the road That leads me to the
Lord? Where is the soul's re - fresh - ing view Of Je - sus and His
still! But they have left an ach - ing void The world can nev - er
rest! I hate the sins that made Thee mourn, And drove Thee from my
be, Help me to tear it from Thy throne, And wor - ship on - ly
frame; So pur - er light shall mark the road That leads me to the

Lamb, A light to shine up - on the road That leads me to the Lamb!
Word, Where is the soul's re - fresh - ing view Of Je - sus and His Word?
fill, But they have left an ach - ing void The world can nev - er fill.
breast, I hate the sins that made Thee mourn, And drove Thee from my breast.
Thee, Help me to tear it from Thy throne, And wor - ship on - ly Thee.
Lamb, So pur - er light shall mark the road That leads me to the Lamb.

O FOR A CLOSER WALK WITH GOD

words by
William Cowper (1731-1800)

BEATITUDO
music by
John Bacchus Dykes (1823-1876)

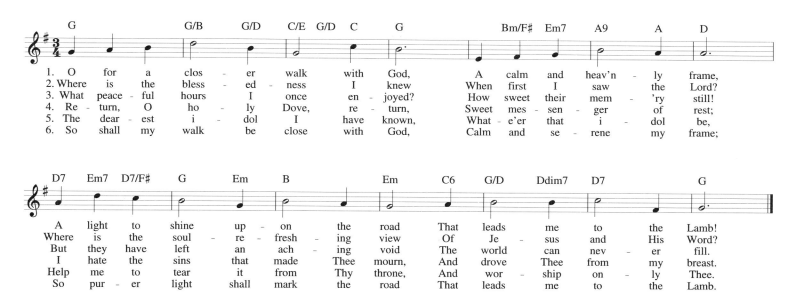

1. O for a clos - er walk with God, A calm and heav'n - ly frame,
2. Where is the bless - ed - ness I knew When first I saw the Lord?
3. What peace - ful hours I once en - joyed? How sweet their mem - 'ry still!
4. Re - turn, O ho - ly Dove, re - turn, Sweet mes - sen - ger of rest;
5. The dear - est i - dol I have known, What - e'er that i - dol be,
6. So shall my walk be close with God, Calm and se - rene my frame;

A light to shine up - on the road That leads me to the Lamb!
Where is the soul re - fresh - ing view Of Je - sus and His Word?
But they have left an ach - ing void The world can nev - er fill.
I hate the sins that made Thee mourn, And drove Thee from my breast.
Help me to tear it from Thy throne, And wor - ship on - ly Thee.
So pur - er light shall mark the road That leads me to the Lamb.

O FOR A HEART TO PRAISE MY GOD

words by
Charles Wesley, 1742

RICHMOND
music by
Thomas Haweis, 1792

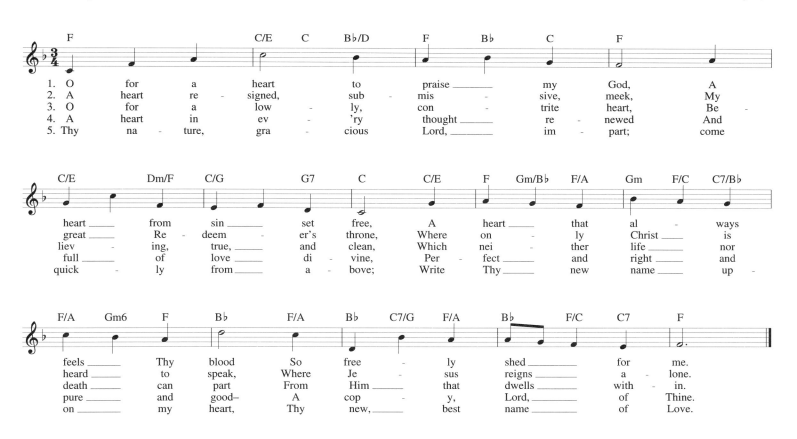

1. O for a heart to praise my God, A
2. A heart re - signed, sub - mis - sive, meek, My
3. O for a low - ly, con - trite heart, Be -
4. A heart in ev - 'ry thought re - newed And
5. Thy na - ture, gra - cious Lord, im - part; come

heart from sin set free, A heart that al - ways
great Re - deem - er's throne, Where on - ly Christ is
liev - ing, true, and clean, Which nei - ther life nor
full of love di - vine, Per - fect and right and
quick - ly from a - bove; Write Thy new name up -

feels Thy blood So free - ly shed for me.
heard to speak, Where Je - sus reigns a - lone.
death can part From Him that dwells with - in.
pure and good— A cop - y, Lord, of Thine.
on my heart, Thy new, best name of Love.

O FOR A THOUSAND TONGUES TO SING

AZMON
music by
Carl Gläser, 1828
arr. by Lowell Mason, 1830

words by
Charles Wesley, 1739

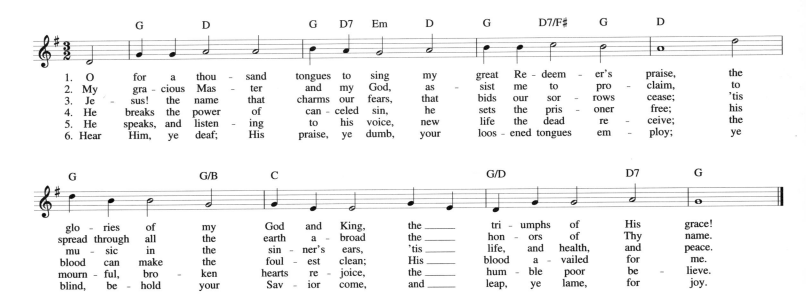

1. O for a thou - sand tongues to sing my great Re - deem - er's praise, the
2. My gra - cious Mas - ter and my God, as - sist me to pro - claim, to
3. Je - sus! the name that charms our fears, that bids our sor - rows cease; 'tis
4. He breaks the power of can - celed sin, he sets the pris - oner free; his
5. He speaks, and listen - ing to his voice, new life the dead re - ceive; the
6. Hear Him, ye deaf; His praise, ye dumb, your loos - ened tongues em - ploy; ye

glo - ries of my God and King, the _____ tri - umphs of His grace!
spread through all the earth a - broad the _____ hon - ors of Thy name.
mu - sic in the sin - ner's ears, 'tis _____ life, and health, and peace.
blood can make the foul - est clean; His _____ blood a - vailed for me.
mourn - ful, bro - ken hearts re - joice, the _____ hum - ble poor be - lieve.
blind, be - hold your Sav - ior come, and _____ leap, ye lame, for joy.

O FOR A THOUSAND TONGUES TO SING

BEATITUDO
music by
John B. Dykes (1823-1876)

words by
Charles Wesley (1707-1788)

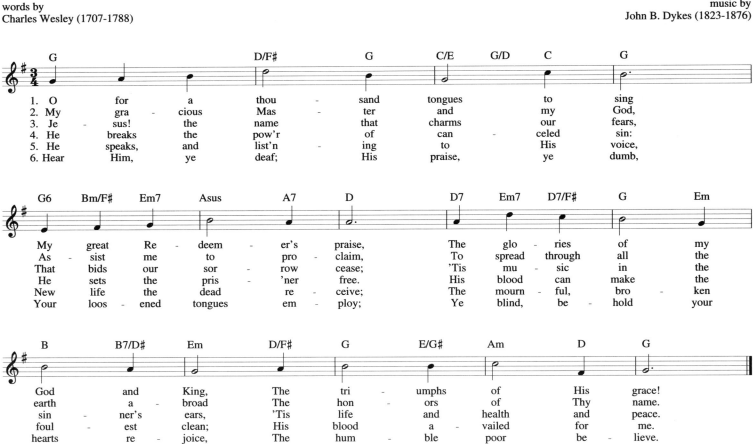

1. O for a thou - sand tongues to sing
2. My gra - cious Mas - ter and my God,
3. Je - sus! the name that charms our fears,
4. He breaks the pow'r of can - celed sin:
5. He speaks, and list'n - ing to His voice,
6. Hear Him, ye deaf; His praise, ye dumb,

My great Re - deem - er's praise, The glo - ries of my
As - sist me to pro - claim, To spread through all the
That bids our sor - row cease; 'Tis mu - sic in the
He sets the pris - 'ner free. His blood can make the
New life the dead re - ceive; The mourn - ful, bro - ken
Your loos - ened tongues em - ploy; Ye blind, be - hold your

God and King, The tri - umphs of His grace!
earth a - broad The hon - ors of Thy name.
sin - ner's ears, 'Tis life and health and peace.
foul - est clean; His blood a - vailed for me.
hearts re - joice, The hum - ble poor be - lieve.
Sav - ior come, And leap, ye lame, for joy.

O GLADSOME LIGHT

Ancient Greek text
tr. by Robert S. Bridges, 1899

LE CANTIQUE DE SIMÉON
music by
Louis Bourgeois, 1547

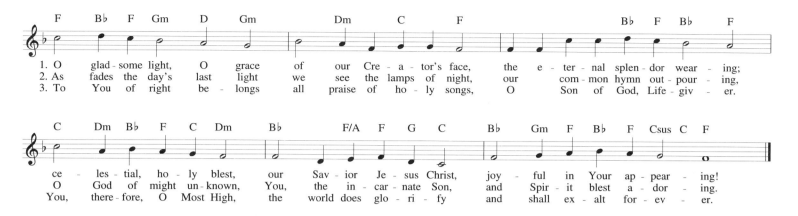

1. O glad-some light, O grace of our Cre - a - tor's face, the e - ter - nal splen - dor wear - ing;
2. As fades the day's last light we see the lamps of night, our com - mon hymn out - pour - ing,
3. To You of right be - longs all praise of ho - ly songs, O Son of God, Life - giv - er.

ce - les - tial, ho - ly blest, our Sav - ior Je - sus Christ, joy - ful in Your ap - pear - ing!
O God of might un - known, You, the in - car - nate Son, and Spir - it blest a - dor - ing.
You, there - fore, O Most High, the world does glo - ri - fy and shall ex - alt for - ev - er.

O GOD OF GOD, O LIGHT OF LIGHT

words by
John Julian, 1883

O GROSSER GOTT
music from
Schlag-Gesang- und Notenbuch, Stuttgart, 1744

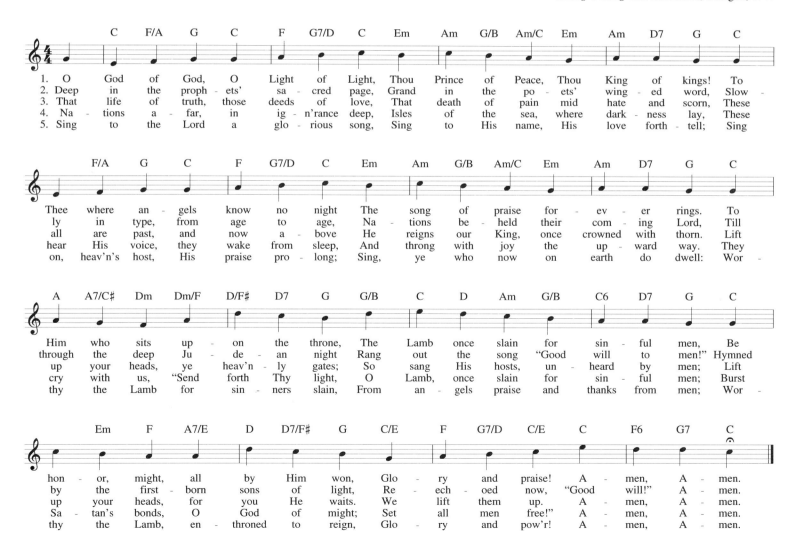

1. O God of God, O Light of Light, Thou Prince of Peace, Thou King of kings! To
2. Deep in the proph - ets' sa - cred page, Grand in the po - ets' wing - ed word, Slow -
3. That life of truth, those deeds of love, That death of pain mid hate and scorn, These
4. Na - tions a - far, in ig - n'rance deep, Isles of the sea, where dark - ness lay, These
5. Sing to the Lord a glo - rious song, Sing to His name, His love forth - tell; Sing

Thee where an - gels know no night The song of praise for - ev - er rings. To
ly in type, from age to age, Na - tions be - held their com - ing Lord, Till
all are past, and now a - bove He reigns our King, once crowned with thorn. Lift
hear His voice, and they wake from sleep, And throng with joy the up - ward way. They
on, heav'n's host, His praise pro - long; Sing, ye who now on earth do dwell: Wor -

Him who sits up - on the throne, The Lamb once slain for sin - ful men, Be
through the deep Ju - de - an night The Rang out the song "Good will to men!" Hymned
up your heads, ye heav'n - ly gates; So sang His hosts, un - heard by men; Lift
cry with us, "Send forth Thy light, O Lamb, once slain for sin - ful men; Burst
thy the Lamb for sin - ners slain, From an - gels praise and thanks from men; Wor -

hon - or, might, all by Him won, Glo - ry and praise! A - men, A - men.
by the first - born sons of light, Re - ech - oed now, "Good will!" A - men, A - men.
up your heads, for you He waits. We lift them up. A - men, A - men.
Sa - tan's bonds, O God of might; Set all men free!" A - men, A - men.
thy the Lamb, en - throned to reign, Glo - ry and pow'r! A - men, A - men.

O GOD OF JACOB, BY WHOSE HAND

ST. PETER
music by
Alexander R. Reinagle (1799-1877)

words by
Philip Doddridge (1702-1751)
alt. by John Logan, 1781

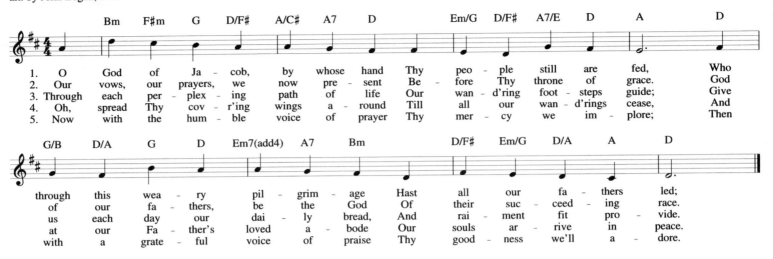

1. O God of Ja-cob, by whose hand Thy peo-ple still are fed, Who
2. Our vows, our prayers, we now pre-sent Be-fore Thy throne of grace. God
3. Through each per-plex-ing path of life Our wan-d'ring foot-steps guide; Give
4. Oh, spread Thy cov-'ring wings a-round Till all our wan-d'rings cease, And
5. Now with the hum-ble voice of prayer Thy mer-cy we im-plore; Then

through this wea-ry pil-grim-age Hast all our fa-thers led;
of our fa-thers, be the God Of their suc-ceed-ing race.
us each day our dai-ly bread, And rai-ment fit pro-vide.
at our Fa-ther's loved a-bode Our souls ar-rive in peace.
with a grate-ful voice of praise Thy good-ness we'll a-dore.

O GOD OF LOVE, O KING OF PEACE

ACK, BLIV HOS OSS
music from
Koralpsalmboken, Stockholm, 1697

words by
Henry W. Baker (1821-1877)

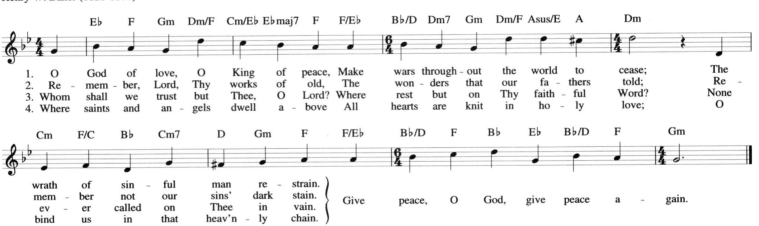

1. O God of love, O King of peace, Make wars through-out the world to cease; The
2. Re-mem-ber, Lord, Thy works of old, The won-ders that our fa-thers told; Re-
3. Whom shall we trust but Thee, O Lord? Where rest but on Thy faith-ful Word? None
4. Where saints and an-gels dwell a-bove All hearts are knit in ho-ly love; O

wrath of sin-ful man re-strain. }
mem-ber not our sins' dark stain. } Give peace, O God, give peace a-gain.
ev-er called on Thee in vain. }
bind us in that heav'n-ly chain. }

O GOD OF LOVE, O KING OF PEACE

TALLIS' CANON
music by
Thomas Tallis (c. 1505-1585)

words by
Henry W. Baker (1821-1877)

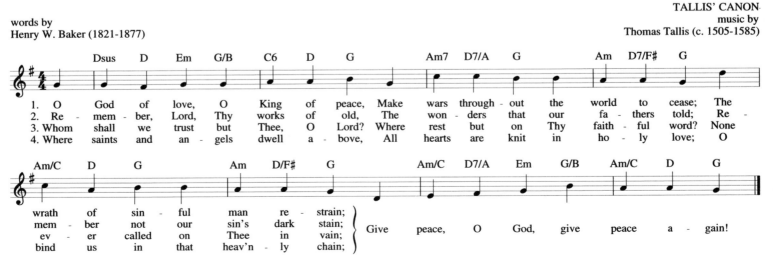

1. O God of love, O King of peace, Make wars through-out the world to cease; The
2. Re-mem-ber, Lord, Thy works of old, The won-ders that our fa-thers told; Re-
3. Whom shall we trust but Thee, O Lord? Where rest but on Thy faith-ful word? None
4. Where saints and an-gels dwell a-bove, All hearts are knit in ho-ly love; O

wrath of sin-ful man re-strain; }
mem-ber not our sin's dark stain; } Give peace, O God, give peace a-gain!
ev-er called on Thee in vain; }
bind us in that heav'n-ly chain; }

O GOD OF LOVE, O KING OF PEACE

words by
Henry Williams Baker, 1860

DU MEINER SEELEN
music from
Cantica Spiritualia, 1847

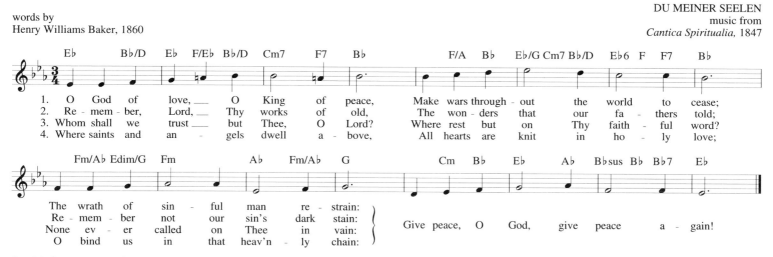

1. O God of love, ___ O King of peace, Make wars through - out the world to cease;
2. Re - mem - ber, Lord, ___ Thy works of old, The won - ders that our fa - thers told;
3. Whom shall we trust ___ but Thee, O Lord? Where rest but on Thy faith - ful word?
4. Where saints and an - gels dwell a - bove, All hearts are knit in ho - ly love;

The wrath of sin - ful man re - strain:
Re - mem - ber not our sin's dark stain:
None ev - er called on Thee in vain:
O bind us in that heav'n - ly chain:

Give peace, O God, give peace a - gain!

O GOD OF MERCY, GOD OF MIGHT

words by
G. Thring (1823-1903)

JUST AS I AM
music by
J. Barnby (1838-1896)

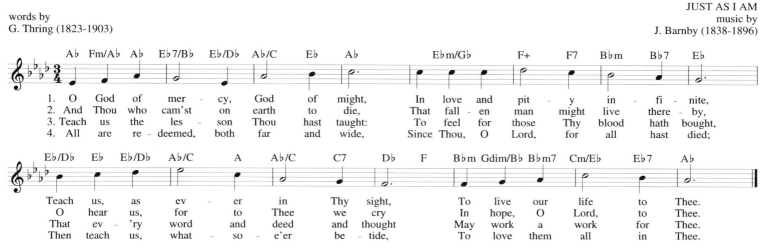

1. O God of mer - cy, God of might, In love and pit - y in - fi - nite,
2. And Thou who cam'st on earth to die, That fall - en man might live there - by,
3. Teach us the les - son Thou hast taught: To feel for those Thy blood hath bought,
4. All are re - deemed, both far and wide, Since Thou, O Lord, for all hast died;

Teach us, as ev - er in Thy sight, To live our life to Thee.
O hear us, for to Thee we cry In hope, O Lord, to Thee.
That ev - 'ry word and deed and thought May work a work for Thee.
Then teach us, what - so - e'er be - tide, To love them all in Thee.

O GOD, OUR HELP IN AGES PAST

words by
Isaac Watts (1674-1748)
para. of Psalm 90:1-5

ST. ANNE
music by
William Croft (1678-1727)

1. O God, our help in a - ges past, Our hope for years to come, Our
2. Un - der the shad - ow of Thy throne Thy saints have dwelt se - cure; Suf -
3. Be - fore the hills in or - der stood, Or earth re - ceived her frame, From
4. A thou - sand a - ges in Thy sight Are like an eve - ning gone; Short
5. Time, like an ev - er roll - ing stream, Bears all our years a - way; They
6. O God, our help in a - ges past, Our hope for years to come, Be

shel - ter from the storm - y blast, And our e - ter - nal home:
fi - cient is Thine arm a - lone, And our de - fense is sure.
ev - er - last - ing Thou art God, To end - less years the same.
as the watch that ends the night Be - fore the ris - ing sun.
fly, for - got - ten, as a dream Dies at the o - p'ning day.
Thou our guide while life shall last, And our e - ter - nal home.

O GOD, THOU FAITHFUL GOD

words by
J. Heermann (1585-1647)
tr. by Catherine Winkworth (1827-1878)

O GOTT, DU FROMMER GOTT
music from
Neu-vermehrtes Gesangbuch, Meiningen, 1693

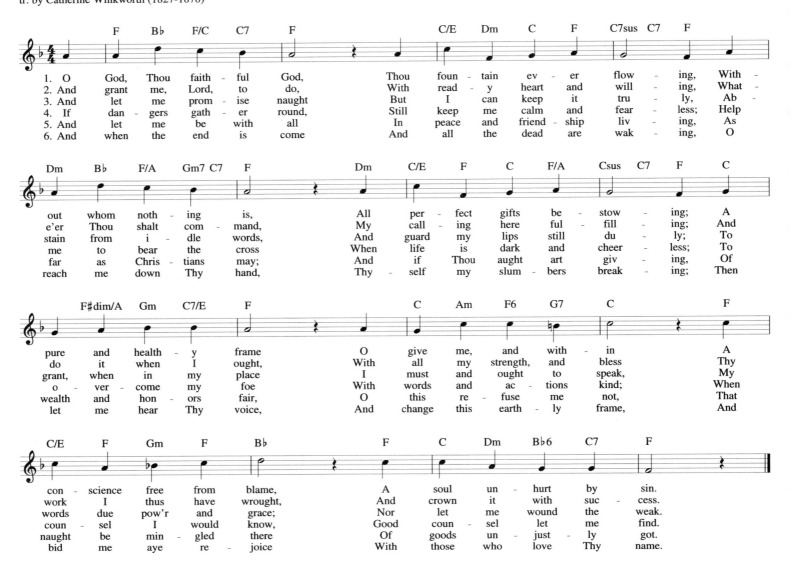

O GOD, UNSEEN YET EVER NEAR

words by
Edward Osler (1798-1863)

ST. FLAVIAN
music from
Day's *Psalter*, 1562

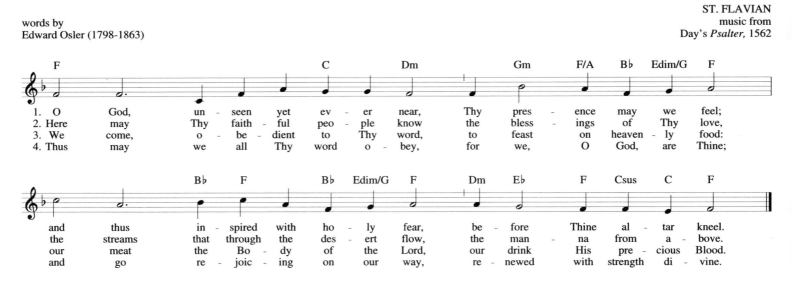

O GOD, THOU FAITHFUL GOD

WAS FRAG ICH NACH DER WELT
music by
Ahasuerus Fritsch (1629-1701)

words by
Johann Heermann (1585-1647)
tr. by Catherine Winkworth (1827-1878)

1. O God, Thou faith - ful God, Thou foun - tain ev - er flow - ing, With
2. And grant me, Lord, to do, With read - y heart and will - ing, What
3. And let me prom - ise naught But I can keep it tru - ly, Ab -
4. If dan - gers gath - er round, Still keep me calm and fear - less; Help
5. And let me be with all In peace and friend - ship liv - ing, As
6. And when the end is come And all the dead are wak - ing, O

out whom noth - ing is, All per - fect gifts be - stow - ing: A
e'er Thou shalt com - mand, My call - ing here ful - fill - ing; And
stain from i - dle words, And guard my lips still du - ly; And
me to bear the cross When life is dark and cheer - less; To
far as Chris - tians may; And if Thou aught are giv - ing Of
reach me down Thy hand, Thy - self my slum - bers break - ing; Then

pure and health - y frame, O give me, and with - in A
do it when I ought, With all my strength, and bless The
grant, when in my place I must and ought to speak, My
o - ver - come my foe With words and ac - tions kind; When
wealth and hon - ors fair, O this re - fuse me not, That
let me hear Thy voice, And change this earth - ly frame, And

con - science free from blame, A soul un - hurt by sin.
work I thus have wrought, And crown it with suc - cess.
words due pow'r and grace, Nor let me wound the weak.
coun - sel I would know, Good coun - sel let me find.
naught be min - gled there Of goods un - just - ly got.
bid me aye re - joice With those who love Thy name.

O GOD, WHOM NEITHER TIME NOR SPACE

LONDON NEW
music from
The Psalmes of David in Prose and Meeter, 1635

words by
Horace Smith (1836-1922)

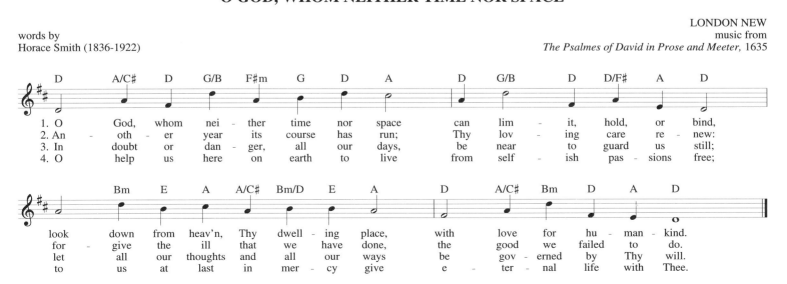

1. O God, whom nei - ther time nor space can lim - it, hold, or bind;
2. An - oth - er year its course has run; Thy lov - ing care re - new:
3. In doubt or dan - ger, all our days, be near to guard us still;
4. O help us here on earth to live from self - ish pas - sions free;

look down from heav'n, Thy dwell - ing place, with love for hu - man - kind.
for - give the ill that we have done, the good we failed to do.
let all our thoughts and all our ways be gov - erned by Thy will.
to us at last in mer - cy give e - ter - nal life with Thee.

O HAPPY DAY THAT FIXED MY CHOICE

HAPPY DAY

words by
Philip Doddridge (1702-1751)

music by
Edward F. Rimbault (1816-1876)

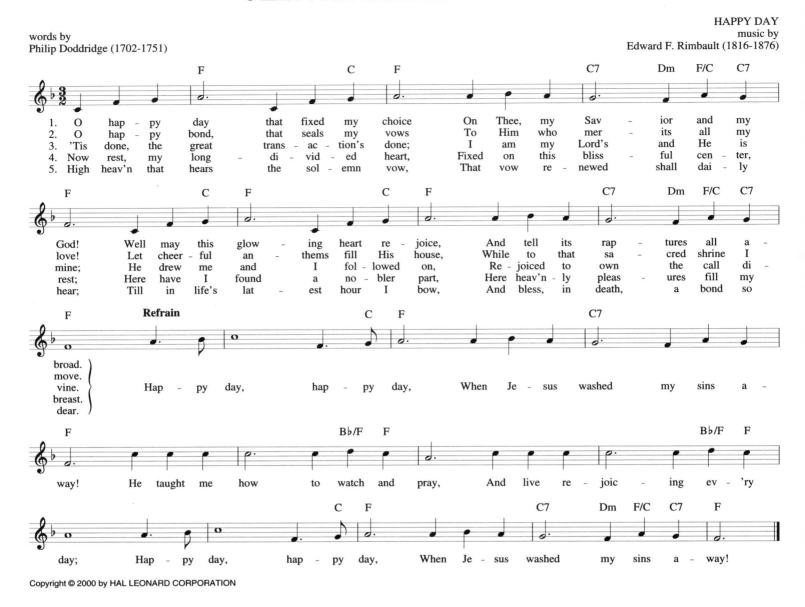

1. O hap - py day that fixed my choice On Thee, my Sav - ior and my
2. O hap - py bond, that seals my vows To Him who mer - its all my
3. 'Tis done, the great trans - ac - tion's done; I am my Lord's and He is
4. Now rest, my long - di - vid - ed heart, Fixed on this bliss - ful cen - ter,
5. High heav'n that hears the sol - emn vow, That vow re - newed shall dai - ly

God! Well may this glow - ing heart re - joice, And tell its rap - tures all a -
love! Let cheer - ful an - thems fill His house, While to that sa - cred shrine I
mine; He drew me and I fol - lowed on, Re - joiced to own the call di -
rest; Here have I found a no - bler part, Here heav'n - ly pleas - ures fill my
hear; Till in life's lat - est hour I bow, And bless, in death, a bond so

Refrain

broad.
move.
vine.
breast.
dear.

Hap - py day, hap - py day, When Je - sus washed my sins a -

way! He taught me how to watch and pray, And live re - joic - ing ev - 'ry

day; Hap - py day, hap - py day, When Je - sus washed my sins a - way!

O HOW I LOVE JESUS

words by
Frederick Whitfield (1829-1904)

Traditional American melody

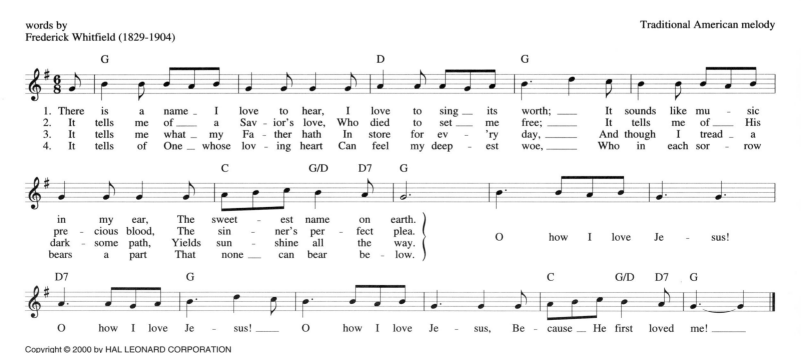

1. There is a name I love to hear, I love to sing its worth; It sounds like mu - sic
2. It tells me of a Sav - ior's love, Who died to set me free; It tells me of His
3. It tells me what my Fa - ther hath In store for ev - 'ry day, And though I tread a
4. It tells of One whose lov - ing heart Can feel my deep - est woe, Who in each sor - row

in my ear, The sweet - est name on earth.
pre - cious blood, The sin - ner's per - fect plea.
dark - some path, Yields sun - shine all the way.
bears a part That none can bear be - low.

O how I love Je - sus!

O how I love Je - sus! O how I love Je - sus, Be - cause He first loved me!

O HOLY SPIRIT, ENTER IN

words by
M. Schirmer (1606-1673)
tr. by C. Winkworth (1827-1878)

WIE SCHÖN LEUCHTET
music by
P. Nicolai (1556-1608)

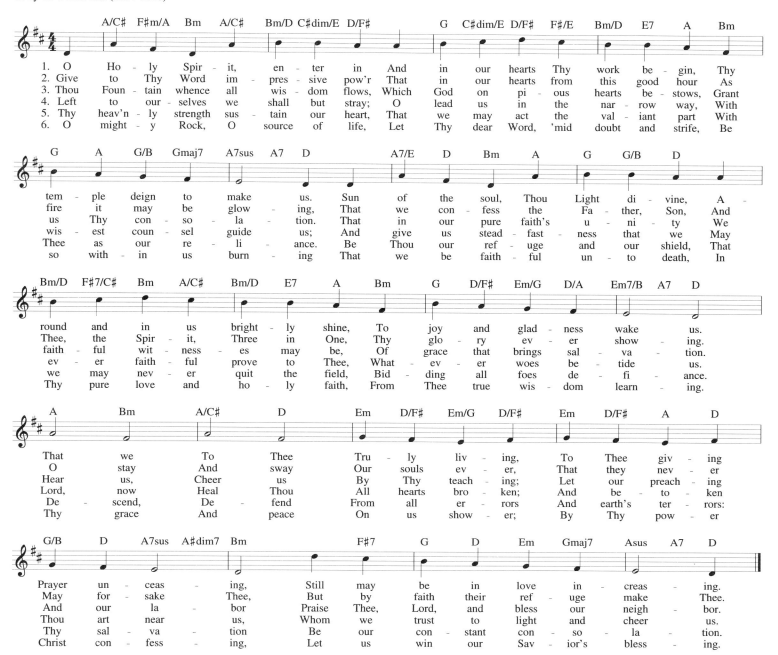

1. O Holy Spir - it, en - ter in And in our hearts Thy work be - gin, Thy
2. Give to Thy Word im - pres - sive pow'r That in our hearts from this good hour As
3. Thou Foun - tain whence all wis - dom flows, Which God on pi - ous hearts be - stows, Grant
4. Left to our - selves we shall but stray; O lead us in the nar - row way, With
5. Thy heav'n - ly strength sus - tain our heart, That we may act the val - iant part With
6. O might - y Rock, O source of life, Let Thy dear Word, 'mid doubt and strife, Be

tem - ple deign to make us. Sun of the soul, Thou Light di - vine, A
fire it may be glow - ing, That we con - fess the Fa - ther, Son, And
us Thy con - so - la - tion. That in our pure faith's u - ni - ty We
wis - est coun - sel guide us; And give us stead - fast - ness that we May
Thee as our re - li - ance. Be Thou our ref - uge and our shield, That
so with - in us burn - ing That we be faith - ful un - to death, In

round and in us bright - ly shine, To joy and glad - ness wake us.
Thee, the Spir - it, Three in One, Thy glo - ry ev - er show - ing.
faith - ful wit - ness - es may be, Of grace that brings sal - va - tion.
ev - er faith - ful prove to Thee, What - ev - er woes be - tide us.
we may nev - er quit the field, Bid - ding all foes de - fi - ance.
Thy pure love and ho - ly faith, From Thee true wis - dom learn - ing.

That we To Thee Tru - ly liv - ing, To Thee giv - ing
O stay us, And Cheer sway us Our souls ev - er, That they nev - er
Hear us, And Heal Thou us All hearts bro - ken; And be - to - ken
Lord, now De - scend, De - fend All er - rors And earth's ter - rors:
Thy grace And peace On us show - er; By Thy pow - er

Prayer un - ceas - ing, Still may be in love in - creas - ing.
May for - sake Thee, But by faith their ref - uge make Thee.
And our la - bor us, Praise Thee, Lord, and bless our neigh - bor.
Thou art near us, Whom we trust to light and cheer us.
Thy sal - va - tion Be our con - stant con - so - la - tion.
Christ con - fess - ing, Let us win our Sav - ior's bless - ing.

O JESUS, BLESSED LORD, TO THEE

words by
T.H. Kingo (1634-1703)
tr. by A.J. Mason (1851-1928)

OLD HUNDREDTH
music by
Louis Bourgeois (1510-1561)

1. O Je - sus, bless - ed Lord, to Thee My heart - felt thanks for - ev - er be, Who
2. Break forth, my soul, for joy and say: What wealth is come to me this day! My

hast so lov - ing - ly be - stowed On me Thy bod - y and Thy blood.
Sav - ior dwells with - in me now: How blest am I! How good art Thou!

O JESUS, I HAVE PROMISED

words by
John E. Bode, 1868

ANGEL'S STORY
music by
Arthur H. Mann, 1883

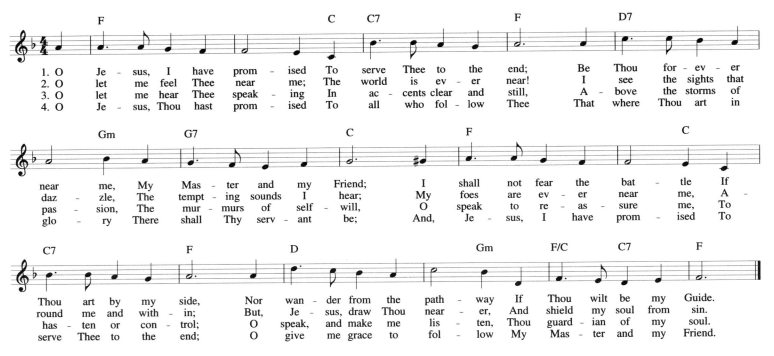

O JESUS, I HAVE PROMISED

words by
John Ernest Bode, 1866

NYLAND
Finnish folk melody

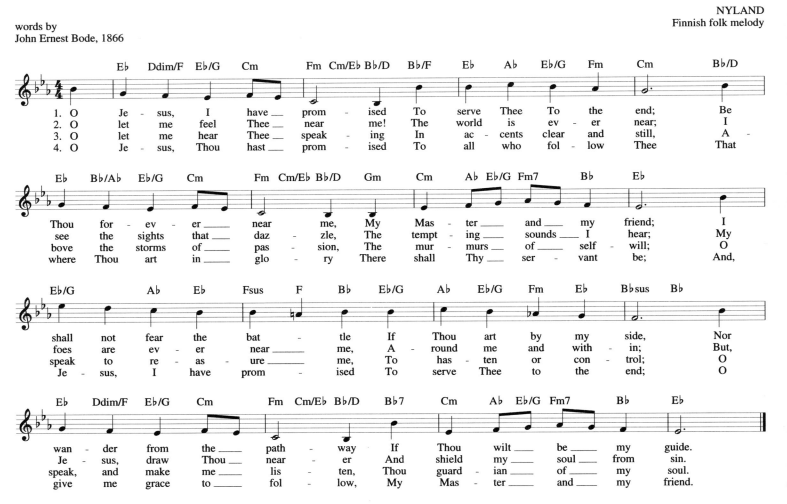

O JESUS, CRUCIFIED FOR MAN

words by
William W. How (1823-1897)

SEFTON
music by
Jean Baptiste Calkin (1827-1905)

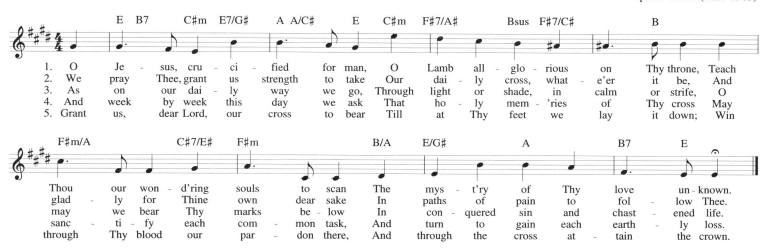

1. O Je - sus, cru - ci - fied for man, O Lamb all - glo - rious on Thy throne, Teach
2. We pray Thee, grant us strength to take Our dai - ly cross, what - e'er it be, And
3. As on our dai - ly way we go, Through light or shade, in calm or strife, O
4. And week by week this day we ask That ho - ly mem - 'ries of Thy cross May
5. Grant us, dear Lord, our cross to bear Till at Thy feet we lay it down; Win

Thou our won - d'ring souls to scan The mys - t'ry of Thy love un - known.
glad - ly for Thine own dear sake In paths of pain to fol - low Thee.
may we bear Thy marks be - low In con - quered sin and chast - ened life.
sanc - ti - fy each com - mon task, And turn to gain each earth - ly loss.
through Thy blood our par - don there, And through the cross at - tain the crown.

O JESUS, KING MOST WONDERFUL

words by
Bernard of Clairvaux (1090-1153)
tr. by E. Caswall (1814-1878)

ST. AGNES
music by
J.B. Dykes (1823-1876)

1. O Je - sus, King most won - der - ful, Thou Con - quer - or re - nowned,
2. When once Thou vis - it - est the heart, Then truth be - gins to shine,
3. O Je - sus, Light of all be - low, Thou Fount of life and fire,
4. May ev - 'ry heart con - fess Thy name, And ev - er Thee a - dore,
5. Thee may our tongues for - ev - er bless, Thee may we love a - lone,

Thou Sweet - ness most in - ef - fa - ble, In whom all joys are found!
Then earth - ly van - i - ties de - part, Then kin - dles love di - vine.
Sur - pass - ing all the joys we know, All that we can de - sire.
And, seek - ing Thee, it - self in - flame To seek Thee more and more!
And ev - er in our lives ex - press The im - age of Thine own!

O JESUS, SAVIOR, I LONG TO REST

words by
I. Baltzell

JESUS, SAVIOR
music by
I. Baltzell

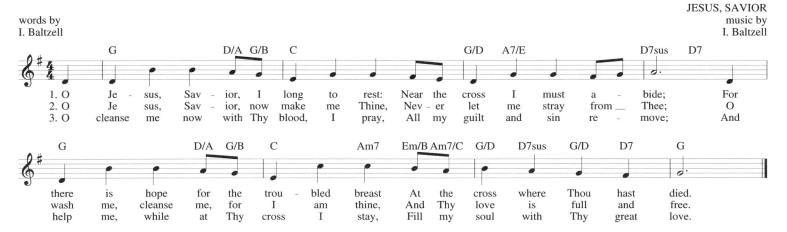

1. O Je - sus, Sav - ior, I long to rest: Near the cross I must a - bide; For
2. O Je - sus, Sav - ior, now make me Thine, Nev - er let me stray from Thee; O
3. O cleanse me now with Thy blood, I pray, All my guilt and sin re - move; And

there is hope for the trou - bled breast At the cross where Thou hast died.
wash me, cleanse me, for I am thine, And Thy love is full and free.
help me, while at Thy cross I stay, Fill my soul with Thy great love.

O JOYFUL SOUND OF GOSPEL GRACE

OLMSTED
Traditional Hymn Tune

words by
Charles Wesley (1707-1788)

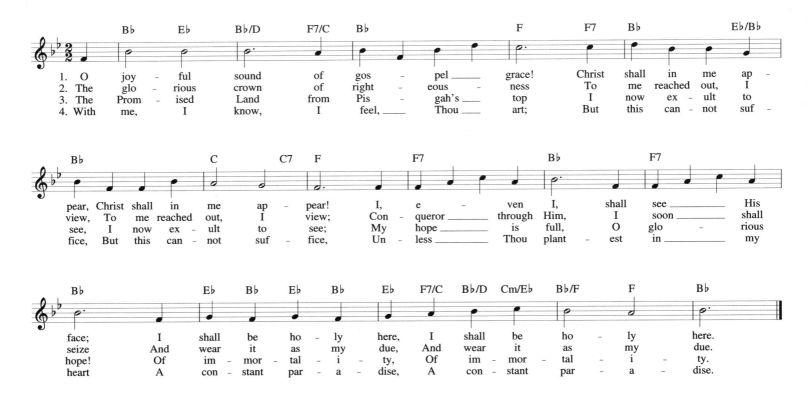

1. O joy - ful sound of gos - pel grace! Christ shall in me ap -
2. The glo - rious crown of right - eous - ness To me reached out, I
3. The Prom - ised Land from Pis - gah's top I now ex - ult to
4. With me, I know, I feel, Thou art; But this can - not suf -

pear, Christ shall in me ap - pear! I, e - ven I, shall see His
view, To me reached out, I view; Con - queror through Him, I soon shall
see, I now ex - ult to see; My hope is full, O glo - rious
fice, But this can - not suf - fice, Un - less Thou plant - est in my

face; I shall be ho - ly here, I shall be ho - ly here.
seize And wear it as my due, And wear it as my due.
hope! Of im - mor - tal - i - ty, Of im - mor - tal - i - ty.
heart A con - stant par - a - dise, A con - stant par - a - dise.

O LAMB OF GOD MOST HOLY

O LAMM GOTTES
music by
Nikolaus Decuis, c. 1541

words by
Nikolaus Decius, c. 1541
tr. by Arthur Tozer Russell (1806-1874)

1. O Lamb of God most ho - ly!
2. O Lamb of God most ho - ly!   Who on the cross did suf - fer, And
3. O Lamb of God most ho - ly!

pa - tient still and low - ly, Your - self to scorn did of - fer; Our sins by You were

tak - en, Or hope had us for - sak - en:
{ Have mer - cy on us, Je - sus!
  Have mer - cy on us, Je - sus!
  Your peace be with us, Je - sus!

O LIVING BREAD FROM HEAVEN

words by
Johann Rist (1607-1667)
tr. by Catherine Winkworth (1827-1878)

NUN LOB, MEIN SEEL
music from
Concentus Novi, Augsburg, 1540

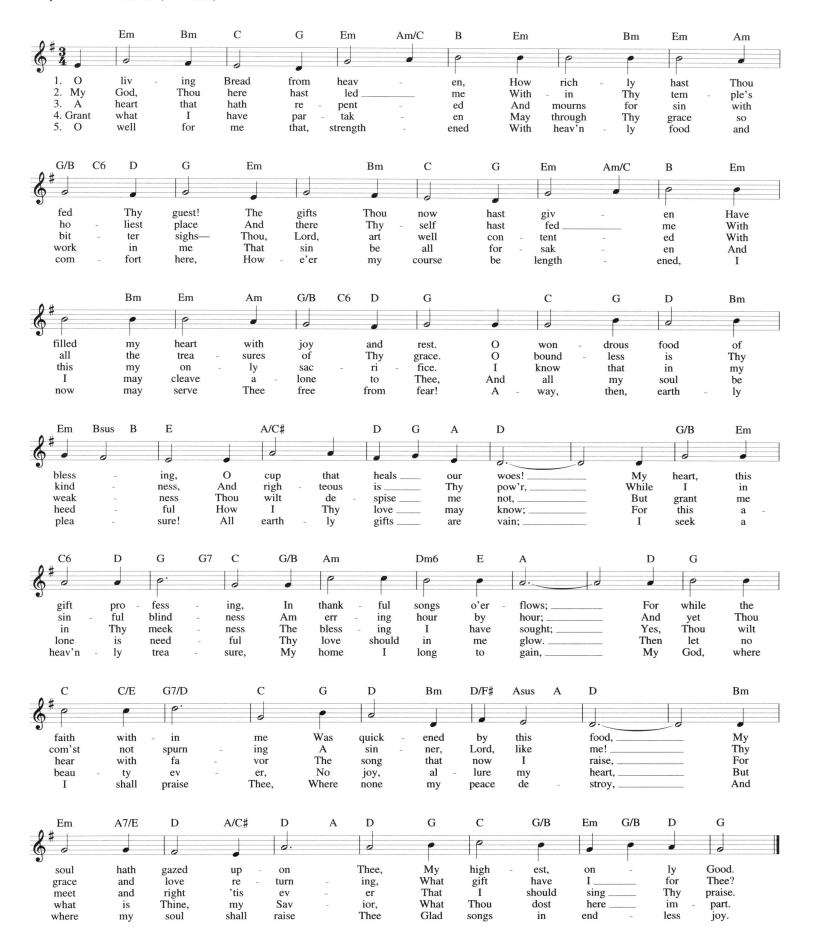

O LITTLE TOWN OF BETHLEHEM

ST. LOUIS
music by
Lewis H. Redner (1831-1908)

words by
Phillips Brooks (1835-1893)

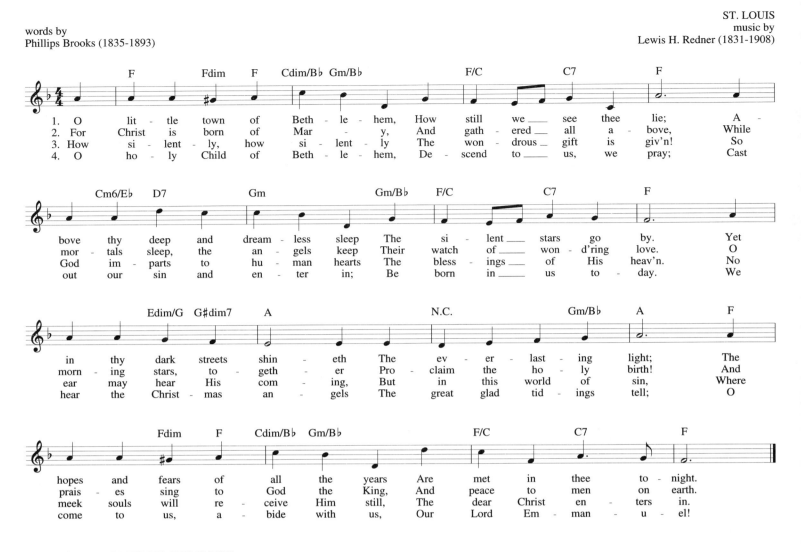

1. O lit-tle town of Beth-le-hem, How still we ___ see thee lie; A-bove thy deep and dream-less sleep The si-lent ___ stars go by. Yet in thy dark streets shin-eth The ev-er-last-ing light; The hopes and fears of all the years Are met in thee to-night.
2. For Christ is born of Mar-y, And gath-ered ___ all a-bove, While mor-tals sleep, the an-gels keep Their watch of ___ won-d'ring love. O morn-ing stars, to-geth-er Pro-claim the ho-ly birth! And prais-es sing to God the King, And peace to men on earth.
3. How si-lent-ly, how si-lent-ly The won-drous ___ gift is giv'n! So God im-parts to hu-man hearts The bless-ings ___ of His heav'n. No ear may hear His com-ing, But in this world of sin, Where meek souls will re-ceive Him still, The dear Christ en-ters in.
4. O ho-ly Child of Beth-le-hem, De-scend to ___ us, we pray; Cast out our sin and en-ter in; Be born in ___ us to-day. We hear the Christ-mas an-gels The great glad tid-ings tell; O come to us, a-bide with us, Our Lord Em-man-u-el!

O LORD OF LIFE, WHERE'ER THEY BE

GELOBT SEI GOTT
music by
Melchior Vulpius, 1609

words by
Frederick Lucian Hosmer, 1888

1. O Lord of life, wher-e'er they be, Safe in Thine own e-ter-ni-ty, Our dead are liv-ing un-to Thee: Al-le-lu-ia! Al-le-lu-ia! Al-le-lu-ia!
2. All souls are life, and here or there, They rest with-in Thy shel-t'ring care; One prov-i-dence a-like they share: Al-le-lu-ia! Al-le-lu-ia! Al-le-lu-ia!
3. Thy word is true, Thy ways are just; A-bove the re-quiem, "Dust to dust," Shall rise our psalm of grate-ful trust: Al-le-lu-ia! Al-le-lu-ia! Al-le-lu-ia!
4. O hap-py they in God who rest, No more by fear and doubt op-pressed; Liv-ing or dy-ing, they are blest: Al-le-lu-ia! Al-le-lu-ia! Al-le-lu-ia!

O LOVE DIVINE, WHAT HAST THOU DONE

words by
Charles Wesley, 1742

SELENA
music by
Isaac B. Woodbury, 1850

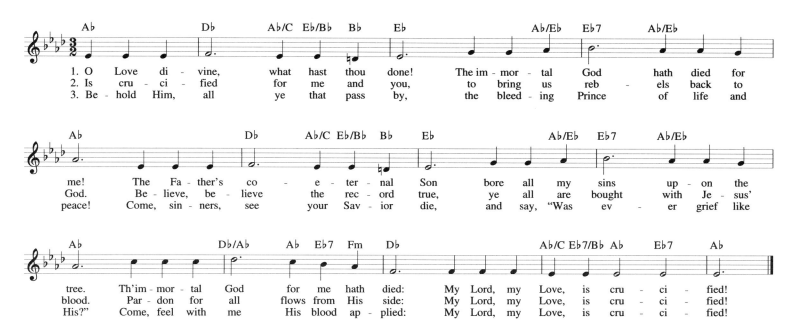

1. O Love di - vine, what hast thou done! The im - mor - tal God hath died for
2. Is cru - ci - fied for me and you, to bring us reb - els back to
3. Be - hold Him, all ye that pass by, the bleed - ing Prince of life and

me! The Fa - ther's co - e - ter - nal Son bore all my sins up - on the
God. Be - lieve, be - lieve the rec - ord true, ye all are bought with Je - sus'
peace! Come, sin - ners, see your Sav - ior die, and say, "Was ev - er grief like

tree. Th'im - mor - tal God for me hath died: My Lord, my Love, is cru - ci - fied!
blood. Par - don for all flows from His side: My Lord, my Love, is cru - ci - fied!
His?" Come, feel with me His blood ap - plied: My Lord, my Love, is cru - ci - fied!

O LOVE, HOW DEEP, HOW BROAD, HOW HIGH

Latin text, 15th century
tr. by Benjamin Webb (1819-1885)

DEUS TUORUM MILITUM
music from *Antiphoner,* 1753
adapt. in *The English Hymnal,* 1906

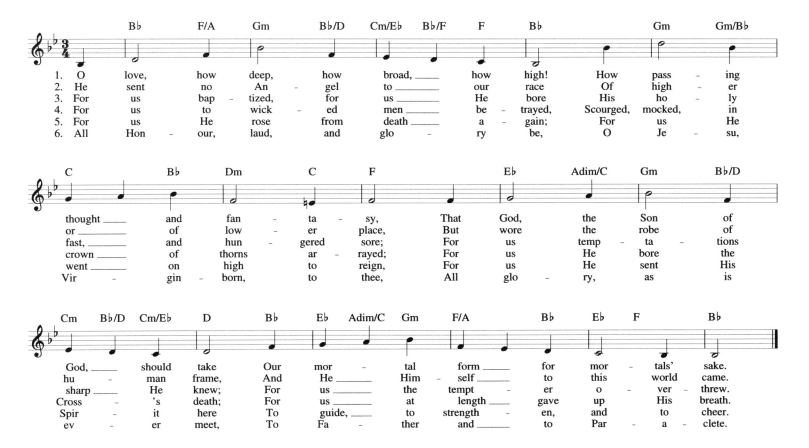

1. O love, how deep, how broad, how high! How pass - ing
2. He sent no An - gel to our race Of high - er
3. For us bap - tized, for us He bore His ho - ly
4. For us to wick - ed men be - trayed, Scourged, mocked, in
5. For us He rose from death a - gain; For us He
6. All Hon - our, laud, and glo - ry be, O Je - su,

thought and fan - ta - sy, That God, the Son of
or of low - er place, But wore the robe of
fast, and hun - gered sore; For us He temp - ta - tions
crown of thorns ar - rayed; For us He bore the
went on high to reign, For us He sent His
Vir - gin - born, to thee, All glo - ry, as is

God, should take Our mor - tal form for mor - tals' sake.
hu - man frame, And He Him - self to this world came.
sharp He knew; For us the tempt - er o - ver - threw.
Cross - 's death; For us at length gave up His breath.
Spir - it here To guide, to strength - en, and to cheer.
ev - er meet, To Fa - ther and to Par - a - clete.

O LORD, MAKE HASTE TO HEAR MY CRY

Author unknown
words based on Psalm 141

CANNONS
music adapt. from
George Frederick Handel, c. 1750

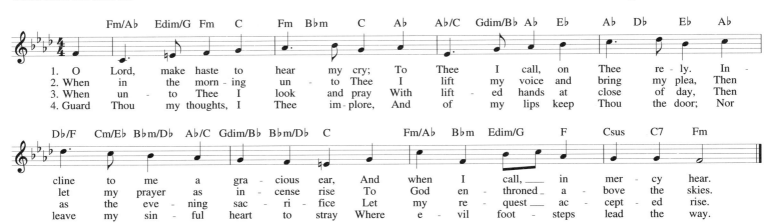

1. O Lord, make haste to hear my cry; To Thee I call, on Thee re - ly. In
2. When in the morn - ing un - to Thee I lift my voice and bring my plea, Then
3. When un - to Thee I look and pray With lift - ed hands at close of day, Then
4. Guard Thou my thoughts, I Thee im - plore, And of my lips keep Thou the door; Nor

cline to me a gra - cious ear, And when I call, ___ in mer - cy hear.
let my prayer as in - cense rise To God en - throned ___ a - bove the skies.
as the eve - ning sac - ri - fice Let my re - quest ___ ac - cept - ed rise.
leave my sin - ful heart to stray Where e - vil foot - steps lead the way.

O LOVE THAT CASTS OUT FEAR

words by
Horatius Bonar (1808-1889)

MOSELEY
music by
Henry Thomas Smart (1813-1879)

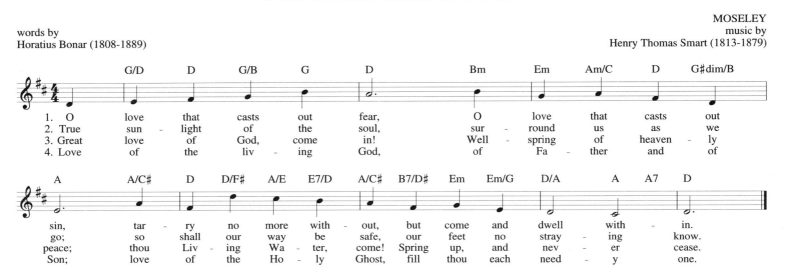

1. O love that casts out fear, O love that casts out
2. True sun - light of the soul, sur - round us as we
3. Great love of God, come in! Well - spring of heaven - ly
4. Love of the liv - ing God, of Fa - ther and of

sin, tar - ry no more with - out, but come and dwell with - in.
go; so shall our way be safe, our feet no stray - ing know.
peace; thou Liv - ing Wa - ter, come! Spring up, and nev - er cease.
Son; love of the Ho - ly Ghost, fill thou each need - y one.

O LOVE THAT WILT NOT LET ME GO

words by
George Matheson, 1882

ST. MARGARET
music by
Albert Lister Peace, 1884

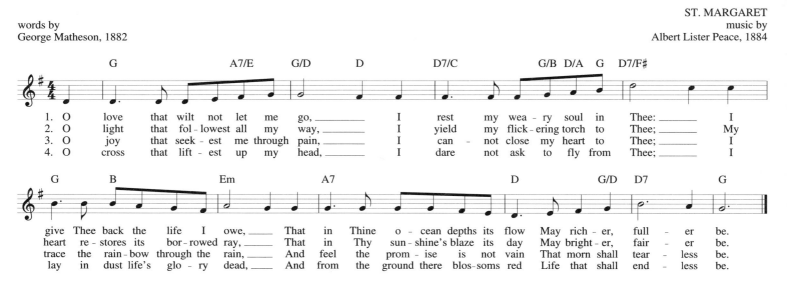

1. O love that wilt not let me go, ___ I rest my wea - ry soul in Thee: ___ I
2. O light that fol - lowest all my way, ___ I yield my flick - ering torch to Thee; ___ My
3. O joy that seek - est me through pain, ___ I can - not close my heart to Thee; ___ I
4. O cross that lift - est up my head, ___ I dare not ask to fly from Thee; ___ I

give Thee back the life I owe, ___ That in Thine o - cean depths its flow May rich - er, full - er be.
heart re - stores its bor - rowed ray, ___ That in Thy sun - shine's blaze its day May bright - er, fair - er be.
trace the rain - bow through the rain, ___ And feel the prom - ise is not vain That morn shall tear - less be.
lay in dust life's glo - ry dead, ___ And from the ground there blos - soms red Life that shall end - less be.

O MASTER, LET ME WALK WITH THEE

words by
Washington Gladden (1836-1918)

MARYTON
music by
H. Percy Smith (1825-1898)

1. O Mas - ter, let me walk with Thee In low - ly
2. Help me the slow of heart to move By some clear,
3. Teach me Thy pa - tience! Still with Thee In clos - er,
4. In hope that sends a shin - ing ray Far down the

paths of serv - ice free; Tell me Thy se - cret;
win - ning word of love; Teach me the way - ward
dear - er com - pa - ny, In work that keeps faith
fu - ture's broad - ening way, In peace that on - ly

help me bear The strain of toil, the fret of care.
feet to stay, And guide them in the home - ward way.
sweet and strong, In trust that tri - umphs o - ver wrong;
Thou canst give, With Thee, O Mas - ter, let me live.

O MY SOUL, BLESS THOU JEHOVAH

Author unkown
based on Psalm 103

STUTTGART
music from
Witt's *Psalmodia Sacra*, 1715
as in *Hymns Ancient and Modern*, 1861

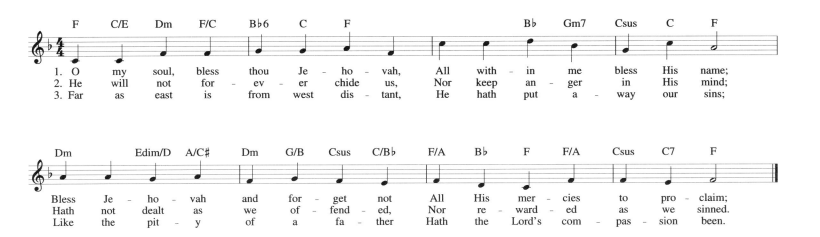

1. O my soul, bless thou Je - ho - vah, All with - in me bless His name;
2. He will not for - ev - er chide us, Nor keep an - ger in His mind;
3. Far as east is from west dis - tant, He hath put a - way our sins;

Bless Je - ho - vah and for - get not All His mer - cies to pro - claim;
Hath not dealt as we of - fend - ed, Nor re - ward - ed as we sinned.
Like the pit - y of a fa - ther Hath the Lord's com - pas - sion been.

O PERFECT LOVE

words by
Dorothy Frances Gurney, 1883

PERFECT LOVE
music by
Joseph Barnby, 1889

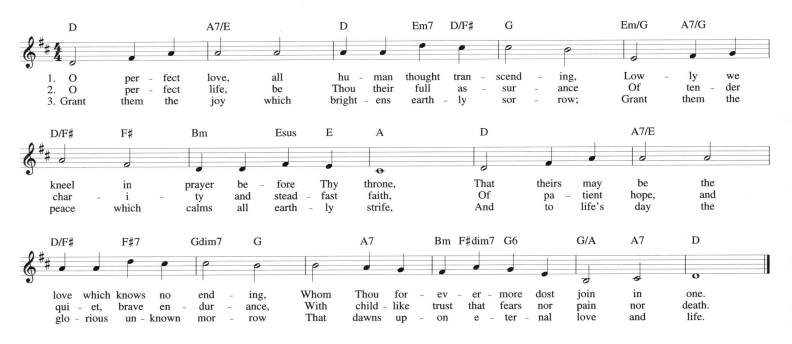

O SACRED HEAD, NOW WOUNDED

words attr. to
Bernard of Clairvaux (1091-1153)
tr. by James Waddell Alexander (1804-1859)

PASSION CHORALE
music by
Hans Leo Hassler (1564-1612)

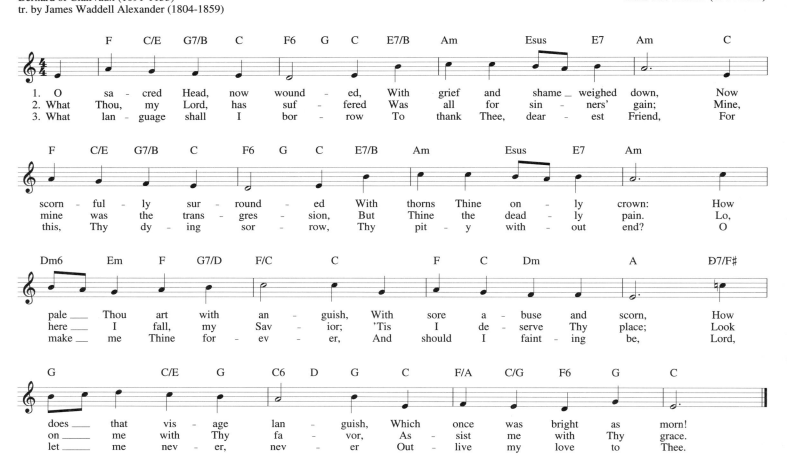

O SAVING VICTIM
(O Salutáris)

words by
Thomas Aquinas (1227-1275)
tr. by Edward Caswall (1814-1878)

DUGUET
music by
Dieudonne Duguet (d. 1767)

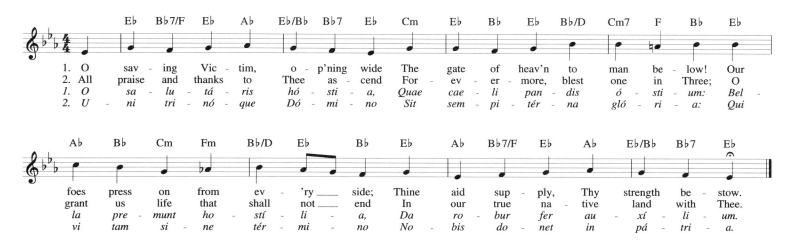

1. O sav-ing Vic-tim, o-p'ning wide The gate of heav'n to man be-low! Our
2. All praise and thanks to Thee as-cend For ev-er-more, blest one in Three; O
1. O sa-lu-tá-ris hó-sti-a, Quae cae-li pan-dis ó-sti-um: Bel-
2. U-ni tri-nó-que Dó-mi-no Sit sem-pi-tér-na gló-ri-a: Qui

foes press on from ev-'ry side; Thine aid sup-ply, Thy strength be-stow.
grant us life that shall not end In our true na-tive land with Thee.
la pre-munt ho-stí-li-a, Da ro-bur fer au-xí-li-um.
vi tam si-ne tér-mi-no No-bis do-net in pá-tri-a.

O SAVIOR, PRECIOUS SAVIOR

words by
Frances R. Havergal (1836-1879)

ANGEL'S STORY
music by
Arthur H. Mann (1850-1929)

1. O Sav-ior, pre-cious Sav-ior, Whom yet un-seen we love; O
2. O Bring-er of sal-va-tion, Who won-drous-ly hast wrought, Thy
3. In Thee all full-ness dwell-eth, All grace and pow'r di-vine; The
4. Oh, grant the con-sum-ma-tion Of this our song a-bove,

Name of might and fa-vor, All oth-er names a-bove: We
self the rev-e-la-tion Of love be-yond our thought: We
glo-ry that ex-cel-leth, O Son of God, is Thine. We
end-less ad-o-ra-tion And ev-er-last-ing love; Then

wor-ship Thee; we bless Thee; To Thee a-lone we sing; We
wor-ship Thee; we bless Thee; To Thee a-lone we sing; We
wor-ship Thee; we bless Thee; To Thee a-lone we sing; We
shall we praise and bless Thee Where per-fect prais-es ring, And

praise Thee and con-fess Thee, Our ho-ly Lord and King.
praise Thee and con-fess Thee, Our gra-cious Lord and King.
praise Thee and con-fess Thee, Our glo-rious Lord and King.
ev-er-more con-fess Thee, Our Sav-ior and our King!

O SAVING VICTIM
(O Salutáris)

words by
Thomas Aquinas (1227-1275)
tr. by Edward Caswall (1814-1878)

HERR JESU CHRIST, DICH ZU UNS WEND
music from
Cantionale Germanicum, 1628

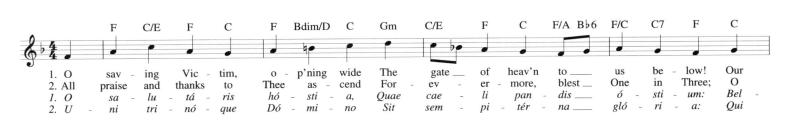

1. O sav-ing Vic-tim, o-p'ning wide The gate of heav'n to us be-low! Our
2. All praise and thanks to Thee as-cend For ev-er-more, blest One in Three; O
1. O sa-lu-tá-ris hó-sti-a, Quae cae-li pan-dis ó-sti-um: Bel
2. U-ni tri-nó-que Dó-mi-no Sit sem-pi-tér-na gló-ri-a: Qui

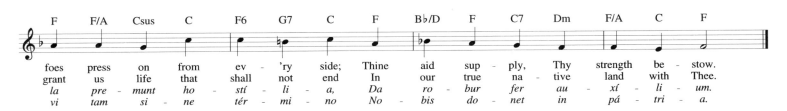

foes press on from ev-'ry side; Thine aid sup-ply, Thy strength be-stow.
grant us life that shall not end In our true na-tive land with Thee.
la pre-munt ho-stí-li-a, Da ro-bur fer au-xí-li-um.
vi-tam si-ne tér-mi-no No-bis do-net in pá-tri-a.

O SOMETIMES THE SHADOWS ARE DEEP

words by
Erastus Johnson (1826-1909)

THE ROCK OF REFUGE
music by
William G. Fischer (1835-1912)

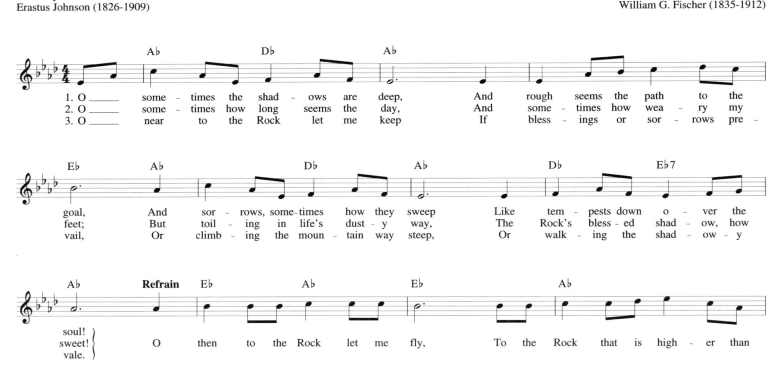

1. O some-times the shad-ows are deep, And rough seems the path to the
2. O some-times how long seems the day, And some-times how wea-ry my
3. O near to the Rock let me keep If bless-ings or sor-rows pre-

goal, And sor-rows, some-times how they sweep Like tem-pests down o-ver the
feet; But toil-ing in life's dust-y way, The Rock's bless-ed shad-ow, how
vail, Or climb-ing the moun-tain way steep, Or walk-ing the shad-ow-y

Refrain

soul!
sweet! } O then to the Rock let me fly, To the Rock that is high-er than
vale.

I; O then to the Rock let me fly, To the Rock that is high-er than I!

O SONS AND DAUGHTERS, LET US SING!

O FILII ET FILIAE
15th century French carol

words attr. to
Jean Tisserand, d. 1494
tr. by John M. Neale (1818-1866)

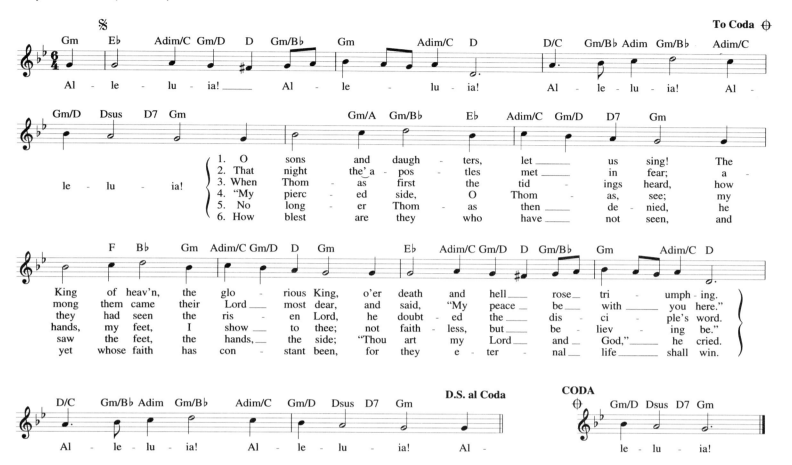

1. O sons and daugh - ters, let us sing! The King of heav'n, the glo - rious King, o'er death and hell rose tri - umph - ing.
2. That night the' a - pos - tles met in fear; The a - mong them came their Lord most dear, and said, "My peace be with you here."
3. When Thom - as first the tid - ings heard, how they had seen the ris - en Lord, he doubt - ed the dis - ci - ple's word.
4. "My pierc - ed side, O Thom - as, see; my hands, my feet, I show to thee; not faith - less, but be - liev - ing be."
5. No long - er Thom - as then de - nied, he saw the feet, the hands, the side; "Thou art my Lord and God," he cried.
6. How blest are they who have not seen, and yet whose faith has con - stant been, for they e - ter - nal life shall win.

Al - le - lu - ia! Al - le - lu - ia! Al - le - lu - ia! Al - le - lu - ia!

D.S. al Coda

Al - le - lu - ia! Al - le - lu - ia! Al -

CODA

le - lu - ia!

O SPIRIT OF THE LIVING GOD

MELCOMBE
music by
Samuel Webbe, 1782

words by
James Montgomery, 1823

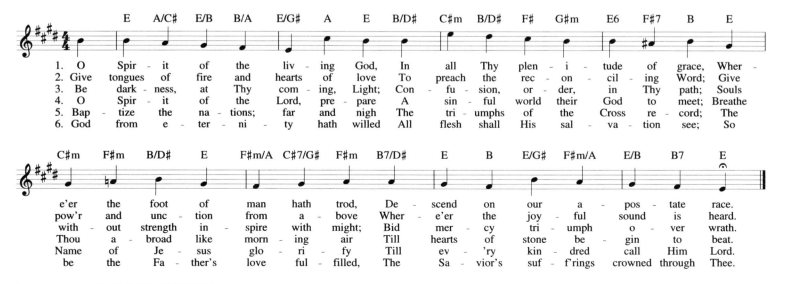

1. O Spir - it of the liv - ing God, In all Thy plen - i - tude of grace, Wher - e'er the foot of man hath trod, De - scend on our a - pos - tate race.
2. Give tongues of fire and hearts of love To preach the rec - on - cil - ing Word; Give pow'r and unc - tion from a - bove, Wher - e'er the joy - ful sound is heard.
3. Be dark - ness, at Thy com - ing, Light; Con - fu - sion, or - der, in Thy path; Souls with - out strength in - spire with might; Bid mer - cy tri - umph o - ver wrath.
4. O Spir - it of the Lord, pre - pare A sin - ful world their God to meet; Breathe Thou a - broad like morn - ing air, Till hearts of stone be - gin to beat.
5. Bap - tize the na - tions; far and nigh The tri - umphs of the Cross re - cord; The Name of Je - sus glo - ri - fy, Till ev - 'ry kin - dred call Him Lord.
6. God from e - ter - ni - ty hath willed All flesh shall His sal - va - tion see; So be the Fa - ther's love ful - filled, The Sa - vior's suf - f'rings crowned through Thee.

O SPIRIT OF THE LIVING GOD

WINCHESTER NEW
music from
Musikalisch Hand-Buch, Hamburg, 1690

words by
James Montgomery, 1823

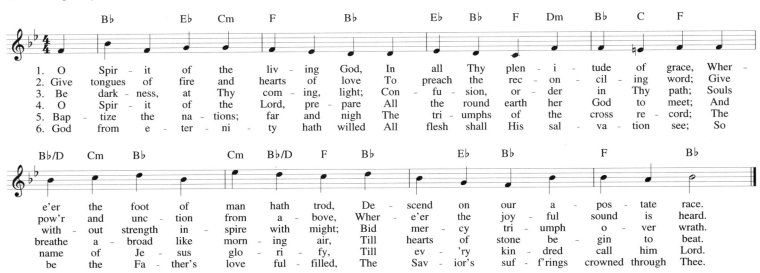

1. O Spir - it of the liv - ing God, In all Thy plen - i - tude of grace, Wher
2. Give tongues of fire and hearts of love To preach the rec - on - cil - ing word; Give
3. Be dark - ness, at Thy com - ing, light; Con - fu - sion, or - der in Thy path; Souls
4. O Spir - it of the Lord, pre - pare All the round earth her God to meet; And
5. Bap - tize the na - tions; far and nigh The tri - umphs of the cross re - cord; The
6. God from e - ter - ni - ty hath willed All flesh shall His sal - va - tion see; So

e'er the foot of man hath trod, De - scend on our a - pos - tate race.
pow'r and unc - tion from a - bove, Wher - e'er the joy - ful sound is heard.
with - out strength in - spire with might; Bid mer - cy tri - umph o - ver wrath.
breathe a - broad like morn - ing air, Till hearts of stone be - gin to beat.
name of Je - sus glo - ri - fy, Till ev - 'ry kin - dred call him Lord.
be the Fa - ther's love ful - filled, The Sav - ior's suf - f'rings crowned through Thee.

O THAT I HAD A THOUSAND VOICES

O DASS ICH TAUSEND ZUNGEN HÄTTE
music by
Cornelius H. Dretzel (1697-1775)

words by
Johann Mentzer (1658-1734)
tr. from *Evangelical Lutheran Hymn-Book,* 1919

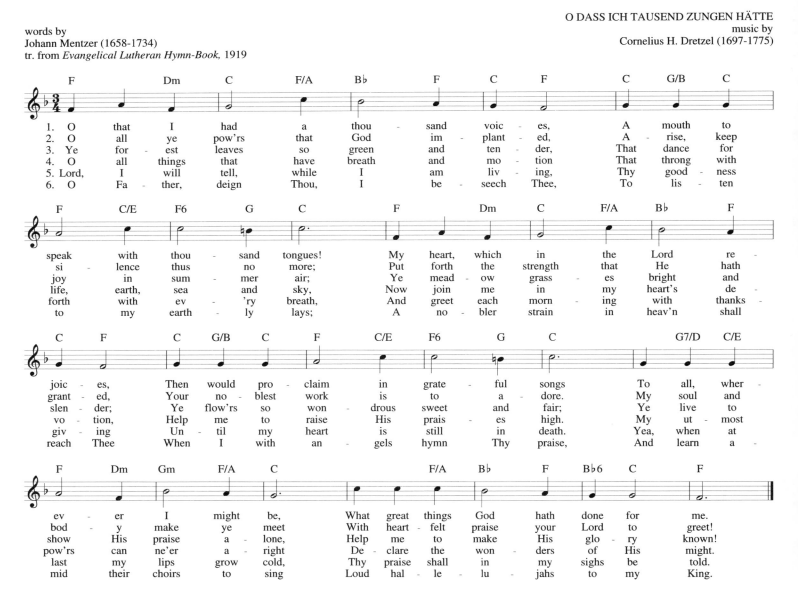

1. O that I had a thou - sand voic - es, A mouth to
2. O all ye pow'rs that God im - plant - ed, A - rise, keep
3. Ye for - est leaves so green and ten - der, That dance for
4. O all things that have breath and mo - tion, That throng with
5. Lord, I will tell, while I am liv - ing, Thy good - ness
6. O Fa - ther, deign Thou, I be - seech Thee, To lis - ten

speak with thou - sand tongues! My heart, which in the Lord re
si - lence thus no more; Put forth the strength that He hath
joy in sum - mer air; Ye mead - ow grass - es bright and
life, earth, sea and sky, Now join me in my heart's de
forth with ev - 'ry breath, And greet each morn - ing with thanks
to my earth - ly lays; A no - bler strain in heav'n shall

joic - es, Then would pro - claim in grate - ful songs To all, wher
grant - ed, Your no - blest work is to a - dore. My soul and
slen - der, Ye flow'rs so won - drous sweet and fair; Ye live to
vo - tion, Help me to raise His prais - es high. My ut - most
giv - ing, Un - til my heart is still in death. Yea, when at
reach Thee When I with an - gels hymn Thy praise, And learn a

ev - er I might be, What great things God hath done for me.
bod - y make ye meet, With heart - felt praise your Lord to greet!
show His praise a - lone, Ye live to make His glo - ry known!
pow'rs can ne'er a - right, De - clare the won - ders of His might.
last my lips grow cold, Thy praise shall in my sighs be told.
mid their choirs to sing Loud hal - le - lu - jahs to my King.

O SPLENDOR OF GOD'S GLORY BRIGHT

words by
Ambrose of Milan, 4th century
tr. by Robert S. Bridges, 1899

WAREHAM
music by
William Knapp, 1738

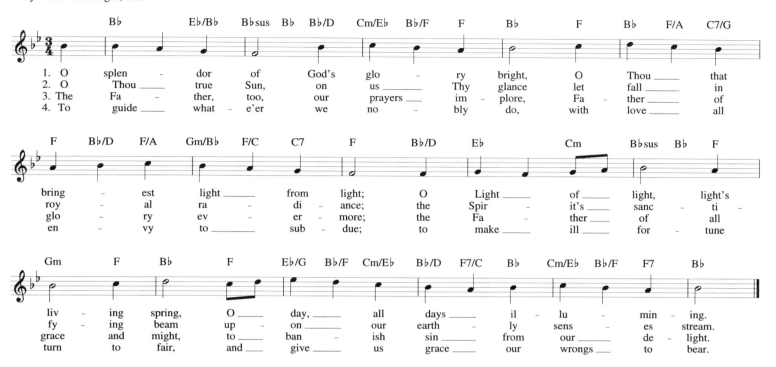

1. O splen - dor of God's glo - ry bright, O Thou that
2. O Thou true of Sun, on us Thy glance let fall in
3. The Fa - ther, too, on our prayers im - plore, Fa - ther of
4. To guide what - e'er we no - bly do, with love all

bring - est light from light; O Light of light, light's
roy - al ra - di - ance; the Spir - it's sanc - ti -
glo - ry ev - er - more; the Fa - ther of all
en - vy to sub - due; to make ill for - tune

liv - ing spring, O day, all days il - lu - min - ing.
fy - ing beam up - on our earth - ly sens - es stream.
grace and might, to ban - ish sin from our de - light.
turn to fair, and give us grace our wrongs to bear.

O THAT I HAD A THOUSAND VOICES

O DASS ICH TAUSEND ZUNGEN HÄTTE
music by
J.B. König (1691-1758)

words by
Johann Mentzer (1658-1734)
tr. from *Evangelical Lutheran Hymn-Book,* 1919

1. O that I had a thou - sand voic - es, A mouth to speak with thou - sand tongues!
2. O all ye pow'rs that God im - plant - ed, A - rise, keep si - lence thus no more;
3. Ye for - est leaves so green and ten - der, That dance for joy in sum - mer air;
4. O all things that have breath and mo - tion, That throng with life, earth, sea and sky,
5. Lord, I will tell, while I am liv - ing, Thy good - ness forth with ev - 'ry breath,
6. O Fa - ther, deign Thou, I be - seech Thee, To lis - ten to my earth - ly lays;

My heart, which in the Lord re - joic - es, Then would pro - claim in grate - ful songs
Put forth the strength that He hath grant - ed, Your no - blest work is to a - dore.
Ye mead - ow grass - es bright and slen - der; Ye flow'rs so won - drous sweet and fair;
Now join me in my heart's de - vo - tion, Help me to raise His prais - es high.
And greet each morn - ing with thanks - giv - ing Un - til my heart is still in death.
A no - bler strain in heav'n shall reach Thee When I with an - gels hymn Thy praise,

To all, wher - ev - er I might be, What great things God hath done for me.
My soul and bod - y make ye meet With heart - felt praise your Lord to greet!
Ye live to show His praise a - lone, Help me to make His glo - ry known!
My ut - most pow'rs can ne'er a - right De - clare the won - ders of His might.
Yea, when at last my lips grow cold, Thy praise shall in my sighs be told.
And learn a - mid their choirs to sing Loud hal - le - lu - jahs to my King.

O THAT THE LORD WOULD GUIDE MY WAYS

EVAN

words by
Isaac Watts (1674-1748)

music by
W.H. Havergal (1793-1870)

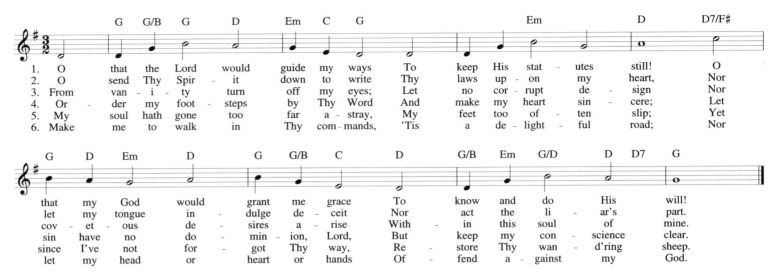

O THE DEEP, DEEP LOVE OF JESUS

BUNESSAN
Traditional Gaelic melody

words by
Samuel Trevor Francis, c. 1890

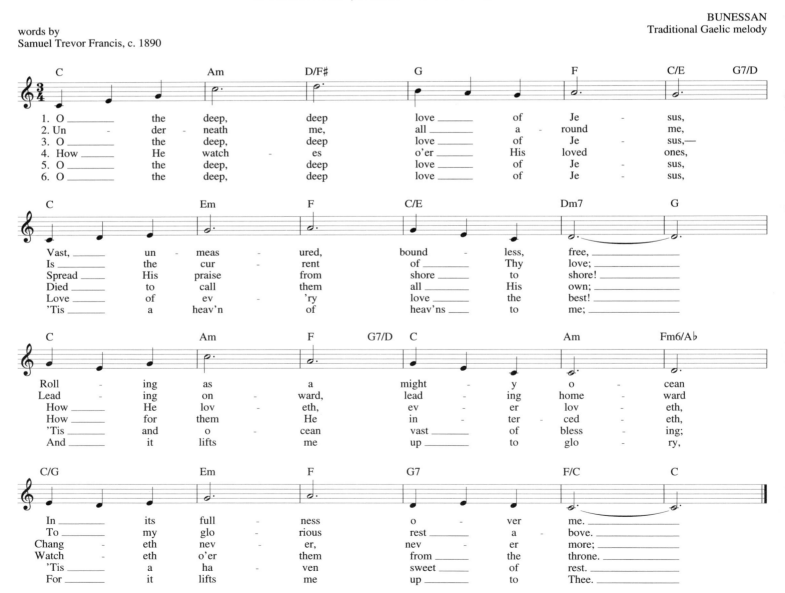

O THAT WILL BE GLORY

words by
Charles H. Gabriel, 1900

GLORY SONG
music by
Charles H. Gabriel, 1900

O THOU IN WHOSE PRESENCE

words by
Joseph Swain, 1791 (v.1-4)
Author for v.5 unknown

DAVIS
music from
Wyeth's *Repository of Sacred Music, Part Second,* 1813
attr. to Freeman Lewis, 1813

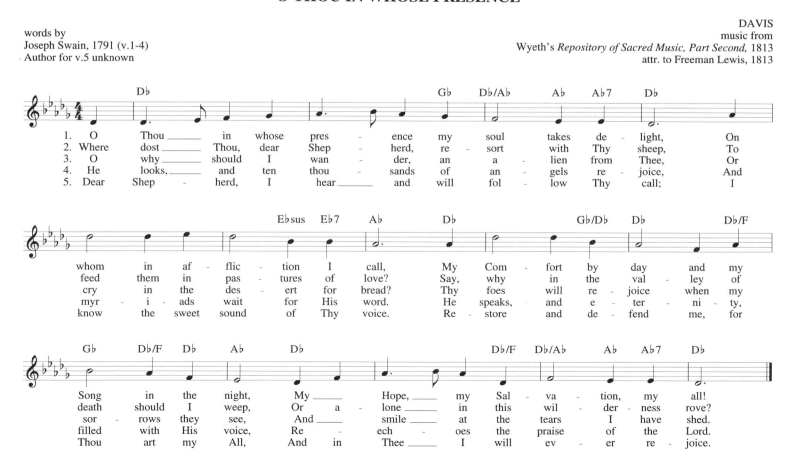

O THOU MY SOUL, BLESS GOD THE LORD

HOWARD
music by
Elizabeth H. Cuthbert, c. 1810

words from
Scottish Psalter, 1650
based on Psalm 103

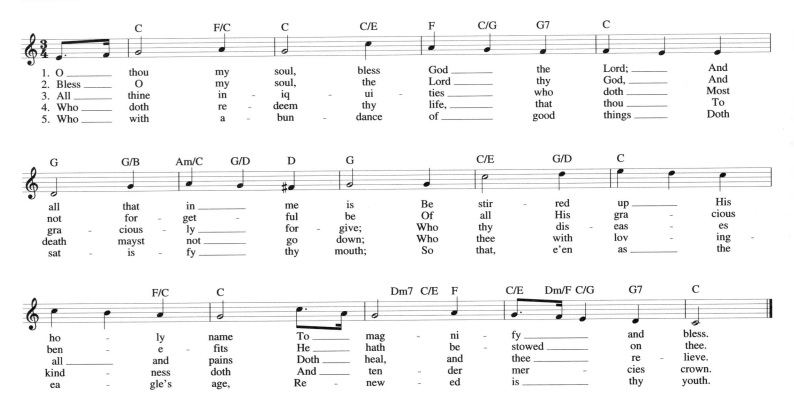

O THE DEEP, DEEP LOVE OF JESUS

EBENEZER
music by
Thomas J. Williams, 1890

words by
Samuel Trevor Francis, c. 1890

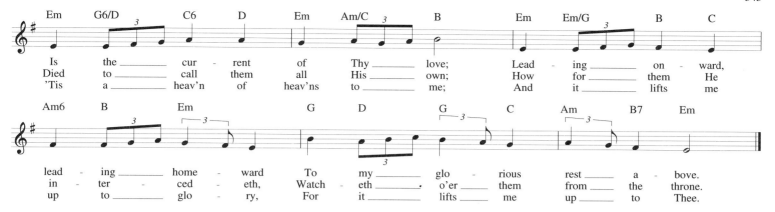

O THOU WHO CAMEST FROM ABOVE

words by
Charles Wesley, 1762

HEREFORD
music by
Samuel Sebastian Wesley, 1872

O VERY GOD OF VERY GOD

words by
John Mason Neale (1818-1866)

BANGOR
music from
A Compleat Melody or Harmony of Zion, 1734

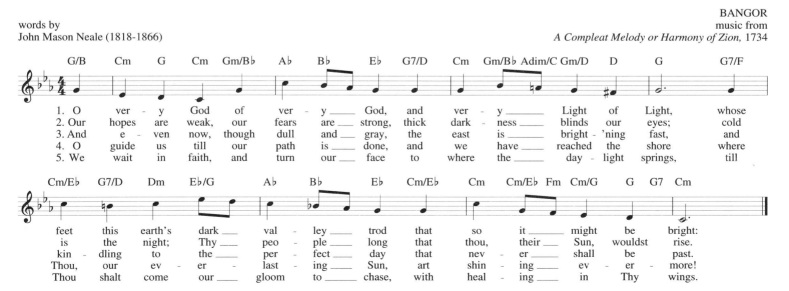

O TO BE LIKE THEE!

words by
Thomas O. Chisholm, 1897

RONDINELLA
music by
William J. Kirkpatrick, 1897

O TRINITY OF BLESSED LIGHT

Latin text, 6th century
v. 1, 2 tr. by John Mason Neale (1818-1866)
v. 3 by Charles Coffin (1676-1749)
tr. by John Chandler (1806-1876)

BROMLEY
music by
Franz Joseph Haydn (1732-1809)

O WHAT THEIR JOY AND THEIR GLORY MUST BE

words by
Peter Abelard, 12th century
tr. by John Mason Neale, 1851

O QUANTA QUALIA
music from
Paris Antiphoner, 1681

1. O what their joy and their glo - ry must be, _____ those end - less
2. Tru - ly, "Je - ru - sa - lem" name we that shore, _____ cit - y of
3. There, where no trou - bles dis - trac - tion can bring, _____ we the sweet
4. Now, in the mean - while, with hearts raised on high, _____ we for that
5. Low be - fore Him with our prais - es we fall, _____ of whom, and

sab - baths the bless - ed ones see; _____ crown for the val - iant, to
peace that brings joy ev - er - more; _____ wish and ful - fill - ment are
an - thems of Zi - on shall sing; _____ while for Thy grace, Lord, their
coun - try must yearn and must sigh; _____ seek - ing Je - ru - sa - lem,
in whom, and through whom are all; _____ of whom, the Fa - ther; and

wea - ry ones rest; _____ God shall be all, and in all ev - er blest.
not sev - ered there, _____ nor do things prayed for come short of the prayer.
voic - es of praise _____ Thy bless - ed peo - ple e - ter - nal - ly raise.
dear na - tive land, _____ through our long ex - ile on Bab - y - lon's strand.
in whom, the Son, _____ through whom, the Spir - it, with them ev - er One.

O WONDROUS SIGHT! O VISION FAIR

words from
Sarum Breviary, 1495
tr. by John Mason Neale, 1851

WAREHAM
music by
William Knapp, 1738

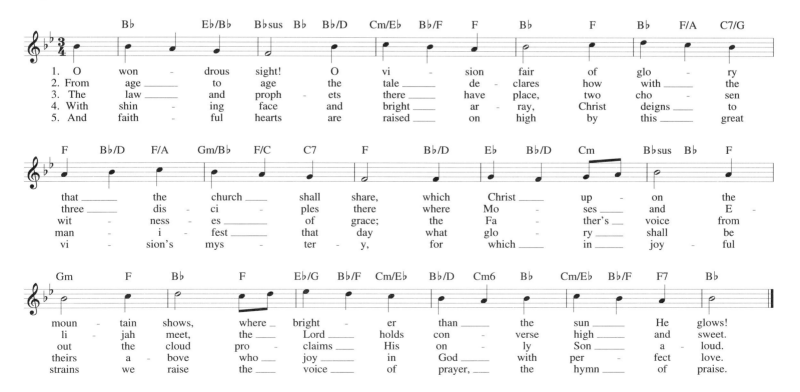

1. O won - drous sight! O vi - sion fair of glo - ry
2. From age to age the tale de - clares how with the
3. The law and proph - ets there have place, two cho - sen
4. With shin - ing face and bright ar - ray, Christ deigns to
5. And faith - ful hearts are raised on high by this great

that the church shall share, which Christ up - on the
three dis - ci - ples there where Mo - ses and E -
wit - ness - es of grace; the Fa - ther's voice from
man - i - fest that day what glo - ry shall be
vi - sion's mys - ter - y, for which in joy - ful

moun - tain shows, where bright - er than the sun He glows!
li - jah meet, the Lord holds con - verse high and sweet.
out the cloud pro - claims His on - ly Son a - loud.
theirs a - bove who joy in God with per - fect love.
strains we raise the voice of prayer, the hymn of praise.

O WORD OF GOD INCARNATE

words by
William W. How (1823-1897)

MUNICH
music from
Neuver mehrtes Gesangbuch, Meiningen, 1693
arr. by Felix Mendelssohn (1809-1847)

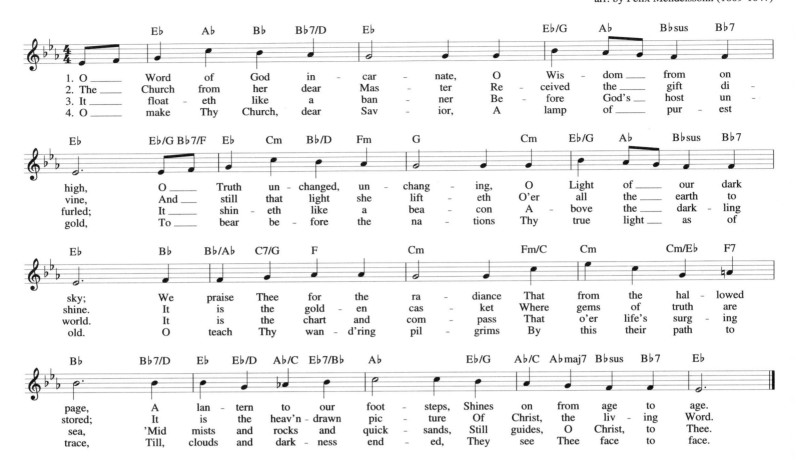

1. O _____ Word of God in - car - nate, O Wis - dom _____ from on
2. The _____ Church from her dear Mas - ter Re - ceived the _____ gift di -
3. It _____ float - eth like a ban - ner Be - fore God's _____ host un -
4. O _____ make Thy Church, dear Sav - ior, A lamp of _____ pur - est

high, O _____ Truth un - changed, un - chang - ing, O Light of _____ our dark
vine, And _____ still that light she lift - eth O'er all the _____ earth to
furled; It _____ shin - eth like a bea - con A - bove the _____ dark - ling
gold, To _____ bear be - fore the na - tions Thy true light _____ as of

sky; We praise Thee for the ra - diance That from the hal - lowed
shine. It is the gold - en cas - ket Where gems of truth are
world. It is the chart and com - pass That o'er life's surg - ing
old. O teach Thy wan - d'ring pil - grims By this their path to

page, A lan - tern to our foot - steps, Shines on from age to age.
stored; It is the heav'n - drawn pic - ture Of Christ, the liv - ing Word.
sea, 'Mid mists and rocks and quick - sands, Still guides, O Christ, to Thee.
trace, Till, clouds and dark - ness end - ed, They see Thee face to face.

O WORSHIP THE KING

words by
Robert Grant (1779-1838)

HANOVER
music by
William Croft (1678-1727)

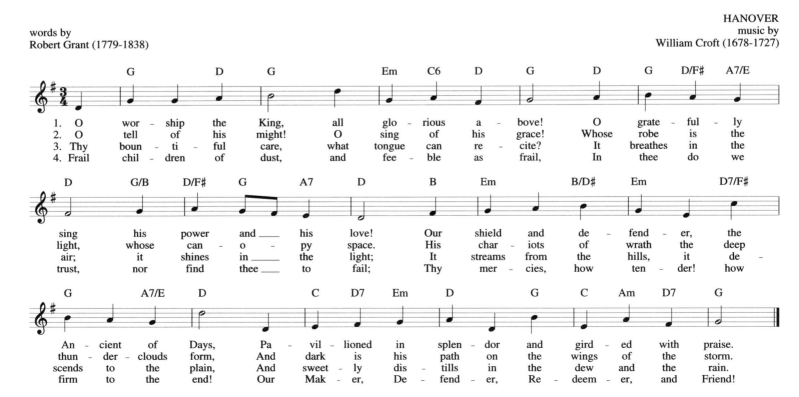

1. O wor - ship the King, all glo - rious a - bove! O grate - ful - ly
2. O tell of his might! O sing of his grace! Whose robe is the
3. Thy boun - ti - ful care, what tongue can re - cite? It breathes in the
4. Frail chil - dren of dust, and fee - ble as frail, In thee do we

sing his power and _____ his love! Our shield and de - fend - er, the
light, whose can - o - py space. His char - iots of wrath the deep
air; it shines in _____ the light; It streams from the hills, it de -
trust, nor find thee _____ to fail; Thy mer - cies, how ten - der! how

An - cient of Days, Pa - vil - lioned in splen - dor and gird - ed with praise.
thun - der - clouds form, And dark is his path on the wings of the storm.
scends to the plain, And sweet - ly dis - tills in the dew and the rain.
firm to the end! Our Mak - er, De - fend - er, Re - deem - er, and Friend!

O WORSHIP THE KING

words by
Robert Grant, 1833

LYONS
music attr. to
Johann Michael Haydn (1737-1806)
arr. by William Gardiner, 1815

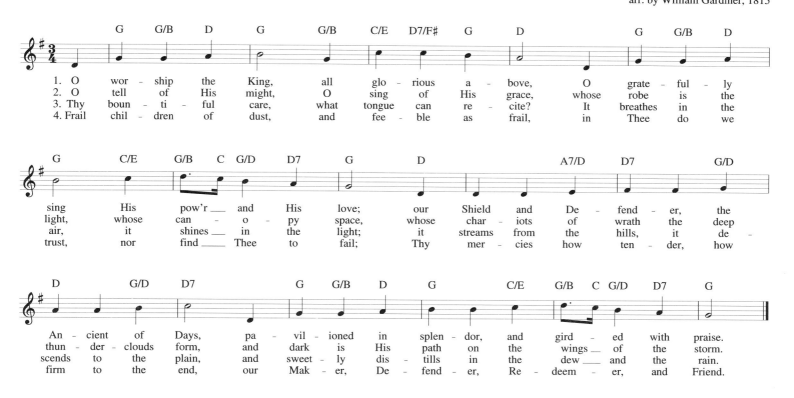

1. O wor - ship the King, all glo - rious a - bove, O grate - ful - ly
2. O tell of His might, O sing of His grace, whose robe is the
3. Thy boun - ti - ful care, what tongue can re - cite? It breathes in the
4. Frail chil - dren of dust, and fee - ble as frail, in Thee do we

sing His pow'r ___ and His love; our Shield and De - fend - er, the
light, whose can - o - py space, whose char - iots of wrath the deep
air, it shines ___ in the light; it streams from the hills, it de -
trust, nor find ___ Thee to fail; Thy mer - cies how ten - der, how

An - cient of Days, pa - vil - ioned in splen - dor, and gird - ed with praise.
thun - der - clouds form, and dark is His path on the wings ___ of the storm.
scends to the plain, and sweet - ly dis - tills in the dew ___ and the rain.
firm to the end, our Mak - er, De - fend - er, Re - deem - er, and Friend.

Copyright © 2000 by HAL LEONARD CORPORATION

O ZION, HASTE

words by
Mary Ann Thomson (1834-1923)

TIDINGS
music by
James Walch (1837-1901)

1. O Zi - on, haste, thy mis - sion high ful - fill - ing, To tell to all the
2. Pro - claim to ev - 'ry peo - ple, tongue, and na - tion That God, in whom they
3. Give of thy sons to bear the mes - sage glo - rious, Give of thy wealth to
4. He comes a - gain! O Zi - on, ere thou meet him, Make known to ev - 'ry

world that God is light; That he who made all na - tions is not will - ing
live and move, is love; Tell how he stooped to save his lost cre - a - tion
speed them on their way, Pour out thy soul for them in prayer vic - to - rious,
heart his sav - ing grace; Let none whom he hath ran - somed fail to greet him,

Refrain

One soul should per - ish, lost in shades of night.
And died on earth that man might live a - bove.
And all thou spend - est Je - sus will re - pay.
Through thy ne - glect, un - fit to see his face.

Pub - lish glad tid - ings,

tid - ings of peace, Tid - ings of Je - sus, re - demp - tion, and re - lease.

Copyright © 2000 by HAL LEONARD CORPORATION

OF THE FATHER'S LOVE BEGOTTEN

DIVINUM MYSTERIUM
13th Century Plainsong
arr. by C. Winfred Douglas, 1916

words by
Aurelius C. Prudentius, 4th Century
tr. by John M. Neale and Henry W. Baker

1. Of the Fa-ther's love be-got-ten, Ere the worlds be-gan to be,
2. O ye heights of heav'n, a-dore Him; An-gel hosts, His prais-es sing;
3. Christ, to Thee with God the Fa-ther, And, O Ho-ly Ghost, to Thee,

He is Al-pha and O-me-ga, He the Source, the End-ing He
Pow'rs, do-min-ions, bow be-fore Him And ex-tol our God and King;
Hymn and chant and high thanks-giv-ing, And un-wear-ied prais-es be:

Of the things that are, that have been, And that fu-ture years shall see,
Let no tongue on earth be si-lent; Ev-ery voice in con-cert ring,
Hon-or, glo-ry, and do-min-ion And e-ter-nal vic-to-ry,

Ev-er-more and ev-er-more.
Ev-er-more and ev-er-more.
Ev-er-more and ev-er-more. A-men.

THE OLD RUGGED CROSS

OLD RUGGED CROSS
music by
Rev. George Bennard, 1913

words by
Rev. George Bennard, 1913

1. On a hill far a-way stood an old rug-ged cross, The em-blem of suf-f'ring and
2. O that old rug-ged cross, so de-spised by the world, Has a won-drous at-trac-tion for
3. In the old rug-ged cross, stained with blood so di-vine, A won-drous beau-ty I
4. To the old rug-ged cross I will ev-er be true, Its shame and re-proach glad-ly

shame. And I love that old cross, where the dear-est and best For a
me. For the dear Lamb of God left His glo-ry a-bove To
see. For 'twas on that old cross Je-sus suf-fered and died To
bear. Then He'll call me some-day to my home far a-way, Where His

world of lost sin-ners was slain. So I'll cher-ish the old rug-ged
bear it to dark Cal-va-ry.
par-don and sanc-ti-fy me.
glo-ry for-ev-er I'll share.

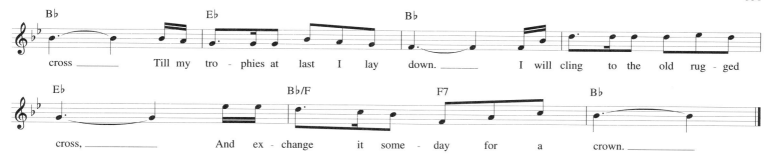

cross _____ Till my tro - phies at last I lay down. _____ I will cling to the old rug - ged

cross, _____ And ex - change it some - day for a crown. _____

ON JORDAN'S BANK THE BAPTIST'S CRY

words by
Charles Coffin, 1736
tr. by John Chandler, 1837

WINCHESTER NEW
music from
Musikalisches Handbuch, 1690

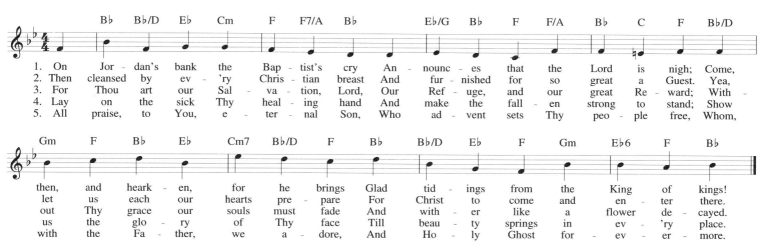

1. On Jor - dan's bank the Bap - tist's cry An - nounc - es that the Lord is nigh; Come,
2. Then cleansed by ev - 'ry Chris - tian breast And fur - nished for so great a Guest. Yea,
3. For Thou art our Sal - va - tion, Lord, Our Ref - uge, and our great Re - ward; With -
4. Lay on the sick Thy heal - ing hand And make the fall - en strong to stand; Show
5. All praise, to You, e - ter - nal Son, Who ad - vent sets Thy peo - ple free, Whom,

then, and heark - en, for he brings Glad tid - ings from the King of kings!
let us each our hearts pre - pare For Christ to come and en - ter there.
out us Thy grace the glo - ry of Thy souls must fade And with - er like a flower de - cayed.
us the glo - ry of Thy face Till beau - ty springs in ev - 'ry place.
with the Fa - ther, we a - dore, And Ho - ly Ghost for - ev - er - more.

ON JORDAN'S STORMY BANKS

words by
Samuel Stennett (1727-1795)

PROMISED LAND
Traditional American melody
arr. by Rigdon M. McIntosh (1836-1899)

1. On _____ Jor - dan's storm - y banks I stand _____ And cast a wish - ful eye To _____
2. All _____ o'er those wide ex - tend - ed plains Shines one e - ter - nal day; There _____
3. No _____ chill - ing winds _____ nor poi - s'nous breath _____ Can reach that health - ful shore; Sick -
4. When _____ shall I reach _____ that hap - py place _____ And be for - ev - er blest? When _____

Ca - naan's _____ fair and hap - py land, Where _____ my pos - ses - sions lie.
God the _____ Son for - ev - er reigns And _____ scat - ters _____ night a - way.
ness and _____ sor - row, pain and death Are _____ felt and _____ feared no more.
shall I _____ see my Fa - ther's face And _____ in His _____ bos - om rest?

I am

bound for the Prom - ised Land, _____ I am bound for the Prom - ised Land. O _____

who will _____ come and go with me? I am bound for the Prom - ised Land.

ON MY HEART IMPRINT THINE IMAGE

DER AM KREUZ

words by
Thomas H. Kingo (1634-1703)
tr. by Peer O. Strömme (1856-1921)

music by
Johann B. König (1691-1758)

ON OUR WAY REJOICING

HERMAS

words by
John S.B. Monsell (1811-1875)

music by
Frances R. Havergal (1836-1879)

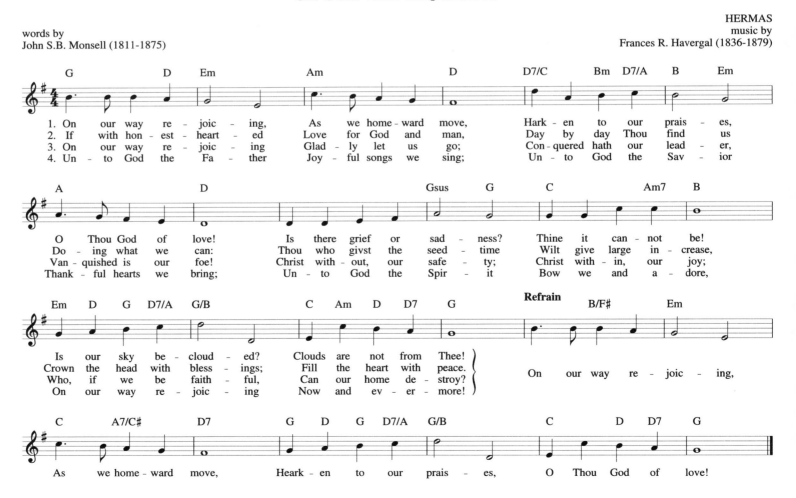

ON THIS DAY, THE FIRST OF DAYS

words from
Le Mans Breviary, 1748
tr. by Henry W. Baker, (1821-1877)

LÜBECK
music from
Freylinghausen's Gesangbuch, 1704

1. On this day, the first of days, God our Mak-er's name we praise;
2. On this day the e - ter - nal Son O - ver death His tri - umph won;
3. Word - made - flesh, all prais - es be! You from sin have set us free;
4. Ho - ly Spir - it, You im - part Gifts of love to ev - 'ry heart;
5. God, the bless - ed Three in One, May Your ho - ly will be done;

Who, cre - a - tion's Lord and Spring, Did the world from dark - ness bring.
On this day the Spir - it came With its gifts of liv - ing flame.
And with You we die and rise Un - to God in sac - ri - fice.
Give us light and grace, we pray, Fill our hearts this ho - ly day.
In Your Word our souls are free, As we praise the Trin - i - ty.

Copyright © 2000 by HAL LEONARD CORPORATION

ONCE TO EVERY MAN AND NATION

words by
James Russel Lowell, 1845

EBENEZER
music by
Thomas J. Williams, 1890

1. Once to ev - 'ry man and na - tion Comes the mo - ment
2. Then to side with truth is no - ble, When we share her
3. By the light of burn - ing mar - tyrs, Christ, Thy bleed - ing
4. Though the cause of e - vil pros - per, Yet the truth a -

to de - cide. In the strife of truth with false - hood,
wretch - ed crust. Ere her cause bring fame and prof - it,
feet we track. Toil - ing up new Cal - v'ries ev - er
lone is strong. Though her por - tion be the scaf - fold,

For the good or e - vil side. Some great cause, some
And 'tis pros - p'rous to be just. Then it is the
With the cross that turns not back. New oc - ca - sions
And up - on the throne be wrong. Yet that scaf - fold

great de - ci - sion, Of - f'ring each the bloom or blight,
brave man choos - es While the cow - ard stands a - side,
teach new du - ties; An - cient val - ues test our youth.
sways the fu - ture, And, be - hind the dim un - known,

And the choice goes by for - ev - er 'Twixt that dark - ness and that light.
Till the mul - ti - tude make vir - tue Of the faith they had de - nied.
They must up - ward still and on - ward, Who would keep a - breast of truth.
Stand - eth God with - in the shad - ow, Keep - ing watch a - bove His own.

Copyright © 2000 by HAL LEONARD CORPORATION

ONCE FOR ALL

words by
Philip P. Bliss (1838-1876)

music by
Philip P. Bliss (1838-1876)

1. Free from the law, O hap-py con-di - tion, Je-sus hath bled, and there is re-
2. Now are we free— there's no con-dem-na - tion, Je-sus pro-vides a per-fect sal-
3. "Chil-dren of God," O glo-ri-ous call - ing, Sure-ly His grace will keep us from

mis - sion; Cursed by the law and bruised by the fall, Grace hath re-deemed us once for
va - tion; "Come un-to me," O hear His sweet call, Come, and He saves us once for
fall - ing; Pass-ing from death to life at His call, Bless-ed sal-va-tion once for

all.
all. Once _ for all, O sin-ner, re-ceive it, Once _ for all, O broth-er, be-
all.

lieve it; Cling to the Cross, the bur-den will fall, Christ hath re-deemed us once for all.

ONCE HE CAME IN BLESSING

GOTTES SOHN IST KOMMEN
music attr. to
M. Weisse (c. 1480-1534)

words by
J. Horn (c. 1490-1547)
tr. by C. Winkworth (1827-1878)

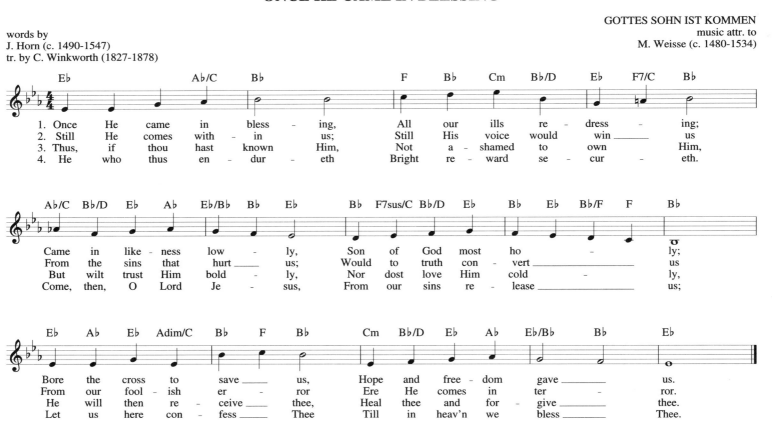

1. Once He came in bless - ing, All our ills re-dress - ing;
2. Still He comes with-in us, Still His voice would win ___ us
3. Thus, if thou hast known Him, Not a-shamed to own Him,
4. He who thus en-dur-eth Bright re-ward se-cur - eth.

Came in like-ness low - ly, Son of God most ho - ly;
From the sins that hurt ___ us; Would to truth con-vert ___ us
But wilt trust Him bold - ly, Nor dost love Him cold - ly,
Come, then, O Lord Je - sus, From our sins re-lease ___ us;

Bore the cross to save ___ us, Hope and free-dom gave ___ us.
From our fool-ish er - ror, Ere He comes in ter - ror.
He will then re-ceive ___ thee, Heal thee and for-give ___ thee.
Let us here con-fess ___ Thee Till in heav'n we bless ___ Thee.

ON WHAT HAS NOW BEEN SOWN

words by
John Newton (1725-1807)

DARWALL'S 148TH
music by
John Darwall (1731-1789)

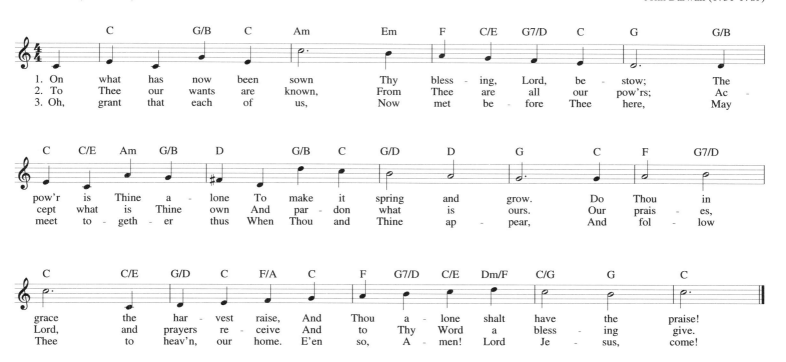

1. On what has now been sown Thy bless - ing, Lord, be - stow; The
2. To Thee our wants are known, From Thee are all our pow'rs; The Ac -
3. Oh, grant that each of us, Now met be - fore Thee here, May

pow'r is Thine a - lone To make it spring and grow. Do Thou in
cept what is Thine own And par - don what is ours. Our prais - es,
meet to - geth - er thus When Thou and Thine ap - pear, And fol - low

grace the har - vest raise, And Thou a - lone shalt have the praise!
Lord, and prayers re - ceive And Thou to Thy Word a bless - ing give.
Thee to heav'n, our home. E'en so, A - men! Lord Je - sus, come!

ONCE IN ROYAL DAVID'S CITY

words by
Cecil F. Alexander (1818-1895)

IRBY
music by
Henry J. Gauntlett (1805-1876)

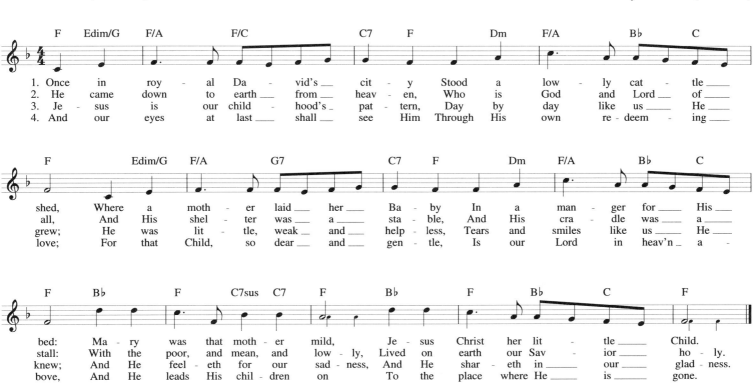

1. Once in roy - al Da - vid's cit - y Stood a low - ly cat - tle
2. He came down to earth from heav - en, Who is God and Lord of
3. Je - sus is our child - hood's pat - tern, Day by day like us He
4. And our eyes at last shall see Him Through His own re - deem - ing

shed, Where a moth - er laid her Ba - by In a man - ger for His
all, And His shel - ter was a sta - ble, And His cra - dle was a
grew; He was lit - tle, weak and help - less, Tears and smiles like us He
love; For that Child, so dear and gen - tle, Is our Lord in heav'n a -

bed: Ma - ry was that moth - er mild, Je - sus Christ her lit - tle Child.
stall: With the poor, and mean, and low - ly, Lived on earth our Sav - ior ho - ly.
knew; And He feel - eth for our sad - ness, And He shar - eth in our glad - ness.
bove, And He leads His chil - dren on To the place where He is gone.

ONE THERE IS, ABOVE ALL OTHERS

AMEN SJUNGE HVARJE TUNGA

words by
John Newton (1725-1807)

music by
Andreas P. Berggren (1801-1880)

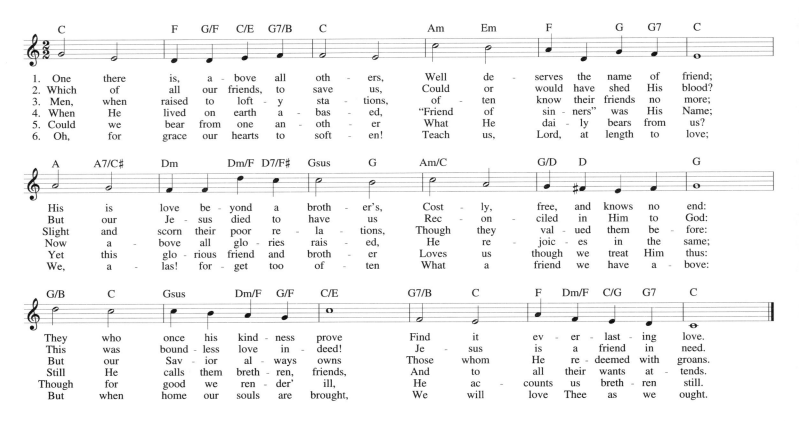

1. One there is, a - bove all oth - ers, Well de - serves the name of friend;
2. Which of all our friends, to save us, Could or would have shed His blood?
3. Men, when raised to loft - y sta - tions, of - ten know their friends no more;
4. When He lived on earth a - bas - ed, "Friend of sin - ners" was His Name;
5. Could we bear from one an - oth - er What He dai - ly bears from us?
6. Oh, for grace our hearts to soft - en! Teach us, Lord, at length to love;

His is love be - yond a broth - er's, Cost - ly, free, and knows no end:
But our Je - sus died to have us Rec - on - ciled in Him to God:
Slight and scorn their poor re - la - tions, Though they val - ued them be - fore:
Now a - bove all glo - ries rais - ed, He re - joic - es in the same;
Yet this glo - rious friend and broth - er Loves us though we treat Him thus:
We, a - las! for - get too of - ten What a friend we have a - bove:

They who once his kind - ness prove Find it ev - er - last - ing love.
This was bound - less love in - deed! Je - sus is a friend in need.
But our Sav - ior al - ways owns Those whom He re - deemed with groans.
Still He calls them breth - ren, friends, And to all their wants at - tends.
Though for good we ren - der' ill, He ac - counts us breth - ren still.
But when home our souls are brought, We will love Thee as we ought.

ONE DAY

words by
J. Wilbur Chapman, 1910

music by
Charles H. Marsh, 1910

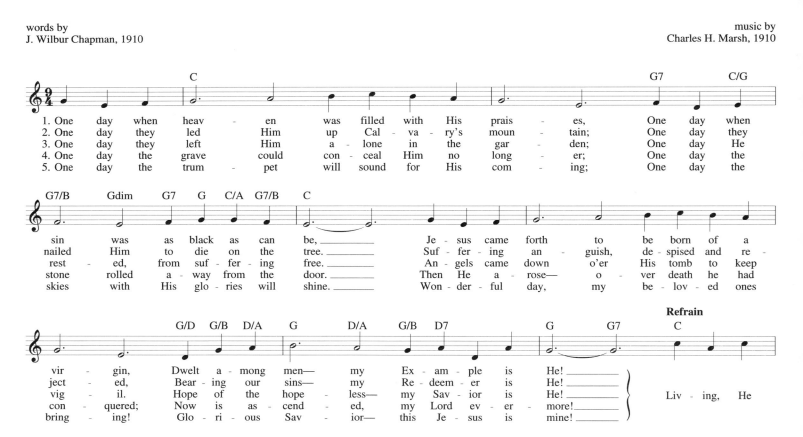

1. One day when heav - en was filled with His prais - es, One day when
2. One day they led Him up Cal - va - ry's moun - tain; One day they
3. One day they left Him a - lone in the gar - den; One day He
4. One day the grave could con - ceal Him no long - er; One day the
5. One day the trum - pet will sound for His com - ing; One day the

sin was as black as can be, _____ Je - sus came forth to be born of a
nailed Him to die on the tree. _____ Suf - fer - ing an - guish, de - spised and re -
rest - ed, from suf - fer - ing free. _____ An - gels came down o'er His tomb to keep
stone rolled a - way from the door. _____ Then He a - rose— o - ver death he had
skies with His glo - ries will shine. _____ Won - der - ful day, my be - lov - ed ones

Refrain

vir - gin, Dwelt a - mong men— my Ex - am - ple is He! _____
ject - ed, Bear - ing our sins— my Re - deem - er is He! _____
vig - il. Hope of the hope - less— my Sav - ior is He! _____
con - quered; Now is as - cend - ed, my Lord ev - er - more! _____
bring - ing! Glo - ri - ous Sav - ior— this Je - sus is mine! _____

Liv - ing, He

loved me; Dy-ing, He saved me; Bur-ied, He car-ried my sins far a-way; _____ Ris-ing, He jus-ti-fied free-ly for-ev-er; One day He's com-ing— O glo-ri-ous day! _____

ONLY A SINNER

words by
James M. Gray (1851-1935)

music by
David B. Towner (1850-1919)

1. Naught have I got-ten but what I re-ceived; Grace hath be-stowed it since I have be-lieved;
2. Once I was fool-ish, and sin ruled my heart, Caus-ing my foot-steps from God to de-part;
3. Suf-fer a sin-ner whose heart o-ver-flows, Lov-ing his Sav-ior to tell what he knows;

Boast-ing ex-clud-ed, pride I a-base; I'm on-ly a sin-ner saved by grace!
Je-sus hath found me, hap-py my case; I now am a sin-ner saved by grace!
Once more to tell it, would I em-brace– I'm on-ly a sin-ner saved by grace!

On-ly a sin-ner saved by grace! On-ly a sin-ner saved by grace!

This is my sto-ry, to God be the glo-ry, I'm on-ly a sin-ner saved by grace!

ONLY TRUST HIM

words by
John H. Stockton (1813-1877)

MINERVA
music by
John H. Stockton (1813-1877)

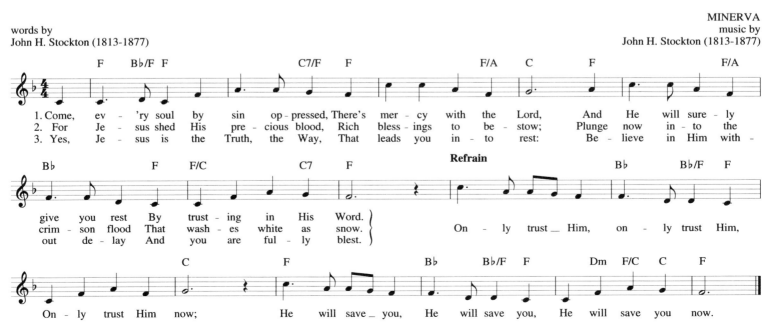

1. Come, ev-'ry soul by sin op-pressed, There's mer-cy with the Lord, And He will sure-ly
2. For Je-sus shed His pre-cious blood, Rich bless-ings to be-stow; Plunge now in-to the
3. Yes, Je-sus is the Truth, the Way, That leads you in-to rest: Be-lieve in Him with-

give you rest By trust-ing in His Word.
crim-son flood That wash-es white as snow.
out de-lay And you are ful-ly blest.

Refrain
On-ly trust _ Him, on-ly trust Him,

On-ly trust Him now; He will save _ you, He will save you, He will save you now.

ONLY A STEP TO JESUS

ONLY A STEP

words by
Fanny J. Crosby (1820-1915)

music by
William H. Doane (1832-1915)

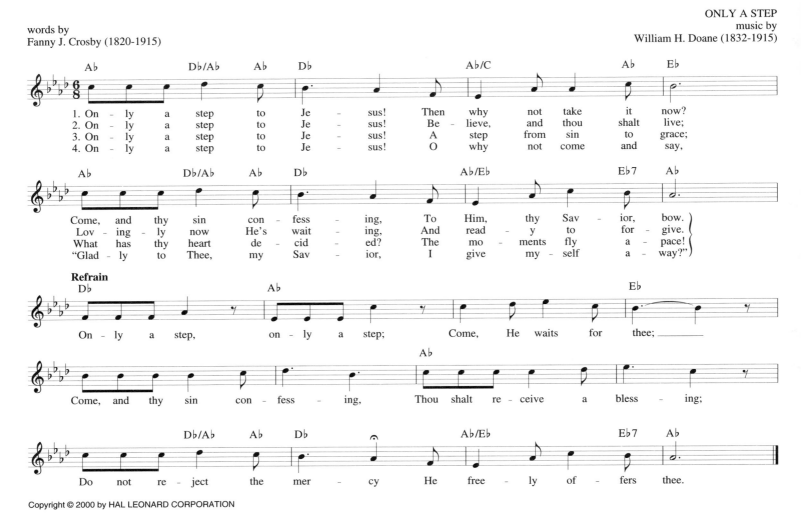

ONLY BELIEVE

words by
Paul Rader (1879-1938)

music by
Paul Rader (1879-1938)

ONLY-BEGOTTEN, WORD OF GOD ETERNAL

Latin text, c. 9th century
tr. by Maxwell Julius Blacker (1822-1888)

ROUEN
music from
Vesperale, 1746

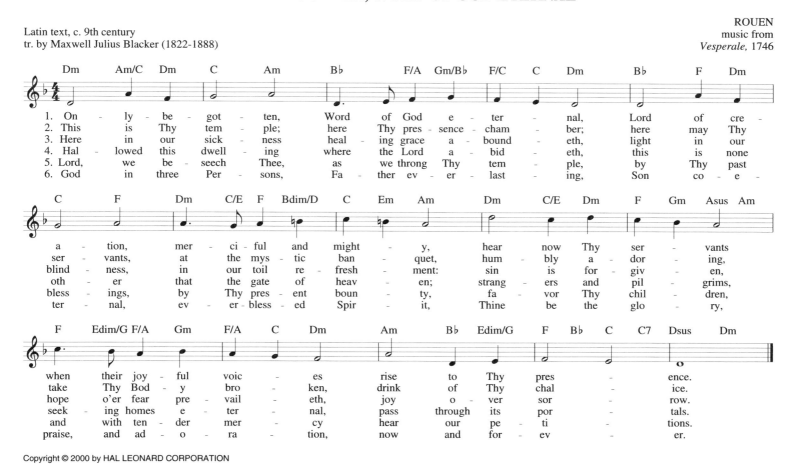

ONWARD, CHRISTIAN SOLDIERS

words by
Sabine Baring-Gould, 1864

ST. GERTRUDE
music by
Arthur S. Sullivan, 1871

OPEN MY EYES, THAT I MAY SEE

words by
Clara H. Scott, 1895

SCOTT
music by
Clara H. Scott, 1895

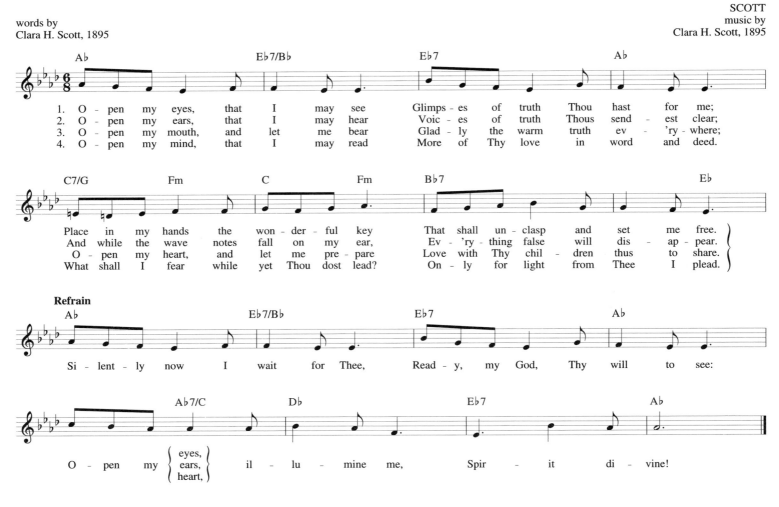

OPEN NOW THY GATES OF BEAUTY

words by
Benjamin Schmolck, 1732
tr. by Catherine Winkworth, 1863

UNSER HERRSCHER
music by
Joachim Neander, 1680

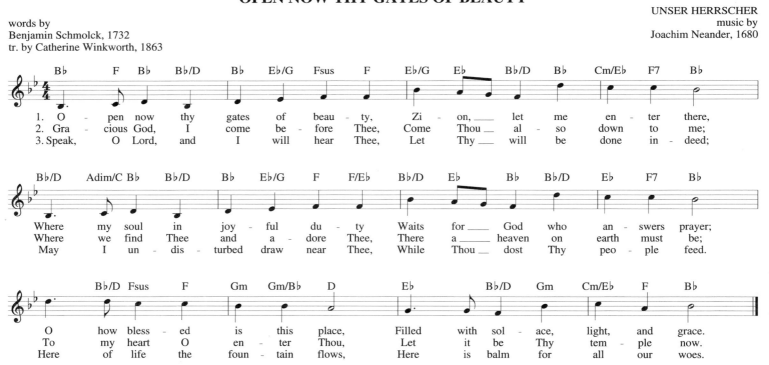

OUR FATHER, THOU IN HEAVEN ABOVE

VATER UNSER

words by
Martin Luther (1483-1546)
tr. by Catherine Winkworth (1827-1878)

music by
Martin Luther (1483-1546)

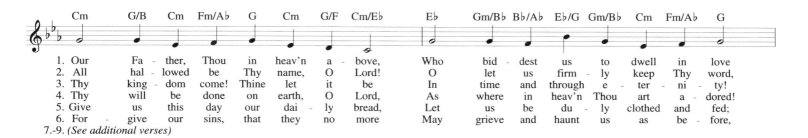

1. Our Fa - ther, Thou in heav'n a - bove, Who bid - dest us to dwell in love
2. All hal - lowed be Thy name, O Lord! O let us firm - ly keep Thy word,
3. Thy king - dom come! Thine let it be! In time and through - e - ter - ni - ty!
4. Thy will be done on earth, O Lord, As where in heav'n Thou art a - dored!
5. Give us this day our dai - ly bread, Let us be du - ly clothed and fed;
6. For - give our sins, that they no more May grieve and haunt us as be - fore,

7.-9. *(See additional verses)*

As breth - ren of one fam - i - ly And cry for all we need to Thee;
And lead, ac - cord - ing to Thy name, A ho - ly life, un - touched by blame;
O let Thy Ho - ly Spir - it dwell With us, to rule and guide us well;
Pa - tience in time of grief be - stow, O - be - dience true in weal and woe;
And keep Thou from our homes a - far Fam - ine and pes - ti - lence and war,
As we for - give their tres - pass - es Who un - to us have done a - miss;

Teach us to mean the words we say, And from the in - most heart to pray.
Let no false teach - ings do us hurt; All poor de - lud - ed souls con - vert.
From Sa - tan's might - y pow'r and rage Pre - serve Thy Church from age to age.
Our sin - ful flesh and blood con - trol That thwart Thy will with - in the soul.
That we may live in god - ly peace Un - vexed be cares and av - a - rice.
Thus let us dwell in char - i - ty And serve each oth - er will - ing - ly.

Additional Verses

7. Into temptation lead us not,
And when the foe doth war and plot
Against our souls on ev'ry hand,
Then armed with faith, O may we stand
Against him as a valiant host
Through comfort of the Holy Ghost.

8. Deliv'rance from all evil give,
For yet in evil days we live.
Redeem us from eternal death,
And, when we yield our dying breath,
Console us, grant us calm release,
And take our souls to Thee in peace.

9. Amen! That is, so let it be!
Strengthen our faith and trust in Thee
That we may doubt not, but believe
That what we ask we shall receive.
Thus in Thy name and at Thy word
We say, "Amen. Now hear us, Lord."

OUR LORD IS RISEN FROM THE DEAD

JORDAN

words by
Charles Wesley (1707-1788)

music by
Joseph Barnby (1838-1896)

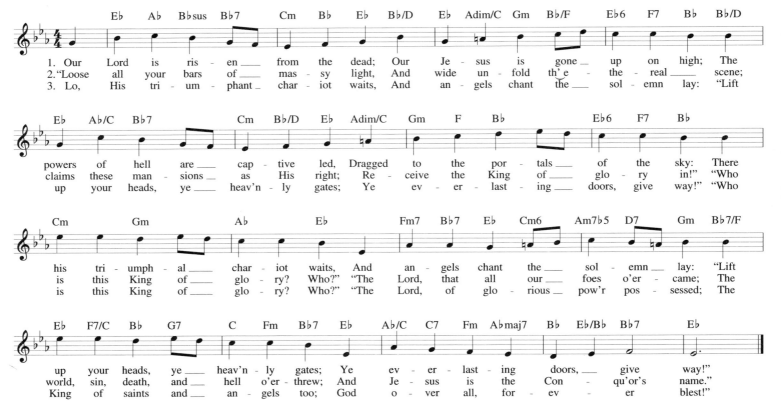

THE PALMS

words by
Charles H. Gabriel (1856-1932)

music by
J. Baptiste Faure (1830-1914)
arr. by Charles H. Gabriel (1856-1932)

PASS ME NOT, O GENTLE SAVIOR

words by
Fanny J. Crosby (1820-1915)

PASS ME NOT
music by
William H. Doane (1832-1915)

1. Pass me not, O gen-tle Sav-ior; Hear my hum-ble cry. While on oth-ers Thou art
2. Let me at the throne of mer-cy Find a sweet re-lief; Kneel-ing there in deep con-
3. Trust-ing on-ly in Thy mer-it, Would I seek Thy face. Heal my wound-ed, bro-ken
4. Thou, the Spring of all my com-fort, More than life to me, Whom have I on earth be-

call-ing, Do not pass me by.
tri-tion, Help my un-be-lief.
spir-it; Save me by Thy grace.
side Thee? Whom in heav'n but Thee?

Sav-ior, Sav-ior,

Hear my hum-ble cry. While on oth-ers Thou art call-ing, Do not pass me by.

PEACE, PERFECT PEACE

words by
Edward H. Bickersteth (1825-1906)

PAX TECUM
music by
George T. Caldbeck (1852-1918)

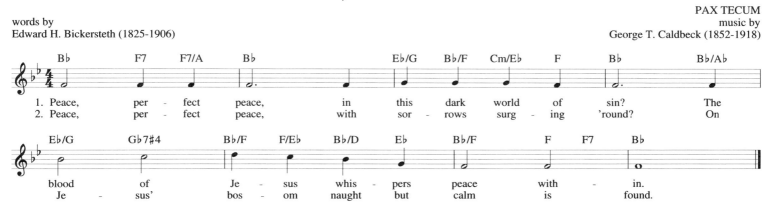

1. Peace, per-fect peace, in this dark world of sin? The
2. Peace, per-fect peace, with this sor-rows surg-ing 'round? On

blood of Je-sus whis-pers peace with-in.
Je-sus' bos-om naught but peace calm is found.

PEACE TO SOOTHE OUR BITTER WOES

words by
N.F.S. Grundtvig (1783-1872)
tr. by G.A.T. Rygh (1860-1942)

FRED TIL BOD
music by
J.P.E. Hartmann (1805-1900)

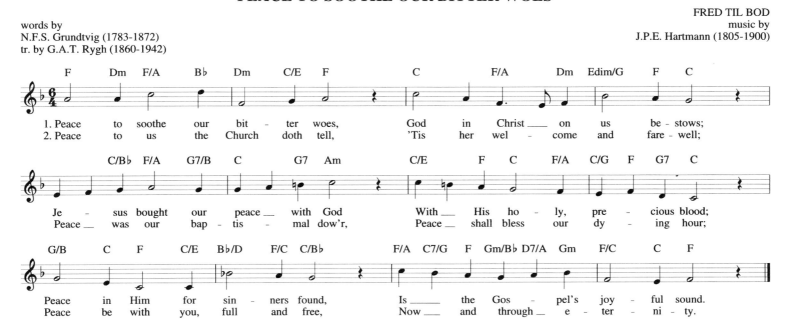

1. Peace to soothe our bit-ter woes, God in Christ___ on us be-stows;
2. Peace to us the Church doth tell, 'Tis her wel-come and fare-well;

Je-sus bought our peace___ with God With___ His ho-ly, pre-cious blood;
Peace___ was our bap-tis-mal dow'r, Peace___ shall bless our dy-ing hour;

Peace in Him for sin-ners found, Is___ the Gos-pel's joy-ful sound.
Peace be with you, full and free, Now___ and through___ e-ter-ni-ty.

PENTECOSTAL POWER

words by
Charlotte G. Homer, 1912

music by
Charles H. Gabriel, 1912

1. Lord, as of old at Pen-te-cost Thou didst Thy pow'r dis-play, With
2. For might-y works for Thee, pre-pare And strength-en ev-'ry heart. Come,
3. All self con-sume; all sin de-stroy! With ear-nest zeal en-due Each
4. Speak, Lord; be-fore Thy throne we wait. Thy prom-ise we be-lieve, And

cleans-ing, pu-ri-fy-ing flame De-scend on us to-day.
take pos-ses-sion of Thine own, And nev-er-more de-part.
wait-ing heart to work for Thee. O Lord, our faith re-new!
will not let Thee go un-til The bless-ing we re-ceive.

Lord, send the old-time pow-er, the Pen-te-cos-tal pow-er! Thy flood-gates of bless-ing on us throw o-pen wide! Lord, send the old-time pow-er, the Pen-te-cos-tal pow-er, That sin-ners be con-vert-ed and Thy name glo-ri-fied!

PRAISE GOD, FROM WHOM ALL BLESSINGS FLOW

words by
Thomas Ken, 1674

OLD HUNDREDTH
music attr. to
Louis Bourgeois, 1551

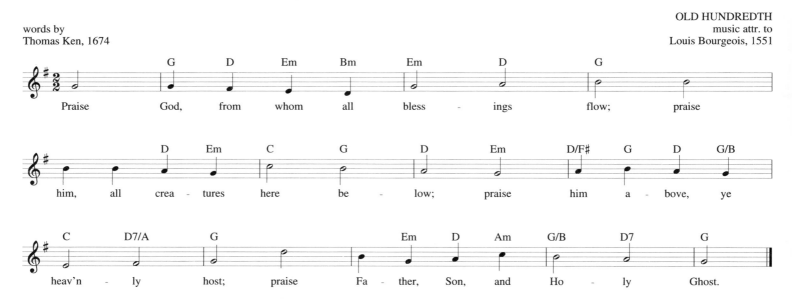

Praise God, from whom all bless-ings flow; praise him, all crea-tures here be-low; praise him a-bove, ye heav'n-ly host; praise Fa-ther, Son, and Ho-ly Ghost.

PRAISE HIM! PRAISE HIM!

JOYFUL SONG

words by
Fanny J. Crosby, 1869

music by
Chester G. Allen, 1869

PRAISE HIM, ALL YE LITTLE CHILDREN

BONNER

Author unknown

music by
Carey Bonner

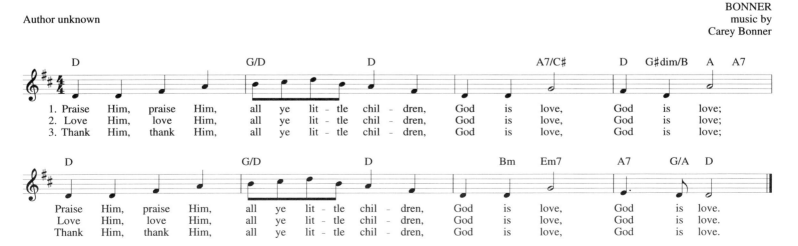

PRAISE, MY SOUL, THE KING OF HEAVEN

LAUDA ANIMA

words by
Henry F. Lyte, 1834

music by
John Goss, 1869

1. Praise, my soul, the King of heav - en, to the throne thy
2. Praise the Lord for grace and fa - vor us; to all peo - ple
3. Fa - ther - like, God tends and spares us; well our fee - ble
4. An - gels in the heights, a - dor - ing, you be - hold God

trib - ute bring; ran - somed, healed, re - stored, for - giv - en,
in dis - tress; praise God, still re - the same as ev - er,
frame God knows; moth - er - like, God gen - tly bears us,
face to face; saints tri - um - phant, now a - dor - ing,

ev - er - more God's prais - es sing. Al - le - lu - ia!
slow to chide, and swift to bless. Al - le - lu - ia!
res - cues us from all our foes. Al - le - lu - ia!
gath - ered in from ev - 'ry race. Al - le - lu - ia!

Al - le - lu - ia! Praise the ev - er - last - ing King.
Al - le - lu - ia! Glo - rious now God's faith - ful - ness.
Al - le - lu - ia! Wide - ly yet God's mer - cy flows.
Al - le - lu - ia! Praise with us the God of grace.

PRAISE THE LORD OF HEAVEN

NOUS ALLONS
Traditional French carol

words by
Thomas B. Browne (1805-1874)

1. Praise ___ the Lord of heav - en! Praise ___ Him in the height;
2. Praise ___ the Lord, you foun - tains Of ___ the deeps and seas,
3. Praise ___ Him, fowl and cat - tle, Prin - ces and all kings;

Praise ___ Him, all you an - gels; Praise ___ Him, stars and light!
Rocks ___ and hills and moun - tains, Ce - dars and all trees!
Praise ___ Him, men and wom - en, All ___ cre - a - ted things;

Praise ___ Him, clouds and wa - ters Which, ___ a - bove the skies,
Praise ___ Him, clouds and va - pors, Snow ___ and hail and fire,
For ___ the Name of God is Ex - cel - lent a - lone

When ___ His word com - mand - ed, Did ___ es - tab - lished rise!
Storm - y wind, ful - fill - ing On - ly His de - sire!
O - ver earth His foot - stool, O - ver heav'n His throne!

PRAISE THE LORD, SING HALLELUJAH

words from
The Book of Psalms, 1831
adapt. by William J. Kirkpatrick (1838-1921)

PRAISE JEHOVAH
music by
William J. Kirkpatrick (1838-1921)

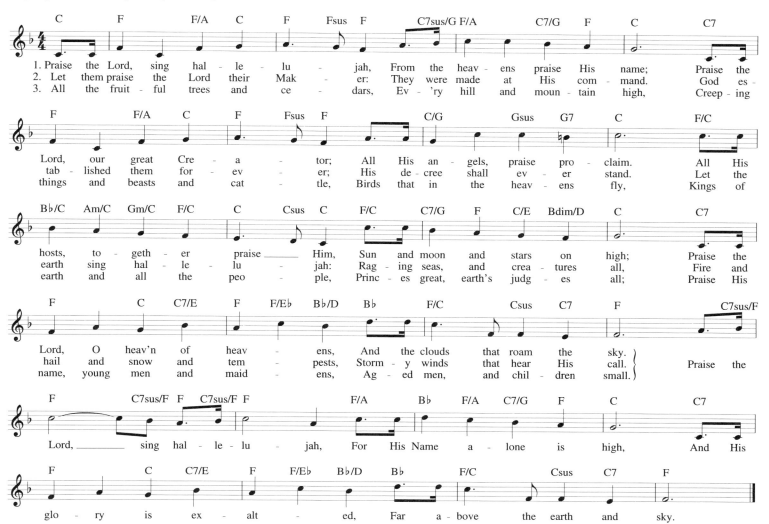

PRAISE THE LORD WHO REIGNS ABOVE

words by
Charles Wesley, 1743

AMSTERDAM
music from
Foundery Collection, 1742

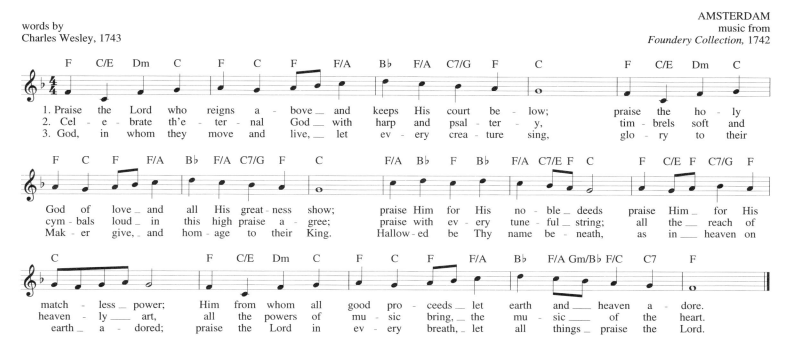

PRAISE THE LORD THROUGH EVERY NATION

WACHET AUF
music by
Hans Sachs (1494-1576)
adapt. by Philipp Nicolai (1556-1608)

words by
Rhijnvis Feith (1753-1824)

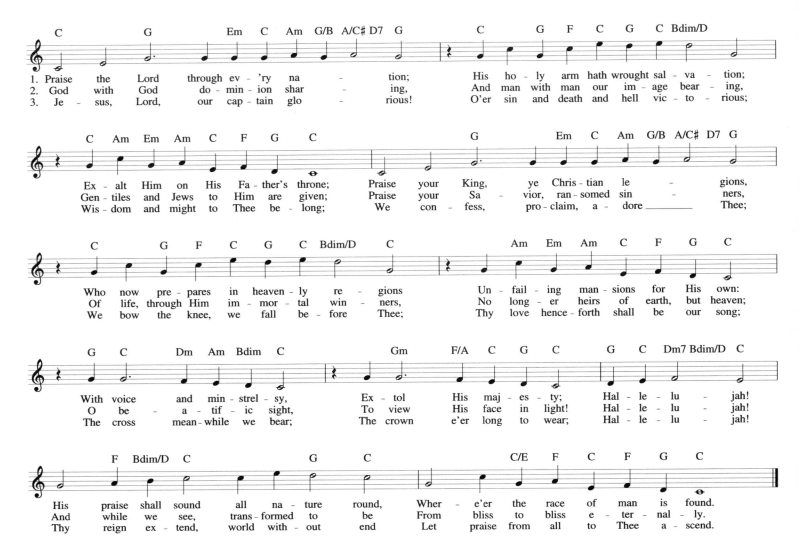

1. Praise the Lord through ev-'ry na - tion; His ho - ly arm hath wrought sal - va - tion;
2. God with God do - min - ion shar - ing, And man with man our im - age bear - ing,
3. Je - sus, Lord, our cap - tain glo - rious! O'er sin and death and hell vic - to - rious;

Ex - alt Him on His Fa - ther's throne; Praise your King, ye Chris - tian le - gions,
Gen - tiles and Jews to Him are given; Praise your Sa - vior, ran - somed sin - ners,
Wis - dom and might to Thee be - long; We con - fess, pro - claim, a - dore Thee;

Who now pre - pares in heaven - ly re - gions Un - fail - ing man - sions for His own:
Of life, through Him im - mor - tal win - ners, No long - er heirs of earth, but heaven;
We bow the knee, we fall be - fore Thee; Thy love hence - forth shall be our song;

With voice and min - strel - sy, Ex - tol His maj - es - ty; Hal - le - lu - jah!
O be - a - tif - ic sight, To view His face in light! Hal - le - lu - jah!
The cross mean - while we bear; The crown e'er long to wear; Hal - le - lu - jah!

His praise shall sound all na - ture round, Wher - e'er the race of man is found.
And while we see, trans - formed to be From bliss to bliss e - ter - nal - ly.
Thy reign ex - tend, world with - out end Let praise from all to Thee a - scend.

PRAISE THE LORD! YE HEAVENS, ADORE HIM

AUSTRIAN HYMN
music by
Franz Joseph Haydn, 1797

words from
Foundling Hospital Collection, 1796 (v. 1,2)
v. 3 by Edward Osler, 1836

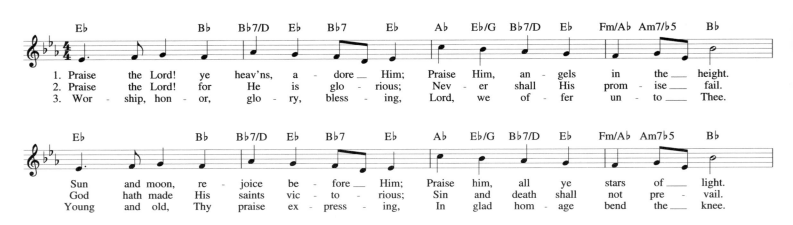

1. Praise the Lord! ye heav'ns, a - dore Him; Praise Him, an - gels in the height.
2. Praise the Lord! for He is glo - rious; Nev - er shall His prom - ise fail.
3. Wor - ship, hon - or, glo - ry, bless - ing, Lord, we of - fer un - to Thee.

Sun and moon, re - joice be - fore Him; Praise him, all ye stars of light.
God hath made His saints vic - to - rious; Sin and death shall not pre - vail.
Young and old, Thy praise ex - press - ing, In glad hom - age bend the knee.

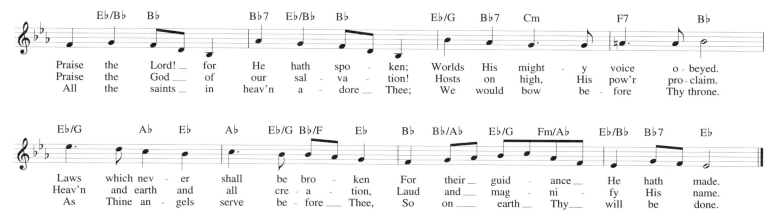

PRAISE THE LORD! YE HEAVENS, ADORE HIM

words based on Psalm 148
v.1,2 from *Foundling Hospital Collection,* 1796
v.3 by Edward Osler, 1836

FABEN
music by
John H. Willcox, 1849

Copyright © 2000 by HAL LEONARD CORPORATION

PRAISE THE SAVIOR, YE WHO KNOW HIM

words by
Thomas Kelly (1769-1855)

ACCLAIM
Traditional German melody

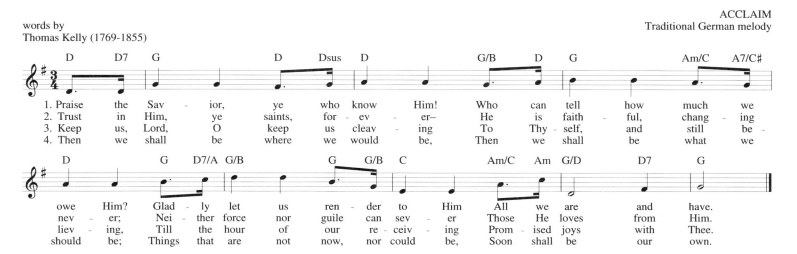

Copyright © 2000 by HAL LEONARD CORPORATION

PRAISE TO GOD, IMMORTAL PRAISE

DIX
music by
Conrad Kocher (1786-1872)

words by
Anna Laetitia Barbauld (1743-1825)

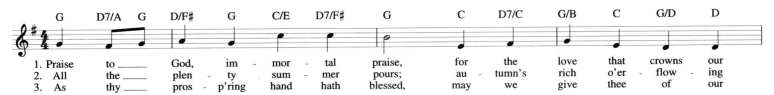

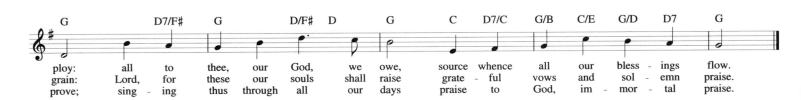

1. Praise to God, im - mor - tal praise, for the love that crowns our
2. All the plen - ty sum - mer pours; au - tumn's rich o'er - flow - ing
3. As thy pros - p'ring hand hath blessed, may we give thee of our

days; boun - te - ous source of ev - 'ry joy, let thy praise our tongues em -
stores; flocks that whit - en all the plain; yel - low sheaves of rip - ened
best; and by deeds of kind - ly love for thy mer - cies grate - ful

ploy: all to thee, our God, we owe, source whence all our bless - ings flow.
grain: Lord, for these our souls shall raise grate - ful vows and sol - emn praise.
prove; sing - ing thus through all our days praise to God, im - mor - tal praise.

PRAISE TO THE FATHER

FLEMMING
music by
Friedrich F. Flemming (1778-1813)

words by
Elizabeth R. Charles (1828-1896)

1. Praise to the Fa - ther for his lov - ing kind - ness, Ten - der - ly
2. Praise to the Sav - ior for His deep com - pas - sion, Gra - cious - ly
3. Praise to the Spir - it, com - fort - er of Is - rael, Sent from the

car - ing for his err - ing chil - dren; Praise Him, all an - gels;
car - ing for His cho - sen peo - ple; Young men and wom - en,
Fa - ther and the Son to bless us! Praise to the Fa - ther,

praise Him in the heav - ens; Praise to the Fa - ther!
ag - ing folk and chil - dren, Praise to the Sav - ior!
Son, and Ho - ly Spir - it! Praise to the Tri - une God!

PRAISE TO THE HOLIEST IN THE HEIGHT

NEWMAN

words by
John Henry Newman (1801-1890)

music by
Richard Runciman Terry (1865-1938)

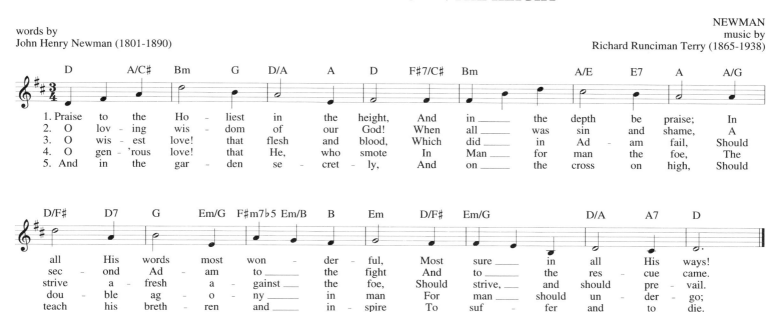

1. Praise to the Ho - liest in the height, And in the depth be praise; In all His words most won - der - ful, Most sure in all His ways!
2. O lov - ing wis - dom of our God! When all was sin and shame, A sec - ond Ad - am to the fight And to the res - cue came.
3. O wis - est love! that flesh and blood, Which did in Ad - am fail, Should strive a - fresh a - gainst the foe, Should strive, and should pre - vail.
4. O gen - 'rous love! that He, who smote In Man for man the foe, The dou - ble ag - o - ny in man For man should un - der - go;
5. And in the gar - den se - cret - ly, And on the cross on high, Should teach his breth - ren and in - spire To suf - fer and to die.

PRAISE TO THE LIVING GOD

LEONI
Traditional Hebrew melody

words from
Medieval Jewish liturgy
tr. by Max Landsberg (1845-1928)
and Newton M. Mann (1836-1926)

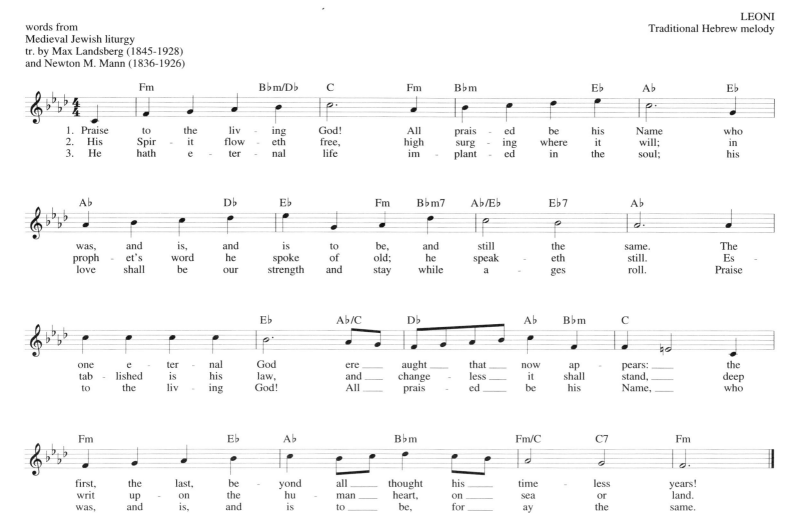

1. Praise to the liv - ing God! All prais - ed be his Name who was, and is, and is to be, and still the same. The one e - ter - nal God ere aught that now ap - pears: the first, the last, be - yond all thought his time - less years!
2. His Spir - it flow - eth free, high surg - ing where it will; in proph - et's word he spoke of old; he speak - eth still. Es - tab - lished is his law, and change - less it shall stand, deep writ up - on the hu - man heart, on sea or land.
3. He hath e - ter - nal life im - plant - ed in the soul; his love shall be our strength and stay while a - ges roll. Praise to the liv - ing God! All prais - ed be his Name, who was, and is, and is to be, for ay the same.

PRAISE TO THE LORD, THE ALMIGHTY

LOBE DEN HERREN
music from
Erneuerten Gesangbuch, 1665

words by
Joachim Neander, 1680
tr. by Catherine Winkworth, 1863

PRAISE WE THE LORD THIS DAY

SWABIA
music by
Johann M. Spiess (1715-1772)

words from
Hymns for the Festivals and Saints' Days, 1846

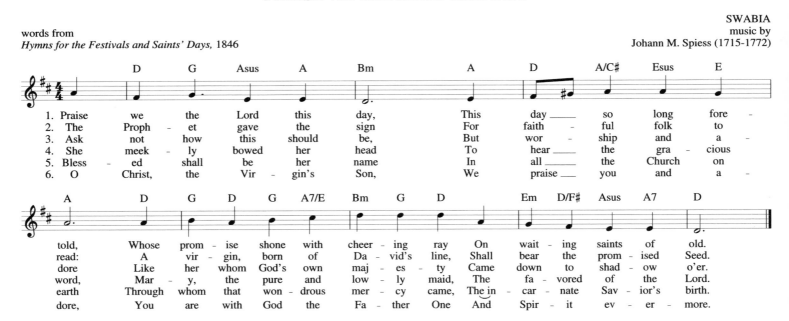

PRAISE YE THE TRIUNE GOD

words by
Elizabeth R. Charles, c. 1859

FLEMMING
music by
Friedrich F. Flemming, 1811

1. Praise ye the Fa - ther for His lov - ing kind - ness; Ten - der - ly
2. Praise ye the Sav - ior great is His com - pas - sion; Gra - cious - ly
3. Praise ye the Spir - it, Com - fort - er of Is - rael, Sent of the

cares ___ He for His err - ing chil - dren. Praise Him, ye an - gels,
cares ___ He for His cho - sen peo - ple. Young men and maid - ens,
Fa - ther and the Son to bless us. Praise ye the Fa - ther,

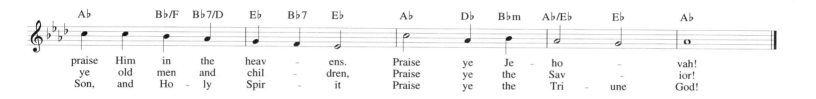

praise Him in the heav - ens. Praise ye Je - ho - vah!
ye old men and chil - dren, Praise ye the Sav - ior!
Son, and Ho - ly Spir - it Praise ye the Tri - une God!

Copyright © 2000 by HAL LEONARD CORPORATION

PRAYER IS THE SOUL'S SINCERE DESIRE

words by
James Montgomery, 1818

CAMPMEETING
Traditional American melody

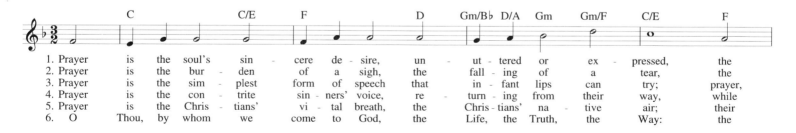

1. Prayer is the soul's sin - cere de - sire, un - ut - tered or ex - pressed, the
2. Prayer is the bur - den of a sigh, the fall - ing of a tear, the
3. Prayer is the sim - plest form of speech that in - fant lips can try; prayer,
4. Prayer is the con - trite sin - ners' voice, re - turn - ing from their way, while
5. Prayer is the Chris - tians' vi - tal breath, the Chris - tians' na - tive air; their
6. O Thou, by whom we come to God, the Life, the Truth, the Way: the

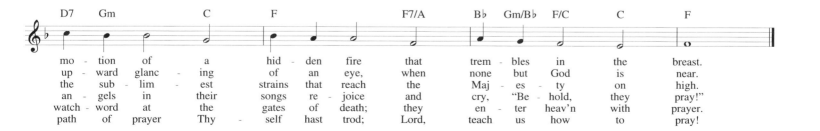

mo - tion of a hid - den fire that trem - bles in the breast.
up - ward glanc - ing of an eye, when none but God is near.
the sub - lim - est strains that reach the Maj - es - ty on high.
an - gels in their songs re - joice and cry, "Be - hold, they pray!"
watch - word at the gates of death; they en - ter heav'n with prayer.
path of prayer Thy - self hast trod; Lord, teach us how to pray!

Copyright © 2000 by HAL LEONARD CORPORATION

PRECIOUS MEMORIES

words by
J.B.F. Wright

music by
J.B.F. Wright

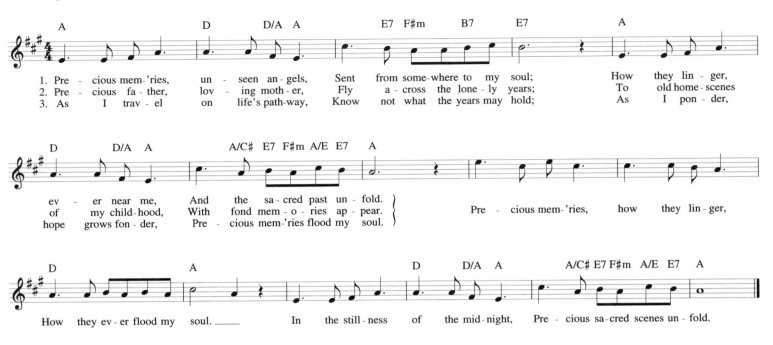

READY

TILLMAN

words by
A.C. Palmer (1845-1882)

music by
Charles D. Tillman, 1903

REDEEMED

words by
Fanny Crosby (1820-1915)

music by
William J. Kirkpatrick (1838-1921)

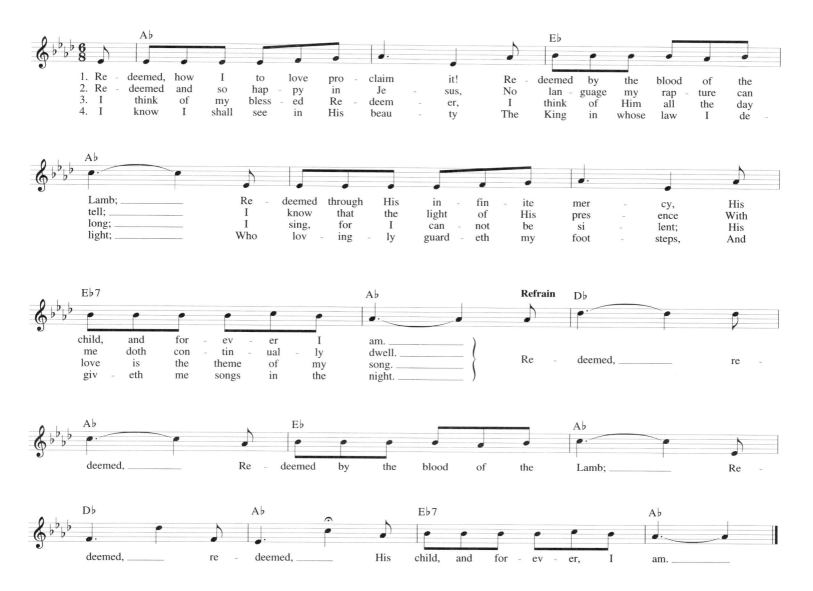

1. Re - deemed, how I to love pro - claim it! Re - deemed by the blood of the
2. Re - deemed and so hap - py in Je - sus, No lan - guage my rap - ture can
3. I think of my bless - ed Re - deem - er, I think of Him all the day
4. I know I shall see in His beau - ty The King in whose law I de -

Lamb; Re - deemed through His in - fin - ite mer - cy, His
tell; I know that His the light of His pres - ence, With
long; I sing, for I can - not be si - lent; His
light; Who lov - ing - ly guard - eth my foot - steps, And

child, and for - ev - er I am. Re - deemed, re -
me doth con - tin - ual - ly dwell.
love is the theme of my song.
giv - eth me songs in the night.

Refrain
deemed, Re - deemed by the blood of the Lamb; Re -

deemed, re - deemed, His child, and for - ev - er, I am.

REJOICE IN THE LORD ALWAYS

words from
Philippians 4:4

REJOICE
Traditional music

① Re - joice in the Lord al - ways, a - gain I say, re - joice! ② Re - joice in the Lord al - ways, a - gain I say, re - joice! ③ Re -

joice, re - joice, a - gain I say, re - joice! ④ Re - joice, re - joice, a - gain I say, re - joice!

*May be sung as a round.

REJOICE, THE LORD IS KING

DARWALL'S 148TH
music by
John Darwall, 1770

words by
Charles Wesley, 1746

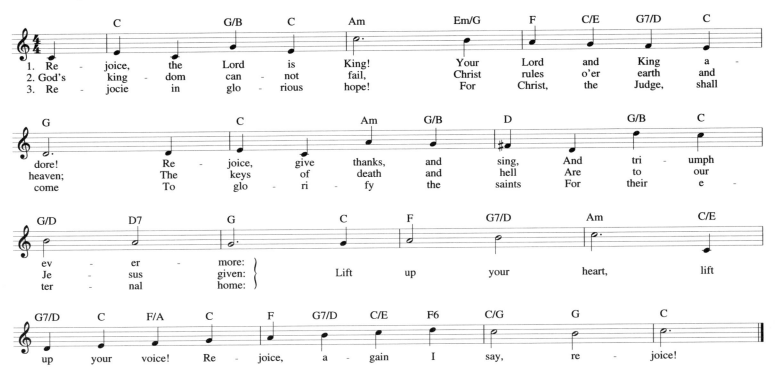

REJOICE, THE LORD IS KING

LAUS REGIS
music by
William E. Fischer (1849-1936)

words by
Charles Wesley (1707-1788)

REJOICE, YE PURE IN HEART

words by
Edward Hayes Plumptre, 1865

MARION
music by
Arthur Henry Messiter, 1883

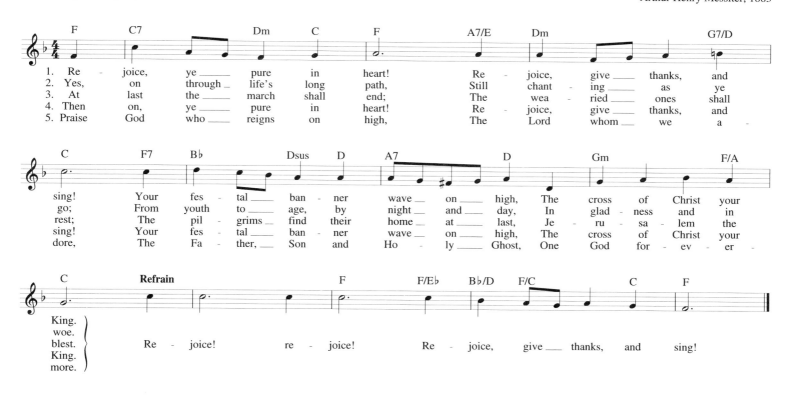

RENEW ME, O ETERNAL LIGHT

words by
Johann F. Ruopp (1672-1708)
tr. by August Crull (1846-1923)

HERR JESU CHRIST, MEINS
music from
As Hymnodus Sacer, Leipzig, 1625

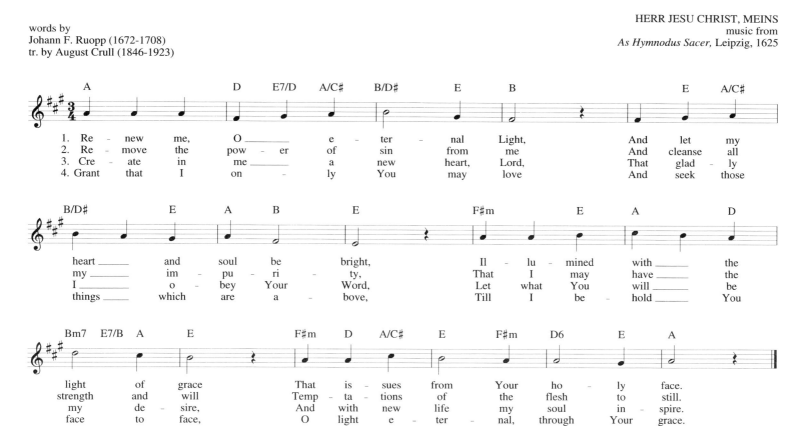

RESCUE THE PERISHING

RESCUE

words by
Fanny J. Crosby, 1869

music by
William H. Doane, 1870

REVIVE US AGAIN

words by
William P. Mackay (1839-1885)

music by
John J. Husband (1760-1825)

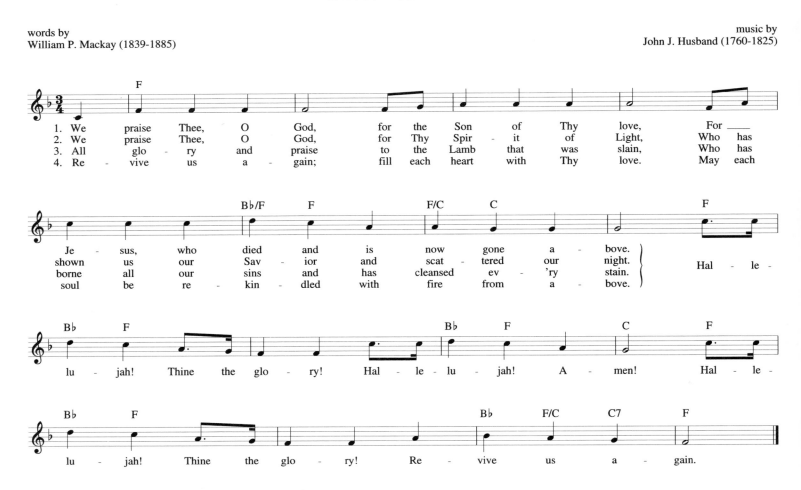

RIDE ON! RIDE ON IN MAJESTY!

ST. DROSTANE
words by
Henry Hart Milman, 1827

music by
John Bacchus Dykes, 1862

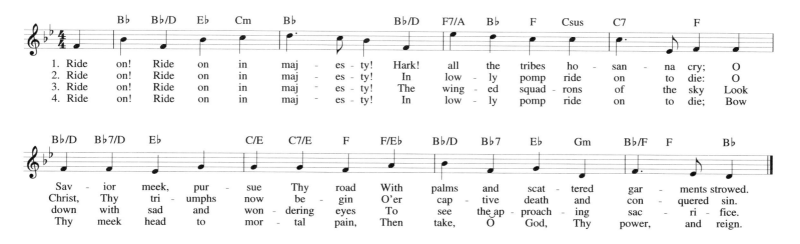

1. Ride on! Ride on in maj - es - ty! Hark! all the tribes ho - san - na cry; O
2. Ride on! Ride on in maj - es - ty! In low - ly pomp ride on to die: O
3. Ride on! Ride on in maj - es - ty! The wing - ed squad - rons of the sky Look
4. Ride on! Ride on in maj - es - ty! In low - ly pomp ride on to die; Bow

Sav - ior meek, pur - sue Thy road With palms and scat - tered gar - ments strowed.
Christ, Thy tri - umphs now be - gin O'er cap - tive death and con - quered sin.
down with sad and won - dering eyes To see the ap - proach - ing sac - ri - fice.
Thy meek head to mor - tal pain, Then take, O God, Thy power, and reign.

RING THE BELLS OF HEAVEN

RING THE BELLS
words by
William O. Cushing, 1866

music by
George F. Root, c. 1866

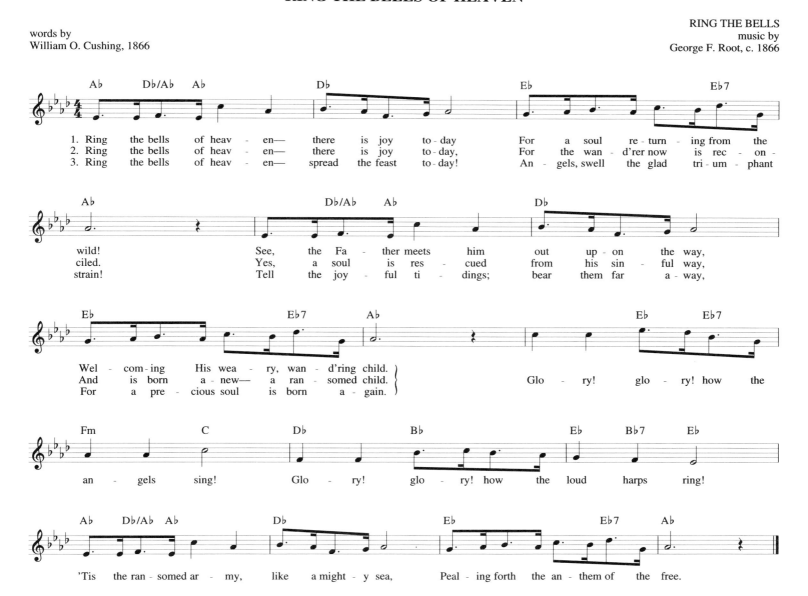

1. Ring the bells of heav - en— there is joy to - day For a soul re - turn - ing from the
2. Ring the bells of heav - en— there is joy to - day, For the wan - d'rer now is rec - on -
3. Ring the bells of heav - en— spread the feast to - day! An - gels, swell the glad tri - um - phant

wild! See, the Fa - ther meets him out up - on the way,
ciled. Yes, a soul is res - cued from his sin - ful way,
strain! Tell the joy - ful ti - dings; bear them far a - way,

Wel - com - ing His wea - ry, wan - d'ring child.
And is born a - new— a ran - somed child. Glo - ry! glo - ry! how the
For a pre - cious soul is born a - gain.

an - gels sing! Glo - ry! glo - ry! how the loud harps ring!

'Tis the ran - somed ar - my, like a might - y sea, Peal - ing forth the an - them of the free.

RISE, MY SOUL, TO WATCH AND PRAY

words by
Johann B. Freystein (1671-1718)
tr. by Catherine Winkworth (1827-1878)

STRAF MICH NICHT
music from
Hundert Geistlicher Arien, Dresden, 1694

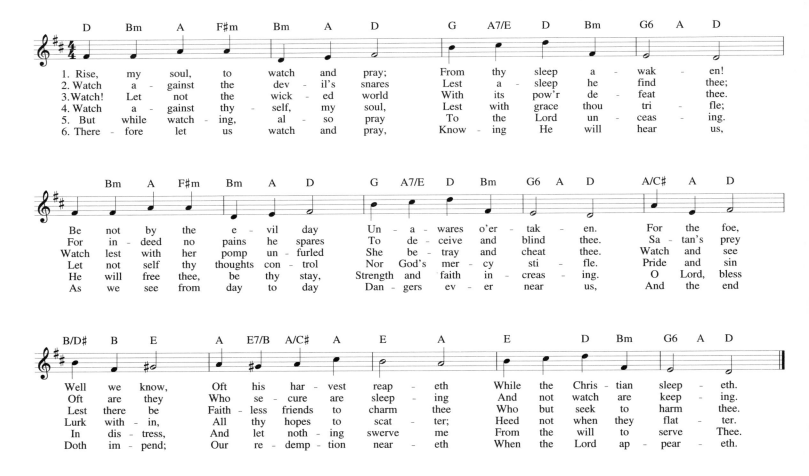

1. Rise, my soul, to watch and pray; From thy sleep a - wak - en!
2. Watch a - gainst the dev - il's snares Lest a - sleep he find thee;
3. Watch! Let not the wick - ed world With its pow'r de - feat thee.
4. Watch a - gainst thy - self, my soul, Lest with grace thou tri - fle;
5. But while watch - ing, al - so pray To the Lord un - ceas - ing.
6. There - fore let us watch and pray, Know - ing He will hear us,

Be not by the e - vil day Un - a - wares o'er - tak - en. For the foe,
For in - deed no pains he spares To de - ceive and blind thee. Sa - tan's prey
Watch lest with her pomp un - furled She be - tray and cheat thee. Watch and see
Let not self thy thoughts con - trol Nor God's mer - cy sti - fle. Pride and sin
He will free thee, be thy stay, Strength and faith in - creas - ing. O Lord, bless
As we see from day to day Dan - gers ev - er near us, And the end

Well we know, Oft his har - vest reap - eth While the Chris - tian sleep - eth.
Oft are they Who se - cure are sleep - ing And not watch are keep - ing.
Lest there be Faith - less friends to charm thee Who but seek to harm thee.
Lurk with - in, All thy hopes to scat - ter; Heed not when they flat - ter.
In dis - tress, And let noth - ing swerve me From the will to serve Thee.
Doth im - pend; Our re - demp - tion near - eth When the Lord ap - pear - eth.

RISE UP, O MEN OF GOD

words by
William Pierson Merrill, 1911

FESTAL SONG
music by
William H. Walter, 1894

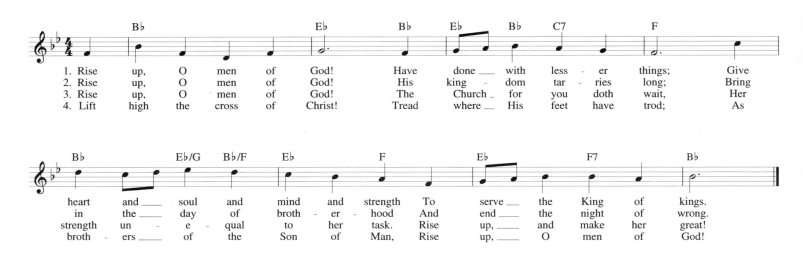

1. Rise up, O men of God! Have done ___ with less - er things; Give
2. Rise up, O men of God! His king - dom tar - ries long; Bring
3. Rise up, O men of God! The Church ___ for you doth wait, Her
4. Lift high the cross of Christ! Tread where ___ His feet have trod; As

heart and ___ soul and mind and strength To serve ___ the King of kings.
in the ___ day of broth - er - hood And end the night of wrong.
strength un - e - qual to her task. Rise up, ___ and make her great!
broth - ers ___ of the Son of Man, Rise up, ___ O men of God!

RISE, YE CHILDREN OF SALVATION

NEANDER

words by
Justus Falckner, 1697
tr. by Emma F. Bevan, 1858

music by
Joachim Neander, 1680

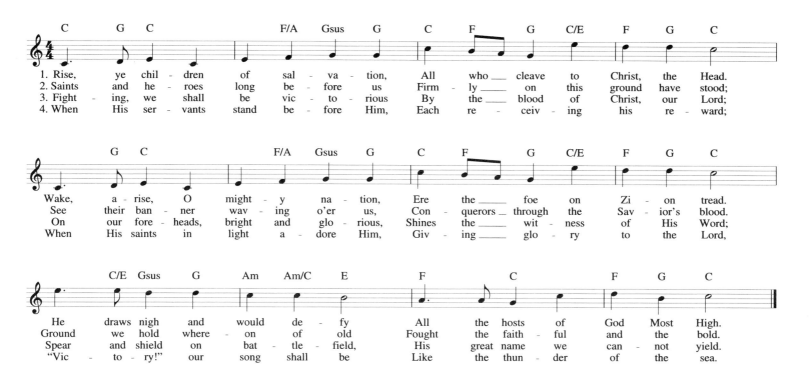

1. Rise, ye chil - dren of sal - va - tion, All who ___ cleave to Christ, the Head.
2. Saints and he - roes long be - fore us Firm - ly ___ on this ground have stood;
3. Fight - ing, we shall be vic - to - rious By the ___ blood of Christ, our Lord;
4. When His ser - vants stand be - fore Him, Each re - ceiv - ing his re - ward;

Wake, a - rise, O might - y na - tion, Ere the ___ foe on Zi - on tread.
See their ban - ner wav - ing o'er us, Con - querors ___ through the Sav - ior's blood.
On our fore - heads, bright and glo - rious, Shines the ___ wit - ness of His Word;
When His saints in light a - dore Him, Giv - ing ___ glo - ry to the Lord,

He draws nigh and would de - fy All the hosts of God Most High.
Ground we hold where - on of old Fought the faith - ful and the bold.
Spear and shield on bat - tle - field, His great name we can - not yield.
"Vic - to - ry!" our song shall be Like the thun - der of the sea.

ROCK OF AGES

TOPLADY

words by
Augustus M. Toplady (1740-1778)
v. 1,2,4 alt. by Thomas Cotterill, 1815

music by
Thomas Hastings (1784-1872)

1. Rock of A - ges, cleft for me, Let me hide my - self in Thee. Let the
2. Could my tears for - ev - er flow, Could my zeal no lan - guor know, These for
3. Noth - ing in my hand I bring; Sim - ply to Thy cross I cling. Na - ked,
4. While I draw this fleet - ing breath, When my eyes shall close in death, When I

wa - ter and the blood From Thy wound - ed side which flowed Be of
sin could not a - tone; Thou must save, and Thou a - lone. In my
come to Thee for dress; Help - less, look to Thee for grace. Foul, I
rise to worlds un - known And be - hold Thee on Thy throne, Rock of

sin the dou - ble cure, Save from wrath and make me pure.
hand no price I bring; Sim - ply to Thy cross I cling.
to the foun - tain fly; Wash me, Sav - ior, or I die!
A - ges, cleft for me, Let me hide my - self in Thee.

ROUND THE LORD IN GLORY SEATED

RUSTINGTON

words by
Richard Mant (1776-1848)

music by
Charles Hubert Hastings Parry (1848-1918)

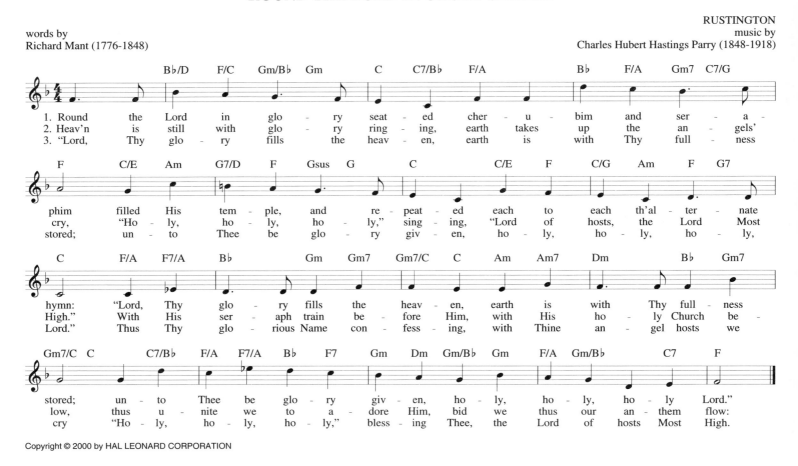

SAFE IN THE ARMS OF JESUS

SAFE

words by
Fanny J. Crosby, 1870

music by
William H. Doane, 1870

SAFELY THROUGH ANOTHER WEEK

SABBATH MORN
music by
Lowell Mason (1792-1827)

words by
John Newton (1725-1807)

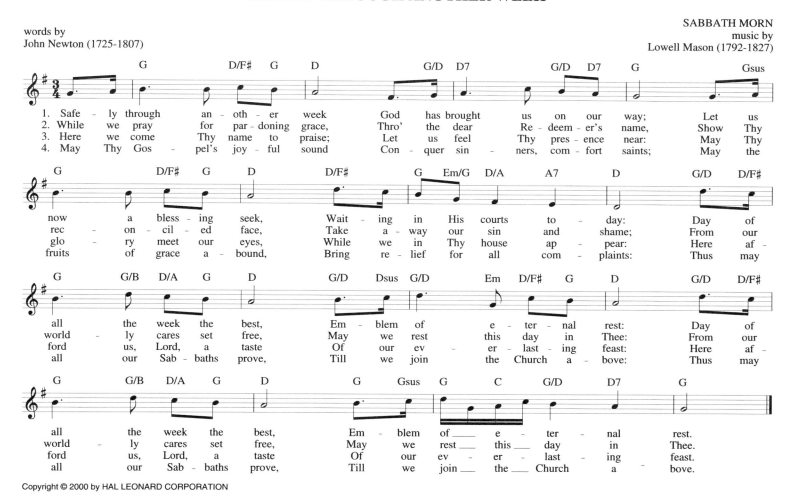

1. Safe - ly through an - oth - er week God has brought us on our way; Let us
2. While we pray for par - don-ing grace, Thro' the dear Re - deem - er's name, Show Thy
3. Here we come Thy name to praise; Let us feel Thy pres - ence near: May Thy
4. May Thy Gos - pel's joy - ful sound Con - quer sin - ners, com - fort saints; May the

now a bless - ing seek, Wait - ing in His courts to - day: Day of
rec - on - cil - ed face, Take a - way our sin and shame; From our
glo - ry meet our eyes, While we in Thy house ap - pear: Here af -
fruits of grace a - bound, Bring re - lief for all com - plaints: Thus may

all the week the best, Em - blem of e - ter - nal rest: Day of
world - ly cares set free, May we rest this day in Thee: From our
ford us, Lord, a taste Of our ev - er - last - ing feast: Here af -
all our Sab - baths prove, Till we join the Church a - bove: Thus may

all the week the best, Em - blem of e - ter - nal rest.
world - ly cares set free, May we rest this day in Thee.
ford us, Lord, a taste Of our ev - er - last - ing feast.
all our Sab - baths prove, Till we join the Church a - bove.

THE SANDS OF TIME ARE SINKING

RUTHERFORD
music by
Chrétien Urhan (1790-1845)

words by
Anne R. Cousin (1824-1906)

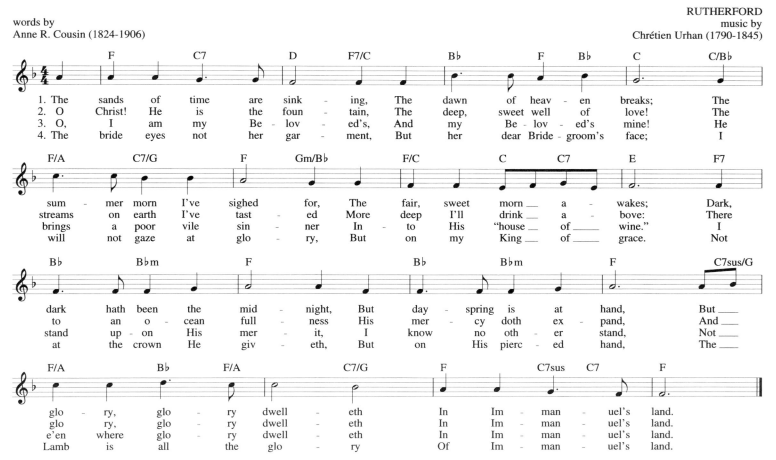

1. The sands of time are sink - ing, The dawn of heav - en breaks; The
2. O Christ! He is the foun - tain, The deep, sweet well of love! The
3. O, I am my Be - lov - ed's, And my Be - lov - ed's mine! He
4. The bride eyes not her gar - ment, But her dear Bride-groom's face; I

sum - mer morn I've sighed for, The fair, sweet morn a - wakes; Dark,
streams on earth I've tast - ed More deep I'll drink a - bove; There
brings a poor vile sin - ner In - to His "house of wine." I
will not gaze at glo - ry, But on my King of grace. Not

dark hath been the mid - night, But day - spring is at hand, But
to an o - cean full - ness His mer - cy doth ex - pand, And
stand up - on His mer - it, I know no oth - er stand, Not
at the crown He giv - eth, But on His pierc - ed hand, The

glo - ry, glo - ry dwell - eth In Im - man - uel's land.
glo - ry, glo - ry dwell - eth In Im - man - uel's land.
e'en where glo - ry dwell - eth In Im - man - uel's land.
Lamb is all the glo - ry Of Im - man - uel's land.

SANCTIFYING POWER

words by
Lelia N. Morris, 1908

music by
Lelia N. Morris, 1908

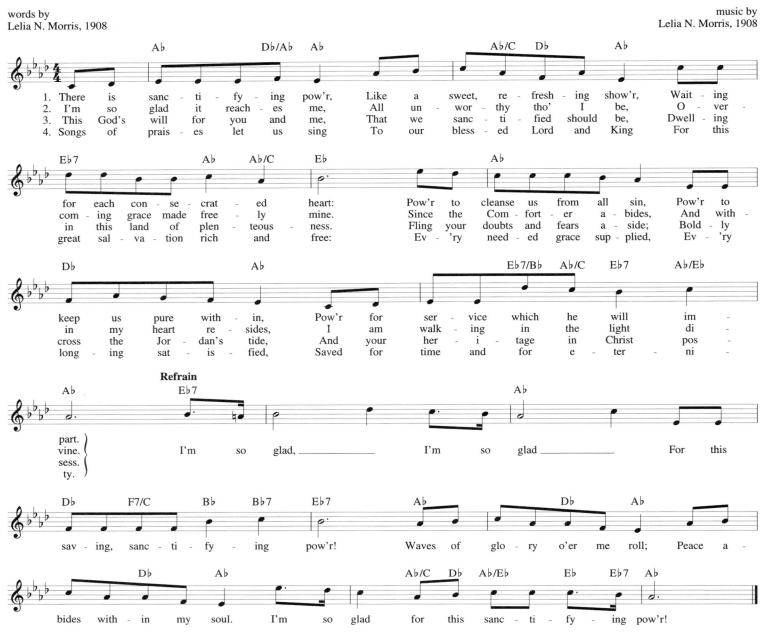

1. There is sanc-ti-fy-ing pow'r, Like a sweet, re-fresh-ing show'r, Wait-ing for each con-se-crat-ed heart: Pow'r to cleanse us from all sin, Pow'r to keep us pure with-in, Pow'r for ser-vice which he will im-

2. I'm so glad it reach-es me, All un-wor-thy tho' I be, O-ver com-ing grace made free-ly mine. Since the Com-fort-er a-bides, And with-in my heart re-sides, I am walk-ing in the light di-

3. This God's will for you and me, That we sanc-ti-fied should be, Dwell-ing in this land of plen-teous-ness. Fling your doubts and fears a-side; Bold-ly cross the Jor-dan's tide, And your her-i-tage in Christ pos-

4. Songs of prais-es let us sing To our bless-ed Lord and King For this great sal-va-tion rich and free: Ev-'ry need-ed grace sup-plied, Ev-'ry long-ing sat-is-fied, Saved for time and for e-ter-ni-

Refrain

part. / vine. / sess. / ty.

I'm so glad, _____ I'm so glad _____ For this sav-ing, sanc-ti-fy-ing pow'r! Waves of glo-ry o'er me roll; Peace a-bides with-in my soul. I'm so glad for this sanc-ti-fy-ing pow'r!

SATISFIED

words by
Clara T. Williams, 1881

music by
Ralph E. Hudson, 1881

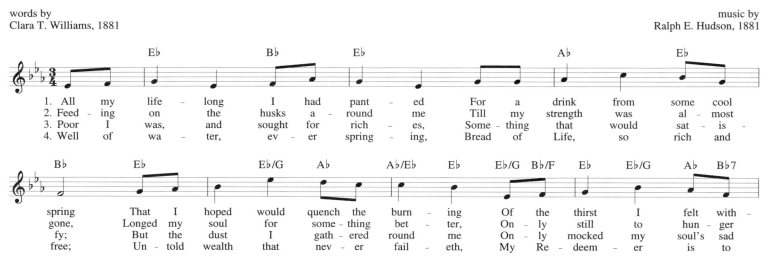

1. All my life-long I had pant-ed For a drink from some cool spring That I hoped would quench the burn-ing Of the thirst I felt with-

2. Feed-ing on the husks a-round me Till my strength was al-most gone, Longed my soul for some-thing bet-ter, On-ly still to hun-ger

3. Poor I was, and sought for rich-es, Some-thing that would sat-is-fy; But the dust I gath-ered round me On-ly mocked my soul's sad

4. Well of wa-ter, ev-er spring-ing, Bread of Life, so rich and free; Un-told wealth that nev-er fail-eth, My Re-deem-er is to

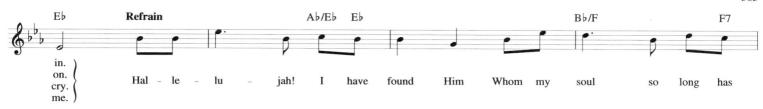

SAVED BY THE BLOOD

GLORY, I'M SAVED

words by
S.J. Henderson, 19th century

music by
Daniel B. Towner (1850-1919)

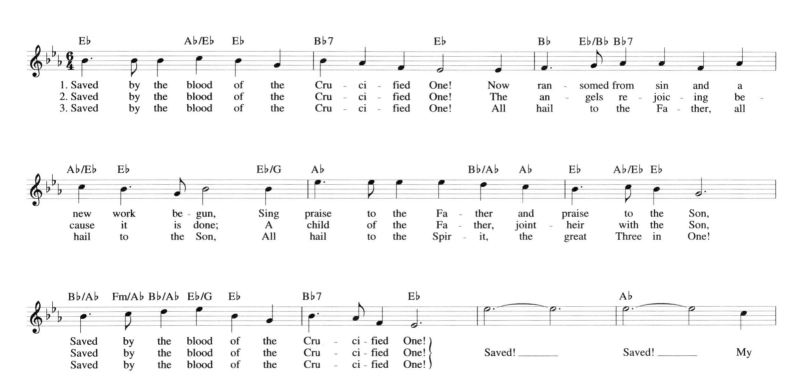

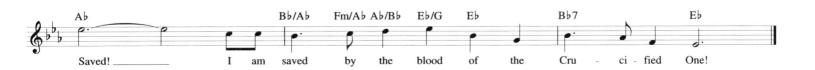

SAVED BY GRACE

words by
Fanny J. Crosby, 1894

music by
George C. Stebbins, 1894

1. Some - day the sil - ver cord will break, And I no more as now shall sing. But, O the
2. Some - day my earth - ly house will fall; I can - not tell how soon 'twill be. But this I
3. Some - day, when fades the gold - en sun Be - neath the ros - y - tint - ed west, My bless - ed
4. Some - day— till then I'll watch and wait, My lamp all trimmed and burn - ing bright, That when my

joy when I shall wake With - in the pal - ace of the King! } And I shall
know— my All in All Has now a place in heav'n for me.
Lord will say, "Well done!" And I shall en - ter in - to rest.
Sav - ior opes the gate, My soul to Him may take its flight.

see Him face to face, And tell the sto - ry— saved by grace. And I shall

see Him face to face, And tell the sto - ry— saved by grace.

Copyright © 2000 by HAL LEONARD CORPORATION

SAVED, SAVED!

RAPTURE

words by
Jack P. Scholfield, 1911

music by
Jack P. Scholfield, 1911

1. I've found a Friend _____ who is all to me; _____ His
2. He saved me from _____ ev - 'ry sin and harm, _____ Se
3. When poor and need - y and all a - lone, _____ In

love is ev - er true. _____ I love to tell _____ how He
cures my soul each day. _____ I'm lean - ing strong _____ on His
love He said to me, _____ "Come un - to Me _____ and I'll

lift - ed me, _____ And what His grace can do for you. }
might - y arm; _____ I know He'll guide me all the way.
lead you home, _____ To live with Me e - ter - nal - ly."

Refrain

Saved _____ by His pow'r di - vine! Saved _____ to new life sub - lime!

Life now is sweet and my joy is com - plete, For I'm saved, saved, saved! _____

Copyright © 2000 by HAL LEONARD CORPORATION

SAVIOR, AGAIN TO THY DEAR NAME WE RAISE

words by
John Ellerton, 1866

ELLERS
music by
Edward John Hopkins, 1869

1. Sav	ior,	a	gain	to	Thy	dear	name	we	raise
2. Grant	us	Thy	peace	up	on	our	home	ward	way;
3. Grant	us	Thy	peace,	Lord,	through	the	com	ing	night;
4. Grant	us	Thy	peace	through	out	our	earth	ly	life,

With one ac-
With Thee be-
Turn Thou for-
Our balm in

cord, our part-ing hymn of praise. We stand to bless Thee
gan, with Thee shall end the day. Guard Thou the lips from
us its dark-ness in to light. From harm and dan-ger
sor - row, and our stay in strife. Then, when Thy voice shall

ere our wor - ship cease; And, now de - part - ing, wait Thy word of peace.
sin, the hearts from shame, That in this house have called up - on Thy name.
keep Thy chil - dren free, For dark and light are both a - like to Thee.
bid our con - flict cease, Call us, O Lord, to Thine e - ter - nal peace.

SAVIOR, LIKE A SHEPHERD LEAD US

words from
Hymns for the Young, 1836
attr. to Dorothy A. Thrupp

BRADBURY
music by
William B. Bradbury, 1859

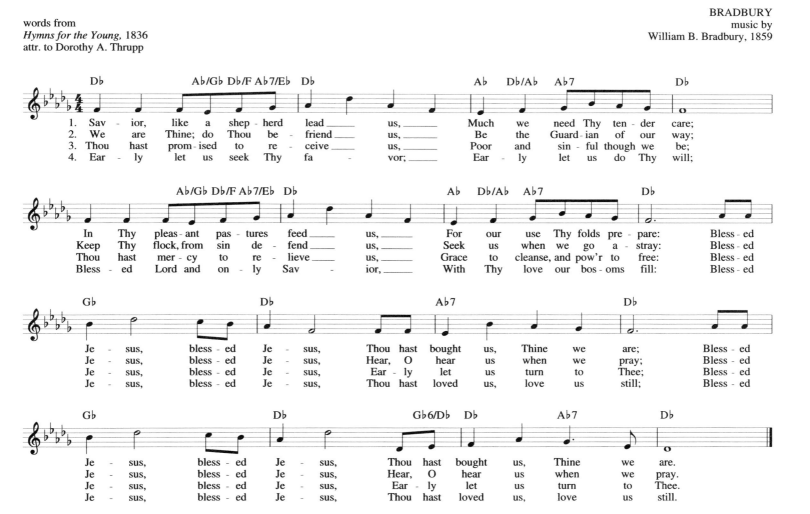

1. Sav - ior, like a shep - herd lead us, Much we need Thy ten - der care;
2. We are Thine; do Thou be - friend us, Be the Guard-ian of our way;
3. Thou hast prom - ised to re - ceive us, Poor and sin - ful though we be;
4. Ear - ly let us seek Thy fa - vor; Ear - ly let us do Thy will;

In Thy pleas-ant pas - tures feed us, For our use Thy folds pre - pare: Bless - ed
Keep Thy flock, from sin de - fend us, Seek us when we go a - stray: Bless - ed
Thou hast mer - cy to re - lieve us, Grace to cleanse, and pow'r to free: Bless - ed
Bless - ed Lord and on - ly Sav - ior, With Thy love our bos - oms fill: Bless - ed

Je - sus, bless - ed Je - sus, Thou hast bought us, Thine we are; Bless - ed
Je - sus, bless - ed Je - sus, Hear, O hear us when we pray; Bless - ed
Je - sus, bless - ed Je - sus, Ear - ly let us turn to Thee; Bless - ed
Je - sus, bless - ed Je - sus, Thou hast loved us, love us still; Bless - ed

Je - sus, bless - ed Je - sus, Thou hast bought us, Thine we are.
Je - sus, bless - ed Je - sus, Hear, O hear us when we pray.
Je - sus, bless - ed Je - sus, Ear - ly let us turn to Thee.
Je - sus, bless - ed Je - sus, Thou hast loved us, love us still.

SAVIOR, LIKE A SHEPHERD LEAD US

SICILIAN MARINERS
Sicilian melody
from *The European Magazine and London Review*, 1792

words attr. to
Dorothy A. Thrupp
from *Hymns for the Young*, 1836

1. Sav - ior, like a shep - herd lead us, Much we need Thy
2. We are Thine; do Thou be - friend us, Be the Guard - ian
3. Thou hast prom - ised to re - ceive us, Poor and sin - ful
4. Ear - ly let us seek Thy fa - vor, Ear - ly let us

ten - der care; In Thy pleas - ant pas - tures feed us;
of our way; Keep Thy flock, from sin de - fend us,
though we be; Thou hast mer - cy to re - lieve us,
do Thy will; Bless - ed Lord and on - ly Sav - ior,

For our use Thy folds pre - pare: Bless - ed Je - sus,
Seek us when we go a - stray: Bless - ed Je - sus,
Grace to cleanse, and pow'r to free: Bless - ed Je - sus,
With Thy love our bos - oms fill: Bless - ed Je - sus,

bless - ed Je - sus, Thou hast bought us, Thine we are.
bless - ed Je - sus, Hear, O hear us when we pray.
bless - ed Je - sus, Ear - ly let us turn to Thee.
bless - ed Je - sus, Thou hast loved us, love us still.

SAVIOR, MORE THAN LIFE TO ME

EVERY DAY AND HOUR

words by
Fanny J. Crosby (1820-1915)

music by
William H. Doane (1832-1915)

1. Sav - ior, more than life to me, I am cling-ing, cling-ing close to Thee; Let Thy
2. Through this chang - ing world be - low, Lead me gen - tly, gen - tly as I go; Trust - ing
3. Let me love Thee more and more, Till this fleet-ing, fleet-ing life is o'er; Till my

pre - cious blood ap - plied, Keep me ev - er, ev - er near Thy side.
Thee, I can - not stray, I can nev - er, nev - er lose my way.
soul is lost in love, In a bright-er, bright-er world a - bove.

Ev - 'ry

day, ev - 'ry hour, Let me feel Thy cleans - ing pow'r; May Thy

ten - der love to me Bind me clos - er, clos - er, Lord, to Thee.

SAVIOR, WHEN IN DUST TO THEE

words by
R. Grant (1779-1838)

ABERYSTWYTH
music by
J. Parry (1841-1903)

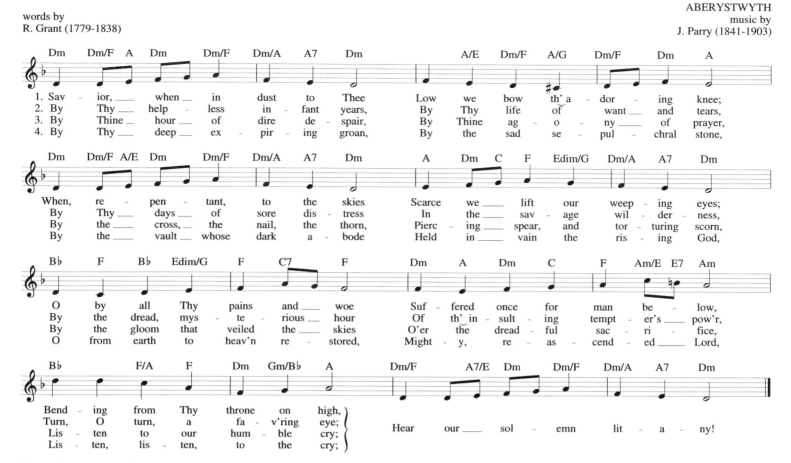

SEE HOW GREAT A FLAME ASPIRES

words by
Charles Wesley, 1749

ARFON (MAJOR)
Traditional Welsh melody

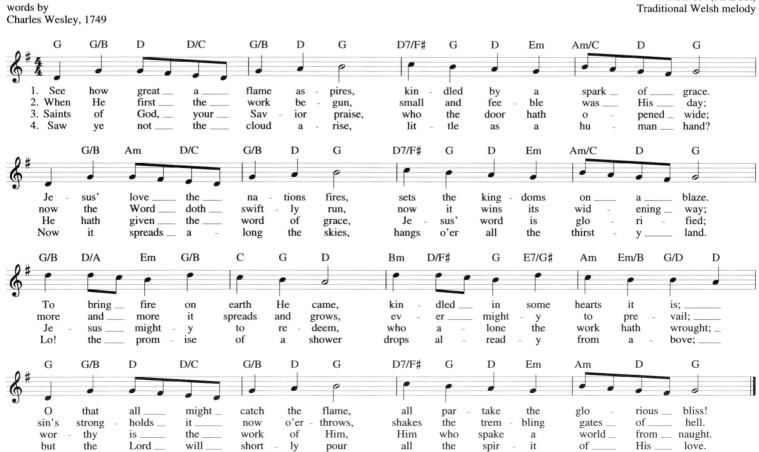

SEND THE LIGHT

words by
Charles H. Gabriel, 1890

McCABE
music by
Charles H. Gabriel, 1890

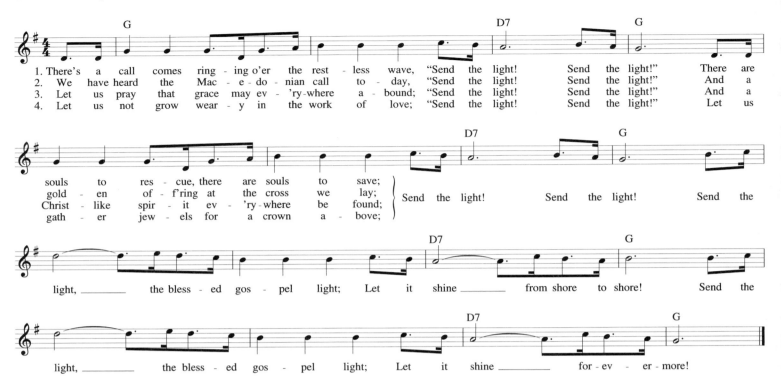

1. There's a call comes ring - ing o'er the rest - less wave, "Send the light! Send the light!" There are
2. We have heard the Mac - e - do - nian call to - day, "Send the light! Send the light!" And a
3. Let us pray that grace may ev - 'ry-where a - bound; "Send the light! Send the light!" And a
4. Let us not grow wear - y in the work of love; "Send the light! Send the light!" Let us

souls to res - cue, there are souls to save;
gold - en of - f'ring at the cross we lay;
Christ - like spir - it ev - 'ry-where be found;   Send the light! Send the light! Send the
gath - er jew - els for a crown a - bove;

light,_____ the bless - ed gos - pel light; Let it shine_____ from shore to shore! Send the

light,_____ the bless - ed gos - pel light; Let it shine_____ for - ev - er - more!

SEE, THE CONQUEROR MOUNTS IN TRIUMPH

words by
Christopher Wordsworth (1807-1885)

IN BABILONE
music from
Oude en Nieuwe Hollantse Boerenlities en Contradanseu, 1710

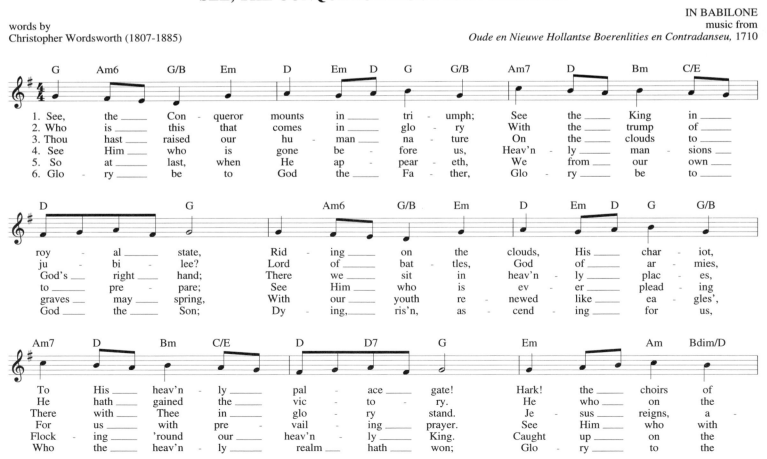

1. See, the_____ Con - queror mounts in_____ tri - umph; See the_____ King in_____
2. Who is_____ this that comes in_____ glo - ry With the_____ trump of_____
3. Thou hast_____ raised our hu - man_____ na - ture On the_____ clouds to_____
4. See Him_____ who is gone be - fore us, Heav'n - ly_____ man - sions_____
5. So at_____ last, when He ap - pear - eth, We from_____ our own_____
6. Glo - ry_____ be to God the_____ Fa - ther, Glo - ry_____ be to

roy - al_____ state, Rid - ing_____ on the clouds, His_____ char - iot,
ju - bi - lee? Lord of_____ bat - tles, God of_____ ar - mies,
God's_____ right_____ hand; There we_____ sit in heav'n - ly_____ plac - es,
to_____ pre - pare; See Him_____ who is ev - er_____ plead - ing
graves_____ may_____ spring, With our_____ youth re - newed like_____ ea - gles',
God the_____ Son; Dy - ing,_____ ris'n, as - cend - ing for us,

To His_____ heav'n - ly_____ pal - ace_____ gate! Hark! the_____ choirs of
He hath_____ gained the_____ vic - to - ry. He who_____ on the
There with_____ Thee in glo - ry stand. See Him_____ who with
For us_____ with pre - vail - ing_____ prayer. Je - sus reigns, a
Flock - ing_____ 'round our_____ heav'n - ly_____ King. Caught up on the
Who the_____ heav'n - ly_____ realm_____ hath_____ won; Glo - ry_____ to the

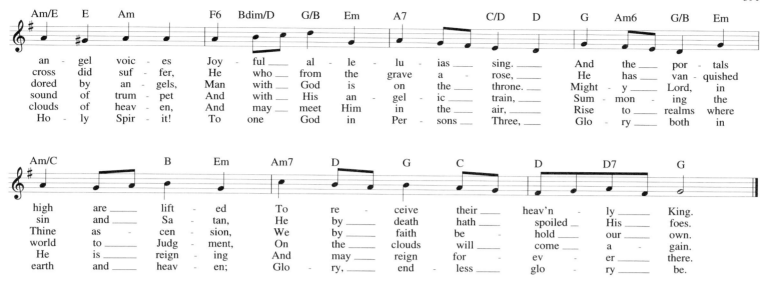

SHALL I CRUCIFY MY SAVIOR?

words by
Carrie Breck, 1896

TULLAR
music by
Grant Colfax Tullar, 1896

SHALL WE GATHER AT THE RIVER?

BEAUTIFUL RIVER

words by
Robert Lowry (1826-1899)

music by
Robert Lowry (1826-1899)

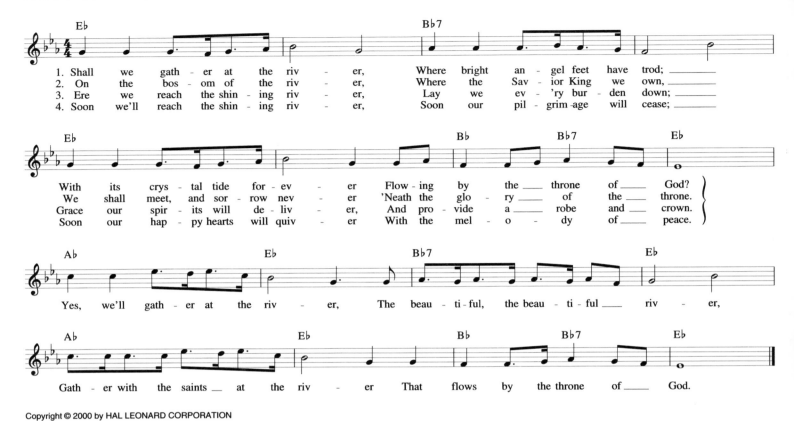

A SHELTER IN THE TIME OF STORM

SHELTER

words by
Vernon J. Charlesworth, c. 1880
adapt. by Ira D. Sankey, 1885

music by
Ira D. Sankey, 1885

SHEPHERD OF SOULS, REFRESH AND BLESS

words by
James Montgomery (1771-1854)

ST. AGNES
music by
John B. Dykes (1823-1876)

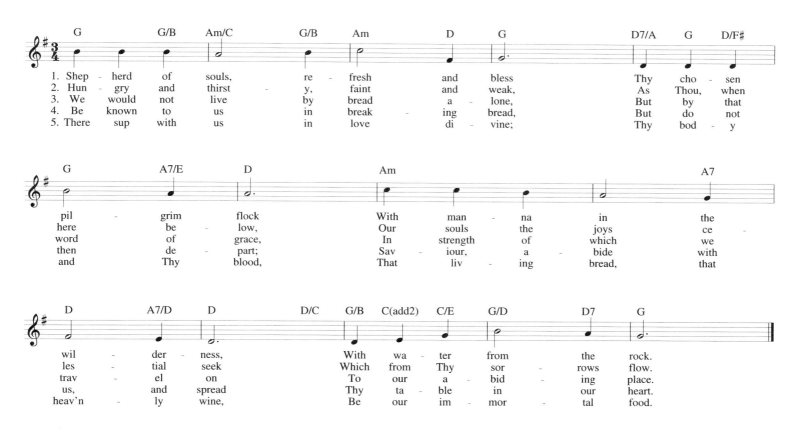

1. Shep - herd of souls, re - fresh and bless
2. Hun - gry and thirst - y, faint and weak,
3. We would not live by bread a - lone,
4. Be known to us in break - ing bread,
5. There sup with us in love di - vine;

pil - grim flock   With man - na in   the
here be - low,   Our souls the   joys   ce -
word of grace,   In strength of   which   we
then de - part;   Sav - iour,   a - bide   with
and Thy blood,   That liv - ing   bread,   that

wil - der - ness,   With wa - ter from   the rock.
les - tial seek   Which from Thy   sor - rows flow.
trav - el on   To our a - bid - ing place.
us, and spread   Thy ta - ble in   our heart.
heav'n - ly wine,   Be our im - mor - tal food.

Copyright © 2000 by HAL LEONARD CORPORATION

SHEPHERD OF TENDER YOUTH

words by
Clement of Alexandria, c. 220 A.D.
tr. by Henry M. Dexter, 1846

KIRBY BEDON
music by
Edward Bunnett, 1887

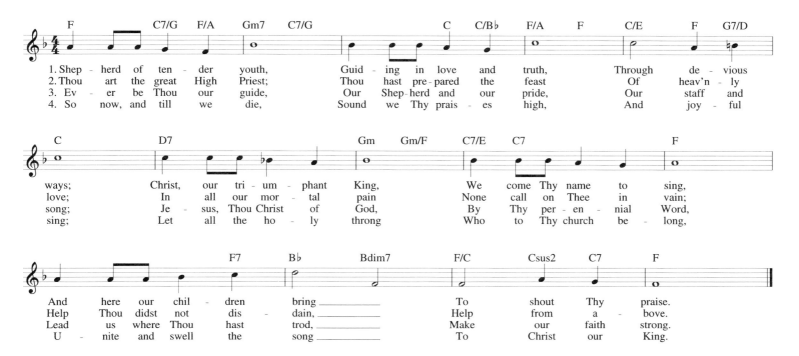

1. Shep - herd of ten - der youth,   Guid - ing in love and truth,   Through de - vious
2. Thou art the great High Priest;   Thou hast pre - pared the feast   Of heav'n - ly
3. Ev - er be Thou our guide,   Our Shep - herd and our pride,   Our staff and
4. So now, and till we die,   Sound we Thy prais - es high,   And joy - ful

ways;   Christ, our tri - um - phant King,   We come Thy name to sing,
love;   In all our mor - tal pain   None call on Thee in vain,
song;   Je - sus, Thou Christ of God,   By Thy per - en - nial Word,
sing;   Let all the ho - ly throng   Who to Thy church be - long,

And here our chil - dren bring ___   To shout Thy praise.
Help Thou didst not dis - dain, ___   Help from a - bove.
Lead us where Thou hast trod, ___   Make our faith strong.
U - nite and swell the song ___   To Christ our King.

Copyright © 2000 by HAL LEONARD CORPORATION

SILENT NIGHT, HOLY NIGHT

STILLE NACHT

words by
Joseph Mohr (1792-1848)
tr. by John F. Young (1820-1885)

music by
Franz X. Gruber (1787-1863)

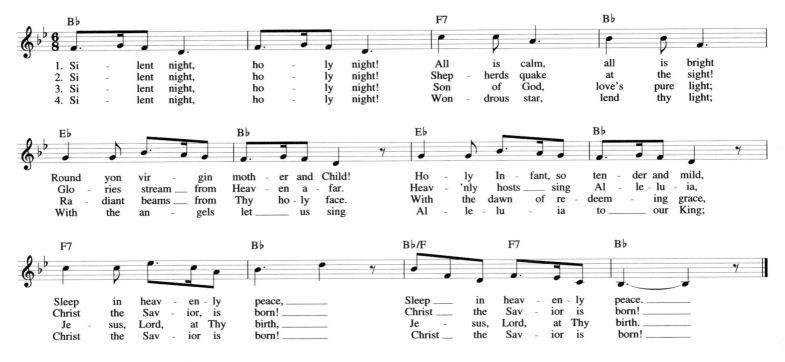

1. Si - lent night, ho - ly night! All is calm, all is bright
2. Si - lent night, ho - ly night! Shep - herds quake at the sight!
3. Si - lent night, ho - ly night! Son of God, love's pure light;
4. Si - lent night, ho - ly night! Won - drous star, lend thy light;

Round yon vir - gin moth - er and Child! Ho - ly In - fant, so ten - der and mild,
Glo - ries stream from Heav - en a - far. Heav - 'nly hosts sing Al - le - lu - ia,
Ra - diant beams from Thy ho - ly face. With the dawn of re - deem - ing grace,
With the an - gels let us sing Al - le - lu - ia to our King;

Sleep in heav - en - ly peace, Sleep in heav - en - ly peace.
Christ the Sav - ior, is born! Christ the Sav - ior is born!
Je - sus, Lord, at Thy birth, Je - sus, Lord, at Thy birth.
Christ the Sav - ior is born! Christ the Sav - ior is born!

SINCE I HAVE BEEN REDEEMED

OTHELLO

words by
Edwin O. Excell, 1884

music by
Edwin O. Excell, 1884

1. I have a song I love to sing, Since I have been re -
2. I have a Christ that sat - is - fies, Since I have been re -
3. I have a wit - ness bright and clear, Since I have been re -
4. I have a home pre - pared for me, Since I have been re -

deemed, Of my Re - deem - er, Sav - ior, King, since I have been re -
deemed, To do His will my high - est prize, Since I have been re -
deemed, Dis - pel - ling ev - ery doubt and fear, Since I have been re -
deemed, Where I shall live e - ter - nal - ly, Since I have been re -

Refrain

deemed.
deemed.
deemed.
deemed.

Since I have been re - deemed, Since I have been re - deemed, I will

glo - ry in His name; Since I have been re - deemed, I will glo - ry in my Sav - ior's name.

SINCE JESUS CAME INTO MY HEART

words by
Rufus H. McDaniel, 1914

McDANIEL
music by
Charles H. Gabriel, 1914

1. What a won-der-ful change in my life has been wrought
2. I have ceased from my wan-d'ring and go-ing a-stray
3. I'm pos-sessed of a hope that is stead-fast and sure,
4. There's a light in the val-ley of death now for me,
5. I shall go there to dwell in that Cit-y, I know,

Since Je-sus came in-to my heart.

I have
And my
And no
And the
And I'm

light in my soul for which long I had sought,
sins, which were man-y, are all washed a-way,
dark clouds of doubt now my path-way ob-scure,
gates of the Cit-y be-yond I can see,
hap-py, so hap-py, as on-ward I go,

Since Je-sus came in-to my heart! Since

Je-sus came in-to my heart, Since Je-sus came in-to my heart, Floods of

joy o'er my soul like the sea bil-lows roll, Since Je-sus came in-to my heart.

SING HALLELUJAH, PRAISE THE LORD!

words by
John Swertner (1746-1813)

BECHLER
music by
John Christian Bechler (1784-1857)

1. Sing hal-le-lu-jah, praise the Lord! Sing with a cheer-ful voice; Ex-
2. There we for all e-ter-ni-ty shall join th'an-gel-ic praise; And

alt our God with one ac-cord, and in His name re-joice. Ne'er
songs in per-fect har-mo-ny to God, our Sav-ior, raise. He

cease to sing, O ran-somed host, praise Fa-ther, Son, and Ho-ly Ghost, Un-
has re-deemed us by His blood, and made us kings and priests to God; For

til in realms of end-less light your prais-es shall u-nite.
us, for us the Lamb was slain! Praise ye the Lord! A-men.

SING, MY SOUL, HIS WONDROUS LOVE

Author unknown, c. 1800

ST. BEES
music by
John Bacchus Dykes (1823-1876)

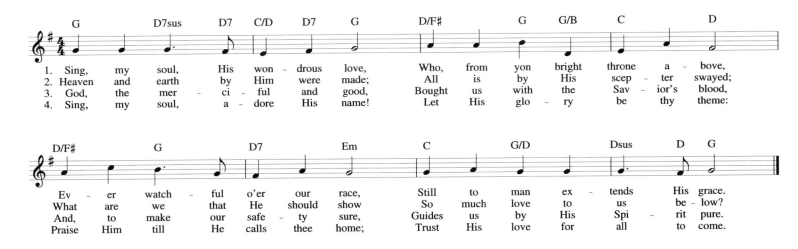

1. Sing, my soul, His won - drous love, Who, from yon bright throne a - bove,
2. Heaven and earth by Him were made; All is by His scep - ter swayed;
3. God, the mer - ci - ful and good, Bought us with the Sav - ior's blood,
4. Sing, my soul, a - dore His name! Let His glo - ry be thy theme:

Ev - er watch - ful o'er our race, Still to man ex - tends His grace.
What are we that He should show So much love to us be - low?
And, to make our safe - ty sure, Guides us by His Spi - rit pure.
Praise Him till He calls thee home; Trust His love for all to come.

SING PRAISE TO GOD, WHO REIGNS ABOVE

words by
Johann J. Schütz (1640-1690)
tr. by Francis E. Cox (1812-1897)

LOBT GOTT DEN HERREN, IHR
music by
Melchior Vulpius (c. 1560-1615)

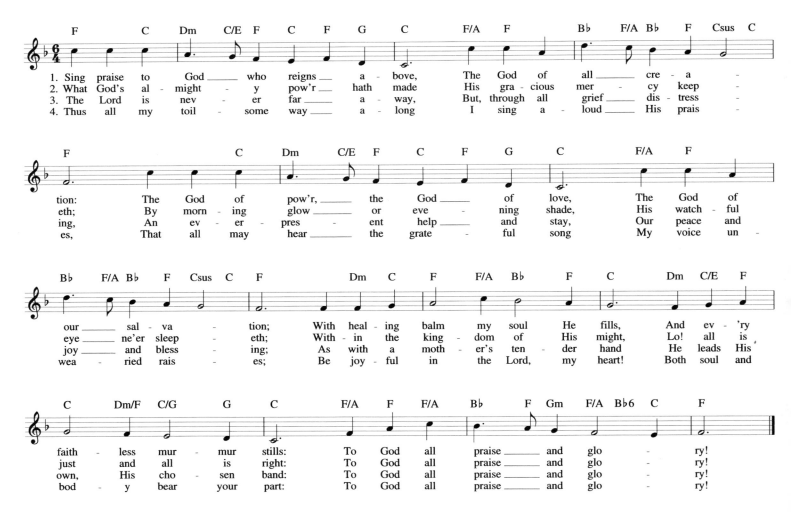

1. Sing praise to God who reigns a - bove, The God of all cre - a -
2. What God's al - might - y pow'r hath made, His gra - cious mer - cy keep
3. The Lord is nev - er far a - way, But, through all grief dis - tress,
4. Thus all my toil - some way a - long I sing a - loud His prais -

tion: The God of pow'r, the God of love, The God of
eth; By morn - ing glow or eve - ning shade, His watch - ful
ing, An ev - er - pres - ent help and stay, Our peace and
es, That all may hear the grate - ful song My voice un -

our sal - va - tion; With heal - ing balm my soul He fills, And ev - 'ry
eye ne'er sleep - eth; With - in the king - dom of His might, Lo! all is
joy and bless - ing; As with a moth - er's ten - der hand He leads His
wea - ried rais - es; Be joy - ful in the Lord, my heart! Both soul and

faith - less mur - mur stills: To God all praise and glo - ry!
just and all is right; To God all praise and glo - ry!
own, His cho - sen band: To God all praise and glo - ry!
bod - y bear your part: To God all praise and glo - ry!

SING, MY TONGUE, THE GLORIOUS BATTLE

words by
Venantius Honorius Fortunatus, 6th century
v. 1-4, 6 tr. by P.D.
v. 5 tr. by John Mason Neale, 1851

PICARDY
Traditional French melody

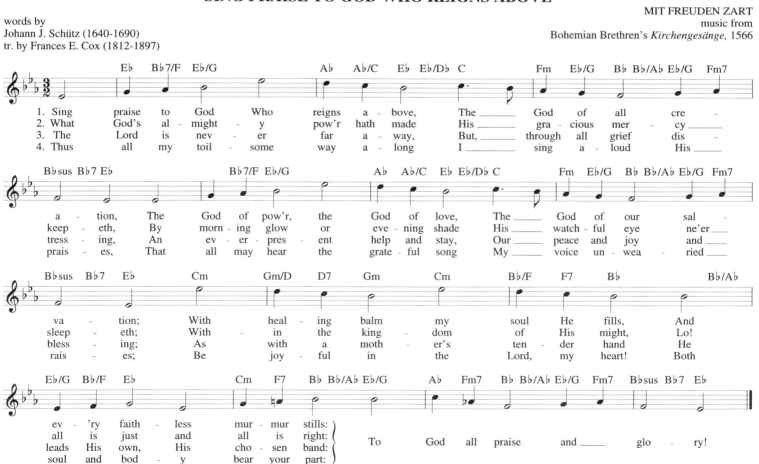

1. Sing, my tongue, the glo - rious ___ bat - tle, Sing the end - ing of the ___ fray;
2. God in pit - y saw man ___ fall - en, Shamed and sunk in mis - er - y,
3. Thus the scheme of our sal - va - tion Was of old in or - der laid,
4. There - fore when th'ap - point - ed ___ full - ness Of the ho - ly time was ___ come,
5. Thir - ty years a - mong us ___ dwell - ing, His ap - point - ed time ful - filled,
6. To the Trin - i - ty be ___ glo - ry Ev - er last - ing, as is ___ meet;

Now a - bove the Cross, the ___ tro - phy, sound the loud tri - um - phant ___ lay:
When he fell on death by ___ tast - ing, Fruit of the for - bid - den ___ tree;
That the man - i - fold de - ceiv - er's Art by art might be out - weighed,
He was sent who mak - eth ___ all things Forth from God's e - ter - nal ___ home;
Born for this He meets His ___ Pas - sion, For that this He free - ly ___ willed,
E - qual to the Fa - ther, ___ e - qual To the Son and Par - a - clete:

Tell how Christ, the world's Re - deem - er, As a Vic - tim won the ___ day.
Then an - oth - er tree was cho - sen Which the world from death should ___ free.
And the lure the foe put for - ward In - to means of heal - ing ___ made.
Thus He came to earth in - car - nate, Off - spring of a maid - en's ___ womb.
On the Cross the Lamb is lift - ed, Where His life - blood shall be ___ spilled.
Tri - nal U - ni - ty, whose prais - es All cre - at - ed things re - peat.

SING PRAISE TO GOD WHO REIGNS ABOVE

words by
Johann J. Schütz (1640-1690)
tr. by Frances E. Cox (1812-1897)

MIT FREUDEN ZART
music from
Bohemian Brethren's *Kirchengesänge*, 1566

1. Sing praise to God Who reigns a - bove, The ___ God of all cre -
2. What God's al - might - y pow'r hath made, His ___ gra - cious mer - cy
3. The Lord is nev - er far a - way, But, ___ through all grief dis -
4. Thus all my toil - some way a - long I ___ sing a - loud His

a - tion, The God of pow'r, the God of love, The ___ God of our sal -
keep - eth, By morn - ing glow or eve - ning shade His ___ watch - ful eye ne'er ___
tress - ing, An ev - er - pres - ent help and stay, Our ___ peace and joy and ___
prais - es, That all may hear the grate - ful song My ___ voice un - wea - ried ___

va - tion; With heal - ing balm my soul He fills, And
sleep - eth; With - in the king - dom of His might, Lo!
bless - ing; As with a moth - er's ten - der hand He
rais - es; Be joy - ful in the Lord, my heart! Both

ev - 'ry faith - less mur - mur stills: }
all is just and all is right: }   To God all praise and ___ glo - ry!
leads His own, His cho - sen band: }
soul and bod - y bear your part: }

SING PRAISES TO GOD

LAUDATE DOMINUM
music by
C. Hubert H. Parry, 1887

words by
Henry Williams Baker, 1875, et al.

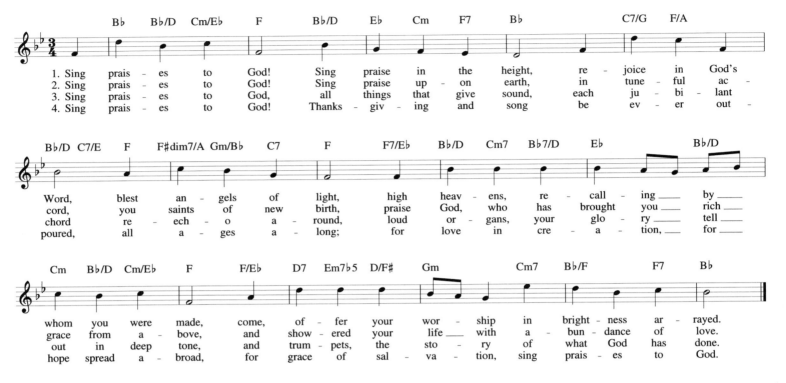

1. Sing prais - es to God! Sing praise in the height, re - joice in God's
2. Sing prais - es to God! Sing praise up - on earth, in tune - ful ac -
3. Sing prais - es to God, all things that give sound, each ju - bi - lant
4. Sing prais - es to God! Thanks - giv - ing and song be ev - er out -

Word, blest an - gels of light, high heav - ens, re - call - ing ___ by ___
cord, you saints of new birth, high praise God, who has brought you ___ rich ___
chord re - ech - o a - round, loud or - gans, your glo - ry ___ tell ___
poured, all a - ges a - long; for love in cre - a - tion, ___ for ___

whom you were made, come, of - fer your wor - ship in bright - ness ar - rayed.
grace from a - bove, and show - ered your life ___ with a - bun - dance of love.
out in deep tone, and trum - pets, the sto - ry of what God has done.
hope spread a - broad, for grace of sal - va - tion, sing prais - es to God.

SING TO THE LORD OF HARVEST

WIE LIEBLICH IST DER MAIEN
music by
J. Steurlein (1546-1613)
from *Himmlische Harpffe Davids*

words by
J.S.B. Monsell (1811-1875)

1. Sing to the Lord ___ of ___ har - vest; Sing songs of love and praise. With
2. By Him the clouds ___ drop ___ good - ness; The des - erts bloom and spring. The
3. Heap on His sa - cred ___ al - tar The gifts His good - ness gave, The

joy - ful hearts ___ and ___ voic - es Your al - le - lu - ias raise. By
hills leap up ___ in ___ glad - ness; The val - leys laugh and sing. He
gold - en sheaves ___ of ___ har - vest, The souls He died to save. Your

Him the roll - ing ___ sea - sons In fruit - ful or - der ___ move; Sing
fill - eth with His ___ full - ness, All things with large ___ in - crease; He
hearts lay down be - fore Him When at His feet ___ ye fall, And

to the Lord ___ of ___ har - vest A song of hap - py love.
crowns the year ___ with ___ good - ness, With plen - ty, and with peace.
with your lives ___ a - dore Him Who gave His life for all.

SING WITH ALL THE SAINTS IN GLORY

words by
William J. Irons, 1873

HYMN TO JOY
music by
Ludwig van Beethoven, 1824
arr. by Edward Hodges, 1864

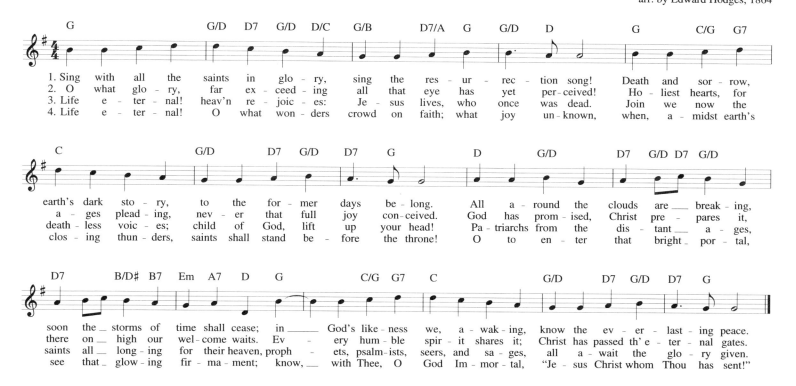

1. Sing with all the saints in glory, sing the res-ur-rec-tion song! Death and sor-row,
2. O what glory, far ex-ceed-ing all that eye has yet per-ceived! Ho-liest hearts, for
3. Life e-ter-nal! heav'n re-joic-es: Je-sus lives, who once was dead. Join we now the
4. Life e-ter-nal! O what won-ders crowd on faith; what joy un-known, when, a-midst earth's

earth's dark sto-ry, to the for-mer days be-long. All a-round the clouds are break-ing,
a-ges plead-ing, nev-er that full joy con-ceived. God has prom-ised, Christ pre-pares it,
death-less voic-es; child of God, lift up your head! Pa-triarchs from the dis-tant a-ges,
clos-ing thun-ders, saints shall stand be-fore the throne! O to en-ter that bright por-tal,

soon the storms of time shall cease; in God's like-ness we, a-wak-ing, know the ev-er-last-ing peace.
there on high our wel-come waits. Ev-ery hum-ble spir-it shares it; Christ has passed th'e-ter-nal gates.
saints all long-ing for their heaven, proph-ets, psalm-ists, seers, and sa-ges, all a-wait the glo-ry given.
see that glow-ing fir-ma-ment; know, with Thee, O God Im-mor-tal, "Je-sus Christ whom Thou has sent!"

SINGING I GO

words by
Eliza E. Hewitt (1851-1920)

music by
William J. Kirkpatrick (1838-1921)

1. The trust-ing heart to Je-sus clings, Nor an-y ill fore-bodes, But
2. The pass-ing days bring man-y cares. "Fear not," I hear Him say; And
3. He tells me of my Fa-ther's love And nev-er-slum-b'ring eye; My
4. When to the throne of grace I flee, I find the prom-ise true: The

at the cross of Cal-v'ry sings, "Praise God for lift-ed loads!"
when my fears are turned to prayers, The bur-dens slip a-way.
ev-er-last-ing King a-bove Will all my needs sup-ply.
might-y arms up-hold-ing me Will bear my bur-dens too.

Refrain

Sing-ing I go a-long life's road, Prais-ing the Lord, prais-ing the Lord;

Sing-ing I go a-long life's road, For Je-sus has lift-ed my load.

SO LET OUR LIPS AND LIVES EXPRESS

HEBRON

words by
Isaac Watts, 1707

music by
Lowell Mason, 1830

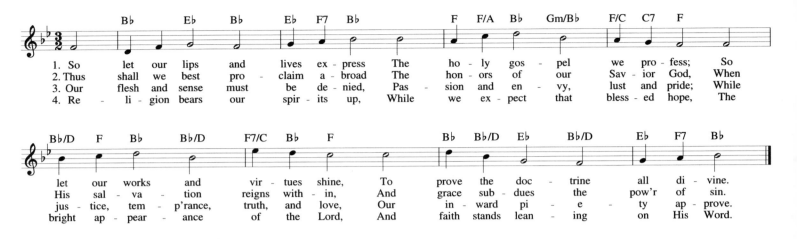

1. So let our lips and lives ex - press The ho - ly gos - pel we pro - fess; So
2. Thus shall we best pro - claim a - broad The hon - ors of our Sav - ior God, When
3. Our flesh and sense must be de - nied, Pas - sion and en - vy, lust and pride; While
4. Re - li - gion bears our spir - its up, While we ex - pect that bless - ed hope, The

let our works and vir - tues shine, To prove the doc - trine all di - vine.
His sal - va - tion reigns with - in, And grace sub - dues the pow'r of sin.
jus - tice, tem - p'rance, truth, and love, Our in - ward pi - e - ty ap - prove.
bright ap - pear - ance of the Lord, And faith stands lean - ing on His Word.

SOFTLY AND TENDERLY

THOMPSON

words by
Will L. Thompson (1847-1909)

music by
Will L. Thompson (1847-1909)

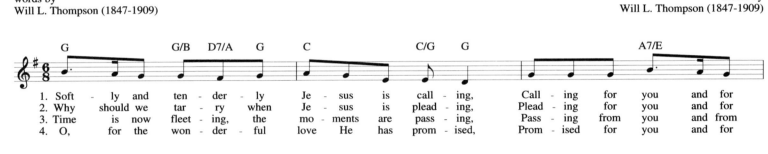

1. Soft - ly and ten - der - ly Je - sus is call - ing, Call - ing for you and for
2. Why should we tar - ry when Je - sus is plead - ing, Plead - ing for you and for
3. Time is now fleet - ing, the mo - ments are pass - ing, Pass - ing from you and from
4. O, for the won - der - ful love He has prom - ised, Prom - ised for you and for

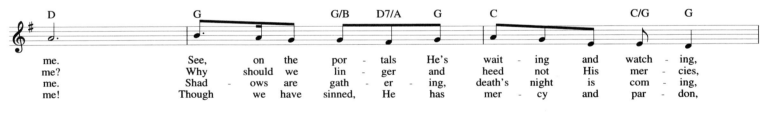

me. See, on the por - tals He's wait - ing and watch - ing,
me? Why should we lin - ger and heed not His mer - cies,
me. Shad - ows are gath - er - ing, death's night is com - ing,
me! Though we have sinned, He has mer - cy and par - don,

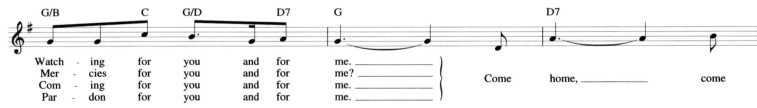

Watch - ing for you and for me. Come home, come
Mer - cies for you and for me?
Com - ing for you and for me.
Par - don for you and for me.

home, Ye who are wear - y, come home.

Earn - est - ly, ten - der - ly, Je - sus is call - ing, Call - ing, O sin - ner, come home!

SOLDIERS OF CHRIST, ARISE

words by
Charles Wesley, 1749

DIADEMATA
music by
George J. Elvey, 1868

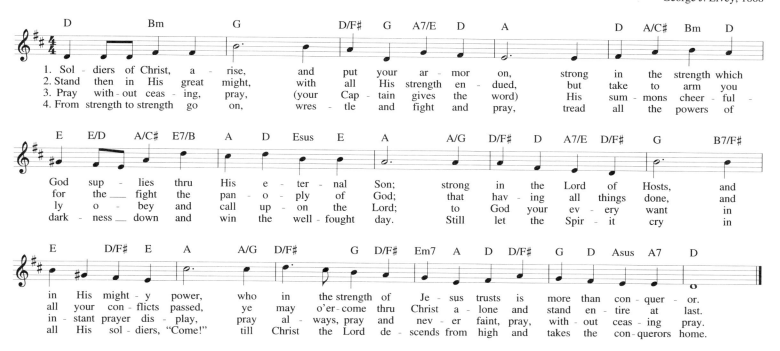

1. Sol - diers of Christ, a - rise, and put your ar - mor on, strong in the strength which
2. Stand then in His great might, with all His strength en - dued, but take to arm you
3. Pray with - out ceas - ing, pray, (your Cap - tain gives the word) His sum - mons cheer - ful -
4. From strength to strength go on, wres - tle and fight and pray, tread all the powers of

God sup - plies thru His e - ter - nal Son; strong in the Lord of Hosts, and
for the ___ fight the pan - o - ply of God; that hav - ing all things done, and
ly o - bey and call up - on the Lord; to God your ev - ery want in
dark - ness ___ down and win the well - fought day. Still let the Spir - it cry in

in His might - y power, who in the strength of Je - sus trusts is more than con - quer - or.
all your con - flicts passed, ye may o'er - come thru Christ a - lone and stand en - tire at last.
in - stant prayer dis - play, pray al - ways, pray and nev - er faint, pray, with - out ceas - ing pray.
all His sol - diers, "Come!" till Christ the Lord de - scends from high and takes the con - querors home.

Copyright © 2000 by HAL LEONARD CORPORATION

SOMEBODY'S KNOCKING AT YOUR DOOR

African-American Spiritual

SOMEBODY'S KNOCKIN'
African-American Spiritual

Some - bod - y's knock - ing at your door, Some - bod - y's knock - ing at your

door. O ___ sin - ner, why don't you an - swer?

Some - bod - y's knock - ing at your door.
1. Knocks like ___ Je - sus.
2. Can't you ___ hear him?
3. An - swer ___ Je - sus.

Some - bod - y's knock - ing at your door.
Knocks like ___ Je - sus,
Can't you ___ hear him?
An - swer ___ Je - sus.

Some - bod - y's knock - ing at your door. O ___ sin - ner,

why don't you an - swer? Some - bod - y's knock - ing at your door.

Copyright © 2000 by HAL LEONARD CORPORATION

SOMETHING FOR THEE

SOMETHING FOR JESUS
music by
Robert Lowry (1826-1899)

words by
Sylvanus D. Phelps (1816-1895)

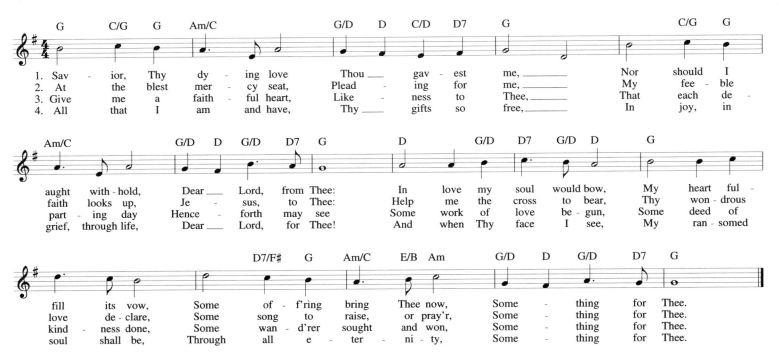

1. Sav - ior, Thy dy - ing love Thou gav - est me, Nor should I
2. At the blest mer - cy seat, Plead - ing for me, My fee - ble
3. Give me a faith - ful heart, Like - ness to Thee, That each de -
4. All that I am and have, Thy gifts so free, In joy, in

aught with - hold, Dear Lord, from Thee: In love my soul would bow, My heart ful -
faith looks up, Je - sus, to Thee: Help me the cross to bear, Thy won - drous
part - ing day Hence - forth may see Some work of love be - gun, Some deed of
grief, through life, Dear Lord, for Thee! And when Thy face I see, My ran - somed

fill its vow, Some of - f'ring bring Thee now, Some - thing for Thee.
love de - clare, Some song to raise, or pray'r, Some - thing for Thee.
kind - ness done, Some wan - d'rer sought and won, Some - thing for Thee.
soul shall be, Through all e - ter - ni - ty, Some - thing for Thee.

SOMETIMES A LIGHT SURPRISES

BLOMSTERTID
music from
Swedish *Koralbox,* 1697

words by
William Cowper (1731-1800)

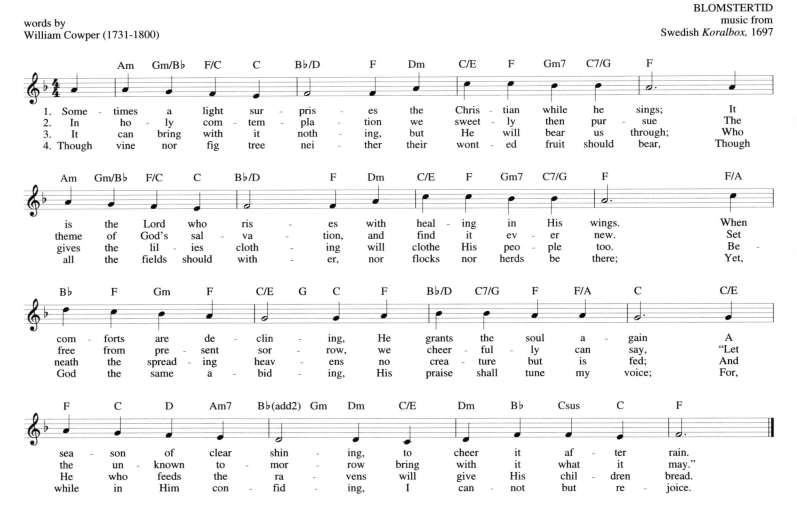

1. Some - times a light sur - pris - es the Chris - tian while he sings; It
2. In ho - ly com - tem - pla - tion we sweet - ly then pur - sue The
3. It can bring with it noth - ing, we but He will bear us through; Who
4. Though vine nor fig tree nei - ther their wont - ed fruit should bear, Though

is the Lord who ris - es with heal - ing in His wings. When
theme of God's sal - va - tion, and find it ev - er new. Set
gives the lil - ies cloth - ing will clothe His peo - ple too. Be -
all the fields should with - er, nor flocks nor herds be there; Yet,

com - forts are de - clin - ing, He grants the soul a - gain A
free from pre - sent sor - row, we cheer - ful - ly can say, "Let
neath the spread - ing heav - ens no crea - ture but is fed; And
God the same a - bid - ing, His praise shall tune my voice; For,

sea - son of clear shin - ing, to cheer it af - ter rain.
the un - known to - mor - row bring with it what it may."
He who feeds the ra - vens will give His chil - dren bread.
while in Him con - fid - ing, I can - not but re - joice.

SOMETIMES A LIGHT SURPRISES

words by
William Cowper (1731-1800)

LIGHT
music from
The Christian Lyre, 1830

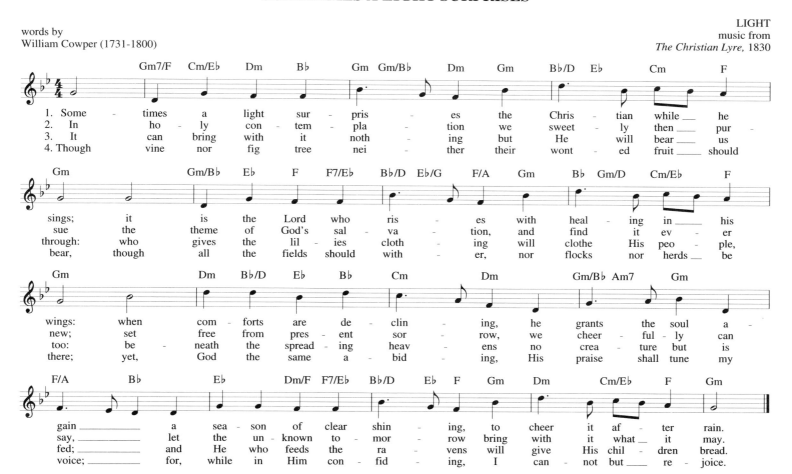

THE SON OF GOD GOES FORTH TO WAR

words by
R. Heber (1783-1826)

ALL SAINTS NEW
music by
H.S. Cutler (1824-1902)

SOUL, ADORN THYSELF WITH GLADNESS

SCHMÜCKE DICH

words by
J. Franck (1618-1677)
tr. by C. Winkworth (1827-1878)

music by
J. Crüger (1598-1662)

1. Soul, a - dorn thy - self with glad - ness, Leave be - hind all gloom and sad - ness,
2. Hast - en as a bridge to meet Him, And with lov - ing rev - 'rence greet Him,
3. Hu - man rea - son, though it pon - der, Can - not fath - om this great won - der,
4. Je - sus, Sun of Life, my Spen - dor, Je - sus, Thou my Friend most ten - der,
5. Lord, by love and mer - cy driv - en, Thou hast left Thy throne in heav - en,
6. Je - sus, Bread of Life, I pray Thee, Let me glad - ly here o - bey Thee.

Come in - to the day - light's spen - dor; There with joy thy prais - es ren - der
For with words of life im - mor - tal Now He knock - eth at thy por - tal.
That Christ's bod - y e'er re - main - eth Though it count - less souls sus - tain - eth,
Je - sus, joy of my de - sir - ing, Fount of life, my soul in - spir - ing,
On the cross for us to lan - guish And to die in bit - ter an - guish,
By Thy love I am in - vit - ed, Be Thy love with love re - quit - ed;

Un - to Him whose grace un - bound - ed Hath this won - drous Sup - per found - ed.
Haste to ope the gates be - fore Him, Say - ing, while thou dost a - dore Him:
And that He His blood is giv - ing With the wine we are re - ceiv - ing.
At Thy feet I cry, my Mak - er, Let me be a fit par - tak - er
To fore - go all joy and glad - ness And to shed Thy blood in sad - ness.
From this Sup - per let me meas - ure, Lord, how vast and deep love's treas - ure.

High o'er all the heav'ns he reign - eth, Yet to dwell with thee He deign - eth.
Suf - fer, Lord, that I re - ceive Thee, And I nev - er - more will leave Thee.
These great mys - ter - ies un - sound - ed Are by God a - lone ex - pound - ed.
Of this bless - ed food from heav - en, For our good, Thy glo - ry, giv - en.
By this blood, re - deemed and liv - ing, Lord, I praise Thee with thanks - giv - ing.
Through the gifts Thou here dost give me, As Thy guest in heav'n re - ceive me.

SOUL OF MY SAVIOR

ANIMA CHRISTI

v. 1, 2 attr. to Pope John XXII (1249-1334)
tr. by Edward Caswall (1814-1878)
v. 3 from *The Parish Hymnal*, 1915

music by
W.J. Maher (1823-1877)

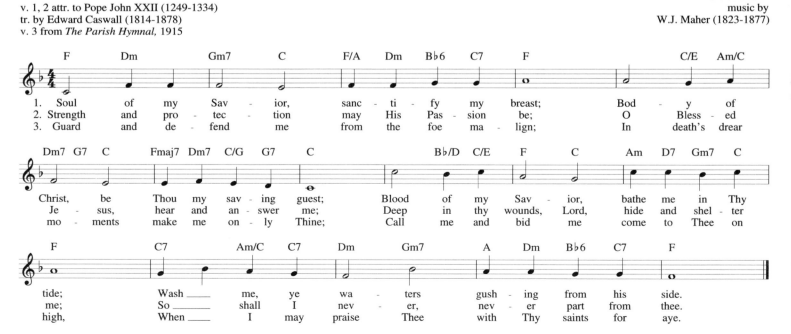

1. Soul of my Sav - ior, sanc - ti - fy my breast; Bod - y of
2. Strength and pro - tec - tion may His Pas - sion be; O Bless - ed
3. Guard and de - fend me from the foe ma - lign; In death's drear

Christ, be Thou my sav - ing guest; Blood of my Sav - ior, bathe me in Thy
Je - sus, hear and an - swer me; Deep in thy wounds, Lord, hide and shel - ter
mo - ments make me on - ly Thine; Call me and bid me come to Thee on

tide; Wash me, ye wa - ters gush - ing from his side.
me; So shall I nev - er, nev - er part from thee.
high, When I may praise Thee with Thy saints for aye.

SOUND THE BATTLE CRY

words by
William F. Sherwin, 1869

SHERWIN
music by
William F. Sherwin, 1869

1. Sound the bat - tle cry! See, the foe is nigh. Raise the stan - dard high
2. Strong to meet the foe, March - ing on we go, While our cause, we know,
3. O Thou God of all, hear us when we call; help us one and all

For the ___ Lord. Gird your ar - mor on; Stand firm, ev - 'ry - one. Rest your cause up - on His
Must pre - vail. Shield and ban - ner bright Gleam - ing in the light; Bat - tling for the right, We
By Thy grace. When the bat - tle's done, And the vic - t'ry's won, May we wear the crown Be -

ho - ly Word. }
ne'er can fail. } Rouse, then, sol - diers; ral - ly round the ban - ner.
fore Thy face. }

Refrain

Read - y, stead - y, pass the word a - long. On - ward, for - ward,

shout a - loud, "Ho - san - na!" Christ is Cap - tain of the might - y throng.

SPIRIT DIVINE, ATTEND OUR PRAYERS

NUN DANKET ALL' UND BRINGET EHR'

words by
Andrew Reed, 1829

music by
Johann Crüger, 1647

1. Spir - it di - vine, at - tend our prayers, And make this
2. Come as the light: to us re - veal ___ Our sin - ful -
3. Come as the fire: and purge our hearts ___ Like sac - ri -
4. Come as the wind, with rush - ing sound, ___ With pen - te -
5. Come as the dove: and spread Thy wings, ___ The wings of

house Thy home; De - scend with all Thy
ness and woe; And lead us in those
fi - cial flame; Let our whole soul an
cos - tal grace; And make the great sal -
peace - ful love; And let Thy church on

gra - cious powers; ___ O come, great Spir - it, come!
paths of life ___ Where all the right - eous go.
of - fering be known ___ To our re - deem - er's name.
va - tion known ___ Wide as the hu - man race.
earth be - come ___ Blest as Thy church a - bove.

THE SPACIOUS FIRMAMENT ON HIGH

CREATION
music by
Franz Joseph Haydn (1732-1809)
from *The Creation*

words by
Joseph Addison (1672-1719)
para. of Psalm 19:1-6

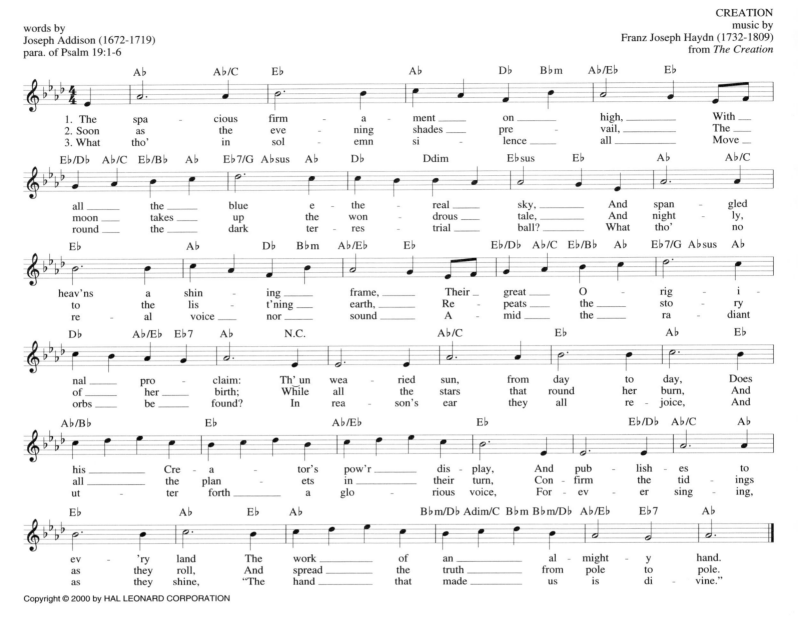

1. The spa - cious firm - a - ment on high, With
2. Soon as the eve - ning shades pre - vail, The
3. What tho' in sol - emn si - lence all Move

all the blue e - the - real sky, And span - gled
moon takes up the won - drous tale, And night - ly,
round the dark ter - res - trial ball? What tho' no

heav'ns a shin - ing frame, Their great O - rig - i -
to the lis - t'ning earth, Re - peats the sto - ry
re - al voice nor sound A - mid the ra - diant

nal pro - claim: Th' un wea - ried sun, from day to day, Does
of her birth; While all the stars that round her burn, And
orbs be found? In rea - son's ear they all re - joice, And

his Cre - a - tor's pow'r dis - play, And pub - lish - es to
all the plan - ets in their turn, Con - firm the tid - ings
ut - ter forth a glo - rious voice, For - ev - er sing - ing,

ev - 'ry land The work of an al - might - y hand.
as they roll, And spread the truth from pole to pole.
as they shine, "The hand that made us is di - vine."

SPIRIT OF FAITH, COME DOWN

BEALOTH
music from
Sacred Harp (Mason), 1840

words by
Charles Wesley, 1746

1. Spir - it of faith, come down, re - veal the things of God, and make to us the
2. No one can tru - ly say that Je - sus is the Lord, un - less Thou take the
3. O that the world might know the all - a - ton - ing Lamb! Spir - it of faith, de -
4. In - spire the liv - ing faith (which who - so - e'er re - ceive, the wit - ness in them -

God - head known, and wit - ness with the blood. 'Tis Thine the blood to ap - ply and
veil a - way and breath the liv - ing Word. Then, on - ly then, we feel our
scend and show the vir - tue of His name; the grace which all may find, the
selves they have and con - scious - ly be - lieve), the faith that con - quers all, and

give us eyes to see, who did for ev - ery sin - ner die hath sure - ly died for me.
in - terest in His blood, and cry with joy un - speak - a - ble, "Thou art my Lord, my God!"
sav - ing power, im - part, and tes - ti - fy to hu - man - kind, and speak in ev - ery heart.
doth the moun - tain move, and saves who - e'er on Je - sus call, and per - fects them in love.

SPIRIT OF GOD, DESCEND UPON MY HEART

MORECAMBE

words by
George Croly, 1854

music by
Frederick Cook Atkinson, 1870

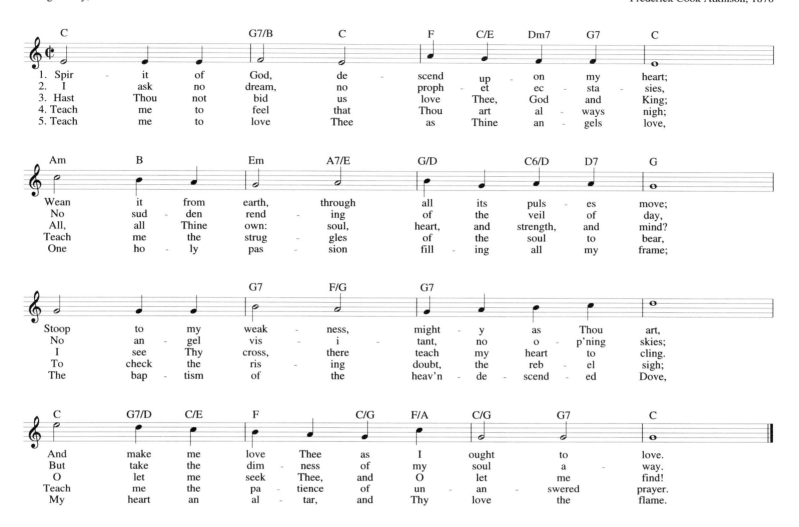

1. Spir - it of God, de - scend up - on my heart;
2. I ask no dream, no proph - et ec - sta - sies,
3. Hast Thou not bid us love Thee, God and King;
4. Teach me to feel that Thou art al - ways nigh;
5. Teach me to love Thee as Thine an - gels love,

Wean it from earth, through all its puls - es move;
No sud - den rend - ing of the veil of day,
All, all Thine own: soul, heart, and strength, and mind?
Teach me the strug - gles of the soul to bear,
One ho - ly pas - sion fill - ing all my frame;

Stoop to my weak - ness, might - y as Thou art,
No an - gel vis - i - tant, no o - p'ning skies;
I see Thy cross, there teach my heart to cling.
To check the ris - ing doubt, the reb - el sigh;
The bap - tism of the heav'n - de - scend - ed Dove,

And make me love Thee as I ought to love.
But take the dim - ness of my soul a - way.
O let me seek Thee, and O let me find!
Teach me the pa - tience of un - an - swered prayer.
My heart an al - tar, and Thy love the flame.

STAND UP AND BLESS THE LORD

CARLISLE

words by
James Montgomery, 1824

music by
Charles Lockhart, 1769

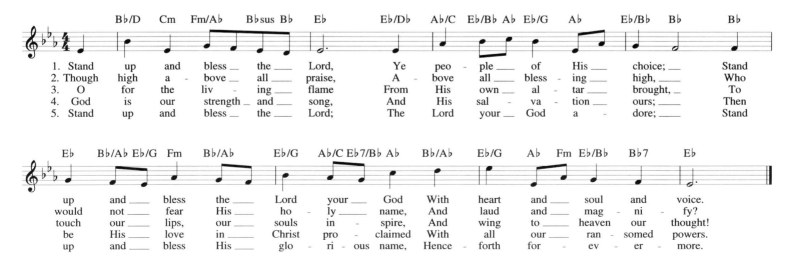

1. Stand up and bless the Lord, Ye peo - ple of His choice; Stand
2. Though high a - bove all praise, A - bove all bless - ing high, Who
3. O for the liv - ing flame From His own al - tar brought, To
4. God is our strength and song, And His sal - va - tion ours; Then
5. Stand up and bless the Lord; The Lord your God a - dore; Stand

up and bless the Lord your God With heart and soul and voice.
would not fear His ho - ly name, And laud and mag - ni - fy?
touch our lips, our souls in - spire, And wing to heaven our thought!
be His love in Christ pro - claimed With all our ran - somed powers.
up and bless His glo - ri - ous name, Hence - forth for - ev - er - more.

STAND UP AND BLESS THE LORD

words by
James Montgomery (1771-1854)

ST. MICHAEL
music from
Genevan Psalter, 1551
adapt. by William Crotch, 1836

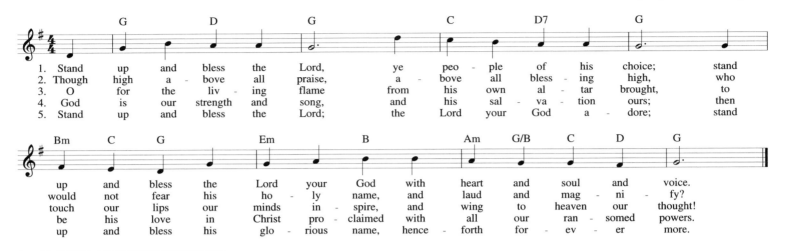

1. Stand up and bless the Lord, ye peo - ple of his choice; stand
2. Though high a - bove all praise, a - bove all bless - ing high, who
3. O for the liv - ing flame, from his own al - tar brought, to
4. God is our strength and song, and his sal - va - tion ours; then
5. Stand up and bless the Lord; the Lord your God a - dore; stand

up and bless the Lord your God with heart and soul and voice.
would not fear his ho - ly name, and laud and mag - ni - fy?
touch our lips our minds in - spire, and wing to heaven our thought!
be his love in Christ pro - claimed with all our ran - somed powers.
up and bless his glo - rious name, hence - forth for - ev - er more.

STAND UP, STAND UP FOR JESUS

words by
George Duffield, Jr., 1858

GEIBEL
music by
Adam Geibel, 1901

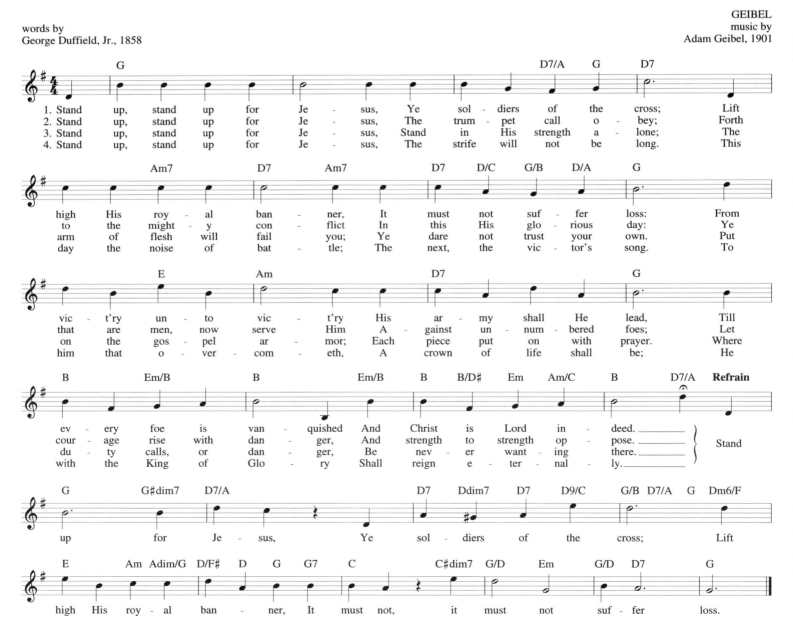

1. Stand up, stand up for Je - sus, Ye sol - diers of the cross; Lift
2. Stand up, stand up for Je - sus, The trum - pet call o - bey; Forth
3. Stand up, stand up for Je - sus, Stand in His strength a - lone; The
4. Stand up, stand up for Je - sus, The strife will not be long. This

high His roy - al ban - ner, It must not suf - fer loss: From
to the might - y con - flict, In this His glo - rious day: Ye
arm of flesh will fail you; Ye dare not trust your own. Put
day the noise of bat - tle; The next, the vic - tor's song. To

vic - t'ry un - to vic - t'ry His ar - my shall He lead, Till
that are men, now serve Him A - gainst un - num - bered foes; Let
on the gos - pel ar - mor; Each piece put on with prayer. Where
him that o - ver - com - eth, A crown of life shall be; He

ev - ery foe is van - quished And Christ is Lord in - deed. _____
cour - age rise with dan - ger, And strength to strength op - pose. _____ } Stand
du - ty calls, or dan - ger, Be nev - er want - ing there. _____
with the King of Glo - ry Shall reign e - ter - nal - ly. _____

Refrain

up for Je - sus, Ye sol - diers of the cross; Lift

high His roy - al ban - ner, It must not, it must not suf - fer loss.

STAND UP, STAND UP FOR JESUS

words by
George Duffield, Jr., 1858

WEBB
music by
George J. Webb, 1830

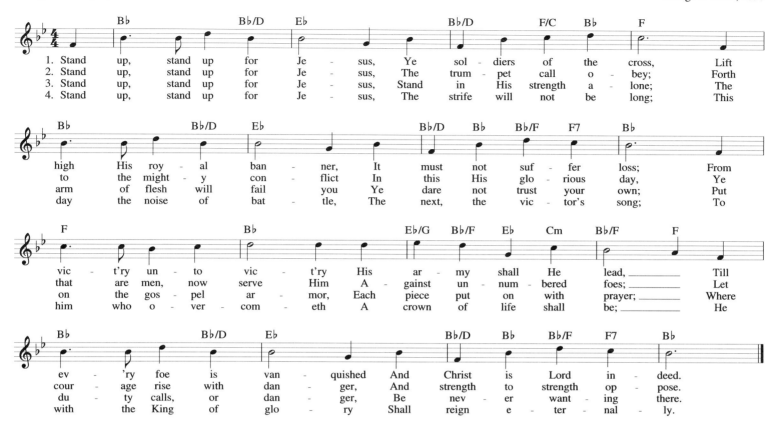

1. Stand up, stand up for Je - sus, Ye sol - diers of the cross, Lift
2. Stand up, stand up for Je - sus, The trum - pet call o - bey; Forth
3. Stand up, stand up for Je - sus, Stand in His strength a - lone; The
4. Stand up, stand up for Je - sus, The strife will not be long; This

high His roy - al ban - ner, It must not suf - fer loss; From
to the might - y con - flict In this His glo - rious day, Ye
arm of flesh will fail you Ye dare not trust your own; Put
day the noise of bat - tle, The next, the vic - tor's song; To

vic - t'ry un - to vic - t'ry His ar - my shall He lead, Till
that are men, now serve Him A - gainst un - num - bered foes; Let
on the gos - pel ar - mor, Each piece put on with prayer; Where
him who o - ver - com - eth A crown of life shall be; He

ev - 'ry foe is van - quished And Christ is Lord in - deed.
cour - age rise with dan - ger, And strength to strength op - pose.
du - ty calls, or dan - ger, Be nev - er want - ing there.
with the King of glo - ry Shall reign e - ter - nal - ly.

STANDING ON THE PROMISES

PROMISES
words by
R. Kelso Carter, 1886

music by
R. Kelso Carter, 1886

1. Stand - ing on the prom - is - es of Christ my King,
2. Stand - ing on the prom - is - es that can - not fail,
3. Stand - ing on the prom - is - es of Christ the Lord,
4. Stand - ing on the prom - is - es I can - not fall,

Thro' e - ter - nal a - ges let His prais - es ring;
When the howl - ing storms of doubt and fear as - sail,
Bound to Him e - ter - nal - ly by love's strong cord,
Lis - t'ning ev - ery mo - ment to the Spir - it's call,

Glo - ry in the high - est, I will shout and sing,
By the liv - ing Word of God I shall pre - vail,
O - ver - com - ing dai - ly with the Spir - it's sword,
Rest - ing in my Sav - ior as my all in all,

Stand - ing on the prom - is - es of God.

Refrain

Stand - ing, stand - ing, Stand - ing on the prom - is - es of God my Sav - ior;

Stand - ing, stand - ing, I'm stand - ing on the prom - is - es of God.

STANDING IN THE NEED OF PRAYER

African-American Spiritual

PENITENT
African-American Spiritual

It's me, it's me, O Lord, ___ stand-ing in the need of prayer. It's me, it's me, O Lord, ___ stand-ing in the need of prayer.

1. Not my broth-er, not my sis-ter, but it's me, O Lord, ___ stand-ing in the need of prayer. Not my
2. Not the preach-er, not the dea-con, but it's me, O Lord, ___ stand-ing in the need of prayer. Not the
3. Not my fa-ther, not my moth-er, but it's me, O Lord, ___ stand-ing in the need of prayer. Not my

broth-er, not my sis-ter, but it's me, O Lord, ___ stand-ing in the need of prayer. It's
preach-er, not the dea-con, but it's me, O Lord, ___ stand-ing in the need of prayer. It's
fa-ther, not my moth-er, but it's me, O Lord, ___ stand-ing in the need of prayer. It's

stand-ing in the need of prayer. It's

stand-ing in the need of prayer.

THE STAR-SPANGLED BANNER

words by
Francis Scott Key (1779-1843)

NATIONAL ANTHEM
music attr. to
John Stafford Smith (1750-1836)

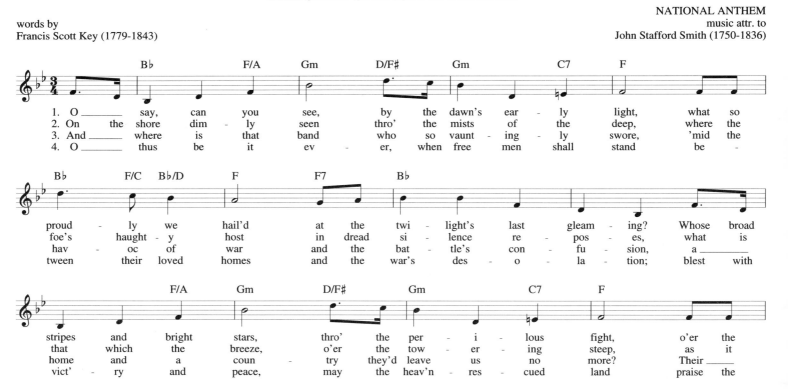

1. O ___ say, can you see, by the dawn's ear-ly light, what so
2. On the shore dim-ly seen thro' the mists of the deep, where the
3. And ___ where is that band who so vaunt-ing-ly swore, 'mid the
4. O ___ thus be it ev-er, when free men shall stand be-

proud-ly we hail'd at the twi-light's last gleam-ing? Whose broad
foe's haught-y host in dread si-lence re-pos-es, what is
hav-oc of war and the bat-tle's con-fu-sion, a ___
tween their loved homes and the war's des-o-la-tion; blest with

stripes and bright stars, thro' the per-i-lous fight, o'er the
that which the breeze, o'er the tow-er-ing steep, as it
home and a coun-try they'd leave us no more? Their ___
vict'-ry and peace, may the heav'n res-cued land praise the

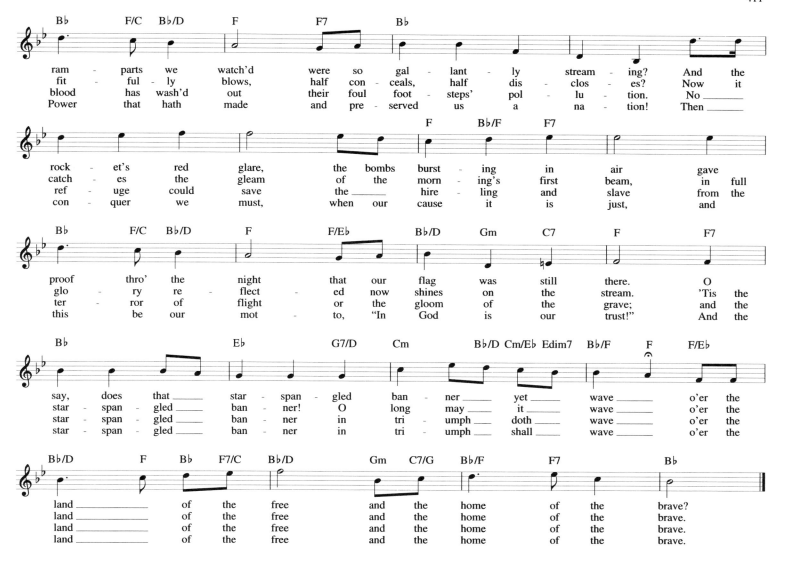

STEAL AWAY TO JESUS

Traditional Spiritual

STEAL AWAY
Traditional Spiritual

STILL, STILL WITH THEE

CONSOLATION

words by
Harriet B. Stowe (1812-1896)

music by
Felix Mendelssohn (1809-1847)

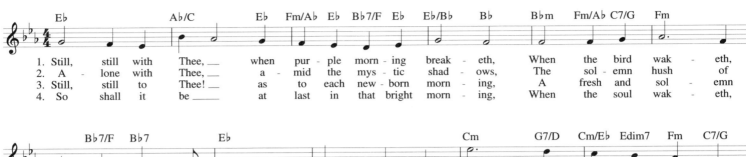
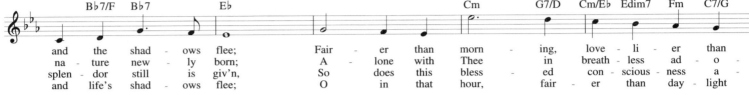
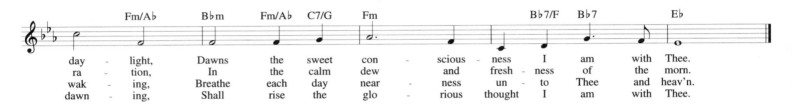

STEPPING IN THE LIGHT

BEAUTIFUL TO WALK

words by
Eliza E. Hewitt, 1890

music by
William J. Kirkpatrick, 1890

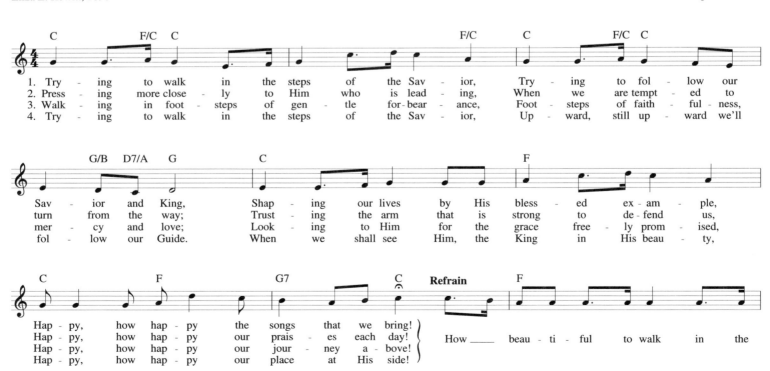

STILL SWEETER EVERY DAY

words by
W.C. Martin, 1899

music by
C. Austin Miles, 1899

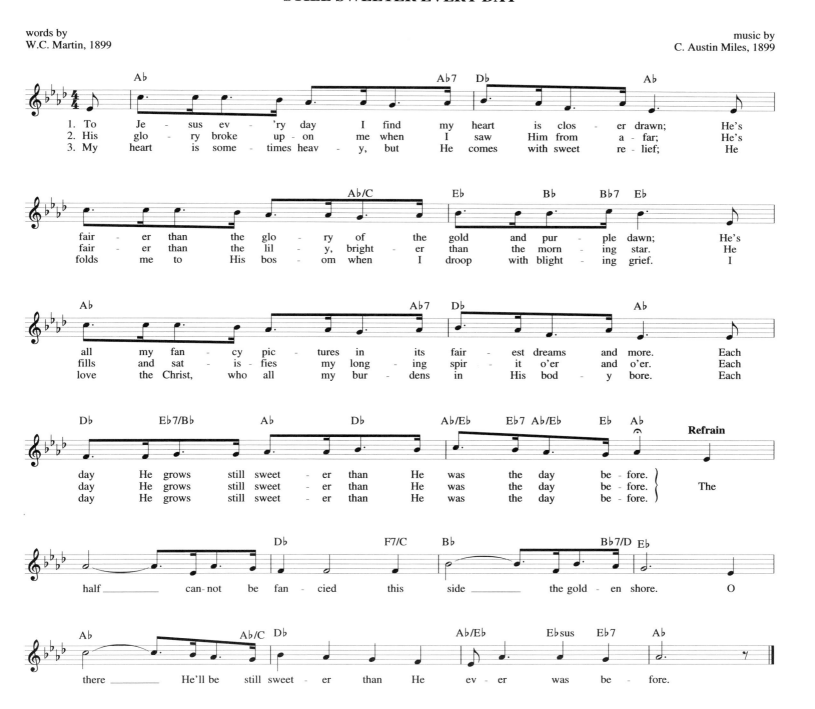

THE STRIFE IS O'ER, THE BATTLE DONE

Traditional Latin text, c. 1695
tr. by Francis Pott, 1861

VICTORY
music by
Giovanni P. da Palestrina, 1591

SUNLIGHT IN MY SOUL

words by
Judson W. Van DeVenter, 1897

music by
Winfield S. Weeden, 1897

SUNSHINE IN MY SOUL

words by
Eliza E. Hewitt, 1887

SUNSHINE
music by
John R. Sweney, 1887

SWEET BY AND BY

words by
Sanford F. Bennett (1836-1898)

music by
Joseph P. Webster (1819-1875)

SWEET HOUR OF PRAYER

SWEET HOUR

words by
William W. Walford (1772-1850)

music by
William B. Bradbury (1816-1868)

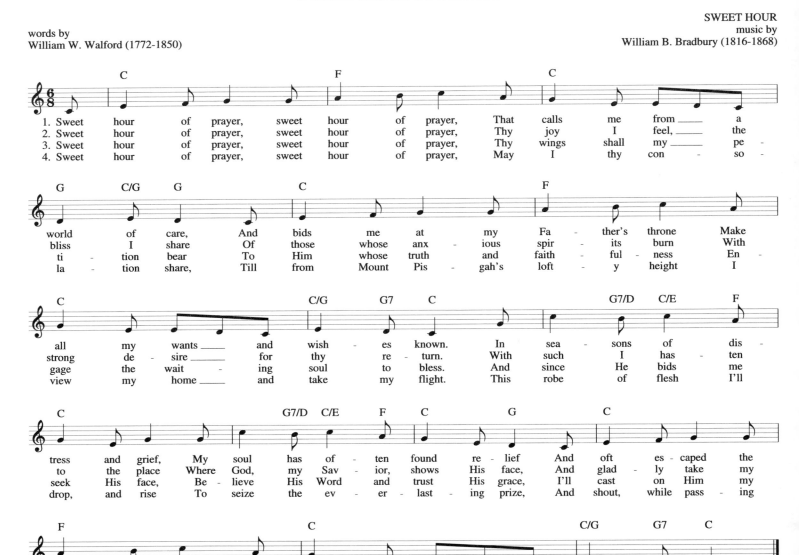

1. Sweet hour of prayer, sweet hour of prayer, That calls me from a world of care, And bids me at my Fa - ther's throne Make all my wants and wish - es known. In sea - sons of dis - tress and grief, My soul has of - ten found re - lief And oft es - caped the tempt - er's snare By thy re - turn, sweet hour of prayer.

2. Sweet hour of prayer, sweet hour of prayer, Thy joy I feel, the bliss I share Of those whose anx - ious spir - its burn With strong de - sire for thy re - turn. With such I has - ten to the place Where God, my Sav - ior, shows His face, And glad - ly take my sta - tion there And wait for thee, sweet hour of prayer.

3. Sweet hour of prayer, sweet hour of prayer, Thy wings shall my pe - ti - tion bear To Him whose truth and faith - ful - ness En gage the wait - ing soul to bless. And since He bids me seek His face, Be - lieve His Word and trust His grace, I'll cast on Him my ev - 'ry care And wait for thee, sweet hour of prayer.

4. Sweet hour of prayer, sweet hour of prayer, May I thy con - so - la - tion share, Till from Mount Pis - gah's loft - y height I view my home and take my flight. This robe of flesh I'll drop, and rise To seize the ev - er - last - ing prize, And shout, while pass - ing through the air, "Fare - well, fare - well, sweet hour of prayer!"

Copyright © 2000 by HAL LEONARD CORPORATION

SWEET WILL OF GOD

SWEET WILL

words by
Lelia N. Morris, 1900

music by
Lelia N. Morris, 1900

1. My stub - born will at last hath yield - ed; I would be Thine, and Thine a - lone. And this the prayer my lips are

2. I'm tired of sin, foot - sore and wea - ry; The dark - some path hath drea - ry grown. But now a light has ris'n to

3. Thy pre - cious will, O con - qu'ring Sav - ior, Doth now em - brace and com - pass me; All dis - cords hushed, my peace a

4. Shut in with Thee, O Lord, for - ev - er, My way - ward feet no more to roam; What pow'r from Thee my soul can

Copyright © 2000 by HAL LEONARD CORPORATION

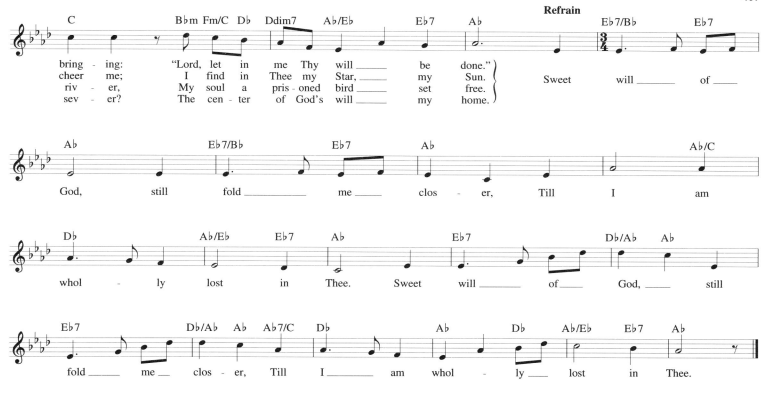

SWING LOW, SWEET CHARIOT

Traditional Spiritual

SWING LOW
Traditional Spiritual

SUN OF MY SOUL

words by
John Keble (1792-1866)

HURSLEY
music from
Katholisches Gesangbuch, Vienna, c. 1774

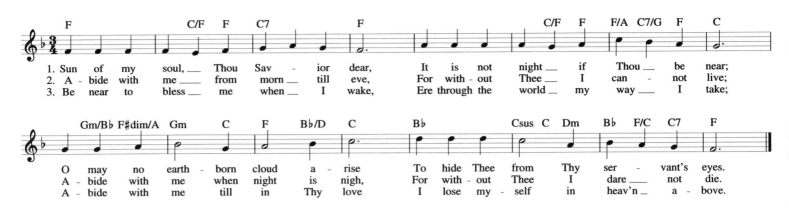

1. Sun of my soul, ___ Thou Sav - ior dear, It is not night ___ if Thou ___ be near;
2. A - bide with me ___ from morn ___ till eve, For with - out Thee ___ I can - not live;
3. Be near to bless ___ me when ___ I wake, Ere through the world ___ my way ___ I take;

O may no earth - born cloud a - rise To hide Thee from Thy ser - vant's eyes.
A - bide with me when night is nigh, For with - out Thee I dare ___ not die.
A - bide with me till in Thy love I lose my - self in heav'n ___ a - bove.

SWEETER AS THE YEARS GO BY

words by
Lelia N. Morris, 1912

SWEETER
music by
Lelia N. Morris, 1912

1. Of Je - sus' love that sought me When I was lost in sin; Of
2. He trod in old Ju - de - a Life's path - way long a - go; The
3. 'Twas won - drous love which led Him For us to suf - fer loss— To

won - drous grace that bro't me Back to His fold a - gain; Of ___
peo - ple thronged a - bout Him, His sav - ing grace to know. He ___
bear with - out a mur - mur The an - guish of the cross. With ___

heights and depths of mer - cy, Far deep - er than the sea, ___ And
healed the bro - ken - heart - ed, And caused the blind to see; ___ And
saints re - deemed in glo - ry, Let us our voic - es raise, ___ Till

high - er than the heav - ens, My theme shall ev - er be.
still His great heart yearn - eth, In love for e - ven me.
heav'n and earth re - ech - o With our Re - deem - er's praise.

Refrain

Sweet - er as the years go by, ___ Sweet - er as the years go by;

Rich - er, full - er, deep - er, Je - sus' love is sweet - er, Sweet - er as the years go by.

TAKE MY LIFE AND LET IT BE

CONSECRATION HYMN

words by
Frances B. Havergal (1836-1879)

music by
William H. Jude (1851-1922)

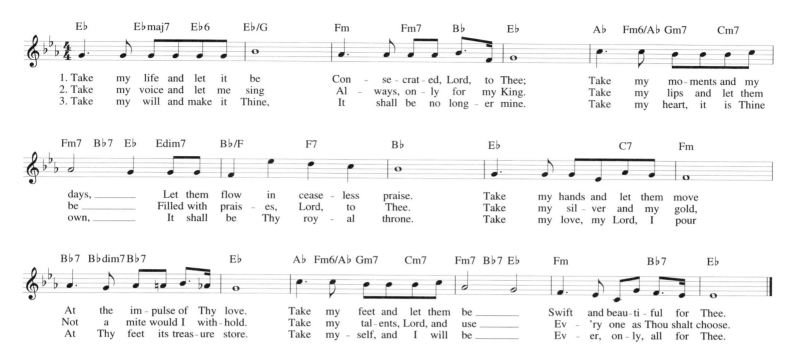

TAKE MY LIFE AND LET IT BE

HENDON

words by
Frances R. Havergal, 1874

music by
Henry A. César Malan, 1827

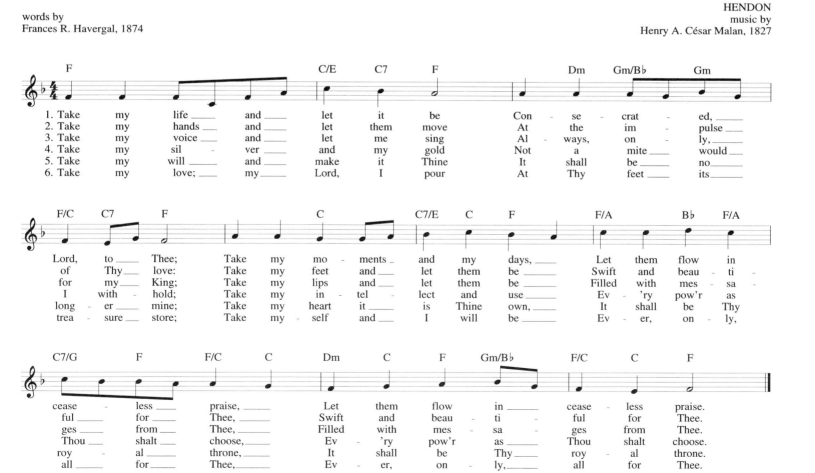

TAKE MY LIFE AND LET IT BE

MESSIAH
music by
Louis J.F. Hérold, 1839
arr. by George Kingsley, 1839

words by
Frances R. Havergal, 1874

TAKE MY LIFE AND LET IT BE

MOZART (II)
music attr. to
Wolfgang A. Mozart, *Twelfth Mass*, 1821

words by
Frances R. Havergal, 1874

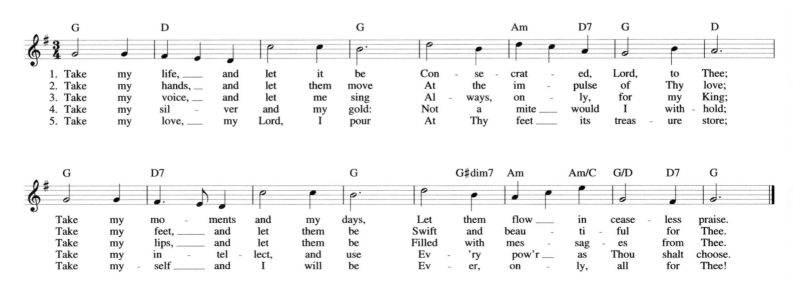

TAKE MY LIFE AND LET IT BE

words by
Frances R. Havergal (1836-1879)

YARBROUGH
music by
William B. Bradbury (1816-1868)

1. Take my life and let it be Con-se-crat-ed, Lord, to Thee; Take my
2. Take my feet and let them be Swift and beau-ti-ful for Thee; Take my
3. Take my sil-ver and my gold, Not a mite would I with-hold; Take my
4. Take my will and make it Thine, It shall be no lon-ger mine; Take my

hands and let them move At the im-pulse of Thy love.
voice, and let me sing, Al-ways, on-ly, for my King.
mo-ments and my days, Let them flow in cease-less praise.
heart, it is Thine own, It shall be Thy roy-al throne.

Lord, I give my life to

Thee, Thine for-ev-er more to be; Lord, I give my life to Thee, Thine for-ev-er more to be.

TAKE THE NAME OF JESUS WITH YOU

words by
Lydia Baxter (1809-1874)

PRECIOUS NAME
music by
William H. Doane (1832-1915)

1. Take the name of Je-sus with you, Child of sor-row and of woe;
2. Take the name of Je-sus ev-er As a shield from ev-'ry snare;
3. O the precious name of Je-sus! How it thrills our souls with joy,
4. At the name of Je-sus bow-ing, Fall-ing pros-trate at His feet,

It will joy and com-fort give you, Take it then, where'er you go.
If temp-ta-tions round you gath-er Breathe that ho-ly name in prayer,
When His lov-ing arms re-ceive us, And His songs our tongues em-ploy!
King of kings in Heav'n we'll crown Him, When our jour-ney is com-plete.

Pre-cious

name, O how sweet! Hope of earth and joy of Heav'n; Pre-cious

name, O how sweet! Hope of earth and joy of Heav'n.

TAKE THOU OUR MINDS, DEAR LORD

HALL
music by
Calvin Weiss Laufer, 1918

words by
William H. Foulkes, c. 1918

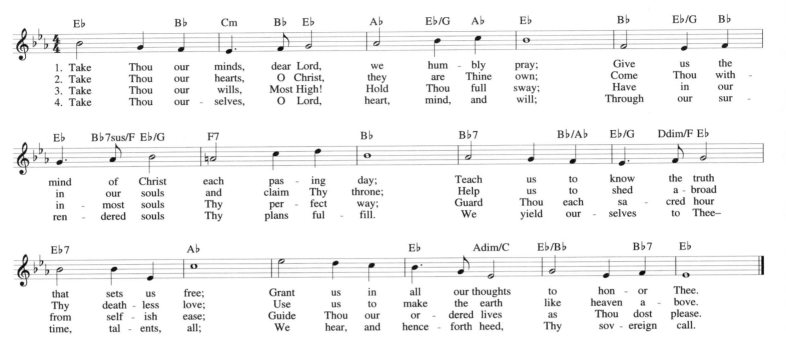

1. Take Thou our minds, dear Lord, we hum - bly pray; Give us the
2. Take Thou our hearts, O Christ, they are Thine own; Come Thou with
3. Take Thou our wills, Most High! Hold Thou full sway; Have in our
4. Take Thou our - selves, O Lord, heart, mind, and will; Through our sur -

mind of Christ each pas - ing day; Teach us to know the truth
in our souls and claim Thy throne; Help us to shed a - broad
in - most souls Thy per - fect way; Guard Thou each sa - cred hour
ren - dered souls Thy plans ful - fill. We yield our - selves to Thee—

that sets us free; Grant us in all our thoughts to hon - or Thee.
Thy death - less love; Use us to make the earth like heaven a - bove.
from self - ish ease; Guide Thou our or - dered lives as Thou dost please.
time, tal - ents, all; We hear, and hence - forth heed, Thy sov - ereign call.

TAKE TIME TO BE HOLY

HOLINESS
music by
George C. Stebbins, 1890

words by
William D. Longstaff, c. 1882

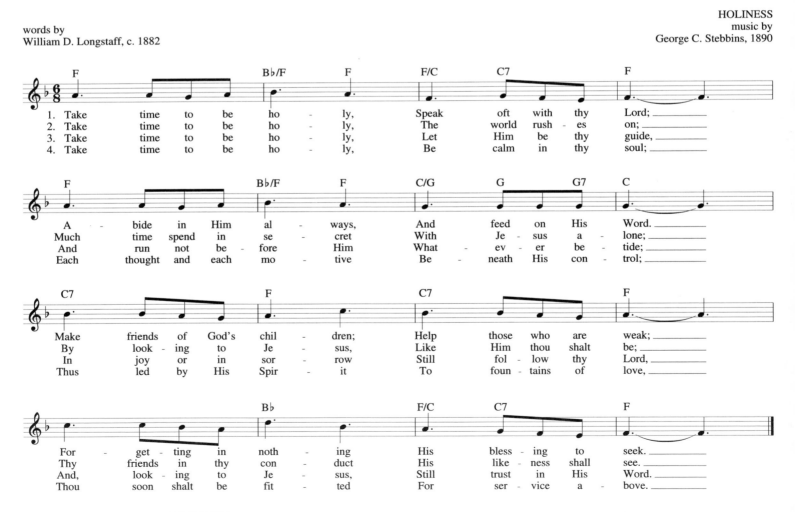

1. Take time to be ho - ly, Speak oft with thy Lord; _____
2. Take time to be ho - ly, The world rush - es on; _____
3. Take time to be ho - ly, Let Him be thy guide, _____
4. Take time to be ho - ly, Be calm in thy soul; _____

A - bide in Him al - ways, And feed on His Word. _____
Much time spend in se - cret With Je - sus a - lone; _____
And run not be - fore Him What - ev - er be - tide; _____
Each thought and each mo - tive Be - neath His con - trol; _____

Make friends of God's chil - dren; Help those who are weak; _____
By look - ing to Je - sus, Like Him thou shalt be; _____
In joy or in sor - row Still fol - low thy Lord, _____
Thus led by His Spir - it To foun - tains of love, _____

For - get - ting in noth - ing His bless - ing to seek. _____
Thy friends in thy con - duct His like - ness shall see. _____
And, look - ing to Je - sus, Still trust in His Word. _____
Thou soon shalt be fit - ted For ser - vice a - bove. _____

TAKE TIME TO BE HOLY

SLANE
Irish Folk melody

words by
William D. Longstaff, 1882

1. Take time to be ho - ly, Speak of - ten with God; Find rest in Him
2. Take time to be ho - ly, The world rush - es on; Much time spend in
3. Take time to be ho - ly, Let Him be thy guide, And run not be -

al - ways And feed on His Word. Make friends of ___ God's ___ chil - dren; Help
se - cret With Je - sus a - lone. By look - ing ___ to ___ Je - sus, Like
fore Him, What - ev - er be - tide. In joy or ___ in ___ sor - row, Still

those who are weak, For - get - ting in noth - ing His ___ bless - ing to seek.
Him thou shalt be; Thy friends in thy con - duct His ___ like - ness shall see.
fol - low thy Lord, And, look - ing to Je - sus, Still ___ trust in His Word.

TAKE UP THY CROSS, THE SAVIOR SAID

BOURBON
music attr. to
Freeman Lewis (1780-1859)

words by
Charles W. Everest, 1833

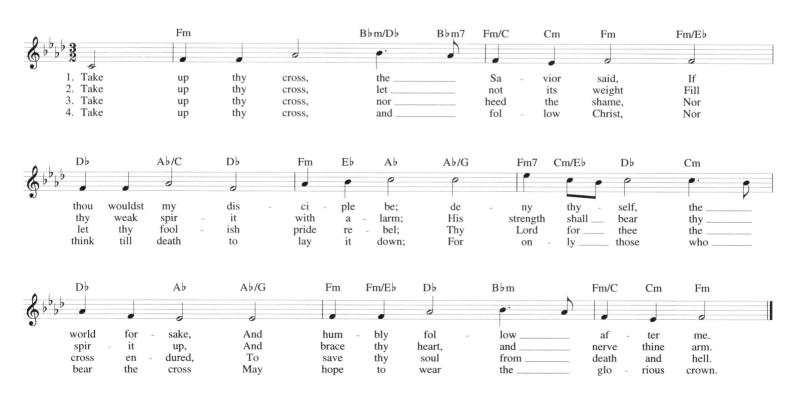

1. Take up thy cross, the ___ Sa - vior said, If
2. Take up thy cross, let ___ not its weight Fill
3. Take up thy cross, nor ___ heed the shame, Nor
4. Take up thy cross, and ___ fol - low Christ, Nor

thou wouldst my dis - ci - ple be; de - ny thy - self, the ___
thy weak spir - it with a - larm; His strength shall ___ bear thy ___
let thy fool - ish pride re - bel; Thy Lord for ___ thee the ___
think till death to lay it down; For on - ly ___ those who ___

world for - sake, And hum - bly fol - low ___ af - ter me.
spir - it up, And brace thy heart, and ___ nerve thine arm.
cross en - dured, To save thy soul from ___ death and hell.
bear the cross May hope to wear the ___ glo - rious crown.

TAKE UP THY CROSS, THE SAVIOR SAID

words by
Charles W. Everest, 1833

GERMANY
music from
William Gardiner's *Sacred Melodies*, 1815

"Take up thy cross," the Sav - ior said, "if thou wouldst
"Take up thy cross," let not its weight fill thy weak
"Take up thy cross," nor heed the shame, nor let thy
"Take up thy cross," and fol - low Christ, nor think till

my dis - ci - ple be; de - ny thy - self, the
spir - it with a - larm; His strength shall bear thy
fool - ish pride re - bel; thy Lord for thee the
death to lay it down; for on - ly those who

world for - sake, and hum - bly fol - low af - ter me."
spir - it up, and brace thy heart and nerve thine arm.
cross en - dured, to save thy soul from death and hell.
bear the cross may hope to wear the glo - rious crown.

TALK WITH US, LORD

words by
Charles Wesley (1707-1788)

SOHO
music by
Joseph Barnby (1838-1896)

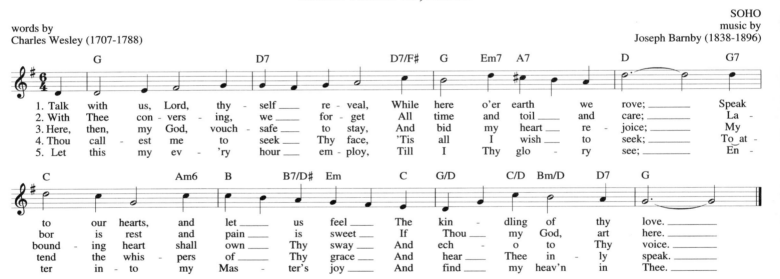

1. Talk with us, Lord, thy - self re - veal, While here o'er earth we rove; Speak
2. With Thee con - vers - ing, we for - get All time and toil and care; La -
3. Here, then, my God, vouch - safe to stay, And bid my heart re - joice; My
4. Thou call - est me to seek Thy face, 'Tis all I wish to seek; To at -
5. Let this my ev - 'ry hour em - ploy, Till I Thy glo - ry see; En -

to our hearts, and let us feel The kin - dling of thy love.
bor is rest and pain is sweet If Thou my God, art here.
bound - ing heart shall own Thy sway And ech - o to Thy voice.
tend the whis - pers of Thy grace And hear Thee in - ly speak.
ter in - to my Mas - ter's joy And find my heav'n in Thee.

TEACH ME, MY GOD AND KING

words by
George Herbert (1593-1633)

CARLISLE
music by
Charles Lockhart (1745-1815)

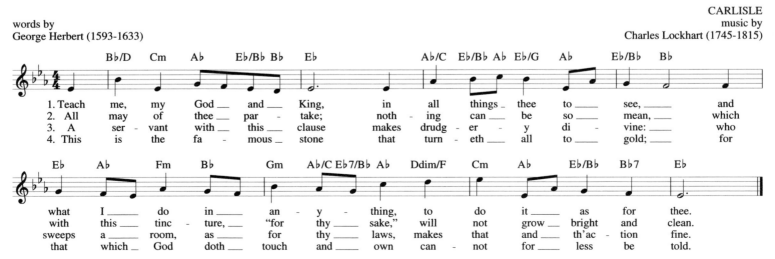

1. Teach me, my God and King, in all things thee to see, and
2. All may of thee par - take; noth - ing can be so mean, which
3. A ser - vant with this clause makes drudg - er - y di - vine: who
4. This is the fa - mous stone that turn - eth all to gold; for

what I do in an - y - thing, to do it as for thee.
with this tinc - ture, "for thy sake," will not grow bright and clean.
sweeps a room, as for thy laws, makes that and th'ac - tion fine.
that which God doth touch and own can - not for less be told.

TEACH ME THY WAY, O LORD

words by
B. Mansell Ramsey, 1919

CAMACHA
music by
B. Mansell Ramsey, 1919

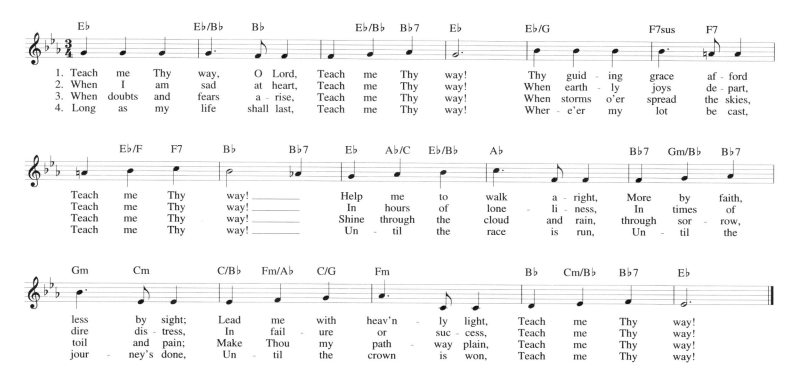

TELL IT TO JESUS

words by
Jeremiah E. Rankin, 1876

DAYTON
music by
Edmund S. Lorenz, 1877

TELL ME THE OLD, OLD STORY

words by
A. Catherine Hankey, 1866

EVANGEL
music by
William H. Doane, 1869

TELL ME THE STORIES OF JESUS

words by
William H. Parker, 1885

STORIES OF JESUS
music by
Frederic A. Challinor, 1903

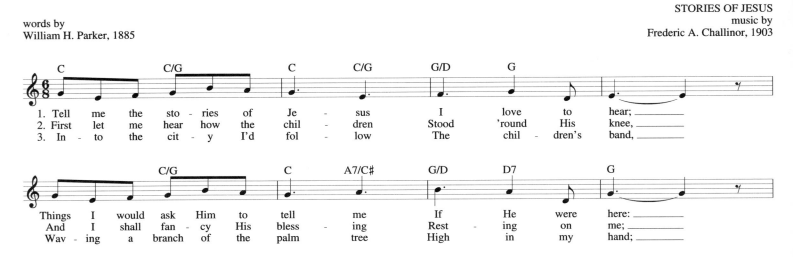

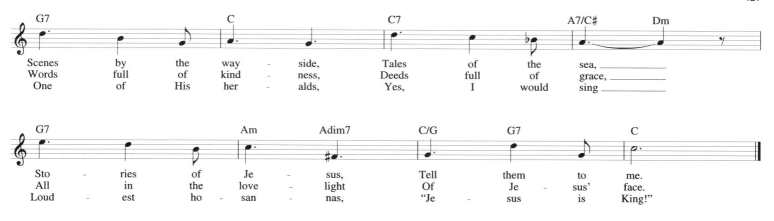

TELL ME THE STORY OF JESUS

STORY OF JESUS

words by
Fanny J. Crosby, 1880

music by
John R. Sweney, 1880

THAT BEAUTIFUL NAME

BEAUTIFUL NAME

words by
Jean Perry, 1916

music by
Mabel Johnston Camp, 1916

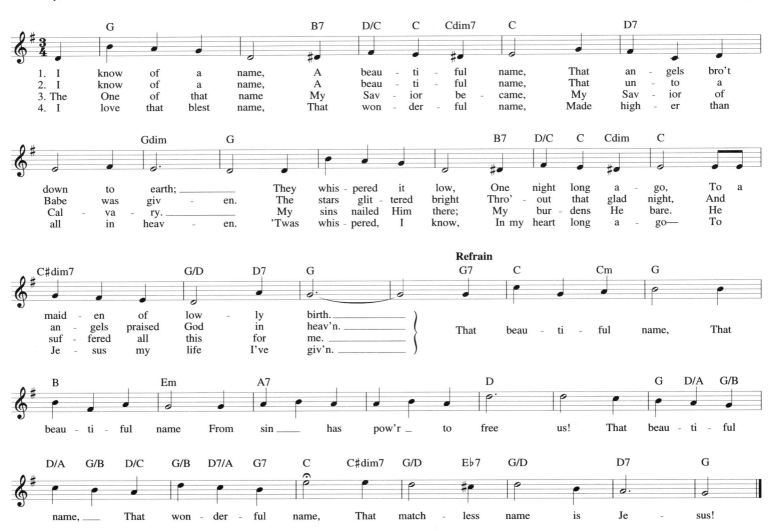

1. I know of a name, A beau-ti-ful name, That an-gels bro't
2. I know of a name, A beau-ti-ful name, That un-to a
3. The One of that name My Sav-ior be-came, My Sav-ior of
4. I love that blest name, That won-der-ful name, Made high-er than

down to earth; They whis-pered it low, One night long a-go, To a
Babe was giv-en. The stars glit-tered bright Thro' out that glad night, And
Cal-va-ry. My sins nailed Him there; My bur-dens He bare. He
all in heav-en. 'Twas whis-pered, I know, In my heart long a-go— To

Refrain

maid-en of low-ly birth.
an-gels praised God in heav'n. } That beau-ti-ful name, That
suf-fered all this for me.
Je-sus my life I've giv'n.

beau-ti-ful name From sin has pow'r to free us! That beau-ti-ful

name, That won-der-ful name, That match-less name is Je-sus!

THEE WE ADORE, O HIDDEN SAVIOR

ADORO TE DEVOTE

words by
Thomas Aquinas (1227-1274)
tr. by James R. Woodford (1820-1885)

music from
Processionale, Paris, 1697

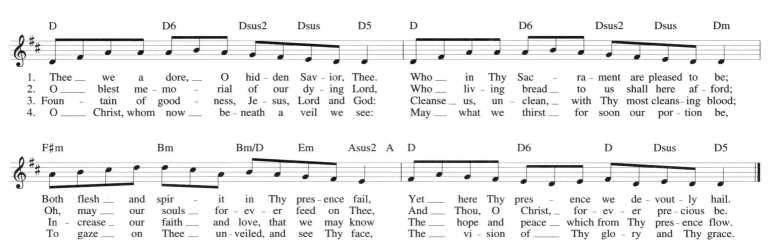

1. Thee we a-dore, O hid-den Sav-ior, Thee. Who in Thy Sac-ra-ment are pleased to be;
2. O blest me-mo-rial of our dy-ing Lord, Who liv-ing bread to us shall here af-ford;
3. Foun-tain of good-ness, Je-sus, Lord and God: Cleanse us, un-clean, with Thy most cleans-ing blood;
4. O Christ, whom now be-neath a veil we see: May what we thirst for soon our por-tion be,

Both flesh and spir-it in Thy pres-ence fail, Yet here Thy pres-ence we de-vout-ly hail.
Oh, may our souls for-ev-er feed on Thee, And Thou, O Christ, for-ev-er pre-cious be.
In-crease our faith and love, that we may know The hope and peace which from Thy pres-ence flow.
To gaze on Thee un-veiled, and see Thy face, The vi-sion of Thy glo-ry and Thy grace.

THEE WE ADORE, ETERNAL LORD

Latin text, 4th or 5th century
tr. by Thomas Cotterill (1779-1823)

MENDON
music by
F.D. Allen, *New York Selections*, 1822

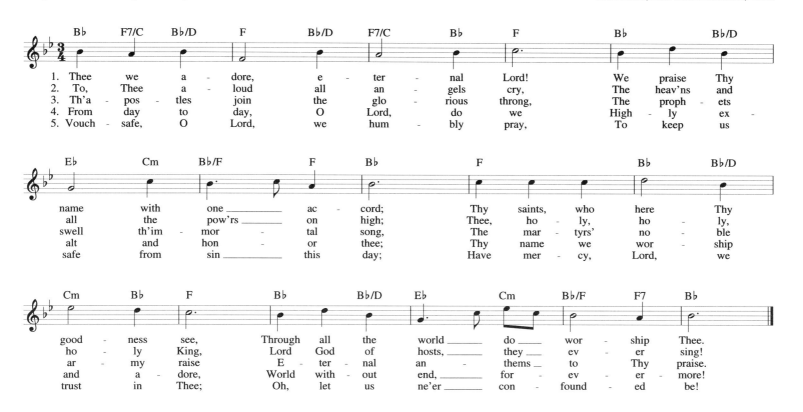

1. Thee we a - dore, e - ter - nal Lord! We praise Thy
2. To, Thee a - loud all an - gels cry, The heav'ns and
3. Th'a - pos - tles join the glo - rious throng, The proph - ets
4. From day to day, O Lord, do we High - ly ex -
5. Vouch - safe, O Lord, we hum - bly pray, To keep us

name with one _____ ac - cord; Thy saints, who here Thy
all the pow'rs _____ on high; Thee, ho - ly, ho -
swell th'im - mor - tal song, The mar - tyrs' no - ble
alt and hon - or thee; Thy name we wor - ship
safe from sin _____ this day; Have mer - cy, Lord, we

good - ness see, Through all the world _____ do _____ wor - ship Thee.
ho - ly King, Lord God of hosts, _____ they _____ ev - er sing!
ar - my raise E - ter - nal an - thems ____ to Thy praise.
and a - dore, World with - out end, _____ for - ev - er - more!
trust in Thee; Oh, let us ne'er _____ con - found - ed be!

THEE WILL I LOVE, MY STRENGTH

words by
Johann Scheffler (1624-1677)
tr. by John Wesley (1703-1791)

ICH WILL DICH LIEBEN
music by
J.B. König, *Harmonischer Lieder-Schatz*, 1738

1. Thee will I love, my strength, my tow'r; _____ Thee will I love, my joy, my crown!
2. I thank Thee, un - cre - a - ted sun, _____ That Thy bright beams on me have shined;
3. Up - hold me in the doubt - ful race, _____ Nor suf - fer me a - gain to stray;
4. Thee will I love, my joy, my crown; _____ Thee will I love, my Lord, my God!

Thee will I love with all my pow - er, In all Thy works, and Thee a - lone;
I thank Thee, who hast o - ver - thrown _____ My foes and healed my wound - ed mind;
Strength - en my feet with stead - y pace _____ Still to press for - ward in Thy way,
Thee will I love, be - neath Thy frown _____ Or smile, Thy scep - ter or Thy rod.

Thee will I love, till the pure fire Fills all my soul with chaste de - sire.
I thank Thee, whose en - liv - 'ning voice Bids my freed heart in Thee re - joice.
That all my pow'rs, with all their might, In Thy sole glo - ry may u - nite.
What though my flesh and heart de - cay? Thee shall I love in end - less day!

THERE IS A BALM IN GILEAD

BALM IN GILEAD
African-American Spiritual

African-American Spiritual

1. Some times I feel dis - cour - aged, And think my work's in
2. Don't ev - er feel dis - cour - aged, For Je - sus is your
3. If you can - not preach like Pe - ter, If you can - not pray like

vain, But then the Ho - ly Spir - it Re - vives my soul a - gain. ____
friend, And if you lack for know - ledge, He'll not re - fuse to lend. ____
Paul, You can tell the love of Je - sus And say, "He died for all." ____

THERE IS A FOUNTAIN

CLEANSING FOUNTAIN
Traditional American melody
arr. by Lowell Mason (1792-1872)

words by
William Cowper (1731-1800)

1. There is a foun - tain filled with blood Drawn from Im - man - uel's veins, And
2. The dy - ing thief re - joiced to see That foun - tain in his day, And
3. Dear dy - ing Lamb, Thy pre - cious blood Shall nev - er lose its pow'r, Till
4. E'er since, by faith, I saw the stream Thy flow - ing wounds sup - ply, Re -
5. When this poor lisp - ing, stam - m'ring tongue Lies si - lent in the grave, Then

sin - ners plunged be - neath that flood Lose all their guilt - y stains, Lose
there may I, though vile as he, Wash all my sins a - way, Wash
all the ran - somed Church of God Be saved to sin no more, Be
deem - ing love has been my theme And shall be till I die, And
in a no - bler, sweet - er song I'll sing Thy pow'r to save, I'll

all their guilt - y stains, _____ Lose all their guilt - y ____ stains; And
all my sins a - way, _____ Wash all my sins ____ a - way; And
saved to sin no more, _____ Be saved to sin ____ no ____ more; Till
shall be till I die, _____ And shall be till ____ I ____ die; Re -
sing Thy pow'r to save, _____ I'll sing Thy pow'r ____ to ____ save; Then

sin - ners plunged be - neath that flood Lose all their guilt - y stains.
there may I, though vile as he, Wash all my sins a - way.
all the ran - somed Church of God Be saved to sin no more.
deem - ing love has been my theme And shall be till I die.
in a no - bler, sweet - er song I'll sing Thy pow'r to save.

THERE IS A FOUNTAIN

words by
W. Cowper (1731-1800)

HORSLEY
music by
W. Horsley (1774-1858)

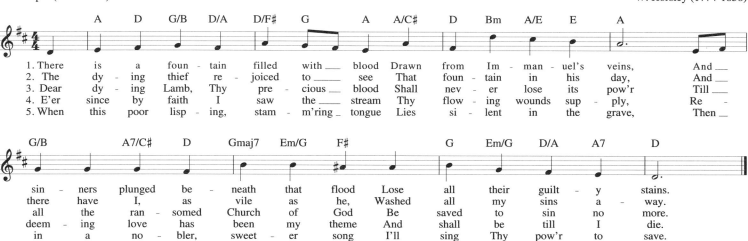

1. There is a foun - tain filled with ___ blood Drawn from Im - man - uel's veins, And ___
2. The dy - ing thief re - joiced to ___ see That foun - tain in his day, And ___
3. Dear dy - ing Lamb, Thy pre - cious ___ blood Shall nev - er lose its pow'r Till ___
4. E'er since by faith I saw the ___ stream Thy flow - ing wounds sup - ply, Re -
5. When this poor lisp - ing, stam - m'ring ___ tongue Lies si - lent in the grave, Then ___

sin - ners plunged be - neath that flood Lose all their guilt - y stains.
there have I, as vile as he, Washed all my sins a - way.
all the ran - somed Church of God Be saved to sin no more.
deem - ing love has been my theme And shall be till I die.
in a no - bler, sweet - er song I'll sing Thy pow'r to save.

THERE IS A GREEN HILL FAR AWAY

words by
Cecil Frances Alexander (1818-1895)

HORSLEY
music by
William Horsley (1774-1858)

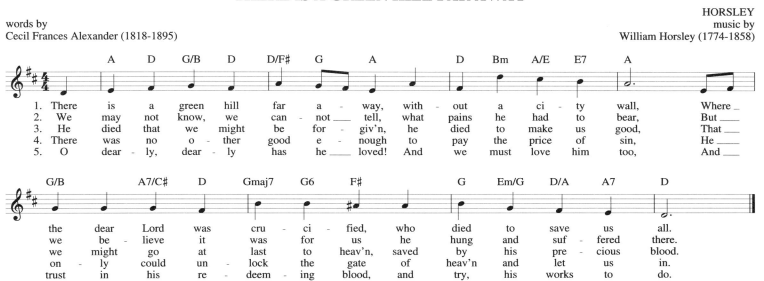

1. There is a green hill far a - way, with - out a ci - ty wall, Where ___
2. We may not know, we can - not ___ tell, what pains he had to bear, But ___
3. He died that we might be for - giv'n, he died to make us good, That ___
4. There was no o - ther good e - nough to pay the price of sin, He ___
5. O dear - ly, dear - ly has he ___ loved! And we must love him too, And ___

the dear Lord was cru - ci - fied, who died to save us all.
we be - lieve it was for us he hung and suf - fered there.
we might go at last to heav'n, saved by his pre - cious blood.
on - ly could un - lock the gate of heav'n and let us in.
trust in his re - deem - ing blood, and try, his works to do.

THERE IS A GREEN HILL FAR AWAY

words by
Cecil F. Alexander (1823-1895)

WINDSOR
music from
Daman's *Booke of Musicke,* 1591

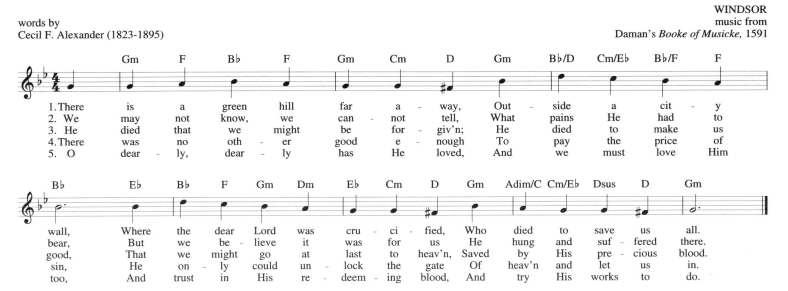

1. There is a green hill far a - way, Out - side a cit - y
2. We may not know, we can - not tell, What pains He had to
3. He died that we might be for - giv'n; He died to make us
4. There was no oth - er good e - nough To pay the price of
5. O dear - ly, dear - ly has He loved, And we must love Him

wall, Where the dear Lord was cru - ci - fied, Who died to save us all.
bear, But we be - lieve it was for us He hung and suf - fered there.
good, That we might go at last to heav'n, Saved by His pre - cious blood.
sin, He on - ly could un - lock the gate Of heav'n and let us in.
too, And trust in His re - deem - ing blood, And try His works to do.

THERE IS A LAND OF PURE DELIGHT

VARINA

words by
Isaac Watts (1674-1748)

music by
George F. Root (1820-1895)

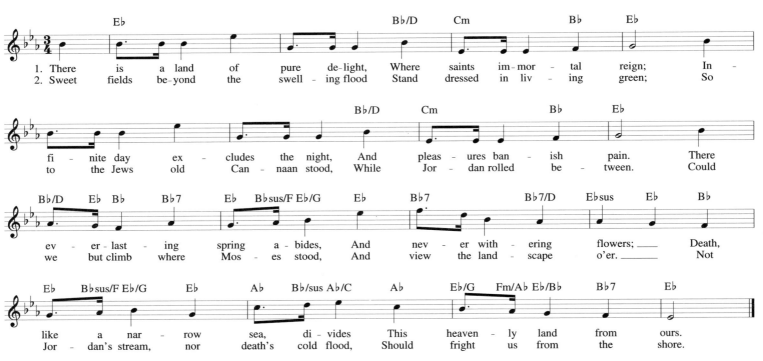

1. There is a land of pure de-light, Where saints im-mor-tal reign; In-
2. Sweet fields be-yond the swell-ing flood Stand dressed in liv-ing green; So

fi - nite day ex - cludes the night, And pleas - ures ban - ish pain. There
to the Jews old Can - naan stood, While Jor - dan rolled be - tween. Could

ev - er-last - ing spring a - bides, And nev - er with - ering flowers;____ Death,
we but climb where Mos - es stood, And view the land - scape o'er.____ Not

like a nar - row sea, di - vides, This heaven - ly land from ours.
Jor - dan's stream, nor death's cold flood, Should fright us from the shore.

THERE IS POWER IN THE BLOOD

POWER IN THE BLOOD

words by
Lewis E. Jones, 1899

music by
Lewis E. Jones, 1899

1. Would you be free from your bur - den of sin?
2. Would you be free from your pas - sion and pride?
3. Would you be whit - er, much whit - er than snow?
4. Would you do ser - vice for Je - sus, your King?

There's pow'r in the blood, pow'r in the blood.

Would you o'er e - vil a vic - to - ry win?
Come for a cleans - ing to Cal - va - ry's tide.
Sin - stains are lost in its life - giv - ing flow.
Would you live dai - ly His prais - es to sing?

There's won - der - ful pow'r in the blood. There is

pow'r, pow'r, won - der - work - ing pow'r in the blood of the Lamb. There is

pow'r, pow'r, won - der - work - ing pow'r in the pre - cious blood of the Lamb.

THERE SHALL BE SHOWERS OF BLESSING

words by
Daniel W. Whittle (1840-1901)
based on Ezekiel 34:26

SHOWERS OF BLESSING
music by
James McGranahan (1840-1907)

THERE'S A GREAT DAY COMING

words by
Will L. Thompson (1847-1909)

GREAT DAY COMING
music by
Will L. Thompson (1847-1909)

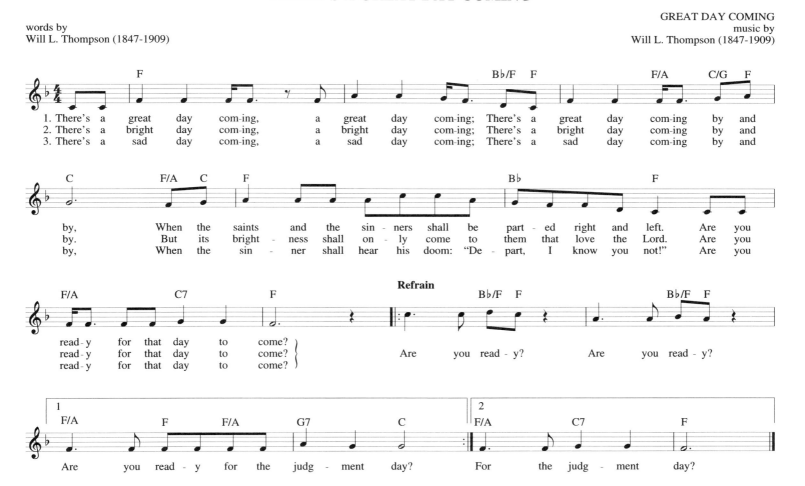

THERE'S A WIDENESS IN GOD'S MERCY

words by
Frederick William Faber, 1854

IN BABILONE
Dutch Folk Tune, 18th century

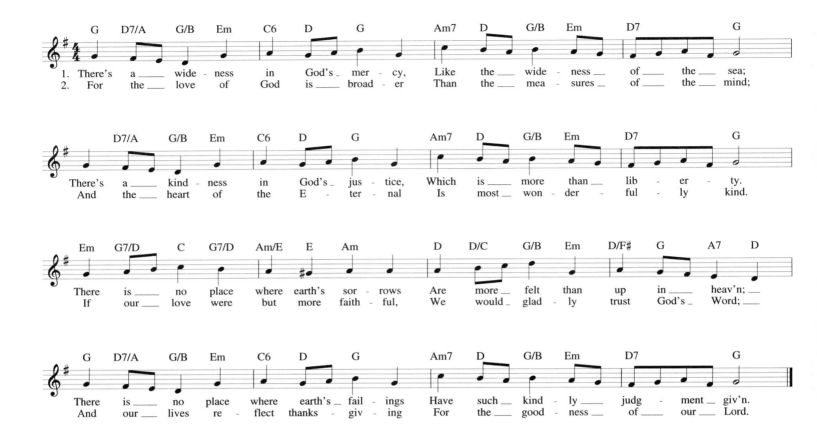

THERE'S A WIDENESS IN GOD'S MERCY

words by
Frederick W. Faber, 1854

WELLESLEY
music by
Lizzie S. Tourjee, 1877

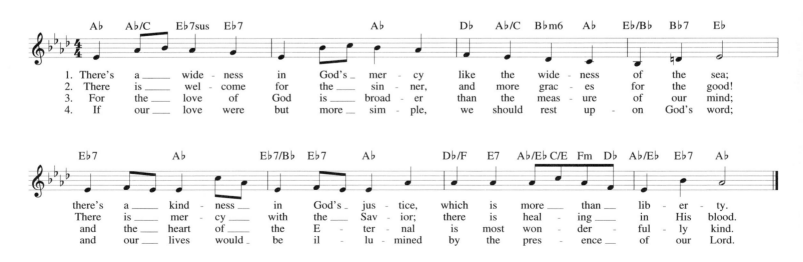

THERE IS NO NAME SO SWEET ON EARTH

GOLDEN CHAIN (Refrain only)

words by
George W. Bethune (1805-1862)

music by
William B. Bradbury (1816-1868)

I love to sing of Christ, {my / our} King, And hail Him, bless-ed Je-sus; For
there's no word ear ev-er heard So dear, so sweet as "Je-sus." We "Je-sus." _____

THINE IS THE GLORY

MACCABEUS

words by
Edmund Louis Budry, 1884
tr. by Richard Birch Hoyle

music by
George Frederick Handel, 1748

1. Thine is the glo-ry, Ris-en, _____ con-quering Son;
2. Lo! Je-sus meets us, Ris-en _____ from the tomb;
3. No more we doubt Thee, Glo-rious _____ Prince of life!

End-less _____ is the vic-tory Thou o'er death hast won.
Lov-ing-ly He greets us, Scat-ters fear and gloom.
Life _____ is _____ nought with-out Thee, Aid us in our strife.

An-gels _____ in bright rai-ment Rolled the stone a-way,
Let _____ the _____ church with glad-ness Hymns of tri-umph sing,
Make _____ us _____ more than con-querors Through Thy death-less love;

Kept _____ the _____ fold-ed grave-clothes Where thy _____ bod-y lay.
For _____ the _____ Lord now liv-eth; Death hath _____ lost its sting.
Bring _____ us _____ safe through Jor-dan To Thy _____ home a-bove.

Refrain (last time only)

Thine is the glo-ry, Ris-en, _____ con-quering Son;

End-less _____ is the vic-tory Thou o'er death hast won.

THINE ARM, O LORD, IN DAYS OF OLD

ST. MATTHEW

words by
Edward Hayes Plumptre (1821-1891)

music by
William Croft (1678-1727)

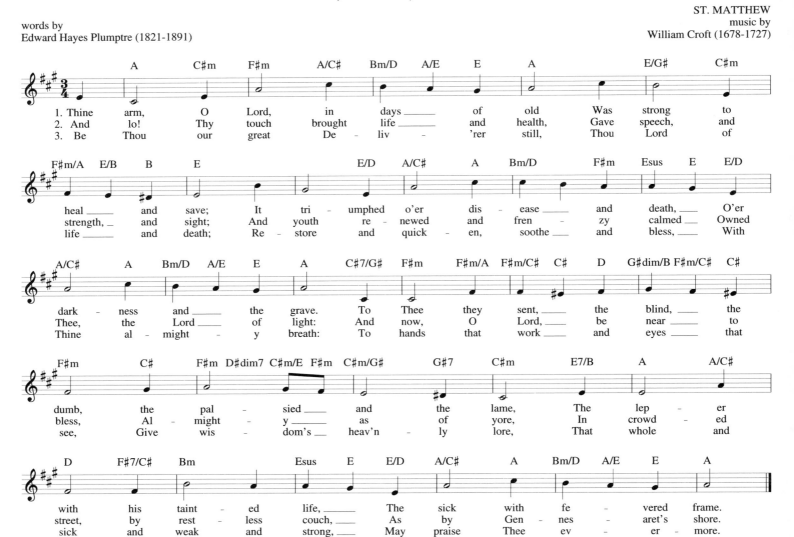

1. Thine arm, O Lord, in days of old Was strong to
2. And lo! Thy touch brought life and health, Gave speech, and
3. Be Thou our great De - liv - 'rer still,

heal and save; It tri - umphed o'er dis - ease and death, O'er
strength, and sight; And youth re - newed and fren - zy calmed Owned
life and death; Re - store and quick - en, soothe and bless, With

dark - ness and the grave. To Thee they sent, the blind, the
Thee, the Lord of light: And now, O Lord, be near to
Thine al - might - y breath: To hands that work and eyes that

dumb, the pal - sied and the lame, The lep - er
bless, Al - might - y as of yore, In crowd - ed
see, Give wis - dom's heav'n - ly lore, That whole and

with his taint - ed life, The sick with fe - vered frame.
street, by rest - less couch, As by Gen - nes - aret's shore.
sick and weak and strong, May praise Thee ev - er - more.

THIS IS LIKE HEAVEN TO ME

LIKE HEAVEN TO ME

words by
J.E. French, 1903

music by
J.E. French, 1903

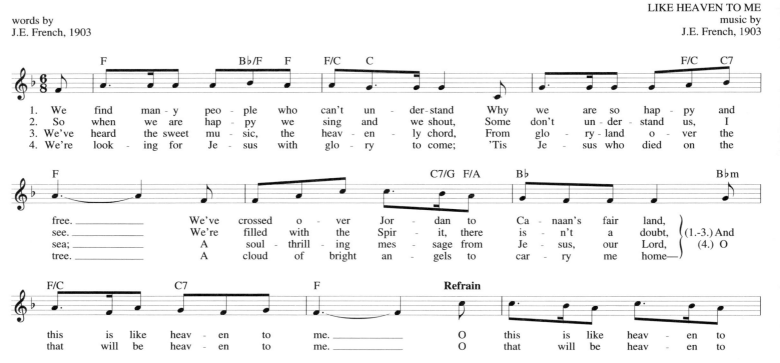

1. We find man - y peo - ple who can't un - der-stand Why we are so hap - py and
2. So when we are hap - py we sing and we shout, Some don't un - der - stand us, I
3. We've heard the sweet mu - sic, the heav - en - ly chord, From glo - ry - land o - ver the
4. We're look - ing for Je - sus with glo - ry to come; 'Tis Je - sus who died on the

free. We've crossed o - ver Jor - dan to Ca - naan's fair land,
see. We're filled with the Spir - it, there is - n't a doubt, (1.-3.) And
sea; A soul - thrill - ing mes - sage from Je - sus, our Lord, (4.) O
tree. A cloud of bright an - gels to car - ry me home—

this is like heav - en to me. O this is like heav - en to
that will be heav - en to me. O that will be heav - en to

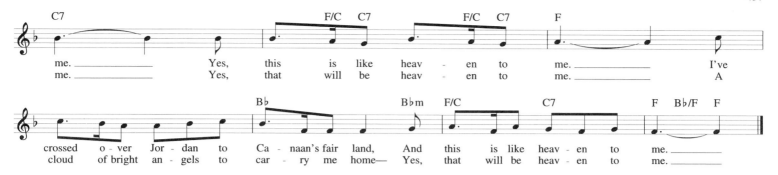

me. ___ Yes, this is like heav - en to me. ___ I've
me. ___ Yes, that will be heav - en to me. ___ A

crossed o - ver Jor - dan to Ca - naan's fair land, And this is like heav - en to me. ___
cloud of bright an - gels to car - ry me home— Yes, that will be heav - en to me. ___

THIS IS MY FATHER'S WORLD

TERRA BEATA

words by
Maltbie D. Babcock, 1901

music by
Franklin L. Sheppard, 1915

1. This ___ is my Fa - ther's world, And ___ to my lis - t'ning ears All
2. This ___ is my Fa - ther's world, The ___ birds their car - ols raise, The
3. This ___ is my Fa - ther's world, O ___ let me ne'er for - get That

na - ture sings, and ___ round me rings The mu - sic of the ___ spheres. This
morn - ing light, the ___ lil - y white, De - clare ___ their Mak - er's ___ praise. This
though the wrong seems ___ oft so strong, God is ___ the Rul - er ___ yet. This

is my Fa - ther's world: I ___ rest me in the thought Of
is my Fa - ther's world: He ___ shines in all that's fair; In the
is my Fa - ther's world: The ___ bat - tle is not done; Je -

rocks and trees, of ___ skies and seas His hand ___ the won - ders ___ wrought.
rus - tling grass I ___ hear Him pass, He speaks ___ to me ev - 'ry - where.
sus who died shall be sat - is - fied, And earth ___ and heav'n be ___ one.

THIS IS THE DAY THE LORD HATH MADE

ARLINGTON

words by
Isaac Watts (1674-1748)

music by
Thomas A. Arne (1710-1778)

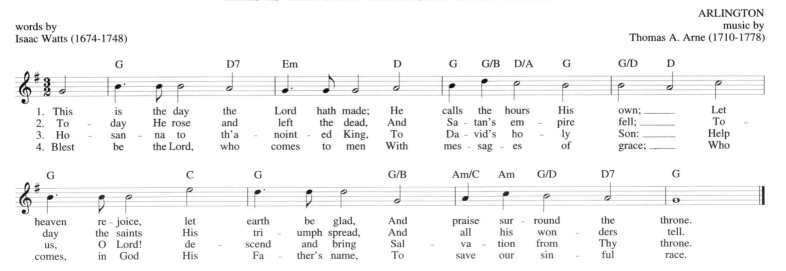

1. This is the day the Lord hath made; He calls the hours His own; ___ Let
2. To - day He rose and left the dead, And Sa - tan's em - pire fell; ___ To -
3. Ho - san - na to th'a - noint - ed King, To Da - vid's ho - ly Son: ___ Help
4. Blest be the Lord, who comes to men With mes - sag - es of grace; ___ Who

heaven re - joice, let earth be glad, And praise sur - round the throne.
day the saints His tri - umph spread, And all his won - ders tell.
us, O Lord! de - scend and bring Sal - va - tion from Thy throne.
comes, in God His Fa - ther's name, To save our sin - ful race.

THIS IS THE DAY THE LORD HATH MADE

NUN DANKET ALL' UND BRINGET EHR'

words by
Isaac Watts, 1719

music by
Johann Crüger, 1647

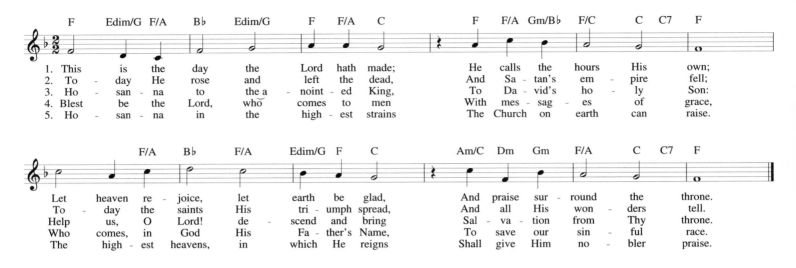

1. This is the day the Lord hath made; He calls the hours His own;
2. To-day He rose and left the dead, And Satan's em-pire fell.
3. Ho-san-na to the a-noint-ed King, To Da-vid's ho-ly Son:
4. Blest be the Lord, who comes to men With mes-sag-es of grace,
5. Ho-san-na in the high-est strains The Church on earth can raise.

Let heaven re-joice, let earth be glad, And praise sur-round the throne.
To-day the saints His tri-umph spread, And all His won-ders tell.
Help us, O Lord! de-scend and bring Sal-va-tion from Thy throne.
Who comes, in God His Fa-ther's Name, To save our sin-ful race.
The high-est heavens, in which He reigns Shall give Him no-bler praise.

THIS IS THY WILL, I KNOW

TRENTHAM

words by
Charles Wesley, 1749

music by
Robert Jackson, 1894

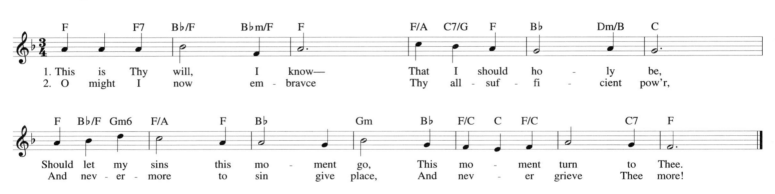

1. This is Thy will, I know— That I should ho-ly be,
2. O might I now em-brace Thy all-suf-fi-cient pow'r,

Should let my sins this mo-ment go, This mo-ment turn to Thee.
And nev-er-more to sin give place, And nev-er grieve Thee more!

THIS JOYFUL EASTERTIDE

VRUECHTEN

words by
George R. Woodward (1848-1934)

music from
Davids Psalmen, Amsterdam, 1684

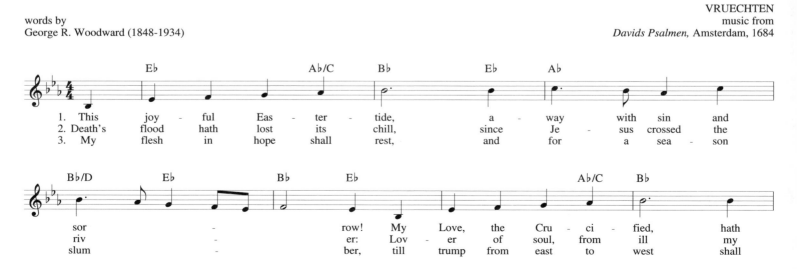

1. This joy-ful Eas-ter-tide, a-way with sin and
2. Death's flood hath lost its chill, since Je-sus crossed the
3. My flesh in hope shall rest, and for a sea-son

sor - row! My Love, the Cru-ci-fied, hath
riv - er: Lov-er of soul, from ill my
slum - ber, till trump from east to west shall

THOU ART THE WAY

words by
George Washington Doane (1799-1859)

DUNDEE
music from
The CL Psalms of David, Edinburgh, 1615

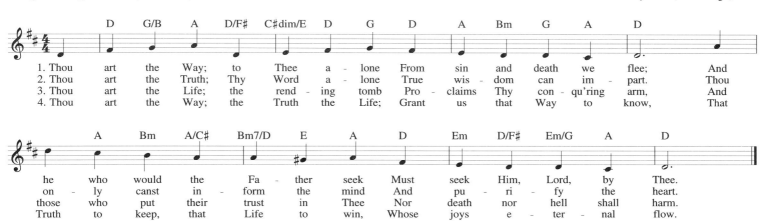

THOU ART THE WAY

words by
George Washington Doane (1799-1859)

ST. JAMES
music by
Raphael Courteville (d. 1735)

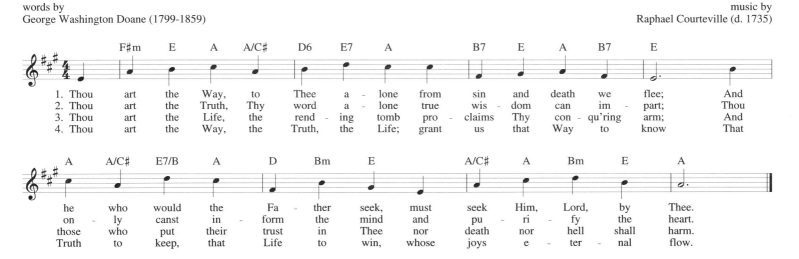

THOU HALLOWED CHOSEN MORN OF PRAISE

MACH'S MIT MIR, GOTT
music by
Bartholomäus Gesius (c. 1555-1613)

words by
John of Damascus, 8th century
tr. by John Mason Neale (1818-1866)

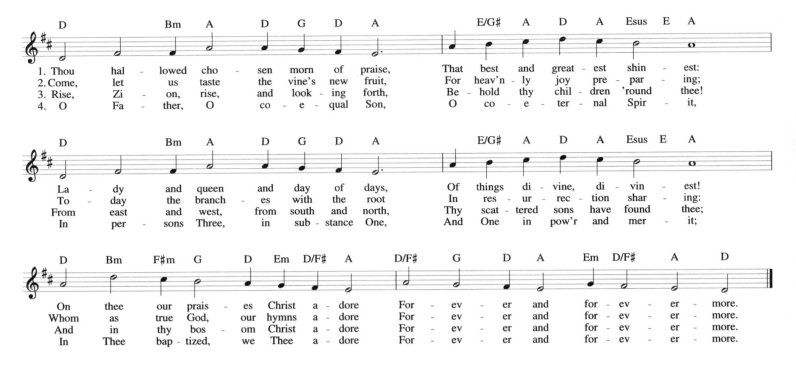

1. Thou hallowed chosen morn of praise, That best and greatest shinest:
2. Come, let us taste the vine's new fruit, For heav'nly joy preparing;
3. Rise, Zion, rise, and looking forth, Behold thy children 'round thee!
4. O Father, O co-equal Son, O co-eternal Spirit,

Lady and queen and day of days, Of things divine, divinest!
Today the branches with the root In resurrection sharing:
From east and west, from south and north, Thy scattered sons have found thee;
In persons Three, in substance One, And One in pow'r and merit;

On thee our praises Christ adore For ever and for evermore.
Whom as true God, our hymns adore For ever and for evermore.
And in thy bosom Christ adore For ever and for evermore.
In Thee baptized, we Thee adore For ever and for evermore.

THOU HIDDEN LOVE OF GOD

VATER UNSER
music from
Geistliche Lieder, 1539

words by
Gerhard Tersteegen, 1729
tr. by John Wesley, 1749

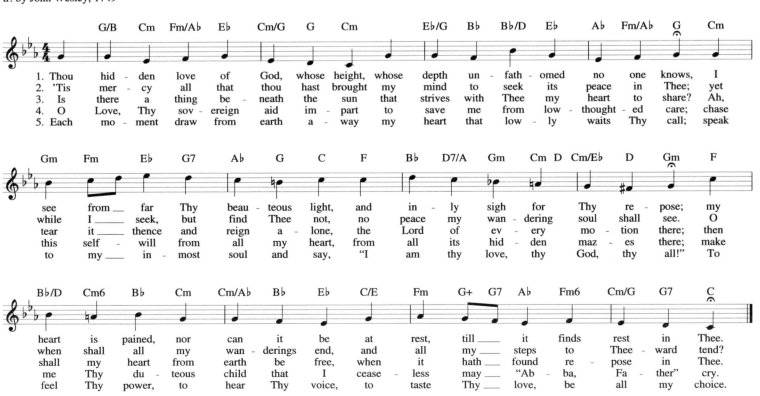

1. Thou hidden love of God, whose height, whose depth unfathomed no one knows, I
2. 'Tis mercy all that thou hast brought my mind to seek its peace in Thee; yet
3. Is there a thing beneath the sun that strives with Thee my heart to share? Ah,
4. O Love, Thy sovereign aid impart to save me from low-thoughted care; chase
5. Each moment draw from earth away my heart that lowly waits Thy call; speak

see from far Thy beauteous light, and inly sigh for Thy repose; my
while I seek, but find Thee not, no peace my wandering soul shall see. O
tear it thence and reign alone, the Lord of ev'ry motion there; then
this self-will from all my heart, from all its hidden mazes there; make
to my inmost soul and say, "I am thy love, thy God, thy all!" To

heart is pained, nor can it be at rest, till it finds rest in Thee.
when shall all my wanderings end, and all my steps to Thee-ward tend?
shall my heart from earth be free, when it hath found repose in Thee.
me Thy duteous child that I cease-less may "Abba, Father" cry.
feel Thy power, to hear Thy voice, to taste Thy love, be all my choice.

THOU HIDDEN SOURCE OF CALM REPOSE

words by
Charles Wesley, 1749

ST. PETERSBURG
music attr. to
Dimitri S. Bortniansky, 1825

1. Thou hid - den source of calm ___ re - pose, Thou all - suf - fi - cient love ___ di -
2. Thy might - y name sal - va - tion is, and keeps ___ my hap - py soul a -
3. Je - sus, my all in all ___ Thou art, my rest ___ in toil, my ease ___ in
4. In want my plen - ti - ful ___ sup - ply, in weak - ness my al - might - y

vine, my help and ref - uge from ___ my foes, se - cure ___ I am if Thou ___ art
bove; com - fort it brings, and power ___ and peace, and joy ___ and ev - er - last - ing
pain, the heal - ing of my bro - ken heart, in war ___ my peace, in loss ___ my
power, in bonds my per - fect lib - er - ty, my light ___ in Sa - tan's dark - est

mine; and lo! from sin and grief ___ and shame ___ I hide ___ me, Je - sus, in Thy name.
love; to me with Thy dear name ___ are given ___ par - don ___ and ho - li - ness and heaven.
gain, my smile be - neath the ty - rant's frown, ___ in shame ___ my glo - ry and my crown,
hour, in grief my joy un - speak - a - ble, ___ my life ___ in death, my heaven in hell.

THOUGH TROUBLES ASSAIL AND DANGERS AFFRIGHT

words by
John Newton (1725-1807)

COBERN
music by
Henry J. Gauntlett (1805-1876)

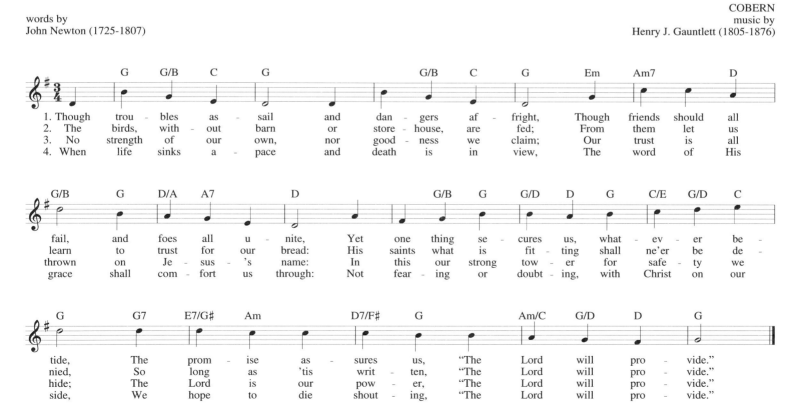

1. Though trou - bles as - sail and dan - gers af - fright, Though friends should all
2. The birds, with - out barn or store - house, are fed; From them should let us
3. No strength of our own, nor good - ness we claim; Our trust is all
4. When life sinks a - pace and death is in view, The word of His

fail, and foes all u - nite, Yet one thing se - cures us, what - ev - er be
learn to trust for our bread: His saints what is fit - ting shall ne'er be de -
thrown on Je - sus 's name: In this our strong tow - er for safe - ty we
grace shall com - fort us through: Not fear - ing or doubt - ing, with Christ on our

tide, The prom - ise as - sures us, "The Lord will pro - vide."
nied, So long as 'tis writ - ten, "The Lord will pro - vide."
hide; The Lord is our pow - er, "The Lord will pro - vide."
side, We hope to die shout - ing, "The Lord will pro - vide."

THOU, WHOSE ALMIGHTY WORD

ITALIAN HYMN

words by
John Marriott (1780-1825)

music by
Felice de Giardini (1716-1796)

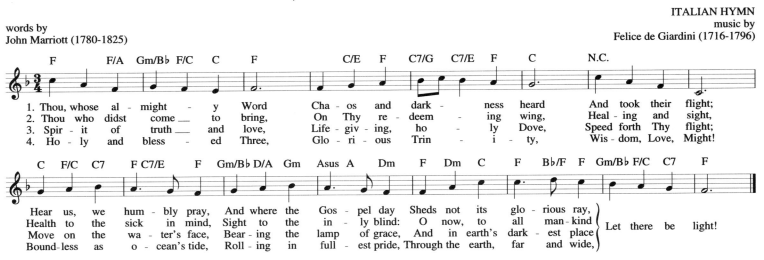

1. Thou, whose al - might - y Word Cha - os and dark - ness heard And took their flight;
2. Thou who didst come to bring, On Thy re - deem - ing wing, Heal - ing and sight,
3. Spir - it of truth and love, Life - giv - ing, ho - ly Dove, Speed forth Thy flight;
4. Ho - ly and bless - ed Three, Glo - ri - ous Trin - i - ty, Wis - dom, Love, Might!

Hear us, we hum - bly pray, And where the Gos - pel day Sheds not its glo - rious ray,
Health to the sick in mind, Sight to the in - ly blind: O now, to all man - kind
Move on the wa - ter's face, Bear - ing the lamp of grace, And in earth's dark - est place
Bound - less as o - cean's tide, Roll - ing in full - est pride, Through the earth, far and wide,

Let there be light!

THRONED UPON THE AWFUL TREE

ARFON
French and Welsh melody

words by
John Ellerton, 1875

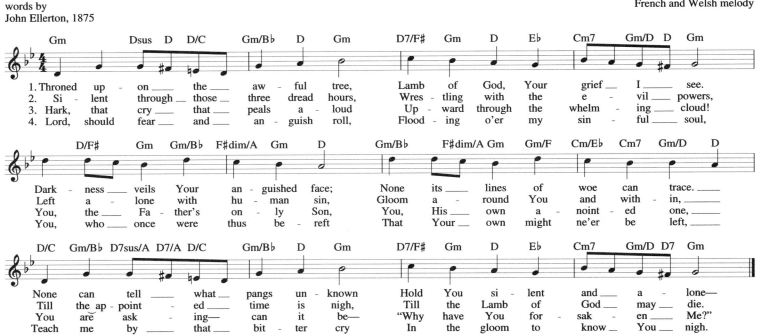

1. Throned up - on the aw - ful tree, Lamb of God, Your grief I see.
2. Si - lent through those three dread hours, Wres - tling with the e - vil powers,
3. Hark, that cry that peals a - loud! Up - ward through the whelm - ing cloud!
4. Lord, should fear and an - guish roll, Flood - ing o'er my sin - ful soul,

Dark - ness veils Your an - guished face; None its lines of woe can trace.
Left a - lone with hu - man sin, Gloom a - round You and with - in,
You, the Fa - ther's on - ly Son, You, His own a - noint - ed one,
You, who once were thus be - reft That Your own might ne'er be left,

None can tell what pangs un - known Hold You si - lent and a - lone—
Till the ap - point - ed time is nigh, Till the Lamb of God may die.
You are ask - ing— can it be— "Why have You for - sak - en Me?"
Teach me by that bit - ter cry In the gloom to know You nigh.

THY KINGDOM COME, O GOD!

ST. CECILIA
music by
Leighton George Hayne (1836-1883)

words by
Lewis Hensley (1824-1905)

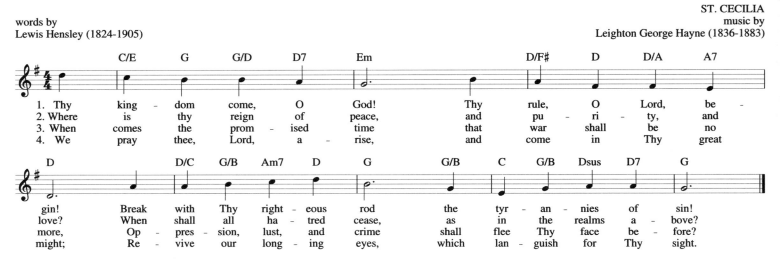

1. Thy king - dom come, O God! Thy rule, O Lord, be -
2. Where is thy reign of peace, and pu - ri - ty, and
3. When comes the prom - ised time that war shall be no
4. We pray thee, Lord, a - rise, and come in Thy great

gin! Break with Thy right - eous rod the tyr - an - nies of sin!
love? When shall all ha - tred cease, as in the realms a - bove?
more, Op - pres - sion, lust, and crime shall flee Thy face be - fore?
might; Re - vive our long - ing eyes, which lan - guish for Thy sight.

"THY KINGDOM COME!" ON BENDED KNEE

words by
Frederick Lucian Hosmer (1840-1929)

ST. FLAVIAN
music from
Day's *Psalter,* 1562

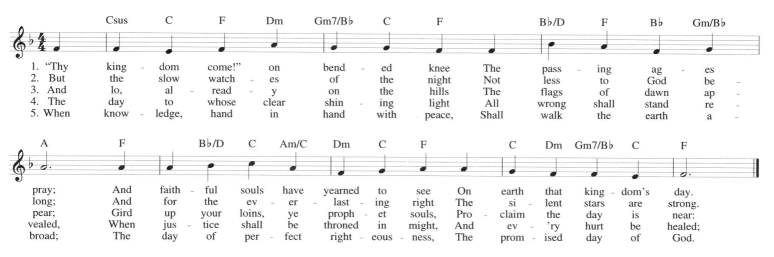

THY MERCY AND THY TRUTH, O LORD

Author unknown
based on Psalm 36

TALLIS' ORDINAL
music by
Thomas Tallis, c. 1567

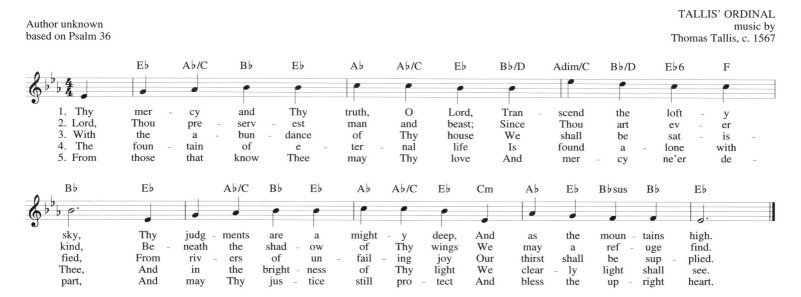

'TIS FINISHED! THE MESSIAH DIES

words by
Charles Wesley, 1762

OLIVE'S BROW
music by
William Bradbury, 1853

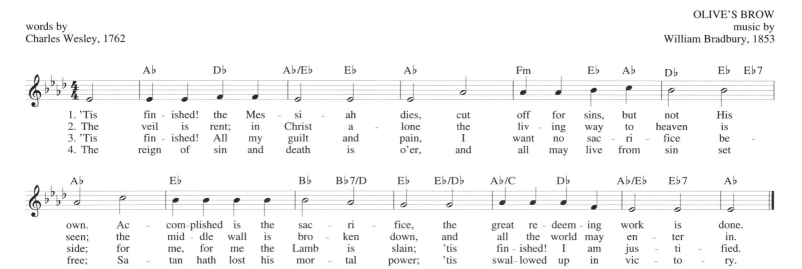

'TIS MIDNIGHT, AND ON OLIVE'S BROW

OLIVE'S BROW

words by
William B. Tappan (1794-1849)

music by
William B. Bradbury (1816-1868)

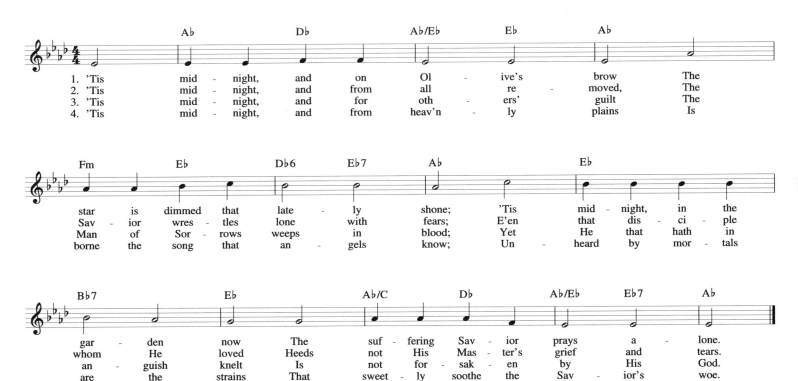

1. 'Tis mid - night, and on Ol - ive's brow The star is dimmed that late - ly shone; 'Tis mid - night, in the gar - den now The suf - fering Sav - ior prays a - lone.
2. 'Tis mid - night, and from all re - moved, The Sav - ior wres - tles lone with fears; E'en that dis - ci - ple whom He loved Heeds not His Mas - ter's grief and tears.
3. 'Tis mid - night, and for oth - ers' guilt The Man of Sor - rows weeps in blood; Yet He that hath in an - guish knelt Is not for - sak - en by His God.
4. 'Tis mid - night, and from heav'n - ly plains Is borne the song that an - gels know; Un - heard by mor - tals are the strains That sweet - ly soothe the Sav - ior's woe.

'TIS SO SWEET TO TRUST IN JESUS

TRUST IN JESUS

words by
Louisa M.R. Stead (1850-1917)

music by
William J. Kirkpatrick (1838-1921)

1. 'Tis so sweet to trust in Je - sus, Just to take Him at His Word, Just to rest up - on His prom - ise, Just to know: "Thus saith the Lord."
2. O how sweet to trust in Je - sus, Just to trust His cleans - ing blood, Just in sim - ple faith to plunge me 'Neath the heal - ing, cleans - ing flood!
3. Yes, 'tis sweet to trust in Je - sus, Just from sin and self to cease, Just from Je - sus sim - ply tak - ing Life and rest, and joy and peace.
4. I'm so glad I learned to trust Thee, Pre - cious Je - sus, Sav - ior, Friend; And I know that Thou art with me, Wilt be with me to the end.

Je - sus, Je - sus, how I trust Him! How I've proved Him o'er and o'er! Je - sus, Je - sus, pre - cious Je - sus! O for grace to trust Him more!

TO BE LIKE JESUS

Traditional words

Traditional music

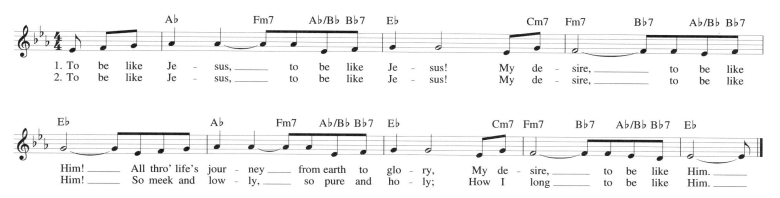

1. To be like Je - sus, _____ to be like Je - sus! My de - sire, _____ to be like
2. To be like Je - sus, _____ to be like Je - sus! My de - sire, _____ to be like

Him! _____ All thro' life's jour - ney _____ from earth to glo - ry, My de - sire, _____ to be like Him. _____
Him! _____ So meek and low - ly, _____ so pure and ho - ly; How I long _____ to be like Him. _____

TO BLESS THE EARTH

words from
The Psalter, 1912
based on Psalm 65

CHRISTUS, DER IST MEIN LEBEN
music by
Melchoir Vulpius, 1609

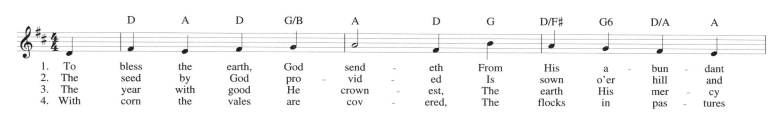

1. To bless the earth, God send - eth From His a - bun - dant
2. The seed by God pro - vid - ed Is sown o'er hill and
3. The year with good He crown - est, The earth His mer - cy
4. With corn the vales are cov - ered, The flocks in pas - tures

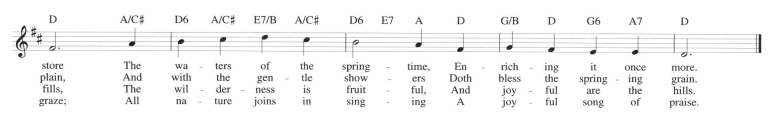

store The wa - ters of the spring - time, En - rich - ing it once more.
plain, And with the gen - tle show - ers Doth bless the spring - ing grain.
fills, The wil - der - ness is fruit - ful, And joy - ful are the hills.
graze; All na - ture joins in sing - ing A joy - ful song of praise.

TO CHRIST, THE PRINCE OF PEACE

words from
Paris Breviary, 1736
tr. by Edward Caswall (1814-1876)

NARENZA
music from
Liesentritt's *Catholicum Hymnologium Germanicum,* 1584
adapt. by William H. Havergal (1793-1870)

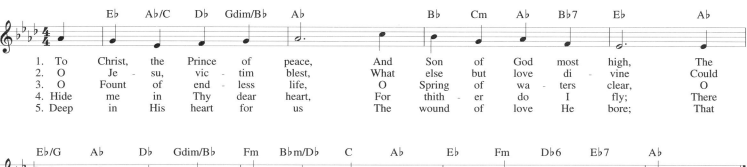

1. To Christ, the Prince of peace, And Son of God most high, The
2. O Je - su, vic - tim blest, What else but love di - vine Could
3. O Fount of end - less life, O Spring of wa - ters clear, O
4. Hide me in Thy dear heart, For thith - er do I fly; There
5. Deep in His heart for us The wound of love He bore; That

Fa - ther of the world to come, Sing we with ho - ly joy.
Thee con - strain to o - pen thus That sa - cred heart of Thine?
Flame ce - les - tial, cleans - ing all Who un - to Thee draw near!
seek Thy grace through life, in death Thine im - mor - al - i - ty.
love which still He kin - dles in The hearts that Him a - dore.

'TIS THE GIFT TO BE SIMPLE
(Simple Gifts)

SIMPLE GIFTS
Traditional Shaker melody

Shaker song, 18th century

"Tis the gift to be sim - ple, 'tis the gift to be free, 'tis the gift to come down where we ought to be, and when we find our - selves in the place just right, 'twill be in the val - ley of love and de - light. When true sim - plic - i - ty is gained to bow and to bend we shan't be a-shamed, to turn, turn, will be our de - light till by turn - ing, turn - ing we come round right.

TO GOD BE THE GLORY

words by
Fanny J. Crosby (1820-1915)

music by
William H. Doane (1832-1915)

1. To God be the glo - ry, great things He hath done! So loved He the
2. O per - fect re - demp - tion, the pur - chase of blood; To ev - 'ry be -
3. Great things He hath taught us, great things He hath done, And great our re -

world that He gave us His Son, Who yield - ed His life an a -
liev - er, the prom - ise of God. The vil - est of - fend - er who
joic - ing through Je - sus, the Son. But pur - er and high - er and

tone - ment for sin And o - pened the life - gate that all may go in. } Praise the
tru - ly be - lieves, That mo - ment from Je - sus a par - don re - ceives. }
great - er will be Our won - der, our trans - port, when Je - sus we see. }

Lord! Praise the Lord! Let the earth hear His voice! Praise the Lord! Praise the

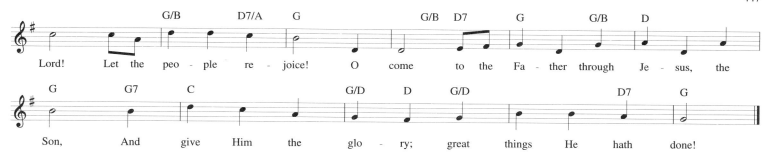

TO THE NAME OF OUR SALVATION

Latin text, 15th century
tr. in *Hymns Ancient and Modern,* 1861

ORIEL
music by
Caspar Ett (1788-1847)

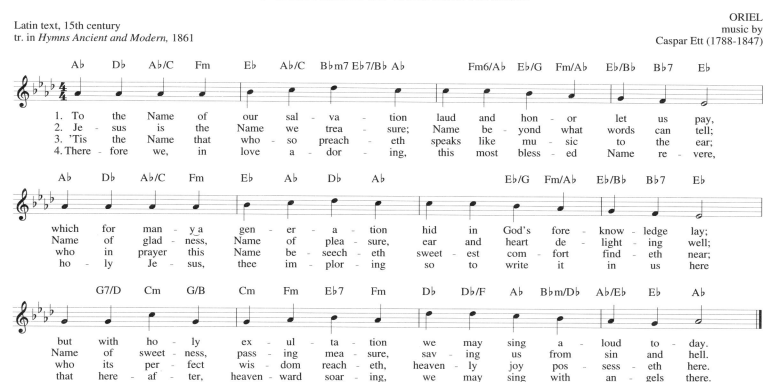

TODAY THY MERCY CALLS US

words by
Oswald Allen, 1861

ANTHES
music by
Friedrich K. Anthes, 1847

TRUST AND OBEY

words by
John H. Sammis, 1887

music by
Daniel B. Towner, 1887

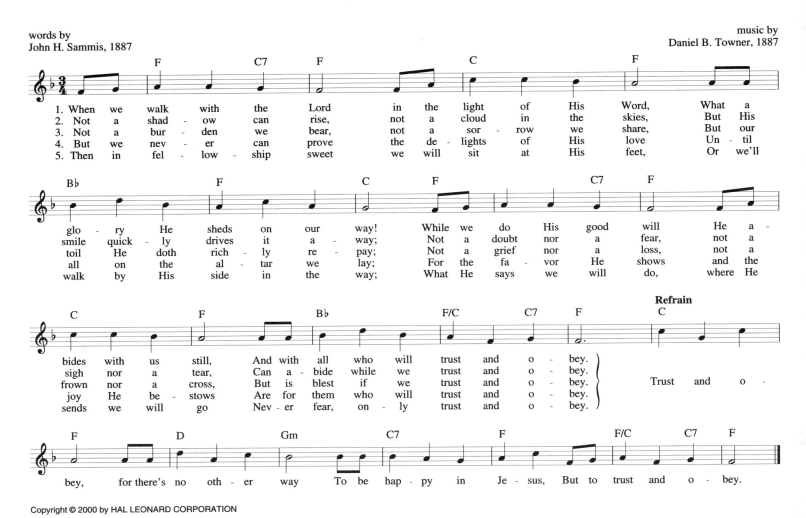

TRUSTING JESUS

words by
Edgar Page Stites (1836-1921)

music by
Ira D. Sankey (1840-1908)

TURN YOUR EYES UPON JESUS

words by
Helen H. Lemmel, 1922

LEMMEL
music by
Helen H. Lemmel, 1922

'TWAS ON THAT DARK, THAT DOLEFUL NIGHT

words by
Isaac Watts (1674-1748)

ST. CROSS
music by
John B. Dykes (1823-1876)

THE UNCLOUDED DAY

words by
J.K. Alwood

music by
J.K. Alwood

1. O they tell me of a home far be-yond the skies, O they tell me of a home far a-way; O they
2. O they tell me of a home where my friends have gone, O they tell me of that land far a-way, Where the
3. O they tell me of a King in His beau-ty there, And they tell me that mine eyes shall be-hold Where He
4. O they tell me that He smiles on His chil-dren there, And His smile _ drives their sor-rows all a-way; And they

tell me of a home where no storm-clouds rise, O they tell me of an un-cloud-ed day.
tree _ of _ life in e-ter-nal bloom Sheds its fra-grance through the un-cloud-ed day.
sits _ on the throne that is whit-er than snow, In the cit-y that is made of _ gold.
tell me that no tears ev-er come a-gain In that love-ly land of un-cloud-ed day.

O the land of cloud-less day! O the land of an un-cloud-ed day! O they

tell me of a home where no storm-clouds rise, O they tell me of an un-cloud-ed day.

UNTO THE HILLS

words by
John Campbell (1845-1914)

SANDON
music by
Charles H. Purday (1799-1885)

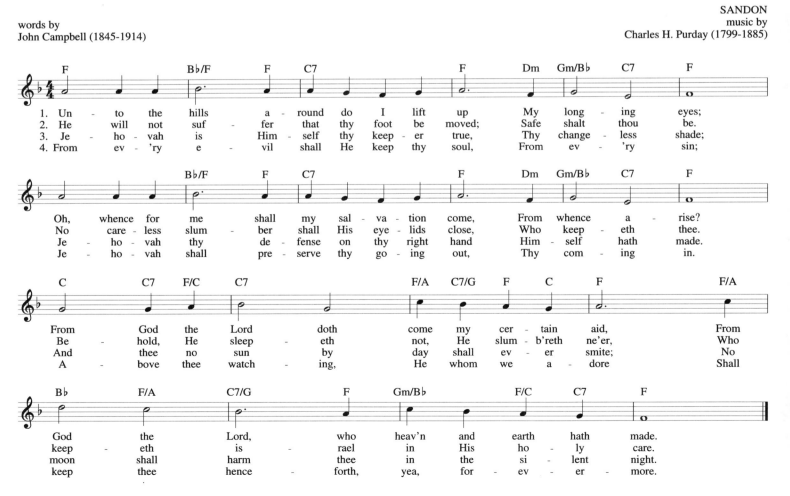

1. Un-to the hills a-round do I lift up My long-ing eyes;
2. He will not suf-fer that thy foot be moved; Safe shalt thou be.
3. Je-ho-vah is Him-self thy keep-er true, Thy change-less shade;
4. From ev-'ry e-vil shall He keep thy soul, From ev-'ry sin;

Oh, whence for me shall my sal-va-tion come, From whence a-rise?
No care-less slum-ber shall His eye-lids close, Who keep-eth thee.
Je-ho-vah thy de-fense on thy right hand Him-self hath made.
Je-ho-vah shall pre-serve thy go-ing out, Thy com-ing in.

From God the Lord doth come my cer-tain aid, From
Be-hold, He sleep-eth not, He slum-b'reth ne'er, Who
And thee no sun by day shall ev-er smite; No
A-bove thee watch-ing, He whom we a-dore Shall

God the Lord, who heav'n and earth hath made.
keep-eth is-rael in His ho-ly care.
moon shall harm thee in the si-lent night.
keep thee hence-forth, yea, for ev-er-more.

UNDER HIS WINGS

words by
William O. Cushing, 1896

HINGHAM
music by
Ira D. Sankey, 1896

1. Un - der His wings I am safe - ly a - bid - ing. Tho' the night deep - ens and
2. Un - der His wings, what a ref - uge in sor - row! How the heart yearn - ing - ly
3. Un - der His wings, O what pre - cious en - joy - ment! There will I hide till life's

tem - pests are wild, Still I can trust Him; I know He will keep me. He has re - deemed me, and
turns to His rest! Of - ten when earth has no balm for my heal - ing, There I find com - fort, and
tri - als are o'er; Shel - tered, pro - tect - ed, no e - vil can harm me. Rest - ing in Je - sus, I'm

Refrain

I am His child.)
there I am blest.} Un - der His wings, un - der His wings, Who from His love ___ can
safe ev - er - more.)

sev - er? ___ Un - der His wings my soul shall a - bide, Safe - ly a - bide ___ for - ev - er.

Copyright © 2000 by HAL LEONARD CORPORATION

UNSEARCHABLE RICHES

words by
Fanny J. Crosby (1820-1915)

music by
John R. Sweney (1837-1899)

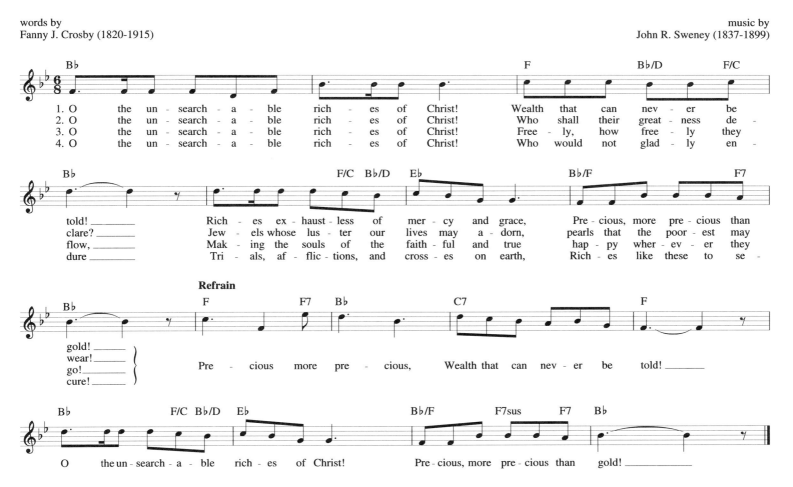

1. O the un - search - a - ble rich - es of Christ! Wealth that can nev - er be
2. O the un - search - a - ble rich - es of Christ! Who shall their great - ness de -
3. O the un - search - a - ble rich - es of Christ! Free - ly, how free - ly they
4. O the un - search - a - ble rich - es of Christ! Who would not glad - ly en -

told! ___ Rich - es ex - haust - less of mer - cy and grace, Pre - cious, more pre - cious than
clare? ___ Jew - els whose lus - ter our lives may a - dorn, pearls that the poor - est may
flow, ___ Mak - ing the souls of the faith - ful and true hap - py wher - ev - er they
dure ___ Tri - als, af - flic - tions, and cross - es on earth, Rich - es like these to se -

Refrain

gold! ___
wear! ___
go! ___ } Pre - cious more pre - cious, Wealth that can nev - er be told! ___
cure! ___ }

O the un - search - a - ble rich - es of Christ! Pre - cious, more pre - cious than gold! ___

Copyright © 2000 by HAL LEONARD CORPORATION

THE UNVEILED CHRIST

words by
N.B. Herrell (1877-1954)

music by
N.B. Herrell (1877-1954)

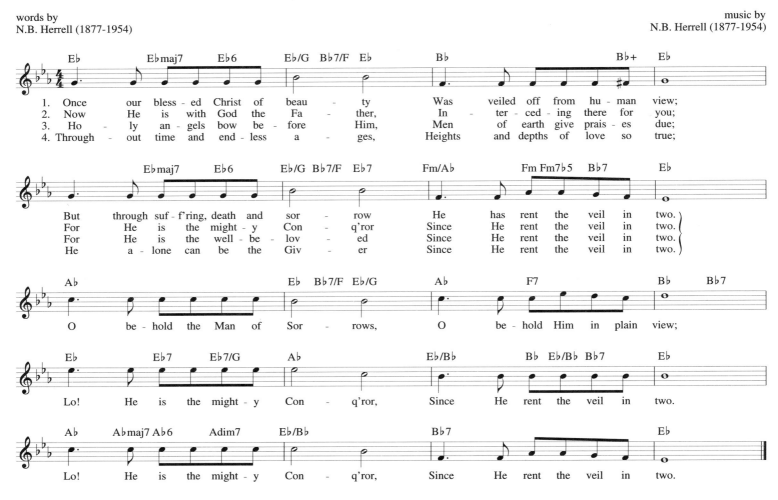

1. Once our bless-ed Christ of beau - ty Was veiled off from hu-man view;
2. Now He is with God the Fa - ther, In - ter-ced-ing there for you;
3. Ho - ly an-gels bow be - fore Him, Men of earth give prais - es due;
4. Through - out time and end-less a - ges, Heights and depths of love so true;

But through suf-f'ring, death and sor - row He has rent the veil in two.
For He is the might-y Con - q'ror Since He rent the veil in two.
For He is the well-be - lov - ed Since He rent the veil in two.
He a - lone can be the Giv - er Since He rent the veil in two.

O be-hold the Man of Sor - rows, O be-hold Him in plain view;

Lo! He is the might - y Con - q'ror, Since He rent the veil in two.

Lo! He is the might - y Con - q'ror, Since He rent the veil in two.

VERILY, VERILY, I SAY UNTO YOU

VERILY

words by
James McGranahan (1840-1907)

music by
James McGranahan (1840-1907)

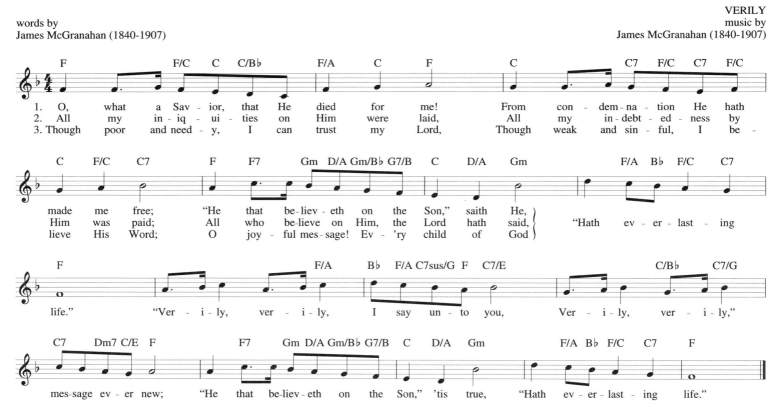

1. O, what a Sav - ior, that He died for me! From con - dem-na - tion He hath
2. All my in-iq-ui-ties on Him were laid, All my in-debt-ed-ness by
3. Though poor and need - y, I can trust my Lord, Though weak and sin-ful, I be -

made me free; "He that be-liev-eth on the Son," saith He,
Him was paid; All who be-lieve on Him, the Lord hath said,
lieve His Word; O joy-ful mes-sage! Ev-'ry child of God

"Hath ev-er-last-ing

life." "Ver - i-ly, ver - i-ly, I say un-to you, Ver - i-ly, ver - i-ly,"

mes-sage ev - er new; "He that be-liev-eth on the Son," 'tis true, "Hath ev-er-last-ing life."

VICTIM DIVINE, THY GRACE WE CLAIM

words by
Charles Wesley (1707-1788)

DAS NEUGEBORNE KINDELEIN
music by
Melchior Vulpius (c. 1560-1615)

1. Vic - tim Di - vine, _____ Thy grace _____ we claim, While thus Thy pre - cious death we show; Once of - fered up, _____ a spot - less Lamb, In Thy great tem - ple here be - low, Thou didst for all _____ man - kind _____ a - tone; And stand - est now _____ be - fore the throne.
2. Thou stand - est in _____ the ho - liest place, As now Thy guilt - y sin - ners slain; Thy blood of sprin - kling speaks _____ and prays All - prev - a - lent for help - less man; Thy Blood is still _____ our ran - som found, And spreads sal - va - tion all _____ a - round.
3. We need not now _____ go up _____ to heaven To bring the long - sought Sav - ior down; Thou art to all _____ al - read - y given, Thou dost e'en now Thy ban - quet crown: To ev - 'ry faith - ful soul _____ ap - pear, And show Thy re - al Pres - ence here.

Copyright © 2000 by HAL LEONARD CORPORATION

VICTORY ALL THE TIME

words by
Lelia N. Morris, 1901

music by
Lelia N. Morris, 1901

1. They who know the Sav - ior shall in Him be strong, Might - y in the con - flict of the right 'gainst wrong. This is bless - ed prom - ise giv - en in God's Word, Do - ing won - drous ex - ploits, they who know the Lord.
2. In the midst of bat - tle be thou not dis - mayed, Tho' the pow'rs of dark - ness 'gainst thee are ar - rayed. God, thy Strength, is with thee, caus - ing thee to stand; Heav - en's al - lied ar - mies wait at thy com - mand.
3. Brave to bear life's test - ing, strong the foe to meet, Walk - ing like a he - ro midst the fur - nace heat, Do - ing won - drous ex - ploits with the Spir - it's Sword, Win - ning souls for Je - sus, praise, O praise the Lord!

Refrain

Vic - to - ry! vic - to - ry! bless - ed, blood-bo't vic - to - ry! Vic - to - ry! vic - to - ry! vic - t'ry all the time! As Je - ho - vah liv - eth, Strength di - vine He giv - eth Un - to those who know Him vic - t'ry all the time!

Copyright © 2000 by HAL LEONARD CORPORATION

THE VOICE OF GOD IS CALLING

MEIRIONYDD

words by
John Haynes Holmes, 1913

music by
William Lloyd, 1840

1. The voice of God is calling its summons in our day; Isaiah heard in
2. "I hear my people crying in slum and mine and mill; no field or mart is
3. We heed, O Lord, Your summons, and answer: Here are we! Send us upon your
4. From ease and plenty save us; from pride of place absolve; purge us of low de-

Zion, and we now hear God say: "Whom shall I send to succor my people in their
silent, no city street is still. I see my people falling in darkness and de-
errand, let us your servants be. Our strength is dust and ashes, our years a passing
sire; lift us to high resolve; take us, and make us holy; teach us Your will and

need? Whom shall I send to loosen the bonds of shame and greed?
spair. Whom shall I send to shatter the fetters which they bear?"
hour; but you can use our weakness to magnify your power.
way. Speak, and behold! we answer; command, and we obey!

WAKE, AWAKE, FOR NIGHT IS FLYING

WACHET AUF

words by
Philipp Nicolai, 1599
tr. by Catherine Winkworth, 1858

music by
Philipp Nicolai, 1599

1. Wake, awake, for night is flying; the watchmen on the heights are cry-
2. Zion hears the watchmen singing, and all her heart with joy is spring-
3. Now let all the heavens adore Thee, and saints and angels sing be-fore

ing: A-wake, Jerusalem, at last! Midnight hears the welcome voic-
ing; she wakes, she rises from her gloom; for her Lord comes down all-glo-
thee, with harp and cymbal's clearest tone; of one pearl each shining por-

es and at the thrilling cry rejoices; come forth, ye virgins,
rious, the strong in grace, in truth victorious. Her Star is risen; her
tal, where we are with the choir immortal of angels round Thy

night is past; the Bridegroom comes, awake; your lamps with gladness take: Al-
Light is come. Ah come, Thou blessed One, God's own beloved Son: Al-
dazzling throne; nor eye hath seen, nor ear hath yet attained to hear what

le-lu-ia! And for his marriage feast prepare, for ye must go and meet him there.
le-lu-ia! We follow till the halls we see where Thou hast bid us sup with Thee.
there is ours; but we rejoice and sing to Thee our hymn of joy eternally.

WALKING IN THE KING'S HIGHWAY

KING'S HIGHWAY

words by
Florence Horton, 1906

music by
Florence Horton, 1906

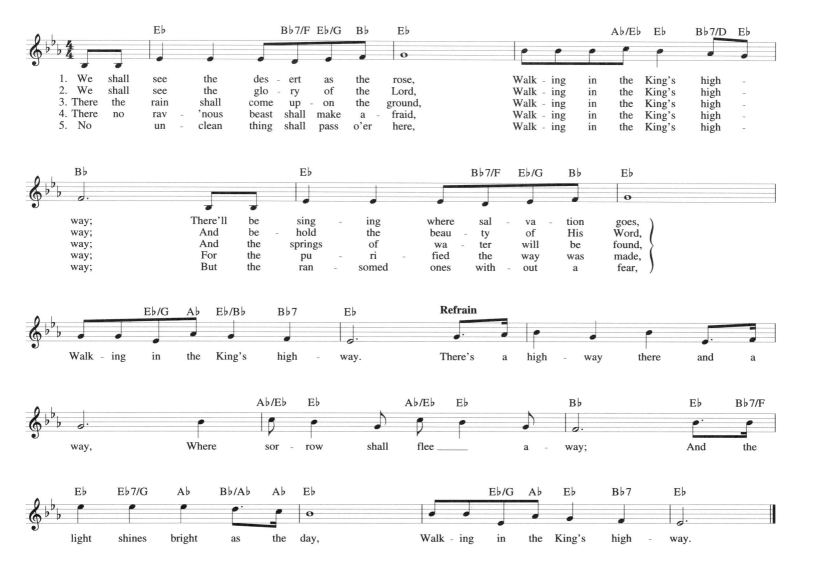

1. We shall see the desert as the rose, Walk-ing in the King's high-
2. We shall see the glo-ry of the Lord, Walk-ing in the King's high-
3. There the rain shall come up-on the ground, Walk-ing in the King's high-
4. There no rav-'nous beast shall make a-fraid, Walk-ing in the King's high-
5. No un-clean thing shall pass o'er here, Walk-ing in the King's high-

way; There'll be sing-ing where sal-va-tion goes,
way; And be-hold-ing the beau-ty of His Word,
way; And the springs of wa-ter will be found,
way; For the pu-ri-fied the way was made,
way; But the ran-somed ones with-out a fear,

Walk-ing in the King's high-way. There's a high-way there and a way, Where sor-row shall flee ____ a-way; And the light shines bright as the day, Walk-ing in the King's high-way.

Refrain

Copyright © 2000 by HAL LEONARD CORPORATION

WALKING WITH JESUS

Traditional words

Traditional music

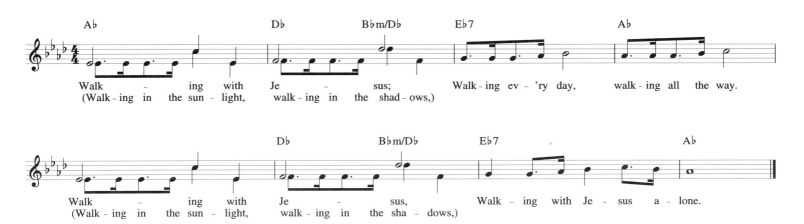

Walk - ing with Je - sus;
(Walk-ing in the sun-light, walk-ing in the shad-ows,)
Walk-ing ev-'ry day, walk-ing all the way.

Walk - ing with Je - sus,
(Walk-ing in the sun-light, walk-ing in the sha-dows,)
Walk-ing with Je-sus a-lone.

Copyright © 2000 by HAL LEONARD CORPORATION

THE WAY OF THE CROSS LEADS HOME

WAY OF THE CROSS

words by
Jessie B. Pounds, 1906

music by
Charles H. Gabriel, 1906

WAYFARING STRANGER

Southern American Folk Text

Southern American Folk Melody

WE ALL BELIEVE IN ONE TRUE GOD

words by
Tobias Clausnitzer, 1668
tr. by Catherine Winkworth, 1863

WIR GLAUBEN ALL' AN EINEN GOTT
music from
Kirchengesangbuch, Darmstadt, 1699
As in *Allgemeines Choral-Melodienbuch,* 1793

1. We all be-lieve in one true God, Fa-ther, Son, and Ho-ly Ghost,
2. And we be-lieve in Je-sus Christ, Son of man and Son of God;
3. And we con-fess the Ho-ly Ghost, Who from both for-ev-er flow;

Strong De-liv-'rer in our need Praised by all the heaven-ly host,
Who, to raise us up to heaven, Left his throne and bore our load,
Who up-holds and com-forts us In the midst of fears and woes.

By whose might-y power a-lone All is made and wrought and done.
By whose cross and death are we Res-cued from our mis-er-y.
Blest and ho-ly Trin-i-ty, Praise shall aye be brought to Thee!

WE ARE CLIMBING JACOB'S LADDER

Traditional Spiritual

JACOB'S LADDER
Traditional Spiritual

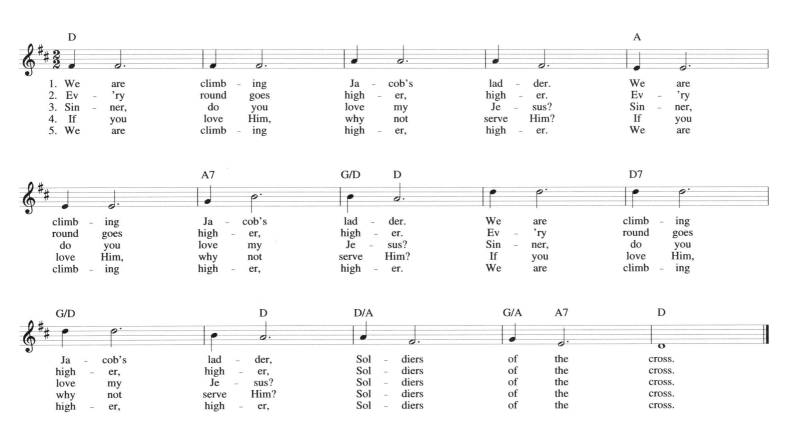

1. We are climb-ing Ja-cob's lad-der. We are
2. Ev-'ry round goes high-er, high-er. Ev-'ry
3. Sin-ner, do you love my Je-sus? Sin-ner,
4. If you love Him, why not serve Him? If you
5. We are climb-ing high-er, high-er. We are

climb-ing Ja-cob's lad-der. We are climb-ing
round goes high-er, high-er. Ev-'ry round goes
do you love my Je-sus? Sin-ner, do you
love Him, why not serve Him? If you love Him,
climb-ing high-er, high-er. We are climb-ing

Ja-cob's lad-der, Sol-diers of the cross.
high-er, high-er, Sol-diers of the cross.
love my Je-sus? Sol-diers of the cross.
why not serve Him? Sol-diers of the cross.
high-er, high-er, Sol-diers of the cross.

WE GATHER TOGETHER

KREMSER
Netherlands Folk melody
arr. by Edward Kremser, 1877

words from
Nederlandtsch Gedenckclanck, 1626
tr. by Theodore Baker, 1894

1. We gath-er to-geth-er to ask the Lord's bless-ing; He chas-tens and
2. Be-side us to guide us, our God with us join-ing, Or-dain-ing, main-
3. We all do ex-tol Thee, Thou Lead-er tri-um-phant, And pray that Thou

has-tens His will to make known; The wick-ed op-press-ing now cease from dis-
tain-ing His king-dom di-vine; So from the be-gin-ing the fight we were
still our De-fend-er wilt be. Let Thy con-gre-ga-tion es-cape trib-u-

tress-ing, Sing prais-es to His name He for-gets not His own.
win-ning; Thou, Lord, wast at our side, all glo-ry be Thine!
la-tion: Thy name be ev-er praised! O Lord, make us free!

WE GIVE THEE BUT THINE OWN

SCHUMANN
music from
Mason and Webb's *Cantica Lauda,* 1850

words by
William W. How (1823-1897)

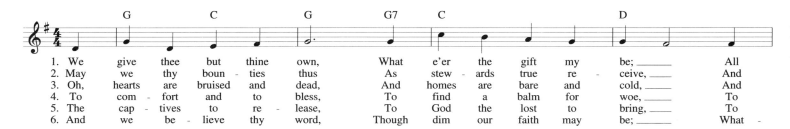

1. We give thee but thine own, What e'er the gift my be; ___ All
2. May we thy boun-ties thus As stew-ards true re-ceive, ___ And
3. Oh, hearts are bruised and dead, And homes are bare and cold, ___ And
4. To com-fort and to bless, To find a balm for woe, ___ To
5. The cap-tives to re-lease, To God the lost to bring, ___ To
6. And we be-lieve thy word, Though dim our faith may be; ___ What

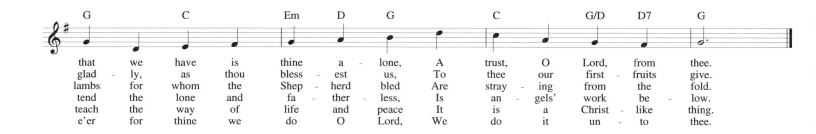

that we have is thine a-lone, A trust, O Lord, from thee.
glad-ly, as thou bless-est us, To thee our first-fruits give.
lambs for whom the Shep-herd bled, Are stray-ing from the fold.
tend the lone and fa-ther-less, Is an-gels' work be-low.
teach the way of life and peace It is a Christ-like thing.
e'er for thine we do O Lord, We do it un-to thee.

WE BELIEVE IN ONE TRUE GOD

words by
Tobias Clausnitzer, 1668
tr. by Catherine Winkworth, 1863

RATISBON
music from
J.G. Werner's *Choralbuch,* 1815
arr. by William H. Havergal, 1861

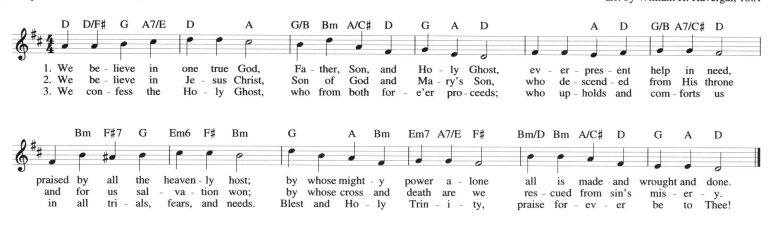

1. We be-lieve in one true God, Fa-ther, Son, and Ho-ly Ghost, ev-er-pres-ent help in need,
2. We be-lieve in Je-sus Christ, Son of God and Ma-ry's Son, who de-scend-ed from His throne
3. We con-fess the Ho-ly Ghost, who from both for-e'er pro-ceeds; who up-holds and com-forts us

praised by all the heaven-ly host; by whose might-y power a-lone all is made and wrought and done.
and for us sal-va-tion won; by whose cross and death are we res-cued from sin's mis-er-y.
in all tri-als, fears, and needs. Blest and Ho-ly Trin-i-ty, praise for-ev-er be to Thee!

WE HAVE AN ANCHOR

ANCHOR
music by
William J. Kirkpatrick, 1882

words by
Priscilla J. Owens, 1882

1. Will your an-chor hold in the storms of life, When the clouds un-fold their ___
2. It is safe-ly moored; 'twill the storm with-stand, For 'tis well-se-cured by the
3. When our eyes be-hold thro' the gath-'ring night The cit-y of gold, our ___

wings of strife? When the strong tides lift, and the ca-bles strain, Will your
Sav-ior's hand. Tho' the tem-pest rage and the wild winds blow, Not an
har-bor bright, We shall an-chor fast by the heav'n-ly shore, With the

an-chor drift ___ or firm re-main? }
an-gry wave ___ shall our bark o'er-flow. } We have an an-chor that
storms all past ___ for-ev-er-more. }

Refrain

keeps the soul Stead-fast and sure while the bil-lows roll, Fas-tened to the Rock which

can-not move, Ground-ed firm and deep in the Sav-ior's love.

WE PRAISE THEE, O GOD, OUR REDEEMER

KREMSER
Netherlands Folk Song
arr. by Edward Kremser, 1877

words by
Julia C. Cory, 1902

1. We praise Thee, O God, our Re - deem - er, Cre - a - tor; In
2. We wor - ship Thee, God of our fa - thers; we bless Thee. Thro'
3. With voic - es u - nit - ed our prais - es we of - fer, And

grate - ful de - vo - tion our trib - ute we bring. We
life's storm and tem - pest our guide Thou hast been. When
glad - ly our songs of true wor - ship we raise. Thy

lay it be - fore Thee; we kneel _____ and a - dore Thee. We
per - ils o'er - take us, Thou wilt _____ not for - sake us, And
strong arm will guide us; our God _____ is be - side us. To

bless Thy ho - ly name; _____ glad prais - es we sing.
with Thy help, O Lord, _____ life's bat - tles we win.
Thee, our great Re - deem - er, for - ev - er we praise.

WE PLOW THE FIELDS AND SCATTER

WIR PFLÜGEN
music by
Johann A.P. Schultz (1747-1800)

words by
Matthias Claudius (1740-1815)
tr. by Jane M. Campbell (1817-1878)

1. We plow the fields and scat - ter The good seed on the land; But
2. He on - ly is the mak - er Of all things near and far; He
3. We thank Thee then, O Fa - ther, For all things bright and good, The

it is fed and wa - tered By God's al - might - y hand. He
paints the way - side flow - er, He lights the eve - ning star. The
seed - time and the har - vest, Our life, our health, our food. Ac

sends the snow in win - ter, The warmth to swell the grain, The
winds and waves o - bey Him; By Him the birds are fed. Much
cept the gifts we of - fer For all Thy love im - parts, And

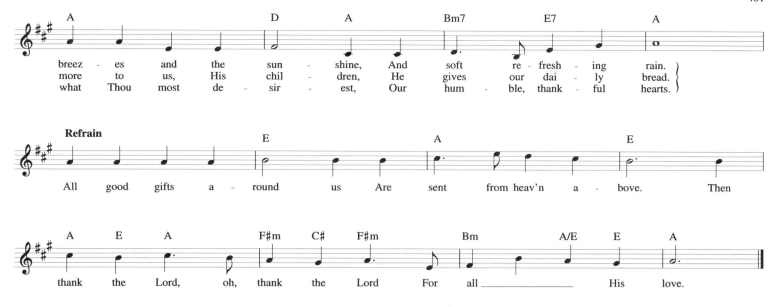

WE SING THE GLORIOUS CONQUEST

words by
John Ellerton (1826-1893)

MUNICH
music from
Neu-vermehrtes Gesangbuch, Meiningen, 1693

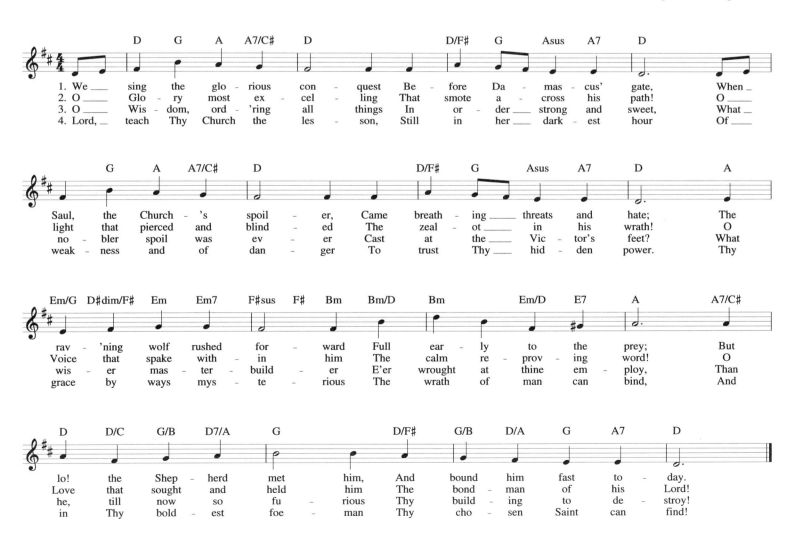

WE SHALL SEE THE KING SOMEDAY

SEE THE KING

words by
Lewis E. Jones, 1906

music by
Lewis E. Jones, 1906

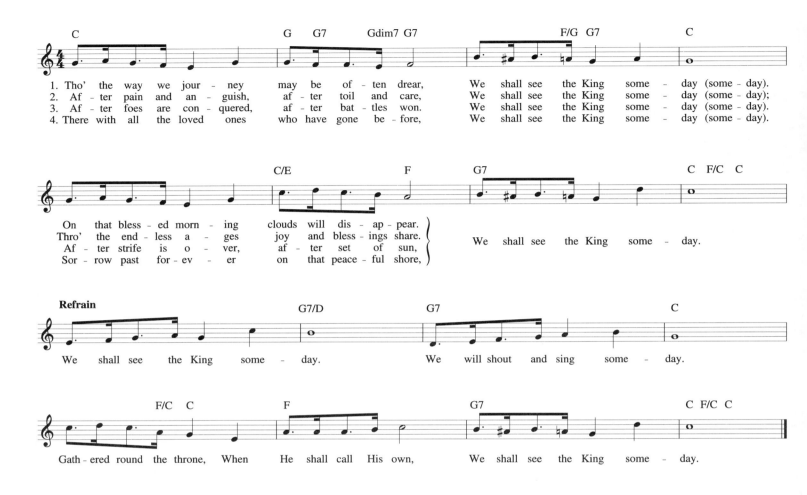

1. Tho' the way we jour-ney may be of-ten drear, We shall see the King some-day (some-day).
2. Af-ter pain and an-guish, af-ter toil and care, We shall see the King some-day (some-day);
3. Af-ter foes are con-quered, af-ter bat-tles won. We shall see the King some-day (some-day).
4. There with all the loved ones who have gone be-fore, We shall see the King some-day (some-day).

On that bless-ed morn-ing clouds will dis-ap-pear.
Thro' the end-less a-ges joy and bless-ings share.
Af-ter strife is o-ver, af-ter set of sun,
Sor-row past for-ev-er on that peace-ful shore,
We shall see the King some-day.

Refrain

We shall see the King some-day. We will shout and sing some-day.

Gath-ered round the throne, When He shall call His own, We shall see the King some-day.

WE SING THE PRAISE OF HIM WHO DIED

WINDHAM

words by
Thomas Kelly (1769-1855)

music attr. to
Daniel Read (1757-1836)

1. We sing the praise of Him who died, Of Him who died up-on the cross. The
2. In-scribed up-on the cross we see In shin-ing let-ters, "God is love." He
3. The cross! It takes our guilt a-way; It holds the faint-ing spir-it up; It
4. It makes the cow-ard spir-it brave And nerves the fee-ble arm for fight; It
5. The balm of life, the cure of woe, The meas-ure and the pledge of love, The

sin-ner's hope let all de-ride; For this we count the world but loss.
bears our sins up-on the tree; He brings us mer-cy from a-bove.
cheers with hope the gloom-y day And sweet-ens ev-'ry bit-ter cup.
takes the ter-ror from the grave And gilds the bed of death with light.
sin-ner's ref-uge here be-low, The an-gel's theme in heav'n a-bove.

WE THREE KINGS OF ORIENT ARE

KINGS OF ORIENT

words by
John H. Hopkins, Jr. (1820-1891)

music by
John H. Hopkins, Jr. (1820-1891)

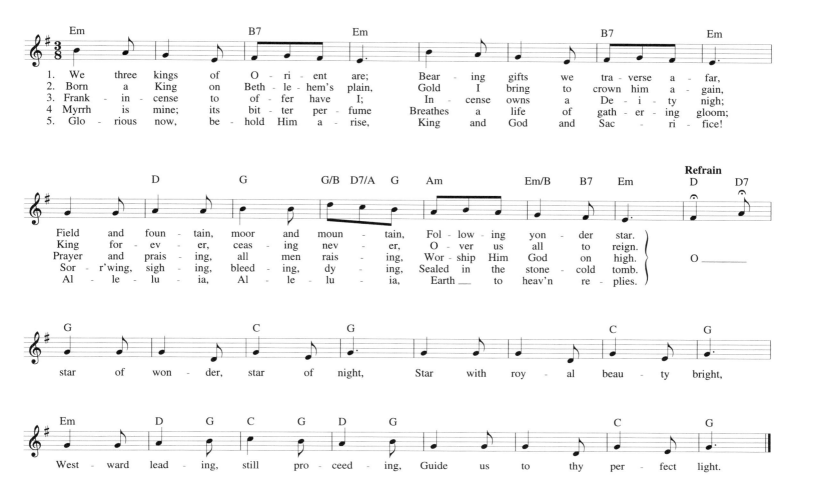

1. We three kings of O - ri - ent are; Bear - ing gifts we tra - verse a - far,
2. Born a King on Beth - le - hem's plain, Gold I bring to crown him a - gain,
3. Frank - in - cense to of - fer have I; In - cense owns a De - i - ty nigh;
4. Myrrh is mine; its bit - ter per - fume Breathes a life of gath - er - ing gloom;
5. Glo - rious now, be - hold Him a - rise, King and God and Sac - ri - fice!

Field and foun - tain, moor and moun - tain, Fol - low - ing yon - der star.
King for - ev - er, ceas - ing nev - er, O - ver us all to reign.
Prayer and prais - ing, all men rais - ing, Wor - ship Him God on high.
Sor - r'wing, sigh - ing, bleed - ing, dy - ing, Sealed in the stone - cold tomb.
Al - le - lu - ia, Al - le - lu - ia, Earth to heav'n re - plies.

Refrain

O _____

star of won - der, star of night, Star with roy - al beau - ty bright,

West - ward lead - ing, still pro - ceed - ing, Guide us to thy per - fect light.

WE WORSHIP AND ADORE YOU

WORSHIP AND ADORE

Traditional words

Traditional music

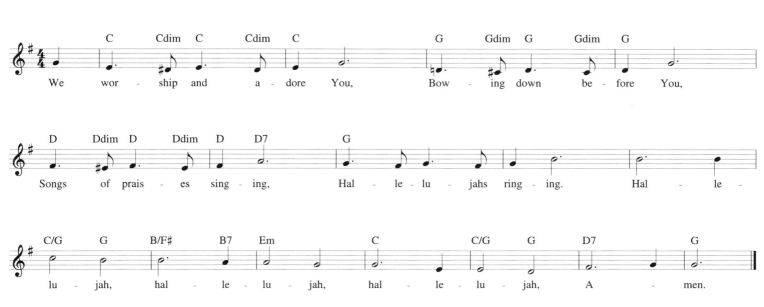

We wor - ship and a - dore You, Bow - ing down be - fore You,

Songs of prais - es sing - ing, Hal - le - lu - jahs ring - ing. Hal - le -

lu - jah, hal - le - lu - jah, hal - le - lu - jah, A - men.

WE WOULD SEE JESUS

words by
Anna B. Warner

music by
Franklin E. Belden

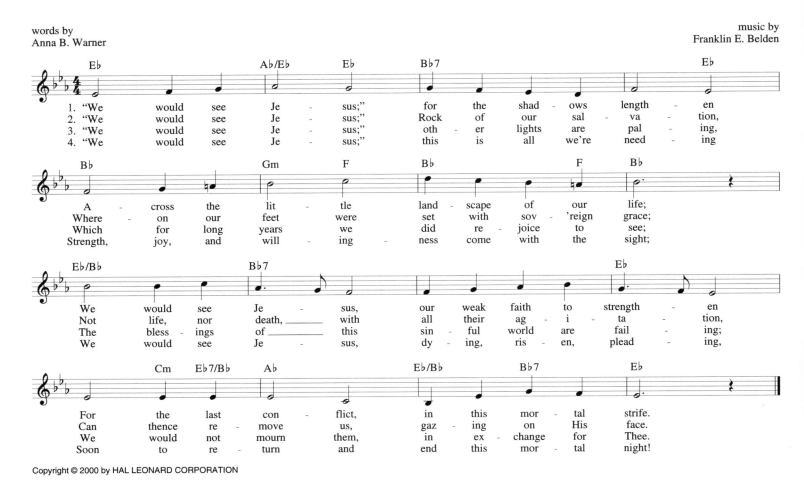

WE'LL UNDERSTAND IT BETTER BY AND BY

BY AND BY

words by
Charles A. Tindley

music by
Charles A. Tindley

WE'LL WORK TILL JESUS COMES

words by
Elizabeth Mills, 19th century

O LAND OF REST
music by
William Miller, 19th century

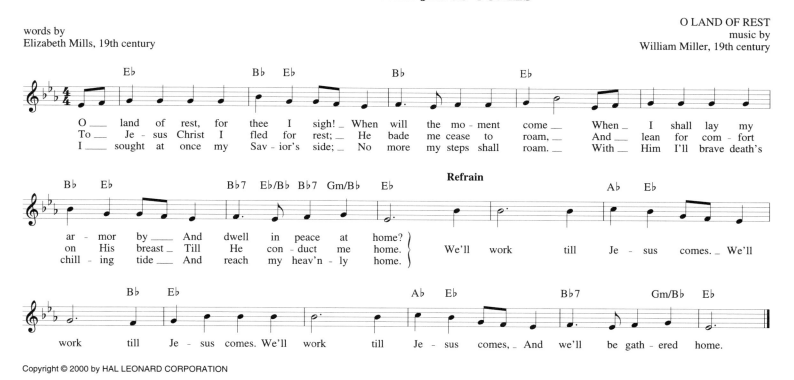

O __ land of rest, for thee I sigh! When will the mo-ment come __ When __ I shall lay my
To __ Je-sus Christ I fled for rest; __ He bade me cease to roam, __ And __ I lean for com-fort
I __ sought at once my Sav-ior's side; No more my steps shall roam. __ With __ Him I'll brave death's

ar-mor by __ And dwell in peace at home?
on His breast __ Till He con-duct me home.
chill-ing tide __ And reach my heav'n-ly home.

We'll work till Je-sus comes. __ We'll

work till Je-sus comes. We'll work till Je-sus comes, __ And we'll be gath-ered home.

WE'RE MARCHING TO ZION

words by Isaac Watts, 1707 (verses)
and Robert Lowry, 1867 (refrain)

MARCHING TO ZION
music by
Robert Lowry, 1867

1. Come, we that love __ the Lord, And let our joys __ be known, __ Join
2. Let those re-fuse __ to sing Who nev-er knew __ our God; __ But
3. The hill of Zi-on yields A thou-sand sa-cred sweets, __ Be-
4. Then let our songs __ a-bound, And ev-'ry tear __ be dry; __ We're

in a song with sweet ac-cord, Join in a song with sweet ac-cord, And
chil-dren of the heav'n-ly King, But chil-dren of the heav'n-ly King, May
fore we reach the heav'n-ly fields, Be-fore we reach the heav'n-ly fields, Or
march-ing thru Im-man-uel's ground, We're march-ing thru Im-man-uel's ground, To

thus sur-round the throne, And thus sur-round the throne. __
speak their joys a-broad, May speak their joys a-broad. __
walk the gold-en streets, Or walk the gold-en streets. __
fair-er worlds on high, To fair-er worlds on high. __

We're

march-ing to Zi-on, beau-ti-ful, beau-ti-ful Zi-on; We're

march-ing up-ward to Zi-on, __ The beau-ti-ful ci-ty of God. __

WE'VE A STORY TO TELL TO THE NATIONS

MESSAGE

words by
H. Ernest Nichol, 1896

music by
H. Ernest Nichol, 1896

1. We've a sto - ry to tell to the na - tions That shall turn their hearts to the
2. We've a song to be sung to the na - tions That shall lift their hearts to the
3. We've a mes - sage to give to the na - tions That the Lord who reign - eth a -
4. We've a Sav - ior to show to the na - tions Who the path of sor - row hath

right, A sto - ry of truth and _____ mer - cy, A
Lord, A song that shall con - quer _____ e - vil, And
bove, Hath sent us His Son to _____ save us, And
trod, That all of the world's great _____ peo - ples Might

sto - ry of peace and light, _____ A sto - ry of peace and light.
shat - ter the spear and sword, _____ And shat - ter the spear and sword.
show us that God is love, _____ And show us that God is love.
come to the truth of God, _____ Might come to the truth of God.

Refrain

For the

dark - ness shall turn to dawn - ing, And the dawn - ing to noon - day bright, And

Christ's great king - dom shall come to earth, The king - dom of love and light.

WELCOME, HAPPY MORNING!

FORTUNATUS

words by
Venantius Fortunatus, 590
tr. by John Ellerton, 1868

music by
Arthur S. Sullivan, 1872

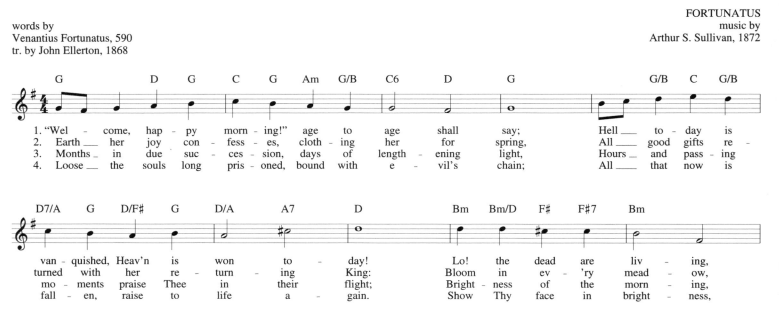

1. "Wel - come, hap - py morn - ing!" age to age shall say; Hell _____ to - day is
2. Earth _____ her joy con - fess - es, cloth - ing her for spring, All _____ good gifts re -
3. Months _____ in due suc - ces - sion, days of length - ening light, Hours _____ and pass - ing
4. Loose _____ the souls long pris - oned, bound with e - vil's chain; All _____ that now is

van - quished, Heav'n is won to - day! Lo! the dead are liv - ing,
turned with her re - turn - ing King: Bloom in ev - 'ry mead - ow,
mo - ments praise Thee in their flight; Bright - ness of the morn - ing,
fall - en, raise to life a - gain. Show Thy face in bright - ness,

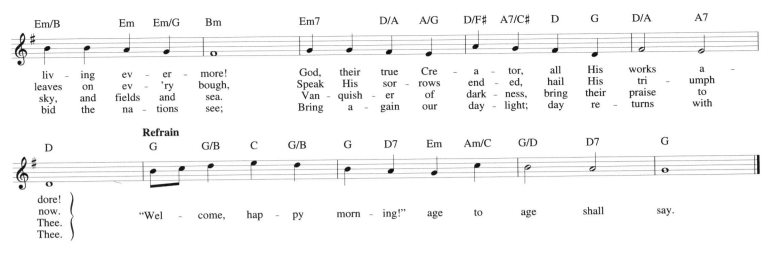

Em/B		Em	Em/G	Bm		Em7	D/A	A/G	D/F#	A7/C#	D	G	D/A	A7

liv - ing ev - er - more! God, their true Cre - a - tor, all His works a -
leaves on ev - 'ry bough, Speak His sor - rows end - ed, hail His tri - umph
sky, and fields and sea. Van - quish - er of dark - ness, bring their praise to
bid the na - tions see; Bring a - gain our day - light; day re - turns with

Refrain

D		G	G/B	C	G/B	G	D7	Em	Am/C	G/D	D7	G

dore!
now.
Thee. } "Wel - come, hap - py morn - ing!" age to age shall say.
Thee.

WELCOME, WELCOME

WELCOME
music by
Daniel Read

words by
Lelia N. Morris

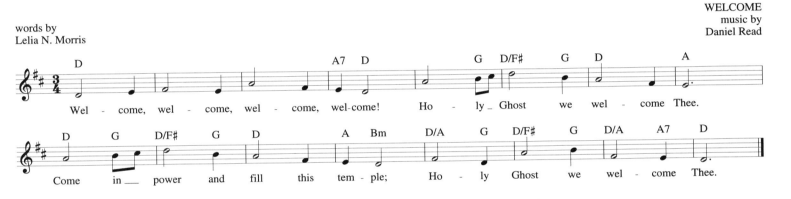

D				A7	D		G	D/F#	G	D		A

Wel - come, wel - come, wel - come, wel-come! Ho - ly Ghost we wel - come Thee.

D	G	D/F#	G	D		A	Bm	D/A	G	D/F#	G	D/A	A7	D

Come in power and fill this tem - ple; Ho - ly Ghost we wel - come Thee.

WERE YOU THERE?

Traditional Spiritual

Traditional Spiritual

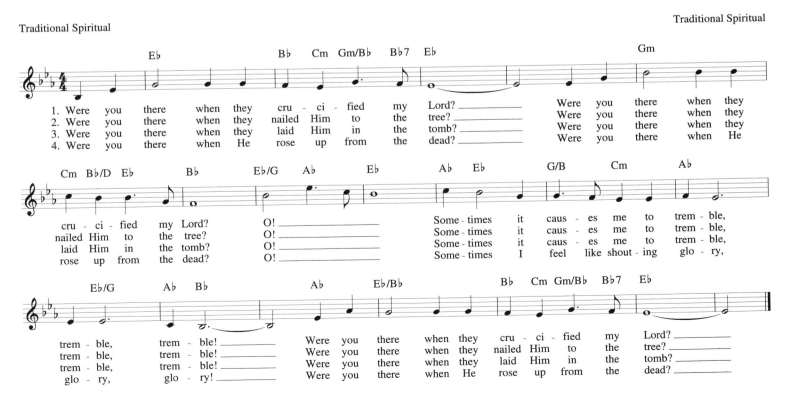

	Eb			Bb	Cm	Gm/Bb	Bb7	Eb			Gm

1. Were you there when they cru - ci - fied my Lord? _____ Were you there when they
2. Were you there when they nailed Him to the tree? _____ Were you there when they
3. Were you there when they laid Him in the tomb? _____ Were you there when they
4. Were you there when He rose up from the dead? _____ Were you there when He

Cm	Bb/D	Eb		Bb		Eb/G	Ab		Eb		Ab	Eb		G/B	Cm		Ab

cru - ci - fied my Lord? O! _____ Some - times it caus - es me to trem - ble,
nailed Him to the tree? O! _____ Some - times it caus - es me to trem - ble,
laid Him in the tomb? O! _____ Some - times it caus - es me to trem - ble,
rose up from the dead? O! _____ Some - times I feel like shout - ing glo - ry,

Eb/G		Ab	Bb			Ab		Eb/Bb		Bb	Cm	Gm/Bb	Bb7	Eb

trem - ble, trem - ble! _____ Were you there when they cru - ci - fied my Lord? _____
trem - ble, trem - ble! _____ Were you there when they nailed Him to the tree? _____
trem - ble, trem - ble! _____ Were you there when they laid Him in the tomb? _____
glo - ry, glo - ry! _____ Were you there when He rose up from the dead? _____

WHAT A FRIEND WE HAVE IN JESUS

words by
Joseph M. Scriven (1820-1886)

CONVERSE
music by
Charles C. Converse (1832-1918)

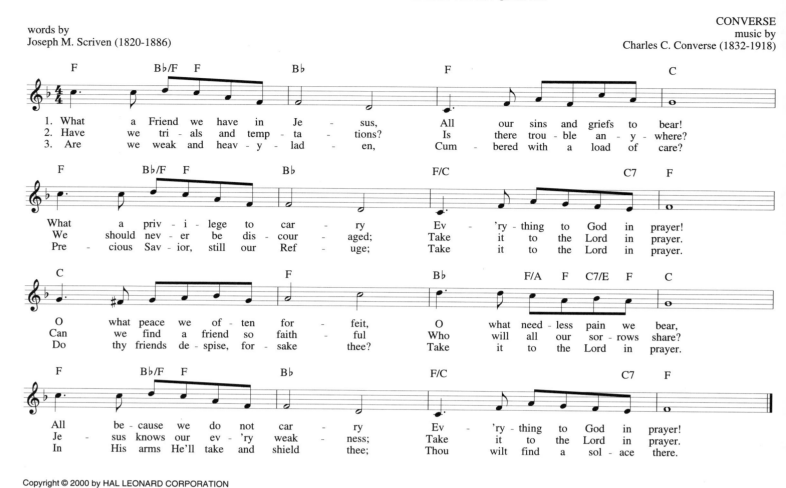

WHAT A WONDERFUL SAVIOR!

words by
Elisha A. Hoffman, 1891

BENTON HARBOR
music by
Elisha A. Hoffman, 1891

WHAT A MIGHTY GOD WE SERVE

Author unknown

MIGHTY GOD
Composer unknown

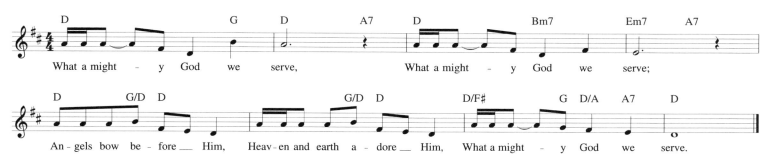

What a might - y God we serve, What a might - y God we serve;
An - gels bow be - fore __ Him, Heav - en and earth a - dore __ Him, What a might - y God we serve.

WHAT CHILD IS THIS?

GREENSLEEVES
Traditional English melody, 16th century

words by
William C. Dix (1837-1898)

1. What Child is this, _____ who, laid to rest, _____ On
2. Why lies He in _____ such mean es - tate _____ Where
3. So bring Him in - cense, gold and myrrh; _____ Come,

Mar - y's lap _____ is sleep - ing? Whom
ox and ass _____ are feed - ing? Good
peas - ant king, _____ to own Him. The

an - gels greet _____ with an - thems sweet _____ While
Chris - tian, fear, _____ for sin - ners here _____ The
King of kings _____ sal - va - tion brings; _____ Let

shep - herds watch _____ are keep - ing?
si - lent Word _____ is plead - ing. This,
lov - ing hearts _____ en - throne Him.

this _____ is Christ the King, _____ Whom shep - herds

guard _____ and an - gels sing: Haste haste _____ to

bring him laud, _____ The Babe, _____ the Son _____ of Mar - y.

WHAT IF IT WERE TODAY

SECOND COMING
music by
Lelia N. Morris (1862-1929)

words by
Lelia N. Morris (1862-1929)

1. Je - sus is com - ing to earth a - gain— What if it were to - day? ____
2. Sa - tan's do - min - ion will then be o'er— O that it were to - day! ____
3. Faith - ful and true would He find us here, If He should come to - day? ____

Com - ing in pow - er and love to reign— What if it were to - day? ____
Sor - row and sigh - ing shall be no more— O that it were to - day! ____
Watch - ing in glad - ness and not in fear, If He should come to - day? ____

Com - ing to claim ___ His cho - sen Bride, All the re - deemed ___ and pu - ri - fied.
Then shall the dead ___ in Christ a - rise, Caught up to meet ___ Him in the skies;
Signs of His com - ing mul - ti - ply, Morn - ing light breaks ___ in east - ern sky;

O - ver this whole earth scat - tered wide, ___ What if it were to - day? ____
When shall these glo - ries meet our eyes? ___ What if it were to - day? ____
Watch, for the time is draw - ing nigh, ___ What if it were to - day? ____

Glo - ry, glo - ry! Joy to my heart 'twill bring, ___ Glo - ry, glo - ry!

When we shall crown Him King; ___ Glo - ry, glo - ry! Haste to pre - pare the

way; ___ Glo - ry, glo - ry! Je - sus will come some day. ____

WHAT WONDROUS LOVE IS THIS

WONDROUS LOVE
music from
William Walker's *Southern Harmony,* 1835

American Folk Hymn Text

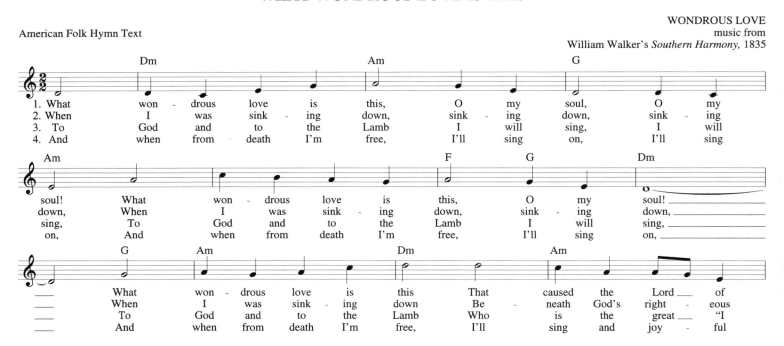

1. What won - drous love is this, O my soul, O my
2. When I was sink - ing down, sink - ing down, sink - ing
3. To God and to the Lamb I will sing, I will
4. And when from death I'm free, I'll sing on, I'll sing

soul! What won - drous love is this, O my soul! ____
down, When I was sink - ing down, sink - ing down, ____
sing, To God and to the Lamb I will sing, ____
on, And when from death I'm free, I'll sing on, ____

____ What won - drous love is this That caused the Lord ___ of
____ When I was sink - ing down Be - neath God's right - eous
____ To God and to the Lamb Who is the great ___ "I
____ And when from death I'm free, I'll sing and joy - ful

bliss, To bear the dread - ful curse for my soul, for my
frown, Christ laid a - side His crown for my soul, for my
Am," While mil - lions join the theme, I will sing, I will
be, And thro' e - ter - ni - ty I'll sing on, I'll sing

soul, To bear the dread - ful curse for my soul. _____
soul, Christ laid a - side His crown for my soul. _____
sing, While mil - lions join the theme, I will sing. _____
on, And thro' e - ter - ni - ty I'll sing on. _____

WHEN ALL THY MERCIES, O MY GOD

words by
Joseph Addison (1672-1719)

WINCHESTER OLD
music attr. to
George Kirbye (c. 1560-1634)

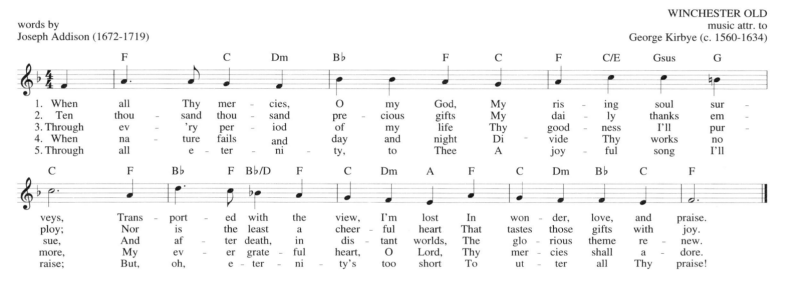

1. When all Thy mer - cies, O my God, My ris - ing soul sur -
2. Ten thou - sand thou - sand pre - cious gifts My dai - ly thanks em -
3. Through ev - 'ry per - iod of my life Thy good - ness I'll pur -
4. When na - ture fails and day and night Di - vide Thy works no
5. Through all e - ter - ni - ty, to Thee A joy - ful song I'll

veys, Trans - port - ed with the view, I'm lost In won - der, love, and praise.
ploy; Nor is the least a cheer - ful heart That tastes those gifts with joy.
sue, And af - ter death, in dis - tant worlds, The glo - rious theme re - new.
more, My ev - er grate - ful heart, O Lord, Thy mer - cies shall a - dore.
raise; But, oh, e - ter - ni - ty's too short To ut - ter all Thy praise!

WHEN I CAN READ MY TITLE CLEAR

words by
Isaac Watts (1674-1748)

PISGAH
Traditional American melody
from *Kentucky Harmony,* 1816

1. When I can read my ti - tle clear To man - sions in the skies, _____ I'll bid fare - well to _____
2. Should earth a - gainst my soul en - gage, And fi - ery darts be hurled, _____ Then I can smile at _____
3. Let cares like a wild de - luge come, And storms of sor - row fall! _____ May I but safe - ly _____
4. There shall I bathe my wea - ry soul In seas of heav'n - ly rest, _____ And not a wave of _____

ev - 'ry fear And wipe my weep - ing eyes. And wipe my weep - ing eyes, _____ And
Sa - tan's rage And face a frown - ing world. And face a frown - ing world, _____ And
reach my home, My God, my heav'n, my all. My God, my heav'n, my all, _____ My
trou - ble roll A - cross my peace - ful breast. A - cross my peace - ful breast, _____ A -

wipe my weep - ing eyes, _____ I'll bid fare - well to ev - 'ry fear And wipe my weep - ing eyes.
face a frown - ing world, _____ Then I can smile at Sa - tan's rage And face a frown - ing world.
God, my heav'n, my all, _____ May I but safe - ly reach my home, My God, my heav'n, my all.
cross my peace - ful breast, _____ And not a wave of trou - ble roll A - cross my peace - ful breast.

WHEN I SEE THE BLOOD

PASSOVER

words by
John Foote, 19th century

music by
John Foote, 19th century

WHEN I SURVEY THE WONDROUS CROSS

HAMBURG

words by
Isaac Watts (1674-1748)

music arr. by
Lowell Mason (1792-1872)
based on plainsong

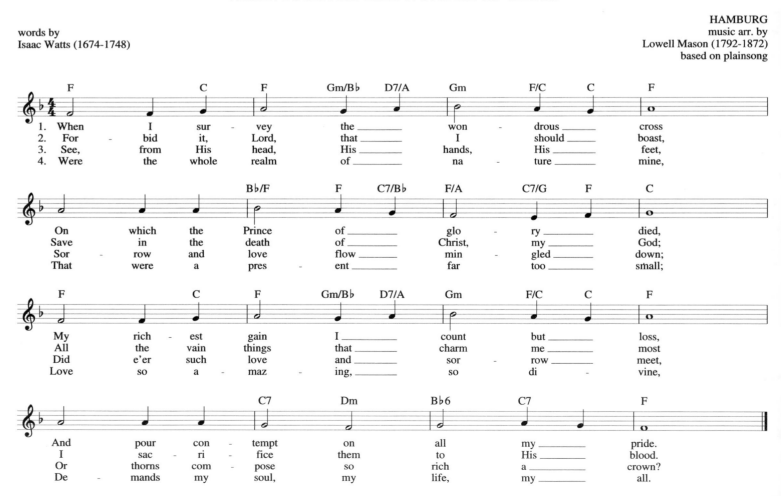

WHEN I SURVEY THE WONDROUS CROSS

ROCKINGHAM
music from
Second Supplement to Psalmody in Miniature, 1783
arr. by Edward Miller, 1790

words by
Isaac Watts, 1707

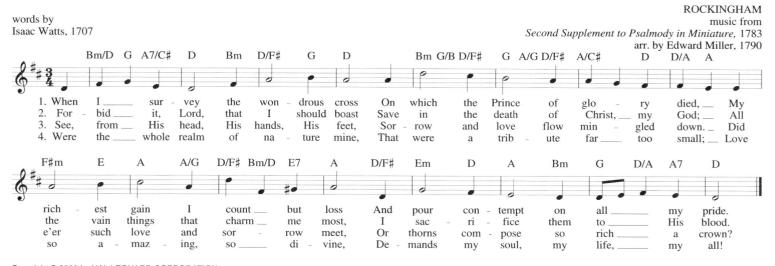

1. When I sur - vey the won - drous cross On which the Prince of glo - ry died, __ My
2. For - bid __ it, Lord, that I should boast Save in the death of Christ, __ my God; All
3. See, from __ His head, His hands, His feet, Sor - row and love flow min - gled down. __ Did
4. Were the __ whole realm of na - ture mine, That were a trib - ute far __ too small; __ Love

rich - est gain I count __ but loss, And pour con - tempt on all __ my pride.
the vain things that charm __ me most, I sac - ri - fice them to __ His blood.
e'er such love and sor - row meet, Or thorns com - pose so rich __ a crown?
so a - maz - ing, so __ di - vine, De - mands my soul, my life, __ my all!

WHEN IN THE HOUR OF UTMOST NEED

WENN WIR IN HÖCHSTEN NÖTEN SEIN
music by
L. Bourgeois (c. 1510-c. 1561)

words by
P. Eber (1511-1569)
tr. by C. Winkworth (1827-1878)

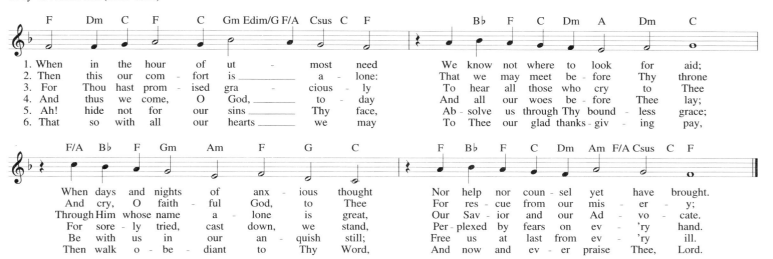

1. When in the hour of ut - most need We know not where to look for aid;
2. Then this our com - fort is __ a - lone: That we may meet be - fore Thy throne
3. For Thou hast prom - ised gra - cious - ly To hear all those who cry to Thee
4. And thus we come, O God, __ to - day And all our woes be - fore Thee lay;
5. Ah! hide not for our sins __ Thy face, Ab - solve us through Thy bound - less grace;
6. That so with all our hearts __ we may To Thee our glad thanks - giv - ing pay,

When days and nights of anx - ious thought Nor help nor coun - sel yet have brought.
And cry, O faith - ful God, to Thee For res - cue from our mis - er - y;
Through Him whose name a - lone is great, Our Sav - ior and our Ad - vo - cate.
For sore - ly tried, cast down, we stand, Per - plexed by fears on ev - 'ry hand.
Be with us in our an - guish still; Free us at last from ev - 'ry ill.
Then walk o - be - diant to Thy Word, And now and ev - er praise Thee, Lord.

WHEN IN THE NIGHT I MEDITATE

ST. FLAVIAN
music from
Day's *Psalter,* 1562

words from
The Psalter, 1912
based on Psalm 16

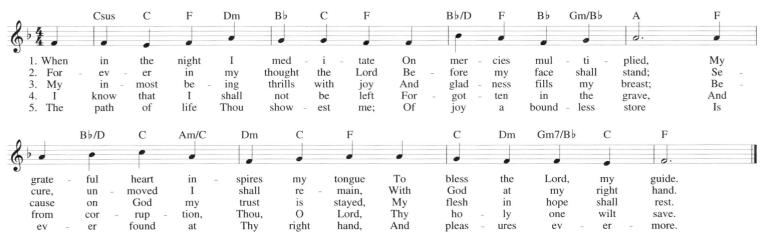

1. When in the night I med - i - tate On mer - cies mul - ti - plied, My
2. For - ev - er in my thought the Lord Be - fore my face shall stand; Se -
3. My in - most be - ing thrills with joy And glad - ness fills my breast; Be -
4. I know that I shall not be left For - got - ten in the grave, And
5. The path of life Thou show - est me; Of joy a bound - less store Is

grate - ful heart in - spires my tongue To bless the Lord, my guide.
cure, un - moved I shall re - main, With God at my right hand.
cause on God my trust is stayed, My flesh in hope shall rest.
from cor - rup - tion, Thou, O Lord, Thy ho - ly one wilt save.
ev - er found at Thy right hand, And pleas - ures ev - er - more.

WHEN ISRAEL WAS IN EGYPT'S LAND
(Go Down, Moses)

GO DOWN, MOSES
African-American Spiritual

African-American Spiritual

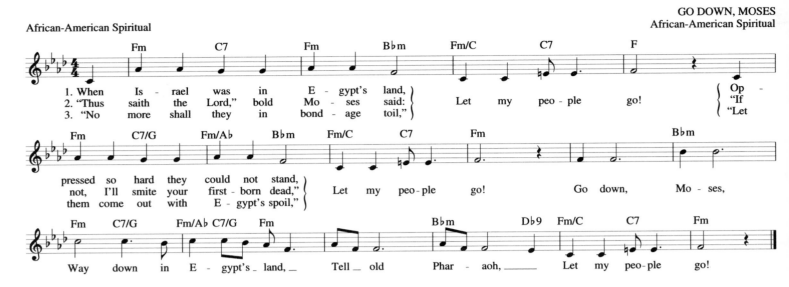

1. When Is - rael was in E - gypt's land,
2. "Thus saith the Lord," bold Mo - ses said:
3. "No more shall they in bond - age toil,"

Let my peo - ple go!

Op
"If
"Let

pressed so hard they could not stand,
not, I'll smite your first - born dead,"
them come out with E - gypt's spoil,"

Let my peo - ple go!

Go down, Mo - ses,

Way down in E - gypt's land, __ Tell __ old Phar - aoh, _____ Let my peo-ple go!

WHEN JESUS WEPT

words by
William Billings, 1770

music by
William Billings, 1770

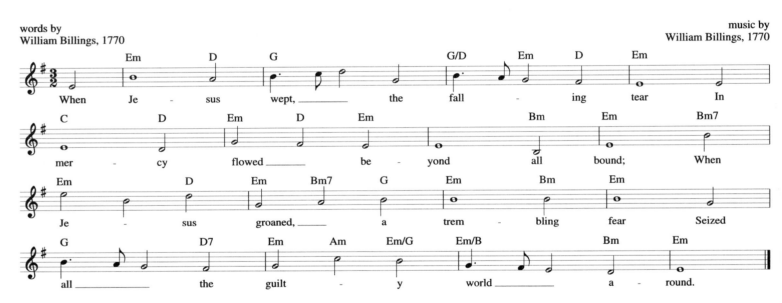

When Je - sus wept, _____ the fall - ing tear In

mer - cy flowed _____ be - yond all bound; When

Je - sus groaned, _____ a trem - bling fear Seized

all _____ the guilt - y world _____ a - round.

WHEN MORNING GILDS THE SKIES

LAUDES DOMINI

words from
Katholisches Gesangbuch, Würzburg, 1828
tr. by Edward Caswall (1814-1878)

music by
Joseph Barnby, 1868

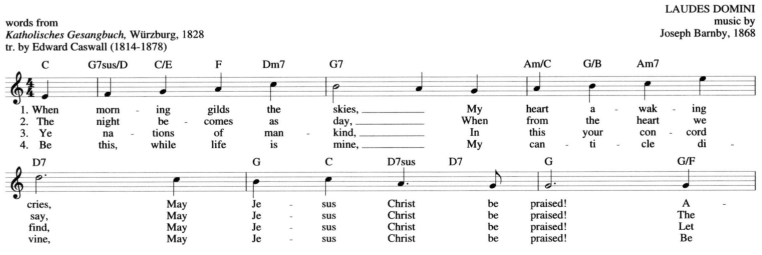

1. When morn - ing gilds the skies, _____ My heart a - wak - ing
2. The night be - comes as day, _____ When from the heart we
3. Ye na - tions of man - kind, _____ In this your con - cord
4. Be this, while life is mine, _____ My can - ti - cle di -

cries, May Je - sus Christ be praised! A
say, May Je - sus Christ be praised! The
find, May Je - sus Christ be praised! Let
vine, May Je - sus Christ be praised! Be

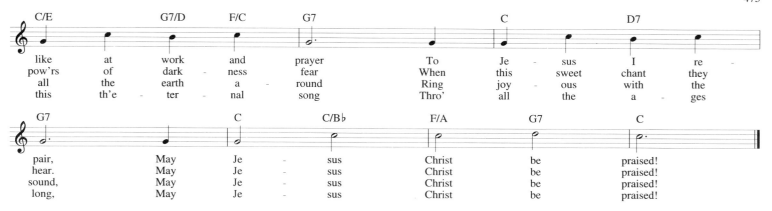

C/E		G7/D	F/C	G7			C		D7	

like at work and prayer To Je - sus I re -
pow'rs of dark - ness fear When this sweet chant with they
all the earth a - round Ring joy - ous with the
this th'e - ter - nal song Thro' all the a - ges

G7		C	C/B♭	F/A	G7	C

pair, May Je - sus Christ be praised!
hear. May Je - sus Christ be praised!
sound, May Je - sus Christ be praised!
long, May Je - sus Christ be praised!

WHEN MORNING LIGHTS THE EASTERN SKIES

ST. STEPHEN
words from
The Psalter, 1912
based on Psalm 143

music by
William Jones, 1789

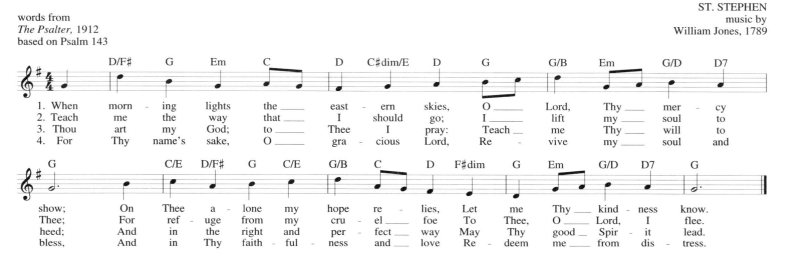

D/F#	G	Em	C		D	C#dim/E	D	G	G/B	Em	G/D	D7

1. When morn - ing lights the ___ east - ern skies, O ___ Lord, Thy ___ mer - cy
2. Teach me the way that ___ I should go; I ___ lift my ___ soul to
3. Thou art my God; to ___ Thee I pray; Teach me Thy ___ will to
4. For Thy name's sake, O ___ gra - cious Lord, Re - vive my ___ soul and

G		C/E	D/F#	G	C/E	G/B	C		D	F#dim	G	Em	G/D	D7	G

show; On Thee a - lone my hope re - lies, Let me Thy ___ kind - ness know.
Thee; For ref - uge from my cru - el ___ foe To Thee, O ___ Lord, I flee.
heed; And in the right and per - fect ___ way May Thy good ___ Spir - it lead.
bless, And in Thy faith - ful - ness and ___ love Re - deem me ___ from dis - tress.

WHEN WE ALL GET TO HEAVEN

HEAVEN
words by
Eliza E. Hewitt, 1898

music by
Emily D. Wilson, 1898

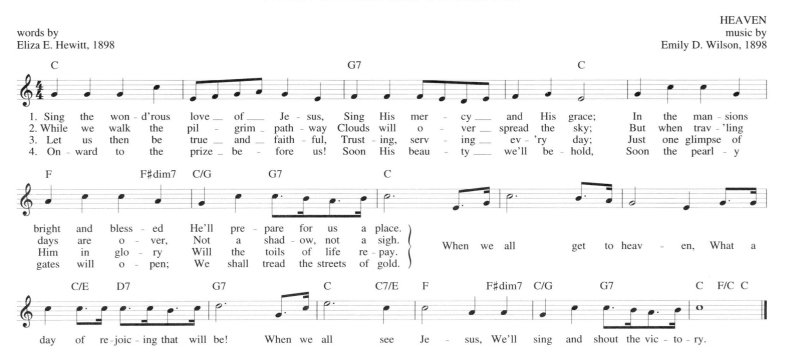

C			G7			C		

1. Sing the won - d'rous love ___ of ___ Je - sus, Sing His mer - cy ___ and His grace; In the man - sions
2. While we walk the pil - grim path - way Clouds will o - ver - spread the sky; But when trav - 'ling
3. Let us then be true ___ and ___ faith - ful, Trust - ing, serv - ing ___ ev - 'ry day; Just one glimpse of
4. On - ward to the prize ___ be - fore us! Soon His beau - ty ___ we'll be - hold, Soon the pearl - y

F		F#dim7	C/G	G7		C	

bright and bless - ed He'll pre - pare for us a place. ⎫
days are o - ver, Not a shad - ow, not a sigh. ⎪
Him in glo - ry Will the toils of life re - pay. ⎬ When we all get to heav - en, What a
gates will o - pen; We shall tread the streets of gold. ⎭

C/E	D7		G7		C	C7/E	F	F#dim7	C/G	G7		C	F/C	C

day of re - joic - ing that will be! When we all see Je - sus, We'll sing and shout the vic - to - ry.

WHEN THE ROLL IS CALLED UP YONDER

ROLL CALL

words by
James M. Black, 1892

music by
James M. Black, 1892

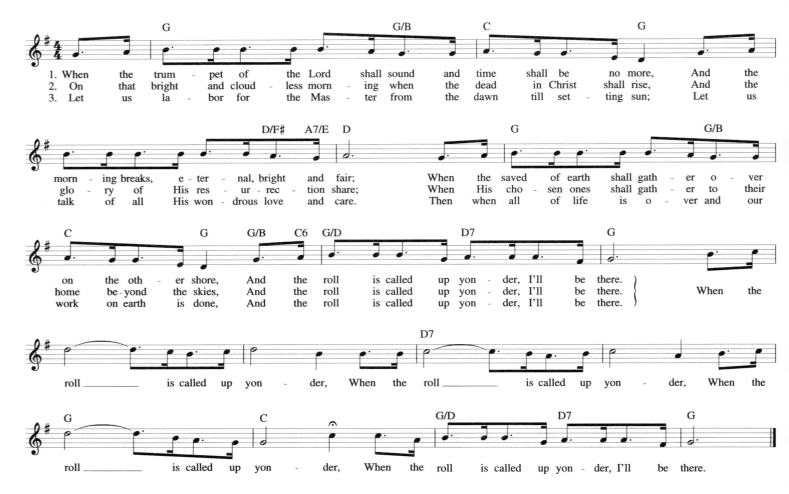

1. When the trum - pet of the Lord shall sound and time shall be no more, And the
2. On that bright and cloud - less morn - ing when the dead in Christ shall rise, And the
3. Let us la - bor for the Mas - ter from the dawn till set - ting sun; Let us

morn - ing breaks, e - ter - nal, bright and fair; When the saved of earth shall gath - er o - ver
glo - ry of His res - ur - rec - tion share; When His cho - sen ones shall gath - er to their
talk of all His won - drous love and care. Then when all of life is o - ver and our

on the oth - er shore, And the roll is called up yon - der, I'll be there.
home be - yond the skies, And the roll is called up yon - der, I'll be there.
work on earth is done, And the roll is called up yon - der, I'll be there. When the

roll _____ is called up yon - der, When the roll _____ is called up yon - der, When the

roll _____ is called up yon - der, When the roll is called up yon - der, I'll be there.

WHERE CROSS THE CROWDED WAYS OF LIFE

GERMANY

words by
Frank Mason North, 1903

music from
William Gardiner's *Sacred Melodies*, 1815

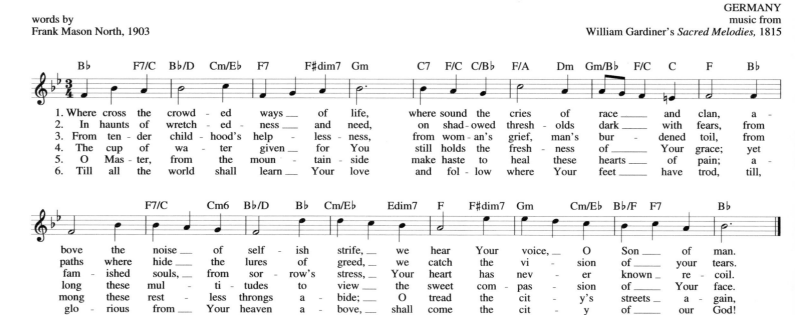

1. Where cross the crowd - ed ways _____ of life, where sound the cries of race _____ and clan, a -
2. In haunts of wretch - ed - ness _____ and need, on shad - owed thresh - olds dark _____ with fears, from
3. From ten - der child - hood's help - less - ness, from wom - an's grief, man's bur - dened toil, from
4. The cup of wa - ter given _____ for You still holds the fresh - ness of _____ Your grace; yet
5. O Mas - ter, from the moun - tain - side make haste to heal these hearts _____ of pain; a -
6. Till all the world shall learn _____ Your love and fol - low where Your feet _____ have trod, till,

bove the noise _____ of self - ish strife, _____ we hear Your voice, _____ O Son of man.
paths where hide _____ the lures of greed, _____ we catch the vi - sion of _____ your tears.
fam - ished souls, _____ from sor - row's stress, _____ Your heart has nev - er known _____ re - coil.
long these mul - ti - tudes to view _____ the sweet com - pas - sion of _____ Your face.
mong these rest - less throngs a - bide; _____ O tread the cit - y's streets _____ a - gain,
glo - rious from _____ Your heaven a - bove, _____ shall come the cit - y of _____ our God!

WHERE HE LEADS I'LL FOLLOW

words by
William A. Ogden, 1885

OGDEN
music by
William A. Ogden, 1885

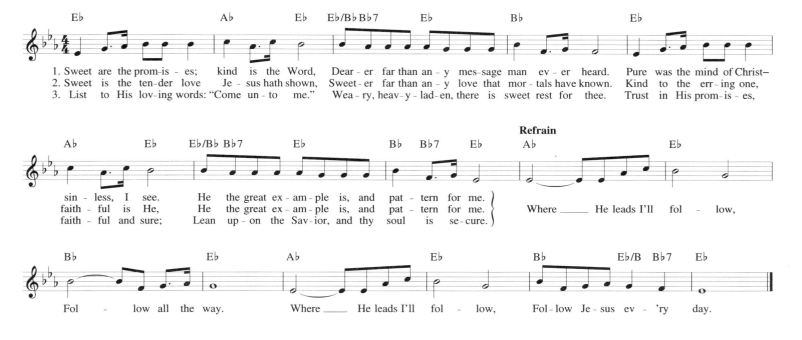

1. Sweet are the prom-is-es; kind is the Word, Dear-er far than an-y mes-sage man ev-er heard. Pure was the mind of Christ—
2. Sweet is the ten-der love Je-sus hath shown, Sweet-er far than an-y love that mor-tals have known. Kind to the err-ing one,
3. List to His lov-ing words: "Come un-to me." Wea-ry, heav-y-lad-en, there is sweet rest for thee. Trust in His prom-is-es,

Refrain

sin-less, I see. He the great ex-am-ple is, and pat-tern for me.
faith-ful is He, He the great ex-am-ple is, and pat-tern for me.   Where ____ He leads I'll fol-low,
faith-ful and sure; Lean up-on the Sav-ior, and thy soul is se-cure.

Fol-low all the way. Where ____ He leads I'll fol-low, Fol-low Je-sus ev-'ry day.

WHERE HE LEADS ME I WILL FOLLOW

words by
E.W. Blandy, 19th century

NORRIS
music by
J.S. Norris (1849-1907)

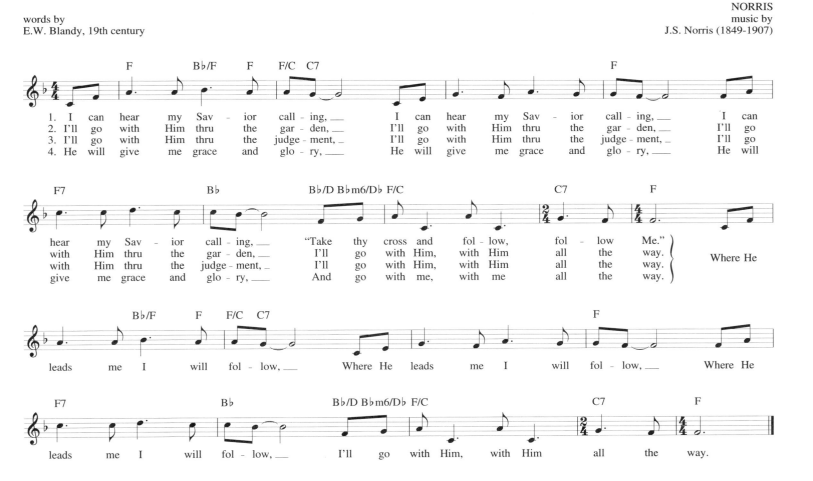

1. I can hear my Sav-ior call-ing, ____ I can hear my Sav-ior call-ing, ____ I can
2. I'll go with Him thru the gar-den, ____ I'll go with Him thru the gar-den, ____ I'll go
3. I'll go with Him thru the judge-ment, ____ I'll go with Him thru the judge-ment, ____ I'll go
4. He will give me grace and glo-ry, ____ He will give me grace and glo-ry, ____ He will

hear my Sav-ior call-ing, ____ "Take thy cross and fol-low, fol-low Me."
with Him thru the gar-den, ____ I'll go with Him, with Him all the way.
with Him thru the judge-ment, ____ I'll go with Him, with Him all the way.   Where He
give me grace and glo-ry, ____ And go with me, with me all the way.

leads me I will fol-low, ____ Where He leads me I will fol-low, ____ Where He

leads me I will fol-low, ____ I'll go with Him, with Him all the way.

WHERE THEY NEED NO SUN

NO SUN

words by
Haldor Lillenas, 1912

music by
Haldor Lillenas, 1912

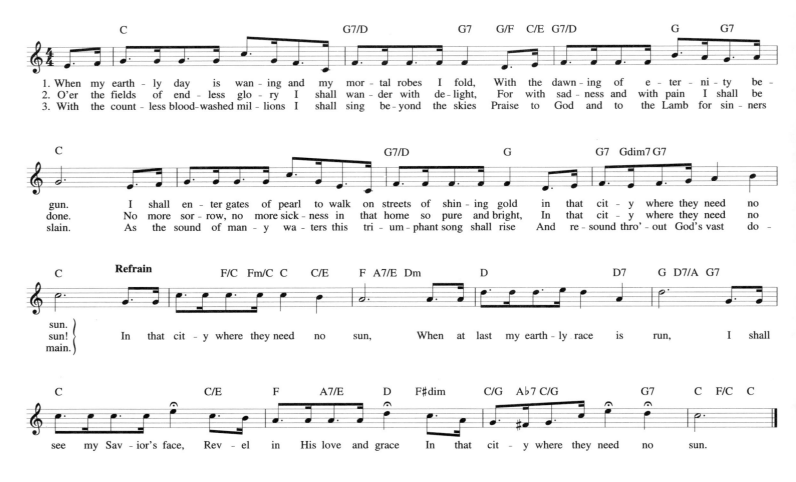

1. When my earth - ly day is wan - ing and my mor - tal robes I fold, With the dawn - ing of e - ter - ni - ty be -
2. O'er the fields of end - less glo - ry I shall wan - der with de - light, For with sad - ness and with pain I shall be
3. With the count - less blood-washed mil - lions I shall sing be - yond the skies Praise to God and to the Lamb for sin - ners

gun. I shall en - ter gates of pearl to walk on streets of shin - ing gold in that cit - y where they need no
done. No more sor - row, no more sick - ness in that home so pure and bright, In that cit - y where they need no
slain. As the sound of man - y wa - ters this tri - um - phant song shall rise And re - sound thro' - out God's vast do -

Refrain

sun. }
sun! } In that cit - y where they need no sun, When at last my earth - ly race is run, I shall
main. }

see my Sav - ior's face, Rev - el in His love and grace In that cit - y where they need no sun.

WHEREFORE, O FATHER, WE THY HUMBLE SERVANTS

LOBET DEN HERREN

words by
William Henry Hammond Jervois (1852-1905)

music by
Johann Crüger (1598-1662)

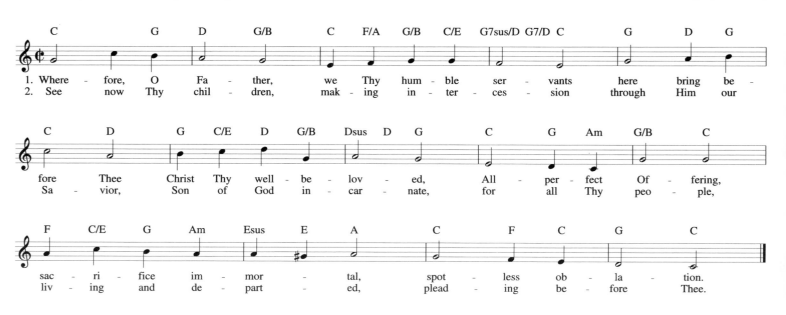

1. Where - fore, O Fa - ther, we Thy hum - ble ser - vants here bring be -
2. See now Thy chil - dren, mak - ing in - ter - ces - sion through Him our

fore Thee Christ Thy well - be - lov - ed, All - per - fect Of - fering,
Sa - vior, Son of God in - car - nate, for all Thy peo - ple,

sac - ri - fice im - mor - tal, spot - less ob - la - tion.
liv - ing and de - part - ed, plead - ing be - fore Thee.

WHEREWITH, O LORD, SHALL I DRAW NEAR

words by
Charles Wesley (1707-1788)

RIVAULX
music by
John B. Dykes (1823-1876)

1. Where - with, O Lord, shall I draw near, And bow my - self be - fore Thy
2. Who - e'er to Thee them - selves ap - prove Must take the path Thy - self hast
3. But though my life hence - forth be Thine, Pres - ent for past can ne'er a -
4. What have I then where - in to trust? I noth - ing have, I noth - ing
5. Guilt - y I stand be - fore Thy face; On me I feel Thy wrath a -

face? How in Thy pur - er eyes ap - pear? What shall I bring to gain Thy grace?
showed: Jus - tice pur - sue, and mer - cy love, And hum - bly walk by faith with God.
tone; Though I to Thee the whole re - sign, I on - ly give Thee back Thine own.
am; Ex - clud - ed is my ev - 'ry boast, My glo - ry swal - lowed up in shame.
bide; 'Tis just the sen - tence should take place, 'Tis just, but O, Thy Son hath died!

WHILE JESUS WHISPERS TO YOU

words by
W.E. Witter

COME, SINNER, COME
music by
Horatio R. Palmer (1834-1907)

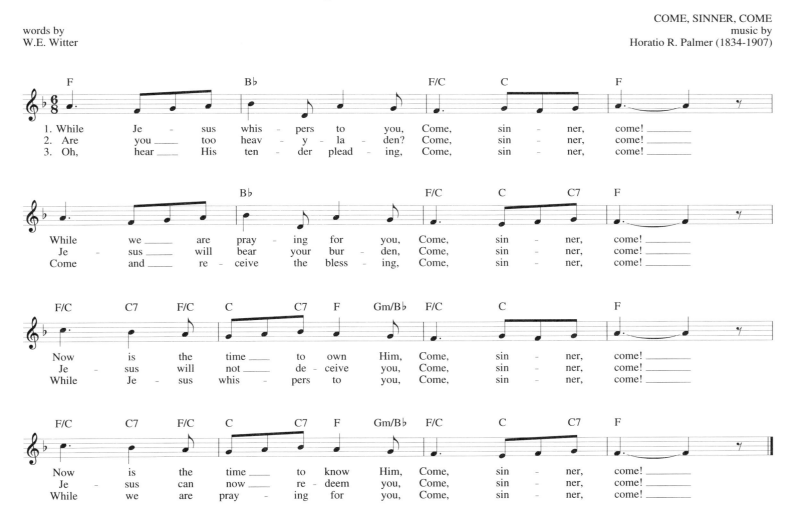

1. While Je - sus whis - pers to you, Come, sin - ner, come! _____
2. Are you too heav - y - la - den? Come, sin - ner, come! _____
3. Oh, hear His ten - der plead - ing, Come, sin - ner, come! _____

While we are pray - ing for you, Come, sin - ner, come! _____
Je - sus will bear your bur - den, Come, sin - ner, come! _____
Come and re - ceive the bless - ing, Come, sin - ner, come! _____

Now is the time to own Him, Come, sin - ner, come! _____
Je - sus will not de - ceive you, Come, sin - ner, come! _____
While Je - sus whis - pers to you, Come, sin - ner, come! _____

Now is the time to know Him, Come, sin - ner, come! _____
Je - sus can now re - deem you, Come, sin - ner, come! _____
While we are pray - ing for you, Come, sin - ner, come! _____

WHISPER A PRAYER

PRAYER
Traditional music

Traditional words

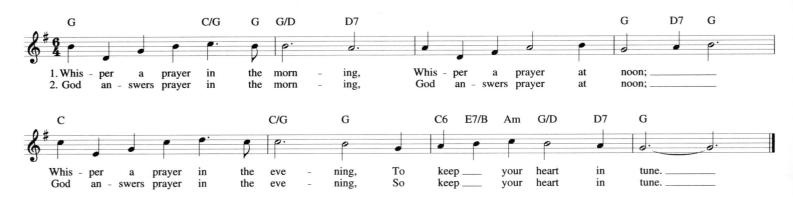

1. Whis - per a prayer in the morn - ing, Whis - per a prayer at noon;____
2. God an - swers prayer in the morn - ing, God an - swers prayer at noon;____

Whis - per a prayer in the eve - ning, To keep ____ your heart in tune. ____
God an - swers prayer in the eve - ning, So keep ____ your heart in tune. ____

WHITER THAN SNOW

FISCHER
music by
William G. Fischer (1835-1912)

words by
James L. Nicholson (1828-1876)

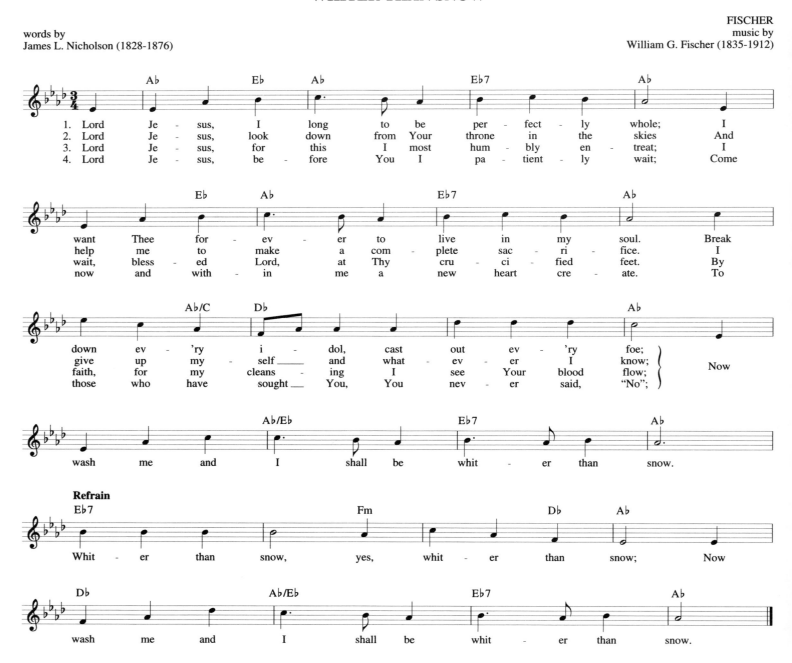

1. Lord Je - sus, I long to be per - fect - ly whole; I
2. Lord Je - sus, look down from Your throne in the skies And
3. Lord Je - sus, for this I most hum - bly en - treat; I
4. Lord Je - sus, be - fore You I pa - tient - ly wait; Come

want Thee for - ev - er to live in my soul. Break
help me to make a com - plete sac - ri - fice. I
wait, bless - ed Lord, at Thy cru - ci - fied feet. By
now and with - in me a new heart cre - ate. To

down ev - 'ry i - dol, cast out ev - 'ry foe;
give up my - self ____ and what - ev - er I know; } Now
faith, for my cleans - ing I see Your blood flow;
those who have sought ____ You, You nev - er said, "No";

wash me and I shall be whit - er than snow.

Refrain

Whit - er than snow, yes, whit - er than snow; Now

wash me and I shall be whit - er than snow.

WHILE SHEPHERDS WATCHED THEIR FLOCKS

CHRISTMAS

words by
Nahum Tate (1652-1715)

music by
George Frederick Handel (1685-1759)
from Weyman's *Melodia Sacra,* 1815

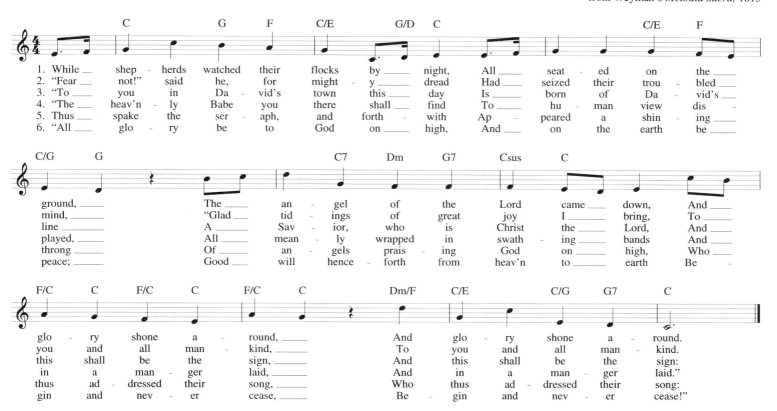

1. While shep - herds watched their flocks by night, All seat - ed on the ground, The an - gel of the Lord came down, And glo - ry shone a - round, And glo - ry shone a - round.
2. "Fear not!" said he, for might - y dread Had seized their trou - bled mind, "Glad tid - ings of great joy I bring, To you and all man - kind, To you and all man - kind.
3. "To you in Da - vid's town this day Is born of Da - vid's line A Sav - ior, who is Christ the Lord, And this shall be the sign, And this shall be the sign:
4. "The heav'n - ly Babe you there shall find To hu - man view dis - played, All mean - ly wrapped in swath - ing bands And in a man - ger laid, And in a man - ger laid."
5. Thus spake the ser - aph, and forth - with Ap - peared a shin - ing throng Of an - gels prais - ing God on high, Who thus ad - dressed their song, Who thus ad - dressed their song,
6. "All glo - ry be to God on high, And on the earth be peace; Good will hence - forth from heav'n to earth Be - gin and nev - er cease, Be - gin and nev - er cease!"

Copyright © 1992 by HAL LEONARD CORPORATION

WHO ARE THESE LIKE STARS APPEARING

ZEUCH MICH, ZEUCH MICH

words by
Theobald Heinrich Schenck (1656-1727)
tr. by Frances Elizabeth Cox (1812-1897)

music from
Geistreiches Gesang-buch, 1698

1. Who are these, like stars ap - pear - ing, These be - fore God's throne who stand? Each a gold - en crown is wear - ing; Who are all this glo - rious band? Al - le - lu - ya, hark! they sing, Prais - ing loud their heaven - ly King.
2. Who are these of daz - zling bright - ness, These in God's own truth ar - rayed, Clad in robes of pur - est white - ness, Robes whose lus - tre ne'er shall fade, Ne'er be touched by time's rude hand— Whence comes all this glo - rious band?
3. These are they who have con - tend - ed For their Sa - vior's hon - or long, Wres - tling on till life was end - ed, Fol - lowing not the sin - ful throng; These, who well the fight sus - tained, Tri - umph through the Lamb have gained.
4. These are they whose hearts were riv - en, Sore with woe and an - guish tried, Who in prayer full oft have striv - en with the God they glo - ri - fied; Now, their pain - ful con - flict o'er, God has bid them weep no more.
5. These like priests have watched and wait - ed, of - fering up to Christ their will, Soul and bod - y con - se - crat - ed, Day and night to serve Him still: Now, in God's most ho - ly place, Blest they stand be - fore His face.

Copyright © 2000 by HAL LEONARD CORPORATION

WHISPERING HOPE

words by
Alice Hawthorne, 1868

music by
Septimus Winner, 1868

1. Soft as the voice of an an - gel Breath - ing a les - son un -
2. If, in the dusk of the twi - light, Dim be the re - gion a -
3. Hope, as an an - chor so stead - fast, Rends the dark veil for the

heard, _____ Hope with a gen - tle per - sua - sion
far, _____ Will not the deep - en - ing dark - ness
soul, _____ Whith - er the Mas - ter has en - tered,

Whis - pers her com - fort - ing word: _____ Wait till the dark - ness is
Bright - en the glim - mer - ing star? _____ Then when the night is up -
Rob - bing the grave of it's goal. _____ Come then, O come, glad fru -

o - ver, Wait till the tem - pest is done, _____
on us, Why should the heart sink a - way? _____
i - tion, Come to my sad wear - y heart. _____

Hope for the sun - shine to - mor - row Aft - er the show - er is
When the dark mid - night is o - ver, Watch for the break - ing of
Come, O Thou blest hope of glo - ry, Nev - er, O nev - er de -

gone. _____
day. _____
part. _____

Whis - per - ing hope, _____ O how

wel - come Thy voice, _____ Mak - ing my

heart _____ in its sor - row re - joice. _____

WHO IS ON THE LORD'S SIDE?

ARMAGEDDON

words by
Frances Ridley Havergal (1836-1879)

music by
C. Luise Reichardt (1780-1826)

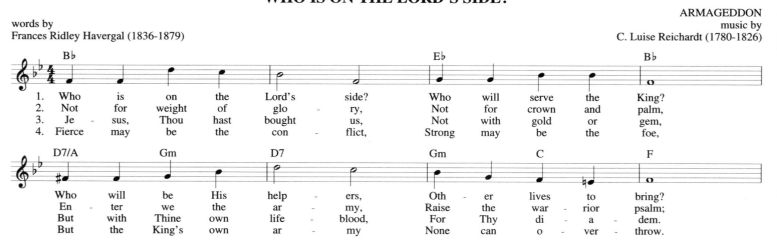

1. Who is on the Lord's side? Who will serve the King?
2. Not for weight of glo - ry, Not for crown and palm,
3. Je - sus, Thou hast bought us, Not with gold or gem,
4. Fierce may be the con - flict, Strong may be the foe,

Who will be His help - ers, Oth - er lives to bring?
En - ter we the ar - my, Raise the war - rior psalm;
But with Thine own life - blood, For Thy di - a - dem.
But the King's own ar - my None can o - ver - throw.

WHO TRUSTS IN GOD, A STRONG ABODE

WAS MEIN GOTT WILL
music by
Claude de Sermisy (c. 1490-1562)

v. 1 by Joachim Magdeburg (c.1525-c.1583)
v. 2, 3 from *Harmonia Cantorium,* Leipzig, 1597
tr. by Benjamin H. Kennedy (1804-1899)

"WHOSOEVER" MEANETH ME

words by
J. Edwin McConnell, 1914

McCONNELL
music by
J. Edwin McConnell, 1914

1. I am hap-py to-day and the sun shines bright, The clouds have been rolled a-way; For the
2. All my hopes have been raised, O His name be praised, His glo-ry has filled my soul; I've been
3. O what won-der-ful love, O what grace di-vine, That Je-sus should die for me; I was

Sav-ior said, "Who-so-ev-er will," May come with Him to stay.
lift-ed up and from sin set free, His blood hath made me whole.
lost in sin, for the world I pined, But now I am set free.

"Who-so-ev-er" sure-ly mean-eth me, Sure-ly mean-eth me, O sure-ly mean-eth me;

"Who-so-ev-er" sure-ly mean-eth me, "Who-so-ev-er" mean-eth me.

WHOSOEVER WILL

words by
Philip P. Bliss (1838-1876)

WHOSOEVER
music by
Philip P. Bliss (1838-1876)

1. "Who-so-ev-er hear-eth," shout, shout the sound! Spread the bless-ed tid-ings all the world a-round;
2. Who-so-ev-er com-eth need not de-lay, Now the door is o-pen, en-ter while you may;
3. "Who-so-ev-er will," the prom-ise is se-cure; "Who-so-ev-er will," for-ev-er must en-dure;

Tell the joy-ful news wher-ev-er man is found. "Who-so-ev-er will may come."
Je-sus is the true, the on-ly Liv-ing Way: "Who-so-ev-er will may come."
"Who-so-ev-er will," 'tis life for-ev-er-more; "Who-so-ev-er will may come."

"Who-so-ev-er will, who-so-ev-er will!" Send the proc-la-ma-tion o-ver land and hill;

'Tis a lov-ing Fa-ther calls the wan-d'rer home; "Who-so-ev-er will may come."

WIDE OPEN ARE THY HANDS

LEOMINSTER

words attr. to
Bernard of Clairvaux (1091-1153)
tr. by Charles Porterfield Krauth (1823-1883)

music by
George W. Martin (1828-1881)

1. Wide o - pen are Thy hands Pay - ing with more than gold The
2. Wide o - pen are Thine arms, A fall - en world t'em - brace, To
3. Draw all my mind and heart Up to Thy throne on high, And

aw - ful debt of guilt - y men, For - ev - er and of old. Ah,
take to love and end - less rest Our whole for - sak - en race. Lord,
let Thy sa - cred Cross ex - alt My spir - it to the sky. To

let me grasp those hands, That we may nev - er part, And
I am sad and poor, But bound - less is Thy grace; Give
these, Thy might - y hands, My spir - it I re - sign. Liv -

let the pow - er of their blood Sus - tain my faint - ing heart.
me the soul - trans - form - ing joy For which I seek Thy face.
ing, I live a - lone to Thee; And dy - ing, I am Thine.

WILL JESUS FIND US WATCHING

DOANE

words by
Fanny J. Crosby (1820-1915)

music by
William H. Doane (1832-1915)

1. When Je - sus comes to re - ward His ser - vants, Wheth - er it be noon or night,
2. If, at the dawn of the ear - ly morn - ing, He shall call us one by one,
3. Have we been true to the trust He left us? Do we seek to do our best?
4. Bless - ed are those whom the Lord finds watch - ing, In His glo - ry they shall share;

Faith - ful to Him will He find us watch - ing, With our lamps all trimmed and bright?
When to the Lord we re - store our tal - ents, Will he an - swer you, "Well done"?
If in our hearts there is naught con - demns us, We shall have a glo - rious rest.
If He shall come at the dawn or mid - night, Will He find us watch - ing there?

O can we say we are read - y, broth - er? Read - y for the soul's bright home?

Say, will He find you and me still watch - ing, Wait - ing, wait - ing when the Lord shall come?

WILL YOU NOT TELL IT TODAY?

IN THE NAME OF THE SAVIOR

words by
Jessie Brown Pounds, 1887

music by
James H. Fillmore, 1887

1. If the name of the Sav-ior is pre-cious to you, If His
2. If your faith in the Sav-ior has brought its re-ward, If a
3. If the souls all a-round you are liv-ing in sin, If the

care has been con-stant and ten-der and true, If the light of His pres-ence has
strength you have found in the strength of your Lord, If the hope of a rest in His
Mas-ter has told you to bid them come in, If the sweet in-vi-ta-tion they

Refrain

bright-ened your way, O will you not tell of your glad-ness to-day? O
pal-ace is sweet, O will you not, broth-er, the sto-ry re-peat?
nev-er have heard, O will you not tell them the cheer-bring-ing word?

will you not tell it to-day? Will you not tell it to-day? If the

light of His pre-sence has bright-ened your way, O will you not tell it to-day?

Copyright © 2000 by HAL LEONARD CORPORATION

WONDERFUL PEACE

words by
W.D. Cornell, 19th century

music by
W.G. Cooper, 19th century

1. Far a-way in the depths of my spir-it to-night Rolls a
2. What a treas-ure I have in this won-der-ful peace, Bur-ied
3. I am rest-ing to-night in this won-der-ful peace, Rest-ing
4. And me-thinks when I rise to that cit-y of peace, Where the
5. Ah, soul, are you here with-out com-fort or rest, March-ing

mel-o-dy sweet-er than psalm; In ce-les-tial-like strains it un-
deep in the heart of my soul; So se-cure that no pow-er can
sweet-ly in Je-sus' con-trol; For I'm kept from all dan-ger by
Au-thor of peace I shall see, That one strain of the song which the
down the rough path-way of time? Make Je-sus your friend ere the

ceas-ing-ly falls O'er my soul like an in-fi-nite calm.
mine it a-way, While the years of e-ter-ni-ty roll.
night and by day, And His glo-ry is flood-ing my soul.
ran-somed will sing, In that heav-en-ly king-dom will be:
shad-ows grow dark; O ac-cept of this peace so sub-lime.

Copyright © 2000 by HAL LEONARD CORPORATION

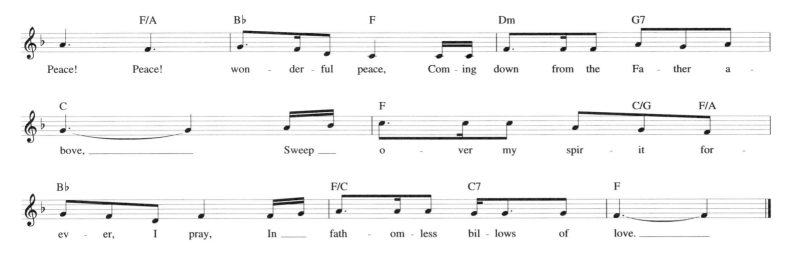

Peace! Peace! won-der-ful peace, Com-ing down from the Fa-ther a-

bove, _____ Sweep ___ o - ver my spir - it for -

ev - er, I pray, In ___ fath - om - less bil - lows of love. _____

WONDERFUL GRACE OF JESUS

WONDERFUL GRACE

words by
Haldor Lillenas, 1918

music by
Haldor Lillenas, 1918

1. Won - der - ful grace of Je - sus, Great - er than all my sin. How shall my tongue de - scribe it?
2. Won - der - ful grace of Je - sus, Reach - ing to all the lost. By it I have been par - doned,
3. Won - der - ful grace of Je - sus, Reach - ing the most de - filed. By its trans - form - ing pow - er,

Where shall its praise be - gin? Tak - ing a - way my bur - den, Set - ting my spir - it free; _____
Saved to the ut - ter - most. Chains have been torn a - sun - der, Giv - ing me lib - er - ty; _____ } For the
Mak - ing him God's dear child. Pur - chas - ing peace and heav - en For all e - ter - ni - ty; _____

won - der - ful grace of Je - sus reach - es me. Won - der - ful the match - less grace of

Je - sus; Deep - er than the might - y roll - ing sea. High - er than the moun - tain; spar - kling like a foun - tain;

All suf - fi - cient grace for e - ven me. Broad - er than the scope of my trans - gres - sions;

Great - er far than all my sin and shame. O mag - ni - fy the pre - cious name of Je - sus; Praise His name!

WILT THOU FORGIVE THAT SIN

words by
John Donne (1573-1631)

DONNE
music by
John Hilton (c. 1599-1657)

1. Wilt Thou for-give that sin, where I be-gun, Which is my sin, though it were done be-fore? Wilt Thou for-give those sins through which I run, And do run still, though still I do de-plore? When Thou hast done, Thou hast not done, For I have more.

2. Wilt Thou for-give that sin, by which I've won Oth-ers to sin, and made my sin their door? Wilt Thou for-give that sin which I did shun A year or two, but wal-lowed in a score? When Thou hast done, Thou hast not done, For I have more.

3. I have a sin of fear that when I've spun My last thread, I shall per-ish on that shore; Swear by Thy-self, that at my death Thy Son Shall shine as He shines now, and here-to-fore. And hav-ing done that, Thou hast done, I fear no more.

WONDERFUL SAVIOR

words by
J.M. Harris, 1905

music by
J.M. Harris, 1905

1. Je-sus, my King, my won-der-ful Sav-ior, All of my life is giv-en to Thee. ___ I am re-joic-ing in Thy sal-va-tion; Thy pre-cious blood now mak-eth me free. ___

2. Free-dom from sin, O won-der-ful sto-ry— All of its stains washed whit-er than snow! ___ Je-sus has come to live in His tem-ple, And with His love my heart is a-glow. ___

3. Je-sus, my Lord, I'll ev-er a-dore Thee, Lay at Thy feet my treas-ures of love. ___ Lead me in ways to show forth Thy glo-ry, Ways that will end in heav-en a-bove. ___

4. When in that bright and beau-ti-ful cit-y I shall be-hold Thy glo-ries un-told, ___ I shall be like Thee, won-der-ful Sav-ior, And I will sing while a-ges un-fold. ___

Refrain

Won-der-ful Sav-ior, won-der-ful Sav-ior, Thou art so near, so pre-cious to me! ___ Won-der-ful Sav-ior, won-der-ful Sav-ior, My heart is filled with prais-es to Thee! ___

WONDERFUL STORY OF LOVE

STORY OF LOVE

words by
J.M. Driver, 19th century

music by
J.M. Driver, 19th century

1. Won-der-ful sto-ry of love! ___ Tell it to me a-gain. ___
2. Won-der-ful sto-ry of love! ___ Tho' you are far a-way— ___
3. Won-der-ful sto-ry of love! ___ Je-sus pro-vides a rest— ___

Won-der-ful sto-ry of love! ___ Wake the im-mor-tal strain! ___ An-gels with rap-ture an-
Won-der-ful sto-ry of love! ___ Still He doth call to-day: ___ Call-ing from Cal-va-ry's
Won-der-ful sto-ry of love! ___ For all the pure and blest. ___ Rest in those man-sions a-

nounce it; Shep-herds with won-der re-ceive it; Sin-ner, O won't you be-lieve it?
moun-tain, Down from the crys-tal-bright foun-tain, E'en from the dawn of cre-a-tion—
bove us, With those who've gone on be-fore us, Sing-ing the rap-tur-ous cho-rus:

Refrain

Won-der-ful sto-ry of love! ___ Won-der-ful! ___ Won-der-

ful! ___ Won-der-ful! ___ Won-der-ful sto-ry of love! ___

Copyright © 2000 by HAL LEONARD CORPORATION

WONDERFUL, WONDERFUL JESUS

NEW ORLEANS

words by
Anna B. Russell

music by
Ernest O. Sellers

1. There is nev-er a day so drear-y, There is nev-er a night so
2. There is nev-er a cross so heav-y, There is nev-er a weight so
3. There is nev-er a care or bur-den, There is nev-er a grief or
4. There is nev-er a guilt-y sin-ner, There is nev-er a wan-d'ring

long, ___ But the soul that is trust-ing Je-sus Will some-where find a
woe, ___ But that Je-sus will help ___ to car-ry Be-cause ___ He lov-eth
loss, ___ But that Je-sus in love ___ will light-en When car-ried to the
one, ___ But that God can in mer-cy par-don Thro' Je-sus Christ, His

Refrain

song. ___ Won-der-ful, won-der-ful Je-sus, In the heart He im-plant-eth a song, ___
so. ___
cross. ___
Son. ___

song of de-liv-'rance, of cour-age, of strength; In the heart He im-plant-eth a song. ___

Copyright © 2000 by HAL LEONARD CORPORATION

WORK, FOR THE NIGHT IS COMING

WORK SONG

words by
Annie Coghill (1836-1907)

music by
Lowell Mason (1792-1872)

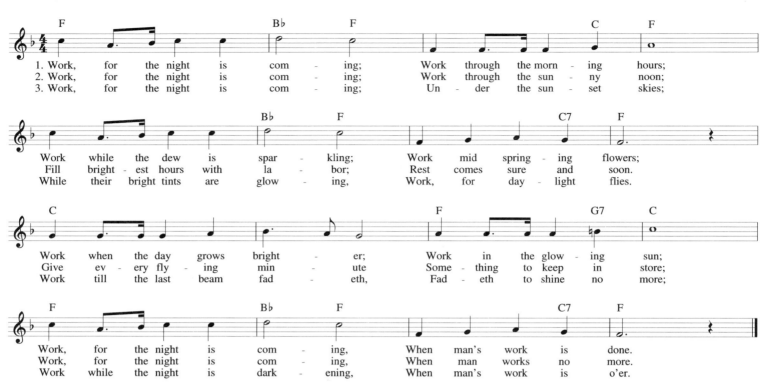

1. Work, for the night is com - ing; Work through the morn - ing hours;
2. Work, for the night is com - ing; Work through the sun - ny noon;
3. Work, for the night is com - ing; Un - der the sun - set skies;

Work while the dew is spar - kling; Work mid spring - ing flowers;
Fill bright - est hours with la - bor; Rest comes sure and soon.
While their bright tints are glow - ing, Work, for day - light flies.

Work when the day grows bright - er; Work in the glow - ing sun;
Give ev - ery fly - ing min - ute Some - thing to keep in store;
Work till the last beam fad - eth, Fad - eth to shine no more;

Work, for the night is com - ing, When man's work is done.
Work, for the night is com - ing, When man works no more.
Work while the night is dark - ening, When man's work is o'er.

THE WORLD IS VERY EVIL

EWING

words by
Bernard of Cluny, (Morlas) 12th century
tr. by John M. Neale (1818-1866)

music by
Alexander C. Ewing (1830-1895)

1. The world is ver - y e - vil, The times are wax - ing late; Be so - ber and keep
2. A - rise, a - rise, good Chris - tian, Let right to wrong suc - ceed; Let pen - i - ten - tial
3. Brief life is here our por - tion; Brief sor - row, short - lived care; The life that knows no
4. And now we fight the bat - tle, But then shall wear the crown Of full and ev - er
5. But He whom now we trust in Shall then be seen and known; And they that know and
6. O sweet and bless - ed coun - try, The home of God's e - lect! O sweet and bless - ed

vig - il, The Judge is at the gate; The Judge that comes in mer - cy, The
sor - row To heav'n - ly glad - ness lead To light that hath no eve - ning, That
end - ing, The tear - less life, is there. O hap - py ret - ri - bu - tion: Short
last - ing And pas - sion - less re - nown; And now we watch and strug - gle, And
see - ing Him Shall have him for their own. And there is Da - vid's foun - tain And
coun - try That ea - ger hearts ex - pect! O sweet and bless - ed

Judge that comes with might, To ter - mi - nate the e - vil, To di - a - dem the right.
knows no moon nor sun, The light so new and gold - en, The light that is but one.
toil, e - ter - nal rest, For mor - tals and for sin - ners A man - sion with the blest!
now we live in hope, And Zi - on in her an - guish With Bab - y - lon must cope.
life in full - est glow, And there the light is gold - en, And milk and hon - ey flow.
that dear land of rest, Who are, with God the Fa - ther And Spir - it, ev - er blest.

WONDERFUL WORDS OF LIFE

words by
Philip P. Bliss (1838-1876)

WORDS OF LIFE
music by
Philip P. Bliss (1838-1876)

1. Sing them o - ver a - gain to me, Won - der - ful words of Life; ____
2. Christ, the bless - ed One, gives to all Won - der - ful words of Life; ____
3. Sweet - ly ech - o the gos - pel call, Won - der - ful words of Life; ____

Let me more of their beau - ty see, Won - der - ful words of Life.____
Sin - ner, list to the lov - ing call, Won - der - ful words of Life.____
Of - fer par - don and peace to all, Won - der - ful words of Life.____

Words of life ____ and beau - ty, Teach me faith ____ and du - ty;
All so free - ly giv - en, Woo - ing us ____ to Heav - en;
Je - sus, on - ly Sav - ior, Sanc - ti - fy ____ for - ev - er:

Refrain

Beau - ti - ful words, won - der - ful words, Won - der - ful words of Life. ____

Beau - ti - ful words, won - der - ful words, Won - der - ful words of Life. ____

WOUNDED FOR ME

words by W.G. Ovens (v. 1)
and Gladys W. Roberts (v. 2-5)

FOR ME
music by
W.G. Ovens

1. Wound - ed for me, wound - ed for me, There on the
2. Dy - ing for me, dy - ing for me, There on the
3. Ris - en for me, ris - en for me, Up from the
4. Liv - ing for me, liv - ing for me, Up in the
5. Com - ing for me, com - ing for me, One day to

cross He was wound - ed for me; Gone my trans - gres - sions, and
cross He was dy - ing for me; Now in His death my re -
grave He has ris - en for me; Now ev - er - more from death's
skies He is liv - ing for me; Dai - ly He's plead - ing and
earth He is com - ing for me; When with what joy His dear

now I am free, All be - cause Je - sus was wound - ed for me.
demp - tion I see, All be - cause Je - sus was dy - ing for me.
sting I am free, All be - cause Je - sus has ris - en for me.
pray - ing for me, O, how I praise Him, He's liv - ing for me.
face I shall see, O, how I praise Him, He's com - ing for me!

YE HOLY ANGELS BRIGHT

DARWALL'S 148TH

words by
Richard Baxter (1615-1691)
rev. by John Hampden Gurney (1802-1862)

music by
John Darwall (1715-1789)

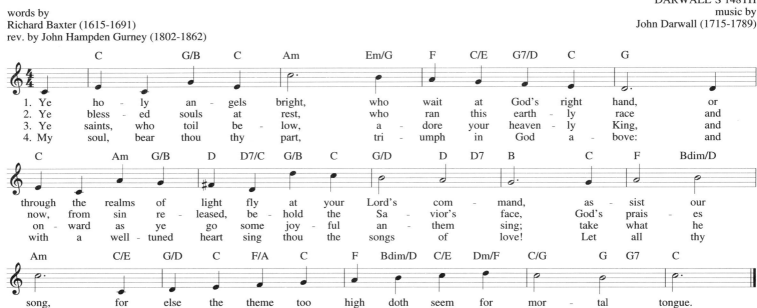

1. Ye ho-ly an-gels bright, who wait at God's right hand, or through the realms of light fly at your Lord's com-mand, as-sist our song, for else the theme too high doth seem for mor-tal tongue.
2. Ye bless-ed souls at rest, who ran this earth-ly race and now, from sin re-leased, be-hold the Sa-vior's face, God's prais-es sound, as in his sight with sweet de-light ye do a-bound.
3. Ye saints, who toil be-low, a-dore your heaven-ly King, and on-ward as ye go some joy-ful an-them sing, take what he gives and praise him still, through good or ill, who ev-er lives!
4. My soul, bear thou thy part, tri-umph in God a-bove: and with a well-tuned heart sing thou the songs of love! Let all thy days till life shall end, what-e'er he send, be filled with praise.

YESTERDAY, TODAY, FOREVER

HYACK

words by
Albert B. Simpson (1843-1919)
based on Hebrews 13:8

music by
James H. Burke, 19th Century

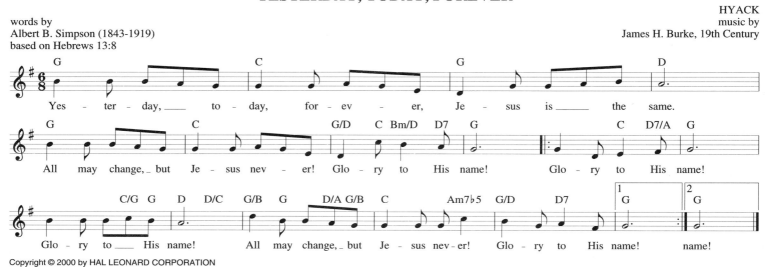

Yes-ter-day, to-day, for-ev-er, Je-sus is the same.
All may change, but Je-sus nev-er! Glo-ry to His name!
Glo-ry to His name!
Glo-ry to His name! All may change, but Je-sus nev-er! Glo-ry to His name! name!

YIELD NOT TO TEMPTATION

PALMER

words by
Horatio R. Palmer, 1868

music by
Horatio R. Palmer, 1868

1. Yield not to temp-ta-tion, For yield-ing is sin; Each vic-to-ry will help you Some oth-er to win; Fight man-ful-ly on-ward, Dark pas-sions sub-due;
2. Shun e-vil com-pan-ions, Bad lan-guage dis-dain, God's name hold in rev-er-ence, Nor take it in vain; Be thought-ful and ear-nest, Kind heart-ed and true;
3. To him that o'er-com-eth God giv-eth a crown, Through faith we shall con-quer, Though oft-en cast down; He, who is our Sav-ior, Our strength will re-new;

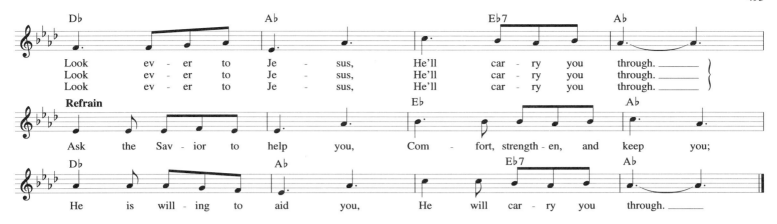

YE RANSOMED SINNERS, HEAR

LENOX

words by
Charles Wesley, 1742

music by
Lewis Edson, 1782

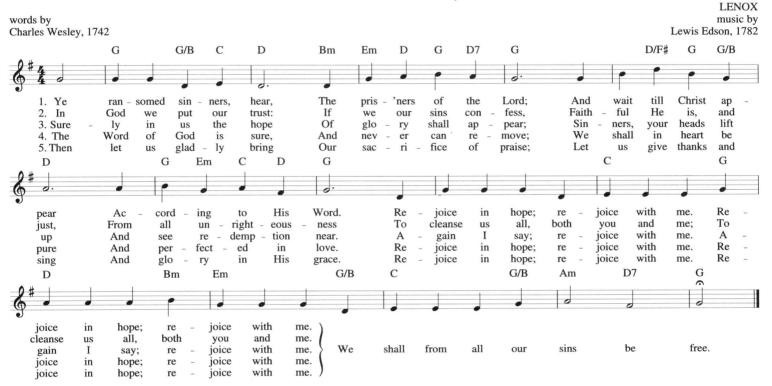

1. Ye ran-somed sin-ners, hear, The pris-'ners of the Lord; And wait till Christ ap-
2. In God we put our trust: If we our sins con-fess, Faith-ful He is, and
3. Sure-ly in us the hope Of glo-ry shall ap-pear, Sin-ners, your heads lift
4. The Word of God is sure, And nev-er can re-move; We shall in heart be
5. Then let us glad-ly bring Our sac-ri-fice of praise; Let us give thanks and

pear Ac-cord-ing to His Word. Re-joice in hope; re-joice with me. Re-
just, From all un-right-eous-ness To cleanse us all, both you and me; To
up And see re-demp-tion near. A-gain I say; re-joice with me. A-
pure And per-fect-ed in love. Re-joice in hope; re-joice with me. Re-
sing And glo-ry in His grace. Re-joice in hope; re-joice with me. Re-

joice in hope; re-joice with me. } We shall from all our sins be free.
cleanse us all, both you and me.
gain I say; re-joice with me.
joice in hope; re-joice with me.
joice in hope; re-joice with me.

YE SERVANTS OF GOD

PADERBORN

words by
Charles Wesley (1707-1788)

music from
Catolisch-Paderbornisches Gesang-buch, 1765

1. Ye ser-vants of God, your Mas-ter pro-claim, And pub-lish a-
2. God rul-eth on high, al-might-y to save; And still He is
3. "Sal-va-tion to God who sits on the throne," Lets all cry a-
4. Then let us a-dore, and give Him His right; All glo-ry and

broad His won-der-ful Name; The Name all-vic-to-rious of
nigh: His pres-ence we have. The great con-gre-ga-tion His
loud, and hon-or the Son. The prais-es of Je-sus the
power, all wis-dom and might, All hon-or and bless-ing, with

Je-sus ex-tol: His king-dom is glo-rious; He rules o-ver all.
tri-umph shall sing, As-crib-ing sal-va-tion to Je-sus our King.
an-gels pro-claim, Fall down on their fac-es, and wor-ship the Lamb.
an-gels a-bove, And thanks nev-er ceas-ing and in-fi-nite love.

YE SERVANTS OF GOD

HANOVER
music by
William Croft (1678-1727)

words by
Charles Wesley (1707-1788)

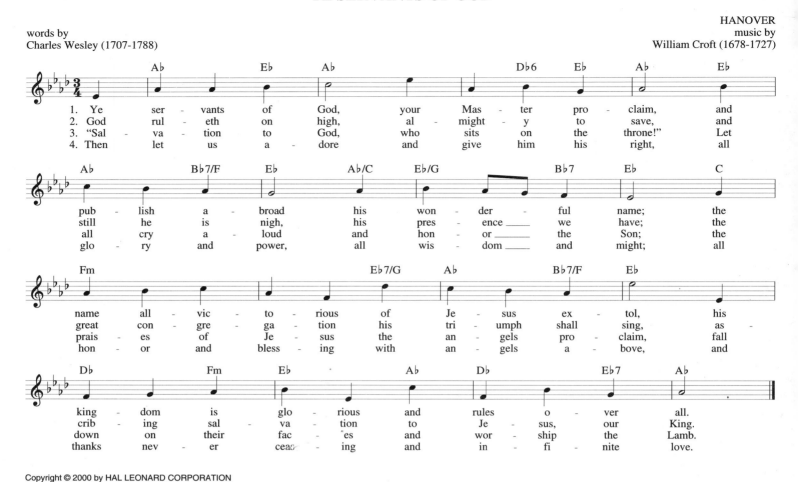

YE WATCHERS AND YE HOLY ONES

LASST UNS ERFREUEN
music from
Geistliche Kirchengesänge, 1623

words by
John Athelstan Laurie Riley, 1906